Family Maps
of
Poweshiek County, Iowa
Deluxe Edition

With Homesteads, Roads, Waterways, Towns, Cemeteries, Railroads, and More

Family Maps
of
Poweshiek County, Iowa
Deluxe Edition

With Homesteads, Roads, Waterways, Towns, Cemeteries, Railroads, and More

by Gregory A. Boyd, J.D.

Homesteads & Other Land Patents

Roads

Rivers, Creeks & Railroads

Featuring **3** *Maps Per Township...*

Arphax Publishing Co.
www.arphax.com

Family Maps of Poweshiek County, Iowa, Deluxe Edition: With Homesteads, Roads, Waterways, Towns, Cemeteries, Railroads, and More.
by Gregory A. Boyd, J.D.

ISBN 1-4203-1558-7

Published by Arphax Publishing Co., 2210 Research Park Blvd., Norman, Oklahoma, USA 73069
www.arphax.com

First Edition

ATTENTION HISTORICAL & GENEALOGICAL SOCIETIES, UNIVERSITIES, COLLEGES, CORPORATIONS, FAMILY REUNION COORDINATORS, AND PROFESSIONAL ORGANIZATIONS: Quantity discounts are available on bulk purchases of this book. For information, please contact Arphax Publishing Co., at the address listed above, or at (405) 366-6181, or visit our web-site at www.arphax.com and contact us through the "Bulk Sales" link.

This book is dedicated to my wonderful family:

Vicki, Jordan, & Amy Boyd

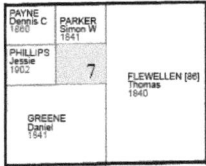

Contents

- Part I -

The Big Picture

- Part II -

Township Map Groups

(each Map Group contains a Patent Index, Patent Map, Road Map, & Historical Map)

Appendices

Preface

The quest for the discovery of my ancestors' origins, migrations, beliefs, and life-ways has brought me rewards that I could never have imagined. The *Family Maps* series of books is my first effort to share with historical and genealogical researchers, some of the tools that I have developed to achieve my research goals. I firmly believe that this effort will allow many people to reap the same sorts of treasures that I have.

Our Federal government's General Land Office of the Bureau of Land Management (the "GLO") has given genealogists and historians an incredible gift by virtue of its enormous database housed on its web-site at glorecords.blm.gov. Here, you can search for and find millions of parcels of land purchased by our ancestors in about thirty states.

This GLO web-site is one of the best FREE on-line tools available to family researchers. But, it is not for the faint of heart, nor is it for those unwilling or unable to to sift through and analyze the thousands of records that exist for most counties.

My immediate goal with this series is to spare you the hundreds of hours of work that it would take you to map the Land Patents for this county. Every Poweshiek County homestead or land patent that I have gleaned from public GLO databases is mapped here. Consequently, I can usually show you in an instant, where your ancestor's land is located, as well as the names of nearby land-owners.

Originally, that was my primary goal. But after speaking to other genealogists, it became clear that there was much more that they wanted. Taking their advice set me back almost a full year, but I think you will agree it was worth the wait. Because now, you can learn so much more.

Now, this book answers these sorts of questions:

- Are there any variant spellings for surnames that I have missed in searching GLO records?
- Where is my family's traditional home-place?
- What cemeteries are near Grandma's house?
- My Granddad used to swim in such-and-such-Creek—where is that?
- How close is this little community to that one?
- Are there any other people with the same surname who bought land in the county?
- How about cousins and in-laws—did they buy land in the area?

And these are just for starters!

The rules for using the *Family Maps* books are simple, but the strategies for success are many. Some techniques are apparent on first use, but many are gained with time and experience. Please take the time to notice the roads, cemeteries, creek-names, family names, and unique first-names throughout the whole county. You cannot imagine what YOU might be the first to discover.

I hope to learn that many of you have answered age-old research questions within these pages or that you have discovered relationships previously not even considered. When these sorts of things happen to you, will you please let me hear about it? I would like nothing better. My contact information can always be found at www.arphax.com.

One more thing: please read the "How To Use This Book" chapter; it starts on the next page. This will give you the very best chance to find the treasures that lie within these pages.

My family and I wish you the very best of luck, both in life, and in your research.   Greg Boyd

How to Use This Book - A Graphical Summary

Part I
"The Big Picture"

Map A ▸ Counties in the State

Map B ▸ Surrounding Counties

Map C ▸ Congressional Townships (Map Groups) in the County

Map D ▸ Cities & Towns in the County

Map E ▸ Cemeteries in the County

Surnames in the County ▸ Number of Land-Parcels for Each Surname

Surname/Township Index ▸ Directs you to Township Map Groups in Part II

The *Surname/Township Index* can direct you to any number of **Township Map Groups**

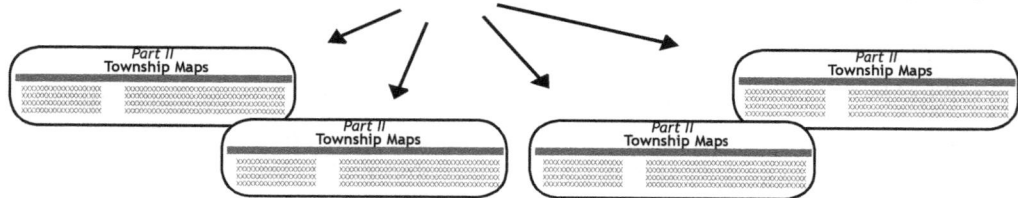

Part II
Township Maps

Part II
Township Maps

Part II
Township Maps

Part II
Township Maps

Part II
Township Map Groups
(1 for each Township in the County)

Each Township Map Group contains all four of of the following tools . . .

Land Patent Index ▸ Every-name Index of Patents Mapped in this Township

Land Patent Map ▸ Map of Patents as listed in above Index

Road Map ▸ Map of Roads, City-centers, and Cemeteries in the Township

Historical Map ▸ Map of Railroads, Lakes, Rivers, Creeks, City-Centers, and Cemeteries

Appendices

Appendix A ▸ Congressional Authority enabling Patents within our Maps

Appendix B ▸ Section-Parts / Aliquot Parts (a comprehensive list)

Appendix C ▸ Multi-patentee Groups (Individuals within Buying Groups)

How to Use This Book

The two "Parts" of this *Family Maps* volume seek to answer two different types of questions. Part I deals with broad questions like: what counties surround Poweshiek County, are there any ASHCRAFTs in Poweshiek County, and if so, in which Townships or Maps can I find them? Ultimately, though, Part I should point you to a particular Township Map Group in Part II.

Part II concerns itself with details like: where exactly is this family's land, who else bought land in the area, and what roads and streams run through the land, or are located nearby. The Chart on the opposite page, and the remainder of this chapter attempt to convey to you the particulars of these two "parts", as well as how best to use them to achieve your research goals.

Part I
"The Big Picture"

Within Part I, you will find five "Big Picture" maps and two county-wide surname tools.

These include:

- Map A - Where Poweshiek County lies within the state
- Map B - Counties that surround Poweshiek County
- Map C - Congressional Townships of Poweshiek County (+ Map Group Numbers)
- Map D - Cities & Towns of Poweshiek County (with Index)
- Map E - Cemeteries of Poweshiek County (with Index)
- Surnames in Poweshiek County Patents (with Parcel-counts for each surname)
- Surname/Township Index (with Parcel-counts for each surname by Township)

The five "Big-Picture" Maps are fairly self-explanatory, yet should not be overlooked. This is particularly true of Maps "C", "D", and "E", all of which show Poweshiek County and its Congressional Townships (and their assigned Map Group Numbers).

Let me briefly explain this concept of Map Group Numbers. These are a device completely of our own invention. They were created to help you quickly locate maps without having to remember the full legal name of the various Congressional Townships. It is simply easier to remember "Map Group 1" than a legal name like: "Township 9-North Range 6-West, 5th Principal Meridian." But the fact is that the TRUE legal name for these Townships IS terribly important. These are the designations that others will be familiar with and you will need to accurately record them in your notes. This is why both Map Group numbers AND legal descriptions of Townships are almost always displayed together.

Map "C" will be your first intoduction to "Map Group Numbers", and that is all it contains: legal Township descriptions and their assigned Map Group Numbers. Once you get further into your research, and more immersed in the details, you will likely want to refer back to Map "C" from time to time, in order to regain your bearings on just where in the county you are researching.

Remember, township boundaries are a completely artificial device, created to standardize land descriptions. But do not let them become a boundary in your mind when choosing which townships to research. Your relative's in-laws, children, cousins, siblings, and mamas and papas, might just as easily have lived in the township next to the one your grandfather lived in—rather than in the one where he actually lived. So Map "C" can be your guide to which other Townships/ Map Groups you likewise ought to analyze.

Of course, the same holds true for County lines; this is the purpose behind Map "B". It shows you surrounding counties that you may want to consider for further reserarch.

Map "D", the Cities and Towns map, is the first map with an index. Map "E" is the second (Cemeteries). Both, Maps "D" and "E" give you broad views of City (or Cemetery) locations in the County. But they go much further by pointing you toward pertinent Township Map Groups so you can locate the patents, roads, and waterways located near a particular city or cemetery.

Once you are familiar with these *Family Maps* volumes and the county you are researching, the "Surnames In Poweshiek County" chapter (or its sister chapter in other volumes) is where you'll likely start your future research sessions. Here, you can quickly scan its few pages and see if anyone in the county possesses the surnames you are researching. The "Surnames in Poweshiek County" list shows only two things: surnames and the number of parcels of land we have located for that surname in Poweshiek County. But whether or not you immediately locate the surnames you are researching, please do not go any further without taking a few moments to scan ALL the surnames in these very few pages.

You cannot imagine how many lost ancestors are waiting to be found by someone willing to take just a little longer to scan the "Surnames In Poweshiek County" list. Misspellings and typographical errors abound in most any index of this sort. Don't miss out on finding your Kinard that was written Rynard or Cox that was written Lox. If it looks funny or wrong, it very often is. And one of those little errors may well be your relative.

Now, armed with a surname and the knowledge that it has one or more entries in this book, you are ready for the "Surname/Township Index." Unlike the "Surnames In Poweshiek County", which has only one line per Surname, the "Surname/Township Index" contains one line-item for each Township Map Group in which each surname is found. In other words, each line represents a different Township Map Group that you will need to review.

Specifically, each line of the Surname/Township

Index contains the following four columns of information:

1. Surname
2. Township Map Group Number (these Map Groups are found in Part II)
3. Parcels of Land (number of them with the given Surname within the Township)
4. Meridian/Township/Range (the legal description for this Township Map Group)

The key column here is that of the Township Map Group Number. While you should definitely record the Meridian, Township, and Range, you can do that later. Right now, you need to dig a little deeper. That Map Group Number tells you where in Part II that you need to start digging.

But before you leave the "Surname/Township Index", do the same thing that you did with the "Surnames in Poweshiek County" list: take a moment to scan the pages of the Index and see if there are similarly spelled or misspelled surnames that deserve your attention. Here again, is an easy opportunity to discover grossly misspelled family names with very little effort. Now you are ready to turn to . . .

Part II
"Township Map Groups"

You will normally arrive here in Part II after being directed to do so by one or more "Map Group Numbers" in the Surname/Township Index of Part I.

Each Map Group represents a set of four tools dedicated to a single Congressional Township that is either wholly or partially within the county. If you are trying to learn all that you can about a particular family or their land, then these tools should usually be viewed in the order they are presented.

These four tools include:

1. a Land Patent Index
2. a Land Patent Map
3. a Road Map, and
4. an Historical Map

As I mentioned earlier, each grouping of this sort is assigned a Map Group Number. So, let's now move on to a discussion of the four tools that make up one of these Township Map Groups.

Land Patent Index

Each Township Map Group's Index begins with a title, something along these lines:

MAP GROUP 1: Index to Land Patents
Township 16-North Range 5-West (2nd PM)

The Index contains seven (7) columns. They are:

1. ID (a unique ID number for this Individual and a corresponding Parcel of land in this Township)
2. Individual in Patent (name)
3. Sec. (Section), and
4. Sec. Part (Section Part, or Aliquot Part)
5. Date Issued (Patent)
6. Other Counties (often means multiple counties were mentioned in GLO records, or the section lies within multiple counties).
7. For More Info . . . (points to other places within this index or elsewhere in the book where you can find more information)

While most of the seven columns are self-explanatory, I will take a few moments to explain the "Sec. Part." and "For More Info" columns.

The "Sec. Part" column refers to what surveryors and other land professionals refer to as an Aliquot Part. The origins and use of such a term mean little to a non-surveyor, and I have chosen to simply call these sub-sections of land what they are: a "Section Part". No matter what we call them, what we are referring to are things like a quarter-section or half-section or quarter-quarter-section. See Appendix "B" for most of the "Section Parts" you will come across (and many you will not) and what size land-parcel they represent.

The "For More Info" column of the Index may seem like a small appendage to each line, but please

recognize quickly that this is not so. And to understand the various items you might find here, you need to become familiar with the Legend that appears at the top of each Land Patent Index.

Here is a sample of the Legend . . .

LEGEND

"For More Info . . . " column

A = Authority (Legislative Act, See Appendix "A")
B = Block or Lot (location in Section unknown)
C = Cancelled Patent
F = Fractional Section
G = Group (Multi-Patentee Patent, see Appendix "C")
V = Overlaps another Parcel
R = Re-Issued (Parcel patented more than once)

Most parcels of land will have only one or two of these items in their "For More Info" columns, but when that is not the case, there is often some valuable information to be gained from further investigation. Below, I will explain what each of these items means to you you as a researcher.

A = Authority
(Legislative Act, See Appendix "A")

All Federal Land Patents were issued because some branch of our government (usually the U.S. Congress) passed a law making such a transfer of title possible. And therefore every patent within these pages will have an "A" item next to it in the index. The number after the "A" indicates which item in Appendix "A" holds the citation to the particular law which authorized the transfer of land to the public. As it stands, most of the Public Land data compiled and released by our government, and which serves as the basis for the patents mapped here, concerns itself with "Cash Sale" homesteads. So in some Counties, the law which authorized cash sales will be the primary, if not the only, entry in the Appendix.

B = Block or Lot (location in Section unknown)
A "B" designation in the Index is a tip-off that the EXACT location of the patent within the map is not apparent from the legal description. This Patent will nonetheless be noted within the proper

Section along with any other Lots purchased in the Section. Given the scope of this project (many states and many Counties are being mapped), trying to locate all relevant plats for Lots (if they even exist) and accurately mapping them would have taken one person several lifetimes. But since our primary goal from the onset has been to establish relationships between neighbors and families, very little is lost to this goal since we can still observe who all lived in which Section.

C = Cancelled Patent

A Cancelled Patent is just that: cancelled. Whether the original Patentee forfeited his or her patent due to fraud, a technicality, non-payment, or whatever, the fact remains that it is significant to know who received patents for what parcels and when. A cancellation may be evidence that the Patentee never physically re-located to the land, but does not in itself prove that point. Further evidence would be required to prove that. *See also*, Re-issued Patents, *below*.

F = Fractional Section

A Fractional Section is one that contains less than 640 acres, almost always because of a body of water. The exact size and shape of land-parcels contained in such sections may not be ascertainable, but we map them nonetheless. Just keep in mind that we are not mapping an actual parcel to scale in such instances. Another point to consider is that we have located some fractional sections that are not so designated by the Bureau of Land Management in their data. This means that not all fractional sections have been so identified in our indexes.

G = Group
(Multi-Patentee Patent, see Appendix "C")

A "G" designation means that the Patent was issued to a GROUP of people (Multi-patentees). The "G" will always be followed by a number. Some such groups were quite large and it was impractical if not impossible to display each individual in our maps without unduly affecting readability. EACH person in the group is named in the Index, but they won't all be found on the Map. You will find the name of the first person in such a Group

on the map with the Group number next to it, enclosed in [square brackets].

To find all the members of the Group you can either scan the Index for all people with the same Group Number or you can simply refer to Appendix "C" where all members of the Group are listed next to their number.

V = Overlaps another Parcel

An Overlap is one where PART of a parcel of land gets issued on more than one patent. For genealogical purposes, both transfers of title are important and both Patentees are mapped. If the ENTIRE parcel of land is re-issued, that is what we call it, a Re-Issued Patent (*see below*). The number after the "V" indicates the ID for the overlapping Patent(s) contained within the same Index. Like Re-Issued and Cancelled Patents, Overlaps may cause a map-reader to be confused at first, but for genealogical purposes, all of these parties' relationships to the underlying land is important, and therefore, we map them.

R = Re-Issued (Parcel patented more than once)

The label, "Re-issued Patent" describes Patents which were issued more than once for land with the EXACT SAME LEGAL DESCRIPTION. Whether the original patent was cancelled or not, there were a good many parcels which were patented more than once. The number after the "R" indicates the ID for the other Patent contained within the same Index that was for the same land. A quick glance at the map itself within the relevant Section will be the quickest way to find the other Patentee to whom the Parcel was transferred. They should both be mapped in the same general area.

I have gone to some length describing all sorts of anomalies either in the underlying data or in their representation on the maps and indexes in this book. Most of this will bore the most ardent reseracher, but I do this with all due respect to those researchers who will inevitably (and rightfully) ask: *"Why isn't so-and-so's name on the exact spot that the index says it should be?"*

In most cases it will be due to the existence of a Multi-Patentee Patent, a Re-issued Patent, a Cancelled Patent, or Overlapping Parcels named in separate Patents. I don't pretend that this discussion will answer every question along these lines, but I hope it will at least convince you of the complexity of the subject.

Not to despair, this book's companion web-site will offer a way to further explain "odd-ball" or errant data. Each book (County) will have its own web-page or pages to discuss such situations. You can go to www.arphax.com to find the relevant web-page for Poweshiek County.

Land Patent Map

On the first two-page spread following each Township's Index to Land Patents, you'll find the corresponding Land Patent Map. And here lies the real heart of our work. For the first time anywhere, researchers will be able to observe and analyze, on a grand scale, most of the original land-owners for an area AND see them mapped in proximity to each one another.

We encourage you to make vigorous use of the accompanying Index described above, but then later, to abandon it, and just stare at these maps for a while. This is a great way to catch misspellings or to find collateral kin you'd not known were in the area.

Each Land Patent Map represents one Congressional Township containing approximately 36-square miles. Each of these square miles is labeled by an accompanying Section Number (1 through 36, in most cases). Keep in mind, that this book concerns itself solely with Poweshiek County's patents. Townships which creep into one or more other counties will not be shown in their entirety in any one book. You will need to consult other books, as they become available, in order to view other countys' patents, cities, cemeteries, etc.

But getting back to Poweshiek County: each Land Patent Map contains a Statistical Chart that looks like the following:

Township Statistics

Parcels Mapped	:	173
Number of Patents	:	163
Number of Individuals	:	152
Patentees Identified	:	151
Number of Surnames	:	137
Multi-Patentee Parcels	:	4
Oldest Patent Date	:	11/27/1820
Most Recent Patent	:	9/28/1917
Block/Lot Parcels	:	0
Parcels Re-Issued	:	3
Parcels that Overlap	:	8
Cities and Towns	:	6
Cemeteries	:	6

This information may be of more use to a social statistician or historian than a genealogist, but I think all three will find it interesting.

Most of the statistics are self-explanatory, and what is not, was described in the above discussion of the Index's Legend, but I do want to mention a few of them that may affect your understanding of the Land Patent Maps.

First of all, Patents often contain more than one Parcel of land, so it is common for there to be more Parcels than Patents. Also, the Number of Individuals will more often than not, not match the number of Patentees. A Patentee is literally the person or PERSONS named in a patent. So, a Patent may have a multi-person Patentee or a single-person patentee. Nonetheless, we account for all these individuals in our indexes.

On the lower-righthand side of the Patent Map is a Legend which describes various features in the map, including Section Boundaries, Patent (land) Boundaries, Lots (numbered), and Multi-Patentee Group Numbers. You'll also find a "Helpful Hints" Box that will assist you.

One important note: though the vast majority of Patents mapped in this series will prove to be reasonably accurate representations of their actual locations, we cannot claim this for patents lying along state and county lines, or waterways, or that have been platted (lots).

Shifting boundaries and sparse legal descriptions in the GLO data make this a reality that we have nonetheless tried to overcome by estimating these patents' locations the best that we can.

Road Map

On the two-page spread following each Patent Map you will find a Road Map covering the exact same area (the same Congressional Township).

For me, fully exploring the past means that every once in a while I must leave the library and travel to the actual locations where my ancestors once walked and worked the land. Our Township Road Maps are a great place to begin such a quest.

Keep in mind that the scaling and proportion of these maps was chosen in order to squeeze hundreds of people-names, road-names, and place-names into tinier spaces than you would traditionally see. These are not professional road-maps, and like any secondary genealogical source, should be looked upon as an entry-way to original sources— in this case, original patents and applications, professionally produced maps and surveys, etc.

Both our Road Maps and Historical Maps contain cemeteries and city-centers, along with a listing of these on the left-hand side of the map. I should note that I am showing you city center-points, rather than city-limit boundaries, because in many instances, this will represent a place where settlement began. This may be a good time to mention that many cemeteries are located on private property, Always check with a local historical or genealogical society to see if a particular cemetery is publicly accessible (if it is not obviously so). As a final point, look for your surnames among the road-names. You will often be surprised by what you find.

Historical Map

The third and final map in each Map Group is our attempt to display what each Township might have looked like before the advent of modern roads. In frontier times, people were usually more determined to settle near rivers and creeks than they were near roads, which were often few and

far between. As was the case with the Road Map, we've included the same cemeteries and city-centers. We've also included railroads, many of which came along before most roads.

While some may claim "Historical Map" to be a bit of a misnomer for this tool, we settled for this label simply because it was almost as accurate as saying "Railroads, Lakes, Rivers, Cities, and Cemeteries," and it is much easier to remember.

In Closing . . .

By way of example, here is *A Really Good Way to Use a Township Map Group*. First, find the person you are researching in the Township's Index to Land Patents, which will direct you to the proper Section and parcel on the Patent Map. But before leaving the Index, scan all the patents within it, looking for other names of interest. Now, turn to the Patent Map and locate your parcels of land. Pay special attention to the names of patent-holders who own land surrounding your person of interest. Next, turn the page and look at the same Section(s) on the Road Map. Note which roads are closest to your parcels and also the names of nearby towns and cemeteries. Using other resources, you may be able to learn of kin who have been buried here, plus, you may choose to visit these cemeteries the next time you are in the area.

Finally, turn to the Historical Map. Look once more at the same Sections where you found your research subject's land. Note the nearby streams, creeks, and other geographical features. You may be surprised to find family names were used to name them, or you may see a name you haven't heard mentioned in years and years—and a new research possibility is born.

Many more techniques for using these *Family Maps* volumes will no doubt be discovered. If from time to time, you will navigate to Poweshiek County's web-page at www.arphax.com (use the "Research" link), you can learn new tricks as they become known (or you can share ones you have employed). But for now, you are ready to get started. So, go, and good luck.

– Part I –

The Big Picture

Map A - Where Poweshiek County, Iowa Lies Within the State

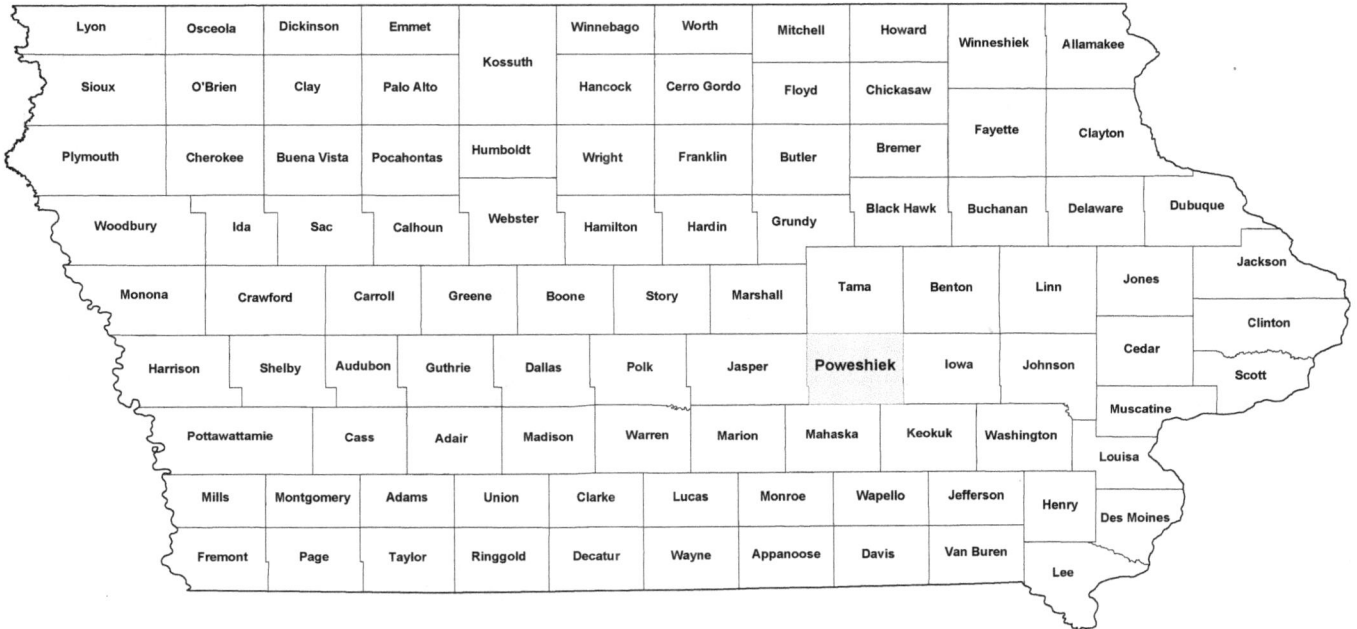

Lyon	Osceola	Dickinson	Emmet	Kossuth	Winnebago	Worth	Mitchell	Howard	Winneshiek	Allamakee
Sioux	O'Brien	Clay	Palo Alto		Hancock	Cerro Gordo	Floyd	Chickasaw		
Plymouth	Cherokee	Buena Vista	Pocahontas	Humboldt	Wright	Franklin	Butler	Bremer	Fayette	Clayton
Woodbury	Ida	Sac	Calhoun	Webster	Hamilton	Hardin	Grundy	Black Hawk	Buchanan	Delaware	Dubuque
Monona	Crawford	Carroll	Greene	Boone	Story	Marshall	Tama	Benton	Linn	Jones	Jackson
Harrison	Shelby	Audubon	Guthrie	Dallas	Polk	Jasper	Poweshiek	Iowa	Johnson	Cedar	Clinton
Pottawattamie	Cass	Adair	Madison	Warren	Marion	Mahaska	Keokuk	Washington	Muscatine	Scott
Mills	Montgomery	Adams	Union	Clarke	Lucas	Monroe	Wapello	Jefferson	Henry	Louisa
Fremont	Page	Taylor	Ringgold	Decatur	Wayne	Appanoose	Davis	Van Buren	Lee	Des Moines

Legend
— State Boundary
— County Boundaries
☐ Poweshiek County, Iowa

Helpful Hints

1 We start with Map "A" which simply shows us where within the State this county lies.

2 Map "B" zooms in further to help us more easily identify surrounding Counties.

3 Map "C" zooms in even further to reveal the Congressional Townships that either lie within or intersect Poweshiek County.

Map B - Poweshiek County, Iowa and Surrounding Counties

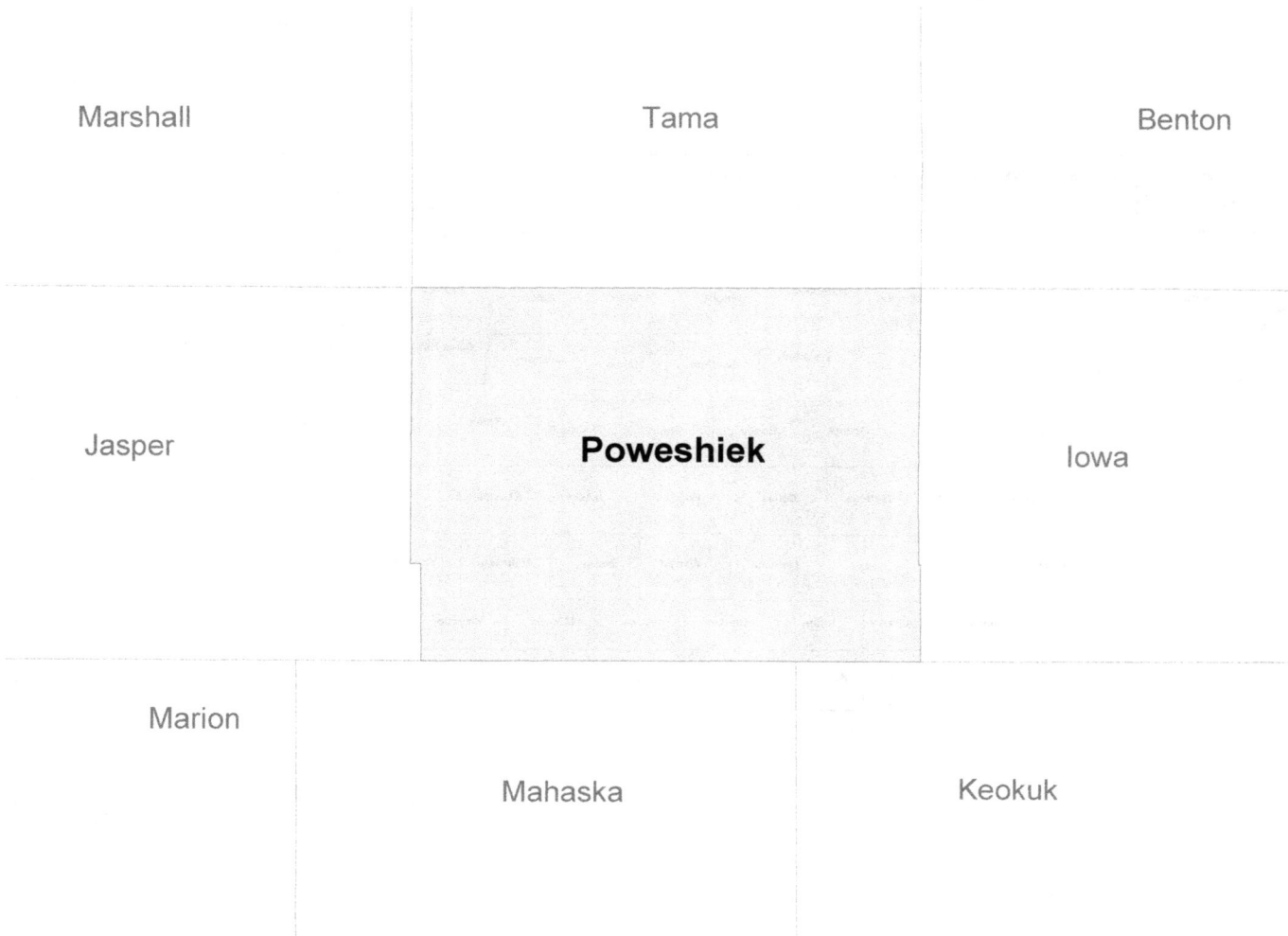

Marshall

Tama

Benton

Jasper

Poweshiek

Iowa

Marion

Mahaska

Keokuk

—— Legend ——

—— State Boundaries (when applicable)

—— County Boundaries

———— Helpful Hints ————

1 Many Patent-holders and their families settled across county lines. It is always a good idea to check nearby counties for your families.

2 Refer to Map "A" to see a broader view of where this County lies within the State, and Map "C" to see which Congressional Townships lie within Poweshiek County.

Map C - Congressional Townships of Poweshiek County, Iowa

Map Group 1 Township 81-N Range 16-W	**Map Group 2** Township 81-N Range 15-W	**Map Group 3** Township 81-N Range 14-W	**Map Group 4** Township 81-N Range 13-W
Map Group 5 Township 80-N Range 16-W	**Map Group 6** Township 80-N Range 15-W	**Map Group 7** Township 80-N Range 14-W	**Map Group 8** Township 80-N Range 13-W
Map Group 9 Township 79-N Range 16-W	**Map Group 10** Township 79-N Range 15-W	**Map Group 11** Township 79-N Range 14-W	**Map Group 12** Township 79-N Range 13-W
Map Group 13 Township 78-N Range 16-W	**Map Group 14** Township 78-N Range 15-W	**Map Group 15** Township 78-N Range 14-W	**Map Group 16** Township 78-N Range 13-W

——— Legend ———

☐ Poweshiek County, Iowa

☐ Congressional Townships

——— Helpful Hints ———

1. Many Patent-holders and their families settled across county lines. It is always a good idea to check nearby counties for your families (See Map "B").

2. Refer to Map "A" to see a broader view of where this county lies within the State, and Map "B" for a view of the counties surrounding Poweshiek County.

Map D Index: Cities & Towns of Poweshiek County, Iowa

The following represents the Cities and Towns of Poweshiek County (along with the corresponding Map Group in which each is found). Cities and Towns are displayed in both the Road and Historical maps in the Group.

City/Town	Map Group No.
Arbor Lake Mobile Home Community	5
Brooklyn	7
Brownsville	14
Carnforth	8
Deep River	16
Dresden	16
Ewart	10
Grinnell	5
Guernsey	12
Hartwick	4
Jacobs	9
Lone Pine Mobile Home Court	7
Malcom	6
Montezuma	14
Searsboro	13
Sheridan	2
Stillwell	13
Tilton	16
Westfield	5
Willows Mobile Home Court	5

Map D - Cities & Towns of Poweshiek County, Iowa

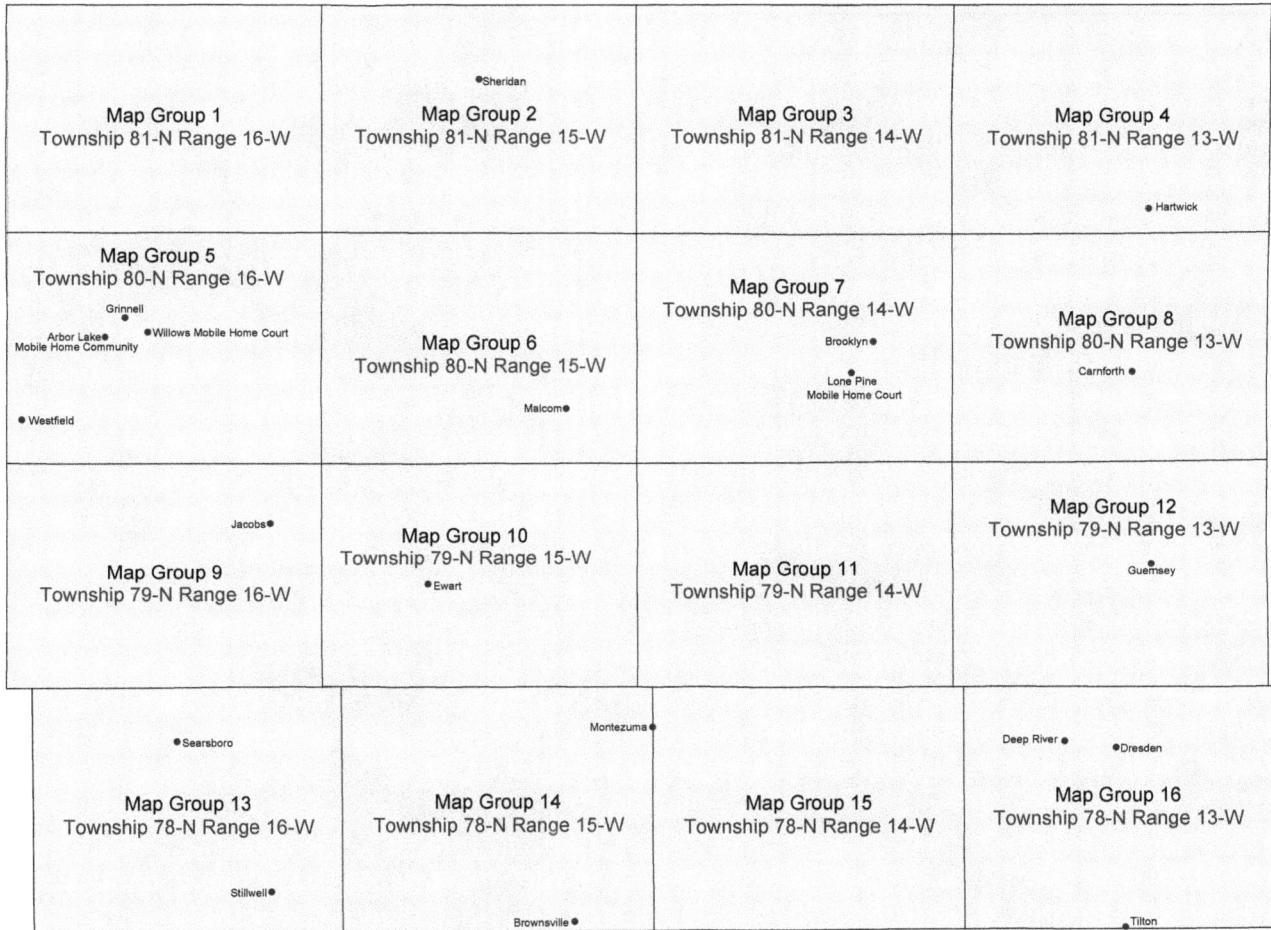

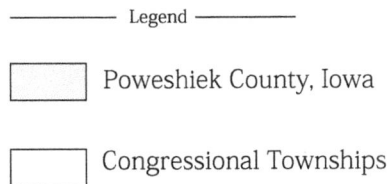

Map Group 1 Township 81-N Range 16-W	●Sheridan Map Group 2 Township 81-N Range 15-W	Map Group 3 Township 81-N Range 14-W	Map Group 4 Township 81-N Range 13-W ● Hartwick
Map Group 5 Township 80-N Range 16-W Grinnell ● Arbor Lake● ●Willows Mobile Home Court Mobile Home Community ● Westfield	Map Group 6 Township 80-N Range 15-W Malcom●	Map Group 7 Township 80-N Range 14-W Brooklyn ● ● Lone Pine Mobile Home Court	Map Group 8 Township 80-N Range 13-W Carnforth ●
Jacobs● Map Group 9 Township 79-N Range 16-W	Map Group 10 Township 79-N Range 15-W ● Ewart	Map Group 11 Township 79-N Range 14-W	Map Group 12 Township 79-N Range 13-W Guernsey ●
● Searsboro Map Group 13 Township 78-N Range 16-W Stillwell●	Montezuma ● Map Group 14 Township 78-N Range 15-W Brownsville ●	Map Group 15 Township 78-N Range 14-W	Deep River ● ●Dresden Map Group 16 Township 78-N Range 13-W ●Tilton

─── Helpful Hints ───

1 Cities and towns are marked only at their center-points as published by the USGS and/or NationalAtlas.gov. This often enables us to more closely approximate where these might have existed when first settled.

2 To see more specifically where these Cities & Towns are located within the county, refer to both the Road and Historical maps in the Map-Group referred to above. See also, the Map "D" Index on the opposite page.

Map E Index: Cemeteries of Poweshiek County, Iowa

The following represents many of the Cemeteries of Poweshiek County, along with the corresponding Township Map Group in which each is found. Cemeteries are displayed in both the Road and Historical maps in the Map Groups referred to below.

Cemetery	Map Group No.
Beason Cem.	14
Blake Cem.	4
Bone Cem.	14
Calvary Cem.	7
Cem. Hill Cem.	13
Chester Cem.	1
Chester Cem.	1
Deep River Cem.	16
Dresden Cem.	16
Ewart Cem.	10
Forest Home Cem.	14
Guernsey Cem.	12
Gwin Cem.	8
Harmony Cem.	12
Harper Cem.	15
Hayes Cem.	9
Hazelwood Cem.	5
International Order of Odd Fellows	7
Ivy Hill Cem.	6
Jackson Township Cem.	14
Kent Cem.	3
Light Cem.	16
Lisor Cem.	15
Little Mount Baptist Cem.	14
Lower Blue Point Cem.	9
Lytle Cem.	11
Masonic IOOF Cem.	14
McCoy Cem.	14
McDonald Cem.	14
Mill Grove Cem.	13
Morrison Cem.	12
Norwegian Lutheran Cem.	5
Searsboro International Order of Oddfellows	13
Sheley Cem.	14
Sheridan Cem.	2
Squires Cem.	3
Sugar Creek Cem.	9
Trinity Cem.	6
Union Cem.	4
Upper Blue Point Cem.	9
West Liberty Cem.	13
Westfield Cem.	5
Wilson Cem.	8
Winslow Cem.	4

Map E - Cemeteries of Poweshiek County, Iowa

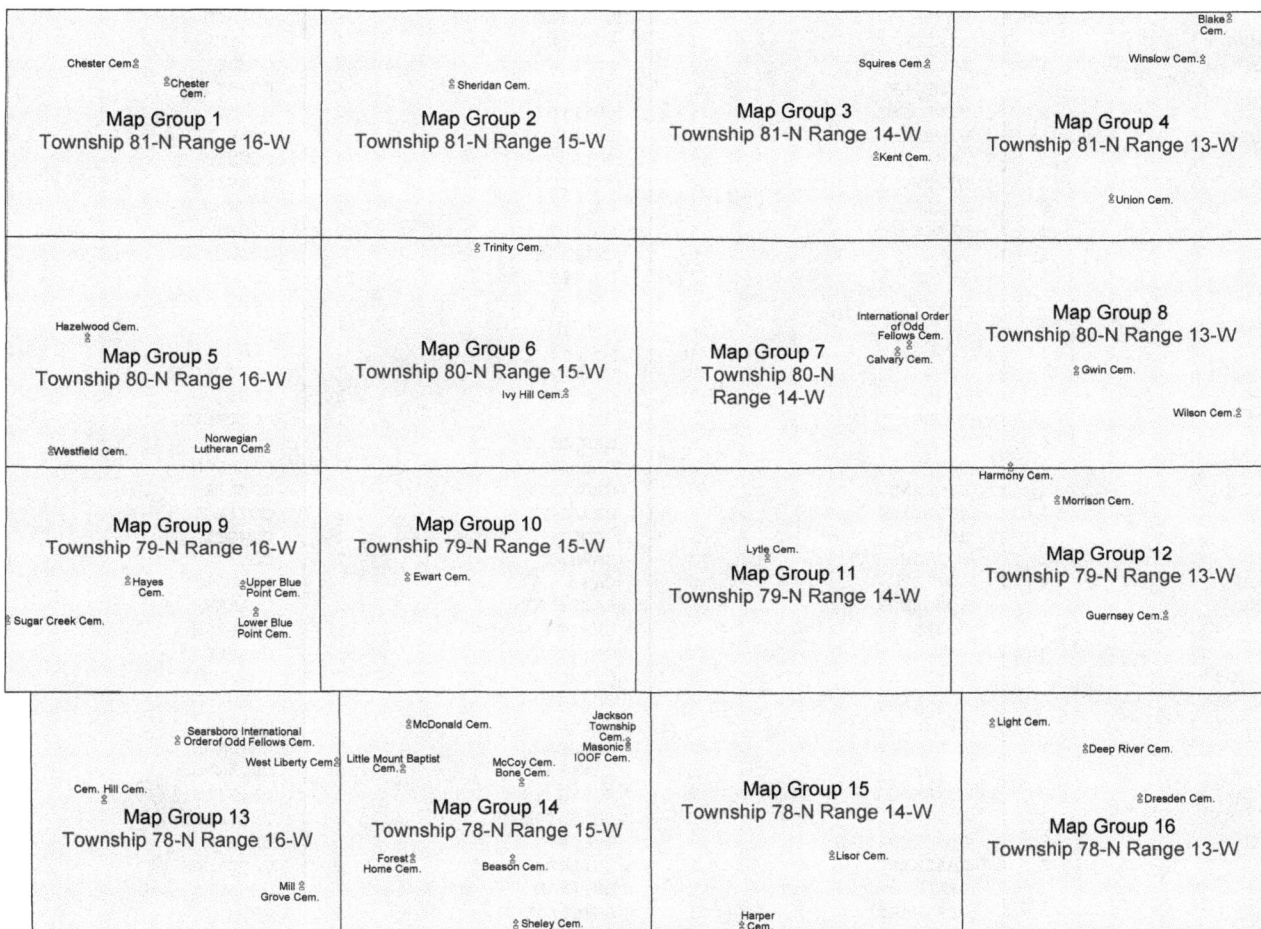

Chester Cem. ⚱ Chester Cem.	⚱ Sheridan Cem.	Squires Cem. ⚱	Blake ⚱ Cem. Winslow Cem. ⚱
Map Group 1 Township 81-N Range 16-W	**Map Group 2** Township 81-N Range 15-W	**Map Group 3** Township 81-N Range 14-W ⚱ Kent Cem.	**Map Group 4** Township 81-N Range 13-W ⚱ Union Cem.
Hazelwood Cem. ⚱	⚱ Trinity Cem. **Map Group 6** Township 80-N Range 15-W Ivy Hill Cem. ⚱	International Order of Odd Fellows Cem. ⚱ Calvary Cem. **Map Group 7** Township 80-N Range 14-W	**Map Group 8** Township 80-N Range 13-W ⚱ Gwin Cem. Wilson Cem. ⚱
Map Group 5 Township 80-N Range 16-W ⚱ Westfield Cem. Norwegian Lutheran Cem. ⚱			
Map Group 9 Township 79-N Range 16-W ⚱ Hayes Cem. ⚱ Upper Blue Point Cem. ⚱ Sugar Creek Cem. ⚱ Lower Blue Point Cem.	**Map Group 10** Township 79-N Range 15-W ⚱ Ewart Cem.	Lytle Cem. ⚱ **Map Group 11** Township 79-N Range 14-W	Harmony Cem. ⚱ ⚱ Morrison Cem. **Map Group 12** Township 79-N Range 13-W Guernsey Cem. ⚱
Searsboro International ⚱ Order of Odd Fellows Cem. West Liberty Cem. ⚱ Cem. Hill Cem. ⚱ **Map Group 13** Township 78-N Range 16-W Mill ⚱ Grove Cem.	⚱ McDonald Cem. Jackson Township Cem. Masonic ⚱ IOOF Cem. Little Mount Baptist Cem. ⚱ McCoy Cem. ⚱ Bone Cem. **Map Group 14** Township 78-N Range 15-W Forest ⚱ Home Cem. Beason Cem. ⚱ ⚱ Sheley Cem.	**Map Group 15** Township 78-N Range 14-W ⚱ Lisor Cem. Harper ⚱ Cem.	⚱ Light Cem. ⚱ Deep River Cem. ⚱ Dresden Cem. **Map Group 16** Township 78-N Range 13-W

———— Legend ————

☐ Poweshiek County, Iowa

☐ Congressional Townships

———— Helpful Hints ————

1 Cemeteries are marked at locations as published by the USGS and/or NationalAtlas.gov.

2 To see more specifically where these Cemeteries are located, refer to the Road & Historical maps in the Map-Group referred to above. See also, the Map "E" Index on the opposite page to make sure you don't miss any of the Cemeteries located within this Congressional township.

Surnames in Poweshiek County, Iowa Patents

The following list represents the surnames that we have located in Poweshiek County, Iowa Patents and the number of parcels that we have mapped for each one. Here is a quick way to determine the existence (or not) of Patents to be found in the subsequent indexes and maps of this volume.

Surname	# of Land Parcels	Surname	# of Land Parcels	Surname	# of Land Parcels	Surname	# of Land Parcels
ADAIR	1	BETTS	8	BURNS	2	COLLINS	2
ADAMS	2	BEVER	1	BURRELL	1	COLVIN	6
ADDLEMAN	1	BIGLER	1	BURTON	4	COLYER	3
ADKINS	1	BILL	10	BUSH	1	COMBE	3
AHERN	4	BINEGAR	1	BUTCHER	1	COMSTOCK	2
AKIN	2	BINFORD	5	BUTLER	3	CONEY	1
ALEXANDER	5	BINGEY	1	BUZZARD	1	CONNELLY	20
ALLEN	12	BIRD	13	BYERS	2	CONNER	2
ALLOWAY	1	BIXBY	2	BYINGTON	7	CONVERS	1
AMMON	3	BIXLER	1	CADWALADER	1	CONWAY	3
ANDERSON	1	BLACK	4	CALDWELL	2	COOK	7
ANDREWS	1	BLAKE	5	CALKINS	1	COOLEY	1
ANGLE	1	BLISH	2	CAMPBELL	13	COOPER	1
ANTHONY	13	BLOUNT	1	CANNON	5	COPE	10
APPLEGATE	4	BLUE	1	CANTRIL	1	CORBIN	5
ARCHER	1	BOGGS	1	CAPLES	1	CORNWELL	4
ARMITAGE	1	BOND	2	CARBERRY	1	CORRELL	3
ARMSTRONG	8	BONE	3	CARBERY	2	COSS	2
ARNOLD	2	BONNEY	1	CAREY	1	COTTRELL	3
ASKEW	4	BOONE	8	CARLETON	3	COUCH	2
ASKINS	1	BOOTH	2	CARNEY	3	COULSON	1
ATCHISON	1	BORLAND	10	CARPENTER	19	COULTER	6
ATWELL	1	BOSLEY	6	CARROLL	2	COVINGTON	1
ATWOOD	4	BOSWELL	2	CARTER	1	COWGILL	1
AUSTIN	2	BOTTOMS	2	CARVER	2	COX	15
BABCOCK	2	BOTTS	6	CASE	2	CRADDOCK	2
BACHTEL	2	BOUGHNER	1	CASSIDAY	2	CRAMER	5
BACON	6	BOWEN	1	CASTOR	1	CRANAGE	1
BADGER	3	BOWMAN	1	CASWELL	1	CRAVER	6
BAGANSTOS	1	BOYD	9	CHAMBERLAIN	2	CRAWFORD	3
BAGENSTOS	3	BOYDSTON	1	CHAMBERLIN	2	CRENSHAW	1
BAGGS	3	BOYER	2	CHANDLER	1	CRILL	2
BAIL	1	BOYLE	1	CHAPMAN	5	CRIPMAN	1
BAILEY	13	BOYNTON	1	CHASE	5	CRISMAN	1
BAILY	3	BRABROOK	7	CHEESMAN	1	CRISPIN	3
BAKER	2	BRACKEN	1	CHESHIRE	5	CROCKER	1
BALDWIN	7	BRACKENRIDGE	3	CHESNUT	1	CROMER	1
BALL	2	BRACKIN	1	CHILDS	2	CROOKHAM	1
BALSLEY	1	BRADY	1	CHIPMAN	2	CROSS	2
BARBER	1	BRAINARD	3	CHITTENDEN	5	CRUM	1
BARBOUR	1	BRAMER	3	CHOUTEAU	9	CULBERSTON	1
BARGAHISER	1	BRANDT	1	CHRISTAIN	1	CULBERTON	1
BARKER	6	BRATTEN	1	CLANEY	3	CULBERTSON	81
BARNES	14	BRAUGHTON	1	CLARK	27	CUMMINGS	1
BARNEY	1	BRAYTON	2	CLARKE	4	CUNNINGHAM	2
BARRETT	3	BREED	6	CLAXTON	1	CURRAN	2
BARTON	8	BREWER	2	CLEAVER	2	CURRY	1
BATES	2	BREWSTER	6	CLEMENS	1	CUSHMAN	29
BATY	1	BRICK	1	CLEMENTS	1	CUTTING	3
BEADLESTON	3	BRIDGES	5	CLEVER	1	CYPHER	2
BEALL	1	BROADBOOKS	1	CLOSE	2	DAINGERFIELD	1
BEAN	3	BROOKS	1	CLOSSEN	1	DALE	1
BEASON	1	BROPLEY	1	CLOUD	7	DALY	2
BEATY	3	BROSS	1	CLUTE	10	DANIELS	3
BECKET	2	BROWN	11	COCHRAN	1	DANN	1
BEEBE	2	BROWNLEE	1	CODDING	1	DARLAND	3
BEELER	3	BRYAN	13	CODDINGTON	1	DAVENFORT	1
BEELERS	2	BRYANT	1	COFFEE	1	DAVENPORT	5
BEEM	1	BUCKINGHAM	2	COFFIN	3	DAVIDSON	3
BENNETT	10	BUDD	9	COLE	1	DAVIE	3
BENT	1	BULLEN	2	COLEY	1	DAVIS	23
BERRYHILL	107	BURNELL	1	COLLIN	1	DAVISON	3

Surname	# of Land Parcels	Surname	# of Land Parcels	Surname	# of Land Parcels	Surname	# of Land Parcels
DEAN	4	FARNHAM	1	GOSNELL	1	HEALD	1
DEARBORN	1	FARQUHAR	3	GOUDY	3	HECK	1
DEEMER	2	FEARING	1	GOUGH	1	HECKMAN	1
DEITRICH	2	FENLON	2	GOWER	73	HEILMAYER	2
DELAHOYDE	9	FENTON	1	GRAHAM	7	HEILMYER	1
DELANO	1	FERGUSON	2	GRANT	1	HERRIMAN	2
DEMENT	2	FISHER	7	GRAVES	1	HERRON	1
DENINGTON	2	FISK	1	GRAYUM	1	HESS	2
DENISON	3	FLANAGAN	5	GREELEY	1	HIATT	10
DENNEY	1	FLATTERY	2	GREEN	1	HICKMAN	1
DEPEW	4	FLESHER	1	GRIDER	1	HIGGINBOTHAM	2
DEVINNAK	1	FLOYD	1	GRIDLEY	1	HIGGINSON	14
DEVRICKSON	1	FOLK	1	GRIER	5	HILL	6
DEWEY	3	FOLSOM	13	GRIFFIN	1	HILLMAN	3
DIBBLE	1	FORBY	1	GRINELL	1	HINER	1
DICKERSON	1	FORD	3	GRINNELL	36	HITCHCOCK	1
DIKEMAN	1	FOREMAN	1	GRISWOLD	10	HOBART	2
DILLON	3	FORSYTHE	7	GROSS	1	HOBSON	2
DINSMOOR	5	FOSS	4	GRUB	1	HODSKIN	2
DIX	10	FOSTER	1	GRUWELL	2	HOKE	1
DOBBIN	1	FOUTS	1	GUILD	5	HOLLENBACK	1
DOBBINS	2	FOWLER	1	GUNNELL	1	HOLLENBECK	11
DOBYNS	2	FOX	2	GURLEY	3	HOLLER	2
DODDS	2	FRAIZER	3	GWIN	12	HOLLEY	3
DONLAN	1	FRANCE	3	GWINN	2	HOLLIDAY	2
DONNEL	10	FRANCIS	3	HADDEN	1	HOLLOPETER	1
DORLING	1	FRANK	3	HAGERTY	1	HOLLY	2
DOUGHTY	3	FRAZIER	4	HAIFLEY	1	HOLMES	1
DOUGLASS	4	FREANER	1	HAINES	2	HOLYOKE	5
DOUNEY	2	FREDERIC	1	HALL	8	HONICON	1
DOWNEY	141	FRENCH	1	HALLETT	2	HONOCOL	1
DRAKE	14	FRIEND	1	HAM	3	HOOK	2
DRUMMOND	4	FRY	4	HAMBLETON	8	HOOPER	1
DRURY	1	FRYAR	1	HAMILTON	3	HOOVER	2
DUFFIELD	4	FULKER	4	HAMLIN	2	HORTON	2
DUGGAR	2	FULLER	5	HAMLINE	1	HOSICK	1
DUNGAN	2	FULTON	1	HAMMOND	1	HOVERSTICK	1
DUNNING	1	FUNK	4	HAND	2	HOWARD	9
DUNTON	4	FURBER	1	HANES	7	HOYT	1
DUPREE	1	GALLAGHER	3	HAPGOOD	4	HUBBARD	4
DWIGHT	1	GALLEHER	1	HARBINE	1	HUDSON	2
DWYER	1	GALLEY	2	HARDEN	1	HULL	1
DYLE	1	GAMBLE	1	HARDING	1	HUME	1
EARLEY	1	GANTZ	2	HARKLEROAD	3	HUMMEL	1
EASLEY	48	GARDINER	2	HARKLOADS	1	HUMPHREY	1
EASLY	1	GARDNER	9	HARMAN	2	HUNT	6
EASON	4	GARRETT	1	HARMON	2	HUNTINGTON	4
EASTER	1	GASKILL	1	HARNER	2	HURDEN	1
EBERHART	2	GATES	13	HARPER	3	HURLEY	1
EBY	2	GATHIELL	1	HARRINGTON	2	HURST	1
EDDY	5	GATLING	26	HARRIS	1	HUTCHENS	1
EDWARDS	30	GATTRELL	2	HARRISON	1	HUTCHESON	2
EGBERT	2	GAUMER	3	HARRY	2	HUTCHINS	7
EGERTON	1	GAUSE	2	HART	2	HYNES	1
EHRET	1	GEETING	4	HARTMAN	4	ILES	1
ELLIOTT	6	GIFFORD	23	HARVEY	1	INGMOND	2
ELLIS	3	GILCHRIST	2	HASE	1	IOWA	16
ELSON	1	GILL	1	HASTINGS	6	IRELAND	1
EMOTT	1	GILLELAND	2	HATFIELD	3	IS-FI-KE	1
ENGLISH	7	GILLETT	6	HATHAWAY	2	JACK	1
ESTES	1	GILMORE	8	HAVELY	1	JACKSON	2
ESTLICK	1	GINN	1	HAVENS	2	JACOB	3
EVANS	2	GIVINN	1	HAWES	1	JAMES	9
EVENS	1	GLADSON	1	HAWKS	3	JAMIESON	1
EWERS	1	GLAZE	3	HAY	4	JAMISON	1
EWING	5	GOLDEN	2	HAYES	6	JARRETT	1
FAHRNEY	7	GOODE	1	HAYS	11	JENKINS	4
FAIRBANK	2	GOODRICH	2	HAYTER	2	JENNINGS	2
FANT	1	GORDON	2	HAYWOOD	2	JEROME	3
FARMER	5	GORMAY	1	HAZLETON	3	JEWETT	2

Surname	# of Land Parcels	Surname	# of Land Parcels	Surname	# of Land Parcels	Surname	# of Land Parcels
JOHNSON	71	LOESCH	1	MCVEY	18	NORRIS	12
JOHNSTON	13	LOGAN	1	MEAD	10	NUSSBAUM	3
JONES	25	LONG	6	MEEKER	2	OGDEN	1
JUDD	13	LOONEY	1	MEIGS	2	OLIPHANT	1
KAPLE	1	LOOSE	10	MEILY	1	ORCUTT	2
KAUFFMAN	4	LORD	3	MENARY	2	ORR	1
KECK	2	LOTT	1	MENDENHALL	1	OSBORN	6
KEENAN	2	LOUD	1	MENETT	1	OTTO	2
KELLOGG	7	LOUGHLIN	1	MERCER	4	PAGE	1
KELLY	1	LOVE	2	MERRETT	1	PARCEL	2
KENNEDY	1	LOWRY	3	MERRITT	4	PARDEE	3
KENT	3	LUCAS	6	MERWIN	1	PARKER	15
KENWORTHY	13	LUCKHART	7	METCALF	1	PARKS	9
KEPPEL	4	LUKECART	2	METHVEN	1	PARMER	1
KERN	2	LYNASON	1	METZGER	1	PAROTT	1
KERSTEN	2	LYNN	1	MICHAEL	2	PARRISH	11
KESTER	1	LYON	1	MIDDLEKAUFF	2	PARSONS	3
KEYS	3	LYTLE	1	MILLAR	14	PASSON	1
KILLIN	1	MACKEY	1	MILLER	10	PATRICK	6
KING	6	MAGILL	1	MILLIKEN	2	PATTEE	7
KINGSMORE	1	MAHAN	1	MILLS	1	PATTERSON	3
KINSEY	2	MAHON	2	MISCHLICH	1	PAUL	1
KIRK	3	MALONE	5	MITCHELL	2	PAYNE	1
KIRKPATRICK	1	MANAT	1	MIX	2	PEARCE	2
KIRKWOOD	20	MANATT	46	MOATES	2	PEASE	1
KNEPPER	5	MANN	1	MOATS	2	PEGRAM	2
KNOTT	1	MARK	4	MONROE	1	PELTON	1
KNOX	3	MARKS	1	MONSON	2	PEOPLES	2
KORN	3	MARPOLE	1	MONTGOMERY	1	PERCY	1
KORNS	6	MARSH	3	MOODY	1	PEREGOY	1
KRIDLER	2	MARSHALL	2	MOORE	2	PERIN	1
KUNKEL	2	MARSON	1	MOREY	4	PERRY	1
KURT	1	MARTIN	6	MORGAN	13	PETERS	1
LADELEY	1	MARVIN	2	MORGANTHALER	1	PETTIBONE	1
LAITON	1	MASAY	1	MORISON	1	PETTIE	1
LALANDER	1	MASUY	1	MORLAND	1	PHELPS	7
LAMBRITE	7	MATHEWS	1	MORRIS	2	PHILLIPS	3
LAMSON	2	MATTESON	1	MORRISON	1	PIERCE	1
LANCEY	1	MAY	1	MORSMAN	3	PIERSOL	1
LANDEN	1	MAYER	1	MORTON	1	PIERSON	1
LANE	4	MCBRIDE	3	MOSELY	12	PIKE	4
LANGFORD	1	MCBURNEY	1	MOSSER	4	PINNEY	11
LAPHAM	1	MCCAGUE	3	MOTHERAL	26	PITT	2
LAREW	1	MCCALL	1	MOUSER	3	PLEAS	2
LARREW	2	MCCARTY	2	MUIRHIRD	1	PLEASANTS	1
LARUE	1	MCCLEIF	1	MUMMA	2	PLUM	1
LATIMER	3	MCCLELLAN	5	MUMMRA	1	PLUMB	1
LAUGHLIN	4	MCCLUNG	1	MURDOCK	2	PLYMPTON	3
LAWLESS	2	MCCLURE	1	MURPHY	1	POCOCK	1
LAWRENCE	6	MCCLUSKY	1	MURRAY	6	POLLARD	1
LAYLANDER	2	MCCORKLE	2	MUSGROVE	4	POOLE	1
LAYTEN	1	MCCORMICK	1	MYERS	6	PORTER	7
LAYTON	4	MCCRACKEN	1	NAYLOR	1	POTTER	1
LEE	3	MCCULLOUGH	1	NEAL	4	POWELL	2
LEHMAN	1	MCCUNE	1	NEFF	3	POWER	5
LEMMON	1	MCCURTAIN	1	NELSON	1	PRESTON	1
LENTZ	1	MCDONALD	4	NETHEROW	2	PRICE	1
LEONARD	3	MCDONNALD	2	NEWELL	1	PROCTOR	2
LESLIE	4	MCDOWELL	7	NEWHALL	1	PROPST	1
LIGHT	3	MCGARVEY	2	NEWKIRK	2	PROSSER	4
LILLEY	2	MCGARY	1	NEWMAN	3	PUFFINBURGER	2
LINN	3	MCKAY	2	NEWSHELL	1	PUGH	2
LINSTED	2	MCKEAN	2	NEWTON	1	PURCEFIELD	1
LISOR	2	MCKENZIE	2	NICHOLAS	1	PURDY	1
LISTON	4	MCKINNEY	5	NICHOLS	2	PUSEY	6
LITTLE	3	MCLAIN	14	NILES	1	PUTNAM	3
LLOYD	1	MCMILLAN	1	NINDE	3	QUACKENBUSH	1
LOCK	2	MCNABB	1	NIXON	1	QUIGGINS	1
LOCKHART	4	MCROY	1	NOBLE	4	RAGADALE	1
LOEBER	2	MCVAY	5	NOLAND	1	RAMAY	1

Surname	# of Land Parcels	Surname	# of Land Parcels	Surname	# of Land Parcels	Surname	# of Land Parcels
RANKIN	2	SHEPARD	2	SWEET	1	WILCOX	1
REDHEAD	2	SHEPHARD	1	SWIFT	1	WILDEN	2
REDMAN	2	SHERMAN	9	SWITZER	4	WILDER	2
REDMOND	3	SHERWOOD	7	SYLVESTER	6	WILDS	2
REED	5	SHEWAKER	1	TALBOT	1	WILLIAMS	30
RENO	100	SHIELDS	1	TALBOTT	15	WILLIAMSON	9
REVERE	1	SHIFFER	2	TARR	1	WILLINGHAM	25
REYNOLDS	9	SHIPLEY	1	TAYLOR	28	WILLIS	1
RHODES	1	SHOALS	2	TEEL	2	WILSEY	1
RHULE	3	SHOEMAKER	4	TERRY	4	WILSON	15
RICE	3	SHOVER	1	THOMAS	4	WILTSE	1
RICHARDSON	1	SHREVE	3	THOMPSON	7	WIMER	1
RICKER	1	SIGAFOOS	4	THORN	4	WINDERS	1
RICKEY	1	SIGLER	2	THORNE	1	WINELAND	1
RIGGS	1	SILPATH	1	TIBBALS	13	WINN	1
RIGHTMYER	4	SIMMONS	1	TICE	1	WINSLOW	4
RILEY	1	SIMPKINS	3	TILL	1	WISDEN	1
RIVERS	10	SIMPSON	3	TIPPIE	3	WITHROW	1
ROARK	1	SKEELS	1	TOLAND	1	WOLCOTT	1
ROBBERTS	1	SKINNER	12	TOMPKINS	2	WOLFE	8
ROBBINS	4	SLACK	2	TOSSE	2	WOOD	6
ROBERTS	7	SLADDEN	1	TOUSEY	17	WOODARD	2
ROBERTSON	3	SMITH	60	TRACY	6	WOODS	1
ROBINS	2	SMOTHERS	2	TRICKER	3	WOODWARD	6
ROBINSON	11	SNODDY	3	TRUMAN	6	WOOLARD	2
ROBISON	1	SNODGRASS	1	TUCKER	1	WOOLVERTON	1
RODGERS	2	SNOOKS	3	TUDOR	1	WRENN	2
ROGERS	4	SNOW	7	TURNER	2	WRIGHT	4
ROHRER	1	SNOWDEN	1	TUTHILL	1	WYATT	1
RORTY	1	SNYDER	14	TUTTLE	5	WYMORE	2
ROSS	5	SOHN	1	TYLER	1	YATES	1
ROUSSEAU	1	SPANGLER	1	TYSON	1	YOUNG	1
ROWLAND	2	SPENCER	11	UNDERWOOD	1	ZEIGLER	2
RUCKER	1	SPERRY	1	UNGER	1	ZIMMERMAN	1
RUSSELL	3	SPONSLER	1	UPDEGRAFF	4	
RUTLEDGE	6	SPRINGER	1	VAN ANTWERP	2	
RYAN	3	SPURRIER	2	VANSCHOYCK	1	
RYEON	3	SQUIRES	2	VERNON	2	
SACKET	2	ST JOHN	4	VESTAL	5	
SAMSON	1	STACY	1	VOUGHT	1	
SANBORN	1	STALLINGS	1	WADDELL	3	
SANDERS	6	STANLEY	4	WADE	2	
SANFORD	2	STEEL	2	WALKER	3	
SANXAY	42	STEELE	4	WALLACK	2	
SARGENT	20	STEPHENS	2	WARD	3	
SARGOOD	3	STERRET	1	WARFIELD	7	
SATCHELL	1	STEVENS	5	WASSON	2	
SATER	1	STEVENSON	1	WATKINS	1	
SAUNDERS	2	STEWART	1	WATSON	27	
SAVILLE	1	STILES	1	WATTS	1	
SAXTON	1	STIVENS	1	WEAVER	1	
SCHIRCLIFF	1	STIX	1	WEBBER	1	
SCHMUCKER	3	STOCKDALE	8	WEISE	1	
SCHNEIDER	1	STODDARD	4	WEISER	1	
SCHOOLEY	1	STOKES	1	WEIST	3	
SCOTT	9	STONEHOCKER	5	WELCH	2	
SCRUGS	1	STRONG	1	WELLER	1	
SEARIGHT	2	STROUSE	1	WELLS	1	
SEARS	7	STROW	2	WENTZ	1	
SELLEW	1	STRUBLE	6	WEST	5	
SEVERANCE	1	STUBBINS	1	WESTCOTT	1	
SEVERNS	2	STUFF	2	WHEATLEY	6	
SEYMOUR	2	STURGEON	1	WHEELER	8	
SHARP	4	SUMMERS	4	WHERRY	7	
SHARRITT	3	SUMNER	11	WHITAKER	3	
SHAUL	3	SUTTON	8	WHITCOMB	2	
SHAY	1	SWAIM	4	WHITE	34	
SHAYLER	1	SWAIN	1	WHITLOCK	1	
SHEFFER	2	SWANEY	2	WHITNEY	1	
SHELEY	2	SWART	2	WICKHAM	2	

Surname/Township Index

This Index allows you to determine which *Township Map Group(s)* contain individuals with the following surnames. Each *Map Group* has a corresponding full-name index of all individuals who obtained patents for land within its Congressional township's borders. After each index you will find the Patent Map to which it refers, and just thereafter, you can view the township's Road Map and Historical Map, with the latter map displaying streams, railroads, and more.

So, once you find your Surname here, proceed to the Index at the beginning of the **Map Group** indicated below.

Surname	Map Group	Parcels of Land	Meridian/Township/Range		
ADAIR	**7**	1	5th PM	80-N	14-W
ADAMS	**15**	1	5th PM	78-N	14-W
" "	**12**	1	5th PM	79-N	13-W
ADDLEMAN	**8**	1	5th PM	80-N	13-W
ADKINS	**5**	1	5th PM	80-N	16-W
AHERN	**9**	4	5th PM	79-N	16-W
AKIN	**1**	2	5th PM	81-N	16-W
ALEXANDER	**1**	3	5th PM	81-N	16-W
" "	**16**	1	5th PM	78-N	13-W
" "	**3**	1	5th PM	81-N	14-W
ALLEN	**9**	5	5th PM	79-N	16-W
" "	**11**	3	5th PM	79-N	14-W
" "	**15**	2	5th PM	78-N	14-W
" "	**14**	1	5th PM	78-N	15-W
" "	**6**	1	5th PM	80-N	15-W
ALLOWAY	**13**	1	5th PM	78-N	16-W
AMMON	**7**	3	5th PM	80-N	14-W
ANDERSON	**8**	1	5th PM	80-N	13-W
ANDREWS	**16**	1	5th PM	78-N	13-W
ANGLE	**4**	1	5th PM	81-N	13-W
ANTHONY	**3**	7	5th PM	81-N	14-W
" "	**6**	4	5th PM	80-N	15-W
" "	**1**	2	5th PM	81-N	16-W
APPLEGATE	**13**	3	5th PM	78-N	16-W
" "	**14**	1	5th PM	78-N	15-W
ARCHER	**10**	1	5th PM	79-N	15-W
ARMITAGE	**13**	1	5th PM	78-N	16-W
ARMSTRONG	**4**	3	5th PM	81-N	13-W
" "	**7**	2	5th PM	80-N	14-W
" "	**3**	2	5th PM	81-N	14-W
" "	**1**	1	5th PM	81-N	16-W
ARNOLD	**13**	2	5th PM	78-N	16-W
ASKEW	**12**	4	5th PM	79-N	13-W
ASKINS	**8**	1	5th PM	80-N	13-W
ATCHISON	**8**	1	5th PM	80-N	13-W
ATWELL	**1**	1	5th PM	81-N	16-W
ATWOOD	**6**	3	5th PM	80-N	15-W
" "	**4**	1	5th PM	81-N	13-W
AUSTIN	**10**	2	5th PM	79-N	15-W
BABCOCK	**6**	1	5th PM	80-N	15-W
" "	**3**	1	5th PM	81-N	14-W
BACHTEL	**7**	2	5th PM	80-N	14-W
BACON	**5**	4	5th PM	80-N	16-W
" "	**15**	1	5th PM	78-N	14-W

Surname	Map Group	Parcels of Land	Meridian/Township/Range
BACON (Cont'd)	**7**	1	5th PM 80-N 14-W
BADGER	**8**	3	5th PM 80-N 13-W
BAGANSTOS	**3**	1	5th PM 81-N 14-W
BAGENSTOS	**3**	3	5th PM 81-N 14-W
BAGGS	**3**	3	5th PM 81-N 14-W
BAIL	**8**	1	5th PM 80-N 13-W
BAILEY	**13**	6	5th PM 78-N 16-W
" "	**5**	4	5th PM 80-N 16-W
" "	**6**	2	5th PM 80-N 15-W
" "	**2**	1	5th PM 81-N 15-W
BAILY	**5**	3	5th PM 80-N 16-W
BAKER	**16**	2	5th PM 78-N 13-W
BALDWIN	**10**	6	5th PM 79-N 15-W
" "	**13**	1	5th PM 78-N 16-W
BALL	**16**	2	5th PM 78-N 13-W
BALSLEY	**12**	1	5th PM 79-N 13-W
BARBER	**6**	1	5th PM 80-N 15-W
BARBOUR	**14**	1	5th PM 78-N 15-W
BARGAHISER	**9**	1	5th PM 79-N 16-W
BARKER	**16**	5	5th PM 78-N 13-W
" "	**12**	1	5th PM 79-N 13-W
BARNES	**15**	7	5th PM 78-N 14-W
" "	**14**	3	5th PM 78-N 15-W
" "	**6**	2	5th PM 80-N 15-W
" "	**3**	1	5th PM 81-N 14-W
" "	**2**	1	5th PM 81-N 15-W
BARNEY	**1**	1	5th PM 81-N 16-W
BARRETT	**3**	2	5th PM 81-N 14-W
" "	**6**	1	5th PM 80-N 15-W
BARTON	**6**	4	5th PM 80-N 15-W
" "	**8**	2	5th PM 80-N 13-W
" "	**7**	2	5th PM 80-N 14-W
BATES	**2**	2	5th PM 81-N 15-W
BATY	**4**	1	5th PM 81-N 13-W
BEADLESTON	**9**	3	5th PM 79-N 16-W
BEALL	**6**	1	5th PM 80-N 15-W
BEAN	**8**	1	5th PM 80-N 13-W
" "	**7**	1	5th PM 80-N 14-W
" "	**2**	1	5th PM 81-N 15-W
BEASON	**14**	1	5th PM 78-N 15-W
BEATY	**4**	3	5th PM 81-N 13-W
BECKET	**3**	2	5th PM 81-N 14-W
BEEBE	**12**	1	5th PM 79-N 13-W
" "	**4**	1	5th PM 81-N 13-W
BEELER	**9**	2	5th PM 79-N 16-W
" "	**14**	1	5th PM 78-N 15-W
BEELERS	**9**	2	5th PM 79-N 16-W
BEEM	**2**	1	5th PM 81-N 15-W
BENNETT	**7**	6	5th PM 80-N 14-W
" "	**3**	3	5th PM 81-N 14-W
" "	**13**	1	5th PM 78-N 16-W
BENT	**9**	1	5th PM 79-N 16-W
BERRYHILL	**16**	16	5th PM 78-N 13-W
" "	**14**	12	5th PM 78-N 15-W
" "	**13**	11	5th PM 78-N 16-W
" "	**15**	10	5th PM 78-N 14-W
" "	**4**	10	5th PM 81-N 13-W
" "	**11**	8	5th PM 79-N 14-W
" "	**3**	8	5th PM 81-N 14-W
" "	**10**	7	5th PM 79-N 15-W

Surname	Map Group	Parcels of Land	Meridian/Township/Range
BERRYHILL (Cont'd)	**7**	6	5th PM 80-N 14-W
" "	**8**	5	5th PM 80-N 13-W
" "	**12**	3	5th PM 79-N 13-W
" "	**6**	3	5th PM 80-N 15-W
" "	**5**	3	5th PM 80-N 16-W
" "	**9**	2	5th PM 79-N 16-W
" "	**2**	2	5th PM 81-N 15-W
" "	**1**	1	5th PM 81-N 16-W
BETTS	**9**	5	5th PM 79-N 16-W
" "	**13**	3	5th PM 78-N 16-W
BEVER	**8**	1	5th PM 80-N 13-W
BIGLER	**8**	1	5th PM 80-N 13-W
BILL	**3**	5	5th PM 81-N 14-W
" "	**4**	3	5th PM 81-N 13-W
" "	**9**	2	5th PM 79-N 16-W
BINEGAR	**14**	1	5th PM 78-N 15-W
BINFORD	**13**	5	5th PM 78-N 16-W
BINGEY	**3**	1	5th PM 81-N 14-W
BIRD	**15**	9	5th PM 78-N 14-W
" "	**11**	4	5th PM 79-N 14-W
BIXBY	**9**	1	5th PM 79-N 16-W
" "	**1**	1	5th PM 81-N 16-W
BIXLER	**13**	1	5th PM 78-N 16-W
BLACK	**9**	3	5th PM 79-N 16-W
" "	**4**	1	5th PM 81-N 13-W
BLAKE	**4**	4	5th PM 81-N 13-W
" "	**2**	1	5th PM 81-N 15-W
BLISH	**9**	2	5th PM 79-N 16-W
BLOUNT	**11**	1	5th PM 79-N 14-W
BLUE	**3**	1	5th PM 81-N 14-W
BOGGS	**8**	1	5th PM 80-N 13-W
BOND	**9**	1	5th PM 79-N 16-W
" "	**1**	1	5th PM 81-N 16-W
BONE	**14**	2	5th PM 78-N 15-W
" "	**11**	1	5th PM 79-N 14-W
BONNEY	**6**	1	5th PM 80-N 15-W
BOONE	**6**	7	5th PM 80-N 15-W
" "	**13**	1	5th PM 78-N 16-W
BOOTH	**9**	1	5th PM 79-N 16-W
" "	**4**	1	5th PM 81-N 13-W
BORLAND	**9**	7	5th PM 79-N 16-W
" "	**7**	2	5th PM 80-N 14-W
" "	**14**	1	5th PM 78-N 15-W
BOSLEY	**8**	4	5th PM 80-N 13-W
" "	**14**	1	5th PM 78-N 15-W
" "	**10**	1	5th PM 79-N 15-W
BOSWELL	**15**	2	5th PM 78-N 14-W
BOTTOMS	**9**	2	5th PM 79-N 16-W
BOTTS	**1**	6	5th PM 81-N 16-W
BOUGHNER	**3**	1	5th PM 81-N 14-W
BOWEN	**3**	1	5th PM 81-N 14-W
BOWMAN	**13**	1	5th PM 78-N 16-W
BOYD	**10**	9	5th PM 79-N 15-W
BOYDSTON	**15**	1	5th PM 78-N 14-W
BOYER	**13**	2	5th PM 78-N 16-W
BOYLE	**16**	1	5th PM 78-N 13-W
BOYNTON	**7**	1	5th PM 80-N 14-W
BRABROOK	**2**	6	5th PM 81-N 15-W
" "	**1**	1	5th PM 81-N 16-W
BRACKEN	**15**	1	5th PM 78-N 14-W

Surname	Map Group	Parcels of Land	Meridian/Township/Range
BRACKENRIDGE	**13**	3	5th PM 78-N 16-W
BRACKIN	**16**	1	5th PM 78-N 13-W
BRADY	**12**	1	5th PM 79-N 13-W
BRAINARD	**13**	3	5th PM 78-N 16-W
BRAMER	**12**	3	5th PM 79-N 13-W
BRANDT	**5**	1	5th PM 80-N 16-W
BRATTEN	**7**	1	5th PM 80-N 14-W
BRAUGHTON	**2**	1	5th PM 81-N 15-W
BRAYTON	**5**	2	5th PM 80-N 16-W
BREED	**9**	4	5th PM 79-N 16-W
" "	**13**	2	5th PM 78-N 16-W
BREWER	**4**	1	5th PM 81-N 13-W
" "	**3**	1	5th PM 81-N 14-W
BREWSTER	**11**	3	5th PM 79-N 14-W
" "	**10**	3	5th PM 79-N 15-W
BRICK	**11**	1	5th PM 79-N 14-W
BRIDGES	**13**	4	5th PM 78-N 16-W
" "	**15**	1	5th PM 78-N 14-W
BROADBOOKS	**7**	1	5th PM 80-N 14-W
BROOKS	**14**	1	5th PM 78-N 15-W
BROPLEY	**14**	1	5th PM 78-N 15-W
BROSS	**3**	1	5th PM 81-N 14-W
BROWN	**9**	4	5th PM 79-N 16-W
" "	**4**	3	5th PM 81-N 13-W
" "	**1**	2	5th PM 81-N 16-W
" "	**7**	1	5th PM 80-N 14-W
" "	**3**	1	5th PM 81-N 14-W
BROWNLEE	**13**	1	5th PM 78-N 16-W
BRYAN	**14**	7	5th PM 78-N 15-W
" "	**11**	3	5th PM 79-N 14-W
" "	**10**	3	5th PM 79-N 15-W
BRYANT	**9**	1	5th PM 79-N 16-W
BUCKINGHAM	**16**	1	5th PM 78-N 13-W
" "	**5**	1	5th PM 80-N 16-W
BUDD	**3**	8	5th PM 81-N 14-W
" "	**1**	1	5th PM 81-N 16-W
BULLEN	**5**	2	5th PM 80-N 16-W
BURNELL	**5**	1	5th PM 80-N 16-W
BURNS	**3**	2	5th PM 81-N 14-W
BURRELL	**8**	1	5th PM 80-N 13-W
BURTON	**6**	3	5th PM 80-N 15-W
" "	**5**	1	5th PM 80-N 16-W
BUSH	**8**	1	5th PM 80-N 13-W
BUTCHER	**3**	1	5th PM 81-N 14-W
BUTLER	**13**	1	5th PM 78-N 16-W
" "	**7**	1	5th PM 80-N 14-W
" "	**1**	1	5th PM 81-N 16-W
BUZZARD	**7**	1	5th PM 80-N 14-W
BYERS	**13**	2	5th PM 78-N 16-W
BYINGTON	**16**	3	5th PM 78-N 13-W
" "	**14**	2	5th PM 78-N 15-W
" "	**13**	2	5th PM 78-N 16-W
CADWALADER	**4**	1	5th PM 81-N 13-W
CALDWELL	**14**	1	5th PM 78-N 15-W
" "	**10**	1	5th PM 79-N 15-W
CALKINS	**2**	1	5th PM 81-N 15-W
CAMPBELL	**10**	5	5th PM 79-N 15-W
" "	**9**	3	5th PM 79-N 16-W
" "	**3**	2	5th PM 81-N 14-W
" "	**2**	2	5th PM 81-N 15-W

Surname	Map Group	Parcels of Land	Meridian/Township/Range		
CAMPBELL (Cont'd)	**15**	1	5th PM	78-N	14-W
CANNON	**12**	5	5th PM	79-N	13-W
CANTRIL	**13**	1	5th PM	78-N	16-W
CAPLES	**4**	1	5th PM	81-N	13-W
CARBERRY	**1**	1	5th PM	81-N	16-W
CARBERY	**15**	2	5th PM	78-N	14-W
CAREY	**12**	1	5th PM	79-N	13-W
CARLETON	**7**	2	5th PM	80-N	14-W
" "	**9**	1	5th PM	79-N	16-W
CARNEY	**2**	3	5th PM	81-N	15-W
CARPENTER	**9**	8	5th PM	79-N	16-W
" "	**14**	7	5th PM	78-N	15-W
" "	**12**	2	5th PM	79-N	13-W
" "	**16**	1	5th PM	78-N	13-W
" "	**13**	1	5th PM	78-N	16-W
CARROLL	**4**	2	5th PM	81-N	13-W
CARTER	**13**	1	5th PM	78-N	16-W
CARVER	**16**	2	5th PM	78-N	13-W
CASE	**13**	2	5th PM	78-N	16-W
CASSIDAY	**10**	2	5th PM	79-N	15-W
CASTOR	**13**	1	5th PM	78-N	16-W
CASWELL	**9**	1	5th PM	79-N	16-W
CHAMBERLAIN	**14**	2	5th PM	78-N	15-W
CHAMBERLIN	**14**	2	5th PM	78-N	15-W
CHANDLER	**9**	1	5th PM	79-N	16-W
CHAPMAN	**8**	5	5th PM	80-N	13-W
CHASE	**14**	3	5th PM	78-N	15-W
" "	**4**	2	5th PM	81-N	13-W
CHEESMAN	**14**	1	5th PM	78-N	15-W
CHESHIRE	**13**	3	5th PM	78-N	16-W
" "	**9**	2	5th PM	79-N	16-W
CHESNUT	**15**	1	5th PM	78-N	14-W
CHILDS	**5**	1	5th PM	80-N	16-W
" "	**1**	1	5th PM	81-N	16-W
CHIPMAN	**11**	2	5th PM	79-N	14-W
CHITTENDEN	**12**	5	5th PM	79-N	13-W
CHOUTEAU	**6**	9	5th PM	80-N	15-W
CHRISTAIN	**15**	1	5th PM	78-N	14-W
CLANEY	**2**	2	5th PM	81-N	15-W
" "	**1**	1	5th PM	81-N	16-W
CLARK	**6**	12	5th PM	80-N	15-W
" "	**16**	10	5th PM	78-N	13-W
" "	**9**	2	5th PM	79-N	16-W
" "	**13**	1	5th PM	78-N	16-W
" "	**11**	1	5th PM	79-N	14-W
" "	**4**	1	5th PM	81-N	13-W
CLARKE	**2**	4	5th PM	81-N	15-W
CLAXTON	**13**	1	5th PM	78-N	16-W
CLEAVER	**16**	1	5th PM	78-N	13-W
" "	**15**	1	5th PM	78-N	14-W
CLEMENS	**11**	1	5th PM	79-N	14-W
CLEMENTS	**11**	1	5th PM	79-N	14-W
CLEVER	**16**	1	5th PM	78-N	13-W
CLOSE	**16**	1	5th PM	78-N	13-W
" "	**12**	1	5th PM	79-N	13-W
CLOSSEN	**2**	1	5th PM	81-N	15-W
CLOUD	**8**	3	5th PM	80-N	13-W
" "	**13**	2	5th PM	78-N	16-W
" "	**9**	2	5th PM	79-N	16-W
CLUTE	**13**	4	5th PM	78-N	16-W

Surname	Map Group	Parcels of Land	Meridian/Township/Range		
CLUTE (Cont'd)	6	4	5th PM	80-N	15-W
" "	7	2	5th PM	80-N	14-W
COCHRAN	10	1	5th PM	79-N	15-W
CODDING	2	1	5th PM	81-N	15-W
CODDINGTON	3	1	5th PM	81-N	14-W
COFFEE	14	1	5th PM	78-N	15-W
COFFIN	7	2	5th PM	80-N	14-W
" "	8	1	5th PM	80-N	13-W
COLE	4	1	5th PM	81-N	13-W
COLEY	12	1	5th PM	79-N	13-W
COLLIN	2	1	5th PM	81-N	15-W
COLLINS	12	1	5th PM	79-N	13-W
" "	7	1	5th PM	80-N	14-W
COLVIN	5	6	5th PM	80-N	16-W
COLYER	9	3	5th PM	79-N	16-W
COMBE	15	2	5th PM	78-N	14-W
" "	14	1	5th PM	78-N	15-W
COMSTOCK	8	1	5th PM	80-N	13-W
" "	1	1	5th PM	81-N	16-W
CONEY	9	1	5th PM	79-N	16-W
CONNELLY	15	8	5th PM	78-N	14-W
" "	7	4	5th PM	80-N	14-W
" "	16	3	5th PM	78-N	13-W
" "	9	3	5th PM	79-N	16-W
" "	8	1	5th PM	80-N	13-W
" "	4	1	5th PM	81-N	13-W
CONNER	9	1	5th PM	79-N	16-W
" "	7	1	5th PM	80-N	14-W
CONVERS	2	1	5th PM	81-N	15-W
CONWAY	1	3	5th PM	81-N	16-W
COOK	16	4	5th PM	78-N	13-W
" "	12	2	5th PM	79-N	13-W
" "	4	1	5th PM	81-N	13-W
COOLEY	12	1	5th PM	79-N	13-W
COOPER	12	1	5th PM	79-N	13-W
COPE	16	4	5th PM	78-N	13-W
" "	15	3	5th PM	78-N	14-W
" "	14	3	5th PM	78-N	15-W
CORBIN	10	5	5th PM	79-N	15-W
CORNWELL	16	4	5th PM	78-N	13-W
CORRELL	6	1	5th PM	80-N	15-W
" "	2	1	5th PM	81-N	15-W
" "	1	1	5th PM	81-N	16-W
COSS	1	2	5th PM	81-N	16-W
COTTRELL	2	3	5th PM	81-N	15-W
COUCH	2	2	5th PM	81-N	15-W
COULSON	2	1	5th PM	81-N	15-W
COULTER	1	5	5th PM	81-N	16-W
" "	9	1	5th PM	79-N	16-W
COVINGTON	8	1	5th PM	80-N	13-W
COWGILL	15	1	5th PM	78-N	14-W
COX	14	4	5th PM	78-N	15-W
" "	13	4	5th PM	78-N	16-W
" "	16	2	5th PM	78-N	13-W
" "	12	1	5th PM	79-N	13-W
" "	9	1	5th PM	79-N	16-W
" "	8	1	5th PM	80-N	13-W
" "	7	1	5th PM	80-N	14-W
" "	3	1	5th PM	81-N	14-W
CRADDOCK	15	2	5th PM	78-N	14-W

Surname	Map Group	Parcels of Land	Meridian/Township/Range		
CRAMER	**9**	3	5th PM	79-N	16-W
" "	**1**	2	5th PM	81-N	16-W
CRANAGE	**16**	1	5th PM	78-N	13-W
CRAVER	**13**	4	5th PM	78-N	16-W
" "	**14**	2	5th PM	78-N	15-W
CRAWFORD	**16**	1	5th PM	78-N	13-W
" "	**4**	1	5th PM	81-N	13-W
" "	**3**	1	5th PM	81-N	14-W
CRENSHAW	**8**	1	5th PM	80-N	13-W
CRILL	**13**	2	5th PM	78-N	16-W
CRIPMAN	**2**	1	5th PM	81-N	15-W
CRISMAN	**13**	1	5th PM	78-N	16-W
CRISPIN	**9**	3	5th PM	79-N	16-W
CROCKER	**4**	1	5th PM	81-N	13-W
CROMER	**9**	1	5th PM	79-N	16-W
CROOKHAM	**14**	1	5th PM	78-N	15-W
CROSS	**16**	1	5th PM	78-N	13-W
" "	**2**	1	5th PM	81-N	15-W
CRUM	**12**	1	5th PM	79-N	13-W
CULBERSTON	**6**	1	5th PM	80-N	15-W
CULBERTON	**14**	1	5th PM	78-N	15-W
CULBERTSON	**9**	20	5th PM	79-N	16-W
" "	**14**	13	5th PM	78-N	15-W
" "	**10**	9	5th PM	79-N	15-W
" "	**16**	8	5th PM	78-N	13-W
" "	**13**	8	5th PM	78-N	16-W
" "	**12**	6	5th PM	79-N	13-W
" "	**4**	5	5th PM	81-N	13-W
" "	**1**	5	5th PM	81-N	16-W
" "	**8**	3	5th PM	80-N	13-W
" "	**15**	1	5th PM	78-N	14-W
" "	**6**	1	5th PM	80-N	15-W
" "	**5**	1	5th PM	80-N	16-W
" "	**2**	1	5th PM	81-N	15-W
CUMMINGS	**9**	1	5th PM	79-N	16-W
CUNNINGHAM	**16**	1	5th PM	78-N	13-W
" "	**8**	1	5th PM	80-N	13-W
CURRAN	**12**	2	5th PM	79-N	13-W
CURRY	**15**	1	5th PM	78-N	14-W
CUSHMAN	**1**	28	5th PM	81-N	16-W
" "	**11**	1	5th PM	79-N	14-W
CUTTING	**12**	2	5th PM	79-N	13-W
" "	**16**	1	5th PM	78-N	13-W
CYPHER	**1**	2	5th PM	81-N	16-W
DAINGERFIELD	**3**	1	5th PM	81-N	14-W
DALE	**10**	1	5th PM	79-N	15-W
DALY	**10**	2	5th PM	79-N	15-W
DANIELS	**7**	3	5th PM	80-N	14-W
DANN	**7**	1	5th PM	80-N	14-W
DARLAND	**15**	3	5th PM	78-N	14-W
DAVENFORT	**3**	1	5th PM	81-N	14-W
DAVENPORT	**3**	3	5th PM	81-N	14-W
" "	**2**	2	5th PM	81-N	15-W
DAVIDSON	**4**	3	5th PM	81-N	13-W
DAVIE	**8**	3	5th PM	80-N	13-W
DAVIS	**12**	10	5th PM	79-N	13-W
" "	**16**	8	5th PM	78-N	13-W
" "	**2**	2	5th PM	81-N	15-W
" "	**14**	1	5th PM	78-N	15-W
" "	**11**	1	5th PM	79-N	14-W

Surname	Map Group	Parcels of Land	Meridian/Township/Range		
DAVIS (Cont'd)	**4**	1	5th PM	81-N	13-W
DAVISON	**6**	2	5th PM	80-N	15-W
" "	**12**	1	5th PM	79-N	13-W
DEAN	**10**	3	5th PM	79-N	15-W
" "	**14**	1	5th PM	78-N	15-W
DEARBORN	**12**	1	5th PM	79-N	13-W
DEEMER	**7**	1	5th PM	80-N	14-W
" "	**5**	1	5th PM	80-N	16-W
DEITRICH	**16**	2	5th PM	78-N	13-W
DELAHOYDE	**6**	9	5th PM	80-N	15-W
DELANO	**7**	1	5th PM	80-N	14-W
DEMENT	**14**	2	5th PM	78-N	15-W
DENINGTON	**12**	2	5th PM	79-N	13-W
DENISON	**8**	2	5th PM	80-N	13-W
" "	**2**	1	5th PM	81-N	15-W
DENNEY	**5**	1	5th PM	80-N	16-W
DEPEW	**11**	2	5th PM	79-N	14-W
" "	**9**	2	5th PM	79-N	16-W
DEVINNAK	**3**	1	5th PM	81-N	14-W
DEVRICKSON	**13**	1	5th PM	78-N	16-W
DEWEY	**13**	3	5th PM	78-N	16-W
DIBBLE	**8**	1	5th PM	80-N	13-W
DICKERSON	**4**	1	5th PM	81-N	13-W
DIKEMAN	**11**	1	5th PM	79-N	14-W
DILLON	**16**	2	5th PM	78-N	13-W
" "	**2**	1	5th PM	81-N	15-W
DINSMOOR	**3**	5	5th PM	81-N	14-W
DIX	**6**	7	5th PM	80-N	15-W
" "	**7**	2	5th PM	80-N	14-W
" "	**5**	1	5th PM	80-N	16-W
DOBBIN	**11**	1	5th PM	79-N	14-W
DOBBINS	**4**	2	5th PM	81-N	13-W
DOBYNS	**10**	2	5th PM	79-N	15-W
DODDS	**16**	2	5th PM	78-N	13-W
DONLAN	**8**	1	5th PM	80-N	13-W
DONNEL	**7**	6	5th PM	80-N	14-W
" "	**5**	4	5th PM	80-N	16-W
DORLING	**15**	1	5th PM	78-N	14-W
DOUGHTY	**4**	3	5th PM	81-N	13-W
DOUGLASS	**9**	2	5th PM	79-N	16-W
" "	**6**	2	5th PM	80-N	15-W
DOUNEY	**16**	2	5th PM	78-N	13-W
DOWNEY	**13**	28	5th PM	78-N	16-W
" "	**16**	25	5th PM	78-N	13-W
" "	**5**	20	5th PM	80-N	16-W
" "	**9**	15	5th PM	79-N	16-W
" "	**14**	11	5th PM	78-N	15-W
" "	**12**	10	5th PM	79-N	13-W
" "	**1**	8	5th PM	81-N	16-W
" "	**8**	5	5th PM	80-N	13-W
" "	**4**	5	5th PM	81-N	13-W
" "	**3**	5	5th PM	81-N	14-W
" "	**7**	4	5th PM	80-N	14-W
" "	**15**	2	5th PM	78-N	14-W
" "	**11**	1	5th PM	79-N	14-W
" "	**6**	1	5th PM	80-N	15-W
" "	**2**	1	5th PM	81-N	15-W
DRAKE	**7**	8	5th PM	80-N	14-W
" "	**3**	4	5th PM	81-N	14-W
" "	**8**	2	5th PM	80-N	13-W

Surname	Map Group	Parcels of Land	Meridian/Township/Range
DRUMMOND	**8**	4	5th PM 80-N 13-W
DRURY	**5**	1	5th PM 80-N 16-W
DUFFIELD	**4**	4	5th PM 81-N 13-W
DUGGAR	**13**	2	5th PM 78-N 16-W
DUNGAN	**13**	2	5th PM 78-N 16-W
DUNNING	**5**	1	5th PM 80-N 16-W
DUNTON	**3**	4	5th PM 81-N 14-W
DUPREE	**13**	1	5th PM 78-N 16-W
DWIGHT	**2**	1	5th PM 81-N 15-W
DWYER	**7**	1	5th PM 80-N 14-W
DYLE	**4**	1	5th PM 81-N 13-W
EARLEY	**10**	1	5th PM 79-N 15-W
EASLEY	**14**	15	5th PM 78-N 15-W
" "	**16**	8	5th PM 78-N 13-W
" "	**11**	5	5th PM 79-N 14-W
" "	**1**	5	5th PM 81-N 16-W
" "	**10**	4	5th PM 79-N 15-W
" "	**6**	3	5th PM 80-N 15-W
" "	**13**	2	5th PM 78-N 16-W
" "	**4**	2	5th PM 81-N 13-W
" "	**3**	2	5th PM 81-N 14-W
" "	**12**	1	5th PM 79-N 13-W
" "	**9**	1	5th PM 79-N 16-W
EASLY	**10**	1	5th PM 79-N 15-W
EASON	**10**	2	5th PM 79-N 15-W
" "	**15**	1	5th PM 78-N 14-W
" "	**14**	1	5th PM 78-N 15-W
EASTER	**9**	1	5th PM 79-N 16-W
EBERHART	**3**	2	5th PM 81-N 14-W
EBY	**13**	2	5th PM 78-N 16-W
EDDY	**5**	2	5th PM 80-N 16-W
" "	**2**	2	5th PM 81-N 15-W
" "	**15**	1	5th PM 78-N 14-W
EDWARDS	**11**	16	5th PM 79-N 14-W
" "	**6**	6	5th PM 80-N 15-W
" "	**13**	3	5th PM 78-N 16-W
" "	**12**	3	5th PM 79-N 13-W
" "	**8**	2	5th PM 80-N 13-W
EGBERT	**7**	2	5th PM 80-N 14-W
EGERTON	**13**	1	5th PM 78-N 16-W
EHRET	**16**	1	5th PM 78-N 13-W
ELLIOTT	**6**	3	5th PM 80-N 15-W
" "	**13**	1	5th PM 78-N 16-W
" "	**8**	1	5th PM 80-N 13-W
" "	**2**	1	5th PM 81-N 15-W
ELLIS	**10**	2	5th PM 79-N 15-W
" "	**2**	1	5th PM 81-N 15-W
ELSON	**3**	1	5th PM 81-N 14-W
EMOTT	**2**	1	5th PM 81-N 15-W
ENGLISH	**13**	5	5th PM 78-N 16-W
" "	**2**	2	5th PM 81-N 15-W
ESTES	**3**	1	5th PM 81-N 14-W
ESTLICK	**3**	1	5th PM 81-N 14-W
EVANS	**9**	1	5th PM 79-N 16-W
" "	**1**	1	5th PM 81-N 16-W
EVENS	**5**	1	5th PM 80-N 16-W
EWERS	**11**	1	5th PM 79-N 14-W
EWING	**3**	3	5th PM 81-N 14-W
" "	**6**	2	5th PM 80-N 15-W
FAHRNEY	**16**	7	5th PM 78-N 13-W

Surname	Map Group	Parcels of Land	Meridian/Township/Range
FAIRBANK	**7**	2	5th PM 80-N 14-W
FANT	**7**	1	5th PM 80-N 14-W
FARMER	**14**	3	5th PM 78-N 15-W
" "	**13**	2	5th PM 78-N 16-W
FARNHAM	**14**	1	5th PM 78-N 15-W
FARQUHAR	**8**	2	5th PM 80-N 13-W
" "	**7**	1	5th PM 80-N 14-W
FEARING	**5**	1	5th PM 80-N 16-W
FENLON	**2**	1	5th PM 81-N 15-W
" "	**1**	1	5th PM 81-N 16-W
FENTON	**3**	1	5th PM 81-N 14-W
FERGUSON	**12**	2	5th PM 79-N 13-W
FISHER	**16**	5	5th PM 78-N 13-W
" "	**9**	1	5th PM 79-N 16-W
" "	**3**	1	5th PM 81-N 14-W
FISK	**8**	1	5th PM 80-N 13-W
FLANAGAN	**2**	4	5th PM 81-N 15-W
" "	**1**	1	5th PM 81-N 16-W
FLATTERY	**16**	2	5th PM 78-N 13-W
FLESHER	**6**	1	5th PM 80-N 15-W
FLOYD	**11**	1	5th PM 79-N 14-W
FOLK	**7**	1	5th PM 80-N 14-W
FOLSOM	**12**	3	5th PM 79-N 13-W
" "	**10**	3	5th PM 79-N 15-W
" "	**3**	3	5th PM 81-N 14-W
" "	**11**	2	5th PM 79-N 14-W
" "	**8**	1	5th PM 80-N 13-W
" "	**5**	1	5th PM 80-N 16-W
FORBY	**12**	1	5th PM 79-N 13-W
FORD	**9**	3	5th PM 79-N 16-W
FOREMAN	**3**	1	5th PM 81-N 14-W
FORSYTHE	**2**	7	5th PM 81-N 15-W
FOSS	**13**	4	5th PM 78-N 16-W
FOSTER	**7**	1	5th PM 80-N 14-W
FOUTS	**4**	1	5th PM 81-N 13-W
FOWLER	**13**	1	5th PM 78-N 16-W
FOX	**9**	2	5th PM 79-N 16-W
FRAIZER	**9**	3	5th PM 79-N 16-W
FRANCE	**3**	2	5th PM 81-N 14-W
" "	**2**	1	5th PM 81-N 15-W
FRANCIS	**1**	3	5th PM 81-N 16-W
FRANK	**3**	3	5th PM 81-N 14-W
FRAZIER	**10**	2	5th PM 79-N 15-W
" "	**9**	1	5th PM 79-N 16-W
" "	**6**	1	5th PM 80-N 15-W
FREANER	**10**	1	5th PM 79-N 15-W
FREDERIC	**5**	1	5th PM 80-N 16-W
FRENCH	**9**	1	5th PM 79-N 16-W
FRIEND	**13**	1	5th PM 78-N 16-W
FRY	**8**	4	5th PM 80-N 13-W
FRYAR	**4**	1	5th PM 81-N 13-W
FULKER	**13**	4	5th PM 78-N 16-W
FULLER	**3**	4	5th PM 81-N 14-W
" "	**2**	1	5th PM 81-N 15-W
FULTON	**8**	1	5th PM 80-N 13-W
FUNK	**16**	4	5th PM 78-N 13-W
FURBER	**1**	1	5th PM 81-N 16-W
GALLAGHER	**12**	3	5th PM 79-N 13-W
GALLEHER	**7**	1	5th PM 80-N 14-W
GALLEY	**16**	2	5th PM 78-N 13-W

Surname	Map Group	Parcels of Land	Meridian/Township/Range		
GAMBLE	**2**	1	5th PM	81-N	15-W
GANTZ	**16**	2	5th PM	78-N	13-W
GARDINER	**12**	2	5th PM	79-N	13-W
GARDNER	**8**	7	5th PM	80-N	13-W
" "	**16**	2	5th PM	78-N	13-W
GARRETT	**1**	1	5th PM	81-N	16-W
GASKILL	**2**	1	5th PM	81-N	15-W
GATES	**9**	4	5th PM	79-N	16-W
" "	**8**	4	5th PM	80-N	13-W
" "	**4**	3	5th PM	81-N	13-W
" "	**1**	2	5th PM	81-N	16-W
GATHIELL	**2**	1	5th PM	81-N	15-W
GATLING	**15**	22	5th PM	78-N	14-W
" "	**11**	4	5th PM	79-N	14-W
GATTRELL	**2**	2	5th PM	81-N	15-W
GAUMER	**4**	3	5th PM	81-N	13-W
GAUSE	**13**	2	5th PM	78-N	16-W
GEETING	**3**	4	5th PM	81-N	14-W
GIFFORD	**12**	13	5th PM	79-N	13-W
" "	**16**	6	5th PM	78-N	13-W
" "	**8**	2	5th PM	80-N	13-W
" "	**6**	2	5th PM	80-N	15-W
GILCHRIST	**6**	2	5th PM	80-N	15-W
GILL	**12**	1	5th PM	79-N	13-W
GILLELAND	**3**	2	5th PM	81-N	14-W
GILLETT	**7**	4	5th PM	80-N	14-W
" "	**9**	2	5th PM	79-N	16-W
GILMORE	**5**	6	5th PM	80-N	16-W
" "	**1**	2	5th PM	81-N	16-W
GINN	**10**	1	5th PM	79-N	15-W
GIVINN	**8**	1	5th PM	80-N	13-W
GLADSON	**2**	1	5th PM	81-N	15-W
GLAZE	**4**	2	5th PM	81-N	13-W
" "	**3**	1	5th PM	81-N	14-W
GOLDEN	**5**	2	5th PM	80-N	16-W
GOODE	**11**	1	5th PM	79-N	14-W
GOODRICH	**2**	2	5th PM	81-N	15-W
GORDON	**16**	2	5th PM	78-N	13-W
GORMAY	**9**	1	5th PM	79-N	16-W
GOSNELL	**13**	1	5th PM	78-N	16-W
GOUDY	**2**	3	5th PM	81-N	15-W
GOUGH	**12**	1	5th PM	79-N	13-W
GOWER	**13**	20	5th PM	78-N	16-W
" "	**16**	11	5th PM	78-N	13-W
" "	**14**	7	5th PM	78-N	15-W
" "	**9**	7	5th PM	79-N	16-W
" "	**15**	5	5th PM	78-N	14-W
" "	**11**	5	5th PM	79-N	14-W
" "	**4**	5	5th PM	81-N	13-W
" "	**12**	4	5th PM	79-N	13-W
" "	**3**	4	5th PM	81-N	14-W
" "	**6**	3	5th PM	80-N	15-W
" "	**8**	2	5th PM	80-N	13-W
GRAHAM	**16**	4	5th PM	78-N	13-W
" "	**6**	2	5th PM	80-N	15-W
" "	**14**	1	5th PM	78-N	15-W
GRANT	**8**	1	5th PM	80-N	13-W
GRAVES	**13**	1	5th PM	78-N	16-W
GRAYUM	**2**	1	5th PM	81-N	15-W
GREELEY	**3**	1	5th PM	81-N	14-W

Surname	Map Group	Parcels of Land	Meridian/Township/Range		
GREEN	**12**	1	5th PM	79-N	13-W
GRIDER	**12**	1	5th PM	79-N	13-W
GRIDLEY	**9**	1	5th PM	79-N	16-W
GRIER	**12**	5	5th PM	79-N	13-W
GRIFFIN	**1**	1	5th PM	81-N	16-W
GRINELL	**1**	1	5th PM	81-N	16-W
GRINNELL	**5**	31	5th PM	80-N	16-W
" "	**6**	2	5th PM	80-N	15-W
" "	**1**	2	5th PM	81-N	16-W
" "	**9**	1	5th PM	79-N	16-W
GRISWOLD	**8**	10	5th PM	80-N	13-W
GROSS	**10**	1	5th PM	79-N	15-W
GRUB	**11**	1	5th PM	79-N	14-W
GRUWELL	**2**	2	5th PM	81-N	15-W
GUILD	**8**	4	5th PM	80-N	13-W
" "	**15**	1	5th PM	78-N	14-W
GUNNELL	**5**	1	5th PM	80-N	16-W
GURLEY	**6**	2	5th PM	80-N	15-W
" "	**7**	1	5th PM	80-N	14-W
GWIN	**8**	10	5th PM	80-N	13-W
" "	**7**	2	5th PM	80-N	14-W
GWINN	**8**	2	5th PM	80-N	13-W
HADDEN	**11**	1	5th PM	79-N	14-W
HAGERTY	**15**	1	5th PM	78-N	14-W
HAIFLEY	**9**	1	5th PM	79-N	16-W
HAINES	**13**	2	5th PM	78-N	16-W
HALL	**15**	2	5th PM	78-N	14-W
" "	**14**	2	5th PM	78-N	15-W
" "	**5**	2	5th PM	80-N	16-W
" "	**4**	2	5th PM	81-N	13-W
HALLETT	**4**	2	5th PM	81-N	13-W
HAM	**7**	3	5th PM	80-N	14-W
HAMBLETON	**13**	8	5th PM	78-N	16-W
HAMILTON	**4**	2	5th PM	81-N	13-W
" "	**15**	1	5th PM	78-N	14-W
HAMLIN	**5**	2	5th PM	80-N	16-W
HAMLINE	**5**	1	5th PM	80-N	16-W
HAMMOND	**7**	1	5th PM	80-N	14-W
HAND	**6**	2	5th PM	80-N	15-W
HANES	**8**	5	5th PM	80-N	13-W
" "	**7**	2	5th PM	80-N	14-W
HAPGOOD	**16**	4	5th PM	78-N	13-W
HARBINE	**10**	1	5th PM	79-N	15-W
HARDEN	**15**	1	5th PM	78-N	14-W
HARDING	**1**	1	5th PM	81-N	16-W
HARKLEROAD	**16**	1	5th PM	78-N	13-W
" "	**15**	1	5th PM	78-N	14-W
" "	**12**	1	5th PM	79-N	13-W
HARKLOADS	**8**	1	5th PM	80-N	13-W
HARMAN	**2**	2	5th PM	81-N	15-W
HARMON	**4**	2	5th PM	81-N	13-W
HARNER	**14**	2	5th PM	78-N	15-W
HARPER	**7**	3	5th PM	80-N	14-W
HARRINGTON	**10**	1	5th PM	79-N	15-W
" "	**2**	1	5th PM	81-N	15-W
HARRIS	**13**	1	5th PM	78-N	16-W
HARRISON	**8**	1	5th PM	80-N	13-W
HARRY	**12**	1	5th PM	79-N	13-W
" "	**8**	1	5th PM	80-N	13-W
HART	**14**	1	5th PM	78-N	15-W

Surname	Map Group	Parcels of Land	Meridian/Township/Range		
HART (Cont'd)	**2**	1	5th PM	81-N	15-W
HARTMAN	**7**	3	5th PM	80-N	14-W
" "	**4**	1	5th PM	81-N	13-W
HARVEY	**3**	1	5th PM	81-N	14-W
HASE	**13**	1	5th PM	78-N	16-W
HASTINGS	**7**	4	5th PM	80-N	14-W
" "	**12**	2	5th PM	79-N	13-W
HATFIELD	**10**	3	5th PM	79-N	15-W
HATHAWAY	**14**	1	5th PM	78-N	15-W
" "	**13**	1	5th PM	78-N	16-W
HAVELY	**9**	1	5th PM	79-N	16-W
HAVENS	**2**	2	5th PM	81-N	15-W
HAWES	**2**	1	5th PM	81-N	15-W
HAWKS	**12**	2	5th PM	79-N	13-W
" "	**8**	1	5th PM	80-N	13-W
HAY	**14**	4	5th PM	78-N	15-W
HAYES	**7**	4	5th PM	80-N	14-W
" "	**9**	2	5th PM	79-N	16-W
HAYS	**1**	9	5th PM	81-N	16-W
" "	**14**	1	5th PM	78-N	15-W
" "	**7**	1	5th PM	80-N	14-W
HAYTER	**14**	1	5th PM	78-N	15-W
" "	**13**	1	5th PM	78-N	16-W
HAYWOOD	**3**	2	5th PM	81-N	14-W
HAZLETON	**13**	3	5th PM	78-N	16-W
HEALD	**4**	1	5th PM	81-N	13-W
HECK	**13**	1	5th PM	78-N	16-W
HECKMAN	**3**	1	5th PM	81-N	14-W
HEILMAYER	**13**	2	5th PM	78-N	16-W
HEILMYER	**13**	1	5th PM	78-N	16-W
HERRIMAN	**4**	2	5th PM	81-N	13-W
HERRON	**1**	1	5th PM	81-N	16-W
HESS	**7**	2	5th PM	80-N	14-W
HIATT	**13**	5	5th PM	78-N	16-W
" "	**9**	5	5th PM	79-N	16-W
HICKMAN	**16**	1	5th PM	78-N	13-W
HIGGINBOTHAM	**13**	2	5th PM	78-N	16-W
HIGGINSON	**10**	7	5th PM	79-N	15-W
" "	**6**	3	5th PM	80-N	15-W
" "	**9**	1	5th PM	79-N	16-W
" "	**7**	1	5th PM	80-N	14-W
" "	**4**	1	5th PM	81-N	13-W
" "	**3**	1	5th PM	81-N	14-W
HILL	**11**	2	5th PM	79-N	14-W
" "	**8**	1	5th PM	80-N	13-W
" "	**7**	1	5th PM	80-N	14-W
" "	**2**	1	5th PM	81-N	15-W
" "	**1**	1	5th PM	81-N	16-W
HILLMAN	**12**	3	5th PM	79-N	13-W
HINER	**15**	1	5th PM	78-N	14-W
HITCHCOCK	**13**	1	5th PM	78-N	16-W
HOBART	**13**	2	5th PM	78-N	16-W
HOBSON	**6**	2	5th PM	80-N	15-W
HODSKIN	**5**	2	5th PM	80-N	16-W
HOKE	**13**	1	5th PM	78-N	16-W
HOLLENBACK	**4**	1	5th PM	81-N	13-W
HOLLENBECK	**9**	11	5th PM	79-N	16-W
HOLLER	**4**	2	5th PM	81-N	13-W
HOLLEY	**5**	2	5th PM	80-N	16-W
" "	**13**	1	5th PM	78-N	16-W

Surname	Map Group	Parcels of Land	Meridian/Township/Range
HOLLIDAY	9	2	5th PM 79-N 16-W
HOLLOPETER	13	1	5th PM 78-N 16-W
HOLLY	13	2	5th PM 78-N 16-W
HOLMES	8	1	5th PM 80-N 13-W
HOLYOKE	5	5	5th PM 80-N 16-W
HONICON	1	1	5th PM 81-N 16-W
HONOCOL	1	1	5th PM 81-N 16-W
HOOK	12	1	5th PM 79-N 13-W
" "	8	1	5th PM 80-N 13-W
HOOPER	8	1	5th PM 80-N 13-W
HOOVER	13	2	5th PM 78-N 16-W
HORTON	1	2	5th PM 81-N 16-W
HOSICK	8	1	5th PM 80-N 13-W
HOVERSTICK	13	1	5th PM 78-N 16-W
HOWARD	3	7	5th PM 81-N 14-W
" "	4	2	5th PM 81-N 13-W
HOYT	16	1	5th PM 78-N 13-W
HUBBARD	3	3	5th PM 81-N 14-W
" "	4	1	5th PM 81-N 13-W
HUDSON	9	2	5th PM 79-N 16-W
HULL	3	1	5th PM 81-N 14-W
HUME	6	1	5th PM 80-N 15-W
HUMMEL	11	1	5th PM 79-N 14-W
HUMPHREY	2	1	5th PM 81-N 15-W
HUNT	2	5	5th PM 81-N 15-W
" "	6	1	5th PM 80-N 15-W
HUNTINGTON	9	4	5th PM 79-N 16-W
HURDEN	9	1	5th PM 79-N 16-W
HURLEY	10	1	5th PM 79-N 15-W
HURST	13	1	5th PM 78-N 16-W
HUTCHENS	14	1	5th PM 78-N 15-W
HUTCHESON	15	2	5th PM 78-N 14-W
HUTCHINS	14	4	5th PM 78-N 15-W
" "	10	2	5th PM 79-N 15-W
" "	8	1	5th PM 80-N 13-W
HYNES	3	1	5th PM 81-N 14-W
ILES	16	1	5th PM 78-N 13-W
INGMOND	12	2	5th PM 79-N 13-W
IOWA	16	1	5th PM 78-N 13-W
" "	15	1	5th PM 78-N 14-W
" "	14	1	5th PM 78-N 15-W
" "	13	1	5th PM 78-N 16-W
" "	12	1	5th PM 79-N 13-W
" "	11	1	5th PM 79-N 14-W
" "	10	1	5th PM 79-N 15-W
" "	9	1	5th PM 79-N 16-W
" "	8	1	5th PM 80-N 13-W
" "	7	1	5th PM 80-N 14-W
" "	6	1	5th PM 80-N 15-W
" "	5	1	5th PM 80-N 16-W
" "	4	1	5th PM 81-N 13-W
" "	3	1	5th PM 81-N 14-W
" "	2	1	5th PM 81-N 15-W
" "	1	1	5th PM 81-N 16-W
IRELAND	13	1	5th PM 78-N 16-W
IS-FI-KE	8	1	5th PM 80-N 13-W
JACK	2	1	5th PM 81-N 15-W
JACKSON	9	1	5th PM 79-N 16-W
" "	6	1	5th PM 80-N 15-W
JACOB	9	2	5th PM 79-N 16-W

Surname	Map Group	Parcels of Land	Meridian/Township/Range
JACOB (Cont'd)	**10**	1	5th PM 79-N 15-W
JAMES	**9**	6	5th PM 79-N 16-W
" "	**14**	2	5th PM 78-N 15-W
" "	**16**	1	5th PM 78-N 13-W
JAMIESON	**1**	1	5th PM 81-N 16-W
JAMISON	**12**	1	5th PM 79-N 13-W
JARRETT	**16**	1	5th PM 78-N 13-W
JENKINS	**5**	2	5th PM 80-N 16-W
" "	**9**	1	5th PM 79-N 16-W
" "	**7**	1	5th PM 80-N 14-W
JENNINGS	**11**	1	5th PM 79-N 14-W
" "	**8**	1	5th PM 80-N 13-W
JEROME	**13**	3	5th PM 78-N 16-W
JEWETT	**8**	2	5th PM 80-N 13-W
JOHNSON	**11**	23	5th PM 79-N 14-W
" "	**15**	16	5th PM 78-N 14-W
" "	**12**	13	5th PM 79-N 13-W
" "	**14**	6	5th PM 78-N 15-W
" "	**10**	5	5th PM 79-N 15-W
" "	**13**	3	5th PM 78-N 16-W
" "	**3**	3	5th PM 81-N 14-W
" "	**7**	1	5th PM 80-N 14-W
" "	**6**	1	5th PM 80-N 15-W
JOHNSTON	**6**	6	5th PM 80-N 15-W
" "	**16**	3	5th PM 78-N 13-W
" "	**4**	2	5th PM 81-N 13-W
" "	**10**	1	5th PM 79-N 15-W
" "	**3**	1	5th PM 81-N 14-W
JONES	**1**	12	5th PM 81-N 16-W
" "	**2**	5	5th PM 81-N 15-W
" "	**16**	3	5th PM 78-N 13-W
" "	**13**	2	5th PM 78-N 16-W
" "	**3**	2	5th PM 81-N 14-W
" "	**12**	1	5th PM 79-N 13-W
JUDD	**2**	7	5th PM 81-N 15-W
" "	**4**	5	5th PM 81-N 13-W
" "	**3**	1	5th PM 81-N 14-W
KAPLE	**2**	1	5th PM 81-N 15-W
KAUFFMAN	**7**	2	5th PM 80-N 14-W
" "	**8**	1	5th PM 80-N 13-W
" "	**4**	1	5th PM 81-N 13-W
KECK	**8**	1	5th PM 80-N 13-W
" "	**3**	1	5th PM 81-N 14-W
KEENAN	**1**	2	5th PM 81-N 16-W
KELLOGG	**6**	4	5th PM 80-N 15-W
" "	**5**	2	5th PM 80-N 16-W
" "	**2**	1	5th PM 81-N 15-W
KELLY	**1**	1	5th PM 81-N 16-W
KENNEDY	**8**	1	5th PM 80-N 13-W
KENT	**3**	2	5th PM 81-N 14-W
" "	**4**	1	5th PM 81-N 13-W
KENWORTHY	**13**	8	5th PM 78-N 16-W
" "	**9**	5	5th PM 79-N 16-W
KEPPEL	**4**	2	5th PM 81-N 13-W
" "	**3**	2	5th PM 81-N 14-W
KERN	**8**	2	5th PM 80-N 13-W
KERSTEN	**12**	2	5th PM 79-N 13-W
KESTER	**14**	1	5th PM 78-N 15-W
KEYS	**6**	3	5th PM 80-N 15-W
KILLIN	**10**	1	5th PM 79-N 15-W

Surname	Map Group	Parcels of Land	Meridian/Township/Range		
KING	9	2	5th PM	79-N	16-W
" "	8	2	5th PM	80-N	13-W
" "	6	1	5th PM	80-N	15-W
" "	3	1	5th PM	81-N	14-W
KINGSMORE	5	1	5th PM	80-N	16-W
KINSEY	3	1	5th PM	81-N	14-W
" "	1	1	5th PM	81-N	16-W
KIRK	16	3	5th PM	78-N	13-W
KIRKPATRICK	12	1	5th PM	79-N	13-W
KIRKWOOD	3	9	5th PM	81-N	14-W
" "	8	7	5th PM	80-N	13-W
" "	12	2	5th PM	79-N	13-W
" "	16	1	5th PM	78-N	13-W
" "	4	1	5th PM	81-N	13-W
KNEPPER	12	3	5th PM	79-N	13-W
" "	4	2	5th PM	81-N	13-W
KNOTT	15	1	5th PM	78-N	14-W
KNOX	9	3	5th PM	79-N	16-W
KORN	4	2	5th PM	81-N	13-W
" "	8	1	5th PM	80-N	13-W
KORNS	2	5	5th PM	81-N	15-W
" "	4	1	5th PM	81-N	13-W
KRIDLER	13	2	5th PM	78-N	16-W
KUNKEL	13	2	5th PM	78-N	16-W
KURT	3	1	5th PM	81-N	14-W
LADELEY	16	1	5th PM	78-N	13-W
LAITON	8	1	5th PM	80-N	13-W
LALANDER	4	1	5th PM	81-N	13-W
LAMBRITE	5	5	5th PM	80-N	16-W
" "	7	2	5th PM	80-N	14-W
LAMSON	14	2	5th PM	78-N	15-W
LANCEY	2	1	5th PM	81-N	15-W
LANDEN	15	1	5th PM	78-N	14-W
LANE	12	2	5th PM	79-N	13-W
" "	8	1	5th PM	80-N	13-W
" "	4	1	5th PM	81-N	13-W
LANGFORD	8	1	5th PM	80-N	13-W
LAPHAM	5	1	5th PM	80-N	16-W
LAREW	3	1	5th PM	81-N	14-W
LARREW	3	2	5th PM	81-N	14-W
LARUE	4	1	5th PM	81-N	13-W
LATIMER	5	3	5th PM	80-N	16-W
LAUGHLIN	4	2	5th PM	81-N	13-W
" "	3	2	5th PM	81-N	14-W
LAWLESS	6	2	5th PM	80-N	15-W
LAWRENCE	15	3	5th PM	78-N	14-W
" "	9	2	5th PM	79-N	16-W
" "	5	1	5th PM	80-N	16-W
LAYLANDER	4	2	5th PM	81-N	13-W
LAYTEN	12	1	5th PM	79-N	13-W
LAYTON	12	4	5th PM	79-N	13-W
LEE	8	3	5th PM	80-N	13-W
LEHMAN	12	1	5th PM	79-N	13-W
LEMMON	12	1	5th PM	79-N	13-W
LENTZ	13	1	5th PM	78-N	16-W
LEONARD	9	3	5th PM	79-N	16-W
LESLIE	12	4	5th PM	79-N	13-W
LIGHT	16	3	5th PM	78-N	13-W
LILLEY	9	2	5th PM	79-N	16-W
LINN	4	3	5th PM	81-N	13-W

Surname	Map Group	Parcels of Land	Meridian/Township/Range
LINSTED	**13**	2	5th PM 78-N 16-W
LISOR	**15**	2	5th PM 78-N 14-W
LISTON	**11**	4	5th PM 79-N 14-W
LITTLE	**16**	1	5th PM 78-N 13-W
" "	**4**	1	5th PM 81-N 13-W
" "	**2**	1	5th PM 81-N 15-W
LLOYD	**1**	1	5th PM 81-N 16-W
LOCK	**1**	2	5th PM 81-N 16-W
LOCKHART	**4**	4	5th PM 81-N 13-W
LOEBER	**2**	2	5th PM 81-N 15-W
LOESCH	**2**	1	5th PM 81-N 15-W
LOGAN	**16**	1	5th PM 78-N 13-W
LONG	**14**	4	5th PM 78-N 15-W
" "	**12**	1	5th PM 79-N 13-W
" "	**4**	1	5th PM 81-N 13-W
LOONEY	**14**	1	5th PM 78-N 15-W
LOOSE	**2**	6	5th PM 81-N 15-W
" "	**6**	2	5th PM 80-N 15-W
" "	**1**	2	5th PM 81-N 16-W
LORD	**4**	3	5th PM 81-N 13-W
LOTT	**11**	1	5th PM 79-N 14-W
LOUD	**4**	1	5th PM 81-N 13-W
LOUGHLIN	**4**	1	5th PM 81-N 13-W
LOVE	**8**	1	5th PM 80-N 13-W
" "	**3**	1	5th PM 81-N 14-W
LOWRY	**1**	3	5th PM 81-N 16-W
LUCAS	**16**	5	5th PM 78-N 13-W
" "	**4**	1	5th PM 81-N 13-W
LUCKHART	**3**	5	5th PM 81-N 14-W
" "	**4**	2	5th PM 81-N 13-W
LUKECART	**3**	2	5th PM 81-N 14-W
LYNASON	**6**	1	5th PM 80-N 15-W
LYNN	**15**	1	5th PM 78-N 14-W
LYON	**14**	1	5th PM 78-N 15-W
LYTLE	**15**	1	5th PM 78-N 14-W
MACKEY	**9**	1	5th PM 79-N 16-W
MAGILL	**2**	1	5th PM 81-N 15-W
MAHAN	**4**	1	5th PM 81-N 13-W
MAHON	**12**	2	5th PM 79-N 13-W
MALONE	**10**	4	5th PM 79-N 15-W
" "	**15**	1	5th PM 78-N 14-W
MANAT	**8**	1	5th PM 80-N 13-W
MANATT	**8**	27	5th PM 80-N 13-W
" "	**7**	18	5th PM 80-N 14-W
" "	**4**	1	5th PM 81-N 13-W
MANN	**2**	1	5th PM 81-N 15-W
MARK	**8**	4	5th PM 80-N 13-W
MARKS	**15**	1	5th PM 78-N 14-W
MARPOLE	**4**	1	5th PM 81-N 13-W
MARSH	**5**	2	5th PM 80-N 16-W
" "	**12**	1	5th PM 79-N 13-W
MARSHALL	**14**	2	5th PM 78-N 15-W
MARSON	**9**	1	5th PM 79-N 16-W
MARTIN	**15**	2	5th PM 78-N 14-W
" "	**9**	2	5th PM 79-N 16-W
" "	**14**	1	5th PM 78-N 15-W
" "	**10**	1	5th PM 79-N 15-W
MARVIN	**8**	1	5th PM 80-N 13-W
" "	**4**	1	5th PM 81-N 13-W
MASAY	**14**	1	5th PM 78-N 15-W

Surname	Map Group	Parcels of Land	Meridian/Township/Range		
MASUY	**14**	1	5th PM	78-N	15-W
MATHEWS	**12**	1	5th PM	79-N	13-W
MATTESON	**5**	1	5th PM	80-N	16-W
MAY	**16**	1	5th PM	78-N	13-W
MAYER	**3**	1	5th PM	81-N	14-W
MCBRIDE	**13**	3	5th PM	78-N	16-W
MCBURNEY	**8**	1	5th PM	80-N	13-W
MCCAGUE	**7**	2	5th PM	80-N	14-W
" "	**6**	1	5th PM	80-N	15-W
MCCALL	**3**	1	5th PM	81-N	14-W
MCCARTY	**14**	2	5th PM	78-N	15-W
MCCLEIF	**9**	1	5th PM	79-N	16-W
MCCLELLAN	**9**	5	5th PM	79-N	16-W
MCCLUNG	**1**	1	5th PM	81-N	16-W
MCCLURE	**13**	1	5th PM	78-N	16-W
MCCLUSKY	**4**	1	5th PM	81-N	13-W
MCCORKLE	**10**	2	5th PM	79-N	15-W
MCCORMICK	**9**	1	5th PM	79-N	16-W
MCCRACKEN	**5**	1	5th PM	80-N	16-W
MCCULLOUGH	**16**	1	5th PM	78-N	13-W
MCCUNE	**10**	1	5th PM	79-N	15-W
MCCURTAIN	**10**	1	5th PM	79-N	15-W
MCDONALD	**14**	2	5th PM	78-N	15-W
" "	**13**	2	5th PM	78-N	16-W
MCDONNALD	**14**	1	5th PM	78-N	15-W
" "	**13**	1	5th PM	78-N	16-W
MCDOWELL	**13**	7	5th PM	78-N	16-W
MCGARVEY	**8**	2	5th PM	80-N	13-W
MCGARY	**7**	1	5th PM	80-N	14-W
MCKAY	**5**	2	5th PM	80-N	16-W
MCKEAN	**14**	1	5th PM	78-N	15-W
" "	**13**	1	5th PM	78-N	16-W
MCKENZIE	**2**	1	5th PM	81-N	15-W
" "	**1**	1	5th PM	81-N	16-W
MCKINNEY	**6**	4	5th PM	80-N	15-W
" "	**8**	1	5th PM	80-N	13-W
MCLAIN	**13**	8	5th PM	78-N	16-W
" "	**9**	4	5th PM	79-N	16-W
" "	**8**	2	5th PM	80-N	13-W
MCMILLAN	**1**	1	5th PM	81-N	16-W
MCNABB	**9**	1	5th PM	79-N	16-W
MCROY	**7**	1	5th PM	80-N	14-W
MCVAY	**14**	3	5th PM	78-N	15-W
" "	**11**	2	5th PM	79-N	14-W
MCVEY	**14**	9	5th PM	78-N	15-W
" "	**15**	8	5th PM	78-N	14-W
" "	**4**	1	5th PM	81-N	13-W
MEAD	**16**	4	5th PM	78-N	13-W
" "	**8**	4	5th PM	80-N	13-W
" "	**12**	2	5th PM	79-N	13-W
MEEKER	**12**	2	5th PM	79-N	13-W
MEIGS	**6**	2	5th PM	80-N	15-W
MEILY	**13**	1	5th PM	78-N	16-W
MENARY	**9**	2	5th PM	79-N	16-W
MENDENHALL	**7**	1	5th PM	80-N	14-W
MENETT	**7**	1	5th PM	80-N	14-W
MERCER	**16**	2	5th PM	78-N	13-W
" "	**12**	2	5th PM	79-N	13-W
MERRETT	**6**	1	5th PM	80-N	15-W
MERRITT	**10**	3	5th PM	79-N	15-W

Surname	Map Group	Parcels of Land	Meridian/Township/Range		
MERRITT (Cont'd)	9	1	5th PM	79-N	16-W
MERWIN	3	1	5th PM	81-N	14-W
METCALF	8	1	5th PM	80-N	13-W
METHVEN	1	1	5th PM	81-N	16-W
METZGER	5	1	5th PM	80-N	16-W
MICHAEL	12	1	5th PM	79-N	13-W
" "	7	1	5th PM	80-N	14-W
MIDDLEKAUFF	16	2	5th PM	78-N	13-W
MILLAR	6	8	5th PM	80-N	15-W
" "	5	3	5th PM	80-N	16-W
" "	1	3	5th PM	81-N	16-W
MILLER	9	8	5th PM	79-N	16-W
" "	14	1	5th PM	78-N	15-W
" "	2	1	5th PM	81-N	15-W
MILLIKEN	16	2	5th PM	78-N	13-W
MILLS	9	1	5th PM	79-N	16-W
MISCHLICH	2	1	5th PM	81-N	15-W
MITCHELL	10	1	5th PM	79-N	15-W
" "	5	1	5th PM	80-N	16-W
MIX	5	2	5th PM	80-N	16-W
MOATES	4	2	5th PM	81-N	13-W
MOATS	4	2	5th PM	81-N	13-W
MONROE	3	1	5th PM	81-N	14-W
MONSON	9	1	5th PM	79-N	16-W
" "	6	1	5th PM	80-N	15-W
MONTGOMERY	1	1	5th PM	81-N	16-W
MOODY	13	1	5th PM	78-N	16-W
MOORE	14	2	5th PM	78-N	15-W
MOREY	2	3	5th PM	81-N	15-W
" "	4	1	5th PM	81-N	13-W
MORGAN	4	4	5th PM	81-N	13-W
" "	13	3	5th PM	78-N	16-W
" "	15	2	5th PM	78-N	14-W
" "	12	2	5th PM	79-N	13-W
" "	6	2	5th PM	80-N	15-W
MORGANTHALER	7	1	5th PM	80-N	14-W
MORISON	12	1	5th PM	79-N	13-W
MORLAND	16	1	5th PM	78-N	13-W
MORRIS	12	1	5th PM	79-N	13-W
" "	2	1	5th PM	81-N	15-W
MORRISON	14	1	5th PM	78-N	15-W
MORSMAN	4	2	5th PM	81-N	13-W
" "	14	1	5th PM	78-N	15-W
MORTON	12	1	5th PM	79-N	13-W
MOSELY	3	8	5th PM	81-N	14-W
" "	2	4	5th PM	81-N	15-W
MOSSER	13	4	5th PM	78-N	16-W
MOTHERAL	6	26	5th PM	80-N	15-W
MOUSER	16	3	5th PM	78-N	13-W
MUIRHIRD	8	1	5th PM	80-N	13-W
MUMMA	16	2	5th PM	78-N	13-W
MUMMRA	16	1	5th PM	78-N	13-W
MURDOCK	12	2	5th PM	79-N	13-W
MURPHY	16	1	5th PM	78-N	13-W
MURRAY	15	3	5th PM	78-N	14-W
" "	9	3	5th PM	79-N	16-W
MUSGROVE	15	4	5th PM	78-N	14-W
MYERS	9	3	5th PM	79-N	16-W
" "	16	1	5th PM	78-N	13-W
" "	14	1	5th PM	78-N	15-W

Surname	Map Group	Parcels of Land	Meridian/Township/Range		
MYERS (Cont'd)	**13**	1	5th PM	78-N	16-W
NAYLOR	**7**	1	5th PM	80-N	14-W
NEAL	**4**	2	5th PM	81-N	13-W
" "	**12**	1	5th PM	79-N	13-W
" "	**9**	1	5th PM	79-N	16-W
NEFF	**2**	2	5th PM	81-N	15-W
" "	**1**	1	5th PM	81-N	16-W
NELSON	**15**	1	5th PM	78-N	14-W
NETHEROW	**1**	2	5th PM	81-N	16-W
NEWELL	**1**	1	5th PM	81-N	16-W
NEWHALL	**15**	1	5th PM	78-N	14-W
NEWKIRK	**11**	2	5th PM	79-N	14-W
NEWMAN	**5**	2	5th PM	80-N	16-W
" "	**9**	1	5th PM	79-N	16-W
NEWSHELL	**11**	1	5th PM	79-N	14-W
NEWTON	**13**	1	5th PM	78-N	16-W
NICHOLAS	**7**	1	5th PM	80-N	14-W
NICHOLS	**14**	2	5th PM	78-N	15-W
NILES	**4**	1	5th PM	81-N	13-W
NINDE	**3**	2	5th PM	81-N	14-W
" "	**4**	1	5th PM	81-N	13-W
NIXON	**15**	1	5th PM	78-N	14-W
NOBLE	**9**	2	5th PM	79-N	16-W
" "	**5**	2	5th PM	80-N	16-W
NOLAND	**2**	1	5th PM	81-N	15-W
NORRIS	**5**	5	5th PM	80-N	16-W
" "	**7**	4	5th PM	80-N	14-W
" "	**3**	2	5th PM	81-N	14-W
" "	**4**	1	5th PM	81-N	13-W
NUSSBAUM	**12**	2	5th PM	79-N	13-W
" "	**8**	1	5th PM	80-N	13-W
OGDEN	**14**	1	5th PM	78-N	15-W
OLIPHANT	**16**	1	5th PM	78-N	13-W
ORCUTT	**13**	2	5th PM	78-N	16-W
ORR	**9**	1	5th PM	79-N	16-W
OSBORN	**9**	3	5th PM	79-N	16-W
" "	**4**	2	5th PM	81-N	13-W
" "	**13**	1	5th PM	78-N	16-W
OTTO	**4**	2	5th PM	81-N	13-W
PAGE	**14**	1	5th PM	78-N	15-W
PARCEL	**9**	1	5th PM	79-N	16-W
" "	**5**	1	5th PM	80-N	16-W
PARDEE	**3**	2	5th PM	81-N	14-W
" "	**2**	1	5th PM	81-N	15-W
PARKER	**13**	4	5th PM	78-N	16-W
" "	**7**	4	5th PM	80-N	14-W
" "	**6**	3	5th PM	80-N	15-W
" "	**8**	2	5th PM	80-N	13-W
" "	**15**	1	5th PM	78-N	14-W
" "	**3**	1	5th PM	81-N	14-W
PARKS	**13**	4	5th PM	78-N	16-W
" "	**4**	3	5th PM	81-N	13-W
" "	**9**	2	5th PM	79-N	16-W
PARMER	**4**	1	5th PM	81-N	13-W
PAROTT	**15**	1	5th PM	78-N	14-W
PARRISH	**15**	11	5th PM	78-N	14-W
PARSONS	**16**	2	5th PM	78-N	13-W
" "	**6**	1	5th PM	80-N	15-W
PASSON	**16**	1	5th PM	78-N	13-W
PATRICK	**4**	6	5th PM	81-N	13-W

Surname	Map Group	Parcels of Land	Meridian/Township/Range		
PATTEE	3	4	5th PM	81-N	14-W
" "	2	3	5th PM	81-N	15-W
PATTERSON	11	2	5th PM	79-N	14-W
" "	6	1	5th PM	80-N	15-W
PAUL	9	1	5th PM	79-N	16-W
PAYNE	12	1	5th PM	79-N	13-W
PEARCE	9	1	5th PM	79-N	16-W
" "	5	1	5th PM	80-N	16-W
PEASE	5	1	5th PM	80-N	16-W
PEGRAM	11	2	5th PM	79-N	14-W
PELTON	8	1	5th PM	80-N	13-W
PEOPLES	3	2	5th PM	81-N	14-W
PERCY	9	1	5th PM	79-N	16-W
PEREGOY	4	1	5th PM	81-N	13-W
PERIN	6	1	5th PM	80-N	15-W
PERRY	9	1	5th PM	79-N	16-W
PETERS	12	1	5th PM	79-N	13-W
PETTIBONE	5	1	5th PM	80-N	16-W
PETTIE	3	1	5th PM	81-N	14-W
PHELPS	9	4	5th PM	79-N	16-W
" "	5	2	5th PM	80-N	16-W
" "	2	1	5th PM	81-N	15-W
PHILLIPS	14	1	5th PM	78-N	15-W
" "	4	1	5th PM	81-N	13-W
" "	1	1	5th PM	81-N	16-W
PIERCE	14	1	5th PM	78-N	15-W
PIERSOL	13	1	5th PM	78-N	16-W
PIERSON	7	1	5th PM	80-N	14-W
PIKE	13	3	5th PM	78-N	16-W
" "	14	1	5th PM	78-N	15-W
PINNEY	12	3	5th PM	79-N	13-W
" "	9	3	5th PM	79-N	16-W
" "	2	3	5th PM	81-N	15-W
" "	5	1	5th PM	80-N	16-W
" "	3	1	5th PM	81-N	14-W
PITT	11	2	5th PM	79-N	14-W
PLEAS	13	2	5th PM	78-N	16-W
PLEASANTS	8	1	5th PM	80-N	13-W
PLUM	6	1	5th PM	80-N	15-W
PLUMB	4	1	5th PM	81-N	13-W
PLYMPTON	4	2	5th PM	81-N	13-W
" "	1	1	5th PM	81-N	16-W
POCOCK	4	1	5th PM	81-N	13-W
POLLARD	8	1	5th PM	80-N	13-W
POOLE	4	1	5th PM	81-N	13-W
PORTER	15	2	5th PM	78-N	14-W
" "	11	2	5th PM	79-N	14-W
" "	4	2	5th PM	81-N	13-W
" "	8	1	5th PM	80-N	13-W
POTTER	6	1	5th PM	80-N	15-W
POWELL	16	1	5th PM	78-N	13-W
" "	2	1	5th PM	81-N	15-W
POWER	13	4	5th PM	78-N	16-W
" "	14	1	5th PM	78-N	15-W
PRESTON	16	1	5th PM	78-N	13-W
PRICE	12	1	5th PM	79-N	13-W
PROCTOR	1	2	5th PM	81-N	16-W
PROPST	10	1	5th PM	79-N	15-W
PROSSER	9	3	5th PM	79-N	16-W
" "	5	1	5th PM	80-N	16-W

Surname	Map Group	Parcels of Land	Meridian/Township/Range		
PUFFINBURGER	**8**	2	5th PM	80-N	13-W
PUGH	**16**	2	5th PM	78-N	13-W
PURCEFIELD	**3**	1	5th PM	81-N	14-W
PURDY	**9**	1	5th PM	79-N	16-W
PUSEY	**8**	6	5th PM	80-N	13-W
PUTNAM	**2**	3	5th PM	81-N	15-W
QUACKENBUSH	**14**	1	5th PM	78-N	15-W
QUIGGINS	**9**	1	5th PM	79-N	16-W
RAGADALE	**13**	1	5th PM	78-N	16-W
RAMAY	**9**	1	5th PM	79-N	16-W
RANKIN	**15**	2	5th PM	78-N	14-W
REDHEAD	**7**	2	5th PM	80-N	14-W
REDMAN	**15**	1	5th PM	78-N	14-W
" "	**14**	1	5th PM	78-N	15-W
REDMOND	**15**	3	5th PM	78-N	14-W
REED	**5**	3	5th PM	80-N	16-W
" "	**15**	1	5th PM	78-N	14-W
" "	**13**	1	5th PM	78-N	16-W
RENO	**14**	23	5th PM	78-N	15-W
" "	**4**	13	5th PM	81-N	13-W
" "	**15**	11	5th PM	78-N	14-W
" "	**9**	11	5th PM	79-N	16-W
" "	**1**	10	5th PM	81-N	16-W
" "	**13**	8	5th PM	78-N	16-W
" "	**16**	6	5th PM	78-N	13-W
" "	**12**	6	5th PM	79-N	13-W
" "	**8**	6	5th PM	80-N	13-W
" "	**10**	3	5th PM	79-N	15-W
" "	**5**	2	5th PM	80-N	16-W
" "	**7**	1	5th PM	80-N	14-W
REVERE	**15**	1	5th PM	78-N	14-W
REYNOLDS	**13**	3	5th PM	78-N	16-W
" "	**7**	3	5th PM	80-N	14-W
" "	**11**	2	5th PM	79-N	14-W
" "	**6**	1	5th PM	80-N	15-W
RHODES	**2**	1	5th PM	81-N	15-W
RHULE	**6**	3	5th PM	80-N	15-W
RICE	**9**	2	5th PM	79-N	16-W
" "	**7**	1	5th PM	80-N	14-W
RICHARDSON	**9**	1	5th PM	79-N	16-W
RICKER	**4**	1	5th PM	81-N	13-W
RICKEY	**13**	1	5th PM	78-N	16-W
RIGGS	**5**	1	5th PM	80-N	16-W
RIGHTMYER	**1**	4	5th PM	81-N	16-W
RILEY	**7**	1	5th PM	80-N	14-W
RIVERS	**13**	6	5th PM	78-N	16-W
" "	**14**	4	5th PM	78-N	15-W
ROARK	**14**	1	5th PM	78-N	15-W
ROBBERTS	**9**	1	5th PM	79-N	16-W
ROBBINS	**12**	2	5th PM	79-N	13-W
" "	**9**	2	5th PM	79-N	16-W
ROBERTS	**13**	2	5th PM	78-N	16-W
" "	**11**	2	5th PM	79-N	14-W
" "	**15**	1	5th PM	78-N	14-W
" "	**10**	1	5th PM	79-N	15-W
" "	**1**	1	5th PM	81-N	16-W
ROBERTSON	**14**	1	5th PM	78-N	15-W
" "	**13**	1	5th PM	78-N	16-W
" "	**12**	1	5th PM	79-N	13-W
ROBINS	**14**	1	5th PM	78-N	15-W

Surname	Map Group	Parcels of Land	Meridian/Township/Range
ROBINS (Cont'd)	9	1	5th PM 79-N 16-W
ROBINSON	12	6	5th PM 79-N 13-W
" "	7	4	5th PM 80-N 14-W
" "	11	1	5th PM 79-N 14-W
ROBISON	13	1	5th PM 78-N 16-W
RODGERS	10	2	5th PM 79-N 15-W
ROGERS	2	2	5th PM 81-N 15-W
" "	13	1	5th PM 78-N 16-W
" "	12	1	5th PM 79-N 13-W
ROHRER	16	1	5th PM 78-N 13-W
RORTY	15	1	5th PM 78-N 14-W
ROSS	4	5	5th PM 81-N 13-W
ROUSSEAU	12	1	5th PM 79-N 13-W
ROWLAND	16	2	5th PM 78-N 13-W
RUCKER	14	1	5th PM 78-N 15-W
RUSSELL	15	1	5th PM 78-N 14-W
" "	9	1	5th PM 79-N 16-W
" "	3	1	5th PM 81-N 14-W
RUTLEDGE	5	6	5th PM 80-N 16-W
RYAN	3	2	5th PM 81-N 14-W
" "	11	1	5th PM 79-N 14-W
RYEON	3	2	5th PM 81-N 14-W
" "	4	1	5th PM 81-N 13-W
SACKET	7	2	5th PM 80-N 14-W
SAMSON	4	1	5th PM 81-N 13-W
SANBORN	14	1	5th PM 78-N 15-W
SANDERS	4	2	5th PM 81-N 13-W
" "	16	1	5th PM 78-N 13-W
" "	14	1	5th PM 78-N 15-W
" "	12	1	5th PM 79-N 13-W
" "	10	1	5th PM 79-N 15-W
SANFORD	12	2	5th PM 79-N 13-W
SANXAY	4	14	5th PM 81-N 13-W
" "	7	7	5th PM 80-N 14-W
" "	6	7	5th PM 80-N 15-W
" "	14	6	5th PM 78-N 15-W
" "	12	3	5th PM 79-N 13-W
" "	8	3	5th PM 80-N 13-W
" "	13	1	5th PM 78-N 16-W
" "	11	1	5th PM 79-N 14-W
SARGENT	6	11	5th PM 80-N 15-W
" "	9	3	5th PM 79-N 16-W
" "	8	3	5th PM 80-N 13-W
" "	7	3	5th PM 80-N 14-W
SARGOOD	16	3	5th PM 78-N 13-W
SATCHELL	14	1	5th PM 78-N 15-W
SATER	7	1	5th PM 80-N 14-W
SAUNDERS	14	2	5th PM 78-N 15-W
SAVILLE	14	1	5th PM 78-N 15-W
SAXTON	16	1	5th PM 78-N 13-W
SCHIRCLIFF	4	1	5th PM 81-N 13-W
SCHMUCKER	1	3	5th PM 81-N 16-W
SCHNEIDER	7	1	5th PM 80-N 14-W
SCHOOLEY	16	1	5th PM 78-N 13-W
SCOTT	8	9	5th PM 80-N 13-W
SCRUGS	15	1	5th PM 78-N 14-W
SEARIGHT	15	2	5th PM 78-N 14-W
SEARS	12	5	5th PM 79-N 13-W
" "	2	2	5th PM 81-N 15-W
SELLEW	3	1	5th PM 81-N 14-W

Surname	Map Group	Parcels of Land	Meridian/Township/Range		
SEVERANCE	**6**	1	5th PM	80-N	15-W
SEVERNS	**16**	2	5th PM	78-N	13-W
SEYMOUR	**1**	2	5th PM	81-N	16-W
SHARP	**15**	3	5th PM	78-N	14-W
" "	**14**	1	5th PM	78-N	15-W
SHARRITT	**14**	3	5th PM	78-N	15-W
SHAUL	**16**	3	5th PM	78-N	13-W
SHAY	**13**	1	5th PM	78-N	16-W
SHAYLER	**5**	1	5th PM	80-N	16-W
SHEFFER	**14**	2	5th PM	78-N	15-W
SHELEY	**14**	2	5th PM	78-N	15-W
SHEPARD	**15**	2	5th PM	78-N	14-W
SHEPHARD	**13**	1	5th PM	78-N	16-W
SHERMAN	**1**	7	5th PM	81-N	16-W
" "	**6**	2	5th PM	80-N	15-W
SHERWOOD	**7**	5	5th PM	80-N	14-W
" "	**12**	2	5th PM	79-N	13-W
SHEWAKER	**3**	1	5th PM	81-N	14-W
SHIELDS	**2**	1	5th PM	81-N	15-W
SHIFFER	**14**	2	5th PM	78-N	15-W
SHIPLEY	**9**	1	5th PM	79-N	16-W
SHOALS	**6**	2	5th PM	80-N	15-W
SHOEMAKER	**3**	4	5th PM	81-N	14-W
SHOVER	**4**	1	5th PM	81-N	13-W
SHREVE	**7**	2	5th PM	80-N	14-W
" "	**3**	1	5th PM	81-N	14-W
SIGAFOOS	**7**	4	5th PM	80-N	14-W
SIGLER	**13**	2	5th PM	78-N	16-W
SILPATH	**5**	1	5th PM	80-N	16-W
SIMMONS	**12**	1	5th PM	79-N	13-W
SIMPKINS	**6**	3	5th PM	80-N	15-W
SIMPSON	**8**	3	5th PM	80-N	13-W
SKEELS	**9**	1	5th PM	79-N	16-W
SKINNER	**15**	6	5th PM	78-N	14-W
" "	**10**	5	5th PM	79-N	15-W
" "	**14**	1	5th PM	78-N	15-W
SLACK	**16**	2	5th PM	78-N	13-W
SLADDEN	**1**	1	5th PM	81-N	16-W
SMITH	**3**	17	5th PM	81-N	14-W
" "	**2**	9	5th PM	81-N	15-W
" "	**16**	7	5th PM	78-N	13-W
" "	**15**	4	5th PM	78-N	14-W
" "	**8**	4	5th PM	80-N	13-W
" "	**7**	4	5th PM	80-N	14-W
" "	**14**	3	5th PM	78-N	15-W
" "	**10**	3	5th PM	79-N	15-W
" "	**4**	3	5th PM	81-N	13-W
" "	**13**	2	5th PM	78-N	16-W
" "	**12**	2	5th PM	79-N	13-W
" "	**9**	2	5th PM	79-N	16-W
SMOTHERS	**16**	2	5th PM	78-N	13-W
SNODDY	**13**	3	5th PM	78-N	16-W
SNODGRASS	**13**	1	5th PM	78-N	16-W
SNOOKS	**8**	3	5th PM	80-N	13-W
SNOW	**13**	7	5th PM	78-N	16-W
SNOWDEN	**15**	1	5th PM	78-N	14-W
SNYDER	**12**	5	5th PM	79-N	13-W
" "	**3**	4	5th PM	81-N	14-W
" "	**15**	2	5th PM	78-N	14-W
" "	**2**	2	5th PM	81-N	15-W

Surname	Map Group	Parcels of Land	Meridian/Township/Range
SNYDER (Cont'd)	**7**	1	5th PM 80-N 14-W
SOHN	**14**	1	5th PM 78-N 15-W
SPANGLER	**2**	1	5th PM 81-N 15-W
SPENCER	**7**	9	5th PM 80-N 14-W
" "	**8**	2	5th PM 80-N 13-W
SPERRY	**9**	1	5th PM 79-N 16-W
SPONSLER	**8**	1	5th PM 80-N 13-W
SPRINGER	**6**	1	5th PM 80-N 15-W
SPURRIER	**13**	2	5th PM 78-N 16-W
SQUIRES	**4**	1	5th PM 81-N 13-W
" "	**3**	1	5th PM 81-N 14-W
ST JOHN	**11**	2	5th PM 79-N 14-W
" "	**9**	2	5th PM 79-N 16-W
STACY	**16**	1	5th PM 78-N 13-W
STALLINGS	**9**	1	5th PM 79-N 16-W
STANLEY	**11**	2	5th PM 79-N 14-W
" "	**14**	1	5th PM 78-N 15-W
" "	**1**	1	5th PM 81-N 16-W
STEEL	**14**	2	5th PM 78-N 15-W
STEELE	**14**	4	5th PM 78-N 15-W
STEPHENS	**5**	2	5th PM 80-N 16-W
STERRET	**7**	1	5th PM 80-N 14-W
STEVENS	**7**	2	5th PM 80-N 14-W
" "	**4**	2	5th PM 81-N 13-W
" "	**9**	1	5th PM 79-N 16-W
STEVENSON	**8**	1	5th PM 80-N 13-W
STEWART	**16**	1	5th PM 78-N 13-W
STILES	**4**	1	5th PM 81-N 13-W
STIVENS	**13**	1	5th PM 78-N 16-W
STIX	**14**	1	5th PM 78-N 15-W
STOCKDALE	**12**	8	5th PM 79-N 13-W
STODDARD	**7**	3	5th PM 80-N 14-W
" "	**5**	1	5th PM 80-N 16-W
STOKES	**4**	1	5th PM 81-N 13-W
STONEHOCKER	**14**	5	5th PM 78-N 15-W
STRONG	**1**	1	5th PM 81-N 16-W
STROUSE	**16**	1	5th PM 78-N 13-W
STROW	**3**	2	5th PM 81-N 14-W
STRUBLE	**16**	4	5th PM 78-N 13-W
" "	**7**	2	5th PM 80-N 14-W
STUBBINS	**13**	1	5th PM 78-N 16-W
STUFF	**16**	2	5th PM 78-N 13-W
STURGEON	**5**	1	5th PM 80-N 16-W
SUMMERS	**2**	4	5th PM 81-N 15-W
SUMNER	**4**	11	5th PM 81-N 13-W
SUTTON	**12**	3	5th PM 79-N 13-W
" "	**10**	3	5th PM 79-N 15-W
" "	**14**	2	5th PM 78-N 15-W
SWAIM	**13**	4	5th PM 78-N 16-W
SWAIN	**13**	1	5th PM 78-N 16-W
SWANEY	**13**	2	5th PM 78-N 16-W
SWART	**1**	2	5th PM 81-N 16-W
SWEET	**15**	1	5th PM 78-N 14-W
SWIFT	**11**	1	5th PM 79-N 14-W
SWITZER	**8**	2	5th PM 80-N 13-W
" "	**3**	2	5th PM 81-N 14-W
SYLVESTER	**13**	3	5th PM 78-N 16-W
" "	**14**	1	5th PM 78-N 15-W
" "	**9**	1	5th PM 79-N 16-W
" "	**8**	1	5th PM 80-N 13-W

Surname	Map Group	Parcels of Land	Meridian/Township/Range		
TALBOT	**8**	1	5th PM	80-N	13-W
TALBOTT	**8**	8	5th PM	80-N	13-W
" "	**7**	7	5th PM	80-N	14-W
TARR	**9**	1	5th PM	79-N	16-W
TAYLOR	**1**	15	5th PM	81-N	16-W
" "	**14**	5	5th PM	78-N	15-W
" "	**16**	2	5th PM	78-N	13-W
" "	**8**	2	5th PM	80-N	13-W
" "	**13**	1	5th PM	78-N	16-W
" "	**11**	1	5th PM	79-N	14-W
" "	**9**	1	5th PM	79-N	16-W
" "	**6**	1	5th PM	80-N	15-W
TEEL	**15**	2	5th PM	78-N	14-W
TERRY	**13**	2	5th PM	78-N	16-W
" "	**9**	2	5th PM	79-N	16-W
THOMAS	**1**	3	5th PM	81-N	16-W
" "	**2**	1	5th PM	81-N	15-W
THOMPSON	**13**	5	5th PM	78-N	16-W
" "	**14**	1	5th PM	78-N	15-W
" "	**9**	1	5th PM	79-N	16-W
THORN	**1**	4	5th PM	81-N	16-W
THORNE	**4**	1	5th PM	81-N	13-W
TIBBALS	**11**	7	5th PM	79-N	14-W
" "	**15**	3	5th PM	78-N	14-W
" "	**16**	2	5th PM	78-N	13-W
" "	**10**	1	5th PM	79-N	15-W
TICE	**10**	1	5th PM	79-N	15-W
TILL	**7**	1	5th PM	80-N	14-W
TIPPIE	**5**	3	5th PM	80-N	16-W
TOLAND	**2**	1	5th PM	81-N	15-W
TOMPKINS	**13**	2	5th PM	78-N	16-W
TOSSE	**15**	2	5th PM	78-N	14-W
TOUSEY	**15**	10	5th PM	78-N	14-W
" "	**11**	6	5th PM	79-N	14-W
" "	**8**	1	5th PM	80-N	13-W
TRACY	**11**	2	5th PM	79-N	14-W
" "	**10**	2	5th PM	79-N	15-W
" "	**14**	1	5th PM	78-N	15-W
" "	**8**	1	5th PM	80-N	13-W
TRICKER	**8**	3	5th PM	80-N	13-W
TRUMAN	**13**	6	5th PM	78-N	16-W
TUCKER	**4**	1	5th PM	81-N	13-W
TUDOR	**4**	1	5th PM	81-N	13-W
TURNER	**13**	1	5th PM	78-N	16-W
" "	**9**	1	5th PM	79-N	16-W
TUTHILL	**16**	1	5th PM	78-N	13-W
TUTTLE	**9**	2	5th PM	79-N	16-W
" "	**8**	2	5th PM	80-N	13-W
" "	**3**	1	5th PM	81-N	14-W
TYLER	**4**	1	5th PM	81-N	13-W
TYSON	**6**	1	5th PM	80-N	15-W
UNDERWOOD	**8**	1	5th PM	80-N	13-W
UNGER	**13**	1	5th PM	78-N	16-W
UPDEGRAFF	**12**	4	5th PM	79-N	13-W
VAN ANTWERP	**3**	2	5th PM	81-N	14-W
VANSCHOYCK	**3**	1	5th PM	81-N	14-W
VERNON	**16**	2	5th PM	78-N	13-W
VESTAL	**9**	3	5th PM	79-N	16-W
" "	**14**	2	5th PM	78-N	15-W
VOUGHT	**6**	1	5th PM	80-N	15-W

Surname	Map Group	Parcels of Land	Meridian/Township/Range		
WADDELL	**7**	3	5th PM	80-N	14-W
WADE	**13**	2	5th PM	78-N	16-W
WALKER	**15**	2	5th PM	78-N	14-W
" "	**13**	1	5th PM	78-N	16-W
WALLACK	**4**	2	5th PM	81-N	13-W
WARD	**16**	1	5th PM	78-N	13-W
" "	**12**	1	5th PM	79-N	13-W
" "	**6**	1	5th PM	80-N	15-W
WARFIELD	**6**	3	5th PM	80-N	15-W
" "	**2**	2	5th PM	81-N	15-W
" "	**1**	2	5th PM	81-N	16-W
WASSON	**15**	1	5th PM	78-N	14-W
" "	**11**	1	5th PM	79-N	14-W
WATKINS	**3**	1	5th PM	81-N	14-W
WATSON	**13**	23	5th PM	78-N	16-W
" "	**9**	2	5th PM	79-N	16-W
" "	**14**	1	5th PM	78-N	15-W
" "	**11**	1	5th PM	79-N	14-W
WATTS	**6**	1	5th PM	80-N	15-W
WEAVER	**14**	1	5th PM	78-N	15-W
WEBBER	**15**	1	5th PM	78-N	14-W
WEISE	**4**	1	5th PM	81-N	13-W
WEISER	**12**	1	5th PM	79-N	13-W
WEIST	**12**	3	5th PM	79-N	13-W
WELCH	**12**	2	5th PM	79-N	13-W
WELLER	**12**	1	5th PM	79-N	13-W
WELLS	**14**	1	5th PM	78-N	15-W
WENTZ	**2**	1	5th PM	81-N	15-W
WEST	**8**	2	5th PM	80-N	13-W
" "	**14**	1	5th PM	78-N	15-W
" "	**13**	1	5th PM	78-N	16-W
" "	**10**	1	5th PM	79-N	15-W
WESTCOTT	**1**	1	5th PM	81-N	16-W
WHEATLEY	**13**	5	5th PM	78-N	16-W
" "	**14**	1	5th PM	78-N	15-W
WHEELER	**3**	3	5th PM	81-N	14-W
" "	**7**	2	5th PM	80-N	14-W
" "	**5**	2	5th PM	80-N	16-W
" "	**9**	1	5th PM	79-N	16-W
WHERRY	**12**	5	5th PM	79-N	13-W
" "	**16**	2	5th PM	78-N	13-W
WHITAKER	**2**	3	5th PM	81-N	15-W
WHITCOMB	**14**	1	5th PM	78-N	15-W
" "	**10**	1	5th PM	79-N	15-W
WHITE	**13**	13	5th PM	78-N	16-W
" "	**14**	11	5th PM	78-N	15-W
" "	**12**	4	5th PM	79-N	13-W
" "	**8**	2	5th PM	80-N	13-W
" "	**6**	2	5th PM	80-N	15-W
" "	**15**	1	5th PM	78-N	14-W
" "	**10**	1	5th PM	79-N	15-W
WHITLOCK	**16**	1	5th PM	78-N	13-W
WHITNEY	**13**	1	5th PM	78-N	16-W
WICKHAM	**4**	2	5th PM	81-N	13-W
WILCOX	**9**	1	5th PM	79-N	16-W
WILDEN	**12**	2	5th PM	79-N	13-W
WILDER	**9**	1	5th PM	79-N	16-W
" "	**7**	1	5th PM	80-N	14-W
WILDS	**10**	2	5th PM	79-N	15-W
WILLIAMS	**11**	6	5th PM	79-N	14-W

Surname	Map Group	Parcels of Land	Meridian/Township/Range
WILLIAMS (Cont'd)	8	5	5th PM 80-N 13-W
" "	13	4	5th PM 78-N 16-W
" "	12	4	5th PM 79-N 13-W
" "	1	4	5th PM 81-N 16-W
" "	6	3	5th PM 80-N 15-W
" "	14	2	5th PM 78-N 15-W
" "	9	1	5th PM 79-N 16-W
" "	4	1	5th PM 81-N 13-W
WILLIAMSON	4	6	5th PM 81-N 13-W
" "	8	2	5th PM 80-N 13-W
" "	12	1	5th PM 79-N 13-W
WILLINGHAM	8	11	5th PM 80-N 13-W
" "	16	8	5th PM 78-N 13-W
" "	12	2	5th PM 79-N 13-W
" "	14	1	5th PM 78-N 15-W
" "	9	1	5th PM 79-N 16-W
" "	5	1	5th PM 80-N 16-W
" "	3	1	5th PM 81-N 14-W
WILLIS	9	1	5th PM 79-N 16-W
WILSEY	12	1	5th PM 79-N 13-W
WILSON	16	3	5th PM 78-N 13-W
" "	8	3	5th PM 80-N 13-W
" "	10	2	5th PM 79-N 15-W
" "	6	2	5th PM 80-N 15-W
" "	15	1	5th PM 78-N 14-W
" "	11	1	5th PM 79-N 14-W
" "	9	1	5th PM 79-N 16-W
" "	5	1	5th PM 80-N 16-W
" "	2	1	5th PM 81-N 15-W
WILTSE	13	1	5th PM 78-N 16-W
WIMER	14	1	5th PM 78-N 15-W
WINDERS	4	1	5th PM 81-N 13-W
WINELAND	8	1	5th PM 80-N 13-W
WINN	14	1	5th PM 78-N 15-W
WINSLOW	4	4	5th PM 81-N 13-W
WISDEN	10	1	5th PM 79-N 15-W
WITHROW	3	1	5th PM 81-N 14-W
WOLCOTT	16	1	5th PM 78-N 13-W
WOLFE	6	5	5th PM 80-N 15-W
" "	12	2	5th PM 79-N 13-W
" "	5	1	5th PM 80-N 16-W
WOOD	3	3	5th PM 81-N 14-W
" "	8	2	5th PM 80-N 13-W
" "	15	1	5th PM 78-N 14-W
WOODARD	4	2	5th PM 81-N 13-W
WOODS	1	1	5th PM 81-N 16-W
WOODWARD	14	2	5th PM 78-N 15-W
" "	11	2	5th PM 79-N 14-W
" "	8	1	5th PM 80-N 13-W
" "	1	1	5th PM 81-N 16-W
WOOLARD	13	2	5th PM 78-N 16-W
WOOLVERTON	14	1	5th PM 78-N 15-W
WRENN	7	2	5th PM 80-N 14-W
WRIGHT	14	2	5th PM 78-N 15-W
" "	16	1	5th PM 78-N 13-W
" "	2	1	5th PM 81-N 15-W
WYATT	10	1	5th PM 79-N 15-W
WYMORE	15	1	5th PM 78-N 14-W
" "	14	1	5th PM 78-N 15-W
YATES	16	1	5th PM 78-N 13-W

Surname	Map Group	Parcels of Land	Meridian/Township/Range
YOUNG	**3**	1	5th PM 81-N 14-W
ZEIGLER	**16**	1	5th PM 78-N 13-W
" "	**15**	1	5th PM 78-N 14-W
ZIMMERMAN	**13**	1	5th PM 78-N 16-W

– Part II –

Township Map Groups

Map Group 1: Index to Land Patents

Township 81-North Range 16-West (5th PM)

After you locate an individual in this Index, take note of the Section and Section Part then proceed to the Land Patent map on the pages immediately following. You should have no difficulty locating the corresponding parcel of land.

The "For More Info" Column will lead you to more information about the underlying Patents. See the *Legend* at right, and the "How to Use this Book" chapter, for more information.

```
                      LEGEND
        "For More Info . . . " column
A = Authority (Legislative Act, See Appendix "A")
B = Block or Lot (location in Section unknown)
C = Cancelled Patent
F = Fractional Section
G = Group (Multi-Patentee Patent, see Appendix "C")
V = Overlaps another Parcel
R = Re-Issued (Parcel patented more than once)

(A & G items require you to look in the Appendixes referred
to above. All other Letter-designations followed by a number
require you to locate line-items in this index that possess
the ID number found after the letter).
```

ID	Individual in Patent	Sec.	Sec. Part	Date Issued	Other Counties	For More Info . . .
178	AKIN, Thomas	17	SW	1855-12-15		A1
179	" "	17	W½SE	1855-12-15		A1
161	ALEXANDER, James	15	W½	1855-05-01		A1 G2
162	" "	20	SENE	1855-05-01		A1 G2 R30
163	" "	21	N½	1855-05-01		A1 G2
161	ALEXANDER, Robert	15	W½	1855-05-01		A1 G2
162	" "	20	SENE	1855-05-01		A1 G2 R30
163	" "	21	N½	1855-05-01		A1 G2
106	ANTHONY, John P	28	SESE	1854-12-09		A6
107	" "	28	W½SE	1854-12-09		A6
108	ARMSTRONG, John P	28	NESE	1854-12-09		A6
39	ATWELL, Dorothy J	7	E½SE	1856-01-15		A6 G96
48	BARNEY, James O	10	SWSE	1855-01-01		A6
46	BERRYHILL, James B	26	SWSW	1854-12-01		A1
177	BIXBY, Sumner	30	SE	1855-05-01		A1
121	BOND, Joseph W	11	SE	1857-02-20		A5
186	BOTTS, William S	25	SE	1855-01-01		A6 V185
187	" "	25	SESW	1855-01-01		A6
190	" "	25	W½SW	1855-01-01		A6 G31
189	" "	36	NE	1855-01-01		A6 G30
188	" "	36	NW	1855-01-01		A6
185	" "	25	NESE	1858-11-10		A6 V186
28	BRABROOK, George	13	E½SE	1855-12-15		A1
2	BROWN, Barnard	19	SW	1855-05-01		A1 F
3	" "	30	NW	1855-05-01		A1 F
12	BUDD, Edward	34	N½SE	1855-05-01		A1
55	BUTLER, Jerusha	7	W½SE	1855-12-15		A1
200	CARBERRY, Jonathan	32	E½SE	1855-02-01		A6 G273
184	CHILDS, Ward	31		1854-12-01		A1 F
8	CLANEY, David	1	SE	1855-12-15		A1
98	COMSTOCK, John	5	E½	1855-12-15		A1
116	CONWAY, Joseph	17	E½SE	1855-12-15		A1
117	" "	21	SWSE	1855-12-15		A1
118	" "	8	SE	1855-12-15		A1
153	CORRELL, Paul	8	NE	1855-05-10		A1
99	COSS, John	2	N½NW	1857-03-10		A1 F
100	" "	3	SWNW	1857-03-10		A1 F
84	COULTER, John Alexander	12	N½SE	1857-02-20		A5
85	" "	12	NESW	1857-02-20		A5
87	" "	12	S½NE	1857-02-20		A5 G59
88	" "	12	SENW	1857-02-20		A5 G59
86	" "	2	NE	1857-02-20		A5 F
126	CRAMER, Lois W	12	N½NW	1855-12-15		A1
127	" "	12	SWNW	1855-12-15		A1
90	CULBERTSON, John C	14	S½NW	1855-01-01		A6
91	" "	23	SW	1855-05-01		A1 G77

ID	Individual in Patent	Sec.	Sec. Part	Date Issued	Other Counties	For More Info . . .
92	CULBERTSON, John C (Cont'd)	26	N½SW	1855-05-01		A1 G77
93	" "	26	NW	1855-05-01		A1 G77
94	" "	35	NW	1855-05-01		A1 G77
58	CUSHMAN, Job	10	NESW	1855-01-01		A6
60	" "	10	SESW	1855-01-01		A6
78	" "	9	E½SE	1855-01-01		A6
79	" "	9	E½SW	1855-01-01		A6
81	" "	9	W½SE	1855-01-01		A6
82	" "	9	W½SW	1855-01-01		A6
83	" "	11	NENE	1855-05-01		A6 G84
63	" "	11	SENE	1855-05-01		A6
64	" "	11	W½NE	1855-05-01		A6
57	" "	10	E½SE	1855-05-10		A1
59	" "	10	NWSE	1855-05-10		A1
61	" "	10	W½SW	1855-05-10		A1
66	" "	14	NWNW	1855-05-10		A1
67	" "	15	NE	1855-05-10		A1
80	" "	9	NE	1855-05-10		A1
62	" "	11	E½NW	1855-12-15		A1
65	" "	12	N½NE	1855-12-15		A1
68	" "	18	N½NW	1855-12-15		A1 F
69	" "	18	SE	1855-12-15		A1
70	" "	21	E½SE	1855-12-15		A1
71	" "	21	NESW	1855-12-15		A1
72	" "	21	NWSE	1855-12-15		A1
73	" "	25	NW	1855-12-15		A1
74	" "	26	E½NE	1855-12-15		A1
75	" "	26	N½SE	1855-12-15		A1
76	" "	26	SESW	1855-12-15		A1
77	" "	28	N½NE	1855-12-15		A1
56	" "	1	SESW	1857-04-01		A4
87	CYPHER, Elizabeth	12	S½NE	1857-02-20		A5 G59
88	" "	12	SENW	1857-02-20		A5 G59
35	DOWNEY, Hugh D	36	SE	1854-01-01		A6
34	" "	35	NE	1855-05-01		A1
32	" "	3	N½NW	1855-12-15		A1 F
33	" "	3	SENW	1855-12-15		A1 F
36	" "	6	N½	1855-12-15		A1 F
37	" "	6	NWSW	1855-12-15		A1 F
38	" "	6	SE	1855-12-15		A1
39	" "	7	E½SE	1856-01-15		A6 G96
49	EASLEY, James S	6	SWSW	1855-05-01		A6 F
52	" "	7	W½NW	1855-05-01		A6 F
53	" "	7	W½SW	1855-05-01		A6 F
50	" "	7	E½NW	1855-12-15		A1 F
51	" "	7	E½SW	1855-12-15		A1 F
89	EVANS, George W	21	SWSW	1855-05-01		A1 G293
4	FENLON, Charles M	25	NE	1855-12-15		A1
104	FLANAGAN, John	1	NE	1855-12-15		A1 F
29	FRANCIS, George M	20	E½NW	1855-01-01		A6
30	" "	20	SENE	1855-01-01		A6 R162
31	" "	20	W½NE	1855-03-01		A4 G137
115	FURBER, Joseph B	28	S½NE	1855-05-01		A1
31	GARRETT, Eliza L	20	W½NE	1855-03-01		A4 G137
174	GATES, Simon S	23	SE	1856-05-01		A1
175	" "	26	W½NE	1856-05-01		A1
160	GILMORE, Quincy A	34	W½	1854-12-01		A1
159	" "	34	S½SE	1855-02-01		A6
141	GRIFFIN, Sophia	22	SESW	1855-03-01		A6 G267
122	GRINELL, Josiah B	28	NENW	1855-01-01		A6
123	GRINNELL, Josiah B	21	SESW	1854-12-01		A1
124	" "	28	S½NW	1855-05-01		A1
143	HARDING, Mordecai	8	W½SW	1855-12-15		A1
1	HAYS, Abraham	10	NW	1855-05-10		A1
11	HAYS, Deborah	3	SW	1855-05-10		A1
110	HAYS, John T	4	SW	1855-05-10		A1
111	" "	4	W½SE	1855-05-10		A1
119	HAYS, Joseph	4	E½SE	1855-12-15		A1
120	" "	5	SW	1855-12-15		A1
142	HAYS, Mary Jane	9	NW	1855-05-10		A1
165	HAYS, Samuel	11	SWNW	1855-01-01		A6
164	" "	10	NE	1855-05-10		A1
197	HERRON, Sarah	14	SENE	1855-05-01		A6 G250

ID	Individual in Patent	Sec.	Sec. Part	Date Issued	Other Counties	For More Info . . .
9	HILL, David	13	W½SW	1857-03-10		A1
189	HONICON, Alcey	36	NE	1855-01-01		A6 G30
190	HONOCOL, Aley	25	W½SW	1855-01-01		A6 G31
151	HORTON, Orson W	33	E½SW	1854-12-01		A1 V152
152	" "	33	SW	1854-12-01		A1 V151
176	IOWA, State Of	16		1937-08-26		A3
125	JAMIESON, Maria C	8	E½SW	1857-02-20		A5 G207
19	JONES, George A	23	NE	1855-01-01		A6
21	" "	24	E½NE	1855-01-01		A6
23	" "	24	SE	1855-01-01		A6
24	" "	24	W½NE	1855-01-01		A6
26	" "	26	SESE	1855-01-01		A6
22	" "	24	E½SW	1855-03-01		A4
25	" "	24	W½SW	1855-03-01		A4
16	" "	14	S½	1855-05-01		A1
17	" "	15	SE	1855-05-01		A1
18	" "	22	NE	1855-05-01		A1
20	" "	23	NW	1855-05-01		A1
27	" "	26	SWSE	1855-05-01		A1
180	KEENAN, Thomas	2	NWSW	1857-02-16		A5
181	" "	2	S½NW	1857-02-16		A5 F
201	KELLY, Nancy	32	E½SW	1855-03-01		A4 G274
47	KINSEY, James	19	NW	1855-12-15		A1 F
105	LLOYD, John	18	NE	1855-12-15		A1
182	LOCK, Thomas	12	NWSW	1857-03-10		A1
183	" "	5	N½NW	1857-03-10		A1 F
41	LOOSE, Isaac	2	W½SE	1855-05-01		A6
40	" "	2	E½SE	1855-12-15		A1
101	LOWRY, John F	20	SW	1855-05-01		A1
102	" "	29	NW	1855-05-01		A1
103	" "	30	SW	1855-05-01		A1 F
166	MCCLUNG, Samuel M	2	S½SW	1855-12-15		A1
125	MCKENZIE, Lewis	8	E½SW	1857-02-20		A5 G207
109	MCMILLAN, Margaret	20	NWNW	1855-01-01		A6 G253
54	METHVEN, Janette	5	S½NW	1857-06-01		A5 F
168	MILLAR, Samuel R	28	SW	1854-12-01		A1
169	" "	29	S½	1854-12-01		A1
170	" "	32	N½	1854-12-01		A1
138	MONTGOMERY, Mary	22	NWSW	1855-03-01		A6 G268
15	NEFF, Fleming	12	SESE	1857-03-10		A1
44	NETHEROW, Jacob	1	N½SW	1855-12-15		A1 F
45	" "	1	NW	1855-12-15		A1 F
167	NEWELL, Samuel	1	SWSW	1857-03-10		A1
139	PHILLIPS, Phebe	27	NWSW	1859-08-01		A6 G269
158	PLYMPTON, Peter W L	22	NW	1855-01-01		A6
95	PROCTOR, John C	7	E½NE	1855-12-15		A1
96	" "	8	NW	1855-12-15		A1
144	RENO, Morgan	13	NESE	1855-03-01		A4 C
146	" "	13	SESW	1855-03-01		A4
91	" "	23	SW	1855-05-01		A1 G77
92	" "	26	N½SW	1855-05-01		A1 G77
93	" "	26	NW	1855-05-01		A1 G77
94	" "	35	NW	1855-05-01		A1 G77
147	" "	13	W½SE	1855-12-15		A1
149	" "	17	NW	1857-02-20		A5
148	" "	14	NENW	1857-04-01		A4
145	" "	13	NESW	1914-12-11		A5
156	RIGHTMYER, Peter M	28	NWNW	1855-02-01		A6
154	" "	19	SE	1855-05-01		A1
155	" "	20	SWNW	1855-05-01		A1
157	" "	30	NE	1855-05-01		A1
83	ROBERTS, Mary A	11	NENE	1855-05-01		A6 G84
171	SCHMUCKER, Samuel S	19	NE	1855-05-01		A1
172	" "	20	SE	1855-05-01		A1
173	" "	29	NE	1855-05-01		A1
13	SEYMOUR, Emery T	21	NWSW	1855-12-15		A1
14	" "	4	N½	1855-12-15		A1 F
191	SHERMAN, William	11	SW	1855-05-01		A6
195	" "	14	NENE	1855-05-01		A6
197	" "	14	SENE	1855-05-01		A6 G250
192	" "	12	S½SW	1855-12-15		A1
193	" "	12	SWSE	1855-12-15		A1
194	" "	13	NW	1855-12-15		A1

ID	Individual in Patent	Sec.	Sec. Part	Date Issued	Other Counties	For More Info . . .
196	SHERMAN, William (Cont'd)	14	W½NE	1855-12-15		A1
109	SLADDEN, John	20	NWNW	1855-01-01		A6 G253
112	STANLEY, John W	34	NE	1855-05-01		A1
97	STRONG, Charles	11	NWNW	1857-04-02		A6 G261
97	STRONG, Emily	11	NWNW	1857-04-02		A6 G261
97	STRONG, John C	11	NWNW	1857-04-02		A6 G261
42	SWART, Jackson	6	E½SW	1855-12-15		A1 F
43	"	7	W½NE	1855-12-15		A1
128	TAYLOR, Lorenzo M	22	NESE	1855-03-01		A6
129	" "	22	NESW	1855-03-01		A6
130	" "	22	NWSE	1855-03-01		A6
138	" "	22	NWSW	1855-03-01		A6 G268
131	" "	22	SESE	1855-03-01		A6
141	" "	22	SESW	1855-03-01		A6 G267
132	" "	22	SWSE	1855-03-01		A6
140	" "	22	SWSW	1855-03-01		A6 G270
133	" "	27	NE	1855-03-01		A6
134	" "	27	NESW	1855-03-01		A6
136	" "	27	SESW	1855-03-01		A6
135	" "	27	SE	1857-04-10		A6
139	" "	27	NWSW	1859-08-01		A6 G269
137	" "	27	SWSW	1860-11-01		A6
150	TAYLOR, Oliver D	13	NE	1855-12-15		A1
5	THOMAS, Darius	17	NE	1855-05-10		A1
6	" "	3	NE	1855-05-10		A1 F
7	" "	3	SE	1855-05-10		A1
200	THORN, William	32	E½SE	1855-02-01		A6 G273
198	" "	32	W½SE	1855-02-01		A6 G271
199	" "	32	W½SW	1855-02-01		A6 G272
201	" "	32	E½SW	1855-03-01		A4 G274
113	WARFIELD, John	18	S½NW	1855-05-10		A1 F
114	" "	18	SW	1855-05-10		A1 F
140	WESTCOTT, Sarah	22	SWSW	1855-03-01		A6 G270
198	WILLIAMS, Jesee S	32	W½SE	1855-02-01		A6 G271
200	WILLIAMS, Jesse L	32	E½SE	1855-02-01		A6 G273
199	" "	32	W½SW	1855-02-01		A6 G272
201	" "	32	E½SW	1855-03-01		A4 G274
10	WOODS, David W	2	NESW	1856-01-15		A6
89	WOODWARD, John B	21	SWSW	1855-05-01		A1 G293

Patent Map

T81-N R16-W
5th PM Meridian

Map Group 1

Township Statistics

Parcels Mapped	:	201
Number of Patents	:	179
Number of Individuals	:	96
Patentees Identified	:	90
Number of Surnames	:	86
Multi-Patentee Parcels	:	27
Oldest Patent Date	:	1/1/1854
Most Recent Patent	:	8/26/1937
Block/Lot Parcels	:	0
Parcels Re - Issued	:	1
Parcels that Overlap	:	4
Cities and Towns	:	0
Cemeteries	:	2

Map grid

Section 6
DOWNEY Hugh D 1855
DOWNEY Hugh D 1855
EASLEY James S 1855
SWART Jackson 1855
DOWNEY Hugh D 1855

Section 5
LOCK Thomas 1857
METHVEN Janette 1857
COMSTOCK John 1855
HAYS Joseph 1855

Section 4
SEYMOUR Emery T 1855
HAYS John T 1855
HAYS John T 1855
HAYS Joseph 1855

Section 7
EASLEY James S 1855
EASLEY James S 1855
SWART Jackson 1855
PROCTOR John C 1855
EASLEY James S 1855
EASLEY James S 1855
BUTLER Jerusha 1855
DOWNEY [96] Hugh D 1856

Section 8
PROCTOR John C 1855
CORRELL Paul 1855
HARDING Mordecai 1855
MCKENZIE [207] Lewis 1857
CONWAY Joseph 1855

Section 9
HAYS Mary Jane 1855
CUSHMAN Job 1855
CUSHMAN Job 1855
CUSHMAN Job 1855
CUSHMAN Job 1855
CUSHMAN Job 1855

Section 18
CUSHMAN Job 1855
WARFIELD John 1855
LLOYD John 1855
WARFIELD John 1855
CUSHMAN Job 1855

Section 17
RENO Morgan 1857
AKIN Thomas 1855
AKIN Thomas 1855
CONWAY Joseph 1855

Section 16
THOMAS Darius 1855
IOWA State Of 1937

Section 19
KINSEY James 1855
SCHMUCKER Samuel S 1855
BROWN Barnard 1855
RIGHTMYER Peter M 1855

Section 20
SLADDEN [253] John 1855
RIGHTMYER Peter M 1855
FRANCIS George M 1855
LOWRY John F 1855
SCHMUCKER Samuel S 1855

Section 21
FRANCIS [137] George M 1855
FRANCIS George M 1855
ALEXANDER [2] Robert 1855
ALEXANDER [2] Robert 1855
SEYMOUR Emery T 1855
CUSHMAN Job 1855
CUSHMAN Job 1855
CUSHMAN Job 1855
WOODWARD [293] John B 1855
GRINNELL Josiah B 1854
CONWAY Joseph 1855

Section 30
BROWN Barnard 1855
RIGHTMYER Peter M 1855
LOWRY John F 1855
BIXBY Sumner 1855

Section 29
LOWRY John F 1855
SCHMUCKER Samuel S 1855
MILLAR Samuel R 1854

Section 28
RIGHTMYER Peter M 1855
GRINELL Josiah B 1855
CUSHMAN Job 1855
GRINNELL Josiah B 1855
FURBER Joseph B 1855
MILLAR Samuel R 1854
ANTHONY John P 1854
ARMSTRONG John P 1854
ANTHONY John P 1854

Section 31
CHILDS Ward 1854

Section 32
MILLAR Samuel R 1854
THORN [272] William 1855
THORN [274] William 1855
THORN [271] William 1855
THORN [273] William 1855

Section 33
HORTON Orson W 1854
HORTON Orson W 1854

Section 3
DOWNEY Hugh D 1855
COSS John 1857
DOWNEY Hugh D 1855
THOMAS Darius 1855
HAYS Deborah 1855
THOMAS Darius 1855

Section 2
COSS John 1857
KEENAN Thomas 1857
KEENAN Thomas 1857
WOODS David W 1856
MCCLUNG Samuel M 1855
LOOSE Isaac 1855
LOOSE Isaac 1855

Section 1
NETHEROW Jacob 1855
FLANAGAN John 1855
NETHEROW Jacob 1855
NEWELL Samuel 1857
CUSHMAN Job 1857
CLANEY David 1855

Section 10
HAYS Abraham 1855
HAYS Samuel 1855
CUSHMAN Job 1855
CUSHMAN Job 1855
CUSHMAN Job 1855
BARNEY James O 1855
CUSHMAN Job 1855
CUSHMAN Job 1855
CUSHMAN Job 1855
CUSHMAN Job 1855

Section 11
STRONG [261] John C 1857
HAYS Samuel 1855
CUSHMAN Job 1855
CUSHMAN Job 1855
CUSHMAN [84] Job 1855
CUSHMAN Job 1855
SHERMAN William 1855
BOND Joseph W 1857

Section 12
CRAMER Lois W 1855
CUSHMAN Job 1855
CRAMER Lois W 1855
COULTER [59] John Alexander 1857
COULTER [59] John Alexander 1857
LOCK Thomas 1857
COULTER John Alexander 1857
COULTER John Alexander 1857
SHERMAN William 1855
SHERMAN William 1855
NEFF Fleming 1857

Section 15
ALEXANDER [2] Robert 1855
CUSHMAN Job 1855
JONES George A 1855

Section 14
CUSHMAN Job 1855
RENO Morgan 1857
CULBERTSON John C 1855
SHERMAN William 1855
SHERMAN [250] William 1855
JONES George A 1855

Section 13
SHERMAN William 1855
SHERMAN William 1855
TAYLOR Oliver D 1855
HILL David 1857
RENO Morgan 1914
RENO Morgan 1855
RENO Morgan 1855
RENO Morgan 1855
BRABROOK George 1855

Section 22
PLYMPTON Peter W L 1855
JONES George A 1855
TAYLOR [268] Lorenzo M 1855
TAYLOR Lorenzo M 1855
TAYLOR Lorenzo M 1855
TAYLOR Lorenzo M 1855
TAYLOR [270] Lorenzo M 1855
TAYLOR [267] Lorenzo M 1855
TAYLOR Lorenzo M 1855
TAYLOR Lorenzo M 1855

Section 23
JONES George A 1855
JONES George A 1855
CULBERTSON [77] John C 1855
GATES Simon S 1856

Section 24
JONES George A 1855
JONES George A 1855
JONES George A 1855
JONES George A 1855
JONES George A 1855
JONES George A 1855

Section 27
TAYLOR Lorenzo M 1855
TAYLOR [269] Lorenzo M 1859
TAYLOR Lorenzo M 1855
TAYLOR Lorenzo M 1857
TAYLOR Lorenzo M 1860
TAYLOR Lorenzo M 1855

Section 26
CULBERTSON [77] John C 1855
GATES Simon S 1856
CUSHMAN Job 1855
CULBERTSON [77] John C 1855
CUSHMAN Job 1855
BERRYHILL James B 1854
CUSHMAN Job 1855
JONES George A 1855
JONES George A 1855

Section 25
CUSHMAN Job 1855
FENLON Charles M 1855
BOTTS [31] William S 1855
BOTTS William S 1855
BOTTS William S 1855
BOTTS William S 1858

Section 34
STANLEY John W 1855
BUDD Edward 1855
GILMORE Quincy A 1854
GILMORE Quincy A 1855

Section 35
CULBERTSON [77] John C 1855
DOWNEY Hugh D 1855

Section 36
BOTTS William S 1855
BOTTS [30] William S 1855
DOWNEY Hugh D 1854

Helpful Hints

1. This Map's INDEX can be found on the preceding pages.

2. Refer to Map "C" to see where this Township lies within Poweshiek County, Iowa.

3. Numbers within square brackets [ ] denote a multi-patentee land parcel (multi-owner). Refer to Appendix "C" for a full list of members in this group.

4. Areas that look to be crowded with Patentees usually indicate multiple sales of the same parcel (Re-issues) or Overlapping parcels. See this Township's Index for an explanation of these and other circumstances that might explain "odd" groupings of Patentees on this map.

Legend

— Patent Boundary

— Section Boundary

No Patents Found (or Outside County)

1., 2., 3., ... Lot Numbers (when beside a name)

[ ] Group Number (see Appendix "C")

Scale: Section = 1 mile X 1 mile (generally, with some exceptions)

Road Map

T81-N R16-W
5th PM Meridian

Map Group 1

Cities & Towns
None

Cemeteries
Chester Cemetery
Chester Cemetery

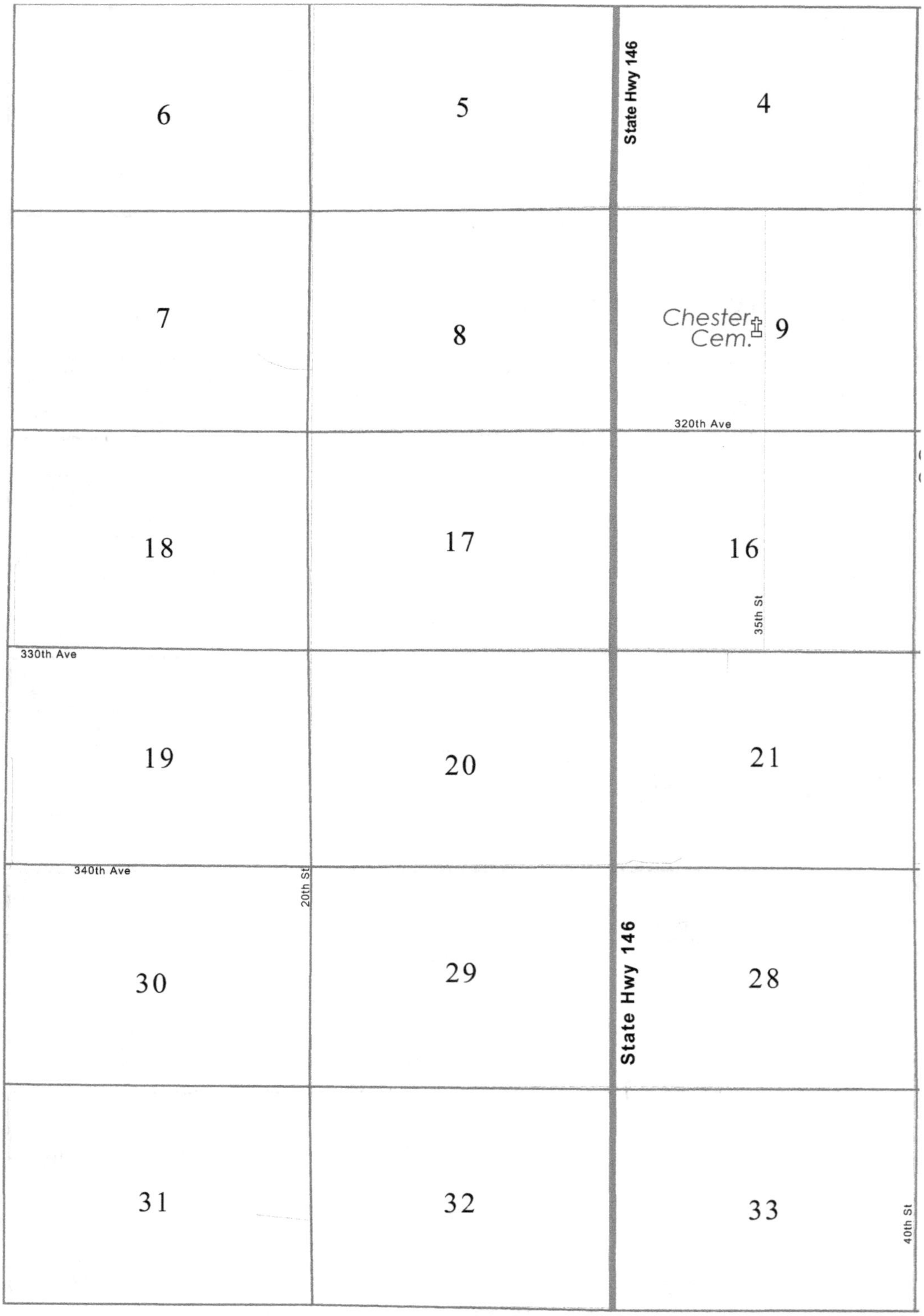

6	5	4
7	8	Chester Cem. 9
18	17	16
19	20	21
30	29	28
31	32	33

State Hwy 146

320th Ave

330th Ave

340th Ave

35th St

20th St

40th St

3	2	1
10	11	12
15	14	13
22	23	24
27	26	25
34	35	36

310th Ave
60th St
Chester Cem.
50th St
322nd Ave
70th St
340th Ave
Newburg Rd
345th Ave
350th Ave
360th Ave

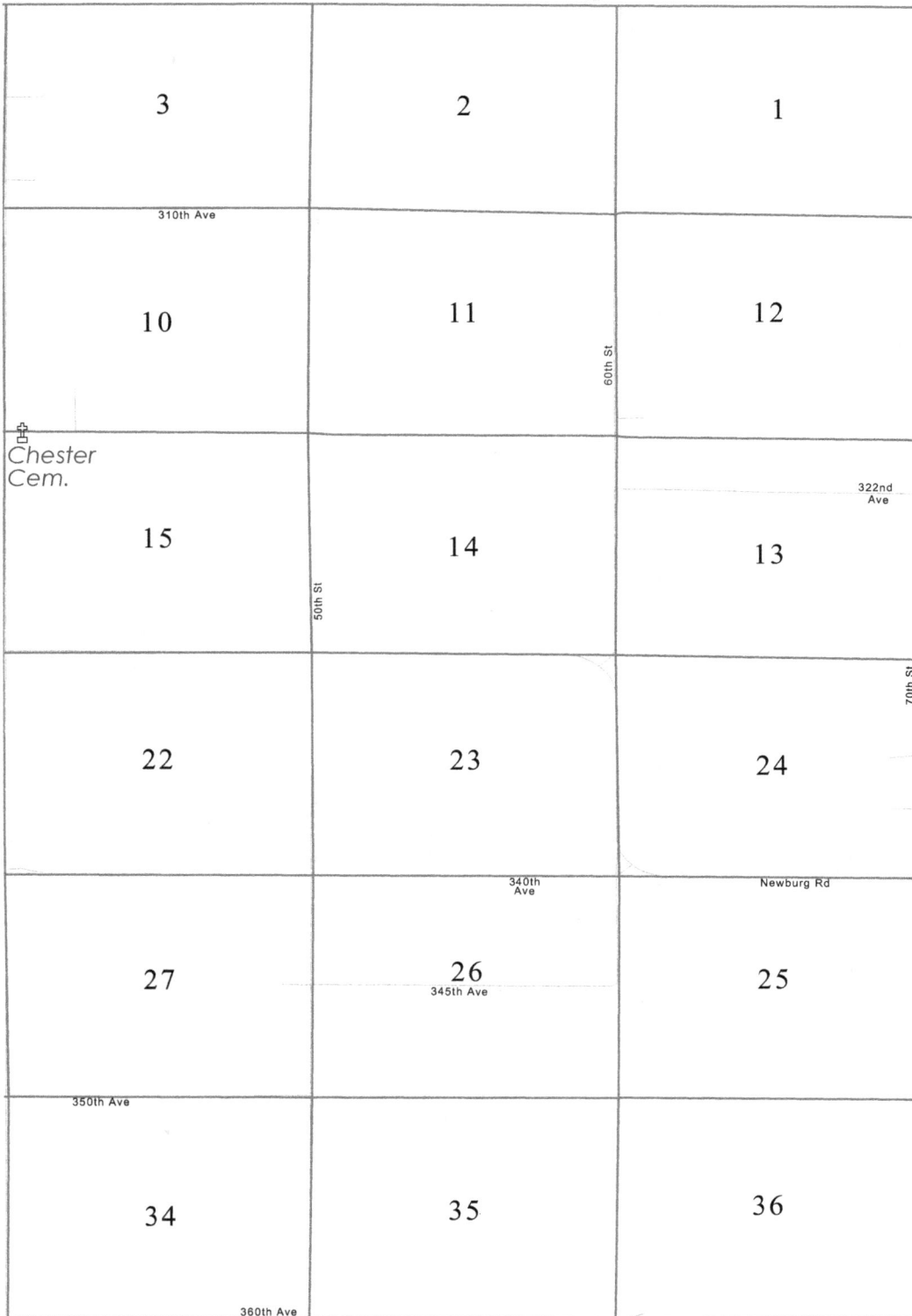

Helpful Hints

1. This road map has a number of uses, but primarily it is to help you: a) find the present location of land owned by your ancestors (at least the general area), b) find cemeteries and city-centers, and c) estimate the route/roads used by Census-takers & tax-assessors.

2. If you plan to travel to Poweshiek County to locate cemeteries or land parcels, please pick up a modern travel map for the area before you do. Mapping old land parcels on modern maps is not as exact a science as you might think. Just the slightest variations in public land survey coordinates, estimates of parcel boundaries, or road-map deviations can greatly alter a map's representation of how a road either does or doesn't cross a particular parcel of land.

Legend

— Section Lines
≡ Interstates
— Highways
— Other Roads
● Cities/Towns
✝ Cemeteries

Scale: Section = 1 mile X 1 mile (generally, with some exceptions)

Historical Map

T81-N R16-W
5th PM Meridian

Map Group 1

Cities & Towns
None

6	5	4
7	8	9 Chester Cem.
18	17	16
19	20	21 Big Bear Crk
30	29	28
31	32	33

Cemeteries
Chester Cemetery
Chester Cemetery

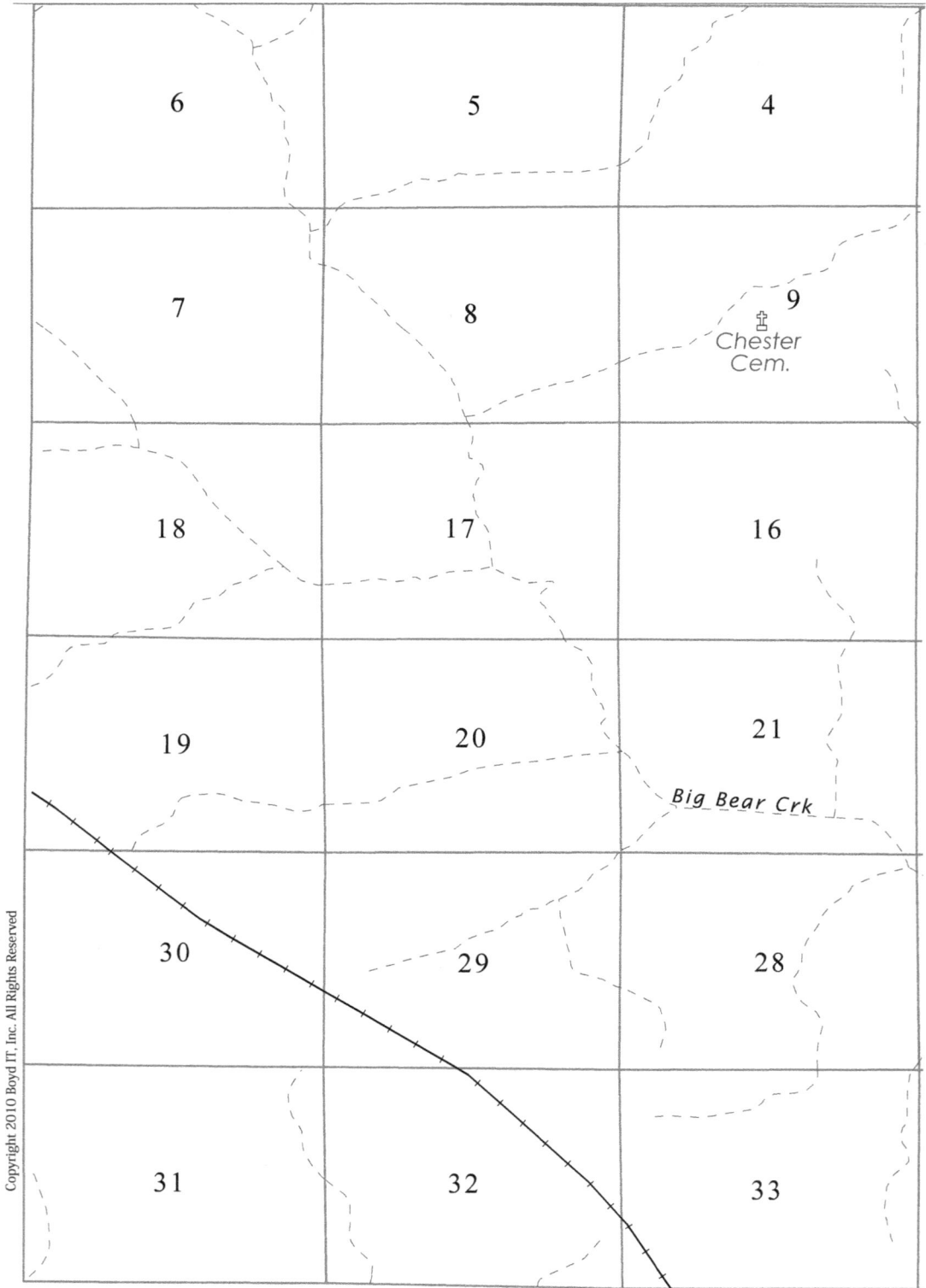

3

2

1

Abes Frk

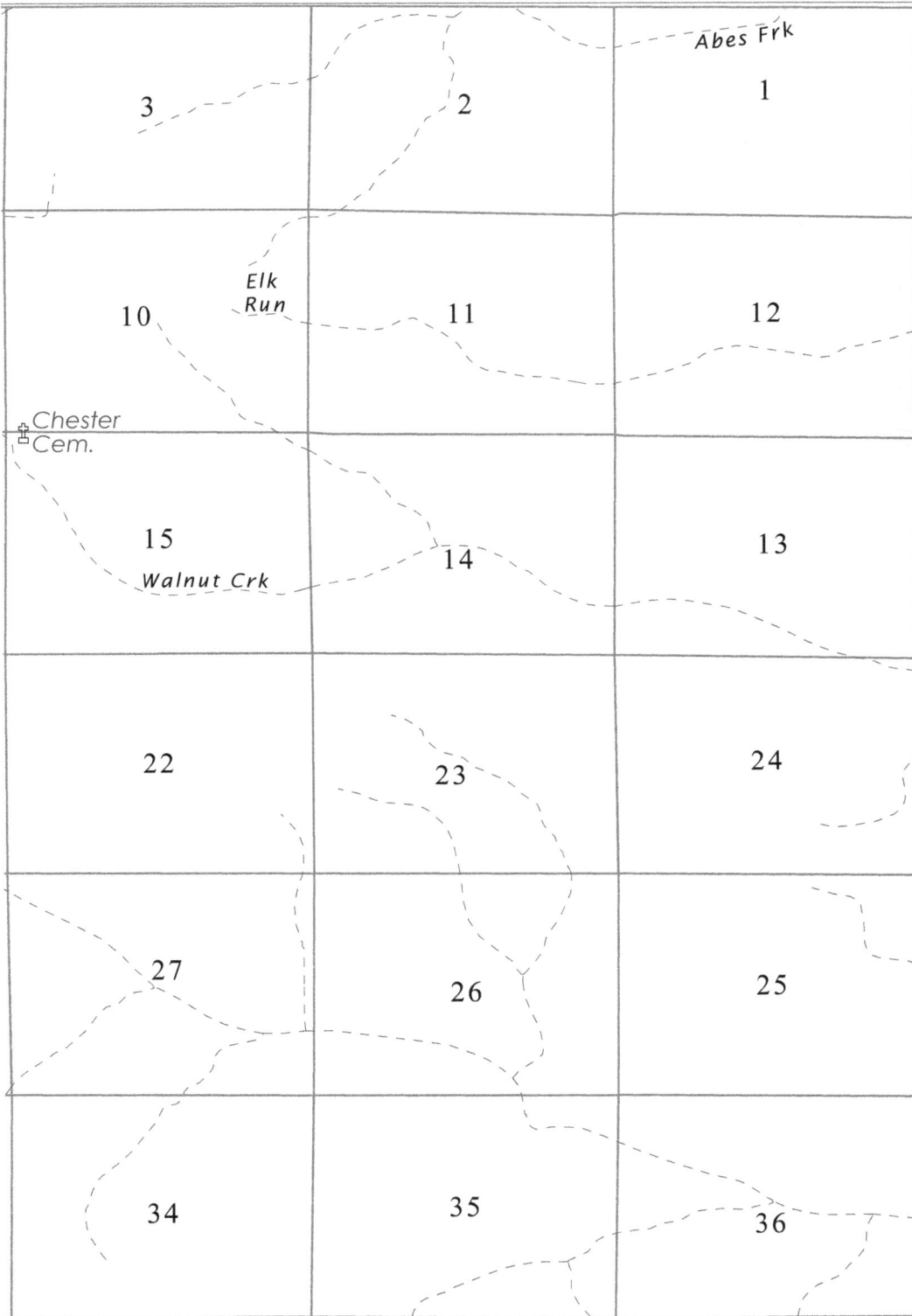

10

Elk
Run

11

12

Chester
Cem.

15

13

Walnut Crk

14

22

23

24

27

26

25

34

35

36

L e g e n d

——————	Section Lines
+++++++	Railroads
▨	Large Rivers & Bodies of Water
- - - - - -	Streams/Creeks & Small Rivers
●	Cities/Towns
⚰	Cemeteries

Scale: Section = 1 mile X 1 mile
(there are some exceptions)

Map Group 2: Index to Land Patents

Township 81-North Range 15-West (5th PM)

After you locate an individual in this Index, take note of the Section and Section Part then proceed to the Land Patent map on the pages immediately following. You should have no difficulty locating the corresponding parcel of land.

The "For More Info" Column will lead you to more information about the underlying Patents. See the *Legend* at right, and the "How to Use this Book" chapter, for more information.

```
                   LEGEND
          "For More Info . . . " column
A = Authority (Legislative Act, See Appendix "A")
B = Block or Lot (location in Section unknown)
C = Cancelled Patent
F = Fractional Section
G = Group  (Multi-Patentee Patent, see Appendix "C")
V = Overlaps another Parcel
R = Re-Issued (Parcel patented more than once)

(A & G items require you to look in the Appendixes referred
to above. All other Letter-designations followed by a number
require you to locate line-items in this index that possess
the ID number found after the letter).
```

ID	Individual in Patent	Sec.	Sec. Part	Date Issued	Other Counties	For More Info . . .
224	BAILEY, Charles E	7	SW	1855-05-01		A1 F
340	BARNES, Maria	34	SWNW	1856-06-16		A6
268	BATES, Calista B	18	W½SW	1856-01-15		A6 G33 F
269	" "	19	W½NW	1856-01-15		A6 G33 F
347	BEAN, Betsy L	29	NW	1855-01-01		A6 G143
347	BEAN, Mary Jane	29	NW	1855-01-01		A6 G143
347	BEAN, Silas T	29	NW	1855-01-01		A6 G143
215	BEEM, Arza B	2	E½	1855-12-15		A1 F
371	BERRYHILL, William D	23	NESE	1855-05-01		A1
372	" "	23	SENE	1855-05-01		A1
349	BLAKE, Patrick H	2	N½NW	1857-03-10		A1 F
266	BRABROOK, George	28	N½NW	1855-12-15		A1
267	" "	28	NWNE	1855-12-15		A1
264	" "	18	E½SW	1856-01-15		A6 F
268	" "	18	W½SW	1856-01-15		A6 G33 F
265	" "	19	E½SW	1856-01-15		A6 F
269	" "	19	W½NW	1856-01-15		A6 G33 F
342	BRAUGHTON, Sarah H	7	SE	1855-05-01		A6 G136
271	CALKINS, George W	24	N½SE	1855-12-15		A1
291	CAMPBELL, Jacob	23	N½SW	1855-01-01		A6
292	" "	23	S½NW	1855-01-01		A6
216	CARNEY, Bartholomew	26	NE	1855-05-01		A1
217	" "	26	W½	1855-05-01		A1
218	" "	28	S½	1855-05-01		A1
305	CLANEY, John	6	SW	1855-12-15		A1 F
306	" "	6	W½SE	1855-12-15		A1
351	CLARKE, Peter	20	N½NE	1857-02-20		A5
352	" "	20	S½NW	1857-02-20		A5
353	" "	28	S½NW	1857-02-20		A5
354	" "	28	SWNE	1857-02-20		A5
286	CLOSSEN, Isaac	12	SW	1855-12-15		A1
357	CODDING, Samuel N	1	N½SE	1855-05-10		A1
341	COLLIN, Mary E	20	N½NW	1856-01-15		A6
230	CONVERS, Daniel C	17	NE	1855-01-01		A6
350	CORRELL, Paul	34	S½SW	1855-05-10		A1
206	COTTRELL, Almon O	15	N½SE	1856-09-01		A1
207	" "	15	W½SW	1856-09-01		A1
208	" "	34	SE	1857-02-16		A5
369	COUCH, Uriah B	18	SE	1855-12-15		A1
370	" "	19	NE	1855-12-15		A1
277	COULSON, Henry	22	SW	1855-12-15		A1
285	CRIPMAN, Ira	8	N½SW	1855-12-15		A1
316	CROSS, John T	8	NW	1856-05-01		A1
304	CULBERTSON, John C	31	SWSW	1857-03-10		A1 F
293	DAVENPORT, Jacob	35	S½SE	1855-12-15		A1
294	" "	35	SESW	1855-12-15		A1

ID	Individual in Patent	Sec.	Sec. Part	Date Issued	Other Counties	For More Info . . .
379	DAVIS, William T	13	N½SE	1855-12-15		A1
380	" "	13	S½NE	1855-12-15		A1
225	DENISON, Charles E	10	NW	1855-12-15		A1
272	DILLON, Hannah S	7	E½SW	1855-03-01		A4
284	DOWNEY, Hugh D	30	E½NW	1855-12-15		A1 F
231	DWIGHT, Daniel	17	SW	1855-12-15		A1
254	EDDY, Franklin	35	N½NW	1855-12-15		A1
255	"	35	SENW	1855-12-15		A1
209	ELLIOTT, Amelia K	33	S½	1855-05-10		A1
329	ELLIS, Joseph S	22	NE	1855-12-15		A1
297	EMOTT, James	34	NWSW	1856-06-16		A6
307	ENGLISH, John	5	SW	1855-12-15		A1
308	"	6	E½SE	1855-12-15		A1
227	FENLON, Charles M	5	NE	1855-12-15		A1 F
309	FLANAGAN, John	28	NENE	1855-12-15		A1
373	FLANAGAN, William	27	N½SW	1855-12-15		A1
374	" "	28	SENE	1855-12-15		A1
375	" "	6	NW	1855-12-15		A1 F
300	FORSYTHE, John A	17	NW	1855-05-01		A6
302	" "	18	NE	1855-05-01		A6
299	" "	15	NE	1855-12-15		A1
301	" "	17	SE	1855-12-15		A1
303	" "	9	NW	1855-12-15		A1
342	FORSYTHE, Mathew	7	SE	1855-05-01		A6 G136
343	FORSYTHE, Matthew	15	NW	1855-12-15		A1
328	FRANCE, Joseph D	13	NENE	1855-12-15		A1
233	FULLER, Dimiris	27	N½NW	1855-12-15		A1
310	GAMBLE, John H	30	E½SE	1855-12-15		A1
288	GASKILL, Israel	22	W½SE	1855-12-15		A1
345	GATHIELL, Nathan	29	SW	1855-03-01		A4
346	GATTRELL, Nathan	20	SW	1855-01-01		A6
347	" "	29	NW	1855-01-01		A6 G143
275	GLADSON, Rebecca	29	NENE	1856-01-15		A6 G226 C R276
276	" "	29	NENE	1857-04-02		A6 G226 R275
318	GOODRICH, John W	2	S½NW	1855-12-15		A1 F
319	" "	2	SW	1855-12-15		A1
202	GOUDY, Abel C	27	E½	1855-05-01		A1
203	" "	29	SE	1855-05-01		A1
204	" "	34	NE	1855-05-01		A1
335	GRAYUM, Polly	12	S½NW	1857-02-20		A5 G255
358	GRUWELL, Sarah	3	NENW	1855-12-15		A1 F
359	" "	3	W½NW	1855-12-15		A1 F
295	HARMAN, Jacob	22	E½SE	1855-05-01		A6
296	" "	23	SWSW	1855-12-15		A1
213	HARRINGTON, Clarissa	24	SWNE	1856-01-15		A6 G164
213	HART, Anson	24	SWNE	1856-01-15		A6 G164
377	HAVENS, William	4	S½	1855-12-15		A1
378	" "	4	S½NE	1855-12-15		A1 F
253	HAWES, Franklin B	8	SE	1855-05-10		A1
249	HILL, Ephraim B	1	NE	1855-05-10		A1 F
355	HUMPHREY, Rollin O	1	S½SE	1855-05-10		A1
330	HUNT, Joshua	35	N½SW	1855-12-15		A1
365	HUNT, Thomas	14	SWSW	1855-12-15		A1
366	" "	15	S½SE	1855-12-15		A1
367	" "	15	SESW	1855-12-15		A1
368	" "	23	NWNW	1855-12-15		A1
364	IOWA, State Of	16		1937-08-26		A3
356	JACK, Samuel	22	NW	1855-12-15		A1
259	JONES, George A	30	NENE	1855-01-01		A6 R260
259	" "	30	NENE	1855-01-01		A6 C R260
260	" "	30	NENE	1855-01-01		A6 R259
260	" "	30	NENE	1855-01-01		A6 C R259
261	" "	30	NWNE	1855-01-01		A6
263	" "	30	SWNE	1855-01-01		A6
258	" "	19	S½	1855-05-01		A1 F
262	" "	30	SENE	1935-10-08		A6
245	JUDD, Eli P	24	S½NW	1855-05-01		A1 G182
246	" "	24	SW	1855-05-01		A1 G182
240	" "	35	N½SE	1855-05-01		A1
241	" "	35	NE	1855-05-01		A1
242	" "	36	N½	1855-05-01		A1
243	" "	36	N½SE	1855-05-01		A1
244	" "	36	N½SW	1855-05-01		A1

ID	Individual in Patent	Sec.	Sec. Part	Date Issued	Other Counties	For More Info . . .
223	KAPLE, Martha	34	NESW	1856-06-16		A6 G199
235	KELLOGG, Edmund B	9	NE	1855-12-15		A1
228	KORNS, Charles W	7	SWSW	1857-03-10		A1 F
229	" "	7	W½NE	1857-03-10		A1
311	KORNS, John	27	S½NW	1855-12-15		A1
312	" "	5	SE	1855-12-15		A1
313	" "	8	N½NE	1855-12-15		A1
234	LANCEY, Dustin	31	SESW	1855-06-01		A6 F
278	LITTLE, Henry	7	NWSW	1857-02-20		A6 F
360	LOEBER, Seigfried	23	S½SE	1855-12-15		A1
361	" "	23	SESW	1855-12-15		A1
279	LOESCH, Henry	18	NW	1855-12-15		A1 G195 F
287	LOOSE, Isaac	32		1855-12-15		A1
323	LOOSE, Joseph B	30	SW	1855-12-15		A1 F
324	" "	30	W½SE	1855-12-15		A1
325	" "	31	N½	1855-12-15		A1 F
326	" "	31	N½SW	1855-12-15		A1 F
327	" "	31	SE	1855-12-15		A1
280	MAGILL, Henry	7	NW	1855-12-15		A1 F
223	MANN, Charles A	34	NESW	1856-06-16		A6 G199
333	MCKENZIE, Lewis	6	N½NE	1856-06-16		A6 F
236	MILLER, Edmund G	30	W½NW	1855-12-15		A1 F
314	MISCHLICH, John	8	S½SW	1855-12-15		A1
210	MOREY, Amos	3	NE	1855-12-15		A1 F
211	" "	3	SENW	1855-12-15		A1 F
212	" "	4	NW	1855-12-15		A1 F
239	MORRIS, Edward W	10	NE	1855-12-15		A1
245	MOSELY, Frederick	24	S½NW	1855-05-01		A1 G182
256	" "	24	S½SE	1855-05-01		A1
246	" "	24	SW	1855-05-01		A1 G182
257	" "	25	W½	1855-05-01		A1
251	NEFF, Fleming	35	SWNW	1857-03-10		A1
252	" "	35	SWSW	1857-03-10		A1
336	NOLAND, Mary	6	S½NE	1856-01-15		A6 G294 F
250	PARDEE, Ephraim	24	SENE	1855-05-10		A1
281	PATTEE, Hiram	1	W½	1855-05-10		A1 F
283	" "	24	N½NW	1855-05-10		A1
282	" "	12	N½NW	1855-12-15		A1
205	PHELPS, Alfred	3	SE	1855-12-15		A1
337	PINNEY, Marcellus	13	NWNE	1857-03-10		A1
338	" "	14	NWSW	1857-03-10		A1
339	" "	23	NENW	1857-03-10		A1
226	POWELL, Charles G	7	E½NE	1855-12-15		A1
275	PUTNAM, Harvey C	29	NENE	1856-01-15		A6 G226 C R276
273	" "	29	SENE	1856-01-15		A6
274	" "	29	W½NE	1856-01-15		A6
276	" "	29	NENE	1857-04-02		A6 G226 R275
214	RHODES, Anthony	3	SW	1855-12-15		A1
331	ROGERS, Joshua	27	S½SW	1855-12-15		A1
332	" "	34	N½NW	1855-12-15		A1
247	SEARS, Elisha	20	S½NE	1855-05-01		A1
248	" "	20	SE	1855-05-01		A1
298	SHIELDS, James	15	NESW	1855-05-01		A6
219	SMITH, Benjamin L	13	S½SE	1855-05-01		A1
220	" "	24	N½NE	1855-05-01		A1
245	" "	24	S½NW	1855-05-01		A1 G182
246	" "	24	SW	1855-05-01		A1 G182
221	" "	25	E½	1855-05-01		A1
222	" "	26	SE	1855-05-01		A1
232	SMITH, Daniel	21	SE	1855-05-01		A1
237	SMITH, Edward	21	SW	1855-05-01		A1
315	SMITH, John S	9	SE	1855-12-15		A1
335	SNYDER, Lewis S	12	S½NW	1857-02-20		A5 G255
334	" "	4	N½NE	1857-03-10		A1 F
279	SPANGLER, Philip	18	NW	1855-12-15		A1 G195 F
317	SUMMERS, John V	13	W½	1855-12-15		A1
362	SUMMERS, Simon	14	E½SW	1855-12-15		A1
363	" "	14	SE	1855-12-15		A1
376	SUMMERS, William H	12	E½	1855-12-15		A1
238	THOMAS, Edward	33	N½	1855-05-01		A1
348	TOLAND, Nicholas S	8	S½NE	1857-03-10		A1
320	WARFIELD, John	36	S½SE	1855-05-10		A1
321	" "	36	S½SW	1855-05-10		A1

ID	Individual in Patent	Sec.	Sec. Part	Date Issued	Other Counties	For More Info . . .
270	WENTZ, George H	21	N½	1855-12-15		A1
289	WHITAKER, Israel	10	SE	1855-12-15		A1
290	" "	14	N½	1855-12-15		A1
322	WHITAKER, John	11		1855-12-15		A1
344	WILSON, Mitchell	5	NW	1855-12-15		A1 F
336	WRIGHT, Lewis	6	S½NE	1856-01-15		A6 G294 F

Patent Map

T81-N R15-W
5th PM Meridian

Map Group 2

Township Statistics

Parcels Mapped	:	179
Number of Patents	:	152
Number of Individuals	:	115
Patentees Identified	:	109
Number of Surnames	:	101
Multi-Patentee Parcels	:	13
Oldest Patent Date	:	1/1/1855
Most Recent Patent	:	8/26/1937
Block/Lot Parcels	:	0
Parcels Re - Issued	:	2
Parcels that Overlap	:	0
Cities and Towns	:	1
Cemeteries	:	1

Section 6
FLANAGAN William 1855
MCKENZIE Lewis 1856 / WRIGHT [294] Lewis 1856
CLANEY John 1855
CLANEY John 1855
ENGLISH John 1855

Section 5
WILSON Mitchell 1855
FENLON Charles M 1855
ENGLISH John 1855
KORNS John 1855

Section 4
MOREY Amos 1855
SNYDER Lewis S 1857
HAVENS William 1855
HAVENS William 1855

Section 7
MAGILL Henry 1855
KORNS Charles W 1857 / POWELL Charles G 1855
LITTLE Henry 1857 / BAILEY Charles E 1855 / FORSYTHE [136] Mathew 1855
KORNS Charles W 1857 / DILLON Hannah S 1855

Section 8
CROSS John T 1856
KORNS John 1855 / TOLAND Nicholas S 1857
CRIPMAN Ira 1855
MISCHLICH John 1855
HAWES Franklin B 1855

Section 9
FORSYTHE John A 1855
KELLOGG Edmund B 1855
SMITH John S 1855

Section 18
LOESCH [195] Henry 1855
FORSYTHE John A 1855
BRABROOK [33] George 1856 / BRABROOK George 1856
COUCH Uriah B 1855

Section 17
FORSYTHE John A 1855
CONVERS Daniel C 1855
DWIGHT Daniel 1855
FORSYTHE John A 1855

Section 16
IOWA State Of 1937

Section 19
BRABROOK [33] George 1856
COUCH Uriah B 1855
BRABROOK George 1856 / JONES George A 1855

Section 20
COLLIN Mary E 1856 / CLARKE Peter 1857
CLARKE Peter 1857 / SEARS Elisha 1855
GATTRELL Nathan 1855
SEARS Elisha 1855

Section 21
WENTZ George H 1855
SMITH Edward 1855 / SMITH Daniel 1855

Section 30
MILLER Edmund G 1855 / DOWNEY Hugh D 1855 / JONES George A 1855 / JONES George A 1855
JONES George A 1855 / JONES George A 1935
LOOSE Joseph B 1855 / LOOSE Joseph B 1855 / GAMBLE John H 1855

Section 29
GATTRELL [143] Nathan 1855
PUTNAM Harvey C 1856
GATHIELL Nathan 1855
GOUDY Abel C 1855

Section 28
PUTNAM [226] Harvey C 1856 / PUTNAM [226] Harvey C 1857 / PUTNAM Harvey C 1856
BRABROOK George 1855 / BRABROOK George 1855 / FLANAGAN John 1855
CLARKE Peter 1857 / CLARKE Peter 1857 / FLANAGAN William 1855
CARNEY Bartholomew 1855

Section 31
LOOSE Joseph B 1855
LOOSE Joseph B 1855
CULBERTSON John C 1857 / LANCEY Dustin 1855 / LOOSE Joseph B 1855

Section 32
LOOSE Isaac 1855

Section 33
THOMAS Edward 1855
ELLIOTT Amelia K 1855

Section 3
GRUWELL Sarah 1855
GRUWELL Sarah 1855
MOREY Amos 1855
MOREY Amos 1855
RHODES Anthony 1855
PHELPS Alfred 1855

Section 2
BLAKE Patrick H 1857
GOODRICH John W 1855
GOODRICH John W 1855

BEEM Arza B 1855

Section 1
PATTEE Hiram 1855
HILL Ephraim B 1855
CODDING Samuel N 1855
HUMPHREY Rollin O 1855

Section 10
DENISON Charles E 1855
MORRIS Edward W 1855
WHITAKER Israel 1855

Section 11
WHITAKER John 1855

Section 12
PATTEE Hiram 1855
SNYDER [255] Lewis S 1857
CLOSSEN Isaac 1855
SUMMERS William H 1855

Section 15
FORSYTHE Matthew 1855
FORSYTHE John A 1855
COTTRELL Almon O 1856
SHIELDS James 1855
COTTRELL Almon O 1856
HUNT Thomas 1855
HUNT Thomas 1855

Section 14
WHITAKER Israel 1855
PINNEY Marcellus 1857
HUNT Thomas 1855
SUMMERS Simon 1855
SUMMERS Simon 1855

Section 13
PINNEY Marcellus 1857
FRANCE Joseph D 1855
DAVIS William T 1855
DAVIS William T 1855
SUMMERS John V 1855
SMITH Benjamin L 1855

Section 22
JACK Samuel 1855
ELLIS Joseph S 1855
COULSON Henry 1855
GASKILL Israel 1855
HARMAN Jacob 1855

Section 23
HUNT Thomas 1855
PINNEY Marcellus 1857
CAMPBELL Jacob 1855
CAMPBELL Jacob 1855
HARMAN Jacob 1855
LOEBER Seigfried 1855
BERRYHILL William D 1855
BERRYHILL William D 1855
LOEBER Seigfried 1855

Section 24
PATTEE Hiram 1855
JUDD [182] Eli P 1855
JUDD [182] Eli P 1855
SMITH Benjamin L 1855
HART [164] Anson 1856
PARDEE Ephraim 1855
CALKINS George W 1855
MOSELY Frederick 1855

Section 27
FULLER Dimiris 1855
KORNS John 1855
FLANAGAN William 1855
GOUDY Abel C 1855
ROGERS Joshua 1855

Section 26
CARNEY Bartholomew 1855
CARNEY Bartholomew 1855
SMITH Benjamin L 1855

Section 25
SMITH Benjamin L 1855
MOSELY Frederick 1855

Section 34
ROGERS Joshua 1855
BARNES Maria 1856
EMOTT James 1856
MANN [199] Charles A 1856
GOUDY Abel C 1855
COTTRELL Almon O 1857
CORRELL Paul 1855

Section 35
EDDY Franklin 1855
NEFF Fleming 1857
EDDY Franklin 1855
HUNT Joshua 1855
NEFF Fleming 1857
DAVENPORT Jacob 1855
JUDD Eli P 1855
JUDD Eli P 1855
DAVENPORT Jacob 1855

Section 36
JUDD Eli P 1855
JUDD Eli P 1855
WARFIELD John 1855
WARFIELD John 1855

Helpful Hints
1. This Map's INDEX can be found on the preceding pages.
2. Refer to Map "C" to see where this Township lies within Poweshiek County, Iowa.
3. Numbers within square brackets [ ] denote a multi-patentee land parcel (multi-owner). Refer to Appendix "C" for a full list of members in this group.
4. Areas that look to be crowded with Patentees usually indicate multiple sales of the same parcel (Re-issues) or Overlapping parcels. See this Township's Index for an explanation of these and other circumstances that might explain "odd" groupings of Patentees on this map.

Copyright 2010 Boyd IT, Inc. All Rights Reserved

Legend
Patent Boundary
Section Boundary
No Patents Found (or Outside County)
1., 2., 3., ... Lot Numbers (when beside a name)
[ ] Group Number (see Appendix "C")

Scale: Section = 1 mile X 1 mile (generally, with some exceptions)

Road Map

T81-N R15-W
5th PM Meridian

Map Group 2

Cities & Towns
Sheridan

Cemeteries
Sheridan Cemetery

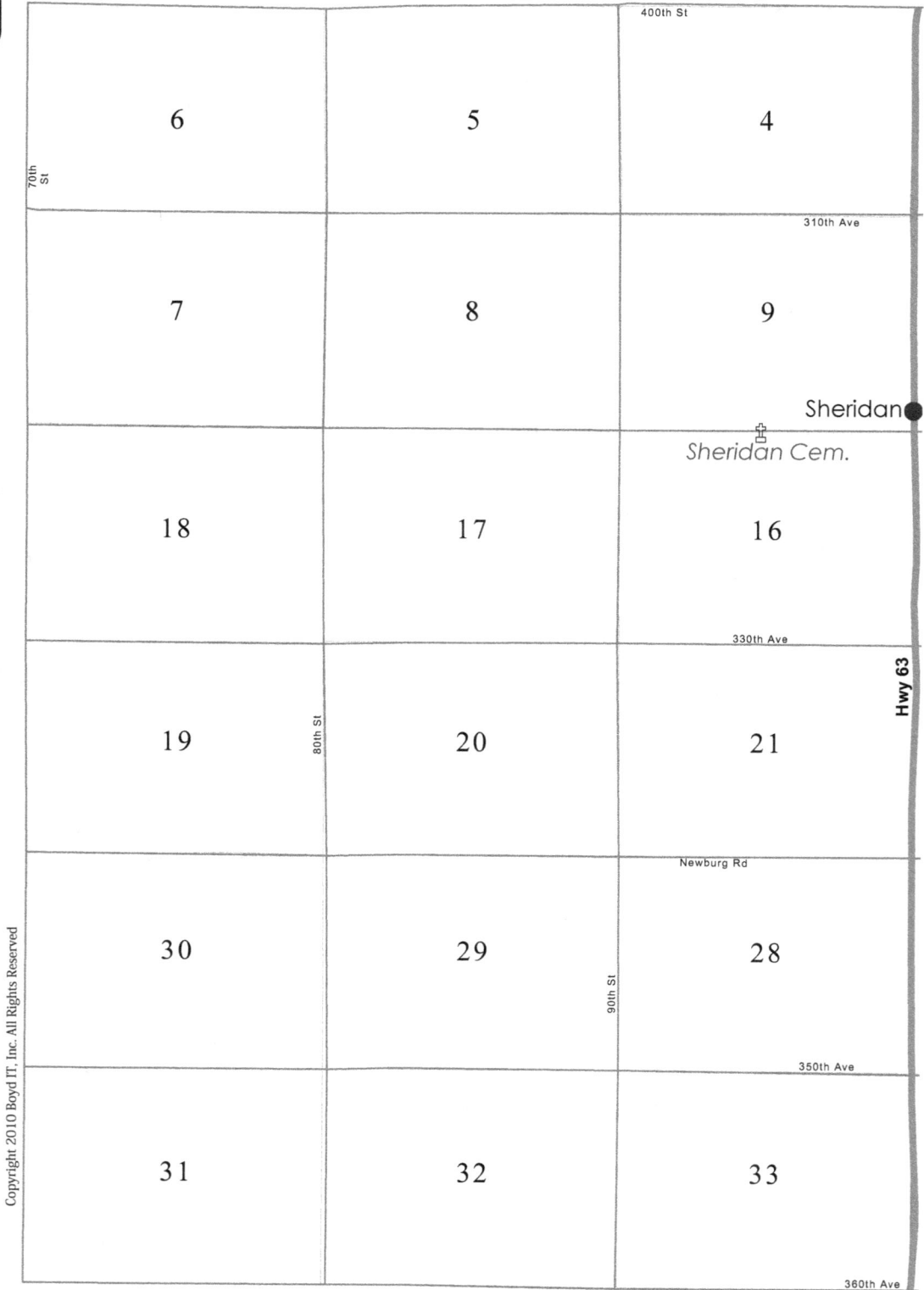

6	5	4
7	8	9
18	17	16
19	20	21
30	29	28
31	32	33

400th St
310th Ave
330th Ave
350th Ave
360th Ave
Newburg Rd
70th St
80th St
90th St
Hwy 63
Sheridan
Sheridan Cem.

400th St

| 3 | 2 | 1 |

| 10 | 11 | 12 |

320th Ave

| 15 | 14 | 13 |

110th St

| 22 | 23 | 24 |

340th Ave

120th St

| 27 | 26 | 25 |

130th St

| 34 | 35 | 36 |

Helpful Hints

1. This road map has a number of uses, but primarily it is to help you: a) find the present location of land owned by your ancestors (at least the general area), b) find cemeteries and city-centers, and c) estimate the route/roads used by Census-takers & tax-assessors.

2. If you plan to travel to Poweshiek County to locate cemeteries or land parcels, please pick up a modern travel map for the area before you do. Mapping old land parcels on modern maps is not as exact a science as you might think. Just the slightest variations in public land survey coordinates, estimates of parcel boundaries, or road-map deviations can greatly alter a map's representation of how a road either does or doesn't cross a particular parcel of land.

Legend

———————— Section Lines

════════ Interstates

━━━━━━━━ Highways

———————— Other Roads

● Cities/Towns

✝ Cemeteries

Scale: Section = 1 mile X 1 mile
(generally, with some exceptions)

Cities & Towns
Sheridan

Cemeteries
Sheridan Cemetery

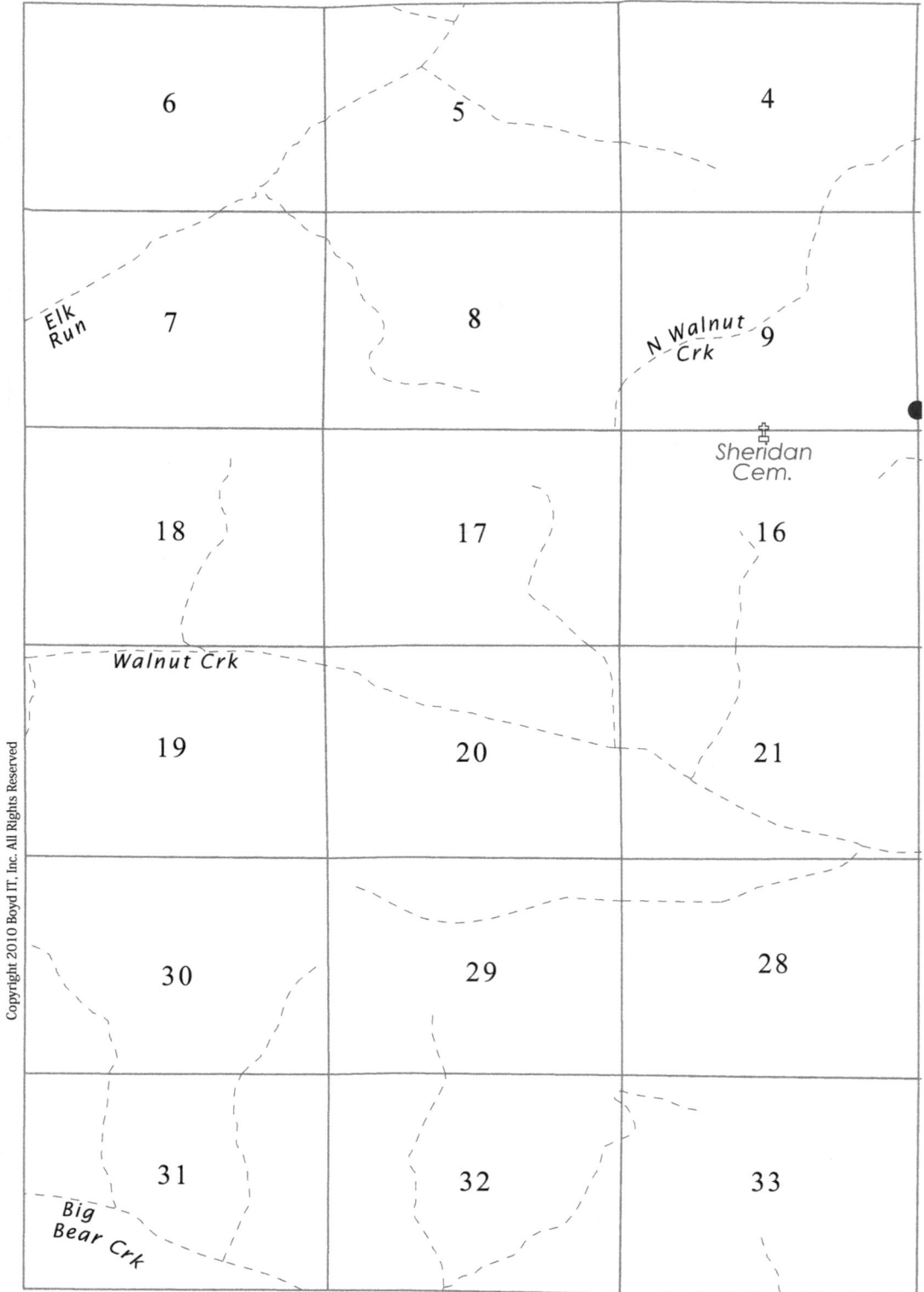

6

5

4

Elk
Run

7

8

N Walnut
Crk

9

☩
Sheridan
Cem.

18

17

16

Walnut Crk

19

20

21

30

29

28

31

Big
Bear Crk

32

33

3

2

1

10

11

12

● Sheridan

15

14

13

22

23

24

27

26

25

34

35

36

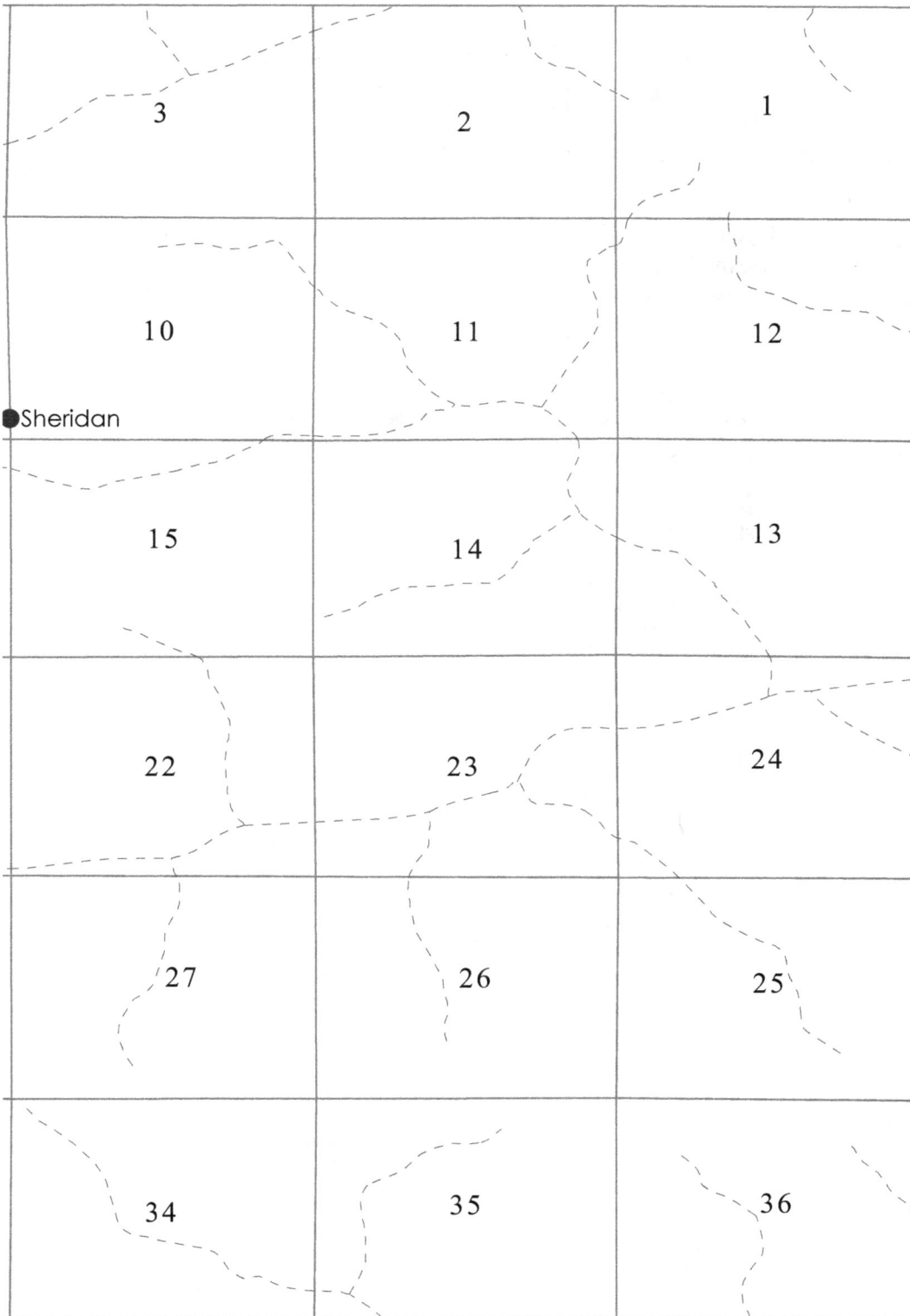

Helpful Hints

1. This Map takes a different look at the same Congressional Township displayed in the preceding two maps. It presents features that can help you better envision the historical development of the area: a) Water-bodies (lakes & ponds), b) Water-courses (rivers, streams, etc.), c) Railroads, d) City/town center-points (where they were oftentimes located when first settled), and e) Cemeteries.

2. Using this "Historical" map in tandem with this Township's Patent Map and Road Map, may lead you to some interesting discoveries. You will often find roads, towns, cemeteries, and waterways are named after nearby landowners: sometimes those names will be the ones you are researching. See how many of these research gems you can find here in Poweshiek County.

L e g e n d

———————— Section Lines

—+—+—+—+— Railroads

▭ Large Rivers & Bodies of Water

- - - - - - - - Streams/Creeks & Small Rivers

● Cities/Towns

⚏ Cemeteries

Scale: Section = 1 mile X 1 mile
(there are some exceptions)

Map Group 3: Index to Land Patents

Township 81-North Range 14-West (5th PM)

After you locate an individual in this Index, take note of the Section and Section Part then proceed to the Land Patent map on the pages immediately following. You should have no difficulty locating the corresponding parcel of land.

The "For More Info" Column will lead you to more information about the underlying Patents. See the *Legend* at right, and the "How to Use this Book" chapter, for more information.

<table>
<tr><td colspan="2" align="center">LEGEND</td></tr>
<tr><td colspan="2" align="center">"For More Info . . . " column</td></tr>
<tr><td>**A**</td><td>= Authority (Legislative Act, See Appendix "A")</td></tr>
<tr><td>**B**</td><td>= Block or Lot (location in Section unknown)</td></tr>
<tr><td>**C**</td><td>= Cancelled Patent</td></tr>
<tr><td>**F**</td><td>= Fractional Section</td></tr>
<tr><td>**G**</td><td>= Group (Multi-Patentee Patent, see Appendix "C")</td></tr>
<tr><td>**V**</td><td>= Overlaps another Parcel</td></tr>
<tr><td>**R**</td><td>= Re-Issued (Parcel patented more than once)</td></tr>
</table>

(A & G items require you to look in the Appendixes referred to above. All other Letter-designations followed by a number require you to locate line-items in this index that possess the ID number found after the letter).

ID	Individual in Patent	Sec.	Sec. Part	Date Issued	Other Counties	For More Info . . .
592	ALEXANDER, Catharine F	25	NENW	1854-02-01		A6 G295
539	ANTHONY, John P	20	SESE	1854-12-09		A6 R540
542	" "	20	SWSE	1854-12-09		A6 R543
540	" "	20	SESE	1855-03-01		A6 R539
541	" "	20	SWNE	1855-03-01		A4
543	" "	20	SWSE	1855-03-01		A6 R542
535	" "	20	E½SW	1855-05-01		A1
538	" "	20	SENE	1855-05-01		A1
536	" "	20	NESE	1856-06-16		A6
537	" "	20	NWSE	1856-06-16		A6
597	ARMSTRONG, Thomas K	24	SESE	1855-05-01		A6 C R598
599	" "	24	SWSE	1855-12-15		A1
598	" "	24	SESE	1855-12-20		A6 R597
446	BABCOCK, George M	32	SE	1855-02-01		A6
465	BAGANSTOS, Henry L	15	W½NW	1855-12-15		A1
466	BAGENSTOS, Henry L	15	SWSW	1855-12-15		A1
467	" "	9	NWSE	1856-01-15		A6
468	" "	9	SWSE	1856-01-15		A6
550	BAGGS, John T	22	SW	1854-12-01		A1
552	" "	27	N½NW	1854-12-01		A1
551	" "	24	NWNW	1855-05-10		A1
425	BARNES, Erastus R	14	SESW	1855-12-15		A1
440	BARRETT, George	3	N½SW	1855-12-15		A1
441	" "	4	N½SW	1855-12-15		A1 R404
618	BECKET, William K	19	N½SE	1855-12-15		A1
619	" "	19	S½NE	1855-12-15		A1
583	BENNETT, Hannah	4	N½NE	1856-06-16		A6 G184 F
584	" "	4	N½NW	1856-06-16		A6 G184 F
585	" "	5	N½NE	1856-06-16		A6 G184 F
403	BERRYHILL, Charles H	34	W½SE	1857-06-01		A5
503	BERRYHILL, James B	22	NWSE	1855-12-15		A1
505	" "	26	NESW	1855-12-15		A1
506	" "	26	SESW	1855-12-15		A1
507	" "	26	SWNE	1855-12-15		A1
504	" "	22	SWNE	1856-09-01		A1
608	BERRYHILL, William D	20	NENW	1855-05-01		A1
607	" "	19	SENW	1855-12-15		A1 F
455	BILL, Harvey A	17	N½SW	1855-05-01		A1
456	" "	17	SESE	1855-05-01		A1
457	" "	17	W½SE	1855-05-01		A1
458	" "	20	S½NW	1855-05-01		A1
459	" "	27	S½NW	1855-05-01		A1
594	BINGEY, Thomas B	2	SE	1855-01-01		A6
530	BLUE, John	1	N½SW	1855-05-01		A1
521	BOUGHNER, James V	6	W½SE	1855-05-01		A6
408	BOWEN, David	6	E½SE	1855-12-15		A1

ID	Individual in Patent	Sec.	Sec. Part	Date Issued	Other Counties	For More Info . . .
553	BREWER, Joseph	24	NENE	1853-11-01		A1
434	BROSS, Gabriel D	29	E½SE	1855-05-01		A1
442	BROWN, George	13	SE	1855-12-15		A1
414	BUDD, Edward	20	NWNE	1855-01-01		A6
417	" "	22	NENW	1855-01-01		A6
418	" "	22	SENW	1855-01-01		A6
420	" "	28	NE	1855-01-01		A6 G41
413	" "	20	NENE	1855-03-01		A4
415	" "	20	W½SW	1855-05-01		A1
416	" "	21	N½NW	1855-05-01		A1
419	" "	22	W½NW	1855-05-01		A1
461	BURNS, Henry	10	N½SE	1855-12-15		A1
462	"	10	NE	1855-12-15		A1
508	BUTCHER, James	26	NENW	1850-04-10		A1
411	CAMPBELL, Ebenezer B	3	S½SW	1855-05-01		A6
412	" "	9	NE	1855-12-15		A1
509	CODDINGTON, James	2	S½NW	1856-01-15		A6 G54 F
596	COX, Thomas J	11	S½SE	1857-05-01		A1
606	CRAWFORD, William	11	N½NW	1855-05-01		A6
450	DAINGERFIELD, Mariah H	21	SE	1855-01-01		A6 G135
476	DAVENFORT, Hewlett	1	NWNE	1855-12-15		A1 F
477	DAVENPORT, Hewlett	1	SENW	1855-05-10		A1 F
478	" "	1	SWNE	1855-05-10		A1 F
479	" "	2	N½NW	1855-12-15		A1 F
469	DEVINNAK, Henry L	1	SWSW	1855-05-10		A1
609	DINSMOOR, William	17	NE	1855-05-01		A1
610	" "	18	NE	1855-05-01		A1
611	" "	27	SW	1855-05-01		A1
612	" "	28	SE	1855-05-01		A1
613	" "	8	SE	1855-05-01		A1
484	DOWNEY, Hugh D	3	S½NW	1855-12-15		A1 F
485	" "	4	S½NE	1855-12-15		A1 F
486	" "	7	E½NW	1855-12-15		A1 F
487	" "	7	NE	1855-12-15		A1
488	" "	8	W½NW	1855-12-15		A1
526	DRAKE, John A	25	NWNW	1855-05-01		A1
527	" "	25	S½NW	1855-05-01		A1
528	" "	27	SENE	1855-05-01		A1
529	" "	27	W½SE	1855-05-01		A1 V621
386	DUNTON, Austin	17	NW	1855-05-01		A1
387	" "	28	SW	1855-05-01		A1
388	" "	32	NE	1855-05-01		A1
389	" "	33	W½	1855-05-01		A1
520	EASLEY, James S	14	SWSE	1855-05-01		A6 G123 R472
519	"	23	NENW	1857-04-01		A4
564	EBERHART, Margaret L	7	N½SW	1856-01-15		A6 G125 F
565	" "	7	W½NW	1856-01-15		A6 G125 F
443	ELSON, George	12	S½NE	1856-04-10		A6
509	ESTES, Beulah	2	S½NW	1856-01-15		A6 G54 F
422	ESTLICK, Elizabeth	24	SENE	1855-07-02		A6 G133
614	EWING, William	21	S½NW	1855-05-01		A1
615	" "	21	SW	1855-05-01		A1
616	" "	28	NW	1855-05-01		A1
532	FENTON, John	9	NW	1855-12-15		A1
450	FISHER, George S	21	SE	1855-01-01		A6 G135
454	FOLSOM, Gilman	35	SW	1854-12-01		A1
452	" "	10	SESE	1856-09-01		A1
453	" "	15	NENE	1856-09-01		A1
620	FOREMAN, William M	4	SW	1855-12-15		A1
554	FRANCE, Joseph D	18	N½SW	1855-12-15		A1 F
555	" "	18	S½NW	1855-12-15		A1 F
587	FRANK, Silas	26	NWNE	1854-05-01		A1
588	" "	26	NWNW	1855-05-01		A1
589	" "	27	NENE	1855-05-01		A1
522	FULLER, Jane	23	SWNE	1853-07-20		A6
523	" "	26	NENE	1854-05-01		A1
524	" "	26	NWSE	1854-12-01		A1
525	" "	26	SENE	1855-12-15		A1
492	GEETING, Jacob	19	SW	1855-12-15		A1 F
493	" "	29	E½SW	1855-12-15		A1
494	" "	31	W½	1855-12-15		A1 F
495	" "	32	N½NW	1855-12-15		A1
384	GILLELAND, Nancy G	13	NWSW	1853-07-20		A6 G181

ID	Individual in Patent	Sec.	Sec. Part	Date Issued	Other Counties	For More Info . . .
385	GILLELAND, Nancy G (Cont'd)	13	SWNW	1853-07-20		A6 G181
381	GLAZE, Adam	23	NWNE	1855-05-01		A1
512	GOWER, James H	23	SENE	1853-07-20		A6
511	" "	15	SWNE	1855-12-15		A1
510	" "	15	SENE	1856-09-01		A1
513	" "	26	SENW	1856-09-01		A1
410	GREELEY, Dennis P	19	NENE	1857-04-10		A6
406	HARVEY, Cyrus W	6	SW	1855-05-10		A1 F
448	HAYWOOD, George P	6	NW	1855-05-10		A1 F
449	" "	6	W½NE	1855-05-10		A1 F
470	HECKMAN, Henry L	15	NWSW	1855-12-15		A1
531	HIGGINSON, John C	36	NW	1855-02-01		A6
444	HOWARD, George	10	SWSW	1855-05-01		A6
445	" "	9	E½SE	1855-12-15		A1
566	HOWARD, Mark	1	SESW	1855-01-01		A6
567	" "	12	NW	1855-05-10		A1
568	" "	12	SE	1855-05-10		A1
569	" "	12	W½SW	1855-05-10		A1
572	HOWARD, Nancy	10	N½SW	1855-12-15		A1
560	HUBBARD, Luther P	1	NWSE	1855-05-10		A1
561	" "	1	S½SE	1855-05-10		A1
562	" "	12	N½NE	1855-05-10		A1
515	HULL, Elizabeth S	24	SWNE	1855-07-02		A6 G190
460	HYNES, Helen	12	E½SW	1855-05-10		A1
591	IOWA, State Of	16		1937-08-26		A3
384	JOHNSON, Archibald	13	NWSW	1853-07-20		A6 G181
385	" "	13	SWNW	1853-07-20		A6 G181
383	" "	14	NESE	1853-07-20		A6
533	JOHNSTON, John	14	SESE	1855-05-10		A1
586	JONES, Leanah	11	N½SE	1857-02-16		A5 G185
605	JONES, Uriah	20	NWNW	1852-07-13		A6
421	JUDD, Eli P	25	N½NE	1855-05-01		A1
390	KECK, Benjamin F	18	N½SE	1855-12-15		A1
557	KENT, Joseph	24	E½NW	1854-03-01		A6
570	KENT, Moses	22	SWSE	1854-05-01		A1
573	KEPPEL, Philip	25	SENE	1853-06-01		A6
574	" "	25	SWNE	1853-06-01		A6
489	KING, Hugh F	24	SWNW	1855-12-15		A1
534	KINSEY, John	14	SENE	1856-09-01		A1
583	KIRKWOOD, Samuel J	4	N½NE	1856-06-16		A6 G184 F
584	" "	4	N½NW	1856-06-16		A6 G184 F
585	" "	5	N½NE	1856-06-16		A6 G184 F
580	" "	5	NWNW	1856-09-01		A1 F
581	" "	6	E½NE	1856-09-01		A1 F
586	" "	11	N½SE	1857-02-16		A5 G185
578	" "	3	N½NE	1857-02-16		A5 F
579	" "	3	N½NW	1857-02-16		A5 F
582	" "	8	E½NW	1857-02-16		A5
571	KURT, Moses	22	E½SE	1854-05-01		A1
490	LAREW, Isaac	25	S½SW	1854-12-01		A1
514	LARREW, James	24	NWNE	1855-07-02		A6
515	" "	24	SWNE	1855-07-02		A6 G190
600	LAUGHLIN, Thomas	14	N½SW	1855-05-01		A1
601	" "	14	S½NW	1855-05-01		A1
422	LOVE, Agnes H	24	SENE	1855-07-02		A6 G133
472	LUCKHART, Henry	14	SWSE	1854-12-01		A1 C R520
471	" "	14	NWSE	1931-09-29		A1
496	LUCKHART, Jacob	13	NENE	1853-11-01		A1
497	" "	13	SWNE	1853-11-01		A1
498	" "	15	SENW	1854-05-01		A1
473	LUKECART, Henry	13	NWNE	1855-12-15		A1
491	LUKECART, Isaiah	13	SENE	1855-05-10		A1
407	MAYER, Daniel	24	N½SE	1854-12-01		A1
447	MCCALL, George	5	S½	1855-12-15		A1
575	MERWIN, Phineas	35	SE	1857-04-01		A4 G210
474	MONROE, Henry	1	E½NE	1854-12-01		A1 F
426	MOSELY, Frederick	26	E½SE	1855-05-01		A1
427	" "	26	SWNW	1855-05-01		A1
428	" "	26	SWSE	1855-05-01		A1
429	" "	26	W½SW	1855-05-01		A1
430	" "	31	E½	1855-05-01		A1
431	" "	34	E½SE	1855-05-01		A1
432	" "	34	NE	1855-05-01		A1

ID	Individual in Patent	Sec.	Sec. Part	Date Issued	Other Counties	For More Info . . .
433	MOSELY, Frederick (Cont'd)	35	N½	1855-05-01		A1
603	NINDE, Thomas	29	W½SE	1855-05-01		A1
602	"	29	E½NW	1855-12-15		A1
382	NORRIS, Adin H	1	N½NW	1855-05-01		A1 F
624	NORRIS, William S	2	NE	1855-05-01		A1 F
424	PARDEE, Ephraim	19	S½SE	1855-05-10		A1
423	PARDEE, Ephraim N	19	SWNW	1855-12-15		A1 F
420	PARKER, Elizabeth H	28	NE	1855-01-01		A6 G41
480	PATTEE, Hiram	18	S½SW	1855-05-10		A1 F
481	" "	18	SWSE	1855-05-10		A1
482	" "	19	N½NW	1855-05-10		A1 F
483	" "	19	NWNE	1855-05-10		A1
544	PEOPLES, John	18	N½NW	1855-12-15		A1 F
545	" "	7	S½SW	1855-12-15		A1 F
451	PETTIE, George W	3	S½NE	1855-12-15		A1 F
563	PINNEY, Marcellus	25	N½SW	1854-12-01		A1
475	PURCEFIELD, Henry	17	S½SW	1853-07-13		A6
402	RUSSELL, Caleb	8	SW	1855-12-15		A1
516	RYAN, James	8	NE	1855-12-15		A1
546	RYAN, John	23	SENW	1855-12-15		A1
517	RYEON, James	13	N½NW	1855-12-15		A1
518	"	13	SWSW	1855-12-15		A1
404	SELLEW, Chauncey B	4	N½SE	1855-12-15		A1 R441
435	SHEWAKER, Gano	14	NENW	1856-05-01		A1
436	SHOEMAKER, Gano	13	E½SW	1856-09-01		A1
437	" "	13	SENW	1856-09-01		A1
438	" "	14	NENE	1856-09-01		A1
439	" "	14	W½NE	1856-09-01		A1
595	SHREVE, Thomas C	34	SW	1855-05-01		A1
391	SMITH, Benjamin L	10	SESW	1855-05-01		A1
392	" "	10	SWSE	1855-05-01		A1
393	" "	15	NENW	1855-05-01		A1
394	" "	15	NWNE	1855-05-01		A1
395	" "	17	NESE	1855-05-01		A1
396	" "	18	SESE	1855-05-01		A1
397	" "	25	SE	1855-05-01		A1
398	" "	29	W½NW	1855-05-01		A1
399	" "	29	W½SW	1855-05-01		A1
400	" "	30		1855-05-01		A1
401	" "	36	NE	1855-05-01		A1
556	SMITH, Joseph D	1	SWNW	1855-12-15		A1 F
564	SMITH, Polly	7	N½SW	1856-01-15		A6 G125 F
565	" "	7	W½NW	1856-01-15		A6 G125 F
576	SMITH, Russell B	5	NENW	1855-12-15		A1 F
577	" "	5	S½NW	1855-12-15		A1 F
604	SMITH, Thomas R	7	SE	1855-12-15		A1
499	SNYDER, Jacob S	14	SWSW	1857-03-10		A1
500	" "	22	SENE	1857-03-10		A1
501	" "	23	NENE	1857-03-10		A1
502	" "	23	W½NW	1857-03-10		A1
593	SQUIRES, Sumner L	1	NESE	1854-12-01		A1
409	STROW, David	14	NWNW	1856-05-01		A1
547	STROW, John	11	S½SW	1856-05-01		A1 G262
547	STROW, Perry	11	S½SW	1856-05-01		A1 G262
548	SWITZER, John	11	N½SW	1855-05-01		A6
549	"	11	S½NW	1855-05-01		A6
590	TUTTLE, Smith	11	NE	1855-05-10		A1
463	VAN ANTWERP, HENRY D	32	S½NW	1855-05-10		A1
464	" "	32	SW	1855-05-10		A1
405	VANSCHOYCK, Cornelius	15	N½SE	1855-05-10		A1
520	WATKINS, Elizabeth	14	SWSE	1855-05-01		A6 G123 R472
621	WHEELER, William P	27	SE	1855-05-01		A1 V529
622	" "	33	E½	1855-05-01		A1
623	" "	34	NW	1855-05-01		A1
625	WILLINGHAM, William W	15	NESW	1855-12-15		A1
575	WITHROW, Mary	35	SE	1857-04-01		A4 G210
558	WOOD, Joseph P	15	S½SE	1861-08-15		A5
559	" "	15	SESW	1861-08-15		A5
617	WOOD, William H	22	NWNE	1857-03-10		A1
592	YOUNG, Stephen	25	NENW	1854-02-01		A6 G295

Patent Map

T81-N R14-W
5th PM Meridian

Map Group 3

Township Statistics

Parcels Mapped	:	245
Number of Patents	:	207
Number of Individuals	:	132
Patentees Identified	:	125
Number of Surnames	:	114
Multi-Patentee Parcels	:	17
Oldest Patent Date	:	4/10/1850
Most Recent Patent	:	8/26/1937
Block/Lot Parcels	:	0
Parcels Re - Issued	:	5
Parcels that Overlap	:	2
Cities and Towns	:	0
Cemeteries	:	2

Section 6
HAYWOOD George P 1855
HAYWOOD George P 1855
KIRKWOOD Samuel J 1856
HARVEY Cyrus W 1855
BOUGHNER James V 1855
BOWEN David 1855

Section 5
KIRKWOOD Samuel J 1856
SMITH Russell B 1855
KIRKWOOD Samuel J 1856
SMITH Russell B 1855
MCCALL George

Section 4
KIRKWOOD [184] Samuel J 1856
KIRKWOOD [184] Samuel J 1856
DOWNEY Hugh D 1855
FOREMAN William M 1855
BARRETT George 1855
SELLEW Chauncey B 1855

Section 7
EBERHART [125] Margaret L 1856
DOWNEY Hugh D 1855
DOWNEY Hugh D 1855
EBERHART [125] Margaret L 1856
SMITH Thomas R 1855
PEOPLES John 1855

Section 8
DOWNEY Hugh D 1855
KIRKWOOD Samuel J 1857
RYAN James 1855
RUSSELL Caleb 1855
DINSMOOR William 1855

Section 9
FENTON John 1855
CAMPBELL Ebenezer B 1855
BAGENSTOS Henry L 1856
HOWARD George 1855
BAGENSTOS Henry L 1856

Section 18
PEOPLES John 1855
FRANCE Joseph D 1855
FRANCE Joseph D 1855
PATTEE Hiram 1855
DINSMOOR William 1855
KECK Benjamin F 1855
PATTEE Hiram 1855
SMITH Benjamin L 1855

Section 17
DUNTON Austin 1855
DINSMOOR William 1855
BILL Harvey A 1855
BILL Harvey A 1855
PURCEFIELD Henry 1853
SMITH Benjamin L 1855
BILL Harvey A 1855

Section 16
IOWA State Of 1937

Section 19
PATTEE Hiram 1855
PATTEE Hiram 1855
GREELEY Dennis P 1857
PARDEE Ephraim N 1855
BERRYHILL William D 1855
BECKET William K 1855
GEETING Jacob 1855
BECKET William K 1855
PARDEE Ephraim 1855

Section 20
JONES Uriah 1852
BERRYHILL William D 1855
BUDD Edward 1855
BUDD Edward 1855
BILL Harvey A 1855
ANTHONY John P 1855
ANTHONY John P 1855
BUDD Edward 1855
ANTHONY John P 1855
ANTHONY John P 1856
ANTHONY John P 1856
ANTHONY John P 1854
ANTHONY John P 1855
ANTHONY John P 1854
ANTHONY John P 1855

Section 21
BUDD Edward 1855
EWING William 1855
EWING William 1855
FISHER [135] George S 1855

Section 30
SMITH Benjamin L 1855

Section 29
SMITH Benjamin L 1855
NINDE Thomas 1855
NINDE Thomas 1855
SMITH Benjamin L 1855
GEETING Jacob 1855
BROSS Gabriel D 1855

Section 28
EWING William 1855
DUNTON Austin 1855
BUDD [41] Edward 1855
DINSMOOR William 1855

Section 31
GEETING Jacob 1855
MOSELY Frederick 1855

Section 32
GEETING Jacob 1855
ANTWERP Henry D Van 1855
DUNTON Austin 1855
ANTWERP Henry D Van 1855
BABCOCK George M 1855

Section 33
DUNTON Austin 1855
WHEELER William P 1855

78

Section 3
KIRKWOOD Samuel J 1857
KIRKWOOD Samuel J 1857
DOWNEY Hugh D 1855
PETTIE George W 1855
BARRETT George 1855
CAMPBELL Ebenezer B 1855

Section 2
DAVENPORT Hewlett 1855
CODDINGTON [54] James 1856

Section 1
NORRIS William S 1855
NORRIS Adin H 1855
DAVENPORT Hewlett 1855
SMITH Joseph D 1855
DAVENPORT Hewlett 1855
DAVENPORT Hewlett 1855
MONROE Henry 1854
BINGEY Thomas B 1855
BLUE John 1855
HUBBARD Luther P 1855
SQUIRES Sumner L 1854
DEVINNAK Henry L 1855
HOWARD Mark 1855
HUBBARD Luther P 1855

Section 10
BURNS Henry 1855
HOWARD Nancy 1855
BURNS Henry 1855
HOWARD George 1855
SMITH Benjamin L 1855
SMITH Benjamin L 1855
FOLSOM Gilman 1856

Section 11
CRAWFORD William 1855
SWITZER John 1855
SWITZER John 1855
STROW [262] John 1856
TUTTLE Smith 1855
KIRKWOOD [185] Samuel J 1857
COX Thomas J 1857

Section 12
HOWARD Mark 1855
HUBBARD Luther P 1855
ELSON George 1856
HOWARD Mark 1855
HYNES Helen 1855
HOWARD Mark 1855

Section 15
BAGANSTOS Henry L 1855
SMITH Benjamin L 1855
SMITH Benjamin L 1855
FOLSOM Gilman 1856
LUCKHART Jacob 1854
GOWER James H 1855
GOWER James H 1856
HECKMAN Henry L 1855
WILLINGHAM William W 1855
VANSCHOYCK Cornelius 1855
WOOD Joseph P 1861
WOOD Joseph P 1861
BAGENSTOS Henry L 1855

Section 14
STROW David 1856
SHEWAKER Gano 1856
SHOEMAKER Gano 1856
LAUGHLIN Thomas 1855
LAUGHLIN Thomas 1855
SHOEMAKER Gano 1856
KINSEY John 1856
LUCKHART Henry 1931
SNYDER Jacob S 1857
BARNES Erastus R 1855
EASLEY [123] James S 1855
LUCKHART Henry
JOHNSON Archibald 1853
JOHNSTON John 1855

Section 13
RYEON James 1855
JOHNSON [181] Archibald 1853
SHOEMAKER Gano 1856
LUKECART Henry 1855
LUCKHART Jacob 1855
LUCKHART Jacob 1853
LUKECART Isaiah 1855
JOHNSON [181] Archibald 1853
BROWN George 1855
RYEON James 1855
SHOEMAKER Gano 1856

Section 22
BUDD Edward 1855
WOOD William H 1857
BUDD Edward 1855
BUDD Edward 1855
BERRYHILL James B 1856
SNYDER Jacob S 1857
BERRYHILL James B 1855
KENT Moses 1854
KURT Moses 1854
BAGGS John T 1854

Section 23
SNYDER Jacob S 1857
EASLEY James S 1857
RYAN John 1855
GLAZE Adam 1855
FULLER Jane 1853
SNYDER Jacob S 1857
GOWER James H 1853

Section 24
BAGGS John T 1855
KING Hugh F 1855
KENT Joseph 1854
LARREW James 1855
BREWER Joseph 1853
LARREW [190] James 1855
ESTLICK [133] Elizabeth 1855
MAYER Daniel 1854
ARMSTRONG Thomas K 1855
ARMSTRONG Thomas K 1855
ARMSTRONG Thomas K 1855

Section 27
BAGGS John T 1854
BILL Harvey A 1855
FRANK Silas 1855
DRAKE John A 1855
DINSMOOR William 1855
DRAKE John A 1855
WHEELER William P 1855

Section 26
FRANK Silas 1855
MOSELY Frederick 1855
BUTCHER James 1850
GOWER James H 1856
FRANK Silas 1854
BERRYHILL James B 1855
FULLER Jane 1854
BERRYHILL James B 1855
FULLER Jane 1854
MOSELY Frederick 1855
BERRYHILL James B 1855
MOSELY Frederick 1855
MOSELY Frederick 1855

Section 25
DRAKE John A 1855
YOUNG [295] Stephen 1854
JUDD Eli P 1855
DRAKE John A 1855
KEPPEL Philip 1853
KEPPEL Philip 1853
PINNEY Marcellus 1854
LAREW Isaac 1854
SMITH Benjamin L 1855

Section 34
WHEELER William P 1855
MOSELY Frederick 1855
SHREVE Thomas C 1855
BERRYHILL Charles H 1857
MOSELY Frederick 1855

Section 35
MOSELY Frederick 1855
FOLSOM Gilman 1854
MERWIN [210] Phineas 1857

Section 36
HIGGINSON John C 1855
SMITH Benjamin L 1855

Helpful Hints

1. This Map's INDEX can be found on the preceding pages.

2. Refer to Map "C" to see where this Township lies within Poweshiek County, Iowa.

3. Numbers within square brackets [ ] denote a multi-patentee land parcel (multi-owner). Refer to Appendix "C" for a full list of members in this group.

4. Areas that look to be crowded with Patentees usually indicate multiple sales of the same parcel (Re-issues) or Overlapping parcels. See this Township's Index for an explanation of these and other circumstances that might explain "odd" groupings of Patentees on this map.

Legend

—— Patent Boundary

━━ Section Boundary

No Patents Found (or Outside County)

1., 2., 3., ... Lot Numbers (when beside a name)

[ ] Group Number (see Appendix "C")

Scale: Section = 1 mile X 1 mile (generally, with some exceptions)

Road Map

T81-N R14-W
5th PM Meridian

Map Group 3

Cities & Towns

None

Cemeteries

Kent Cemetery
Squires Cemetery

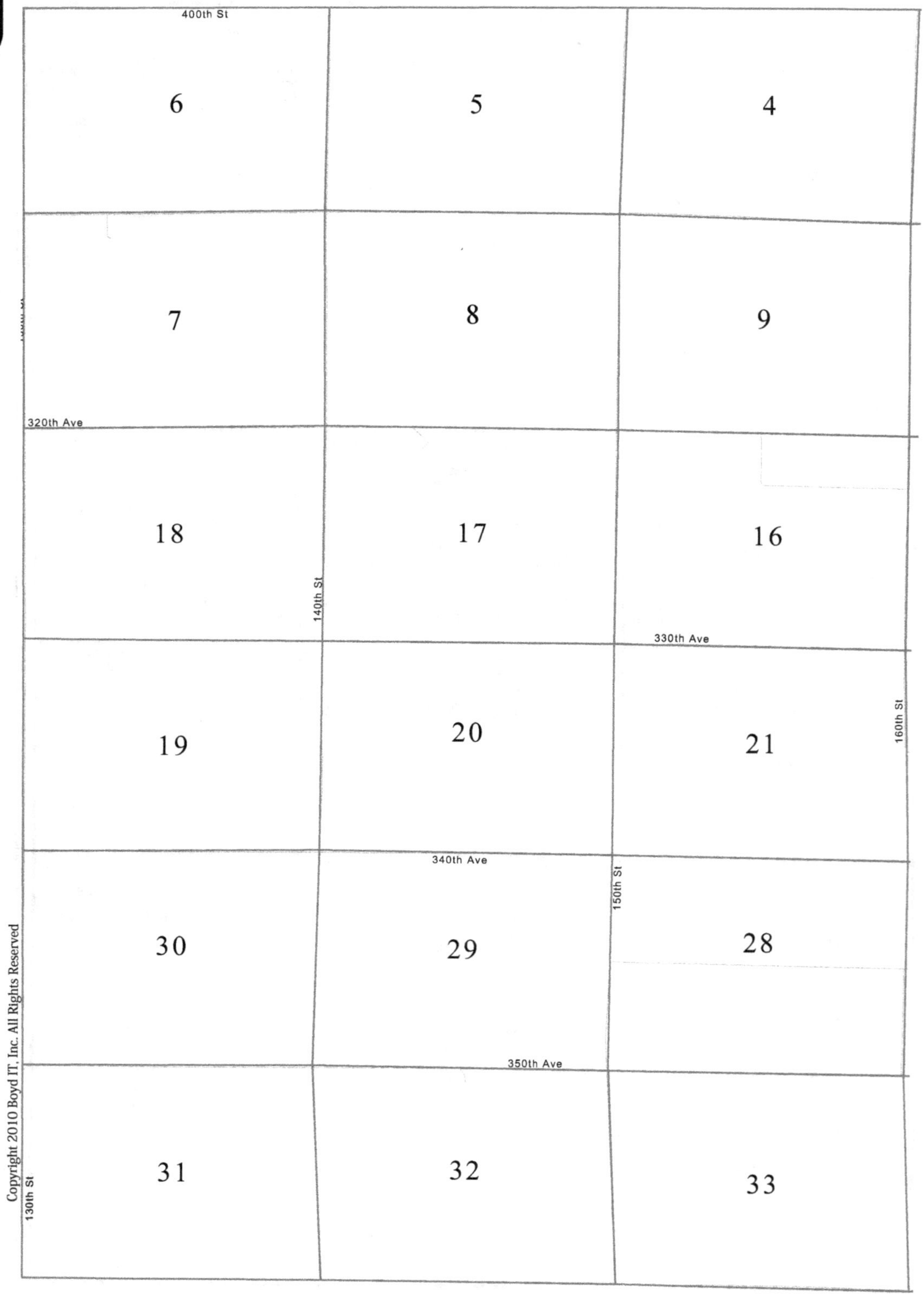

400th St
6
5
4
7
8
9
320th Ave
18
17
16
140th St
330th Ave
19
20
21
160th St
340th Ave
150th St
30
29
28
350th Ave
31
32
33
130th St
Copyright 2010 Boyd IT, Inc. All Rights Reserved

3

2

1

310th Ave

10

11

Squires Cem.

12

190th St

15

14

320th Ave

V18 Rd

13

170th St

Aurora Dr

N Lakeshore Dr

328th Ave

Skyline Dr

Shady Lane Dr

E Park

Woodland Hills Dr

Herbert Tracey Dr Dr

Dee Dr S

Lakeshore

Belaire Dr

Holiday Ln

Lakeshore Dr

E Ridge Dr

Wilson Ave

Franklin Dr

Larry's Dr

NE Lakeshore Dr

Waukonda Dr

Union Dr

Barbara Dr

Caron

22

23

24

Kent Cem.

27

345th Ave

165th St

26

25

350th Ave

34

355th Ave

35

360th Ave

36

Helpful Hints

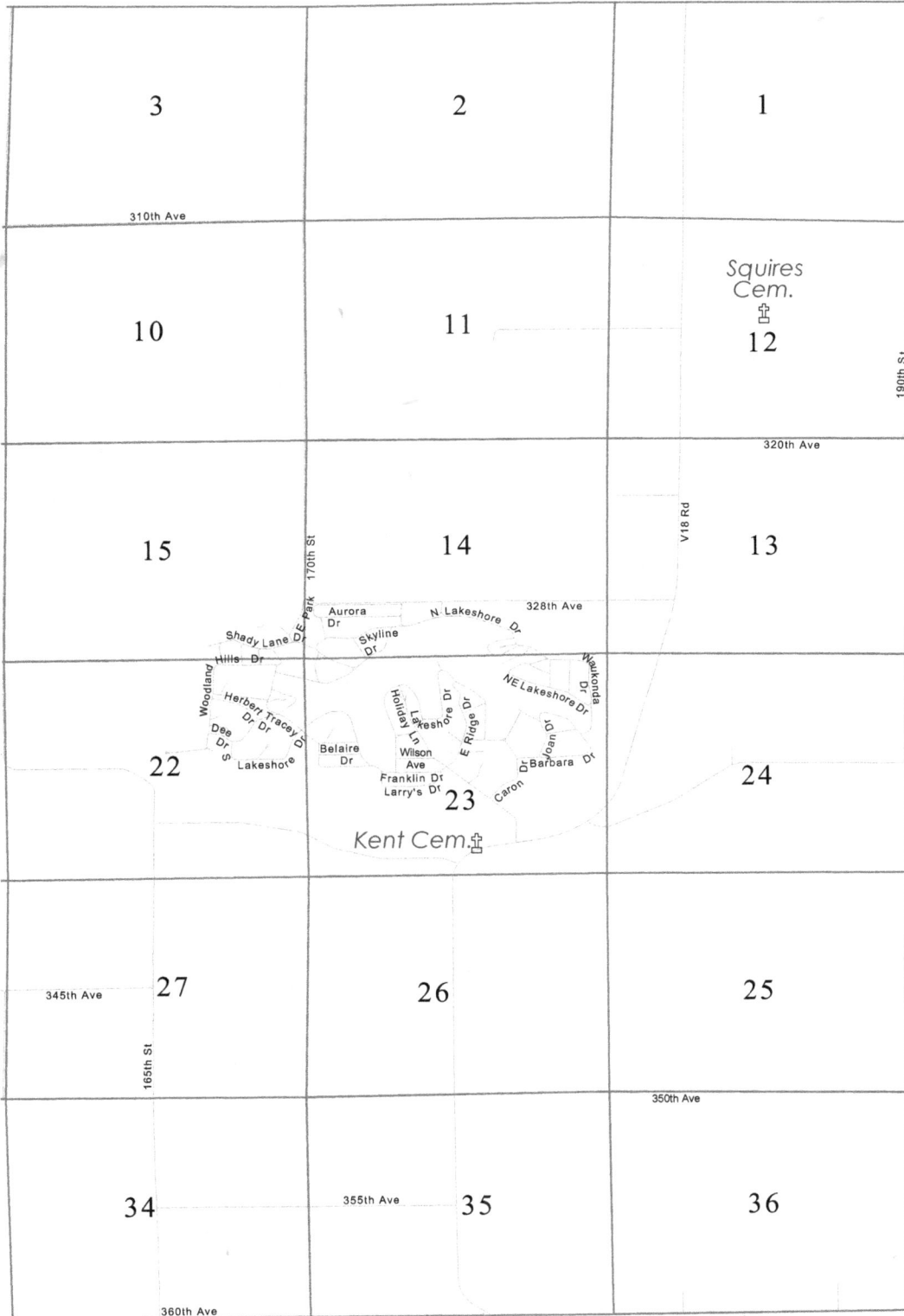

1. This road map has a number of uses, but primarily it is to help you: a) find the present location of land owned by your ancestors (at least the general area), b) find cemeteries and city-centers, and c) estimate the route/roads used by Census-takers & tax-assessors.

2. If you plan to travel to Poweshiek County to locate cemeteries or land parcels, please pick up a modern travel map for the area before you do. Mapping old land parcels on modern maps is not as exact a science as you might think. Just the slightest variations in public land survey coordinates, estimates of parcel boundaries, or road-map deviations can greatly alter a map's representation of how a road either does or doesn't cross a particular parcel of land.

Legend

————	Section Lines
≡≡≡≡	Interstates
▬▬▬▬	Highways
————	Other Roads
●	Cities/Towns
✝	Cemeteries

Scale: Section = 1 mile X 1 mile
(generally, with some exceptions)

Historical Map

T81-N R14-W
5th PM Meridian

Map Group 3

Cities & Towns
None

Cemeteries
Kent Cemetery
Squires Cemetery

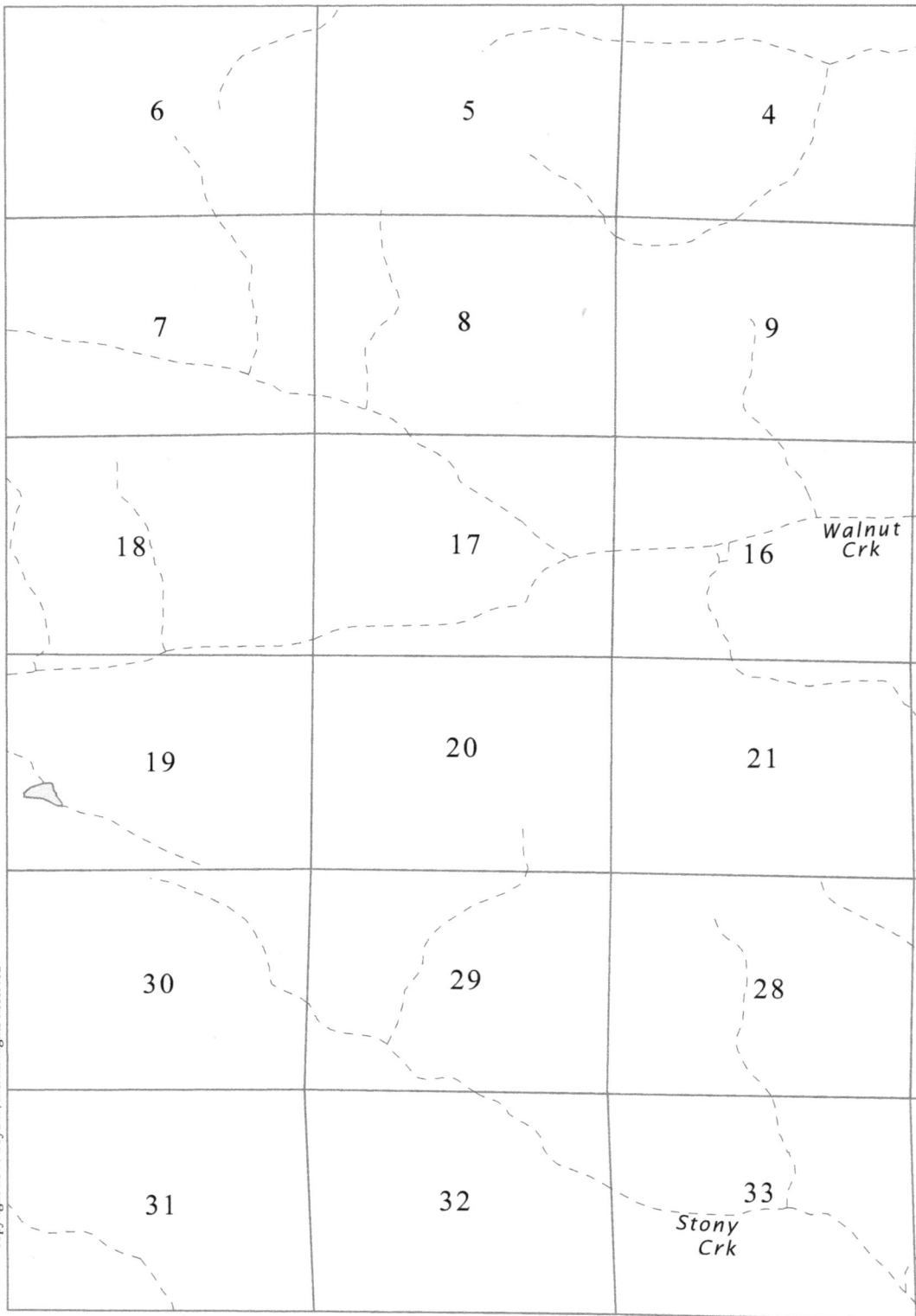

6	5	4
7	8	9
18	17	16 Walnut Crk
19	20	21
30	29	28
31	32	33 Stony Crk

3

2

N Walnut
Crk

1

Helpful Hints

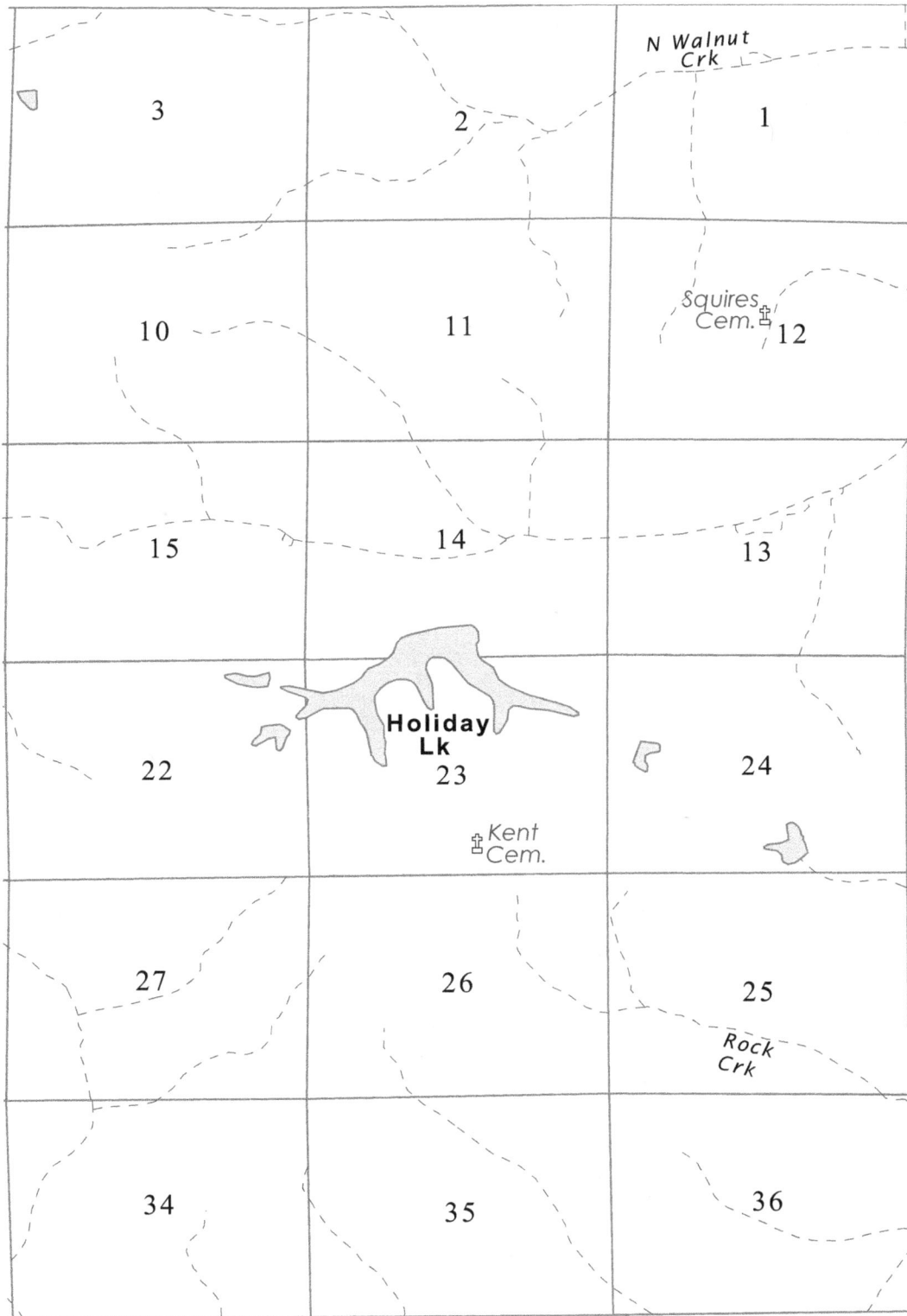

1. This Map takes a different look at the same Congressional Township displayed in the preceding two maps. It presents features that can help you better envision the historical development of the area: a) Water-bodies (lakes & ponds), b) Water-courses (rivers, streams, etc.), c) Railroads, d) City/ town center-points (where they were oftentimes located when first settled), and e) Cemeteries.

2. Using this "Historical" map in tandem with this Township's Patent Map and Road Map, may lead you to some interesting discoveries. You will often find roads, towns, cemeteries, and waterways are named after nearby landowners: sometimes those names will be the ones you are researching. See how many of these research gems you can find here in Poweshiek County.

10

11

Squires
Cem.

12

15

14

13

22

Holiday
Lk

23

Kent
Cem.

24

27

26

25

Rock
Crk

34

35

36

Legend

——————	Section Lines
+++++++	Railroads
▭	Large Rivers & Bodies of Water
- - - - - - -	Streams/Creeks & Small Rivers
●	Cities/Towns
☨	Cemeteries

Scale: Section = 1 mile X 1 mile
(there are some exceptions)

Map Group 4: Index to Land Patents

Township 81-North Range 13-West (5th PM)

After you locate an individual in this Index, take note of the Section and Section Part then proceed to the Land Patent map on the pages immediately following. You should have no difficulty locating the corresponding parcel of land.

The "For More Info" Column will lead you to more information about the underlying Patents. See the *Legend* at right, and the "How to Use this Book" chapter, for more information.

```
                    LEGEND
          "For More Info . . . " column
A = Authority (Legislative Act, See Appendix "A")
B = Block or Lot (location in Section unknown)
C = Cancelled Patent
F = Fractional Section
G = Group (Multi-Patentee Patent, see Appendix "C")
V = Overlaps another Parcel
R = Re-Issued (Parcel patented more than once)

(A & G items require you to look in the Appendixes referred
to above. All other Letter-designations followed by a number
require you to locate line-items in this index that possess
the ID number found after the letter).
```

ID	Individual in Patent	Sec.	Sec. Part	Date Issued	Other Counties	For More Info . . .
637	ANGLE, Charles W	27	E½	1855-05-01		A1
850	ARMSTRONG, Thomas K	18	E½NW	1855-12-15		A1 F
851	" "	18	SENE	1855-12-15		A1
852	" "	18	W½NE	1855-12-15		A1
824	ATWOOD, Nancy	1	E½NE	1853-04-15		A6 G141 F
782	BATY, Marshall	33	W½SW	1855-05-01		A1
780	BEATY, Marshal	28	SESW	1855-12-15		A1 C
781	" "	28	W½NW	1855-12-15		A1 C R784
783	BEATY, Marshall	28	SENW	1909-02-08		A1
784	" "	28	W½NW	1909-02-08		A1 R781
774	BEEBE, Lewis L	9	NWNW	1855-12-15		A1
633	BERRYHILL, Charles H	6	NWSE	1855-12-15		A1
634	" "	6	SWSW	1855-12-15		A1 F
632	" "	21	SE	1857-02-16		A5
713	BERRYHILL, James B	10	NENE	1853-07-13		A6 G21
714	" "	11	NWNW	1853-07-13		A6 G21
712	" "	9	SENW	1853-07-13		A6
865	BERRYHILL, William D	9	NENW	1855-05-01		A1
866	" "	9	NESW	1855-12-15		A1
867	" "	9	NWSE	1855-12-15		A1
868	" "	9	S½SW	1855-12-15		A1
688	BILL, Harvey A	15	S½SW	1855-05-01		A1
689	" "	22	E½NW	1855-05-01		A1
690	" "	22	N½NE	1855-05-01		A1
643	BLACK, Nancy	13	S½SE	1855-01-01		A6 G139
678	BLAKE, George	1	NWNW	1853-11-01		A1 F
679	" "	1	NWSW	1853-11-01		A1
773	BLAKE, Lewis	6	SESW	1854-10-02		A6 G27 F
789	BLAKE, Matilda A	6	NESW	1855-12-15		A1 F
810	BOOTH, Myron	20	N½NW	1856-09-01		A1
715	BREWER, James	7	W½NE	1852-12-30		A6
680	BROWN, George	18	SW	1855-05-01		A1 F
812	BROWN, Norman E	33	NESW	1855-05-01		A1
813	" "	33	SE	1855-05-01		A1
697	CADWALADER, Isaac	12	N½SE	1854-12-01		A1
705	CAPLES, Mary	10	NWNE	1852-10-01		A6 G276
681	CARROLL, George	9	NWSW	1855-12-15		A1
682	" "	9	SWNW	1855-12-15		A1
860	CHASE, Wheten	1	NENW	1852-11-01		A1 F
861	" "	1	SWNW	1852-11-01		A1 F
743	CLARK, Sally	14	SENE	1855-02-01		A6 G223
674	COLE, Addison G	21	NW	1861-11-25		A5 G158 R675
674	COLE, Mary L	21	NW	1861-11-25		A5 G158 R675
646	CONNELLY, Edward	23	N½NW	1855-05-01		A1
755	COOK, John M	18	SE	1855-12-15		A1
821	CRAWFORD, Rebecca	19	NWNW	1854-12-01		A1 F

ID	Individual in Patent	Sec.	Sec. Part	Date Issued	Other Counties	For More Info . . .
779	CROCKER, Dorothy	20	SW	1855-01-01		A6 G178
745	CULBERTSON, John C	10	W½SW	1853-10-01		A6
749	" "	5	SESE	1856-10-10		A2
746	" "	36	NESE	1857-06-01		A5
748	" "	36	W½SE	1857-06-01		A5
747	" "	36	SESE	1860-07-20		A1
862	DAVIDSON, William B	19	NESW	1855-12-15		A1 F
863	" "	19	SWNW	1855-12-15		A1 F
864	" "	19	W½SW	1855-12-15		A1 F
659	DAVIS, Emily	22	SWSW	1855-12-15		A1
658	DICKERSON, Eliza	34	NE	1855-05-01		A1
699	DOBBINS, Jacob	5	NWNW	1855-12-15		A1 F
700	"	6	NENW	1855-12-15		A1 F R735
648	DOUGHTY, Eli M	3	E½SE	1854-12-01		A1
716	DOUGHTY, James H	3	NWSE	1854-12-01		A1
761	DOUGHTY, John W	12	S½SW	1855-12-15		A1
693	DOWNEY, Hugh D	22	NWSW	1856-09-01		A1
692	" "	17	S½NE	1857-03-10		A1
694	" "	7	NESW	1857-03-10		A1 F
695	" "	7	SWSW	1857-03-10		A1 F
696	" "	8	S½NE	1857-03-10		A1
645	DUFFIELD, David M	10	NWSE	1854-05-01		A1
726	DUFFIELD, James R	5	SWSW	1854-02-01		A6
727	" "	6	SESE	1854-02-01		A6
728	" "	17	N½NE	1856-01-15		A6 G113
751	DYLE, John	12	S½SE	1854-12-01		A6
730	EASLEY, James S	22	E½SW	1855-01-01		A6
731	" "	22	W½SE	1855-01-01		A6
869	FOUTS, William D	4	SW	1855-12-15		A1
643	FRYAR, Daniel	13	S½SE	1855-01-01		A6 G139
824	GATES, Samuel	1	E½NE	1853-04-15		A6 G141 F
823	" "	1	SWNE	1853-04-15		A6 F
838	GATES, Simon S	30	NWNE	1855-05-10		A1
825	GAUMER, Samuel	29	S½SW	1855-05-01		A1
826	" "	32	N½SW	1855-05-01		A1
827	" "	32	NW	1855-05-01		A1
627	GLAZE, Adam	5	N½SW	1855-05-01		A1
628	" "	5	S½NW	1855-05-01		A1 F
719	GOWER, James H	23	NWNE	1855-12-15		A1
720	" "	24	W½SW	1855-12-15		A1
717	" "	13	E½NE	1856-09-01		A1
718	" "	13	NWNE	1856-09-01		A1
721	" "	3	NENE	1857-03-10		A1 F
657	HALL, Elisha	12	NWNE	1854-05-01		A1
656	" "	12	NENE	1854-07-01		A6
873	HALLETT, William	8	NWNE	1855-05-10		A1
872	" "	8	NENE	1857-10-30		A2
675	HAMILTON, George A	21	NW	1855-01-01		A6 G160 C R674
676	" "	21	SW	1855-03-01		A4 G159
674	" "	21	NW	1861-11-25		A5 G158 R675
840	HARMON, Stephen N	12	N½SW	1854-05-01		A1
841	" "	12	S½NW	1854-05-01		A1
834	HARTMAN, Sanford F	13	SW	1855-05-01		A1
835	HEALD, Sarah	12	S½NE	1854-12-01		A1
790	HERRIMAN, Melvin C	23	S½NW	1855-05-01		A1
791	" "	25	SENW	1857-03-10		A1 V710
750	HIGGINSON, John C	14	NW	1855-05-01		A1
752	HOLLENBACK, John	1	SE	1854-10-02		A6 G172
814	HOLLER, Peter C	3	E½NW	1855-05-01		A1 F
815	" "	3	W½NE	1855-05-01		A1 F
778	HOWARD, Mark	19	SE	1855-01-01		A6
779	" "	20	SW	1855-01-01		A6 G178
777	HUBBARD, Luther P	7	NWNW	1855-05-10		A1 F
839	IOWA, State Of	16		1937-08-26		A3
753	JOHNSTON, John	7	NENW	1854-05-01		A1
754	" "	7	NWSE	1854-05-01		A1
649	JUDD, Eli P	30	E½NW	1855-05-01		A1 F
650	" "	30	E½SW	1855-05-01		A1 F
651	" "	30	NWNW	1855-05-01		A1 F
652	" "	30	SWSW	1855-05-01		A1 F
653	" "	31	N½	1855-05-01		A1 F
638	KAUFFMAN, Christian	3	SWSE	1855-01-01		A6 G183
769	KENT, Joseph	19	E½NW	1854-03-01		A6 F

ID	Individual in Patent	Sec.	Sec. Part	Date Issued	Other Counties	For More Info . . .
819	KEPPEL, Philip	30	NWSW	1853-06-01		A6 F
820	" "	30	SWNW	1853-06-01		A6 F
828	KIRKWOOD, Samuel J	36	S½SW	1857-02-20		A5 G186
829	KNEPPER, Samuel	24	SE	1855-05-01		A1
830	" "	35	SE	1855-05-01		A1
874	KORN, William	34	NW	1855-05-01		A1
875	" "	34	SE	1855-05-01		A1
770	KORNS, Joseph	32	SE	1855-05-01		A1
724	LALANDER, Mary	28	S½SE	1855-01-01		A6 G191
828	LANE, Miranda	36	S½SW	1857-02-20		A5 G186
698	LARUE, Isaac	5	N½NE	1856-09-01		A1 F
853	LAUGHLIN, Thomas	5	N½SE	1855-05-01		A1
854	" "	5	S½NE	1855-05-01		A1 F
724	LAYLANDER, James	28	S½SE	1855-01-01		A6 G191
723	" "	33	NE	1855-05-01		A1
858	LINN, Timothy	23	SWNE	1855-05-10		A1
857	" "	23	E½NE	1856-09-01		A1
859	" "	24	W½NW	1856-09-01		A1
728	LITTLE, Nancy	17	N½NE	1856-01-15		A6 G113
639	LOCKHART, Conrad	17	NENW	1854-08-01		A6
640	" "	17	NWNW	1854-08-01		A6
641	" "	18	NENE	1854-08-01		A6
642	" "	8	SESW	1854-08-01		A6
775	LONG, Lewis	2	SWNE	1852-09-10		A6 F
786	LORD, Mary G	19	NE	1855-05-10		A1
787	" "	20	SE	1855-05-10		A1
788	" "	20	SENE	1855-05-10		A1
768	LOUD, Joseph F	31	SE	1855-01-01		A6
855	LOUGHLIN, Thomas	5	SWSE	1856-09-01		A1
818	LUCAS, Phebe A	32	S½SW	1855-05-01		A1
701	LUCKHART, Jacob	7	NESE	1854-05-01		A1
702	" "	8	NWSW	1854-05-01		A1
752	MAHAN, Maria	1	SE	1854-10-02		A6 G172
876	MANATT, William	34	SW	1855-05-01		A1
794	MARPOLE, Morgan H	36	NWSW	1884-03-10		A6
638	MARVIN, Olivia	3	SWSE	1855-01-01		A6 G183
744	MCCLUSKY, John A	30	SE	1855-05-10		A1
725	MCVEY, James O	28	NENE	1857-04-10		A6
704	MOATES, Jacob	1	SENW	1853-04-15		A6 F
703	" "	1	NESW	1853-06-01		A6
756	MOATS, John	11	NENW	1854-03-01		A6
757	" "	11	NWNE	1854-11-01		A4
631	MOREY, Amos	4	NW	1855-12-15		A1 F
762	MORGAN, John W	7	NWSW	1855-05-01		A1 F
763	" "	7	S½NW	1855-05-01		A1 F
785	MORGAN, Mary E	15	NE	1855-05-01		A1
836	MORGAN, Sarah Jane	15	SE	1855-05-01		A1
809	MORSMAN, Moses J	6	SWSE	1854-05-01		A1
808	" "	4	S½SE	1855-12-15		A1
764	NEAL, John W	29	N½SW	1855-05-10		A1
765	" "	31	SW	1855-05-10		A1 F
766	NILES, John W	36	NE	1855-01-01		A6
856	NINDE, Thomas	4	N½SE	1856-09-01		A1
629	NORRIS, Adin H	6	NWNW	1855-05-01		A1 F
635	OSBORN, Charles M	20	S½NW	1855-05-10		A1
636	" "	20	W½NE	1855-05-10		A1
713	OTTO, Susanna	10	NENE	1853-07-13		A6 G21
714	" "	11	NWNW	1853-07-13		A6 G21
684	PARKS, George W	15	NWSW	1854-12-01		A1
686	" "	15	SESW	1854-12-01		A6 G216 C
685	" "	15	NESW	1959-05-21		A6 G216
676	PARMER, Jerusha	21	SW	1855-03-01		A4 G159
822	PATRICK, Richard M	25	SW	1855-05-01		A1
843	PATRICK, Stephen	26		1855-05-01		A1
844	" "	27	NW	1855-05-01		A1
845	" "	29	NW	1855-05-01		A1
846	" "	35	NE	1855-05-01		A1
842	" "	25	W½NW	1855-12-15		A1
837	PEREGOY, Sarah T	9	S½SE	1852-05-01		A6
816	PHILLIPS, Peter	11	SWNW	1855-12-15		A1
691	PLUMB, Henry	22	S½NE	1855-05-01		A1
743	PLYMPTON, Jeremiah	14	SENE	1855-02-01		A6 G223
742	" "	14	W½NE	1855-02-01		A6

ID	Individual in Patent	Sec.	Sec. Part	Date Issued	Other Counties	For More Info . . .
654	POCOCK, Elias	13	NW	1855-05-01		A1
773	POOLE, Sarah	6	SESW	1854-10-02		A6 G27 F
870	PORTER, William G	33	SESW	1855-05-01		A1
871	" "	35	W½	1855-05-01		A1
807	RENO, Morgan	2	W½SE	1853-06-10		A6 G237
799	" "	2	E½NE	1854-10-02		A6 F
801	" "	2	NESE	1854-10-02		A6
796	" "	13	N½SE	1855-12-15		A1
805	" "	4	S½NE	1857-02-20		A5 F
795	" "	11	S½SE	1857-03-10		A1
797	" "	13	SWNE	1857-03-10		A1
798	" "	14	NENE	1857-03-10		A1
800	" "	2	N½NW	1857-03-10		A1 F
802	" "	3	NWNW	1857-03-10		A1 F
803	" "	3	SWNW	1857-03-10		A1 F
804	" "	4	N½NE	1857-03-10		A1 F
806	" "	5	NENW	1857-03-10		A1 F
817	RICKER, Peter	8	SE	1856-09-01		A1
877	ROSS, William	11	E½NE	1855-05-01		A1
878	" "	11	NWSE	1855-05-01		A1
879	" "	11	SW	1855-05-01		A1
880	" "	14	S½	1855-05-01		A1
881	" "	2	SESE	1855-05-01		A1
729	RYEON, James	18	W½NW	1855-12-15		A1 F
683	SAMSON, George	28	S½NE	1855-12-15		A1
686	SANDERS, Elizabeth W	15	SESW	1854-12-01		A6 G216 C
685	" "	15	NESW	1959-05-21		A6 G216
660	SANXAY, Frederic	10	SENW	1854-12-01		A6
661	" "	10	W½NW	1854-12-01		A6
672	" "	9	NENE	1854-12-01		A6
662	" "	17	E½SE	1857-02-20		A5
663	" "	17	N½SW	1857-02-20		A5
664	" "	17	NWSE	1857-02-20		A5
665	" "	17	S½NW	1857-02-20		A5
666	" "	17	S½SW	1857-02-20		A5
667	" "	17	SWSE	1857-02-20		A5
668	" "	19	SESW	1857-03-10		A1 F
669	" "	28	NENW	1857-03-10		A1
670	" "	30	SWNE	1857-03-10		A1
671	" "	36	NESW	1857-03-10		A1
673	SANXAY, Frederick	20	NENE	1856-06-16		A6
647	SCHIRCLIFF, Edward L	28	NWNE	1857-05-01		A1
882	SHOVER, William	10	S½SE	1857-03-10		A1
758	SMITH, John P	27	SW	1855-05-01		A1
759	" "	29	E½	1855-05-01		A1
760	" "	32	NE	1855-05-01		A1
847	SQUIRES, Sumner L	6	NWSW	1855-12-15		A1 F
848	STEVENS, Sylvester S	21	E½NE	1855-05-10		A1
849	" "	22	W½NW	1855-05-10		A1
807	STILES, Jerusha	2	W½SE	1853-06-10		A6 G237
675	STOKES, Elinira	21	NW	1855-01-01		A6 G160 C R674
626	SUMNER, Abner	10	NENW	1854-05-01		A1
734	SUMNER, James	3	SW	1853-07-20		A6
732	" "	2	S½NW	1853-11-01		A1 F
733	" "	3	SENE	1853-11-01		A1 F
735	" "	6	NENW	1853-11-01		A1 F R700
736	" "	6	NESE	1853-11-01		A1
737	" "	6	NWNE	1853-11-01		A1 F
738	" "	6	S½NE	1853-11-01		A1
739	" "	6	S½NW	1853-11-01		A1 F
740	" "	7	E½NE	1854-11-01		A4
741	" "	8	W½NW	1854-11-01		A4
767	THORNE, John W	10	E½SW	1854-05-01		A1
705	TUCKER, Jacob T	10	NWNE	1852-10-01		A6 G276
776	TUDOR, Lewis	28	N½SE	1855-12-15		A1
677	TYLER, George B	25	SE	1855-12-15		A1
792	WALLACK, Michael	28	SW	1855-05-01		A1
793	" "	33	NW	1855-05-01		A1
722	WEISE, James H	21	W½NE	1855-12-15		A1
630	WICKHAM, Alpheus	15	W½NW	1854-05-01		A1
655	WICKHAM, Elias	15	E½NW	1854-05-01		A1
811	WILLIAMS, Nathan	30	E½NE	1856-05-01		A1
706	WILLIAMSON, James A	23	E½SE	1855-05-01		A1

ID	Individual in Patent	Sec.	Sec. Part	Date Issued	Other Counties	For More Info . . .
707	WILLIAMSON, James A (Cont'd)	24	E½NW	1855-05-01		A1
708	" "	24	E½SW	1855-05-01		A1
709	" "	24	NE	1855-05-01		A1
710	" "	25	E½NW	1855-05-01		A1 V791
711	" "	25	NE	1855-05-01		A1
687	WINDERS, George W	10	SWNE	1853-07-13		A6
644	WINSLOW, Daniel	2	NWNE	1853-08-01		A1 F
831	WINSLOW, Samuel	11	NESE	1854-05-01		A1
832	" "	11	SENW	1854-05-01		A1
833	" "	11	SWNE	1854-05-01		A1
772	WOODARD, Laughlin	10	SENE	1854-12-01		A1
771	WOODARD, Laughlin H	10	NESE	1856-09-01		A1

Patent Map

T81-N R13-W
5th PM Meridian

Map Group 4

Township Statistics

Parcels Mapped	:	257
Number of Patents	:	204
Number of Individuals	:	148
Patentees Identified	:	140
Number of Surnames	:	129
Multi-Patentee Parcels	:	19
Oldest Patent Date	:	5/1/1852
Most Recent Patent	:	5/21/1959
Block/Lot Parcels	:	0
Parcels Re - Issued	:	3
Parcels that Overlap	:	2
Cities and Towns	:	1
Cemeteries	:	3

Section 6:
NORRIS Adin H 1855; DOBBINS Jacob 1855; SUMNER James 1853; SUMNER James 1853; SUMNER James 1853; SUMNER James 1853; SQUIRES Sumner L 1855; BLAKE Matilda A 1855; BERRYHILL Charles H 1855; SUMNER James 1853; BERRYHILL Charles H 1855; BLAKE [27] Lewis 1855; MORSMAN Moses J 1854; DUFFIELD James R 1854

Section 5:
DOBBINS Jacob 1855; RENO Morgan 1857; LARUE Isaac 1856; GLAZE Adam 1855; LAUGHLIN Thomas 1855; GLAZE Adam 1855; LAUGHLIN Thomas 1855; DUFFIELD James R 1854; LOUGHLIN Thomas 1856; CULBERTSON John C 1856

Section 4:
MOREY Amos 1855; RENO Morgan 1857; RENO Morgan 1857; FOUTS William D 1855; NINDE Thomas 1856; MORSMAN Moses J 1855

Section 7:
HUBBARD Luther P 1855; JOHNSTON John 1854; BREWER James 1852; SUMNER James 1854; MORGAN John W 1855; MORGAN John W 1855; DOWNEY Hugh D 1857; JOHNSTON John 1854; LUCKHART Jacob 1854; DOWNEY Hugh D 1857

Section 8:
SUMNER James 1854; LUCKHART Jacob 1854; LOCKHART Conrad 1854; RICKER Peter 1856

Section 9:
HALLETT William 1855; HALLETT William 1857; BEEBE Lewis L 1855; BERRYHILL William D 1855; SANXAY Frederic 1854; DOWNEY Hugh D 1857; CARROLL George 1855; BERRYHILL James B 1853; CARROLL George 1855; BERRYHILL William D 1855; BERRYHILL William D 1855; BERRYHILL William D 1855; PEREGOY Sarah T 1852

Section 18:
RYEON James 1855; ARMSTRONG Thomas K 1855; ARMSTRONG Thomas K 1855; ARMSTRONG Thomas K 1855; BROWN George 1855; COOK John M 1855

Section 17:
LOCKHART Conrad 1854; LOCKHART Conrad 1854; LOCKHART Conrad 1854; DUFFIELD [113] James R 1856; SANXAY Frederic 1857; DOWNEY Hugh D 1857; SANXAY Frederic 1857; SANXAY Frederic 1857; SANXAY Frederic 1857; SANXAY Frederic 1857

Section 16:
IOWA State Of 1937

Section 19:
CRAWFORD Rebecca 1854; DAVIDSON William B 1855; KENT Joseph 1854; LORD Mary G 1855; DAVIDSON William B 1855; DAVIDSON William B 1855; SANXAY Frederic 1857; HOWARD Mark 1855

Section 20:
BOOTH Myron 1856; OSBORN Charles M 1855; OSBORN Charles M 1855; SANXAY Frederick 1856; LORD Mary G 1855; HOWARD [178] Mark 1855; LORD Mary G 1855

Section 21:
HAMILTON [158] George A 1861; WEISE James H 1855; STEVENS Sylvester S 1855; HAMILTON [160] George A 1855; BERRYHILL Charles H 1857; HAMILTON [159] George A 1855

Section 30:
JUDD Eli P 1855; GATES Simon S 1855; WILLIAMS Nathan 1856; JUDD Eli P 1855; KEPPEL Philip 1853; SANXAY Frederic 1857; KEPPEL Philip 1853; JUDD Eli P 1855; JUDD Eli P 1855; MCCLUSKY John A 1855

Section 29:
PATRICK Stephen 1855; NEAL John W 1855; GAUMER Samuel 1855; SMITH John P 1855

Section 28:
BEATY Marshal 1855; SANXAY Frederic 1857; SCHIRCLIFF Edward L 1857; MCVEY James O 1857; BEATY Marshall 1909; BEATY Marshall 1909; SAMSON George 1855; WALLACK Michael 1855; TUDOR Lewis 1855; BEATY Marshal 1855; LAYLANDER [191] James 1855

Section 31:
JUDD Eli P 1855; NEAL John W 1855; LOUD Joseph F 1855

Section 32:
GAUMER Samuel 1855; SMITH John P 1855; GAUMER Samuel 1855; LUCAS Phebe A 1855; KORNS Joseph 1855

Section 33:
WALLACK Michael 1855; LAYLANDER James 1855; BATY Marshall 1855; BROWN Norman E 1855; PORTER William G 1855; BROWN Norman E 1855

Section 3
- RENO Morgan 1857
- HOLLER Peter C 1855
- HOLLER Peter C 1855
- GOWER James H 1857
- SUMNER James 1853
- RENO Morgan 1857
- DOUGHTY James H 1854
- KAUFFMAN [183] Christian 1855
- DOUGHTY Eli M 1854
- SUMNER James 1853

Section 2
- RENO Morgan 1857
- WINSLOW Daniel 1853
- SUMNER James 1853
- LONG Lewis 1852
- RENO Morgan 1854
- RENO [237] Morgan 1853
- RENO Morgan 1854
- ROSS William 1855

Section 1
- BLAKE George 1853
- CHASE Wheten 1852
- CHASE Wheten 1852
- MOATES Jacob 1853
- GATES Samuel 1853
- GATES [141] Samuel 1853
- BLAKE George 1853
- MOATES Jacob 1853
- HOLLENBACK [172] John 1854

Section 10
- SANXAY Frederic 1854
- SUMNER Abner 1854
- TUCKER [276] Jacob T 1852
- BERRYHILL [21] James B 1853
- SANXAY Frederic 1854
- WINDERS George W 1853
- WOODARD Laughlin 1854
- CULBERTSON John C 1853
- DUFFIELD David M 1854
- WOODARD Laughlin H 1856
- THORNE John W 1854
- SHOVER William 1857

Section 11
- BERRYHILL [21] James B 1853
- MOATS John 1854
- MOATS John 1854
- ROSS William 1855
- PHILLIPS Peter 1855
- WINSLOW Samuel 1854
- WINSLOW Samuel 1854
- ROSS William 1855
- WINSLOW Samuel 1854
- ROSS William 1855
- RENO Morgan 1857

Section 12
- HARMON Stephen N 1854
- HALL Elisha 1854
- HALL Elisha 1854
- HEALD Sarah 1854
- HARMON Stephen N 1854
- CADWALADER Isaac 1854
- DOUGHTY John W 1855
- DYLE John 1854

Section 15
- WICKHAM Alpheus 1854
- MORGAN Mary E 1855
- WICKHAM Elias 1854
- PARKS George W 1854
- PARKS [216] George W 1959
- BILL Harvey A 1855
- PARKS [216] George W 1854
- MORGAN Sarah Jane 1855

Section 14
- HIGGINSON John C 1855
- PLYMPTON Jeremiah 1855
- RENO Morgan 1857
- PLYMPTON [223] Jeremiah 1855
- ROSS William 1855

Section 13
- POCOCK Elias 1855
- GOWER James H 1856
- RENO Morgan 1857
- GOWER James H 1856
- HARTMAN Sanford F 1855
- RENO Morgan 1855
- FRYAR [139] Daniel 1855

Section 22
- STEVENS Sylvester S 1855
- BILL Harvey A 1855
- BILL Harvey A 1855
- PLUMB Henry 1855
- DOWNEY Hugh D 1856
- EASLEY James S 1855
- DAVIS Emily 1855
- EASLEY James S 1855

Section 23
- CONNELLY Edward 1855
- GOWER James H 1855
- LINN Timothy 1856
- HERRIMAN Melvin C 1855
- LINN Timothy 1855
- WILLIAMSON James A 1855
- GOWER James H 1855
- WILLIAMSON James A 1855

Section 24
- LINN Timothy 1856
- WILLIAMSON James A 1855
- WILLIAMSON James A 1855
- KNEPPER Samuel 1855

Section 27
- PATRICK Stephen 1855
- ANGLE Charles W 1855
- SMITH John P 1855

Section 26
- PATRICK Stephen 1855

Section 25
- PATRICK Stephen 1855
- WILLIAMSON James A 1855
- HERRIMAN Melvin C 1857
- WILLIAMSON James A 1855
- PATRICK Richard M 1855
- TYLER George B 1855

Section 34
- KORN William 1855
- DICKERSON Eliza 1855
- MANATT William 1855
- KORN William 1855

Section 35
- PATRICK Stephen 1855
- PORTER William G 1855
- KNEPPER Samuel 1855

Section 36
- NILES John W 1855
- MARPOLE Morgan H 1884
- SANXAY Frederic 1857
- CULBERTSON John C 1857
- KIRKWOOD [186] Samuel J 1857
- CULBERTSON John C 1857
- CULBERTSON John C 1860

Helpful Hints
1. This Map's INDEX can be found on the preceding pages.
2. Refer to Map "C" to see where this Township lies within Poweshiek County, Iowa.
3. Numbers within square brackets [ ] denote a multi-patentee land parcel (multi-owner). Refer to Appendix "C" for a full list of members in this group.
4. Areas that look to be crowded with Patentees usually indicate multiple sales of the same parcel (Re-issues) or Overlapping parcels. See this Township's Index for an explanation of these and other circumstances that might explain "odd" groupings of Patentees on this map.

Legend
- ———— Patent Boundary
- ▬▬▬ Section Boundary
- No Patents Found (or Outside County)
- 1., 2., 3., ... Lot Numbers (when beside a name)
- [ ] Group Number (see Appendix "C")

Scale: Section = 1 mile X 1 mile (generally, with some exceptions)

Road Map

T81-N R13-W
5th PM Meridian

Map Group 4

Cities & Towns
Hartwick

Cemeteries
Blake Cemetery
Union Cemetery
Winslow Cemetery

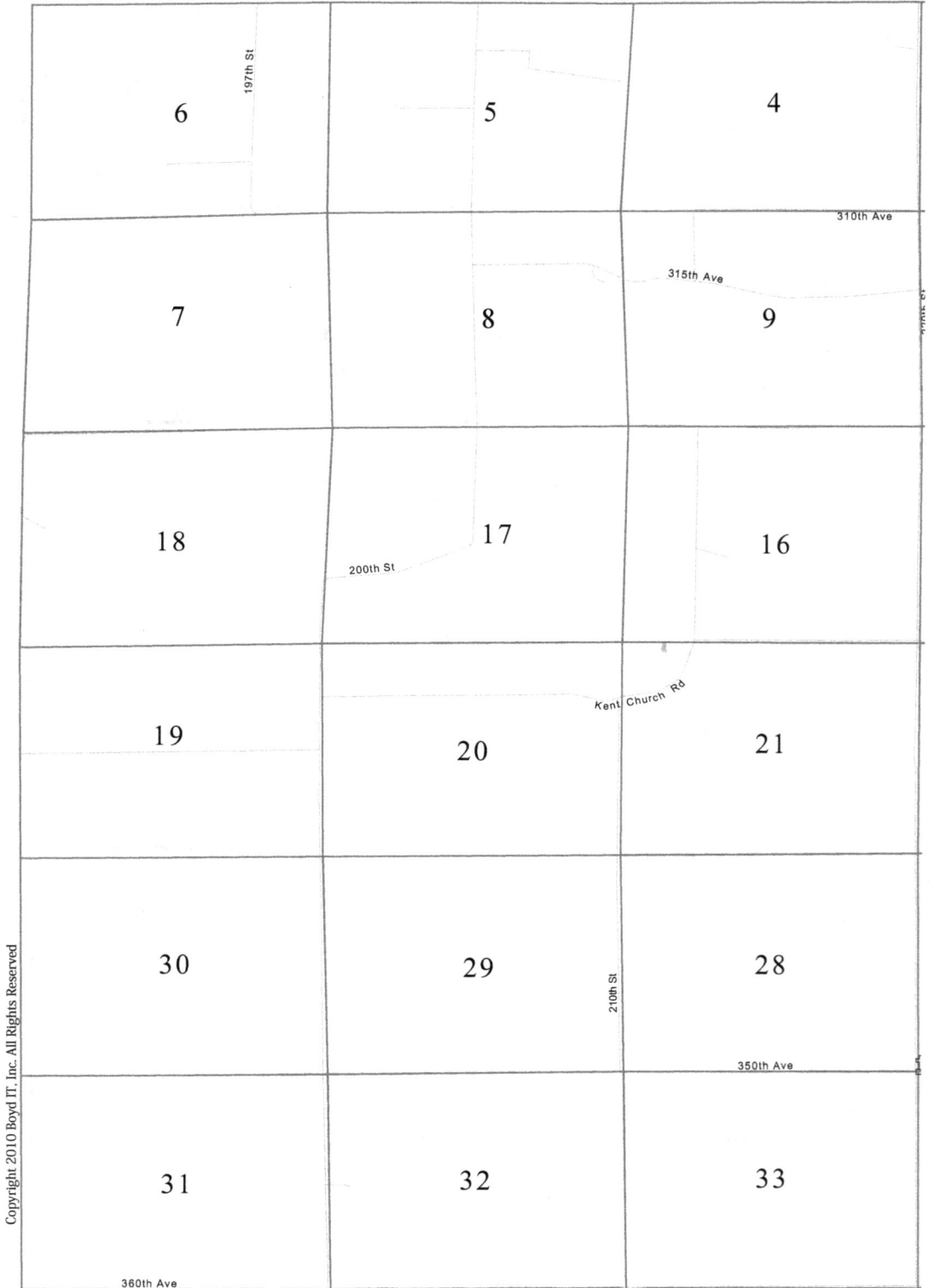

6	5	4
7	8	9
18	17	16
19	20	21
30	29	28
31	32	33

197th St

310th Ave

315th Ave

200th St

Kent Church Rd

210th St

350th Ave

360th Ave

3	2	1

301 Street Ave

✝ *Blake Cem.*

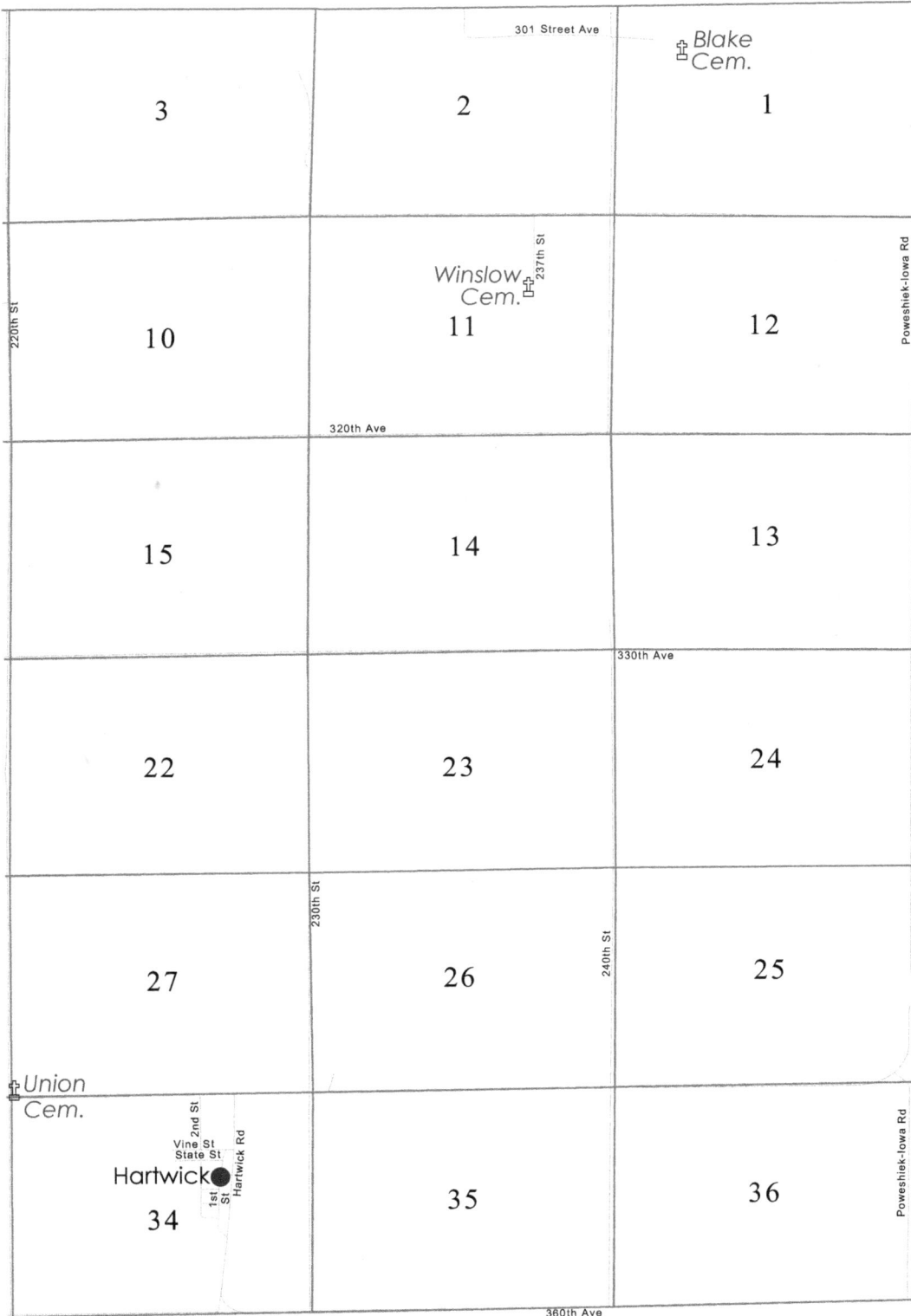

10	11	12

220th St

Winslow Cem.

237th St

320th Ave

Poweshiek-Iowa Rd

15	14	13

330th Ave

22	23	24

230th St

240th St

27	26	25

✝ *Union Cem.*

2nd St
Vine St
State St
1st St
Hartwick Rd

Hartwick ●

34	35	36

360th Ave

Poweshiek-Iowa Rd

Legend

————————	Section Lines
═══════	Interstates
▬▬▬▬▬	Highways
————————	Other Roads
●	Cities/Towns
✝	Cemeteries

Scale: Section = 1 mile X 1 mile
(generally, with some exceptions)

Historical Map

T81-N R13-W
5th PM Meridian

Map Group 4

Cities & Towns
Hartwick

Cemeteries
Blake Cemetery
Union Cemetery
Winslow Cemetery

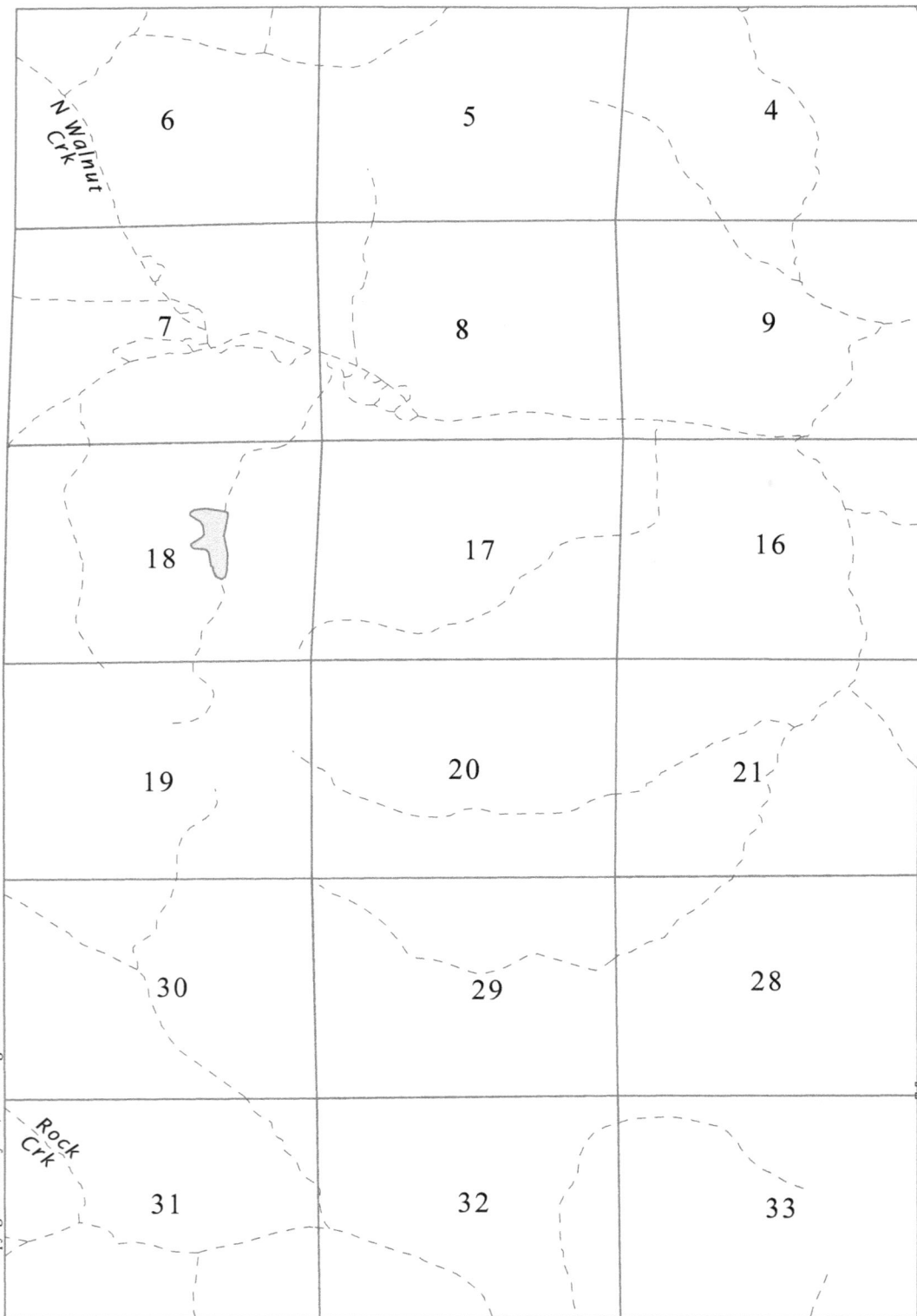

6	5	4
7	8	9
18	17	16
19	20	21
30	29	28
31	32	33

N Walnut Crk

Rock Crk

3

2

🛇 Blake Cem.

1

Walnut Crk

Winslow Cem. 🛇

10

11

12

15

14

13

22

23

24

27

26

25

Union 🛇 Cem.

Hartwick ●

34

35

36

Honey Crk

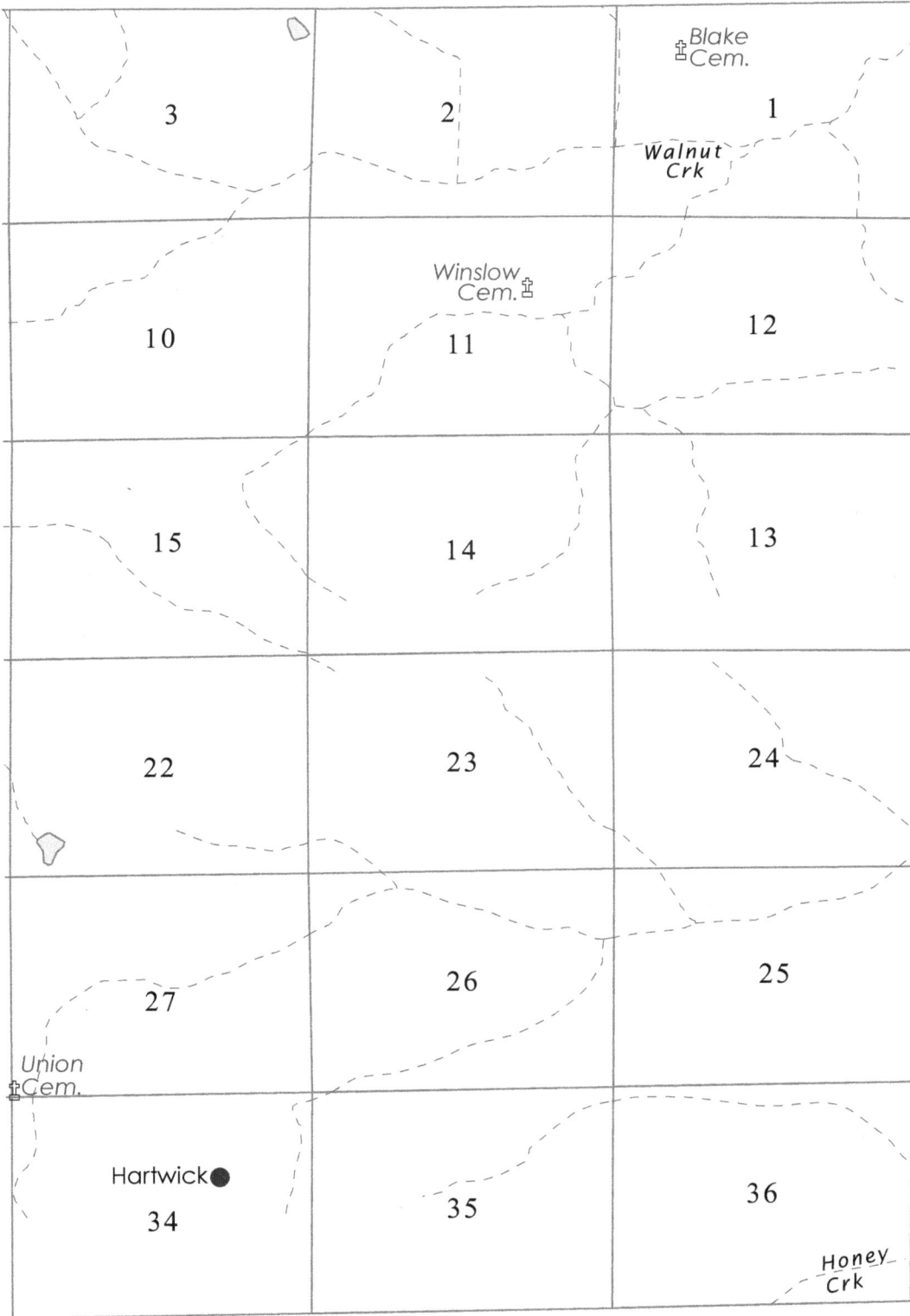

Helpful Hints

1. This Map takes a different look at the same Congressional Township displayed in the preceding two maps. It presents features that can help you better envision the historical development of the area: a) Water-bodies (lakes & ponds), b) Water-courses (rivers, streams, etc.), c) Railroads, d) City/town center-points (where they were oftentimes located when first settled), and e) Cemeteries.

2. Using this "Historical" map in tandem with this Township's Patent Map and Road Map, may lead you to some interesting discoveries. You will often find roads, towns, cemeteries, and waterways are named after nearby landowners: sometimes those names will be the ones you are researching. See how many of these research gems you can find here in Poweshiek County.

Legend

————————	Section Lines
┼┼┼┼┼┼	Railroads
▭	Large Rivers & Bodies of Water
- - - - - - -	Streams/Creeks & Small Rivers
●	Cities/Towns
🛇	Cemeteries

Scale: Section = 1 mile X 1 mile
(there are some exceptions)

Map Group 5: Index to Land Patents

Township 80-North Range 16-West (5th PM)

After you locate an individual in this Index, take note of the Section and Section Part then proceed to the Land Patent map on the pages immediately following. You should have no difficulty locating the corresponding parcel of land.

The "For More Info" Column will lead you to more information about the underlying Patents. See the *Legend* at right, and the "How to Use this Book" chapter, for more information.

```
                        LEGEND
            "For More Info . . . " column
A = Authority (Legislative Act, See Appendix "A")
B = Block or Lot (location in Section unknown)
C = Cancelled Patent
F = Fractional Section
G = Group (Multi-Patentee Patent, see Appendix "C")
V = Overlaps another Parcel
R = Re-Issued (Parcel patented more than once)

(A & G items require you to look in the Appendixes referred
to above. All other Letter-designations followed by a number
require you to locate line-items in this index that possess
the ID number found after the letter).
```

ID	Individual in Patent	Sec.	Sec. Part	Date Issued	Other Counties	For More Info . . .
1016	ADKINS, Mary	20	E½SE	1855-01-01		A6 G227
1062	BACON, William H	33	S½NE	1854-12-01		A1
1063	" "	33	SE	1854-12-01		A1
1064	" "	34	S½NW	1854-12-01		A1
1065	" "	34	SW	1854-12-01		A1
963	BAILEY, John	14	NESE	1855-05-01		A1
964	" "	14	NWSW	1855-05-01		A1
965	" "	2	E½SE	1855-05-01		A1
966	" "	2	S½NE	1855-05-01		A1 F
967	BAILY, John	1	S½	1855-05-01		A1
968	" "	1	S½NE	1855-05-01		A1 F
969	" "	1	S½NW	1855-05-01		A1 F
1061	BERRYHILL, James B	36	SW	1855-12-15		A1 G25
956	" "	33	NWNE	1857-03-10		A1
1060	BERRYHILL, William D	33	SWSW	1853-06-03		A6
1061	" "	36	SW	1855-12-15		A1 G25
1050	BRANDT, Thomas	36	NW	1855-05-01		A1
888	BRAYTON, Benjamin B	32	NENE	1855-02-01		A6 G34
887	" "	33	NWNW	1855-02-01		A6 G35
918	BUCKINGHAM, Hamilton	34	S½NE	1855-02-01		A6
925	BULLEN, Henry L	13	NESE	1854-12-01		A1
926	" "	24		1854-12-01		A1
1049	BURNELL, Strong	13	W½SE	1854-12-01		A1
1059	BURTON, William	36	SE	1855-12-15		A1
1058	CHILDS, Ward	35	NW	1854-12-01		A1
971	COLVIN, John T	25	SW	1854-12-01		A1
972	" "	26	SE	1854-12-01		A1
973	" "	34	NENW	1854-12-01		A1
974	" "	34	NWNE	1854-12-01		A1
975	" "	35	NENE	1854-12-01		A1
976	" "	35	W½NE	1854-12-01		A1
970	CULBERTSON, John C	32	SWNW	1853-07-13		A6
893	DEEMER, Daniel	35	E½SW	1855-05-01		A1
935	DENNEY, Hugh D	22	SE	1854-12-01		A1
962	DIX, John A	13	SESE	1855-01-01		A6
1020	DONNEL, Mary	33	NENE	1855-05-01		A1
1021	" "	33	NENW	1855-05-01		A1
1022	" "	6	N½SE	1855-05-01		A1
1023	" "	6	NESW	1855-05-01		A1 F
938	DOWNEY, Hugh D	17	SE	1854-12-01		A1
941	" "	20	W½SE	1854-12-01		A1
942	" "	21	S½SW	1854-12-01		A1
943	" "	23	SW	1854-12-01		A1
944	" "	28	N½	1854-12-01		A1
952	" "	8	SE	1854-12-01		A1
953	" "	9	S½SE	1854-12-01		A1

ID	Individual in Patent	Sec.	Sec. Part	Date Issued	Other Counties	For More Info . . .
954	DOWNEY, Hugh D (Cont'd)	9	SW	1854-12-01		A1
940	" "	2	NW	1855-02-01		A6 F
948	" "	5	S½SW	1855-02-01		A6
950	" "	6	SESE	1855-02-01		A6
951	" "	6	SWSE	1855-02-01		A6
955	" "	31	SWSW	1855-05-01		A6 G107 F
936	" "	1	N½NE	1855-12-15		A1 F
937	" "	1	N½NW	1855-12-15		A1 F
939	" "	2	N½NE	1855-12-15		A1 F
945	" "	31	NESW	1855-12-15		A1
946	" "	31	NWNW	1855-12-15		A1 F
947	" "	31	SENW	1855-12-15		A1 F
949	" "	6	NE	1856-09-01		A1 F
888	DRURY, Rachael	32	NENE	1855-02-01		A6 G34
961	DUNNING, Abigail P	11	S½SE	1855-03-01		A4 G241
904	EDDY, Edward	29	NENE	1854-12-01		A1
905	" "	29	W½NE	1854-12-01		A1
916	EVENS, George W	7	SENW	1854-05-01		A1 F
906	FEARING, Franklin	2	W½SE	1854-12-01		A1
917	FOLSOM, Gilman	15	NW	1854-12-01		A1
909	FREDERIC, George	36	NE	1855-05-10		A1
1034	GILMORE, Quincy A	27	SW	1854-12-01		A1
1036	" "	11	SESW	1855-02-01		A6 G148
1031	" "	11	SWSW	1855-02-01		A6
1035	" "	28	E½SE	1855-02-01		A6
1032	" "	14	NESW	1855-03-01		A4
1033	" "	14	NWSE	1855-03-01		A4
1042	GOLDEN, Robert	30	NWSW	1854-05-01		A1
1043	" "	30	SWSW	1854-05-01		A1 F
982	GRINNELL, Josiah B	10	NW	1854-12-01		A1
983	" "	10	S½	1854-12-01		A1
984	" "	15	S½	1854-12-01		A1
985	" "	18	NE	1854-12-01		A1
986	" "	19	N½NE	1854-12-01		A1
987	" "	19	N½NW	1854-12-01		A1 F
988	" "	19	S½NE	1854-12-01		A1
989	" "	19	S½NW	1854-12-01		A1 F
991	" "	20	N½NE	1854-12-01		A1
992	" "	20	N½NW	1854-12-01		A1
993	" "	20	S½NE	1854-12-01		A1
994	" "	20	S½NW	1854-12-01		A1
996	" "	21	NE	1854-12-01		A1
997	" "	28	NWSW	1854-12-01		A6
998	" "	3	N½	1854-12-01		A1 F
999	" "	4		1854-12-01		A1 F
1000	" "	5	N½SE	1854-12-01		A1
1001	" "	5	NE	1854-12-01		A1 F
1002	" "	5	S½SE	1854-12-01		A1
1005	" "	7	E½	1854-12-01		A1
1006	" "	7	SW	1854-12-01		A1 F
1007	" "	7	W½NW	1854-12-01		A1 F
1008	" "	8	N½	1854-12-01		A1
1009	" "	8	SW	1854-12-01		A1
1010	" "	9	N½	1854-12-01		A1
1011	" "	9	N½SE	1854-12-01		A1
995	" "	20	SW	1855-01-01		A6
1003	" "	6	E½NW	1855-05-01		A1 F
1004	" "	6	S½SW	1855-12-15		A1 F
1012	" "	17	NW	1866-08-21		A5 G155
990	" "	19	SWSW	1914-11-27		A6 F
1013	GUNNELL, Josiah B	31	SENE	1854-12-01		A6 G156
921	HALL, Harriet S	21	SE	1854-12-01		A1
922	" "	22	SW	1854-12-01		A1
932	HAMLIN, Homer	10	NE	1854-12-01		A1
933	" "	31	NWSE	1854-12-01		A1
934	HAMLINE, Homer	22	NE	1855-03-01		A4
900	HODSKIN, Ebenezer	31	NWSW	1855-05-01		A1 F
901	" "	31	SWNW	1855-05-01		A1 F
930	HOLLEY, Henry W	33	NESW	1854-12-01		A1
931	" "	33	SENW	1854-12-01		A1
1055	HOLYOKE, Thomas	30	NENW	1855-01-01		A6 G177 F
1051	" "	5	N½SW	1855-12-15		A1
1052	" "	5	NENW	1855-12-15		A1 F

ID	Individual in Patent	Sec.	Sec. Part	Date Issued	Other Counties	For More Info . . .
1053	HOLYOKE, Thomas (Cont'd)	5	NWNW	1855-12-15		A1 F
1054	" "	5	S½NW	1855-12-15		A1 F
1048	IOWA, State Of	16		1937-08-26		A3
959	JENKINS, James S	32	NESE	1854-12-01		A1
960	" "	32	SENW	1854-12-01		A1
1037	KELLOGG, Raymond W	34	NENE	1857-03-10		A1
1038	" "	35	SENE	1857-03-10		A1
1055	KINGSMORE, Catharine	30	NENW	1855-01-01		A6 G177 F
977	LAMBRITE, Joseph	11	N½SW	1854-12-01		A1
978	" "	13	SW	1854-12-01		A1
979	" "	2	SW	1854-12-01		A1
980	" "	23	SE	1854-12-01		A1
981	" "	25	N½	1854-12-01		A1
924	LAPHAM, Henry G	11	NW	1855-02-01		A6
1028	LATIMER, Nathaniel	30	NWNW	1850-04-10		A1 F
1029	" "	31	NESE	1854-03-01		A6
1027	LATIMER, Nathaniel J	31	NENW	1854-05-01		A1
927	LAWRENCE, Henry	6	NWNW	1855-05-10		A1 F
919	MARSH, Hammon	19	S½SE	1854-12-01		A1
920	" "	19	SESW	1854-12-01		A1 F
884	MATTESON, Alanson	32	NENW	1853-09-10		A6
923	MCCRACKEN, Henry F	34	NWNW	1855-02-01		A6 C R1047
1047	MCCRACKEN, Samuel S	34	NWNW	1855-11-23		A6 R923
957	MCKAY, James	6	NWSW	1852-12-10		A6 F
958	" "	6	SWNW	1852-12-10		A6 F
915	METZGER, George S	35	W½SE	1855-05-01		A1
1044	MILLAR, Samuel R	12	NE	1854-12-01		A1
1045	" "	12	S½	1854-12-01		A1
1046	" "	26	W½	1854-12-01		A1
887	MITCHELL, Emily	33	NWNW	1855-02-01		A6 G35
907	MIX, George A	11	NE	1854-12-01		A1
908	" "	12	NW	1854-12-01		A1
902	NEWMAN, Edmund B	31	SESW	1854-12-01		A1 F
903	" "	31	SWSE	1854-12-01		A1
928	NOBLE, Henry T	32	SENE	1855-05-01		A1
929	" "	33	SESW	1855-05-01		A1
910	NORRIS, George H	13	NW	1854-12-01		A1
911	" "	17	E½NE	1854-12-01		A1
912	" "	17	SW	1854-12-01		A6
913	" "	17	W½NE	1854-12-01		A6
914	" "	18	W½	1854-12-01		A1 F
955	PARCEL, Jane	31	SWSW	1855-05-01		A6 G107 F
1030	PEARCE, Peter S	32	SWSE	1854-05-01		A1
1026	PEASE, Myron R	26	NE	1854-12-01		A1
885	PETTIBONE, Albert W	11	N½SE	1854-12-01		A1
1017	PHELPS, Loyal C	19	N½SE	1854-12-01		A1
1018	" "	19	N½SW	1854-12-01		A1 F
1019	PINNEY, Marcellus	3	S½	1854-12-01		A1
892	PROSSER, Daniel D	32	SESE	1852-03-10		A1
1014	REED, Julius A	21	N½SW	1854-12-01		A1
1015	" "	22	NW	1854-12-01		A1
1016	" "	20	E½SE	1855-01-01		A6 G227
1024	RENO, Morgan	32	NESW	1854-07-01		A6
1025	" "	32	NWSE	1854-07-01		A6
961	RIGGS, Jetur R	11	S½SE	1855-03-01		A4 G241
895	RUTLEDGE, David M	31	NENE	1850-03-01		A1
898	" "	32	NWNW	1850-03-01		A1
896	" "	31	SWNE	1854-03-01		A6 C R897
894	" "	29	NESE	1855-05-01		A1
899	" "	32	W½NE	1855-05-01		A1
897	" "	31	SWNE	1857-04-04		A6 R896
1066	RUTLEDGE, William	31	NWNE	1852-02-20		A6
1036	SHAYLER, Lucinda	11	SESW	1855-02-01		A6 G148
1013	SILPATH, Julia Ann	31	SENE	1854-12-01		A6 G156
1056	STEPHENS, Thomas	33	NWSW	1854-08-01		A6
1057	" "	33	SWNW	1854-08-01		A6
891	STODDARD, Charles H	29	SENE	1855-02-01		A6
883	STURGEON, Abtil	35	W½SW	1855-05-01		A1
1039	TIPPIE, Reason	28	NESW	1855-03-01		A6
1040	" "	28	SESW	1855-03-01		A6
1041	" "	28	W½SE	1855-05-01		A1
889	WHEELER, Caleb	25	SE	1854-12-01		A1
890	" "	27	N½	1854-12-01		A1

ID	Individual in Patent	Sec.	Sec. Part	Date Issued	Other Counties	For More Info . . .
1067	WILLINGHAM, William W	18	SE	1854-12-01		A1
1012	WILSON, Mary Ann	17	NW	1866-08-21		A5 G155
886	WOLFE, Andrew J	35	E½SE	1855-05-01		A1

Patent Map

T80-N R16-W
5th PM Meridian

Map Group 5

Township Statistics

Parcels Mapped	:	185
Number of Patents	:	150
Number of Individuals	:	80
Patentees Identified	:	78
Number of Surnames	:	76
Multi-Patentee Parcels	:	10
Oldest Patent Date	:	3/1/1850
Most Recent Patent	:	8/26/1937
Block/Lot Parcels	:	0
Parcels Re-Issued	:	2
Parcels that Overlap	:	0
Cities and Towns	:	4
Cemeteries	:	3

Section 6
LAWRENCE Henry 1855
GRINNELL Josiah B 1855
DOWNEY Hugh D 1856
MCKAY James 1852
MCKAY James 1852
DONNEL Mary 1855
DONNEL Mary 1855
GRINNELL Josiah B 1855
DOWNEY Hugh D 1855
DOWNEY Hugh D 1855

Section 5
HOLYOKE Thomas 1855
HOLYOKE Thomas 1855
GRINNELL Josiah B 1854
HOLYOKE Thomas 1855
HOLYOKE Thomas 1855
GRINNELL Josiah B 1854
DOWNEY Hugh D 1855
GRINNELL Josiah B 1854

Section 4
GRINNELL Josiah B 1854

Section 7
GRINNELL Josiah B 1854
EVENS George W 1854
GRINNELL Josiah B 1854
GRINNELL Josiah B 1854

Section 8
GRINNELL Josiah B 1854
GRINNELL Josiah B 1854
DOWNEY Hugh D 1854

Section 9
GRINNELL Josiah B 1854
DOWNEY Hugh D 1854
DOWNEY Hugh D 1854

Section 18
NORRIS George H 1854
GRINNELL Josiah B 1854
WILLINGHAM William W 1854

Section 17
GRINNELL [155] Josiah B 1866
NORRIS George H 1854
NORRIS George H 1854
NORRIS George H 1854
DOWNEY Hugh D 1854

Section 16
IOWA State Of 1937

Section 19
GRINNELL Josiah B 1854
GRINNELL Josiah B 1854
GRINNELL Josiah B 1854
GRINNELL Josiah B 1854
PHELPS Loyal C 1854
PHELPS Loyal C 1854
GRINNELL Josiah B 1914
MARSH Hammon 1854
MARSH Hammon 1854

Section 20
GRINNELL Josiah B 1854
GRINNELL Josiah B 1854
GRINNELL Josiah B 1854
GRINNELL Josiah B 1854
GRINNELL Josiah B 1855
DOWNEY Hugh D 1854
REED [227] Julius A 1855

Section 21
GRINNELL Josiah B 1854
REED Julius A 1854
DOWNEY Hugh D 1854
HALL Harriet S 1854

Section 30
LATIMER Nathaniel 1850
HOLYOKE [177] Thomas 1855
GOLDEN Robert 1854
GOLDEN Robert 1854

Section 29
EDDY Edward 1854
EDDY Edward 1854
STODDARD Charles H 1855
RUTLEDGE David M 1855

Section 28
DOWNEY Hugh D 1854
GRINNELL Josiah B 1854
TIPPIE Reason 1855
TIPPIE Reason 1855
TIPPIE Reason 1855
GILMORE Quincy A 1855

Section 31
DOWNEY Hugh D 1855
LATIMER Nathaniel J 1854
RUTLEDGE William 1852
RUTLEDGE David M 1850
HODSKIN Ebenezer 1855
DOWNEY Hugh D 1855
RUTLEDGE David M 1854
RUTLEDGE David M 1857
GUNNELL [156] Josiah B 1854
HODSKIN Ebenezer 1855
DOWNEY Hugh D 1855
HAMLIN Homer 1854
LATIMER Nathaniel 1854
DOWNEY [107] Hugh D 1855
NEWMAN Edmund B 1854
NEWMAN Edmund B 1854

Section 32
RUTLEDGE David M 1850
MATTESON Alanson 1853
RUTLEDGE David M 1855
BRAYTON [34] Benjamin B 1855
CULBERTSON John C 1853
JENKINS James S 1854
NOBLE Henry T 1855
RENO Morgan 1854
RENO Morgan 1854
JENKINS James S 1854
PEARCE Peter S 1854
PROSSER Daniel D 1852

Section 33
BRAYTON [35] Benjamin B 1855
DONNEL Mary 1855
BERRYHILL James B 1857
DONNEL Mary 1855
STEPHENS Thomas 1854
HOLLEY Henry W 1854
BACON William H 1854
STEPHENS Thomas 1854
HOLLEY Henry W 1854
BERRYHILL William D 1853
NOBLE Henry T 1855
BACON William H 1854

GRINNELL Josiah B 1854 **3** PINNEY Marcellus 1854	DOWNEY Hugh D 1855 **2** LAMBRITE Joseph 1854	DOWNEY Hugh D 1855	DOWNEY Hugh D 1855	DOWNEY Hugh D 1855

Helpful Hints

1. This Map's INDEX can be found on the preceding pages.

2. Refer to Map "C" to see where this Township lies within Poweshiek County, Iowa.

3. Numbers within square brackets [ ] denote a multi-patentee land parcel (multi-owner). Refer to Appendix "C" for a full list of members in this group.

4. Areas that look to be crowded with Patentees usually indicate multiple sales of the same parcel (Re-issues) or Overlapping parcels. See this Township's Index for an explanation of these and other circumstances that might explain "odd" groupings of Patentees on this map.

Legend

———— Patent Boundary

▬▬▬ Section Boundary

No Patents Found
(or Outside County)

1., 2., 3., ... Lot Numbers
(when beside a name)

[ ] Group Number
(see Appendix "C")

Scale: Section = 1 mile X 1 mile
(generally, with some exceptions)

Road Map

T80-N R16-W
5th PM Meridian

Map Group 5

Cities & Towns
Arbor Lake Mobile Home
  Community
Grinnell
Westfield
Willows Mobile Home Court

Cemeteries
Hazelwood Cemetery
Norwegian Lutheran Cemetery
Westfield Cemetery

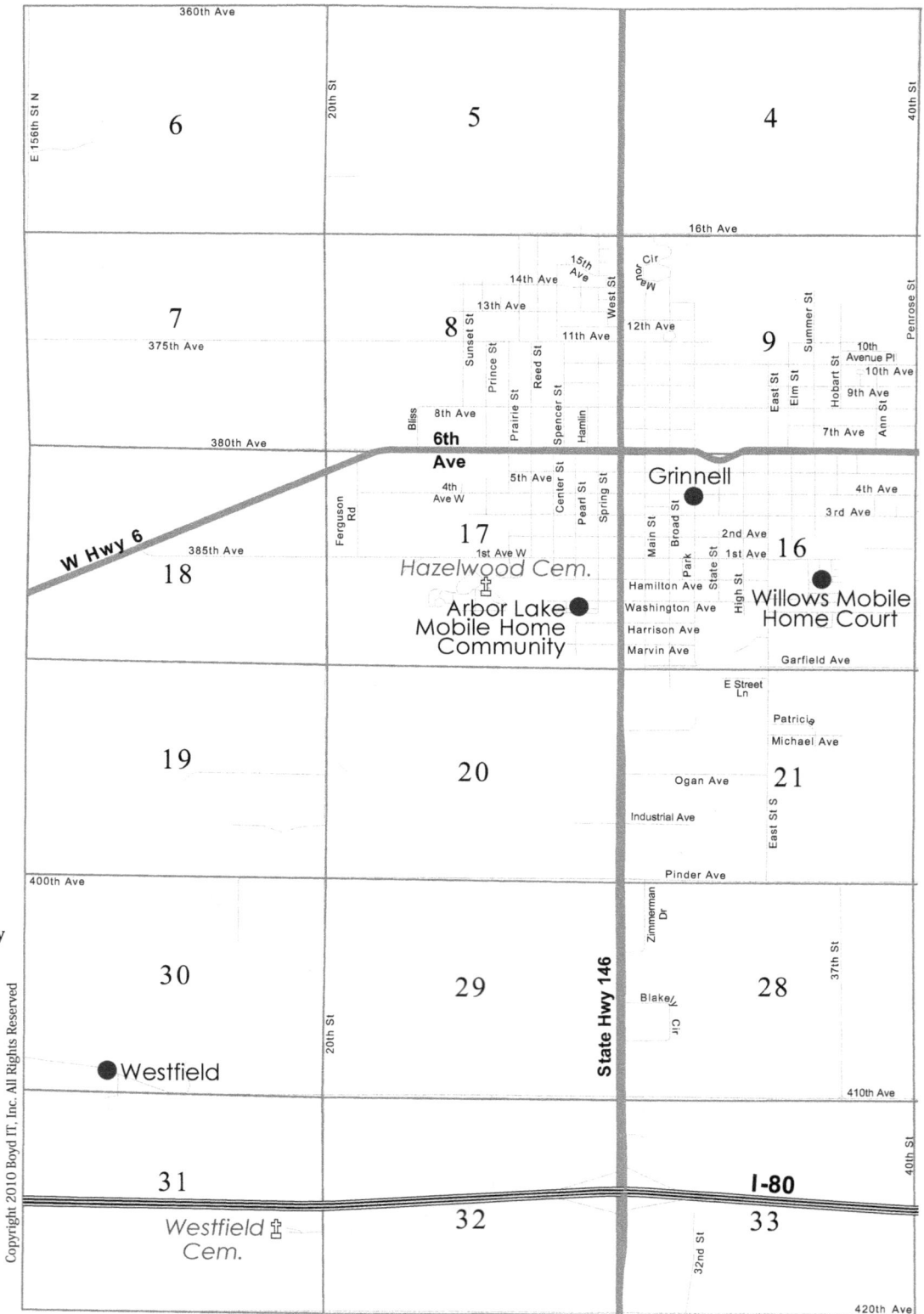

360th Ave

E 156th St N

20th St

40th St

| 6 | 5 | 4 |

16th Ave

7

375th Ave

15th Ave
14th Ave
13th Ave
Manor Cir
West St
11th Ave
12th Ave

8

Sunset St
Prince St
Reed St
Spencer St
Hamlin

9

Summer St
East St
Elm St
Hobart St
10th Avenue Pl
10th Ave
9th Ave
7th Ave
Ann St
Penrose St

380th Ave
Bliss
8th Ave

6th Ave

W Hwy 6

385th Ave

4th Ave W
Ferguson Rd
5th Ave
Center St
Pearl St
Spring St

Grinnell

4th Ave
3rd Ave

17

1st Ave W

Hazelwood Cem.

18

Main St
Broad St
Park
State St
High St
2nd Ave
1st Ave

16

Hamilton Ave
Washington Ave
Harrison Ave
Marvin Ave

Willows Mobile Home Court

Arbor Lake Mobile Home Community

Garfield Ave

E Street Ln

Patricia
Michael Ave

19

20

Ogan Ave

Industrial Ave

East St S

21

Pinder Ave

400th Ave

20th St

30

29

Zimmerman Dr

Blake Cir

28

37th St

State Hwy 146

410th Ave

40th St

Westfield

31

Westfield Cem.

32

I-80

33

32nd St

420th Ave

360th Ave

70th St

3

2

1

45th St

370th Ave

10

11

12

Hwy 6

Oak St

380th Ave

Maple St

15

14

65th St

13

390th Ave

60th St

22

23

24

400th Ave

50th St

27

26

25

35

Norwegian Lutheran Cem.

34

36

Helpful Hints

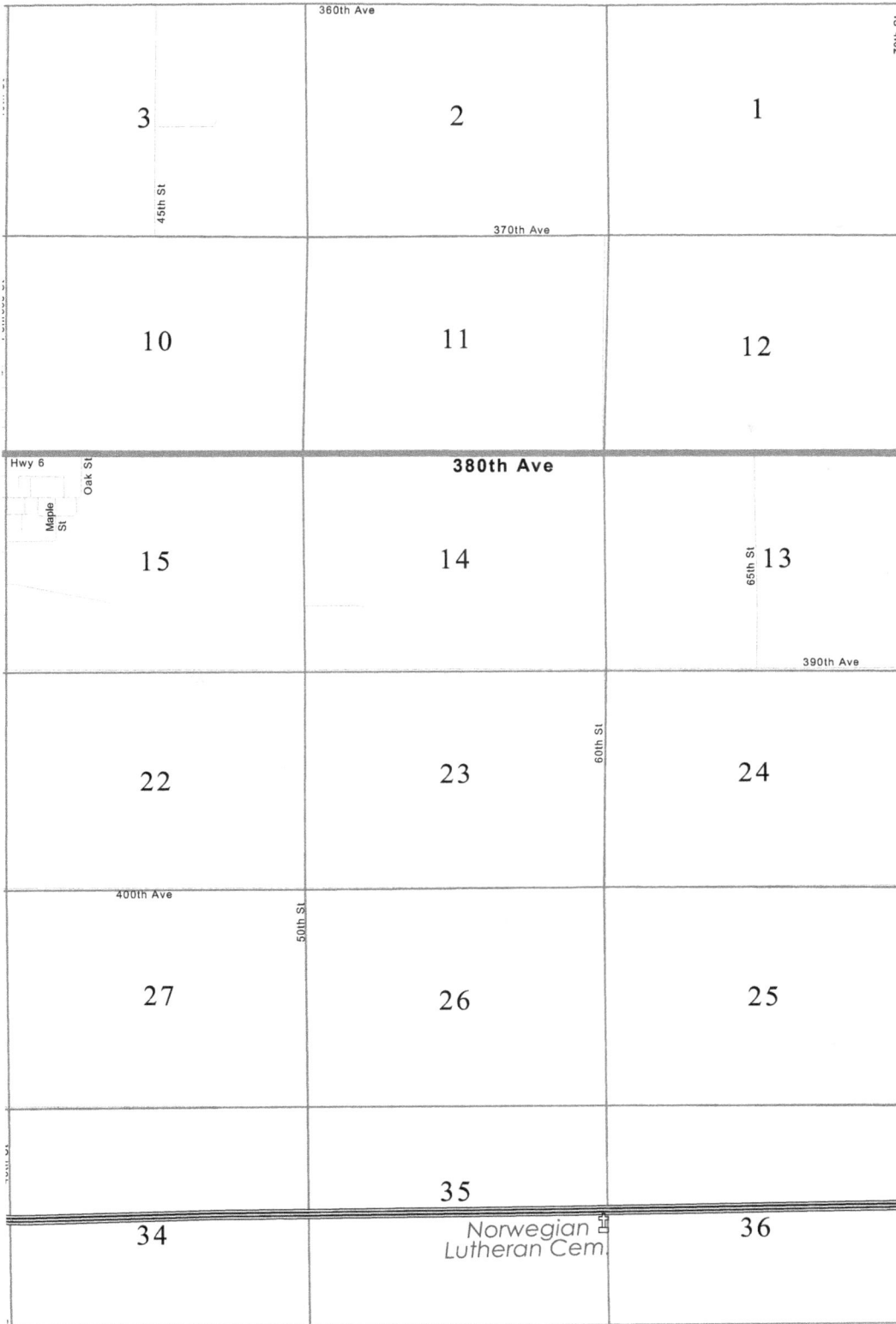

1. This road map has a number of uses, but primarily it is to help you: a) find the present location of land owned by your ancestors (at least the general area), b) find cemeteries and city-centers, and c) estimate the route/roads used by Census-takers & tax-assessors.

2. If you plan to travel to Poweshiek County to locate cemeteries or land parcels, please pick up a modern travel map for the area before you do. Mapping old land parcels on modern maps is not as exact a science as you might think. Just the slightest variations in public land survey coordinates, estimates of parcel boundaries, or road-map deviations can greatly alter a map's representation of how a road either does or doesn't cross a particular parcel of land.

Legend

———————— Section Lines

═══════════ Interstates

━━━━━━━━━ Highways

———————— Other Roads

● Cities/Towns

✝ Cemeteries

Scale: Section = 1 mile X 1 mile
(generally, with some exceptions)

Historical Map

T80-N R16-W
5th PM Meridian

Map Group 5

Cities & Towns
Arbor Lake Mobile Home
 Community
Grinnell
Westfield
Willows Mobile Home Court

Cemeteries
Hazelwood Cemetery
Norwegian Lutheran Cemetery
Westfield Cemetery

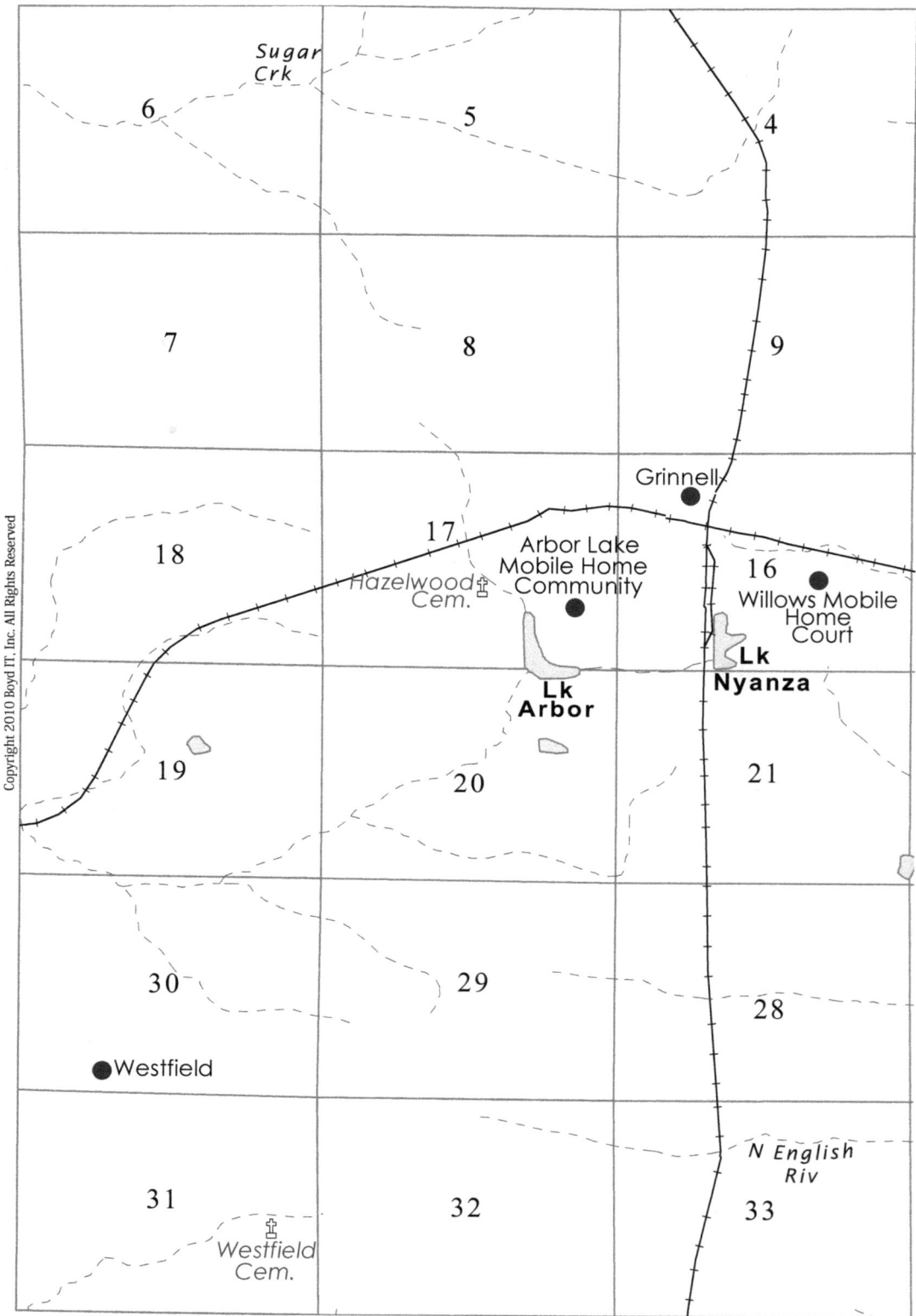

Sugar Crk

6   5   4

7   8   9

Grinnell

17   Arbor Lake Mobile Home Community   16   Willows Mobile Home Court

18   Hazelwood Cem.

Lk Arbor   Lk Nyanza

19   20   21

30   29   28

●Westfield

N English Riv

31   32   33

Westfield Cem.

Copyright 2010 Boyd IT, Inc. All Rights Reserved

104

3　　2　　1

10　　11　　12

15　　14　　13

Little Bear Crk

22　　23　　24

27　　26　　25

34　　35　　36

Norwegian Lutheran Cem.

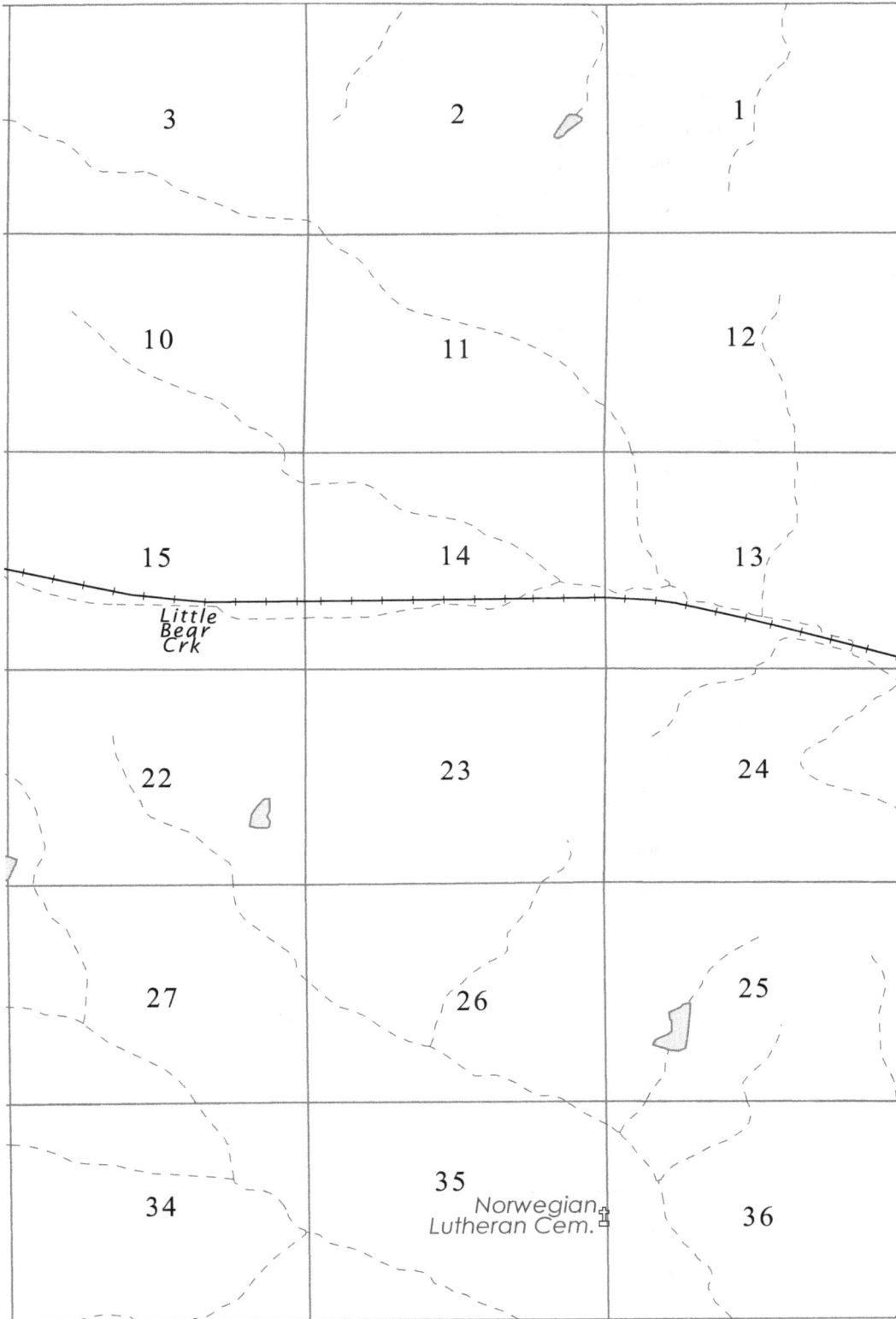

Helpful Hints

1. This Map takes a different look at the same Congressional Township displayed in the preceding two maps. It presents features that can help you better envision the historical development of the area: a) Water-bodies (lakes & ponds), b) Water-courses (rivers, streams, etc.), c) Railroads, d) City/town center-points (where they were oftentimes located when first settled), and e) Cemeteries.

2. Using this "Historical" map in tandem with this Township's Patent Map and Road Map, may lead you to some interesting discoveries. You will often find roads, towns, cemeteries, and waterways are named after nearby landowners: sometimes those names will be the ones you are researching. See how many of these research gems you can find here in Poweshiek County.

Legend

- Section Lines
- Railroads
- Large Rivers & Bodies of Water
- Streams/Creeks & Small Rivers
- Cities/Towns
- Cemeteries

Scale: Section = 1 mile X 1 mile
(there are some exceptions)

105

Map Group 6: Index to Land Patents

Township 80-North Range 15-West (5th PM)

After you locate an individual in this Index, take note of the Section and Section Part then proceed to the Land Patent map on the pages immediately following. You should have no difficulty locating the corresponding parcel of land.

The "For More Info" Column will lead you to more information about the underlying Patents. See the *Legend* at right, and the "How to Use this Book" chapter, for more information.

```
                      LEGEND
            "For More Info . . . " column
A = Authority (Legislative Act, See Appendix "A")
B = Block or Lot (location in Section unknown)
C = Cancelled Patent
F = Fractional Section
G = Group  (Multi-Patentee Patent, see Appendix "C")
V = Overlaps another Parcel
R = Re-Issued (Parcel patented more than once)

(A & G items require you to look in the Appendixes referred
to above. All other Letter-designations followed by a number
require you to locate line-items in this index that possess
the ID number found after the letter).
```

ID	Individual in Patent	Sec.	Sec. Part	Date Issued	Other Counties	For More Info . . .
1297	ALLEN, William T	33	SW	1855-05-01		A1
1176	ANTHONY, John P	13	NESE	1854-12-01		A1
1178	" "	3	S½NE	1854-12-09		A6 F R1121
1179	" "	3	SE	1854-12-09		A6 G4 R1122
1177	" "	27	SW	1855-03-01		A4
1076	ATWOOD, Alpheus	7	NE	1855-12-15		A1
1077	" "	8	NW	1855-12-15		A1
1078	" "	8	W½NE	1855-12-15		A1
1180	BABCOCK, John P	13	W½SW	1855-02-01		A6
1083	BAILEY, Charles E	18	NW	1855-05-01		A1 F
1146	BAILEY, John	4	NESW	1855-05-01		A1
1079	BARBER, Amzi D	7	SE	1855-05-01		A1
1278	BARNES, William B	35	N½NW	1854-12-01		A1
1279	" "	36	N½NW	1854-12-01		A1
1115	BARRETT, Bethiah	29	S½NW	1855-02-01		A6 G247
1096	BARTON, Edwards	12	SESW	1853-11-01		A1
1097	" "	12	SWSE	1853-11-01		A1
1098	" "	24	NENW	1854-05-01		A1
1225	BARTON, Ruth	24	SENW	1855-05-01		A1
1245	BEALL, Thomas M	1	N½SW	1855-05-10		A1
1124	BERRYHILL, James B	24	SENE	1855-05-01		A1
1123	" "	24	NWNW	1855-07-02		A6
1125	" "	24	SWNW	1855-07-02		A6
1161	BONNEY, Lucinda	9	NENE	1855-05-01		A6 G91
1185	BOONE, Joshua J	15	N½	1854-12-01		A1
1186	" "	18	NE	1854-12-01		A1
1187	" "	20	NE	1854-12-01		A1
1188	" "	20	SW	1854-12-01		A1
1189	" "	22	NW	1854-12-01		A1
1190	" "	8	SW	1854-12-01		A1
1191	" "	9	SW	1854-12-01		A1
1280	BURTON, William	5	S½	1855-12-15		A1
1281	" "	5	S½NW	1855-12-15		A1 F
1282	" "	6	E½SE	1855-12-15		A1
1088	CHOUTEAU, Edward A	22	NESE	1854-12-01		A6
1090	" "	22	NWSE	1854-12-01		A6
1091	" "	22	S½SE	1854-12-01		A1
1094	" "	23	NWSW	1854-12-01		A6
1095	" "	23	SWSW	1854-12-01		A6 G49
1087	" "	22	NENE	1855-04-04		A2
1089	" "	22	NWNE	1855-04-04		A2
1092	" "	22	SENE	1855-04-04		A2
1093	" "	22	SWNE	1855-04-04		A2
1196	CLARK, Josiah W	26	NESE	1854-12-01		A6
1197	" "	26	SESE	1854-12-01		A6
1198	" "	34	NESE	1854-12-01		A6

ID	Individual in Patent	Sec.	Sec. Part	Date Issued	Other Counties	For More Info . . .
1199	CLARK, Josiah W (Cont'd)	34	SENE	1854-12-01		A1
1201	" "	34	SESE	1854-12-01		A6 G51
1200	" "	35	S½NW	1854-12-01		A1
1202	" "	35	SW	1854-12-01		A6 G50
1284	CLARK, William	11	SW	1855-01-01		A6
1287	" "	11	W½SE	1855-01-01		A6 G52
1283	" "	11	E½SE	1855-05-01		A1
1285	" "	12	SENE	1855-05-01		A1
1286	" "	13	N½	1855-05-01		A1
1240	CLUTE, Solomon J	25	N½SW	1854-12-01		A6
1239	" "	25	N½NW	1855-01-01		A6
1241	" "	25	S½NW	1855-01-01		A6
1242	" "	25	S½SW	1855-01-01		A6
1213	CORRELL, Paul	3	N½NW	1855-05-10		A1 F
1147	CULBERSTON, John C	22	S½SW	1854-12-01		A1
1148	CULBERTSON, John C	27	N½NW	1854-12-01		A6
1206	DAVISON, Mathew	3	S½NW	1855-05-10		A1 F
1207	" "	4	S½NW	1855-05-10		A1 F
1160	DELAHOYDE, John	10	NENW	1855-03-01		A4 G92
1153	" "	10	NWNW	1855-03-01		A4
1154	" "	10	NWSW	1855-03-01		A4
1155	" "	10	SENW	1855-03-01		A4
1156	" "	10	SWNW	1855-03-01		A4
1157	" "	10	SWSW	1855-05-01		A6
1161	" "	9	NENE	1855-05-01		A6 G91
1158	" "	9	NESE	1855-05-01		A6
1159	" "	9	SENE	1855-05-01		A6
1144	DIX, John A	19	N½SE	1855-03-01		A4 G94
1145	" "	19	S½NE	1855-03-01		A4 G94
1139	" "	19	SESE	1855-03-01		A4
1140	" "	20	S½NW	1855-05-01		A1
1141	" "	21	S½SW	1855-05-01		A1
1143	" "	27	S½NW	1855-05-01		A1
1142	" "	26	SWSE	1857-04-01		A4
1099	DOUGLASS, Elmore	4	S½SW	1852-04-01		A6
1100	" "	9	E½NW	1852-04-01		A6
1118	DOWNEY, Hugh D	31	NE	1855-02-01		A6#
1134	EASLEY, James S	32	NE	1855-01-01		A6 G116
1135	" "	6	W½SE	1855-06-01		A6 G124
1133	" "	6	SWSW	1855-12-15		A1 F
1248	EDWARDS, Thomas M	26	NWSE	1855-01-01		A6
1249	" "	34	NWSE	1855-01-01		A6
1250	" "	34	SWNE	1855-01-01		A6
1251	" "	34	SWSE	1855-01-01		A6
1246	" "	23	SENW	1855-05-01		A6
1247	" "	23	SWNW	1928-07-10		A6
1210	ELLIOTT, Orrin L	4	N½NW	1855-05-10		A1 F
1211	" "	4	NWNE	1855-05-10		A1 F
1212	" "	5	S½NE	1855-05-10		A1
1288	EWING, William	2	S½NW	1855-05-01		A1 F
1289	" "	2	SW	1855-05-01		A1
1216	FLESHER, Lucinda	11	NWNE	1855-05-01		A6 G292
1290	FRAZIER, William	7	W½NW	1855-05-01		A1 F
1137	GIFFORD, Jediah P	23	N½NW	1854-12-01		A1
1138	" "	25	N½NE	1854-12-01		A1
1223	GILCHRIST, Robert W	6	E½SW	1855-05-10		A1 F
1224	" "	7	E½NW	1855-05-10		A1 F
1126	GOWER, James H	12	SWSW	1857-03-10		A1
1127	" "	4	NENE	1857-03-10		A1 F
1128	" "	4	SESE	1857-03-10		A1
1121	GRAHAM, Jacob V B	3	S½NE	1856-01-02		A6 R1178
1122	" "	3	SE	1856-01-02		A6 G154 R1179
1195	GRINNELL, Josiah B	7	NENW	1855-05-01		A1 F
1194	" "	4	NWSW	1855-06-01		A6
1291	GURLEY, William H F	31	NENW	1856-01-15		A6 F
1292	" "	31	SENW	1856-01-15		A6 F
1237	HAND, Seneca L	19	SWSE	1855-02-01		A6 G162
1236	" "	19	SW	1855-05-01		A1 F
1151	HIGGINSON, John C	33	NE	1855-02-01		A6 G168
1149	" "	33	NW	1855-02-01		A6
1150	" "	28	NE	1855-03-01		A6 G167
1080	HOBSON, Benjamin	12	NESW	1850-04-01		A1
1081	" "	12	NWSE	1850-04-01		A1

ID	Individual in Patent	Sec.	Sec. Part	Date Issued	Other Counties	For More Info . . .
1244	HUME, Stephen T	26	SW	1855-05-01		A1
1202	HUNT, Mornan	35	SW	1854-12-01		A6 G50
1243	IOWA, State Of	16		1937-08-26		A3
1134	JACKSON, Elizabeth	32	NE	1855-01-01		A6 G116
1203	JOHNSON, Lemuel	24	NENE	1854-05-01		A1
1165	JOHNSTON, John	21	E½	1854-12-01		A1
1166	" "	21	N½SW	1854-12-01		A1
1167	" "	21	NW	1854-12-01		A1
1168	" "	35	E½	1854-12-01		A1
1169	" "	36	S½NW	1854-12-01		A1
1170	" "	36	SW	1854-12-01		A1
1218	KELLOGG, Raymond M	31	E½SW	1857-02-16		A5 F
1219	" "	31	NWSW	1857-02-16		A5 F
1220	" "	31	SWSW	1857-02-16		A5 F
1221	" "	31	W½NW	1857-02-16		A5 F
1226	KEYS, Samuel	23	NE	1854-05-01		A1
1293	KEYS, William Henry	14	E½SE	1854-05-01		A1
1294	" "	14	W½SE	1854-10-02		A6
1237	KING, Sally	19	SWSE	1855-02-01		A6 G162
1204	LAWLESS, Margaret	8	E½NE	1855-12-15		A1
1205	" "	9	SWNW	1855-12-15		A1
1119	LOOSE, Isaac	5	N½NE	1855-12-15		A1 F
1120	" "	5	N½NW	1855-12-15		A1 F
1179	LYNASON, Jane	3	SE	1854-12-09		A6 G4 R1122
1122	" "	3	SE	1856-01-02		A6 G154 R1179
1252	MCCAGUE, Thomas	34	SW	1855-03-01		A4
1072	MCKINNEY, Alexander F	1	S½SE	1855-12-15		A1
1073	" "	12	E½NW	1855-12-15		A1
1074	" "	12	NENE	1855-12-15		A1
1075	" "	12	W½NE	1855-12-15		A1
1084	MEIGS, Church	14	N½	1855-05-01		A1
1085	" "	34	NW	1855-05-01		A1
1132	MERRETT, James P	12	SESE	1856-01-15		A6
1227	MILLAR, Samuel R	17		1854-12-01		A1
1228	" "	23	E½SW	1854-12-01		A1
1229	" "	23	SE	1854-12-01		A1
1230	" "	26	N½	1854-12-01		A1
1231	" "	27	NE	1854-12-01		A1
1232	" "	27	SE	1854-12-01		A1
1233	" "	33	SE	1854-12-01		A1
1234	" "	34	N½NE	1854-12-01		A1
1117	MONSON, Henry L	32	NW	1855-02-01		A6 G211
1171	MORGAN, John	13	E½SW	1855-12-15		A1
1172	" "	13	W½SE	1855-12-15		A1
1222	MOTHERAL, Robert	15	N½SE	1855-05-01		A1
1255	MOTHERAL, Thomas	10	NENE	1853-11-01		A1
1262	" "	11	SENE	1853-11-01		A1
1268	" "	12	SWNW	1853-11-01		A1
1274	" "	4	SWSE	1853-11-01		A1
1275	" "	9	NWNE	1853-11-01		A1
1276	" "	9	NWNW	1853-11-01		A1
1256	" "	10	NWNE	1854-05-01		A1
1261	" "	11	NWNW	1854-05-01		A1
1263	" "	11	SENW	1854-05-01		A1
1264	" "	11	SWNE	1854-05-01		A1
1266	" "	12	NESE	1854-05-01		A1
1267	" "	12	NWSW	1854-05-01		A1
1271	" "	14	S½SW	1854-05-01		A1
1272	" "	15	S½SE	1854-05-01		A1
1254	" "	10	N½SE	1855-05-01		A1
1257	" "	10	S½NE	1855-05-01		A1
1259	" "	10	SWSE	1855-05-01		A1
1265	" "	11	SWNW	1855-05-01		A1
1270	" "	14	NWSW	1855-05-01		A1
1273	" "	15	SW	1855-05-01		A1
1253	" "	10	E½SW	1855-12-15		A1
1258	" "	10	SESE	1855-12-15		A1
1260	" "	11	NENW	1855-12-15		A1
1269	" "	14	NESW	1855-12-15		A1
1277	" "	9	NWSE	1855-12-15		A1
1129	PARKER, James M	19	S½NW	1854-12-01		A1 F
1130	" "	29	S½	1854-12-01		A1
1131	" "	29	S½NE	1854-12-01		A1

ID	Individual in Patent	Sec.	Sec. Part	Date Issued	Other Counties	For More Info . . .
1150	PARSONS, Nancy	28	NE	1855-03-01		A6 G167
1287	PATTERSON, Rachel	11	W½SE	1855-01-01		A6 G52
1238	PERIN, Simelien	9	SWNE	1855-05-01		A6
1095	PLUM, Catharine	23	SWSW	1854-12-01		A6 G49
1117	POTTER, David W	32	NW	1855-02-01		A6 G211
1117	POTTER, Jesse A	32	NW	1855-02-01		A6 G211
1117	POTTER, Reuben	32	NW	1855-02-01		A6 G211
1181	REYNOLDS, George W	36	E½	1854-05-01		A1 G240
1181	REYNOLDS, John	36	E½	1854-05-01		A1 G240
1070	RHULE, Albert J	3	SW	1855-05-01		A1
1071	" "	4	N½SE	1855-05-01		A1
1086	RHULE, David S	4	S½NE	1855-05-10		A1 F
1102	SANXAY, Frederic	1	SENE	1856-01-15		A6 F
1101	" "	1	N½SE	1857-02-16		A5
1103	" "	1	SWNE	1857-02-16		A5 F
1104	" "	2	NE	1857-02-16		A5 F
1106	" "	2	NWNW	1857-02-16		A5 F
1107	" "	3	N½NE	1857-02-16		A5 F
1105	" "	2	NENW	1857-03-10		A1 F
1108	SARGENT, George B	22	N½SW	1854-12-01		A1
1113	" "	30	SE	1854-12-01		A1
1114	" "	30	W½	1854-12-01		A1 F
1109	" "	28	N½NW	1855-02-01		A6
1111	" "	29	N½NE	1855-02-01		A6
1112	" "	29	N½NW	1855-02-01		A6
1115	" "	29	S½NW	1855-02-01		A6 G247
1110	" "	28	S½NW	1855-03-01		A6
1173	SARGENT, John O	18	S½	1854-12-01		A1 F
1174	" "	19	N½NE	1854-12-01		A1
1175	" "	19	N½NW	1854-12-01		A1 F
1217	SEVERANCE, Ralph A	8	SE	1855-05-01		A1
1295	SHERMAN, William	6	NWSW	1855-12-15		A1 F
1296	" "	6	SWNW	1855-12-15		A1 F
1208	SHOALS, Orin J	24	S½NE	1855-01-01		A6 C
1209	" "	25	S½NE	1914-09-09		A5
1162	SIMPKINS, John F	6	E½NW	1857-03-10		A1 F
1163	" "	6	NE	1857-03-10		A1 F
1164	" "	6	NWNW	1857-03-10		A1 F
1136	SPRINGER, Jarvis W	13	SESE	1854-05-01		A1
1082	TAYLOR, Betsey	30	NE	1854-12-01		A1
1201	TYSON, Ann	34	SESE	1854-12-01		A6 G51
1160	VOUGHT, Jane	10	NENW	1855-03-01		A4 G92
1152	WARD, John C	25	SE	1854-12-01		A1
1182	WARFIELD, John	1	N½NE	1855-05-10		A1 F
1183	" "	1	N½NW	1855-05-10		A1 F
1184	" "	9	S½SE	1855-05-10		A1
1235	WATTS, Samuel	1	S½NW	1857-04-01		A4 F
1135	WHITE, Penelope	6	W½SE	1855-06-01		A6 G124
1151	WHITE, Sarah	33	NE	1855-02-01		A6 G168
1116	WILLIAMS, George C	20	N½NW	1855-05-01		A1
1192	WILLIAMS, Joshua	24	NWNE	1854-05-01		A1
1193	" "	24	SWNE	1854-10-02		A6
1144	WILSON, Matilda J	19	N½SE	1855-03-01		A4 G94
1145	" "	19	S½NE	1855-03-01		A4 G94
1068	WOLFE, Aaron R	1	S½SW	1855-05-01		A6
1069	" "	12	NWNW	1855-05-01		A6
1214	WOLFE, Peter	11	NENE	1855-05-01		A6
1216	" "	11	NWNE	1855-05-01		A6 G292
1215	" "	2	SE	1855-12-15		A1

Patent Map

T80-N R15-W
5th PM Meridian

Map Group 6

Township Statistics

Parcels Mapped	:	230
Number of Patents	:	197
Number of Individuals	:	98
Patentees Identified	:	95
Number of Surnames	:	85
Multi-Patentee Parcels	:	19
Oldest Patent Date	:	4/1/1850
Most Recent Patent	:	8/26/1937
Block/Lot Parcels	:	0
Parcels Re - Issued	:	2
Parcels that Overlap	:	0
Cities and Towns	:	1
Cemeteries	:	2

Section 6
- SIMPKINS John F 1857
- SIMPKINS John F 1857
- SIMPKINS John F 1857
- SHERMAN William 1855
- SHERMAN William 1855
- EASLEY [124] James S 1855
- BURTON William 1855
- EASLEY James S 1855
- GILCHRIST Robert W 1855

Section 5
- LOOSE Isaac 1855
- LOOSE Isaac 1855
- BURTON William 1855
- ELLIOTT Orrin L 1855
- BURTON William 1855

Section 4
- ELLIOTT Orrin L 1855
- ELLIOTT Orrin L 1855
- GOWER James H 1857
- DAVISON Mathew 1855
- RHULE David S 1855
- GRINNELL Josiah B 1855
- BAILEY John 1855
- RHULE Albert J 1855
- DOUGLASS Elmore 1852
- MOTHERAL Thomas 1855
- GOWER James H 1857

Section 7
- FRAZIER William 1855
- GRINNELL Josiah B 1855
- ATWOOD Alpheus 1855
- GILCHRIST Robert W 1855
- BARBER Amzi D 1855

Section 8
- ATWOOD Alpheus 1855
- ATWOOD Alpheus 1855
- LAWLESS Margaret 1855
- BOONE Joshua J 1854
- SEVERANCE Ralph A 1855

Section 9
- MOTHERAL Thomas 1853
- DOUGLASS Elmore 1852
- MOTHERAL Thomas 1853
- DELAHOYDE [91] John 1855
- LAWLESS Margaret 1855
- PERIN Simelien 1855
- DELAHOYDE John 1855
- BOONE Joshua J 1854
- MOTHERAL Thomas 1855
- DELAHOYDE John 1855
- WARFIELD John 1855

Section 18
- BAILEY Charles E 1855
- BOONE Joshua J 1854
- SARGENT John O 1854

Section 17
- MILLAR Samuel R 1854

Section 16
- IOWA State Of 1937

Section 19
- SARGENT John O 1854
- SARGENT John O 1854
- PARKER James M 1854
- DIX [94] John A 1855
- DIX [94] John A 1855
- HAND Seneca L 1855
- HAND [162] Seneca L 1855
- DIX John A 1855

Section 20
- WILLIAMS George C 1855
- DIX John A 1855
- BOONE Joshua J 1854
- BOONE Joshua J 1854

Section 21
- JOHNSTON John 1854
- JOHNSTON John 1854
- JOHNSTON John 1854
- DIX John A 1855

Section 30
- TAYLOR Betsey 1854
- SARGENT George B 1854
- SARGENT George B 1854

Section 29
- SARGENT George B 1855
- SARGENT George B 1855
- SARGENT [247] George B 1855
- PARKER James M 1854
- PARKER James M 1854

Section 28
- SARGENT George B 1855
- SARGENT George B 1855
- HIGGINSON [167] John C 1855

Section 31
- GURLEY William H F 1856
- DOWNEY Hugh D 1855
- KELLOGG Raymond M 1857
- GURLEY William H F 1856
- KELLOGG Raymond M 1857
- KELLOGG Raymond M 1857
- KELLOGG Raymond M 1857

Section 32
- MONSON [211] Henry L 1855
- EASLEY [116] James S 1855
- PARKER James M 1854

Section 33
- HIGGINSON John C 1855
- HIGGINSON [168] John C 1855
- MILLAR Samuel R 1854
- ALLEN William T 1855

Section 3
CORRELL Paul 1855
DAVISON Mathew 1855
ANTHONY John P 1854
GRAHAM Jacob V B 1856
RHULE Albert J 1855
ANTHONY [4] John P 1854
GRAHAM [154] Jacob V B 1856

Section 2
SANXAY Frederic 1857
SANXAY Frederic 1857
SANXAY Frederic 1857
SANXAY Frederic 1857
EWING William 1855
EWING William 1855
WOLFE Peter 1855

Section 1
WARFIELD John 1855
WARFIELD John 1855
WATTS Samuel 1857
SANXAY Frederic 1857
SANXAY Frederic 1856
BEALL Thomas M 1855
SANXAY Frederic 1857
WOLFE Aaron R 1855
MCKINNEY Alexander F 1855

Section 10
DELAHOYDE John 1855
DELAHOYDE [92] John 1855
DELAHOYDE John 1855
DELAHOYDE John 1855
DELAHOYDE John 1855
MOTHERAL Thomas 1855
MOTHERAL Thomas 1854
MOTHERAL Thomas 1853
MOTHERAL Thomas 1855
MOTHERAL Thomas 1855
MOTHERAL Thomas 1855

Section 11
MOTHERAL Thomas 1854
MOTHERAL Thomas 1855
WOLFE [292] Peter 1855
WOLFE Peter 1855
MOTHERAL Thomas 1855
MOTHERAL Thomas 1854
MOTHERAL Thomas 1855
MOTHERAL Thomas 1853
CLARK William 1855
CLARK [52] William 1855
CLARK William 1855

Section 12
WOLFE Aaron R 1855
MCKINNEY Alexander F 1855
MCKINNEY Alexander F 1855
CLARK William 1855
MOTHERAL Thomas 1853
MCKINNEY Alexander F 1855
MOTHERAL Thomas 1854
HOBSON Benjamin 1850
HOBSON Benjamin 1850
MOTHERAL Thomas 1854
GOWER James H 1857
BARTON Edwards 1853
BARTON Edwards 1853
MERRETT James P 1856

Section 15
BOONE Joshua J 1854
MOTHERAL Thomas 1855

Section 14
MEIGS Church 1855
MOTHERAL Robert 1855
MOTHERAL Thomas 1854
MOTHERAL Thomas 1855
MOTHERAL Thomas 1855
MOTHERAL Thomas 1854
KEYS William Henry 1854
KEYS William Henry 1854

Section 13
CLARK William 1855
BABCOCK John P 1855
MORGAN John 1855
MORGAN John 1855
ANTHONY John P 1854
SPRINGER Jarvis W 1854

Section 22
BOONE Joshua J 1854
CHOUTEAU Edward A 1855
CHOUTEAU Edward A 1855
CHOUTEAU Edward A 1855
CHOUTEAU Edward A 1855
SARGENT George B 1854
CHOUTEAU Edward A 1854
CHOUTEAU Edward A 1854
CULBERSTON John C 1854
CHOUTEAU Edward A 1854

Section 23
GIFFORD Jediah P 1854
EDWARDS Thomas M 1928
EDWARDS Thomas M 1855
KEYS Samuel 1854
CHOUTEAU Edward A 1854
CHOUTEAU [49] Edward A 1854
MILLAR Samuel R 1854
MILLAR Samuel R 1854

Section 24
BERRYHILL James B 1855
BARTON Edwards 1854
WILLIAMS Joshua 1854
JOHNSON Lemuel 1854
BERRYHILL James B 1855
BARTON Ruth 1855
WILLIAMS Joshua 1854
BERRYHILL James B 1855
SHOALS Orin J 1855

Section 27
CULBERTSON John C 1854
DIX John A 1855
ANTHONY John P 1855
MILLAR Samuel R 1854
MILLAR Samuel R 1854

Section 26
MILLAR Samuel R 1854
HUME Stephen T 1855
EDWARDS Thomas M 1855
CLARK Josiah W 1854
DIX John A 1857
CLARK Josiah W 1854

Section 25
CLUTE Solomon J 1855
GIFFORD Jediah P 1854
CLUTE Solomon J 1855
SHOALS Orin J 1914
CLUTE Solomon J 1854
WARD John C 1854
CLUTE Solomon J 1854

Section 34
MEIGS Church 1855
MILLAR Samuel R 1854
EDWARDS Thomas M 1855
CLARK Josiah W 1854
EDWARDS Thomas M 1855
CLARK Josiah W 1854
MCCAGUE Thomas 1855
EDWARDS Thomas M 1855
CLARK [51] Josiah W 1854

Section 35
BARNES William B 1854
CLARK Josiah W 1854
CLARK [50] Josiah W 1854
JOHNSTON John 1854

Section 36
BARNES William B 1854
JOHNSTON John 1854
JOHNSTON John 1854
REYNOLDS [240] John 1854

Helpful Hints
1. This Map's INDEX can be found on the preceding pages.
2. Refer to Map "C" to see where this Township lies within Poweshiek County, Iowa.
3. Numbers within square brackets [ ] denote a multi-patentee land parcel (multi-owner). Refer to Appendix "C" for a full list of members in this group.
4. Areas that look to be crowded with Patentees usually indicate multiple sales of the same parcel (Re-issues) or Overlapping parcels. See this Township's Index for an explanation of these and other circumstances that might explain "odd" groupings of Patentees on this map.

Legend
——— Patent Boundary
━━━ Section Boundary
No Patents Found (or Outside County)
1., 2., 3., ... Lot Numbers (when beside a name)
[ ] Group Number (see Appendix "C")

Scale: Section = 1 mile X 1 mile (generally, with some exceptions)

Copyright 2010 Boyd IT, Inc. All Rights Reserved

Road Map

T80-N R15-W
5th PM Meridian

Map Group 6

Cities & Towns
Malcom

Cemeteries
Ivy Hill Cemetery
Trinity Cemetery

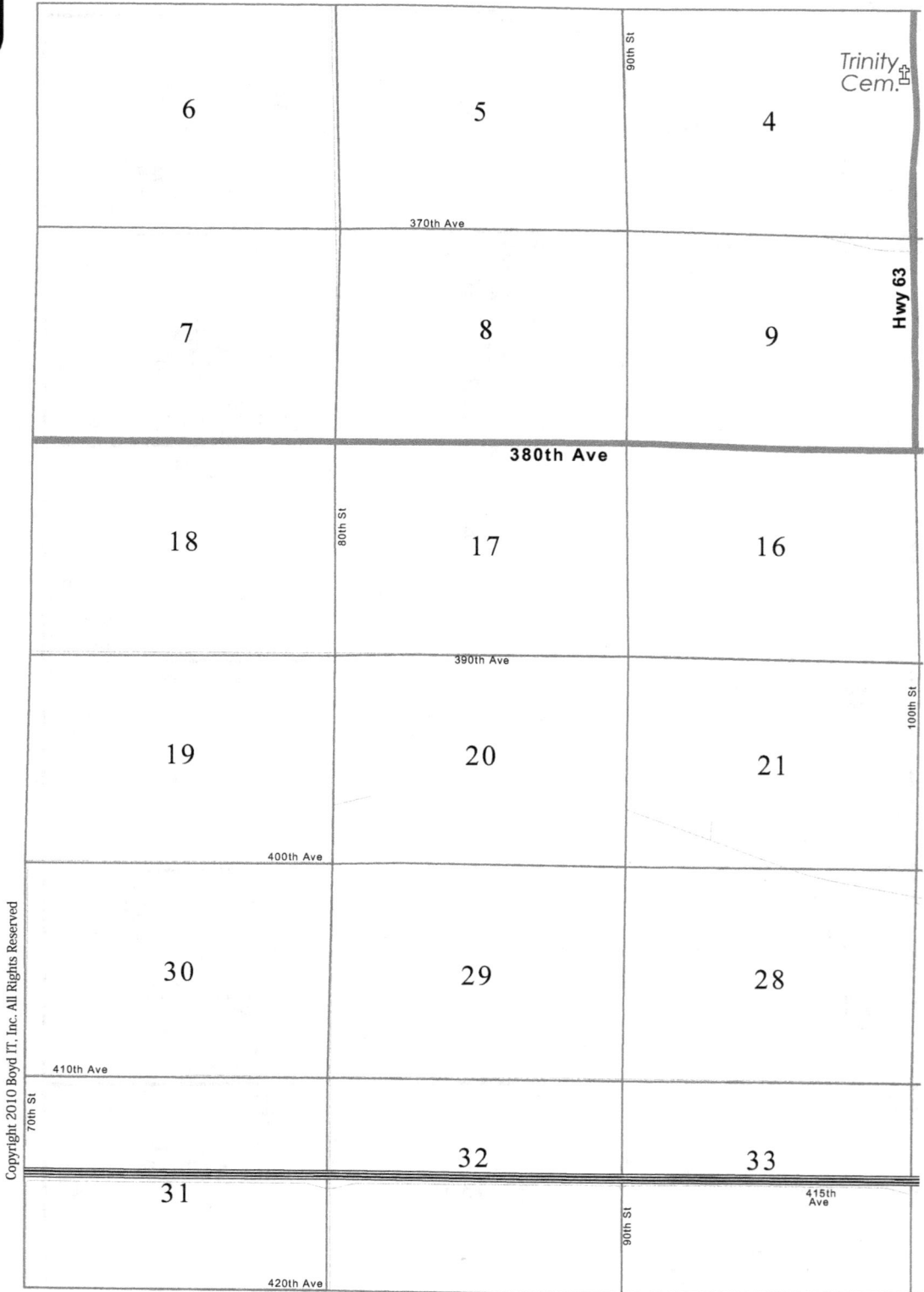

Trinity Cem.

6 5 4

370th Ave

7 8 9

Hwy 63

380th Ave

18 17 16

390th Ave

19 20 21

400th Ave

30 29 28

410th Ave

31 32 33

420th Ave

415th Ave

90th St 80th St 100th St 70th St 90th St

3

2

1

110th St

370th Ave

120th St

10

11

12

380th Ave

15

14

130th St

13

22

23

US Hwy 63

24

Old 6 Rd

Copyright 2010 Boyd IT, Inc. All Rights Reserved

Ivy Hill ⚜ Cem.

400th Ave

Diagonal Rd

Washington St

8th St
7th St
6th St
5th St
4th St

26

Lincoln St
Main St

Malcom ●

3rd St
2nd St
1st St

Clay St

25

27

110th St

S Webster St

115th St

410th Ave

34

I- 80

36

35

420th Ave

L e g e n d

═══════	Section Lines
═══════	Interstates
───────	Highways
───────	Other Roads
●	Cities/Towns
✝	Cemeteries

Scale: Section = 1 mile X 1 mile
(generally, with some exceptions)

Historical Map

T80-N R15-W
5th PM Meridian

Map Group 6

Cities & Towns
Malcom

Cemeteries
Ivy Hill Cemetery
Trinity Cemetery

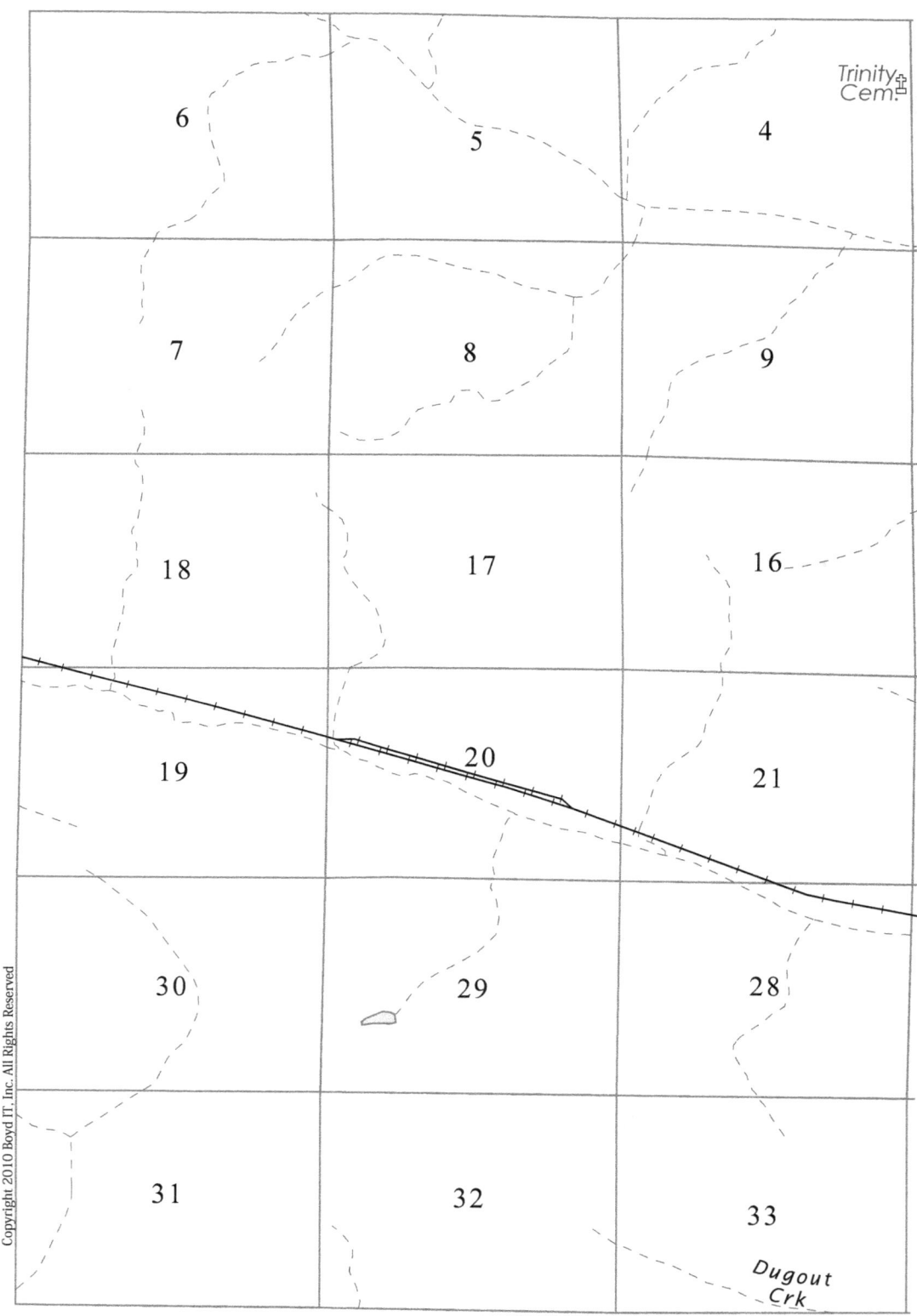

Trinity Cem.

6 5 4

7 8 9

18 17 16

19 20 21

30 29 28

31 32 33

Dugout Crk

114

3

2

1

Big
Bear Crk

10

11

12

15

14

13

22

23

24

✝ Ivy Hill
Cem.

27

26

● Malcom

25

Little
Bear Crk

34

35

◻ 36

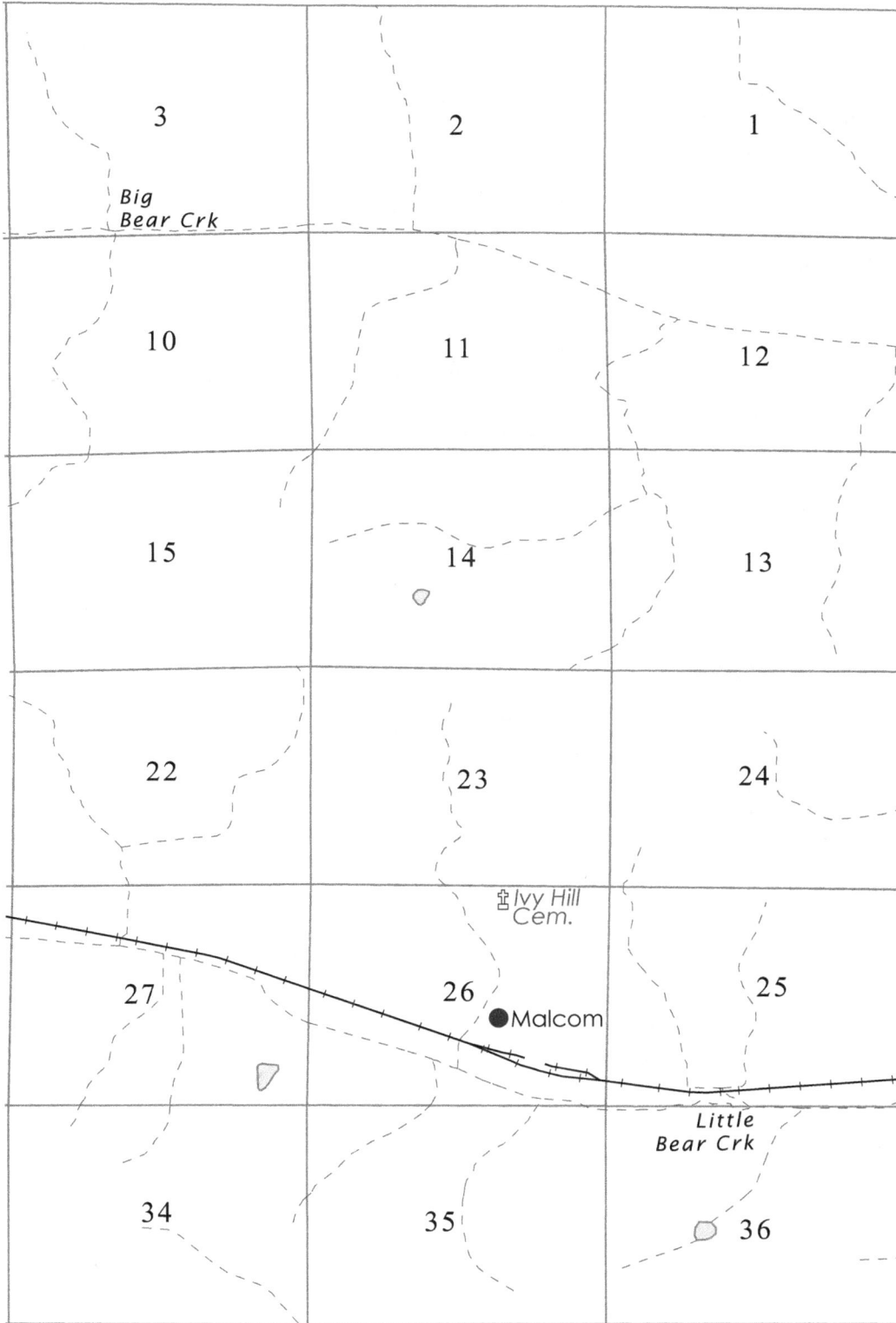

Helpful Hints

1. This Map takes a different look at the same Congressional Township displayed in the preceding two maps. It presents features that can help you better envision the historical development of the area: a) Water-bodies (lakes & ponds), b) Water-courses (rivers, streams, etc.), c) Railroads, d) City/town center-points (where they were oftentimes located when first settled), and e) Cemeteries.

2. Using this "Historical" map in tandem with this Township's Patent Map and Road Map, may lead you to some interesting discoveries. You will often find roads, towns, cemeteries, and waterways are named after nearby landowners: sometimes those names will be the ones you are researching. See how many of these research gems you can find here in Poweshiek County.

L e g e n d

————————	Section Lines
+++++++++	Railroads
▭	Large Rivers & Bodies of Water
- - - - - - - -	Streams/Creeks & Small Rivers
●	Cities/Towns
✝	Cemeteries

Scale: Section = 1 mile X 1 mile
(there are some exceptions)

Map Group 7: Index to Land Patents

Township 80-North Range 14-West (5th PM)

After you locate an individual in this Index, take note of the Section and Section Part then proceed to the Land Patent map on the pages immediately following. You should have no difficulty locating the corresponding parcel of land.

The "For More Info" Column will lead you to more information about the underlying Patents. See the *Legend* at right, and the "How to Use this Book" chapter, for more information.

```
LEGEND
"For More Info . . . " column
A = Authority (Legislative Act, See Appendix "A")
B = Block or Lot (location in Section unknown)
C = Cancelled Patent
F = Fractional Section
G = Group (Multi-Patentee Patent, see Appendix "C")
V = Overlaps another Parcel
R = Re-Issued (Parcel patented more than once)

(A & G items require you to look in the Appendixes referred
to above. All other Letter-designations followed by a number
require you to locate line-items in this index that possess
the ID number found after the letter).
```

ID	Individual in Patent	Sec.	Sec. Part	Date Issued	Other Counties	For More Info . . .
1307	ADAIR, Byers	35	NE	1855-03-01		A6 G1
1307	ADAIR, Samuel C	35	NE	1855-03-01		A6 G1
1362	AMMON, Jacob	7	E½SE	1852-05-01		A6
1363	" "	8	NWSW	1852-05-01		A6
1364	" "	8	SWNW	1852-05-01		A6
1476	ARMSTRONG, Thomas	11	S½SW	1854-05-01		A1
1477	" "	19	N½NE	1854-05-01		A1
1366	BACHTEL, Jacob L	4	N½SW	1856-05-01		A1
1367	" "	4	S½NW	1856-05-01		A1 F
1458	BACON, Samuel	2	SE	1854-12-01		A6
1332	BARTON, Edwards	10	NESE	1852-11-01		A1
1333	" "	7	SENE	1854-05-01		A1
1327	BEAN, Silva	12	NESW	1855-05-01		A6 G55
1406	BENNETT, John L	20	E½	1854-05-01		A1
1433	BENNETT, Joshua B	21	W½	1854-05-01		A1
1486	BENNETT, Uriah P	21	NE	1854-05-01		A1
1487	" "	22	NW	1854-05-01		A1
1488	" "	29	NW	1854-05-01		A1
1489	" "	30	NE	1854-05-01		A1
1368	BERRYHILL, James B	22	SESW	1853-04-15		A6
1369	" "	7	SWNE	1854-10-02		A6
1370	" "	9	NE	1855-05-01		A1
1503	BERRYHILL, William D	6	S½SW	1855-12-15		A1 F
1504	" "	6	SWSE	1855-12-15		A1
1505	" "	7	N½NE	1855-12-15		A1
1371	BORLAND, James	14	NENW	1854-02-01		A6
1372	" "	14	NWNE	1854-02-01		A6
1339	BOYNTON, Flint S	26	E½NW	1854-05-01		A1
1374	BRATTEN, James H	12	NWNW	1855-05-01		A1
1356	BROADBOOKS, Henry	22	NWSE	1854-12-01		A1
1350	BROWN, George	3	NE	1855-05-01		A1 F
1398	BUTLER, John C	27	SW	1855-03-01		A6
1365	BUZZARD, Jacob	18	W½NW	1855-05-10		A1 F
1404	CARLETON, John H	4	S½SW	1857-02-16		A5
1405	" "	5	SESE	1857-02-16		A5
1473	CLUTE, Solomon J	19	SWSW	1855-01-01		A6 F
1474	" "	30	NWNW	1855-01-01		A6 F
1310	COFFIN, Charles B	25	NWNE	1850-03-01		A1
1309	" "	25	E½NE	1854-05-01		A1
1342	COLLINS, Phebe	23	NESW	1854-12-01		A6 G85
1324	CONNELLY, Edward	12	NENE	1855-02-01		A6
1325	" "	12	SENE	1855-02-01		A6
1327	" "	12	NESW	1855-05-01		A6 G55
1326	" "	12	SWNE	1855-05-01		A1
1303	CONNER, Archabel	26	E½	1854-05-01		A1
1483	COX, Thomas J	6	SESE	1857-05-01		A1

ID	Individual in Patent	Sec.	Sec. Part	Date Issued	Other Counties	For More Info . . .
1342	DANIELS, Francis	23	NESW	1854-12-01		A6 G85
1340	" "	23	SESW	1854-12-01		A6
1341	" "	25	NWNW	1854-12-01		A6 G86
1506	DANN, William	11	W½NE	1854-12-01		A1
1318	DEEMER, Daniel	8	N½NW	1855-02-01		A6 G90
1311	DELANO, Charles	30	SWSE	1855-02-01		A6
1396	DIX, John A	30	SESW	1855-03-01		A4 F
1397	" "	30	SWSW	1855-03-01		A4 F
1442	DONNEL, Mary	17	NWSE	1855-05-01		A1
1443	" "	30	SESE	1855-05-01		A1
1444	" "	5	N½	1855-05-01		A1 F
1445	" "	8	NE	1855-05-01		A1
1461	DONNEL, Samuel H	9	NWSW	1855-05-01		A1
1462	" "	9	W½NW	1855-05-01		A1
1358	DOWNEY, Hugh D	15	SWSE	1855-02-01		A6
1359	" "	28	E½SE	1855-05-01		A1
1360	" "	28	W½NE	1855-05-01		A1
1451	DOWNEY, Robert	11	E½NE	1854-12-01		A1
1392	DRAKE, Jesse	17	W½NW	1854-05-01		A1
1393	" "	17	W½SW	1854-05-01		A1
1395	" "	8	SWSW	1854-05-01		A1
1394	" "	18	E½NE	1855-05-10		A1
1399	DRAKE, John C	17	SESW	1854-05-01		A1
1402	" "	8	SE	1854-05-01		A1
1400	" "	18	E½SW	1854-12-01		A1 F
1401	" "	19	N½NW	1854-12-01		A1 F
1511	DWYER, William M	35	SW	1855-05-01		A1
1420	EGBERT, John W	34	SW	1854-05-01		A1
1507	EGBERT, William	33	SE	1854-05-01		A1
1301	FAIRBANK, Betsey	27	W½NW	1854-10-02		A6 G251
1302	" "	28	E½NE	1854-10-02		A6 G251
1509	FANT, William Hamilton	27	NENE	1855-02-01		A6
1480	FARQUHAR, Thomas	12	S½SW	1854-12-01		A1
1308	FOLK, Catharine	18	SE	1853-07-20		A6
1418	FOSTER, John R	32		1854-05-01		A1
1447	GALLEHER, Nudget J	36	SE	1855-05-01		A1
1459	GILLETT, Samuel	25	N½SW	1855-05-01		A1 G147
1460	" "	25	SE	1855-05-01		A1 G147
1465	GILLETT, Samuel N	23	SESE	1854-05-01		A1 G146
1464	" "	23	SWSE	1854-10-02		A6
1459	GILLETT, Simeon	25	N½SW	1855-05-01		A1 G147
1460	" "	25	SE	1855-05-01		A1 G147
1465	GILLETT, Simeon B	23	SESE	1854-05-01		A1 G146
1508	GURLEY, William H F	22	NESW	1855-02-01		A6
1336	GWIN, Elias	7	SWSE	1852-11-01		A1
1373	GWIN, James	7	NWSW	1855-05-01		A1 F
1319	HAM, Daniel	12	NENW	1854-12-01		A1
1320	" "	19	SESW	1854-12-01		A1 F
1321	" "	30	NENW	1854-12-01		A1 F
1355	HAMMOND, George	11	N½SW	1855-05-01		A1 G161
1355	HAMMOND, Hiram	11	N½SW	1855-05-01		A1 G161
1448	HANES, Philip	1	NESE	1854-05-01		A1
1449	" "	1	SESE	1854-05-01		A1
1425	HARPER, Joseph H	5	NESE	1855-05-10		A1
1426	" "	5	SW	1855-05-10		A1
1427	" "	5	W½SE	1855-05-10		A1
1467	HARTMAN, Sanford F	25	S½SW	1855-05-01		A1
1468	" "	34	N½NE	1855-05-01		A1
1469	" "	35	NW	1855-05-01		A1
1493	HASTINGS, Walter	2	N½NW	1854-12-01		A6 G165 F
1491	" "	2	S½NW	1854-12-01		A1 F
1492	" "	2	SW	1854-12-01		A1
1510	HASTINGS, William	11	NW	1854-12-01		A1
1421	HAYES, Jonathan	24	SWSE	1854-05-01		A1
1422	" "	25	NENW	1854-05-01		A1
1423	" "	25	S½NW	1854-05-01		A1
1424	" "	25	SWNE	1854-05-01		A1
1470	HAYS, Sanford	24	S½NW	1854-05-01		A1
1481	HESS, Thomas	12	NWSW	1855-12-15		A1
1482	" "	12	SWNW	1855-12-15		A1
1403	HIGGINSON, John C	9	E½NW	1855-02-01		A6
1463	HILL, Samuel	26	W½NW	1854-10-02		A6 G170
1475	IOWA, State Of	16		1937-08-26		A3

ID	Individual in Patent	Sec.	Sec. Part	Date Issued	Other Counties	For More Info . . .
1306	JENKINS, Benjamin	35	SE	1855-05-01		A1
1439	JOHNSON, Lemuel	8	SENW	1854-05-01		A1
1315	KAUFFMAN, Christian	30	NESW	1854-12-01		A1 F
1316	" "	30	SENW	1854-12-01		A1 F
1429	LAMBRITE, Joseph	8	E½SW	1855-03-01		A6
1428	" "	17	NESW	1855-05-01		A1
1361	MANATT, Irven	7	NWSE	1850-03-01		A1
1379	MANATT, James	10	SESE	1850-03-01		A1
1381	" "	14	NESW	1851-04-01		A1
1383	" "	14	SENW	1851-04-01		A1
1384	" "	14	SWNW	1852-03-10		A1
1380	" "	13	NWNW	1854-12-01		A1
1382	" "	14	NWNW	1854-12-01		A1
1410	MANATT, John	13	E½SW	1850-03-01		A1
1411	" "	24	NENW	1854-05-01		A1
1452	MANATT, Robert	14	SESE	1851-04-01		A1
1453	" "	14	SESW	1851-04-01		A1
1454	" "	24	NWNW	1854-12-01		A1
1455	" "	9	E½SW	1855-05-01		A1
1456	" "	9	W½SE	1855-05-01		A1
1471	MANATT, Scott	14	NESE	1851-04-01		A1
1472	" "	15	SW	1854-12-01		A1
1512	MANATT, William	14	W½SE	1852-03-10		A1
1513	" "	23	N½NE	1854-05-01		A1
1484	MCCAGUE, Thomas	27	S½SE	1855-01-01		A6
1485	" "	29	N½SW	1855-03-01		A4
1385	MCGARY, Elizabeth	7	SWSW	1857-04-10		A6 G258 F
1318	MCROY, Susannah	8	N½NW	1855-02-01		A6 G90
1450	MENDENHALL, Richard C	20	W½	1854-05-01		A1
1457	MENETT, Robert	13	W½SW	1850-03-01		A1
1338	MICHAEL, Ethan	36	N½	1854-05-01		A1
1357	MORGANTHALER, Henry	3	SW	1855-05-01		A1
1466	NAYLOR, Samuel	11	W½SE	1854-12-01		A1
1314	NICHOLAS, Hester	12	NESE	1855-02-01		A6 G260 C R1312
1351	NORRIS, George H	22	W½SW	1854-12-01		A1
1352	" "	28	N½NW	1854-12-01		A1
1353	" "	29	SE	1854-12-01		A1
1354	" "	30	N½SE	1854-12-01		A1
1375	PARKER, James M	19	N½SW	1854-12-01		A1 F
1376	" "	19	S½NE	1854-12-01		A1
1377	" "	19	S½NW	1854-12-01		A1 F
1378	" "	19	SE	1854-12-01		A1
1440	PIERSON, Lewis M	21	SE	1854-05-01		A1
1328	REDHEAD, Edward	30	NWSW	1854-12-01		A1 F
1329	" "	30	SWNW	1854-12-01		A1 F
1446	RENO, Morgan	12	SENW	1857-03-10		A1
1419	REYNOLDS, George W	31		1854-05-01		A1 G240 F
1386	REYNOLDS, James	33	NE	1854-05-01		A1
1387	" "	33	W½	1854-05-01		A1
1419	REYNOLDS, John	31		1854-05-01		A1 G240 F
1317	RICE, Cyrenias	24	SESE	1854-12-01		A1
1463	RILEY, Elcy	26	W½NW	1854-10-02		A6 G170
1388	ROBINSON, James	6	NESW	1855-05-10		A1
1389	" "	6	NWSE	1855-05-10		A1
1390	" "	6	SENW	1855-05-10		A1
1391	" "	6	SWNE	1855-05-10		A1
1334	SACKET, Edwin	34	S½NE	1854-05-01		A1
1335	" "	34	SE	1854-05-01		A1
1343	SANXAY, Frederic	6	E½NE	1857-02-16		A5 F
1346	" "	6	NWNE	1857-02-16		A5 F
1347	" "	6	NWSW	1857-02-16		A5 F
1348	" "	6	W½NW	1857-02-16		A5 F
1349	" "	7	NW	1857-02-16		A5 F
1344	" "	6	NENW	1857-03-10		A1 F
1345	" "	6	NESE	1857-03-10		A1
1415	SARGENT, John O	1	N½	1854-12-01		A1
1416	" "	1	W½SW	1854-12-01		A1
1417	" "	2	NE	1854-12-01		A1 F
1337	SATER, Esrom	24	N½SE	1854-05-01		A6
1341	SCHNEIDER, Catharine	25	NWNW	1854-12-01		A6 G86
1301	SHERWOOD, Albert	27	W½NW	1854-10-02		A6 G251
1302	" "	28	E½NE	1854-10-02		A6 G251
1298	" "	22	SWSE	1854-11-01		A4

ID	Individual in Patent	Sec.	Sec. Part	Date Issued	Other Counties	For More Info . . .
1299	SHERWOOD, Albert (Cont'd)	27	E½NW	1854-11-01		A4
1300	" "	27	NWNE	1854-11-01		A4
1478	SHREVE, Thomas C	10	NW	1855-05-01		A1
1479	" "	3	NW	1855-05-01		A1 F
1515	SIGAFOOS, William	17	E½NE	1854-05-01		A1
1516	" "	17	NESE	1854-05-01		A1
1518	" "	9	SWSW	1854-05-01		A1
1517	" "	17	S½SE	1854-12-01		A1
1435	SMITH, Lander	13	NENW	1855-02-01		A6 G254
1436	" "	13	NWNE	1855-02-01		A6 G254
1437	SMITH, Leander	12	SESE	1855-02-01		A6
1438	" "	12	SWSE	1855-02-01		A6
1441	SNYDER, Lewis S	4	NENE	1857-03-10		A1 F
1494	SPENCER, William A	10	SW	1855-05-01		A1
1495	" "	10	W½SE	1855-05-01		A1
1496	" "	15	NW	1855-05-01		A1
1497	" "	29	S½SW	1855-05-01		A1
1498	" "	4	NENW	1855-05-01		A1 F
1499	" "	4	NWNE	1855-05-01		A1 F
1500	" "	4	S½NE	1855-05-01		A1 F
1501	" "	4	SE	1855-05-01		A1
1502	" "	9	E½SE	1855-05-01		A1
1385	STERRET, James P	7	SWSW	1857-04-10		A6 G258 F
1330	STEVENS, Edward	18	W½SW	1854-05-01		A1 F
1331	" "	7	NESW	1854-05-01		A1 F
1314	STODDARD, Charles H	12	NESE	1855-02-01		A6 G260 C R1312
1313	" "	12	NWSE	1855-02-01		A6
1312	" "	12	NESE	1860-03-15		A2 R1314
1514	STODDARD, William N	4	NWNW	1855-12-15		A1 F
1322	STRUBLE, Daniel	10	NE	1855-05-01		A1
1323	" "	3	SE	1855-05-01		A1
1409	TALBOTT, John M	14	SWNE	1850-03-01		A1
1407	" "	12	NWNE	1854-12-01		A1
1408	" "	14	NENE	1855-05-10		A1
1430	TALBOTT, Joseph	11	E½SE	1854-03-01		A6
1432	" "	24	NE	1854-03-01		A6
1431	" "	13	NENE	1854-05-01		A1
1434	TALBOTT, Joshua C	13	SENE	1850-03-01		A1
1493	TILL, Libby	2	N½NW	1854-12-01		A6 G165 F
1413	WADDELL, John N	18	W½NE	1855-02-01		A6
1412	" "	18	E½NW	1855-06-01		A6 F
1414	" "	7	SESW	1856-01-15		A6 F
1304	WHEELER, Ardon K	27	N½SE	1854-10-02		A6
1305	" "	27	S½NE	1854-10-02		A6
1490	WILDER, Vincen	15	NWSE	1854-05-01		A1
1435	WRENN, Ann	13	NENW	1855-02-01		A6 G254
1436	" "	13	NWNE	1855-02-01		A6 G254

Patent Map

T80-N R14-W
5th PM Meridian

Map Group 7

Township Statistics

Parcels Mapped	:	221
Number of Patents	:	181
Number of Individuals	:	123
Patentees Identified	:	115
Number of Surnames	:	98
Multi-Patentee Parcels	:	18
Oldest Patent Date	:	3/1/1850
Most Recent Patent	:	8/26/1937
Block/Lot Parcels	:	0
Parcels Re-Issued	:	1
Parcels that Overlap	:	0
Cities and Towns	:	2
Cemeteries	:	2

Section 6: SANXAY Frederic 1857; SANXAY Frederic 1857; SANXAY Frederic 1857; SANXAY Frederic 1857; ROBINSON James 1855; ROBINSON James 1855; SANXAY Frederic 1857; ROBINSON James 1855; ROBINSON James 1855; SANXAY Frederic 1857; BERRYHILL William D 1855; BERRYHILL William D 1855; COX Thomas J 1857

Section 5: DONNEL Mary 1855; HARPER Joseph H 1855; HARPER Joseph H 1855; HARPER Joseph H 1855; CARLETON John H 1857

Section 4: STODDARD William N 1855; SPENCER William A 1855; SPENCER William A 1855; SNYDER Lewis S 1857; BACHTEL Jacob L 1856; SPENCER William A 1855; BACHTEL Jacob L 1856; SPENCER William A 1855; CARLETON John H 1857

Section 7: SANXAY Frederic 1857; BERRYHILL William D 1855; BERRYHILL James B 1854; BARTON Edwards 1854; GWIN James 1855; STEVENS Edward 1854; MANATT Irven 1850; STERRET [258] James P 1857; WADDELL John N 1856; GWIN Elias 1852; AMMON Jacob 1852

Section 8: DEEMER [90] Daniel 1855; AMMON Jacob 1852; JOHNSON Lemuel 1854; DONNEL Mary 1855; AMMON Jacob 1852; DRAKE Jesse 1854; DRAKE John C 1854; LAMBRITE Joseph 1855

Section 9: DONNEL Samuel H 1855; HIGGINSON John C 1855; BERRYHILL James B 1855; DONNEL Samuel H 1855; MANATT Robert 1855; MANATT Robert 1855; SIGAFOOS William 1854; SPENCER William A 1855

Section 18: BUZZARD Jacob 1855; WADDELL John N 1855; WADDELL John N 1855; DRAKE Jesse 1855; STEVENS Edward 1854; DRAKE John C 1854; FOLK Catharine 1853

Section 17: DRAKE Jesse 1854; SIGAFOOS William 1854; LAMBRITE Joseph 1855; DONNEL Mary 1855; SIGAFOOS William 1854; DRAKE Jesse 1854; DRAKE John C 1854; SIGAFOOS William 1854

Section 16: IOWA State Of 1937

Section 19: DRAKE John C 1854; ARMSTRONG Thomas 1854; PARKER James M 1854; PARKER James M 1854; PARKER James M 1854; PARKER James M 1854; CLUTE Solomon J 1855; HAM Daniel 1854

Section 20: MENDENHALL Richard C 1854; BENNETT John L 1854

Section 21: BENNETT Joshua B 1854; BENNETT Uriah P 1854; PIERSON Lewis M 1854

Section 30: CLUTE Solomon J 1855; HAM Daniel 1854; REDHEAD Edward 1854; KAUFFMAN Christian 1854; BENNETT Uriah P 1854; REDHEAD Edward 1854; KAUFFMAN Christian 1854; NORRIS George H 1854; DIX John A 1855; DIX John A 1855; DELANO Charles 1855; DONNEL Mary 1855

Section 29: BENNETT Uriah P 1854; MCCAGUE Thomas 1855; NORRIS George H 1854; SPENCER William A 1855

Section 28: NORRIS George H 1854; SHERWOOD [251] Albert 1854; DOWNEY Hugh D 1855; DOWNEY Hugh D 1855

Section 31: REYNOLDS [240] John 1854

Section 32: FOSTER John R 1854

Section 33: REYNOLDS James 1854; REYNOLDS James 1854; EGBERT William 1854

Helpful Hints

1. This Map's INDEX can be found on the preceding pages.

2. Refer to Map "C" to see where this Township lies within Poweshiek County, Iowa.

3. Numbers within square brackets [ ] denote a multi-patentee land parcel (multi-owner). Refer to Appendix "C" for a full list of members in this group.

4. Areas that look to be crowded with Patentees usually indicate multiple sales of the same parcel (Re-issues) or Overlapping parcels. See this Township's Index for an explanation of these and other circumstances that might explain "odd" groupings of Patentees on this map.

Section 3
SHREVE Thomas C 1855
BROWN George 1855
MORGANTHALER Henry 1855
STRUBLE Daniel 1855

Section 2
HASTINGS [165] Walter 1854
HASTINGS Walter 1854
HASTINGS Walter 1854
BACON Samuel 1854

Section 1
SARGENT John O 1854
SARGENT John O 1854
SARGENT John O 1854
HANES Philip 1854
HANES Philip 1854

Section 10
SHREVE Thomas C 1855
STRUBLE Daniel 1855
SPENCER William A 1855
SPENCER William A 1855
BARTON Edwards 1852
MANATT James 1850

Section 11
HASTINGS William 1854
DANN William 1854
DOWNEY Robert 1854
HAMMOND [161] George 1855
ARMSTRONG Thomas 1854
NAYLOR Samuel 1854
TALBOTT Joseph 1854

Section 12
BRATTEN James H 1855
HAM Daniel 1854
TALBOTT John M 1854
CONNELLY Edward 1855
HESS Thomas 1855
RENO Morgan 1857
CONNELLY Edward 1855
CONNELLY Edward 1855
HESS Thomas 1855
CONNELLY [55] Edward 1855
STODDARD Charles H 1855
STODDARD Charles H 1860
STODDARD [260] Charles H 1855
FARQUHAR Thomas 1854
SMITH Leander 1855
SMITH Leander 1855

Section 15
SPENCER William A 1855
WILDER Vincen 1854
DOWNEY Hugh D 1855
MANATT Scott 1854

Section 14
MANATT James 1854
BORLAND James 1854
BORLAND James 1854
TALBOTT John M 1855
MANATT James 1852
MANATT James 1851
TALBOTT John M 1850
MANATT James 1851
MANATT Scott 1851
MANATT Robert 1851
MANATT William 1852
MANATT Robert 1851

Section 13
MANATT James 1854
SMITH [254] Lander 1855
SMITH [254] Lander 1855
TALBOTT Joseph 1854
TALBOTT Joshua C 1850
MENETT Robert 1850
MANATT John 1850

Section 22
BENNETT Uriah P 1854
NORRIS George H 1854
GURLEY William H F 1855
BROADBOOKS Henry 1854
BERRYHILL James B 1853
SHERWOOD Albert 1854

Section 23
MANATT William 1854
DANIELS [85] Francis 1854
DANIELS Francis 1854
GILLETT Samuel N 1854
GILLETT [146] Samuel N 1854

Section 24
MANATT Robert 1854
MANATT John 1854
TALBOTT Joseph 1854
HAYS Sanford 1854
SATER Esrom 1854
HAYES Jonathan 1854
RICE Cyrenias 1854

Section 27
SHERWOOD [251] Albert 1854
SHERWOOD Albert 1854
SHERWOOD Albert 1854
FANT William Hamilton 1855
WHEELER Ardon K 1854
WHEELER Ardon K 1854
MCCAGUE Thomas 1855
BUTLER John C 1855

Section 26
HILL [170] Samuel 1854
BOYNTON Flint S 1854
CONNER Archabel 1854

Section 25
DANIELS [86] Francis 1854
HAYES Jonathan 1854
COFFIN Charles B 1850
COFFIN Charles B 1854
HAYES Jonathan 1854
HAYES Jonathan 1854
GILLETT [147] Samuel 1855
GILLETT [147] Samuel 1855
HARTMAN Sanford F 1855

Section 34
HARTMAN Sanford F 1855
SACKET Edwin 1854
EGBERT John W 1854
SACKET Edwin 1854

Section 35
HARTMAN Sanford F 1855
ADAIR [1] Byers 1855
DWYER William M 1855
JENKINS Benjamin 1855

Section 36
MICHAEL Ethan 1854
GALLEHER Nudget J 1855

Legend

Patent Boundary

Section Boundary

No Patents Found (or Outside County)

1., 2., 3., ...   Lot Numbers (when beside a name)

[ ]   Group Number (see Appendix "C")

Scale: Section = 1 mile X 1 mile (generally, with some exceptions)

Road Map

T80-N R14-W
5th PM Meridian

Map Group 7

Cities & Towns
Brooklyn
Lone Pine Mobile Home Court

Cemeteries
Calvary Cemetery
International Order of Odd
Fellows Cemetery

360th Ave

140th St

160th St

| 6 | 5 | 4 |

| 7 | 8 | 9 |

380 Ave

| 18 | 17 | 16 |

150th St

Old 6 Rd

142nd St

| 19 | 20 | 21 |

400th Ave

140th St

| 30 | 29 | 28 |

160th St

410th Ave

145th St

| 31 | 32 | 33 |

420th Ave

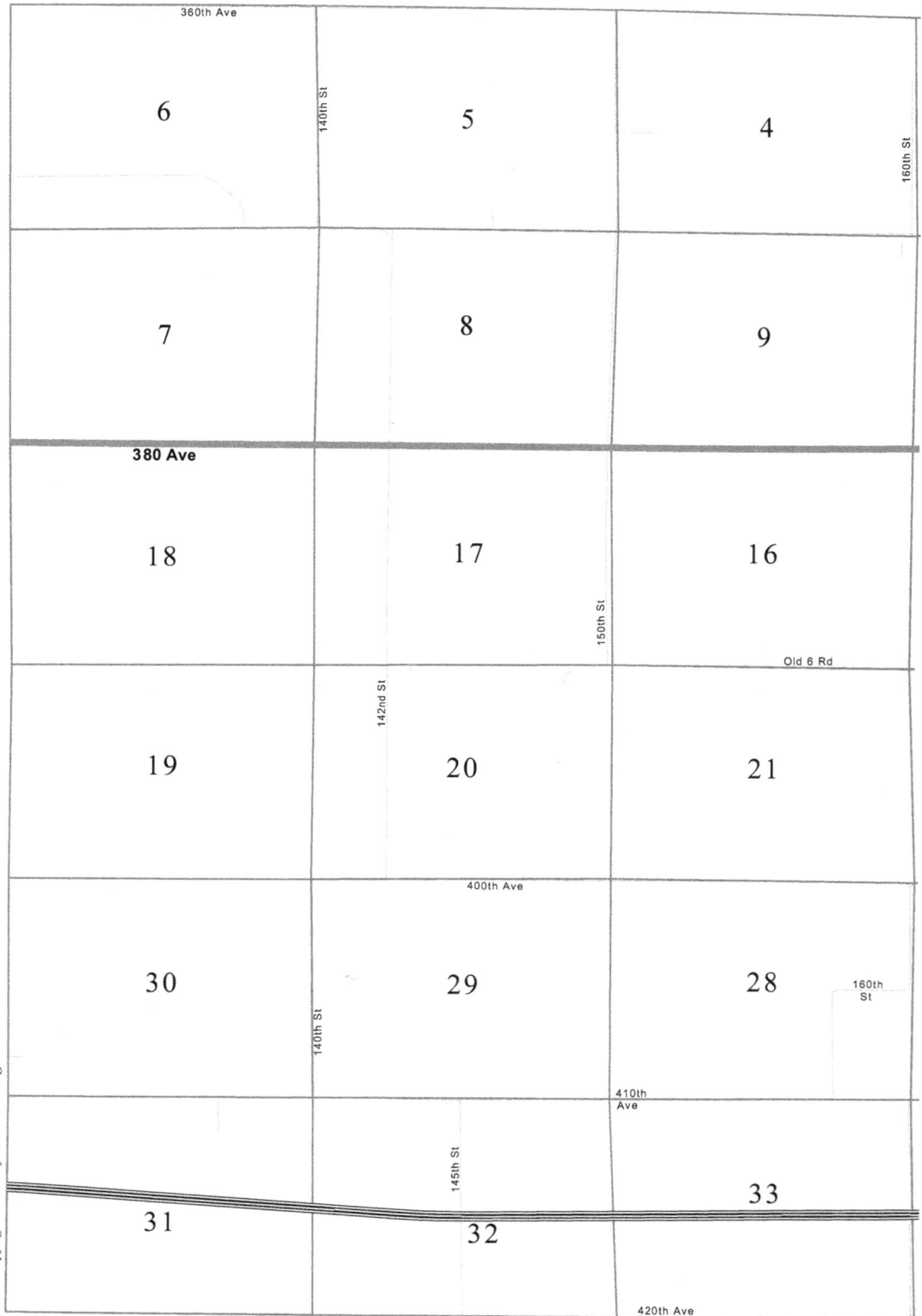

190th St

| 3 | 2 | 1 |

165th St

370th Ave

| 10 | 11 | 12 |

US Hwy 6

380th Ave

| 15 | 14 | 13 |

175th St

185th St

385th Ave

North St

Spring St

Center St

East Ct

Park Ave Co V18

E Des Moines St

E Pershing St

E Main Dr

Boundary St

Brooklyn ●

Pleasant St

Williams St

W Green St

E Green St

✝ *International Order of Odd Fellows Cem.*

✝ Calvary Cem.

E 3rd St

Broadway St

Clay St

High St

Front St

Orchard St

Mills St

| 22 | 23 | 24 |

N Brady St

Ramsey St

Clinton St

Lincoln St

Lone Pine Mobile Home Court ●

Jefferson St

170th St

Old 6 Rd

400th Ave

| 27 | 26 | 25 |

V18 Rd

190th St

| 34 | 35 | **I- 80** |
| | | 36 |

415th Ave

420th Ave

Helpful Hints

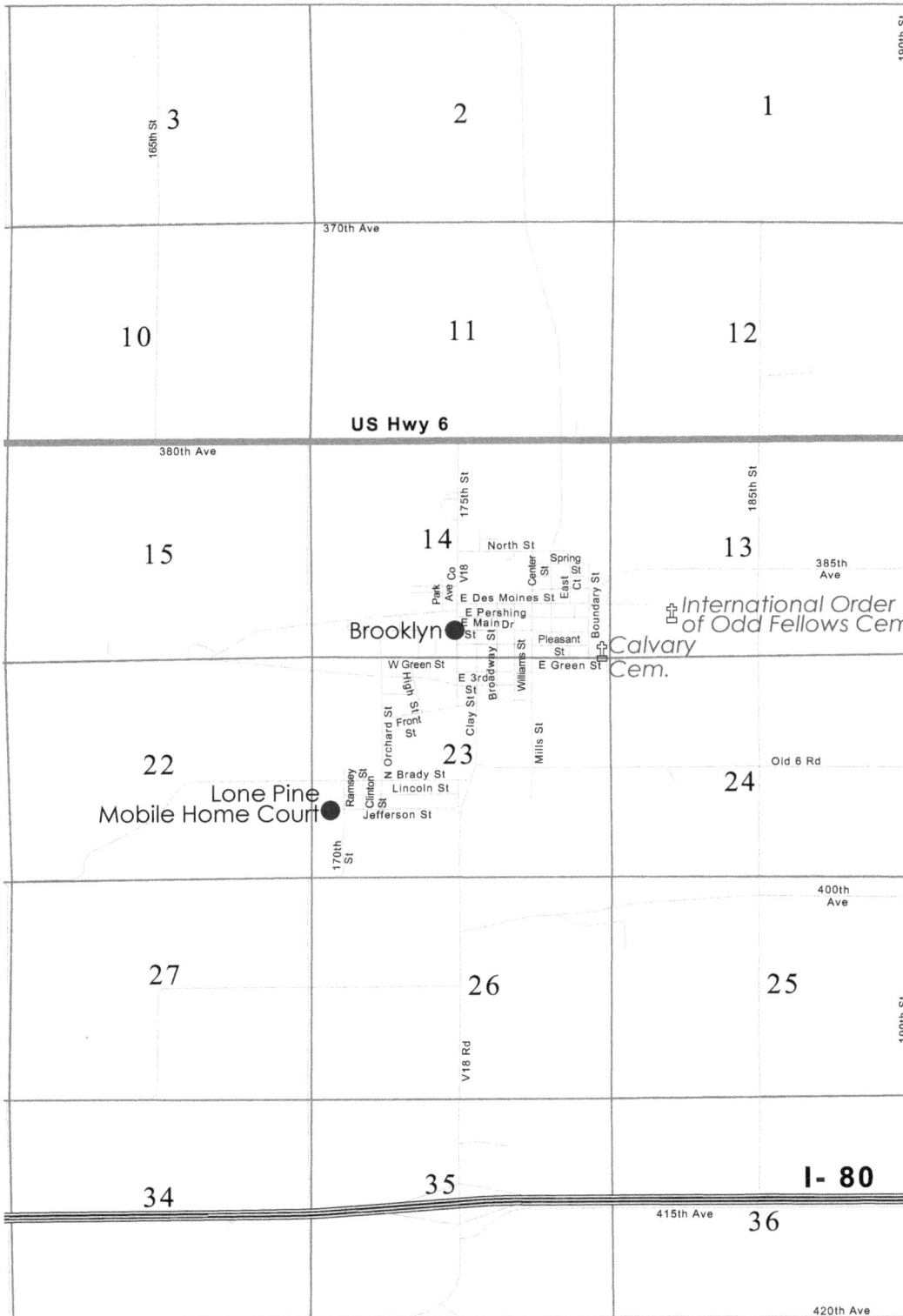

1. This road map has a number of uses, but primarily it is to help you: a) find the present location of land owned by your ancestors (at least the general area), b) find cemeteries and city-centers, and c) estimate the route/roads used by Census-takers & tax-assessors.

2. If you plan to travel to Poweshiek County to locate cemeteries or land parcels, please pick up a modern travel map for the area before you do. Mapping old land parcels on modern maps is not as exact a science as you might think. Just the slightest variations in public land survey coordinates, estimates of parcel boundaries, or road-map deviations can greatly alter a map's representation of how a road either does or doesn't cross a particular parcel of land.

Legend

————	Section Lines
═══════	Interstates
▬▬▬▬▬	Highways
————	Other Roads
●	Cities/Towns
✝	Cemeteries

Scale: Section = 1 mile X 1 mile
(generally, with some exceptions)

123

Historical Map

T80-N R14-W
5th PM Meridian

Map Group 7

Cities & Towns
Brooklyn
Lone Pine Mobile Home Court

Cemeteries
Calvary Cemetery
International Order of Odd
Fellows Cemetery

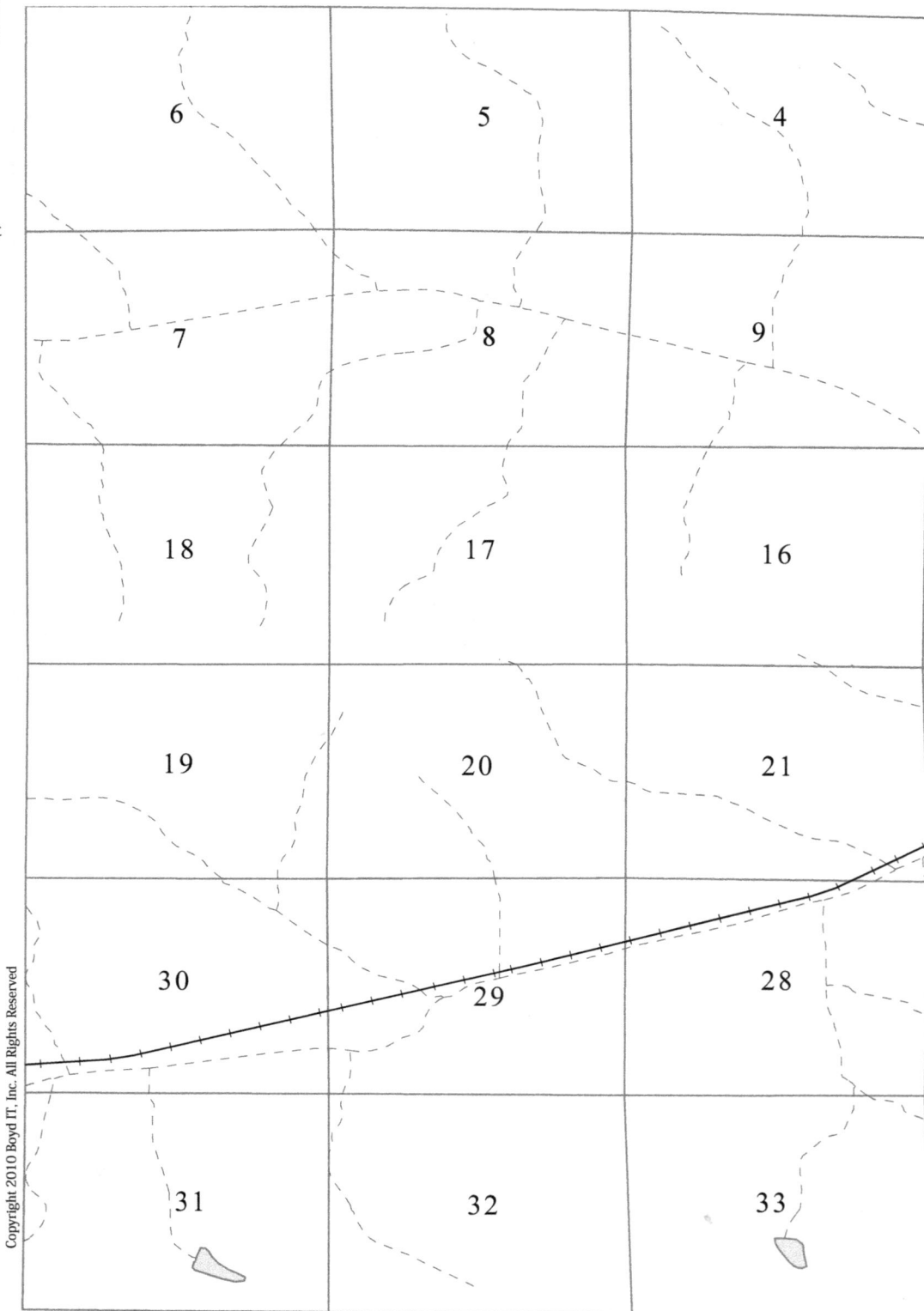

6	5	4
7	8	9
18	17	16
19	20	21
30	29	28
31	32	33

Stony Crk 3	2	1
10	11	12
Big Bear Crk 15	14	13
22	23	24
27	26	25
34	35	36

Brooklyn

International Order of Odd Fellows Cem.

Calvary Cem.

Little Bear Crk

Lone Pine Mobile Home Court

Cub Crk

Helpful Hints

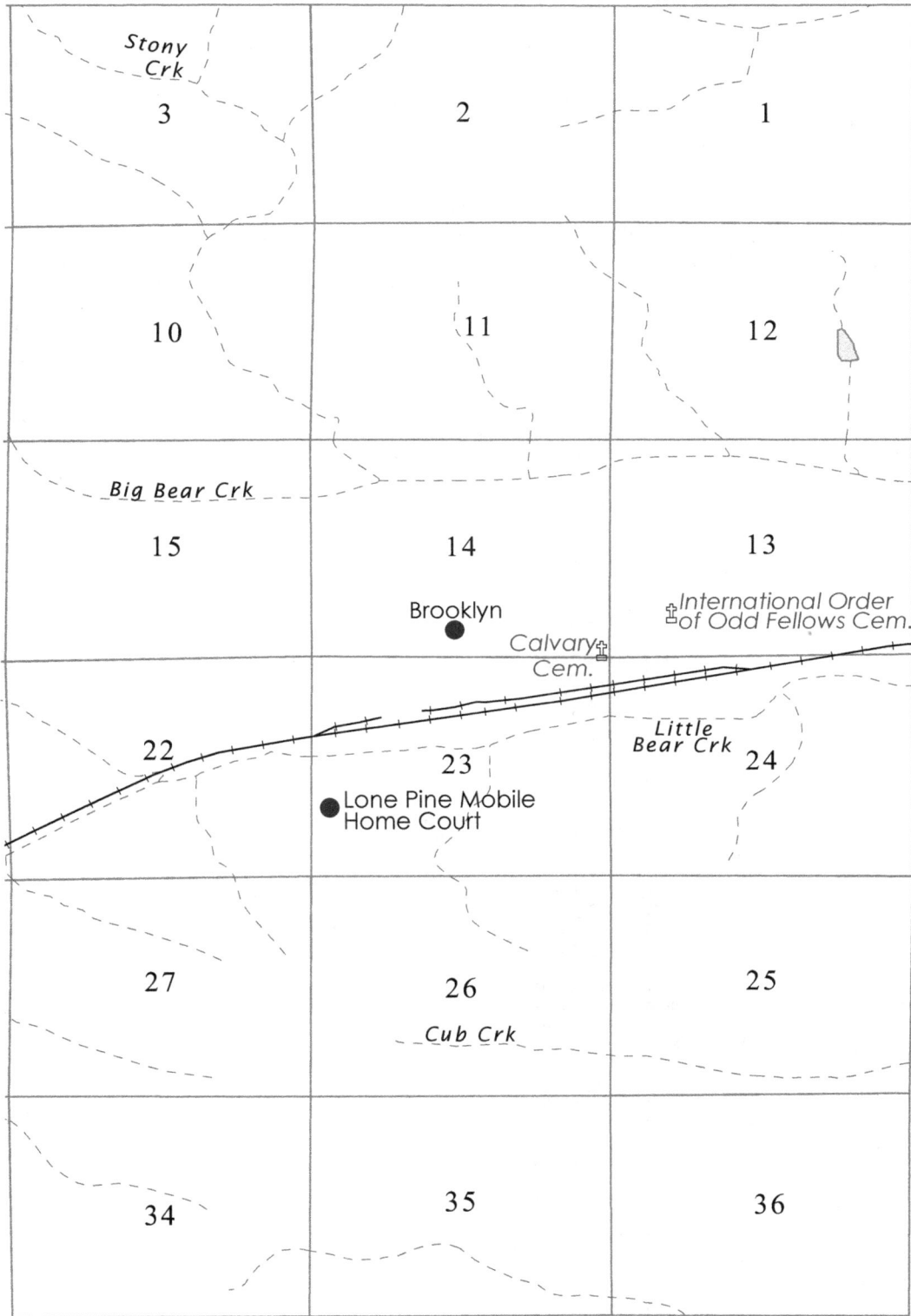

1. This Map takes a different look at the same Congressional Township displayed in the preceding two maps. It presents features that can help you better envision the historical development of the area: a) Water-bodies (lakes & ponds), b) Water-courses (rivers, streams, etc.), c) Railroads, d) City/town center-points (where they were oftentimes located when first settled), and e) Cemeteries.

2. Using this "Historical" map in tandem with this Township's Patent Map and Road Map, may lead you to some interesting discoveries. You will often find roads, towns, cemeteries, and waterways are named after nearby landowners: sometimes those names will be the ones you are researching. See how many of these research gems you can find here in Poweshiek County.

Legend

— Section Lines
+++ Railroads
Large Rivers & Bodies of Water
- - - Streams/Creeks & Small Rivers
● Cities/Towns
✝ Cemeteries

Scale: Section = 1 mile X 1 mile
(there are some exceptions)

Map Group 8: Index to Land Patents

Township 80-North Range 13-West (5th PM)

After you locate an individual in this Index, take note of the Section and Section Part then proceed to the Land Patent map on the pages immediately following. You should have no difficulty locating the corresponding parcel of land.

The "For More Info" Column will lead you to more information about the underlying Patents. See the *Legend* at right, and the "How to Use this Book" chapter, for more information.

```
                          LEGEND
            "For More Info . . . " column
A = Authority (Legislative Act, See Appendix "A")
B = Block or Lot (location in Section unknown)
C = Cancelled Patent
F = Fractional Section
G = Group  (Multi-Patentee Patent, see Appendix "C")
V = Overlaps another Parcel
R = Re-Issued (Parcel patented more than once)

(A & G items require you to look in the Appendixes referred
to above. All other Letter-designations followed by a number
require you to locate line-items in this index that possess
the ID number found after the letter).
```

ID	Individual in Patent	Sec.	Sec. Part	Date Issued	Other Counties	For More Info . . .
1540	ADDLEMAN, David	8	SESW	1856-01-15		A6
1652	ANDERSON, Jane	18	NWNW	1854-03-01		A6 G265 F
1677	ASKINS, Isabella	1	N½NE	1857-02-20		A5 G228 F
1535	ATCHISON, Nancy	33	W½NE	1854-12-09		A6 G8
1670	BADGER, Lewis	3	NWSE	1855-01-01		A6 G5
1668	" "	3	SW	1855-01-01		A6
1669	" "	3	SWSE	1855-05-01		A1
1758	BAIL, Rebecca	36	E½NE	1854-10-02		A6 G224
1545	BARTON, Edwards	26	NESE	1854-05-01		A1
1546	" "	26	SWNE	1854-05-01		A1
1789	BEAN, Mary	34	NWNE	1855-01-01		A6 G285
1535	BERRYHILL, Charles H	33	W½NE	1854-12-09		A6 G8
1534	" "	9	SE	1857-03-10		A1
1591	BERRYHILL, James B	15	E½NE	1855-05-01		A1
1592	" "	25	W½NE	1855-12-15		A1
1593	" "	7	SWSE	1855-12-15		A1 G19
1593	BERRYHILL, William D	7	SWSE	1855-12-15		A1 G19
1706	BEVER, Sampson C	22	S½SW	1852-03-10		A1
1707	BIGLER, Samuel	14	N½SE	1854-05-01		A1
1729	BOGGS, Mary	24	W½SW	1855-05-01		A6 G264
1600	BOSLEY, James J	4	S½NE	1855-05-01		A1 F
1601	" "	4	S½SW	1855-05-01		A1
1602	" "	4	SE	1855-05-01		A1
1603	" "	5	SE	1855-05-01		A1
1519	BURRELL, Alexander	15	E½SE	1855-05-01		A1
1548	BUSH, Enoch	2	NESE	1889-11-04		A1
1634	CHAPMAN, John	10	NW	1854-12-01		A1
1635	" "	10	W½NE	1854-12-01		A1
1636	" "	9	NE	1854-12-01		A1
1761	CHAPMAN, William M C K	10	E½NE	1854-12-01		A1
1762	" "	11	N½	1854-12-01		A1
1569	CLOUD, Henry S	30	NESE	1854-05-01		A1
1570	" "	30	SENE	1854-05-01		A1
1612	CLOUD, James R	30	NWSE	1854-05-01		A1
1530	COFFIN, Charles B	17	NESW	1850-03-01		A1
1531	COMSTOCK, Charles	26	SWSW	1854-05-01		A1
1541	CONNELLY, Edward	29	W½SW	1855-05-01		A1
1676	COVINGTON, Elizabeth	6	SENE	1855-01-01		A6 G229 F
1735	COX, Thomas J	4	NWNW	1857-03-10		A1 F
1786	CRENSHAW, Elizabeth	34	SWNE	1855-01-01		A6 G286
1628	CULBERTSON, John C	21	NWSE	1854-02-01		A6
1630	" "	21	SWSE	1854-02-01		A6 G72
1629	" "	29	SWNW	1855-01-01		A6 G81
1549	CUNNINGHAM, Mary	8	NWNE	1856-01-15		A6 G140
1631	DAVIE, John C	10	E½SW	1854-12-01		A1
1632	" "	10	SE	1854-12-01		A1

ID	Individual in Patent	Sec.	Sec. Part	Date Issued	Other Counties	For More Info . . .
1633	DAVIE, John C (Cont'd)	11	W½SW	1854-12-01		A1
1532	DENISON, Charles E	5	E½SW	1855-12-15		A1
1533	" "	8	NENW	1855-12-15		A1
1751	DIBBLE, William	1	SWNE	1854-05-01		A1 F
1672	DONLAN, Mary Ann	7	NWNW	1855-12-15		A1 F
1577	DOWNEY, Hugh D	23	SWNE	1855-02-01		A6 G111
1575	" "	4	NENW	1857-02-16		A5 F
1576	" "	4	NWNE	1857-02-16		A5 F
1578	" "	23	N½NE	1934-01-20		A2 G105
1579	" "	23	N½NW	1934-01-20		A2 G105
1586	DRAKE, Isaac	30	S½SE	1855-05-01		A1
1587	" "	31	N½NE	1855-05-01		A1
1521	DRUMMOND, Andrew J	14	S½SE	1854-12-01		A1
1671	DRUMMOND, Lucy Ann	27	SESW	1855-12-15		A1
1708	DRUMMOND, Samuel	25	NESE	1854-03-01		A6
1709	" "	25	NENE	1854-07-01		A6 G112
1736	EDWARDS, Thomas M	34	E½SW	1855-01-01		A6
1737	" "	34	NW	1855-01-01		A6
1744	ELLIOTT, Walter H	29	NWNW	1854-05-01		A1
1731	FARQUHAR, Thomas	18	NENE	1854-05-01		A1
1732	" "	7	SWNW	1854-05-01		A1 F
1722	FISK, Solon	2	SESE	1857-03-10		A1
1562	FOLSOM, Gilman	34	SE	1854-12-01		A1
1594	FRY, James	29	NESW	1855-05-01		A1
1637	FRY, John	31	S½NE	1854-05-01		A1
1638	" "	31	SENW	1854-05-01		A1 F
1733	FRY, Thomas	29	SESW	1855-05-01		A1
1549	FULTON, Francis M	8	NWNE	1856-01-15		A6 G140
1681	GARDNER, Newton	31	NWSW	1854-05-01		A1 F
1682	" "	31	SESW	1854-05-01		A1 F
1679	" "	31	E½SE	1854-10-02		A6
1680	" "	31	NESW	1854-10-02		A6
1685	" "	31	W½SE	1854-10-02		A6
1684	" "	31	W½NW	1855-02-01		A6 F
1683	" "	31	SWSW	1855-05-01		A1 F
1718	GATES, Simon S	33	W½SE	1855-05-01		A1
1720	" "	9	NWNW	1855-05-01		A1
1721	" "	9	W½SW	1855-05-01		A1
1719	" "	8	NENE	1856-05-01		A1
1582	GIFFORD, Ira Merritt	17	N½NE	1854-05-01		A1
1583	" "	8	SE	1854-10-02		A6
1618	GIVINN, Jesse	14	N½SW	1855-05-01		A1
1598	GOWER, James H	7	NWNE	1854-12-01		A1
1597	" "	1	SENE	1855-12-15		A1 F
1709	GRANT, Abigail	25	NENE	1854-07-01		A6 G112
1539	GRISWOLD, Cyrus	33	SENE	1854-05-01		A1
1537	" "	29	SENW	1855-05-01		A1
1538	" "	29	SWNE	1855-05-01		A1
1543	GRISWOLD, Edward	28	SESE	1853-11-01		A1
1544	" "	28	SWNE	1854-05-01		A1
1542	" "	28	NWSE	1854-12-01		A1
1723	GRISWOLD, Spencer	22	N½NE	1854-05-01		A1
1726	" "	33	NENE	1854-05-01		A1
1725	" "	28	SWSE	1855-05-01		A1
1724	" "	27	SWSW	1855-12-15		A1
1653	GUILD, Joseph W	5	NWSW	1855-05-01		A6
1655	" "	5	W½NW	1855-05-01		A6 F
1656	" "	6	NENE	1855-05-01		A6 F
1654	" "	5	SENW	1855-05-10		A1 F
1588	GWIN, Jacob	29	NESE	1854-10-02		A6 G157
1620	GWIN, Jesse	23	SWSE	1850-03-01		A1
1621	" "	26	NWNE	1850-03-01		A1
1623	" "	26	NWSW	1850-03-01		A1
1619	" "	14	S½SW	1854-12-01		A1
1622	" "	26	NWSE	1854-12-01		A1
1624	" "	26	SENE	1854-12-01		A1
1639	GWIN, John	26	NESW	1854-05-01		A1
1640	" "	26	SENW	1854-05-01		A1
1734	GWIN, Thomas	19	NWNW	1851-04-01		A1 F
1595	GWINN, James	17	NWSW	1852-09-01		A1
1596	" "	17	S½SW	1852-09-01		A1
1566	HANES, Henry	5	SWNE	1854-05-01		A6 G163
1565	" "	6	W½SW	1854-05-01		A1 F

ID	Individual in Patent	Sec.	Sec. Part	Date Issued	Other Counties	For More Info . . .
1689	HANES, Philip	6	NWSE	1854-10-02		A6
1688	" "	6	NESW	1854-11-01		A4 F
1690	HANES, Phillip	5	NENW	1853-11-01		A1 F
1759	HARKLOADS, William	20	SESE	1852-03-10		A1
1564	HARRISON, Harvey D	19	E½SE	1853-11-01		A1
1617	HARRY, Jane	28	N½NE	1854-08-01		A6
1522	HAWKS, Andrew J	9	SWNW	1857-03-10		A1
1710	HILL, Samuel	7	SENE	1854-10-02		A6 G169
1630	HOLMES, Keren H	21	SWSE	1854-02-01		A6 G72
1667	HOOK, Levi	30	SWNW	1855-05-01		A1 F
1788	HOOPER, Lucinda	34	SENE	1855-01-01		A6 G287
1710	HOSICK, Susan	7	SENE	1854-10-02		A6 G169
1785	HUTCHINS, Caroline R	35	SWNW	1855-01-01		A6 G288
1727	IOWA, State Of	16		1937-08-26		A3
1588	IS-FI-KE,	29	NESE	1854-10-02		A6 G157
1599	JENNINGS, James H	10	SWSW	1856-01-15		A6 G179
1528	JEWETT, Caroline E	21	E½NE	1852-09-10		A6
1529	" "	21	E½SE	1852-09-10		A6
1536	KAUFFMAN, Christian	19	S½SW	1855-01-01		A6 F
1567	KECK, Henry	29	W½SE	1855-05-01		A1
1599	KENNEDY, Mary	10	SWSW	1856-01-15		A6 G179
1578	KERN, Gertrude	23	N½NE	1934-01-20		A2 G105
1579	" "	23	N½NW	1934-01-20		A2 G105
1580	KING, Hugh F	26	SESW	1855-02-01		A6
1581	" "	35	NESE	1855-02-01		A6
1717	KIRKWOOD, Samuel J	1	N½NW	1857-02-20		A5 G186 F
1711	" "	1	NESW	1857-02-20		A5
1712	" "	1	NWSW	1857-02-20		A5
1713	" "	1	S½NW	1857-02-20		A5 F
1714	" "	1	W½SE	1857-02-20		A5
1715	" "	2	N½NE	1857-02-20		A5 F
1716	" "	2	N½NW	1857-02-20		A5 F
1760	KORN, William	3	NW	1855-05-01		A1 F
1665	LAITON, Mercy	33	SW	1854-10-02		A6 G200
1717	LANE, Miranda	1	N½NW	1857-02-20		A5 G186 F
1757	LANGFORD, Naomi R	26	S½SE	1854-10-02		A6 G225
1606	LEE, James	4	N½SW	1855-01-01		A6 G192
1604	" "	4	S½NW	1855-05-01		A1
1605	" "	5	E½NE	1855-05-01		A1 F
1574	LOVE, Hiram W	8	S½NE	1857-03-10		A1
1763	MANAT, Mary Ann	36	W½NE	1854-10-02		A6 G198
1763	MANAT, William	36	W½NE	1854-10-02		A6 G198
1555	MANATT, George	19	NWSE	1854-12-01		A1
1556	" "	19	W½SW	1854-12-01		A1 F
1609	MANATT, James	20	E½NW	1849-04-10		A1
1644	MANATT, John	18	W½NE	1849-04-10		A1
1645	" "	19	E½NW	1849-04-10		A1 F
1646	" "	23	SENE	1854-12-01		A1
1693	MANATT, Robert	17	NW	1849-04-10		A1
1694	" "	18	NWSW	1849-04-10		A1 F
1697	" "	20	E½NE	1850-03-01		A1
1700	" "	21	W½NW	1850-03-01		A1
1698	" "	21	E½NW	1851-04-01		A1
1699	" "	21	W½NE	1851-04-01		A1
1701	" "	22	NWNW	1851-04-01		A1
1702	" "	30	W½NE	1851-04-01		A1
1703	" "	35	E½NE	1854-05-01		A1
1704	" "	36	W½NW	1854-05-01		A1 V1525
1695	" "	2	E½SW	1855-05-01		A1
1696	" "	2	W½SE	1855-05-01		A1
1739	MANATT, Thomas	20	W½NW	1849-04-10		A1
1741	" "	30	NENE	1853-11-01		A1
1738	" "	19	SWSE	1854-12-01		A1
1740	" "	30	N½SW	1855-05-01		A1 F
1764	MANATT, William	18	NESW	1849-04-10		A1 F
1765	" "	18	SENE	1849-04-10		A1
1766	" "	20	NWNE	1851-04-01		A1
1767	" "	36	E½NW	1854-05-01		A1 V1525
1768	" "	4	NENE	1855-05-01		A1 F
1663	MARK, Levi G	32	SE	1854-10-02		A6
1664	" "	33	E½SE	1854-10-02		A6
1665	" "	33	SW	1854-10-02		A6 G200
1666	" "	34	W½SW	1854-10-02		A6 G201

ID	Individual in Patent	Sec.	Sec. Part	Date Issued	Other Counties	For More Info . . .
1691	MARVIN, Rebecca J	12	NE	1855-05-01		A1
1730	MCBURNEY, Temperance	25	SESE	1855-12-15		A1
1563	MCGARVEY, Graham A	28	W½SW	1854-05-01		A1
1769	MCGARVEY, William	29	SESE	1854-12-01		A1
1520	MCKINNEY, Alexander F	13	S½NW	1855-05-10		A1
1610	MCLAIN, James	32	NE	1855-05-01		A1
1611	" "	33	N½NW	1855-05-01		A1
1525	MEAD, Benjamin L	36	S½NW	1855-12-15		A1 G208 V1704, 1767
1526	" "	36	SW	1855-12-15		A1 G208 R1756
1525	MEAD, Enfield S	36	S½NW	1855-12-15		A1 G208 V1704, 1767
1526	" "	36	SW	1855-12-15		A1 G208 R1756
1642	MEAD, John L	1	E½SE	1855-01-01		A6
1643	" "	10	NWSW	1855-01-01		A6
1547	METCALF, Emanuel R	18	SE	1848-05-01		A2
1666	MUIRHIRD, Sarah	34	W½SW	1854-10-02		A6 G201
1686	NUSSBAUM, Nicholas	32	W½	1854-05-01		A1
1607	PARKER, James M	35	S½SE	1854-12-01		A1
1608	" "	35	S½SW	1854-12-01		A1
1670	PELTON, Dolly T	3	NWSE	1855-01-01		A6 G5
1557	PLEASANTS, George W	33	S½NW	1854-12-01		A1
1566	POLLARD, Jane	5	SWNE	1854-05-01		A6 G163
1752	PORTER, William G	6	SWSE	1855-05-01		A1
1568	PUFFINBURGER, Henry	2	S½NW	1857-04-01		A4 F
1589	PUFFINBURGER, Jacob	2	S½NE	1857-04-01		A4 F
1753	PUSEY, William H M	24	E½SW	1854-10-02		A6
1754	" "	24	SE	1854-10-02		A6
1757	" "	26	S½SE	1854-10-02		A6 G225
1755	" "	35	W½NE	1854-10-02		A6
1758	" "	36	E½NE	1854-10-02		A6 G224
1756	" "	36	SW	1854-10-02		A6 R1526
1675	RENO, Morgan	27	N½NW	1853-08-01		A6
1673	" "	15	SESE	1855-01-01		A6 C
1676	" "	6	SENE	1855-01-01		A6 G229 F
1678	" "	3	N½NE	1856-06-16		A6 G239 F
1677	" "	1	N½NE	1857-02-20		A5 G228 F
1674	" "	15	SWSE	1964-03-17		A6
1550	SANXAY, Frederic	15	N½NW	1855-01-01		A6
1551	" "	15	NWNE	1855-05-01		A1
1552	" "	15	NWSE	1855-05-01		A1
1647	SARGENT, John O	11	E½SW	1854-12-01		A1
1648	" "	11	SE	1854-12-01		A1
1649	" "	14	N½	1854-12-01		A1
1770	SCOTT, William	17	S½NE	1850-03-01		A1
1771	" "	17	SE	1850-03-01		A1
1772	" "	22	E½SE	1850-03-01		A1 V1687
1774	" "	23	NESW	1850-03-01		A1
1777	" "	23	W½SW	1850-03-01		A1
1778	" "	27	E½NE	1850-03-01		A1
1773	" "	22	SENE	1854-05-01		A1
1776	" "	23	SWNW	1854-05-01		A1
1775	" "	23	SENW	1854-12-01		A1
1625	SIMPSON, John A	13	N½NW	1855-05-10		A1
1626	" "	15	NWSW	1855-05-10		A1
1627	" "	15	SWNW	1855-05-10		A1
1523	SMITH, Andrew	15	SENW	1855-05-01		A1
1524	" "	15	SWNE	1855-05-01		A1
1742	SMITH, Vincent G	27	N½SE	1848-05-01		A2
1743	" "	27	N½SW	1848-05-01		A2
1571	SNOOKS, Henry	22	N½SW	1850-03-01		A1
1572	" "	22	SWNW	1850-03-01		A1
1573	" "	27	W½NE	1850-03-01		A1
1745	SPENCER, William A	13	N½SE	1855-05-01		A1
1746	" "	13	NE	1855-05-01		A1
1629	SPONSLER, Anna	29	SWNW	1855-01-01		A6 G81
1559	STEVENSON, Mary	13	S½SE	1855-02-01		A6 G290
1728	SWITZER, Tavner B	24	S½NE	1854-10-02		A6
1729	" "	24	W½SW	1855-05-01		A6 G264
1692	SYLVESTER, Richard H	5	NWNE	1855-05-01		A1 F
1641	TALBOT, John J	18	E½NW	1848-06-01		A1 F
1652	TALBOTT, Joseph	18	NWNW	1854-03-01		A6 G265 F
1658	TALBOTT, Joshua C	18	SWNW	1850-12-02		A1 F
1660	" "	5	SWSW	1853-01-15		A6 G266
1661	" "	6	E½SE	1853-01-15		A6 G266

ID	Individual in Patent	Sec.	Sec. Part	Date Issued	Other Counties	For More Info . . .
1662	TALBOTT, Joshua C (Cont'd)	7	NENE	1853-01-15		A6 G266
1659	" "	18	SWSW	1854-11-01		A4 F
1657	" "	18	SESW	1854-12-01		A1 F
1705	TALBOTT, Robert	19	SWNW	1854-05-01		A1 F
1560	TAYLOR, Gilbert T	28	E½SW	1855-02-01		A6
1561	" "	28	S½NW	1855-02-01		A6
1687	TOUSEY, Omer	22	NESE	1855-03-01		A6 V1772
1606	TRACY, Sicha	4	N½SW	1855-01-01		A6 G192
1660	TRICKER, Lucinda	5	SWSW	1853-01-15		A6 G266
1661	" "	6	E½SE	1853-01-15		A6 G266
1662	" "	7	NENE	1853-01-15		A6 G266
1584	TUTTLE, Ira	6	E½NW	1855-12-15		A1 F
1585	" "	6	W½NE	1855-12-15		A1 F
1678	UNDERWOOD, Sarah	3	N½NE	1856-06-16		A6 G239 F
1747	WEST, William B	2	W½SW	1855-05-01		A6 C R1748
1749	" "	3	E½SE	1855-05-01		A6 C R1750
1748	" "	2	W½SW	1860-08-01		A5 R1747
1750	" "	3	E½SE	1860-08-01		A5 R1749
1790	WHITE, William	27	S½SE	1854-12-01		A1
1791	" "	34	NENE	1854-12-01		A1
1527	WILLIAMS, Benjamin	30	E½NW	1854-05-01		A6
1554	WILLIAMS, George C	31	NENW	1855-03-01		A4 F
1553	" "	30	S½SW	1855-05-01		A1 F
1613	WILLIAMS, James	28	N½NW	1854-03-01		A6
1614	" "	30	NWNW	1854-03-01		A6 F
1615	WILLIAMSON, James	1	S½SW	1855-05-01		A1
1616	" "	12	NW	1855-05-01		A1
1779	WILLINGHAM, William W	25	W½SE	1854-02-01		A6
1789	" "	34	NWNE	1855-01-01		A6 G285
1788	" "	34	SENE	1855-01-01		A6 G287
1786	" "	34	SWNE	1855-01-01		A6 G286
1780	" "	35	NENW	1855-01-01		A6
1781	" "	35	NESW	1855-01-01		A6
1782	" "	35	NWNW	1855-01-01		A6
1787	" "	35	NWSE	1855-01-01		A6 G289
1783	" "	35	NWSW	1855-01-01		A6
1784	" "	35	SENW	1855-01-01		A6
1785	" "	35	SWNW	1855-01-01		A6 G288
1577	WILSON, Ann	23	SWNE	1855-02-01		A6 G111
1558	WILSON, George W	24	N½NE	1854-12-01		A1
1559	" "	13	S½SE	1855-02-01		A6 G290
1590	WINELAND, Jacob	6	SESW	1855-05-10		A1 F
1650	WOOD, Joseph P	6	NWNW	1855-12-15		A1 F
1651	" "	6	SWNW	1856-06-16		A6 F
1787	WOODWARD, John P	35	NWSE	1855-01-01		A6 G289

Patent Map

T80-N R13-W
5th PM Meridian

Map Group 8

Township Statistics

Parcels Mapped	:	273
Number of Patents	:	235
Number of Individuals	:	155
Patentees Identified	:	148
Number of Surnames	:	124
Multi-Patentee Parcels	:	37
Oldest Patent Date	:	5/1/1848
Most Recent Patent	:	3/17/1964
Block/Lot Parcels	:	0
Parcels Re - Issued	:	3
Parcels that Overlap	:	5
Cities and Towns	:	1
Cemeteries	:	2

Section 6
WOOD Joseph P 1855
WOOD Joseph P 1856
TUTTLE Ira 1855
TUTTLE Ira 1855
GUILD Joseph W 1855
RENO [229] Morgan 1855
TALBOTT [266] Joshua C 1853
HANES Philip 1854
HANES Philip 1854
HANES Henry 1854
WINELAND Jacob 1855
PORTER William G 1855

Section 5
HANES Phillip 1853
GUILD Joseph W 1855
GUILD Joseph W 1855
SYLVESTER Richard H 1855
HANES [163] Henry 1854
LEE James 1855
GUILD Joseph W 1855
DENISON Charles E 1855
TALBOTT [266] Joshua C 1853
BOSLEY James J 1855

Section 4
COX Thomas J 1857
DOWNEY Hugh D 1857
DOWNEY Hugh D 1857
MANATT William 1855
LEE James 1855
BOSLEY James J 1855
LEE [192] James 1855
BOSLEY James J 1855
BOSLEY James J 1855

Section 7
DONLAN Mary Ann 1855
FARQUHAR Thomas 1854
GOWER James H 1854
TALBOTT [266] Joshua C 1853
HILL [169] Samuel 1854
BERRYHILL [19] James B 1855

Section 8
DENISON Charles E 1855
FULTON [140] Francis M 1856
GATES Simon S 1856
LOVE Hiram W 1857
GIFFORD Ira Merritt 1854
ADDLEMAN David 1856

Section 9
GATES Simon S 1855
HAWKS Andrew J 1857
GATES Simon S 1855
CHAPMAN John 1854
BERRYHILL Charles H 1857

Section 18
TALBOTT [265] Joseph 1854
TALBOT John J 1848
TALBOTT Joshua C 1850
MANATT Robert 1849
MANATT William 1849
TALBOTT Joshua C 1854
TALBOTT Joshua C 1854
MANATT John 1849
FARQUHAR Thomas 1854
MANATT William 1849
METCALF Emanuel R 1848

Section 17
MANATT Robert 1849
GIFFORD Ira Merritt 1854
SCOTT William 1850
GWINN James 1852
COFFIN Charles B 1850
GWINN James 1852
SCOTT William 1850

Section 16
IOWA State Of 1937

Section 19
GWIN Thomas 1851
TALBOTT Robert 1854
MANATT John 1849
MANATT George 1854
MANATT George 1854
KAUFFMAN Christian 1855
HARRISON Harvey D 1853
MANATT Thomas 1854

Section 20
MANATT Thomas 1849
MANATT James 1849
MANATT William 1851
MANATT Robert 1850

Section 21
MANATT Robert 1850
MANATT Robert 1851
MANATT Robert 1851
JEWETT Caroline E 1852
CULBERTSON John C 1854
CULBERTSON [72] John C 1854
JEWETT Caroline E 1852
HARKLOADS William 1852

Section 30
WILLIAMS James 1854
HOOK Levi 1855
MANATT Thomas 1855
WILLIAMS George C 1855
WILLIAMS Benjamin 1854
CLOUD James R 1854
MANATT Robert 1851
MANATT Thomas 1853
CLOUD Henry S 1854
CLOUD Henry S 1854
DRAKE Isaac 1855

Section 29
ELLIOTT Walter H 1854
CULBERTSON [81] John C 1855
CONNELLY Edward 1855
GRISWOLD Cyrus 1855
FRY James 1855
FRY Thomas 1855
GRISWOLD Cyrus 1855
GWIN [157] Jacob 1854
KECK Henry 1855
MCGARVEY William 1854

Section 28
WILLIAMS James 1854
TAYLOR Gilbert T 1855
MCGARVEY Graham A 1854
TAYLOR Gilbert T 1855
HARRY Jane 1854
GRISWOLD Edward 1854
GRISWOLD Edward 1854
GRISWOLD Spencer 1855
GRISWOLD Edward 1853

Section 31
GARDNER Newton 1855
FRY John 1854
GARDNER Newton 1854
GARDNER Newton 1855
WILLIAMS George C 1855
GARDNER Newton 1854
DRAKE Isaac 1855
FRY John 1854
GARDNER Newton 1854
GARDNER Newton 1854

Section 32
NUSSBAUM Nicholas 1854
MCLAIN James 1855
MARK Levi G 1854

Section 33
MCLAIN James 1855
PLEASANTS George W 1854
BERRYHILL [8] Charles H 1854
MARK [200] Levi G 1854
GATES Simon S 1855
GRISWOLD Spencer 1854
GRISWOLD Cyrus 1854
MARK Levi G 1854

Section 3 / 2 / 1 (top row)

KORN William 1855	RENO [239] Morgan 1856 **3**	KIRKWOOD Samuel J 1857	KIRKWOOD Samuel J 1857

RENO [228] Morgan 1857

KIRKWOOD [186] Samuel J 1857

Section 3:
- KORN William 1855
- RENO [239] Morgan 1856
- BADGER Lewis 1855
- BADGER [5] Lewis 1855
- BADGER Lewis 1855
- WEST William B 1860
- WEST William B 1855

Section 2:
- KIRKWOOD Samuel J 1857
- KIRKWOOD Samuel J 1857
- PUFFINBURGER Henry 1857
- PUFFINBURGER Jacob 1857
- WEST William B 1855
- WEST William B 1860
- MANATT Robert 1855
- MANATT Robert 1855
- BUSH Enoch 1889
- FISK Solon 1857
- **2**

Section 1:
- KIRKWOOD [186] Samuel J 1857
- RENO [228] Morgan 1857
- KIRKWOOD Samuel J 1857
- DIBBLE William 1854
- GOWER James H 1855
- KIRKWOOD Samuel J 1857
- KIRKWOOD Samuel J 1857
- MEAD John L 1855
- WILLIAMSON James 1855
- KIRKWOOD Samuel J 1857
- **1**

Sections 10 / 11 / 12

Section 10:
- CHAPMAN John 1854
- CHAPMAN John 1854
- CHAPMAN William M C K 1854
- MEAD John L 1855
- JENNINGS [179] James H 1856
- DAVIE John C 1854
- DAVIE John C 1854
- **10**

Section 11:
- CHAPMAN William M C K 1854
- DAVIE John C 1854
- SARGENT John O 1854
- SARGENT John O 1854
- **11**

Section 12:
- WILLIAMSON James 1855
- MARVIN Rebecca J 1855
- **12**

Sections 15 / 14 / 13

Section 15:
- SANXAY Frederic 1855
- SANXAY Frederic 1855
- BERRYHILL James B 1855
- SIMPSON John A 1855
- SMITH Andrew 1855
- SMITH Andrew 1855
- SIMPSON John A 1855
- SANXAY Frederic 1855
- BURRELL Alexander 1855
- RENO Morgan 1964
- RENO Morgan 1855
- **15**

Section 14:
- SARGENT John O 1854
- GIVINN Jesse 1855
- BIGLER Samuel 1854
- GWIN Jesse 1854
- DRUMMOND Andrew J 1854
- **14**

Section 13:
- SIMPSON John A 1855
- SPENCER William A 1855
- MCKINNEY Alexander F 1855
- SPENCER William A 1855
- WILSON [290] George W 1855
- **13**

Sections 22 / 23 / 24

Section 22:
- MANATT Robert 1851
- GRISWOLD Spencer 1854
- SNOOKS Henry 1850
- SCOTT William 1854
- SNOOKS Henry 1850
- TOUSEY Omer 1855
- BEVER Sampson C 1852
- SCOTT William 1854
- **22**

Section 23:
- DOWNEY [105] Hugh D 1854
- DOWNEY [105] Hugh D 1934
- SCOTT William 1854
- SCOTT William 1854
- DOWNEY [111] Hugh D 1855
- MANATT John 1854
- SCOTT William 1850
- SCOTT William 1850
- GWIN Jesse 1850
- **23**

Section 24:
- WILSON George W 1854
- SWITZER Tavner B 1854
- PUSEY William H M 1854
- PUSEY William H M 1854
- SWITZER [264] Tavner B 1855
- **24**

Sections 27 / 26 / 25

Section 27:
- RENO Morgan 1853
- SNOOKS Henry 1850
- SCOTT William 1850
- SMITH Vincent G 1848
- SMITH Vincent G 1848
- GRISWOLD Spencer 1855
- DRUMMOND Lucy Ann 1855
- WHITE William 1854
- **27**

Section 26:
- GWIN Jesse 1850
- GWIN John 1854
- BARTON Edwards 1854
- GWIN Jesse 1854
- GWIN Jesse 1850
- GWIN John 1854
- GWIN Jesse 1854
- BARTON Edwards 1854
- COMSTOCK Charles 1854
- KING Hugh F 1855
- PUSEY [225] William H M 1854
- **26**

Section 25:
- BERRYHILL James B 1855
- DRUMMOND [112] Samuel 1854
- WILLINGHAM William W 1854
- DRUMMOND Samuel 1854
- MCBURNEY Temperance 1855
- **25**

Sections 34 / 35 / 36

Section 34:
- EDWARDS Thomas M 1855
- WILLINGHAM [285] William W 1855
- WHITE William 1854
- WILLINGHAM [286] William W 1855
- WILLINGHAM [287] William W 1855
- WILLINGHAM [288] William W 1855
- MARK [201] Levi G 1854
- EDWARDS Thomas M 1855
- FOLSOM Gilman 1854
- **34**

Section 35:
- WILLINGHAM William W 1855
- WILLINGHAM William W 1855
- PUSEY William H M 1854
- WILLINGHAM William W 1855
- MANATT Robert 1854
- WILLINGHAM William W 1855
- WILLINGHAM [289] William W 1855
- KING Hugh F 1855
- PARKER James M 1854
- PARKER James M 1854
- **35**

Section 36:
- MANATT Robert 1854
- MANATT William 1854
- MANAT [198] William 1854
- PUSEY [224] William H M 1854
- MEAD [208] Benjamin L 1855
- PUSEY William H M 1854
- MEAD [208] Benjamin L 1855
- **36**

Helpful Hints

1. This Map's INDEX can be found on the preceding pages.

2. Refer to Map "C" to see where this Township lies within Poweshiek County, Iowa.

3. Numbers within square brackets [ ] denote a multi-patentee land parcel (multi-owner). Refer to Appendix "C" for a full list of members in this group.

4. Areas that look to be crowded with Patentees usually indicate multiple sales of the same parcel (Re-issues) or Overlapping parcels. See this Township's Index for an explanation of these and other circumstances that might explain "odd" groupings of Patentees on this map.

Legend

— Patent Boundary

— Section Boundary

No Patents Found (or Outside County)

1., 2., 3., ... Lot Numbers (when beside a name)

[ ] Group Number (see Appendix "C")

Scale: Section = 1 mile X 1 mile (generally, with some exceptions)

Road Map

T80-N R13-W
5th PM Meridian

Map Group 8

Cities & Towns
Carnforth

Cemeteries
Gwin Cemetery
Wilson Cemetery

360th Ave

| 6 | 5 365th Ave | 4 |

370th Ave

220th St

| 7 | 8 | 9 |

US Hwy 6

| 18 385th Ave | 17 | 16 |

Hwy 21

| 19 | 20 | Gwin Cem. 21 |

400th Ave

210th St

| 30 | 29 | 28 |

200th St

| 31 | 32 | 33 |

415th Ave

420th Ave

3

Hartwick Rd

2

240th St

1

10

11

12

Poweshiek-Iowa Rd

380th Ave

15

14

13
385th Ave

388th Ave

390th Ave

22
Carnforth
Old 6 Rd

23

2nd St
3rd St
West
St
4th
St
Union
5th
St

24

400th
Ave

25

Wilson
Cem.

27

26

250th St

410th Ave

230th St

I- 80

34

35

36

Poweshiek-Iowa
Rd

Copyright 2010 Boyd IT, Inc. All Rights Reserved

Helpful Hints

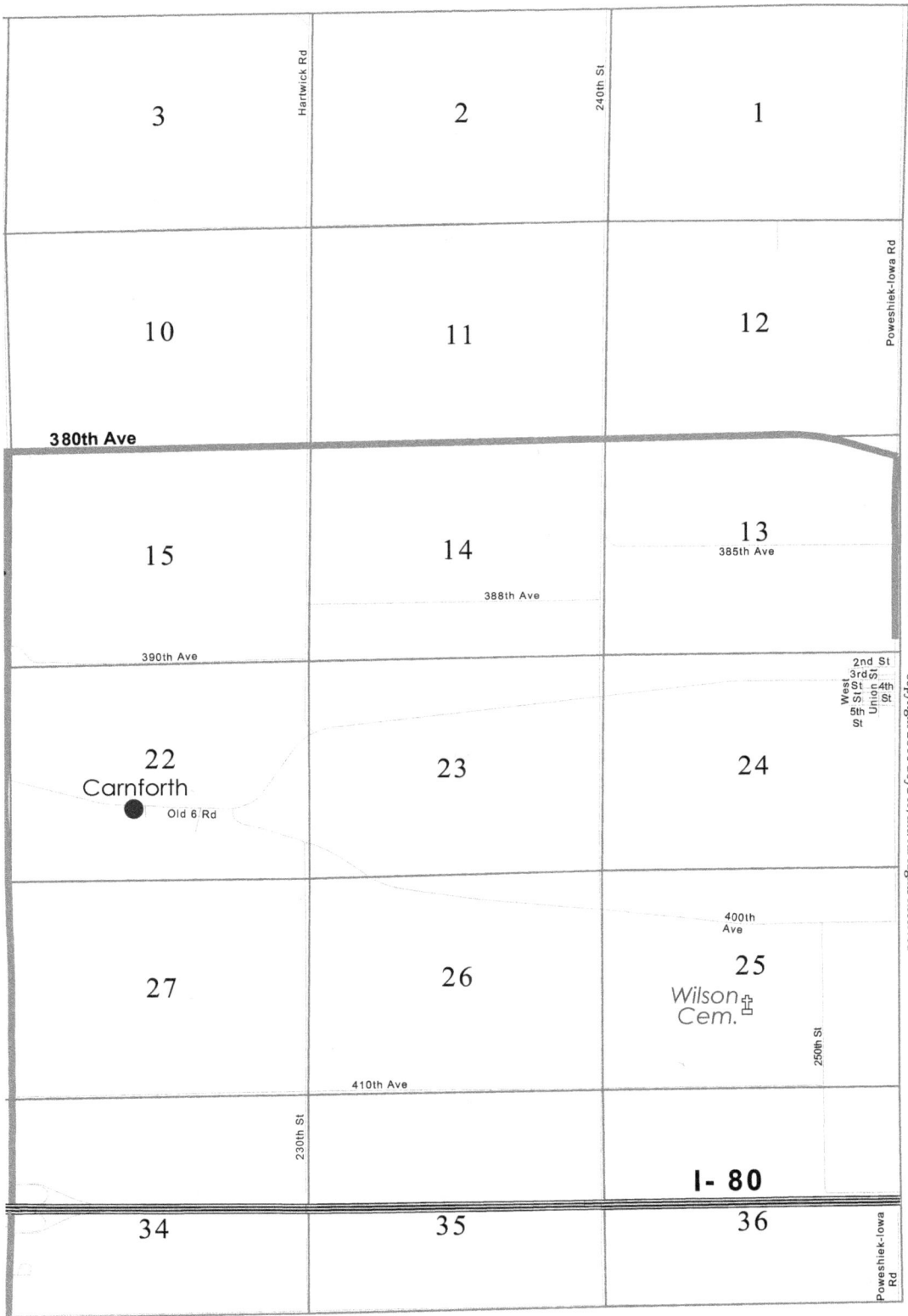

1. This road map has a number of uses, but primarily it is to help you: a) find the present location of land owned by your ancestors (at least the general area), b) find cemeteries and city-centers, and c) estimate the route/roads used by Census-takers & tax-assessors.

2. If you plan to travel to Poweshiek County to locate cemeteries or land parcels, please pick up a modern travel map for the area before you do. Mapping old land parcels on modern maps is not as exact a science as you might think. Just the slightest variations in public land survey coordinates, estimates of parcel boundaries, or road-map deviations can greatly alter a map's representation of how a road either does or doesn't cross a particular parcel of land.

L e g e n d

———————	Section Lines
═══════	Interstates
━━━━━━━	Highways
———————	Other Roads
●	Cities/Towns
✝	Cemeteries

Scale: Section = 1 mile X 1 mile
(generally, with some exceptions)

Historical Map

T80-N R13-W
5th PM Meridian

Map Group 8

Cities & Towns
Carnforth

Cemeteries
Wilson Cemetery
Gwin Cemetery

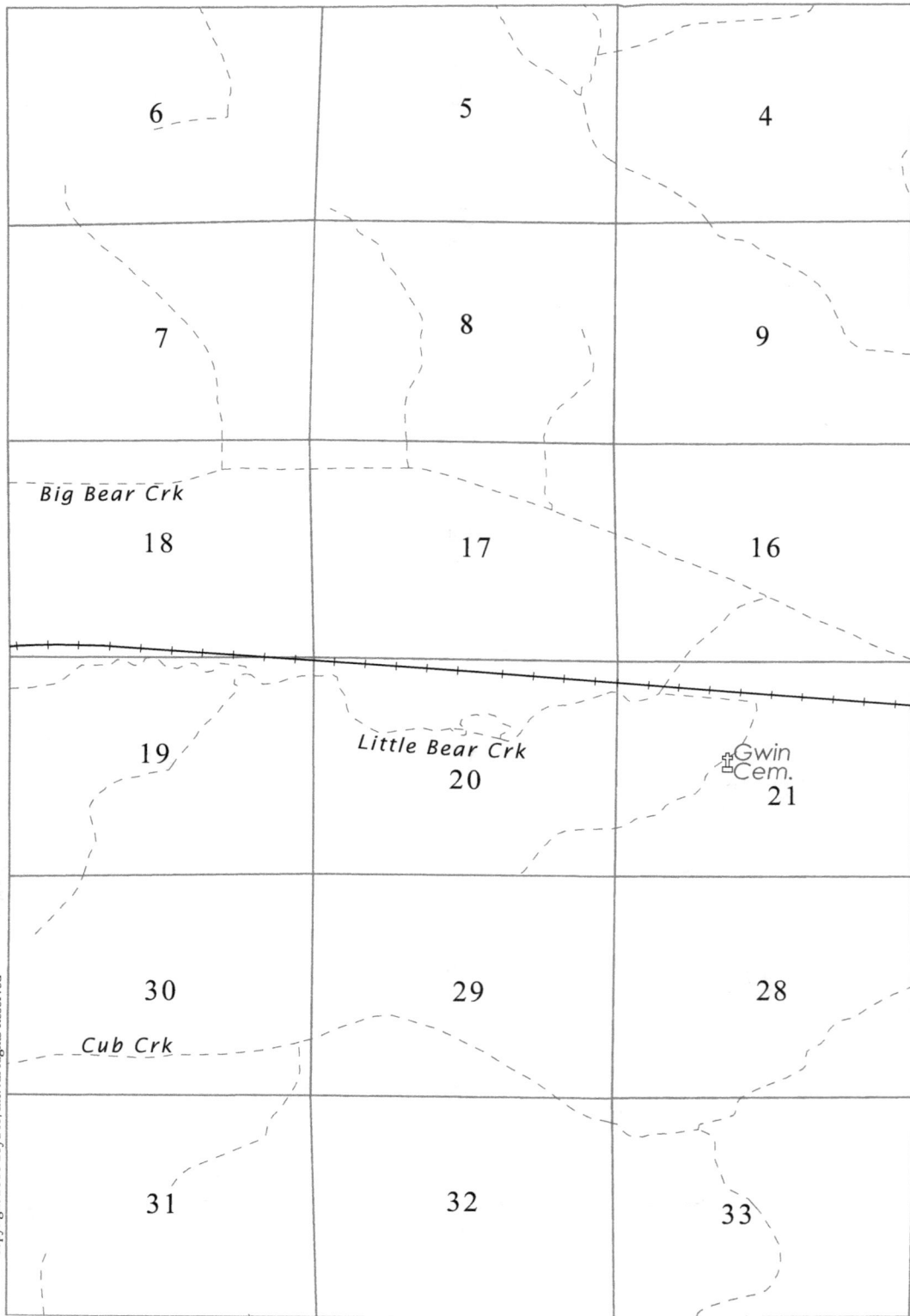

6	5	4
7	8	9
18	17	16
19	20	21
30	29	28
31	32	33

Big Bear Crk

Little Bear Crk

Gwin Cem.

Cub Crk

3

Honey Crk

2

1

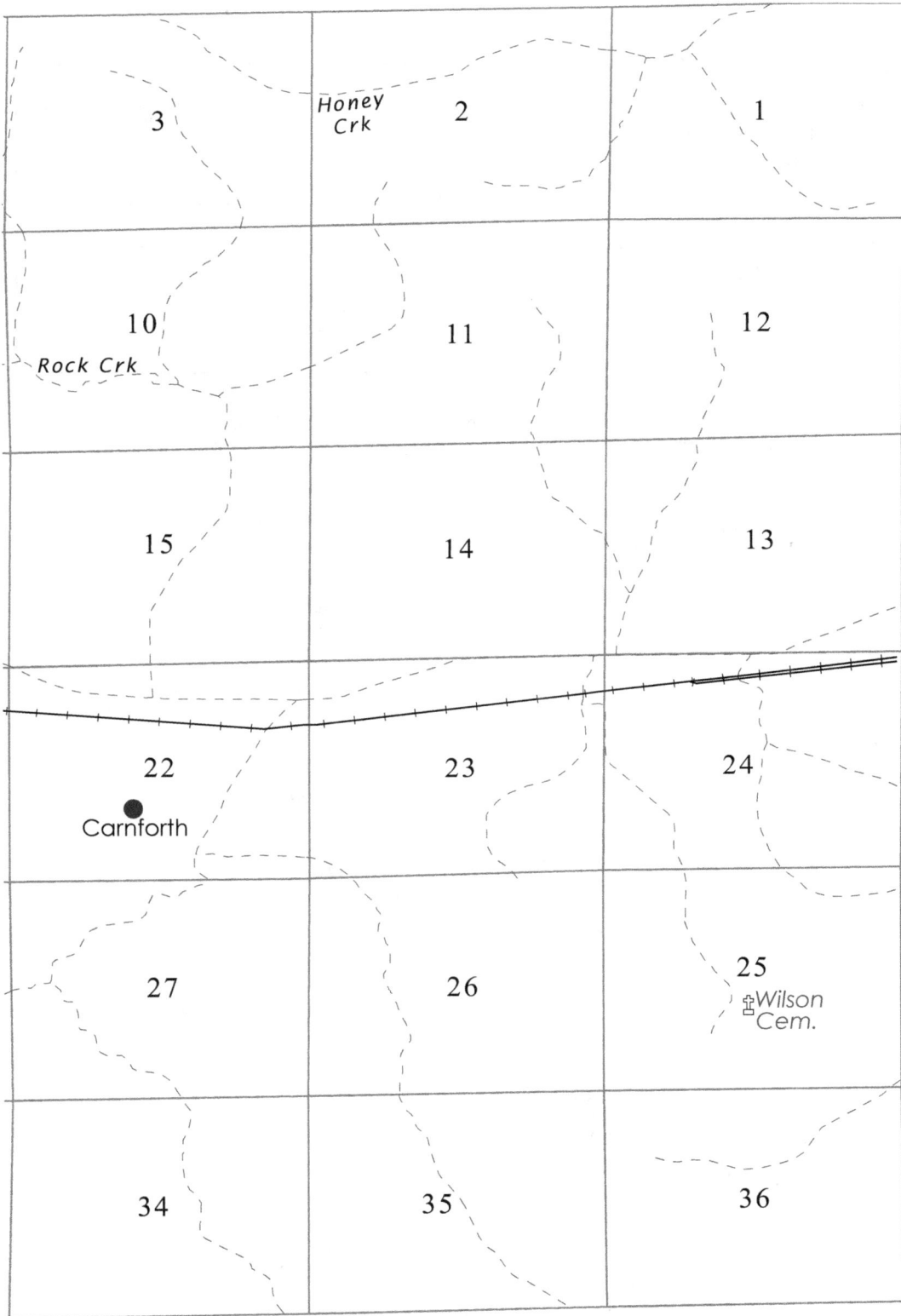

10

Rock Crk

11

12

15

14

13

22

● Carnforth

23

24

27

26

25

⚁ *Wilson Cem.*

34

35

36

Legend

——————	Section Lines
╫╫╫╫╫╫╫	Railroads
�	Large Rivers & Bodies of Water
- - - - - -	Streams/Creeks & Small Rivers
●	Cities/Towns
✝	Cemeteries

Scale: Section = 1 mile X 1 mile
(there are some exceptions)

Map Group 9: Index to Land Patents

Township 79-North Range 16-West (5th PM)

After you locate an individual in this Index, take note of the Section and Section Part then proceed to the Land Patent map on the pages immediately following. You should have no difficulty locating the corresponding parcel of land.

The "For More Info" Column will lead you to more information about the underlying Patents. See the *Legend* at right, and the "How to Use this Book" chapter, for more information.

```
┌─────────────────────────────────────────────────────────┐
│                      LEGEND                               │
│          "For More Info . . . " column                    │
│  A = Authority (Legislative Act, See Appendix "A")        │
│  B = Block or Lot (location in Section unknown)           │
│  C = Cancelled Patent                                     │
│  F = Fractional Section                                   │
│  G = Group  (Multi-Patentee Patent, see Appendix "C")     │
│  V = Overlaps another Parcel                              │
│  R = Re-Issued (Parcel patented more than once)           │
│                                                           │
│  (A & G items require you to look in the Appendixes       │
│  referred to above. All other Letter-designations         │
│  followed by a number require you to locate line-items    │
│  in this index that possess the ID number found after     │
│  the letter).                                             │
└─────────────────────────────────────────────────────────┘
```

ID	Individual in Patent	Sec.	Sec. Part	Date Issued	Other Counties	For More Info . . .
2040	AHERN, Michael H	17	SWNE	1855-12-15		A1
2041	" "	17	SWSE	1855-12-15		A1
2042	" "	20	NENE	1855-12-15		A1
2043	" "	22	W½SE	1855-12-15		A1
1813	ALLEN, Charles	23	SWSE	1854-05-01		A1
1950	ALLEN, John	26	SENE	1855-05-01		A1
2073	ALLEN, Sherwood	36	N½SW	1854-05-01		A1
2074	" "	36	S½NW	1854-05-01		A1
2086	ALLEN, William	17	NESE	1853-10-01		A6
2032	BARGAHISER, Lewis G	29	SE	1855-05-01		A6
1835	BEADLESTON, Ebenezer	10	SWNE	1855-01-01		A6 G6
1833	" "	10	E½SW	1855-03-01		A4 G7
1834	" "	10	W½SE	1855-03-01		A4 G7
1859	BEELER, George M	14	S½SW	1850-04-10		A1
1860	" "	14	SWNW	1854-05-01		A1
1861	BEELERS, George M	14	NWNW	1855-05-01		A1
1862	" "	14	SENW	1855-05-01		A1
1855	BENT, George	3	N½NW	1856-04-01		A1 F
1892	BERRYHILL, James B	2	N½NE	1857-03-10		A1 G19 F
2087	BERRYHILL, William D	4	N½NW	1854-05-01		A1 F
1892	" "	2	N½NE	1857-03-10		A1 G19 F
1792	BETTS, Aaron	19	S½SE	1855-12-15		A1
1793	" "	29	NWNW	1855-12-15		A1
1794	" "	29	S½SW	1855-12-15		A1
1795	" "	30	N½NE	1855-12-15		A1
1796	" "	32	NW	1855-12-15		A1
1864	BILL, Harvey A	1		1855-05-01		A1 F
1865	" "	12	E½NW	1855-05-01		A1
1800	BIXBY, Amos	8	NENW	1855-05-01		A1
1826	BLACK, Dominick	22	SESE	1855-05-10		A1
1827	" "	23	NWSW	1855-05-10		A1
1828	" "	24	SW	1855-05-10		A1
1814	BLISH, Charles C	15	E½SW	1855-03-01		A6
1815	" "	15	W½SE	1855-03-01		A6
1951	BOND, John	13	S½	1855-05-01		A1
2025	BOOTH, Julia	6	SWSE	1856-01-15		A6
1898	BORLAND, James	4	NESW	1854-07-01		A6 G28
1899	" "	4	NWSE	1854-07-01		A6 G28
1895	" "	4	SENW	1854-07-01		A6 F
1896	" "	4	SWNE	1854-07-01		A6 F
1893	" "	3	S½NW	1854-12-01		A1 F
1894	" "	4	SENE	1854-12-01		A1 F
1897	" "	7	NWSE	1855-05-01		A1
1853	BOTTOMS, Mary	10	SENE	1854-03-01		A6 G220
1854	" "	11	SWNW	1854-03-01		A6 G220
2058	BREED, Nathan	31	NESE	1854-12-01		A1

ID	Individual in Patent	Sec.	Sec. Part	Date Issued	Other Counties	For More Info . . .
2059	BREED, Nathan (Cont'd)	32	NESW	1854-12-01		A1
2060	" "	32	NWSE	1854-12-01		A1
2061	" "	32	W½SW	1854-12-01		A1
1952	BROWN, John	6	N½SW	1855-12-15		A1 F
1954	" "	6	SWNW	1855-12-15		A1 F
1955	" "	7	NWNE	1856-09-01		A1
1953	" "	6	NWSE	1857-03-10		A1
2056	BRYANT, Moses	17	NWSE	1854-05-01		A1
1810	CAMPBELL, Carson	7	NENW	1855-05-01		A1 F
1811	" "	7	NWNW	1855-05-01		A1 F
1812	CAMPBELL, Carson H	6	SESW	1855-05-10		A1 F
1816	CARLETON, Charles C	24	NWNW	1855-12-15		A1
1856	CARPENTER, George F	10	NW	1855-12-15		A1
1857	" "	3	W½SW	1855-12-15		A1
1858	" "	4	E½SE	1855-12-15		A1
2027	CARPENTER, Levi	14	N½SW	1852-09-10		A6
2030	" "	26	SWNW	1852-09-10		A6
2029	" "	23	SENW	1855-05-01		A1
2028	" "	23	E½SW	1855-05-10		A1
2070	CARPENTER, Robert	23	NWSE	1854-05-01		A1
1970	CASWELL, Elanor	20	E½NW	1856-01-15		A6 G65
1884	CHANDLER, Margaret	26	SWNE	1854-08-01		A6 G98
2001	CHESHIRE, John W	30	SENE	1854-05-01		A1
2002	" "	33	W½SW	1855-12-15		A1
1889	CLARK, Jackson	17	SWNW	1855-12-15		A1
1890	" "	18	E½NE	1855-12-15		A1
1798	CLOUD, Addison	33	E½SW	1855-12-15		A1
1799	" "	33	W½SE	1855-12-15		A1
1991	COLYER, John L	27	E½SW	1855-12-15		A1
1992	" "	27	NWNE	1855-12-15		A1
1993	" "	27	SENW	1855-12-15		A1
2092	CONEY, William M	32	N½NE	1855-12-15		A1
1837	CONNELLY, Edward	23	NWNE	1855-05-01		A1
1838	" "	25	SWNW	1855-05-01		A1
1839	" "	26	E½SE	1855-05-01		A1
1977	CONNER, John	11	W½SE	1854-08-01		A6
1949	COULTER, John Alexander	17	N½SW	1856-06-16		A6
2083	COX, Thomas J	33	E½SE	1857-02-20		A5
1900	CRAMER, James	20	W½NW	1855-12-15		A1
1901	" "	27	SWNW	1855-12-15		A1 R1929
1902	" "	28	N½NE	1855-12-15		A1
2019	CRISPIN, Joshua	25	SESW	1855-02-01		A6
2020	" "	36	NENW	1855-02-01		A6
2021	" "	36	W½NE	1855-02-01		A6
1986	CROMER, Elizabeth	17	E½NE	1855-05-01		A6 G203 C R1987
1987	" "	17	E½NE	1860-02-07		A6 G203 R1986
1956	CULBERTSON, John C	10	SWSW	1855-05-01		A6 R1917
1974	" "	19	NENE	1855-05-01		A6 G69
1958	" "	19	NENW	1855-05-01		A6 F
1959	" "	19	NWNE	1855-05-01		A6
1960	" "	19	SENE	1855-05-01		A6
1975	" "	19	SWNE	1855-05-01		A6 G82
1969	" "	9	SESE	1855-05-01		A6
1962	" "	26	NWSW	1855-06-01		A6
1963	" "	26	SENW	1855-06-01		A6
1957	" "	14	NENW	1855-12-15		A1
1971	" "	19	W½NW	1856-01-15		A6 G75 F
1970	" "	20	E½NW	1856-01-15		A6 G65
1964	" "	27	SENE	1856-01-15		A6
1965	" "	29	N½SW	1856-01-15		A6
1973	" "	29	NE	1856-01-15		A6 G76
1966	" "	29	S½NW	1856-01-15		A6
1967	" "	32	E½SE	1856-01-15		A6
1972	" "	28	E½SE	1856-06-16		A6 G71
1968	" "	36	E½SE	1857-04-10		A6
1961	" "	25	SE	1857-06-01		A5
1835	CUMMINGS, Elizabeth	10	SWNE	1855-01-01		A6 G6
1928	DEPEW, Jeremiah	27	NWSW	1855-03-01		A6 C
1929	" "	27	SWNW	1855-03-01		A6 C R1901
1911	DOUGLASS, Anne E	24	E½NW	1856-01-15		A6 G150
1912	" "	24	W½NE	1856-01-15		A6 G150
1884	DOWNEY, Hugh D	26	SWNE	1854-08-01		A6 G98
1885	" "	26	W½SE	1854-08-01		A6 G100

ID	Individual in Patent	Sec.	Sec. Part	Date Issued	Other Counties	For More Info . . .
1871	DOWNEY, Hugh D (Cont'd)	15	E½SE	1855-01-01		A6
1881	" "	23	SWNW	1855-01-01		A6 G108
1874	" "	24	E½NE	1855-01-01		A6
1875	" "	28	NWSW	1855-01-01		A6
1879	" "	5	SWSE	1855-03-01		A4
1883	" "	6	NWNW	1855-05-01		A6 G107
1880	" "	8	W½NW	1855-05-10		A1
1872	" "	19	E½SW	1855-12-15		A1 F
1873	" "	19	N½SE	1855-12-15		A1
1876	" "	30	NENW	1855-12-15		A1
1877	" "	31	NWSW	1855-12-15		A1 F
1878	" "	31	SESE	1855-12-15		A1
1882	" "	8	SENW	1856-01-15		A6 G101
1926	EASLEY, James S	21	NWNE	1855-05-01		A6
1852	EASTER,	11	W½SW	1854-02-01		A6 G221
1885	EVANS, Mary	26	W½SE	1854-08-01		A6 G100
1882	FISHER, Hannah L	8	SENW	1856-01-15		A6 G101
1904	FORD, James	32	SESW	1855-12-15		A1
1905	" "	32	SWSE	1855-12-15		A1
1906	" "	35	W½SE	1855-12-15		A1
1817	FOX, Charles	25	E½NW	1855-05-10		A1
1818	" "	25	W½NE	1855-05-10		A1
1844	FRAIZER, Elijah	31	SENW	1855-12-15		A1 C F R1845
1846	" "	31	SESW	1855-12-15		A1 C F R2085
1843	" "	31	NESW	1921-07-08		A1
1845	" "	31	SENW	1921-07-08		A1 R1844
2091	FRAZIER, William	28	W½SE	1855-12-15		A1
1797	FRENCH, Abram S	12	SW	1855-05-01		A1
2076	GATES, Simon S	11	E½SE	1855-05-01		A1
2077	" "	12	W½NW	1855-05-01		A1
2078	" "	2	S½SE	1855-05-01		A1
2082	GATES, Summer E	7	SWNE	1855-12-15		A1
1805	GILLETT, Augustus F	7	SESE	1855-05-10		A1
1806	" "	7	SWSE	1855-05-10		A1
1980	GORMAY, John	8	NWNE	1855-05-10		A1
1913	GOWER, James H	21	E½SW	1856-01-15		A6 G152
1908	" "	21	W½SW	1856-01-15		A6
1911	" "	24	E½NW	1856-01-15		A6 G150
1912	" "	24	W½NE	1856-01-15		A6 G150
1910	" "	31	E½NE	1857-02-20		A5
1907	" "	12	NWNE	1857-03-10		A1
1909	" "	25	NENE	1857-03-10		A1
1974	GRIDLEY, Millicent	19	NENE	1855-05-01		A6 G69
2024	GRINNELL, Josiah B	17	S½SW	1857-03-10		A1
2031	HAIFLEY, Levi	13	E½NW	1855-05-01		A1
1972	HAVELY, Elizabeth	28	E½SE	1856-06-16		A6 G71
1914	HAYES, James	8	E½NE	1855-05-10		A1
1915	" "	8	SWNE	1855-05-10		A1
1801	HIATT, Amos	36	SESW	1855-05-01		A1
1802	" "	36	SWSE	1855-05-01		A1
2010	HIATT, Joseph	12	NENE	1854-05-01		A1
2011	" "	17	SESE	1854-05-01		A1
2012	" "	35	NE	1854-05-01		A1
1976	HIGGINSON, John C	14	NE	1855-05-10		A1
1930	HOLLENBECK, Jerome W	2	NESW	1855-03-01		A4
1931	" "	2	NWSW	1855-03-01		A4
1939	" "	2	SENW	1855-03-01		A4 G175 F
1932	" "	2	SESW	1855-03-01		A4
1934	" "	2	SWSW	1855-03-01		A4
1940	" "	3	NESE	1855-03-01		A4 G176
1937	" "	3	NWSE	1855-03-01		A4 G174
1936	" "	3	SESE	1855-03-01		A4
1938	" "	3	SWSE	1855-03-01		A4 G173
1933	" "	2	SWNW	1855-05-01		A1 F
1935	" "	3	S½NE	1855-05-01		A1 F
1989	HOLLIDAY, John	36	NWSE	1857-03-10		A1
1990	" "	36	SENE	1857-03-10		A1
1831	HUDSON, Dudley D	22	E½SW	1855-12-15		A1
1832	" "	35	NESE	1855-12-15		A1
1847	HUNTINGTON, Frederick D	18	E½SW	1855-05-10		A1 F
1848	" "	18	NESE	1855-05-10		A1
1849	" "	18	SENW	1855-05-10		A1 F
1850	" "	18	W½SE	1855-05-10		A1

ID	Individual in Patent	Sec.	Sec. Part	Date Issued	Other Counties	For More Info . . .
2090	HURDEN, William E	6	NE	1854-12-01		A1 F
2081	IOWA, State Of	16		1937-08-26		A3
1938	JACKSON, Elizabeth	3	SWSE	1855-03-01		A4 G173
1947	JACOB, John A	12	SE	1855-05-01		A1
1948	" "	13	NE	1855-05-01		A1
2013	JAMES, Joseph	15	S½NE	1855-12-15		A1
2014	" "	15	S½NW	1855-12-15		A1
2015	" "	15	W½SW	1855-12-15		A1
2016	" "	20	N½SW	1855-12-15		A1
2017	" "	20	SE	1855-12-15		A1
2018	" "	21	SE	1855-12-15		A1
1927	JENKINS, James S	5	SENE	1854-05-01		A1 F
1941	KENWORTHY, Jesse	30	SWSW	1855-12-15		A1 F
1942	" "	31	NENW	1855-12-15		A1 F
1944	" "	32	S½NE	1855-12-15		A1
1943	" "	31	W½NW	1856-05-01		A1 F
1945	KENWORTHY, Jesse W	30	NWNW	1855-12-15		A1 F
1886	KING, Hugh F	5	SESE	1855-02-01		A6
1887	" "	7	NESE	1855-03-01		A4
1917	KNOX, James	10	SWSW	1855-05-01		A6 C R1956
1918	" "	9	NENE	1855-05-01		A6
1916	" "	10	NWSW	1857-02-17		A6
1867	LAWRENCE, Henry	6	E½SE	1856-09-01		A1
1868	" "	7	E½NE	1856-09-01		A1
2033	LEONARD, Lot B	9	N½SW	1854-12-01		A1
2034	" "	9	NWNW	1854-12-01		A1
2035	" "	9	S½NW	1854-12-01		A1
2096	LILLEY, William W	27	NWSE	1856-01-15		A6 C R2067
2097	" "	27	SWSE	1856-01-15		A6 C R2068
2036	MACKEY, Luddy	25	SENE	1855-12-15		A1
1994	MARSON, John	4	N½NE	1855-05-10		A1 F
2064	MARTIN, Peter	9	SESE	1855-05-10		A1
2065	" "	9	SWSE	1855-05-10		A1
1985	MCCLEIF, Catharine	11	E½SW	1855-01-01		A6 G204
1985	MCCLELLAN, John H	11	E½SW	1855-01-01		A6 G204
1988	" "	11	SENW	1855-03-01		A4 G205
1986	" "	17	E½NE	1855-05-01		A6 G203 C R1987
1981	" "	21	E½NE	1855-05-01		A6 C R1982
1983	" "	22	W½NW	1855-05-01		A6 C R1984
1987	" "	17	E½NE	1860-02-07		A6 G203 R1986
1982	" "	21	E½NE	1860-02-07		A6 R1981
1984	" "	22	W½NW	1860-02-07		A6 R1983
2062	MCCORMICK, Obediah J	28	S½NE	1856-09-01		A1
1919	MCLAIN, James	26	S½SW	1855-05-01		A1
1920	" "	33	N½	1855-05-01		A1
1921	" "	34		1855-05-01		A1
1922	" "	35	W½	1855-05-01		A1
2093	MCNABB, William	23	SESE	1854-12-01		A1
1898	MENARY, Betsy	4	NESW	1854-07-01		A6 G28
1899	" "	4	NWSE	1854-07-01		A6 G28
2094	MERRITT, William	21	SWNE	1855-05-01		A1
1803	MILLER, Andrew B	9	NESE	1857-03-10		A1
1804	" "	9	SENE	1857-03-10		A1
2004	MILLER, Joseph H	30	E½SW	1855-05-10		A1 F
2006	" "	30	NWSW	1855-05-10		A1 F
2007	" "	30	SENW	1855-05-10		A1 F
2008	" "	30	SWNE	1855-05-10		A1
2009	" "	30	SWNW	1855-05-10		A1 F
2005	" "	30	NWSE	1856-05-01		A1
2071	MILLS, Robert	18	W½NE	1855-01-01		A6
1866	MONSON, Henry L	8	SE	1855-01-01		A6
1923	MURRAY, James	11	NE	1855-05-01		A1
1924	" "	3	E½SW	1855-05-01		A1
1925	" "	3	N½NE	1855-12-15		A1 F
1995	MYERS, John	4	SESW	1855-05-01		A1
1996	" "	4	SWSE	1855-05-01		A1
1997	" "	9	NWNE	1855-05-01		A1
2054	NEAL, Milly	30	NESE	1854-10-02		A6 G232
1836	NEWMAN, Edmund B	6	E½NW	1854-12-01		A1 F
1869	NOBLE, Henry T	10	N½NE	1855-05-01		A1
1870	" "	11	N½NW	1855-05-01		A1
2000	ORR, John	22	NESE	1852-03-10		A1
1820	OSBORN, Cornelius Q	17	E½NW	1855-12-15		A1

ID	Individual in Patent	Sec.	Sec. Part	Date Issued	Other Counties	For More Info . . .
1821	OSBORN, Cornelius Q (Cont'd)	17	NWNE	1855-12-15		A1
1822	" "	17	NWNW	1855-12-15		A1
1883	PARCEL, Jane	6	NWNW	1855-05-01		A6 G107
2055	PARKS, Nancy	30	S½SE	1855-01-01		A6 G233
2095	PARKS, William	27	W½SW	1855-12-15		A1
1971	PAUL, Elizabeth D	19	W½NW	1856-01-15		A6 G75 F
2066	PEARCE, Peter S	5	NWNE	1854-05-01		A1 F
1937	PERCY, Content	3	NWSE	1855-03-01		A4 G174
2022	PERRY, Joshua	2	N½NW	1855-05-10		A1 F
1852	PHELPS, Frederick	11	W½SW	1854-02-01		A6 G221
1851	" "	10	E½SE	1854-03-01		A6
1853	" "	10	SENE	1854-03-01		A6 G220
1854	" "	11	SWNW	1854-03-01		A6 G220
2038	PINNEY, Marcellus	28	S½SW	1855-05-01		A6
2037	" "	20	S½SW	1857-02-16		A5
2039	" "	29	NENW	1857-02-16		A5
1824	PROSSER, Daniel D	5	NENE	1852-03-10		A1 F
1823	" "	4	SWNW	1853-07-13		A6 F
1825	" "	5	SWNE	1853-07-13		A6 F
1891	PURDY, Jacob R	9	SWNE	1855-12-15		A1
1973	QUIGGINS, Eliza	29	NE	1856-01-15		A6 G76
1973	QUIGGINS, Mary	29	NE	1856-01-15		A6 G76
1973	QUIGGINS, Nancy	29	NE	1856-01-15		A6 G76
1913	RAMAY, Elizabeth	21	E½SW	1856-01-15		A6 G152
2054	RENO, Morgan	30	NESE	1854-10-02		A6 G232
2044	" "	18	NENW	1855-01-01		A6 F
2055	" "	30	S½SE	1855-01-01		A6 G233
2048	" "	31	W½NE	1855-01-01		A6
2049	" "	31	W½SE	1855-01-01		A6
2050	" "	36	NWNW	1855-01-01		A6
2052	" "	7	SESW	1855-01-01		A6 C F R2053
2051	" "	6	SWSW	1855-05-01		A6 F
2045	" "	23	NESE	1855-12-15		A1
2047	" "	26	NESW	1855-12-15		A1
2046	" "	25	NESW	1857-03-10		A1
2053	" "	7	SESW	1861-04-01		A1 R2052
1833	RICE, Amanda	10	E½SW	1855-03-01		A4 G7
1834	" "	10	W½SE	1855-03-01		A4 G7
1881	RICHARDSON, Bridges	23	SWNW	1855-01-01		A6 G108
1903	ROBBERTS, James F	9	NENW	1852-03-10		A1
1841	ROBBINS, Eli	20	NWNE	1855-12-15		A1
2023	ROBBINS, Joshua	13	W½NW	1855-05-10		A1
1842	ROBINS, Eli	22	W½SW	1855-12-15		A1
2063	RUSSELL, Owen	25	NWNW	1855-05-10		A1
1998	SARGENT, John O	2	N½SE	1855-03-01		A4
1999	" "	2	S½NE	1855-03-01		A4
2057	SARGENT, Nancy Ann	14	SE	1855-05-10		A1
2084	SHIPLEY, Thomas J	27	E½SE	1857-03-10		A1
2026	SKEELS, Leander W	36	NENE	1857-03-10		A1
2067	SMITH, Peter	27	NWSE	1857-05-07		A6 R2096
2068	" "	27	SWSE	1857-05-07		A6 R2097
2072	SPERRY, Samuel Harrison	19	SENW	1856-10-10		A2 F
1829	ST JOHN, DUBOIS	15	N½NE	1855-05-10		A1
1830	"	15	N½NW	1855-05-10		A1
2075	STALLINGS, Silas	28	NESW	1855-12-15		A1
1840	STEVENS, Edwin M	12	S½NE	1855-05-01		A1
2069	SYLVESTER, Richard H	31	SWSW	1855-05-01		A1 F
1939	TARR, Lettice	2	SENW	1855-03-01		A4 G175 F
1975	TAYLOR, Sally	19	SWNE	1855-05-01		A6 G82
2088	TERRY, William D	18	W½NW	1857-02-20		A5 F
2089	" "	7	SWSW	1857-02-20		A5 F
1888	THOMPSON, Israel	19	NWSW	1855-12-15		A1 F
2085	TURNER, Walter	31	SESW	1852-03-10		A1 F R1846
1978	TUTTLE, John F	23	SWSW	1855-12-15		A1
1979	" "	27	N½NW	1855-12-15		A1
1807	VESTAL, Bartholomew	20	S½NE	1853-11-01		A1
1808	" "	25	NWSW	1853-11-01		A1
1809	" "	25	SWSW	1854-05-01		A1
2079	WATSON, Solomon	35	SESE	1855-05-01		A1
2080	" "	36	SWSW	1855-05-01		A1
1819	WHEELER, Charles	9	SWSW	1857-03-10		A1
1863	WILCOX, George W	9	NWSE	1855-12-15		A1
1940	WILDER, Prudence	3	NESE	1855-03-01		A4 G176

ID	Individual in Patent	Sec.	Sec. Part	Date Issued	Other Counties	For More Info . . .
2003	WILLIAMS, John	18	W½SW	1855-12-15		A1 F
2098	WILLINGHAM, William W	27	NENE	1854-08-01		A6
1946	WILLIS, Joel	19	SWSW	1855-12-15		A1 F
1988	WILSON, Maria	11	SENW	1855-03-01		A4 G205

Patent Map

T79-N R16-W
5th PM Meridian

Map Group 9

Township Statistics

Parcels Mapped	:	307
Number of Patents	:	254
Number of Individuals	:	157
Patentees Identified	:	154
Number of Surnames	:	141
Multi-Patentee Parcels	:	33
Oldest Patent Date	:	4/10/1850
Most Recent Patent	:	8/26/1937
Block/Lot Parcels	:	0
Parcels Re - Issued	:	10
Parcels that Overlap	:	0
Cities and Towns	:	1
Cemeteries	:	4

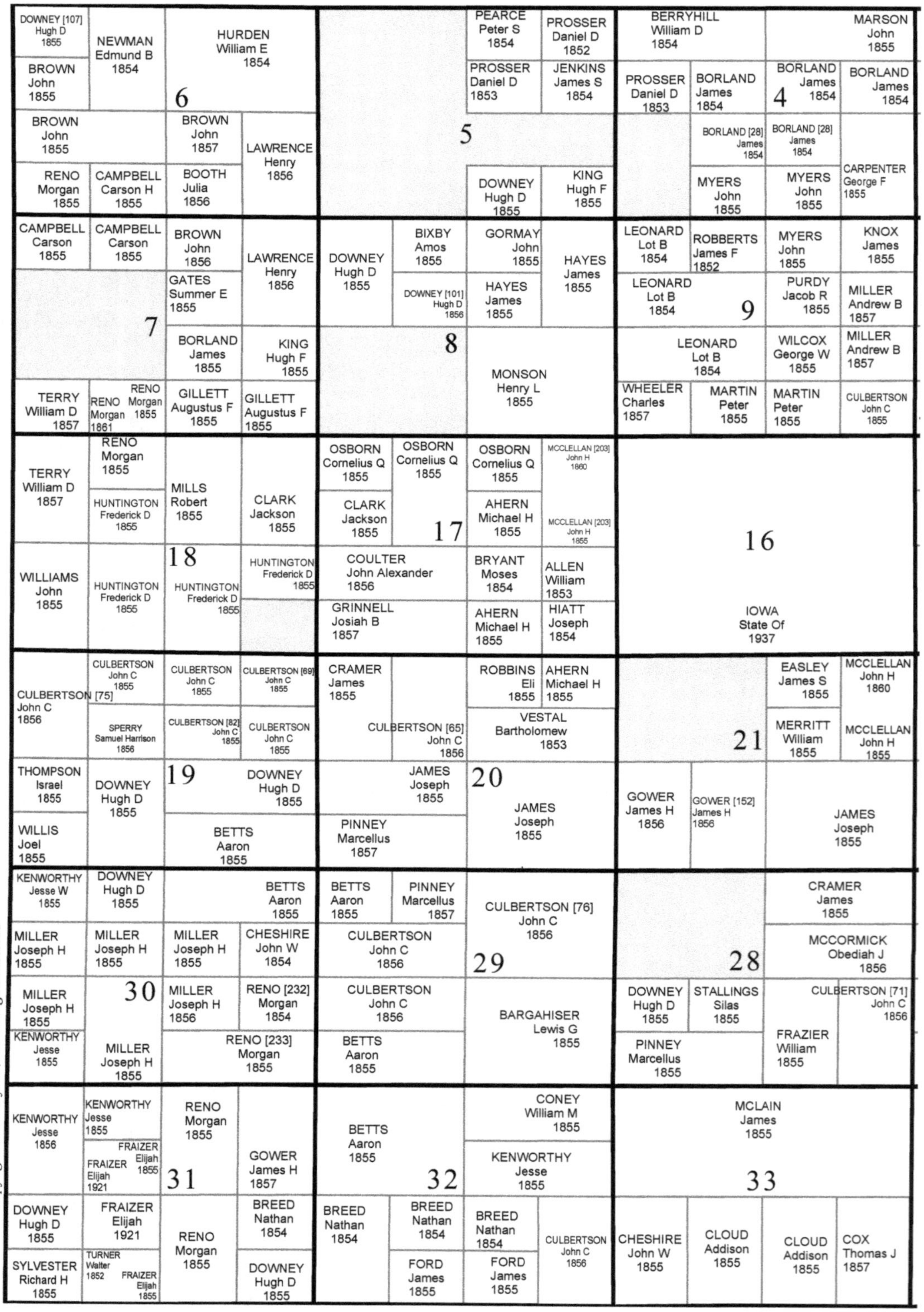

	BENT George 1856	MURRAY James 1855		PERRY Joshua 1855	BERRYHILL [19] James B 1857	
BORLAND James 1854	**3**	HOLLENBECK Jerome W 1855			SARGENT John O 1855	

3 | **2** | **1**

Section 3 / 2 / 1

BENT George 1856	MURRAY James 1855		PERRY Joshua 1855	BERRYHILL [19] James B 1857		
BORLAND James 1854 **3**	HOLLENBECK Jerome W 1855	HOLLENBECK Jerome W 1855	HOLLENBECK [175] Jerome W 1855	SARGENT John O 1855		
CARPENTER George F 1855	MURRAY James 1855	HOLLENBECK [174] Jerome W 1855	HOLLENBECK [176] Jerome W 1855	HOLLENBECK Jerome W 1855	HOLLENBECK Jerome W 1855 **2**	SARGENT John O 1855	**1** BILL Harvey A 1855
		HOLLENBECK [173] Jerome W 1855	HOLLENBECK Jerome W 1855	HOLLENBECK Jerome W 1855	HOLLENBECK Jerome W 1855	GATES Simon S 1855	

Section 10 / 11 / 12

CARPENTER George F 1855	NOBLE Henry T 1855		NOBLE Henry T 1855		MURRAY James 1855	GATES Simon S 1855	BILL Harvey A 1855	GOWER James H 1857 / HIATT Joseph 1854
10	BEADLESTON [6] Ebenezer 1855	PHELPS [220] Frederick 1854	PHELPS [220] Frederick 1854	MCCLELLAN [205] John H 1855				STEVENS Edwin M 1855
KNOX James 1857	BEADLESTON [7] Ebenezer 1855	**11**		CONNER John 1854		**12**		
CULBERTSON John C 1855 / KNOX James 1855	BEADLESTON [7] Ebenezer 1855	PHELPS Frederick 1854	PHELPS [221] Frederick 1854	MCCLELLAN [204] John H 1855	GATES Simon S 1855	FRENCH Abram S 1855	JACOB John A 1855

Section 15 / 14 / 13

JOHN Dubois St 1855	JOHN Dubois St 1855	BEELERS George M 1855	CULBERTSON John C 1855			ROBBINS Joshua 1855	HAIFLEY Levi 1855	JACOB John A 1855
JAMES Joseph 1855 **15**	JAMES Joseph 1855	BEELER George M 1854	BEELERS George M 1855	HIGGINSON John C 1855			
BLISH Charles C 1855	DOWNEY Hugh D 1855	CARPENTER Levi 1852	**14**			**13**	
JAMES Joseph 1855	BLISH Charles C 1855	BEELER George M 1850	SARGENT Nancy Ann 1855	BOND John 1855		

Section 22 / 23 / 24

MCCLELLAN John H 1855			CONNELLY Edward 1855		CARLETON Charles C 1855	GOWER [150] James H 1856	GOWER [150] James H 1856	DOWNEY Hugh D 1855
MCCLELLAN John H 1860 **22**	DOWNEY [108] Hugh D 1855	CARPENTER Levi 1855	**23**			**24**		
ROBINS Eli 1855	HUDSON Dudley D 1855	ORR John 1852	BLACK Dominick 1855	CARPENTER Levi 1855	CARPENTER Robert 1854	RENO Morgan 1855	BLACK Dominick 1855	
	AHERN Michael H 1855	BLACK Dominick 1855	TUTTLE John F 1855		ALLEN Charles 1854	MCNABB William 1854		

Section 27 / 26 / 25

TUTTLE John F 1855	COLYER John L 1855	WILLINGHAM William W 1854				RUSSELL Owen 1855	FOX Charles 1855	GOWER James H 1857
DEPEW Jeremiah 1855 / CRAMER James 1855	COLYER John L 1855 **27**	CULBERTSON John C 1856	CARPENTER Levi 1852	CULBERTSON John C 1855	DOWNEY [98] Hugh D 1855	ALLEN John 1855	CONNELLY Edward 1855	FOX Charles 1855	MACKEY Luddy 1855
DEPEW Jeremiah 1855	SMITH Peter 1857 / LILLEY William W 1856	SHIPLEY Thomas J 1857	CULBERTSON John C 1855	RENO Morgan 1855 **26**	DOWNEY [100] Hugh D 1854	CONNELLY Edward 1855	VESTAL Bartholomew 1853	RENO Morgan 1857	CULBERTSON John C 1857 **25**
PARKS William 1855	COLYER John L 1855	SMITH Peter 1857 / LILLEY William W 1856		MCLAIN James 1855			VESTAL Bartholomew 1854	CRISPIN Joshua 1855	

Section 34 / 35 / 36

34			HIATT Joseph 1854		RENO Morgan 1855	CRISPIN Joshua 1855	SKEELS Leander W 1857
		MCLAIN James 1855 **35**		ALLEN Sherwood 1854	CRISPIN Joshua 1855	HOLLIDAY John 1857	
MCLAIN James 1855		FORD James 1855	HUDSON Dudley D 1855	ALLEN Sherwood 1854 **36**	HOLLIDAY John 1857	
			WATSON Solomon 1855	WATSON Solomon 1855	HIATT Amos 1855	HIATT Amos 1855	CULBERTSON John C 1857

Copyright 2010 Boyd IT, Inc. All Rights Reserved

Helpful Hints

1. This Map's INDEX can be found on the preceding pages.

2. Refer to Map "C" to see where this Township lies within Poweshiek County, Iowa.

3. Numbers within square brackets [ ] denote a multi-patentee land parcel (multi-owner). Refer to Appendix "C" for a full list of members in this group.

4. Areas that look to be crowded with Patentees usually indicate multiple sales of the same parcel (Re-issues) or Overlapping parcels. See this Township's Index for an explanation of these and other circumstances that might explain "odd" groupings of Patentees on this map.

Legend

———— Patent Boundary

━━━━ Section Boundary

No Patents Found (or Outside County)

1., 2., 3., ... Lot Numbers (when beside a name)

[ ] Group Number (see Appendix "C")

Scale: Section = 1 mile X 1 mile (generally, with some exceptions)

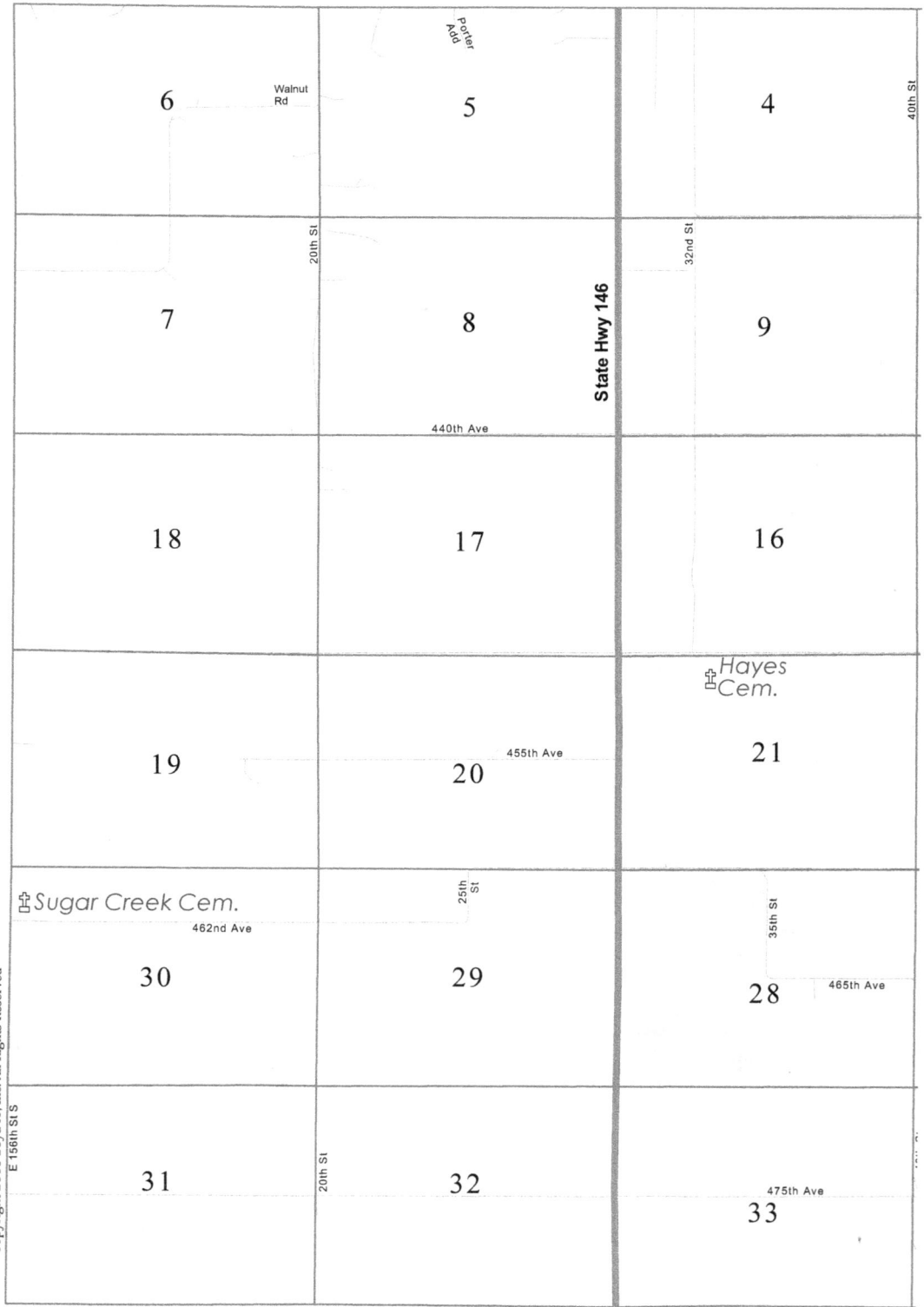

Road Map

T79-N R16-W
5th PM Meridian

Map Group 9

Cities & Towns
Jacobs

Cemeteries
Hayes Cemetery
Lower Blue Point Cemetery
Sugar Creek Cemetery
Upper Blue Point Cemetery

6 Walnut Rd	5 Porter Add	4 40th St
7 20th St	8 440th Ave	9 32nd St / State Hwy 146
18	17	16
19	20 455th Ave	21 Hayes Cem.
30 Sugar Creek Cem. 462nd Ave	29 25th St	28 35th St 465th Ave
31 E 156th St S	32 20th St	33 475th Ave

3	2	1

50th St

430th Ave

10	11	12

60th St

47th St

● Jacobs

15	14	13

450th Ave

Upper Blue ✝
Point Cem.

22	23	24

S 5th St

Lower Blue
Point Cem.
✝

460th Ave

462nd Ave

50th St

27	26	25

472nd
Ave

40th St

60th St

34	35	36

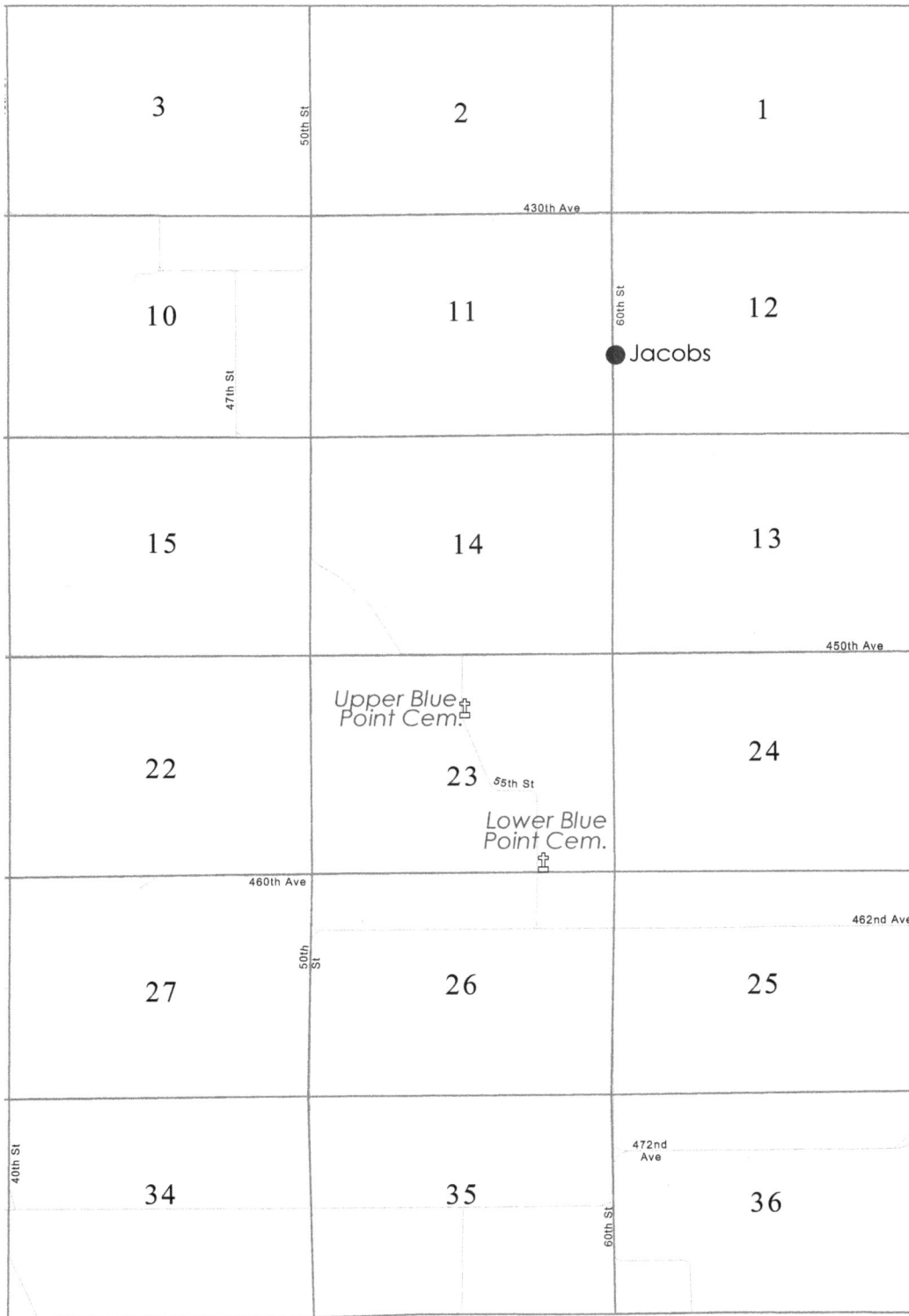

Helpful Hints

1. This road map has a number of uses, but primarily it is to help you: a) find the present location of land owned by your ancestors (at least the general area), b) find cemeteries and city-centers, and c) estimate the route/roads used by Census-takers & tax-assessors.

2. If you plan to travel to Poweshiek County to locate cemeteries or land parcels, please pick up a modern travel map for the area before you do. Mapping old land parcels on modern maps is not as exact a science as you might think. Just the slightest variations in public land survey coordinates, estimates of parcel boundaries, or road-map deviations can greatly alter a map's representation of how a road either does or doesn't cross a particular parcel of land.

Legend

———————	Section Lines
≡≡≡≡≡≡≡	Interstates
━━━━━━━	Highways
———————	Other Roads
●	Cities/Towns
✝	Cemeteries

Scale: Section = 1 mile X 1 mile
(generally, with some exceptions)

Historical Map

T79-N R16-W
5th PM Meridian

Map Group 9

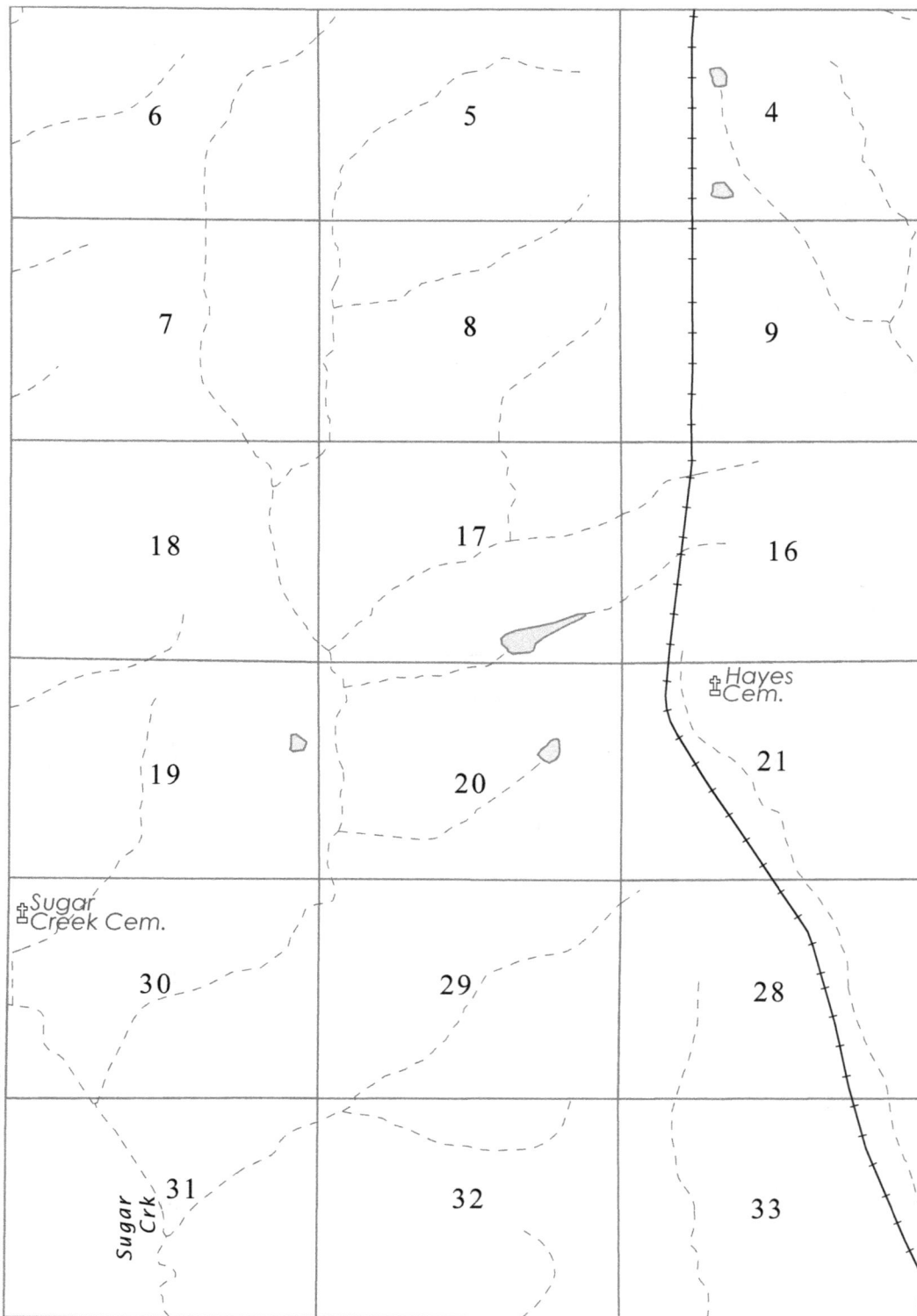

Cities & Towns
Jacobs

Cemeteries
Hayes Cemetery
Lower Blue Point Cemetery
Sugar Creek Cemetery
Upper Blue Point Cemetery

6	5	4
7	8	9
18	17	16
19	20	21
30	29	28
31	32	33

Hayes Cem.
Sugar Creek Cem.
Sugar Crk

3

2

N English
Riv

1

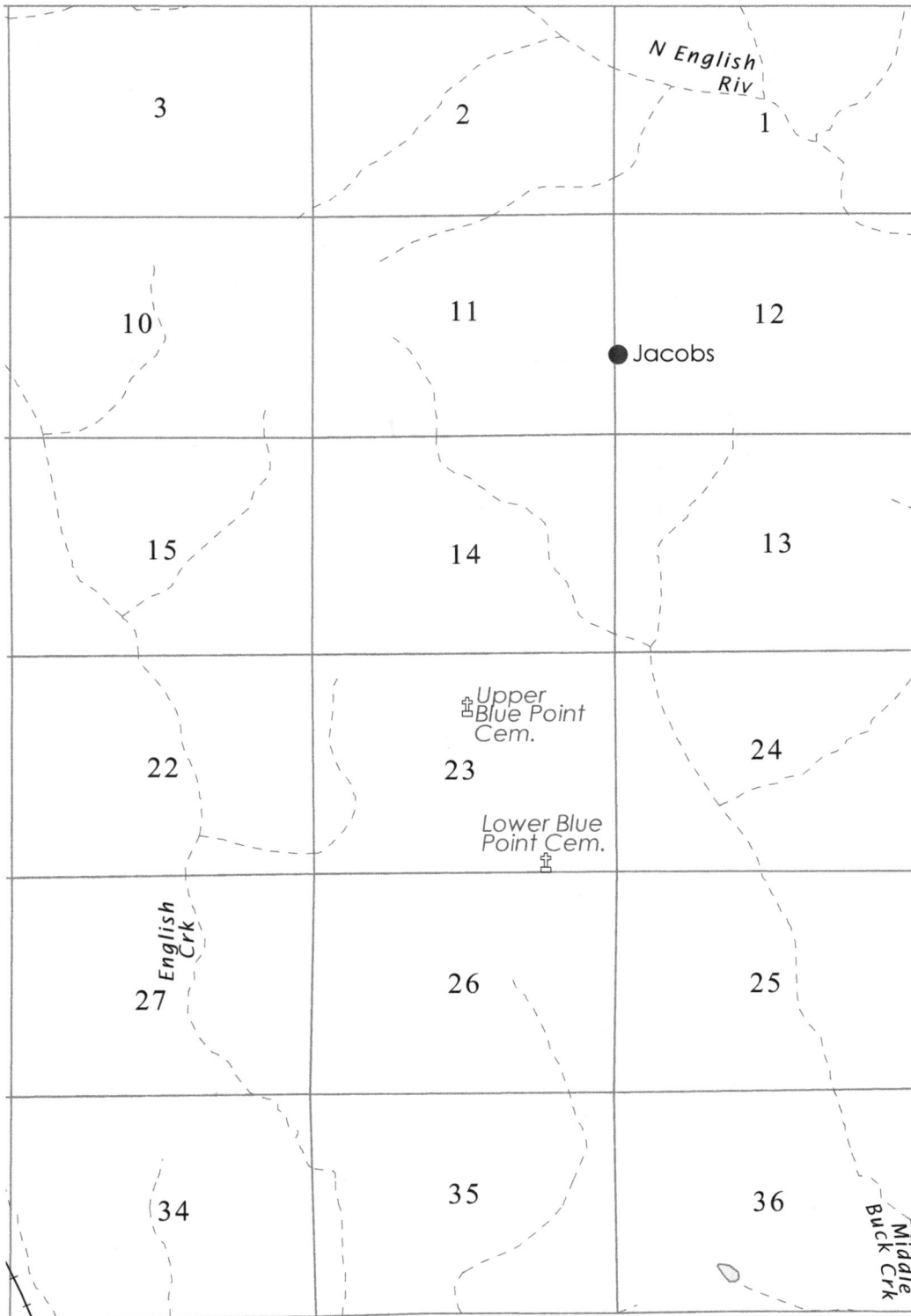

Helpful Hints

1. This Map takes a different look at the same Congressional Township displayed in the preceding two maps. It presents features that can help you better envision the historical development of the area: a) Water-bodies (lakes & ponds), b) Water-courses (rivers, streams, etc.), c) Railroads, d) City/ town center-points (where they were oftentimes located when first settled), and e) Cemeteries.

2. Using this "Historical" map in tandem with this Township's Patent Map and Road Map, may lead you to some interesting discoveries. You will often find roads, towns, cemeteries, and waterways are named after nearby landowners: sometimes those names will be the ones you are researching. See how many of these research gems you can find here in Poweshiek County.

10

11

12

● Jacobs

15

14

13

22

Upper
Blue Point
Cem.

23

Lower Blue
Point Cem.

24

27

English
Crk

26

25

34

35

36

Middle
Buck Crk

Legend

————————	Section Lines
++++++++	Railroads
▓▓▓▓▓▓	Large Rivers & Bodies of Water
- - - - - - - -	Streams/Creeks & Small Rivers
●	Cities/Towns
†	Cemeteries

Scale: Section = 1 mile X 1 mile
(there are some exceptions)

149

Map Group 10: Index to Land Patents

Township 79-North Range 15-West (5th PM)

After you locate an individual in this Index, take note of the Section and Section Part then proceed to the Land Patent map on the pages immediately following. You should have no difficulty locating the corresponding parcel of land.

The "For More Info" Column will lead you to more information about the underlying Patents. See the *Legend* at right, and the "How to Use this Book" chapter, for more information.

```
                        LEGEND
           "For More Info . . . " column
A = Authority (Legislative Act, See Appendix "A")
B = Block or Lot (location in Section unknown)
C = Cancelled Patent
F = Fractional Section
G = Group (Multi-Patentee Patent, see Appendix "C")
V = Overlaps another Parcel
R = Re-Issued (Parcel patented more than once)

(A & G items require you to look in the Appendixes referred
to above. All other Letter-designations followed by a number
require you to locate line-items in this index that possess
the ID number found after the letter).
```

ID	Individual in Patent	Sec.	Sec. Part	Date Issued	Other Counties	For More Info . . .
2104	ARCHER, Mary	11	SW	1855-03-01		A6 G166
2112	AUSTIN, Benjamin D	27	S½NW	1854-05-01		A1
2113	" "	27	W½NE	1854-05-01		A1
2218	BALDWIN, Roger S	11	SE	1855-05-10		A1
2219	" "	12	SW	1855-05-10		A1
2220	" "	7	E½SE	1855-05-10		A1
2221	" "	7	SESW	1855-05-10		A1 F
2222	" "	7	SWSE	1855-05-10		A1
2223	" "	8	SW	1855-05-10		A1
2120	BERRYHILL, Charles H	23	E½NE	1854-05-01		A1
2121	" "	23	E½SE	1854-05-01		A1
2122	" "	24	NESE	1854-10-02		A6
2123	" "	24	SENE	1854-10-02		A6
2118	" "	13	SWSW	1854-11-01		A4
2119	" "	14	SESE	1854-11-01		A4
2150	BERRYHILL, James B	31	NWSW	1855-12-15		A1 G19 F
2150	BERRYHILL, William D	31	NWSW	1855-12-15		A1 G19 F
2156	BOSLEY, James J	17	N½NE	1855-05-01		A1
2197	BOYD, John W	10	NENE	1855-01-01		A6
2199	" "	10	SWNE	1855-01-01		A6
2205	" "	10	NWNE	1855-04-04		A2 G32
2198	" "	10	SENE	1855-05-01		A1
2200	" "	19	E½SE	1855-05-01		A1
2201	" "	19	NE	1855-05-01		A1
2202	" "	30	E½NE	1855-05-01		A1
2203	" "	8	SE	1855-05-01		A1
2204	" "	9	N½	1855-05-01		A1
2151	BREWSTER, James	13	E½SW	1855-01-01		A6
2152	" "	13	NWSW	1855-01-01		A6
2153	" "	14	NESE	1855-01-01		A6
2100	BRYAN, Alanson	36	NESE	1854-05-01		A6 G38
2101	" "	36	SESE	1854-05-01		A6 G40
2149	BRYAN, Jane	14	W½NW	1855-01-01		A6 G45
2188	CALDWELL, John	11	NE	1855-01-01		A6 G44
2145	CAMPBELL, Jacob	14	E½NW	1855-01-01		A6
2148	" "	14	SWSW	1855-01-01		A6
2149	" "	14	W½NW	1855-01-01		A6 G45
2147	" "	14	SESW	1855-03-01		A4
2146	" "	14	N½SW	1855-05-01		A1
2189	CASSIDAY, John	26	E½NE	1854-08-01		A6
2190	" "	26	E½SE	1854-08-01		A6
2210	COCHRAN, Milton B	27	SESW	1855-05-01		A1
2107	CORBIN, Austin	2	N½NE	1855-01-01		A6 F
2108	" "	2	N½NW	1855-01-01		A6 F
2109	" "	2	S½NE	1855-01-01		A6 F
2111	" "	2	SENW	1855-01-01		A6 G58 F

ID	Individual in Patent	Sec.	Sec. Part	Date Issued	Other Counties	For More Info . . .
2110	CORBIN, Austin (Cont'd)	2	SWNW	1855-01-01		A6 F
2173	CULBERTSON, John C	33	E½SE	1855-12-15		A1
2174	" "	34	E½NW	1855-12-15		A1
2175	" "	34	NWSE	1855-12-15		A1
2176	" "	34	SW	1855-12-15		A1
2177	" "	9	S½SE	1855-12-15		A1
2178	" "	31	SWSE	1856-01-15		A6 G70
2171	" "	31	SWSW	1857-04-10		A6 F
2172	" "	31	W½NW	1857-04-10		A6 F
2170	" "	31	E½NW	1858-03-01		A4 F
2125	DALE, David	27	NWSE	1854-07-01		A6
2191	DALY, John	31	NE	1855-12-15		A1
2209	DALY, Michael	30	SE	1855-12-15		A1
2227	DEAN, William A	22	NW	1854-12-01		A1
2228	" "	23	SW	1854-12-01		A1
2229	" "	23	W½SE	1854-12-01		A1
2132	DOBYNS, Duly	18	NESE	1855-03-01		A6 G252 C F
2131	" "	18	NENW	1916-12-02		A6 G252
2100	EARLEY, Andasire	36	NESE	1854-05-01		A6 G38
2163	EASLEY, James S	13	N½NE	1855-03-01		A4
2164	" "	13	N½NW	1855-03-01		A4
2165	" "	14	N½NE	1855-05-01		A6
2166	" "	7	W½SW	1855-06-01		A6 F
2167	EASLY, James S	33	S½NE	1855-03-01		A4
2154	EASON, James	32	SENE	1855-05-01		A6
2155	" "	33	NW	1855-05-01		A1
2124	ELLIS, Chester	32	NENE	1855-05-01		A1
2193	ELLIS, John O	11	NW	1855-01-01		A6
2136	FOLSOM, Gilman	15	NE	1855-05-01		A1
2137	" "	2	S½SE	1855-05-10		A1
2135	" "	10	NESE	1856-09-01		A1
2231	FRAZIER, William	18	SENW	1855-06-01		A6 G138 F
2230	" "	7	NENW	1855-06-01		A6 F
2205	FREANER, William	10	NWNE	1855-04-04		A2 G32
2226	GINN, Jane H	18	N½SE	1855-03-01		A6 G291
2099	GROSS, Aaron	34	E½NE	1855-05-01		A1
2225	HARBINE, Thomas	29	W½	1855-05-01		A1
2178	HARRINGTON, Abigail	31	SWSE	1856-01-15		A6 G70
2102	HATFIELD, Amos F	15	SE	1855-01-01		A6
2104	" "	11	SW	1855-03-01		A6 G166
2103	" "	22	E½	1855-05-10		A1
2179	HIGGINSON, John C	10	NW	1855-01-01		A6
2180	" "	10	W½SW	1855-01-01		A6 R2181
2185	" "	9	N½SE	1855-01-01		A6 R2186
2187	" "	9	SW	1855-01-01		A6
2182	" "	18	SW	1855-05-10		A1 F
2183	" "	18	W½NW	1855-05-10		A1 F
2184	" "	6	W½	1855-05-10		A1 F
2181	" "	10	W½SW	1861-08-15		A5 R2180
2186	" "	9	N½SE	1861-08-15		A5 R2185
2157	HURLEY, James J	32	W½	1855-05-01		A1
2105	HUTCHINS, Asa B	33	N½NE	1855-05-01		A1
2106	" "	34	W½NE	1855-05-01		A1
2224	IOWA, State Of	16		1937-08-26		A3
2168	JACOB, John A	7	NWSE	1855-05-01		A1
2159	JOHNSON, James	23	NW	1854-12-01		A1
2160	" "	23	W½NE	1854-12-01		A1
2158	" "	19	W½SW	1855-05-01		A1 F
2161	" "	30	SW	1855-05-01		A1 F
2162	" "	30	W½NW	1855-05-01		A1 F
2231	JOHNSTON, Margaret	18	SENW	1855-06-01		A6 G138 F
2169	KILLIN, John A	27	NESE	1855-05-01		A1
2114	MALONE, Benjamin	19	E½SW	1854-05-01		A1 F
2115	" "	19	W½SE	1854-05-01		A1
2116	" "	30	E½NW	1854-05-01		A1 F
2117	" "	30	W½NE	1854-05-01		A1 F
2192	MARTIN, John F	12	NW	1855-12-15		A1
2212	MCCORKLE, Milton E	19	E½NW	1855-01-01		A6 G206 F
2211	" "	19	W½NW	1855-05-01		A1 F
2126	MCCUNE, David	29	NE	1855-05-01		A1
2128	MCCURTAIN, Judy	18	S½SE	1856-01-15		A6 G279
2233	MERRITT, William	17	NW	1855-05-01		A1
2234	" "	17	S½NE	1855-05-01		A1

ID	Individual in Patent	Sec.	Sec. Part	Date Issued	Other Counties	For More Info . . .
2235	MERRITT, William (Cont'd)	17	SE	1855-05-01		A1
2101	MITCHELL, Elizabeth	36	SESE	1854-05-01		A6 G40
2212	PROPST, Nancy	19	E½NW	1855-01-01		A6 G206 F
2213	RENO, Morgan	27	NENE	1855-01-01		A6
2214	" "	27	SENE	1855-01-01		A6
2215	" "	31	SESE	1855-05-01		A1
2196	ROBERTS, John	29	SE	1858-01-07		A1
2216	RODGERS, Richard	14	S½NE	1855-01-01		A6
2217	" "	14	W½SE	1855-01-01		A6
2188	SANDERS, William	11	NE	1855-01-01		A6 G44
2129	SKINNER, Franklin	18	E½NE	1855-01-01		A6
2130	" "	18	W½NE	1855-01-01		A6
2132	" "	18	NESW	1855-03-01		A6 G252 C F
2131	" "	18	NENW	1916-12-02		A6 G252
2142	SKINNER, Hannah	17	SW	1855-05-01		A1
2206	SMITH, Josiah F	10	E½SW	1855-05-01		A1
2207	" "	10	NWSE	1855-05-01		A1
2208	" "	8	N½	1855-05-01		A1
2140	SUTTON, Hanibal	27	SESE	1854-07-01		A6
2141	" "	27	SWSE	1858-02-15		A6
2143	SUTTON, Hannibal	29	SWSE	1853-01-01		A6 C
2232	TIBBALS, William J	27	N½NW	1855-05-10		A1
2144	TICE, Henry K	7	NE	1855-05-01		A1
2139	TRACY, Guy	12	SE	1854-12-01		A1
2138	" "	12	NE	1855-12-15		A1
2236	WEST, William	34	W½NW	1855-12-15		A1
2127	WHITCOMB, Edwin F	36	NE	1854-05-01		A1
2128	WHITE, Elias A	18	S½SE	1856-01-15		A6 G279
2194	WILDS, John Q	32	W½NE	1855-05-01		A1
2195	" "	33	W½SE	1855-05-01		A1
2133	WILSON, George N	34	SWSE	1855-05-10		A1
2134	" "	35	N½NE	1857-03-10		A1
2226	WISDEN, Thomas W	18	N½SE	1855-03-01		A6 G291
2111	WYATT, Sally	2	SENW	1855-01-01		A6 G58 F

Patent Map

T79-N R15-W
5th PM Meridian

Map Group 10

Township Statistics

Parcels Mapped	:	138
Number of Patents	:	114
Number of Individuals	:	71
Patentees Identified	:	66
Number of Surnames	:	64
Multi-Patentee Parcels	:	15
Oldest Patent Date	:	1/1/1853
Most Recent Patent	:	8/26/1937
Block/Lot Parcels	:	0
Parcels Re - Issued	:	2
Parcels that Overlap	:	0
Cities and Towns	:	1
Cemeteries	:	1

6
HIGGINSON
John C
1855

5

4

7
FRAZIER
William
1855

TICE
Henry K
1855

EASLEY
James S
1855

JACOB
John A
1855

BALDWIN
Roger S
1855

BALDWIN
Roger S
1855

BALDWIN
Roger S
1855

8
SMITH
Josiah F
1855

BOYD
John W
1855

BALDWIN
Roger S
1855

9
BOYD
John W
1855

HIGGINSON
John C
1855

HIGGINSON
John C
1855

HIGGINSON
John C
1861

CULBERTSON
John C
1855

18
HIGGINSON
John C
1855

SKINNER [252]
Franklin
1916

FRAZIER [138]
William
1855

SKINNER [252]
Franklin
1855

HIGGINSON
John C
1855

SKINNER
Franklin
1855

WISDEN [291]
Thomas W
1855

WHITE [279]
Elias A
1856

SKINNER
Franklin
1855

17
MERRITT
William
1855

SKINNER
Hannah
1855

BOSLEY
James J
1855

MERRITT
William
1855

MERRITT
William
1855

16

IOWA
State Of
1937

19
MCCORKLE
Milton E
1855

MCCORKLE [206]
Milton E
1855

BOYD
John W
1855

JOHNSON
James
1855

MALONE
Benjamin
1854

MALONE
Benjamin
1854

BOYD
John W
1855

20

21

30
JOHNSON
James
1855

MALONE
Benjamin
1854

MALONE
Benjamin
1854

BOYD
John W
1855

JOHNSON
James
1855

DALY
Michael
1855

29
HARBINE
Thomas
1855

MCCUNE
David
1855

ROBERTS
John
1858

SUTTON
Hannibal
1853

28

31
CULBERTSON
John C
1857

CULBERTSON
John C
1858

DALY
John
1855

BERRYHILL [19]
James B
1855

CULBERTSON
John C
1857

CULBERTSON [70]
John C
1858

RENO
Morgan
1855

32
HURLEY
James J
1855

WILDS
John Q
1855

ELLIS
Chester
1855

EASON
James
1855

33
EASON
James
1855

HUTCHINS
Asa B
1855

EASLY
James S
1855

WILDS
John Q
1855

CULBERTSON
John C
1855

154

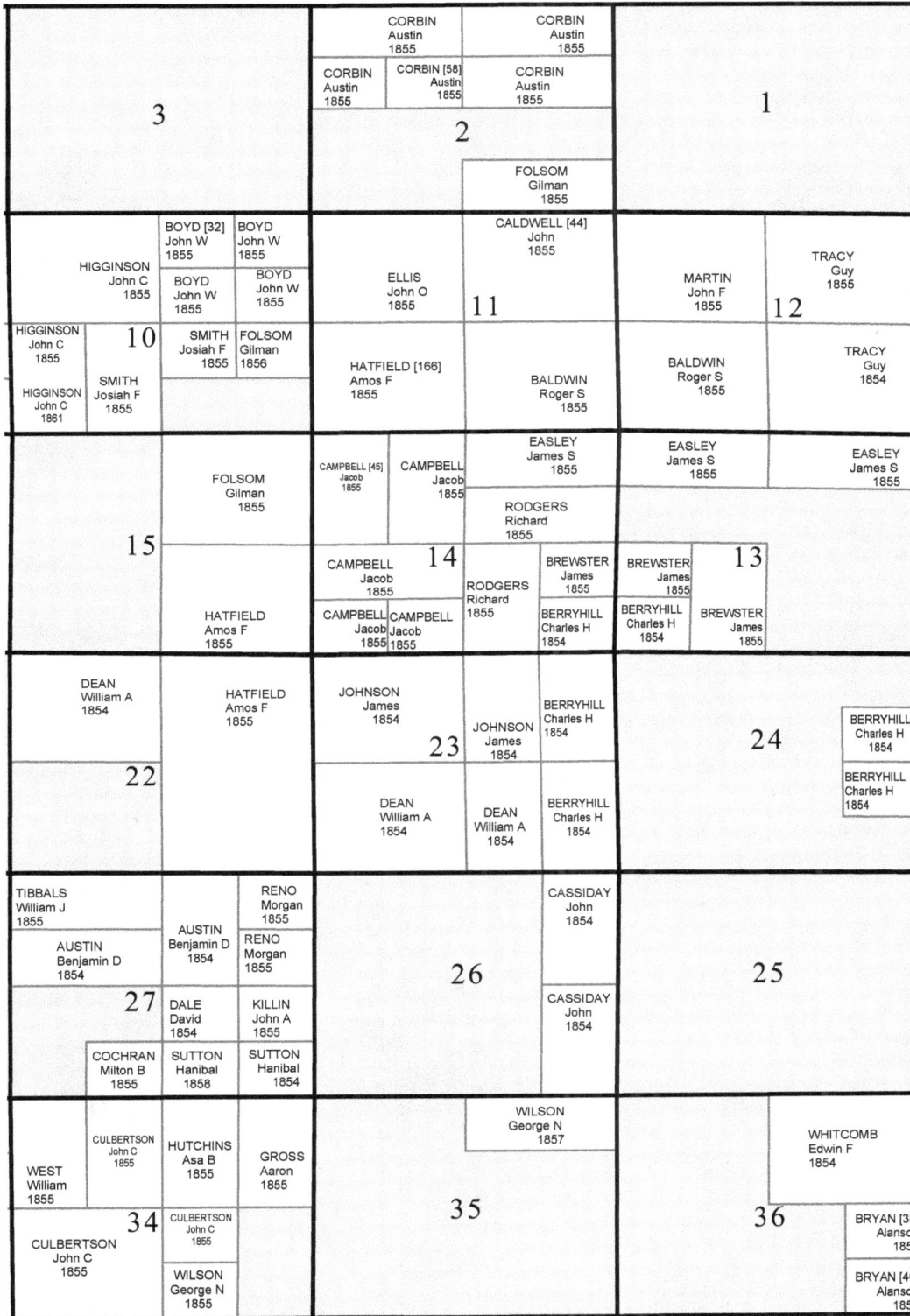

3	CORBIN Austin 1855	CORBIN Austin 1855	1	
	CORBIN Austin 1855	CORBIN [58] Austin 1855	CORBIN Austin 1855	
	2			
	FOLSOM Gilman 1855			

Helpful Hints

1. This Map's INDEX can be found on the preceding pages.

2. Refer to Map "C" to see where this Township lies within Poweshiek County, Iowa.

3. Numbers within square brackets [ ] denote a multi-patentee land parcel (multi-owner). Refer to Appendix "C" for a full list of members in this group.

4. Areas that look to be crowded with Patentees usually indicate multiple sales of the same parcel (Re-issues) or Overlapping parcels. See this Township's Index for an explanation of these and other circumstances that might explain "odd" groupings of Patentees on this map.

Section 10			Section 11	Section 12
HIGGINSON John C 1855	BOYD [32] John W 1855	BOYD John W 1855	CALDWELL [44] John 1855	TRACY Guy 1855
	BOYD John W 1855	BOYD John W 1855	ELLIS John O 1855	MARTIN John F 1855
HIGGINSON John C 1855	SMITH Josiah F 1855	FOLSOM Gilman 1856	11	12
HIGGINSON John C 1861	SMITH Josiah F 1855		HATFIELD [166] Amos F 1855	BALDWIN Roger S 1855	BALDWIN Roger S 1855	TRACY Guy 1854

Section 15			Section 14		Section 13
15	FOLSOM Gilman 1855	CAMPBELL [45] Jacob 1855	CAMPBELL Jacob 1855	EASLEY James S 1855	EASLEY James S 1855	EASLEY James S 1855
			RODGERS Richard 1855		
	HATFIELD Amos F 1855	CAMPBELL Jacob 1855	14	BREWSTER James 1855	BREWSTER James 1855	13
		CAMPBELL Jacob 1855	CAMPBELL Jacob 1855	RODGERS Richard 1855	BERRYHILL Charles H 1854	BERRYHILL Charles H 1854	BREWSTER James 1855

Section 22		Section 23		Section 24
DEAN William A 1854	HATFIELD Amos F 1855	JOHNSON James 1854	BERRYHILL Charles H 1854	24
22		23	JOHNSON James 1854		BERRYHILL Charles H 1854
		DEAN William A 1854	DEAN William A 1854	BERRYHILL Charles H 1854	BERRYHILL Charles H 1854

Section 27			Section 26	Section 25
TIBBALS William J 1855	AUSTIN Benjamin D 1854	RENO Morgan 1855	CASSIDAY John 1854	25
AUSTIN Benjamin D 1854		RENO Morgan 1855	26	
27	DALE David 1854	KILLIN John A 1855		
COCHRAN Milton B 1855	SUTTON Hanibal 1858	SUTTON Hanibal 1854	CASSIDAY John 1854	

Section 34			Section 35	Section 36
WEST William 1855	CULBERTSON John C 1855	HUTCHINS Asa B 1855	GROSS Aaron 1855	WILSON George N 1857	WHITCOMB Edwin F 1854
34	CULBERTSON John C 1855		35	36
CULBERTSON John C 1855	WILSON George N 1855			BRYAN [38] Alanson 1854
				BRYAN [40] Alanson 1854

Legend

Patent Boundary

Section Boundary

No Patents Found (or Outside County)

1., 2., 3., ... Lot Numbers (when beside a name)

[ ] Group Number (see Appendix "C")

Scale: Section = 1 mile X 1 mile (generally, with some exceptions)

Road Map

T79-N R15-W
5th PM Meridian

Map Group 10

Cities & Towns
Ewart

Cemeteries
Ewart Cemetery

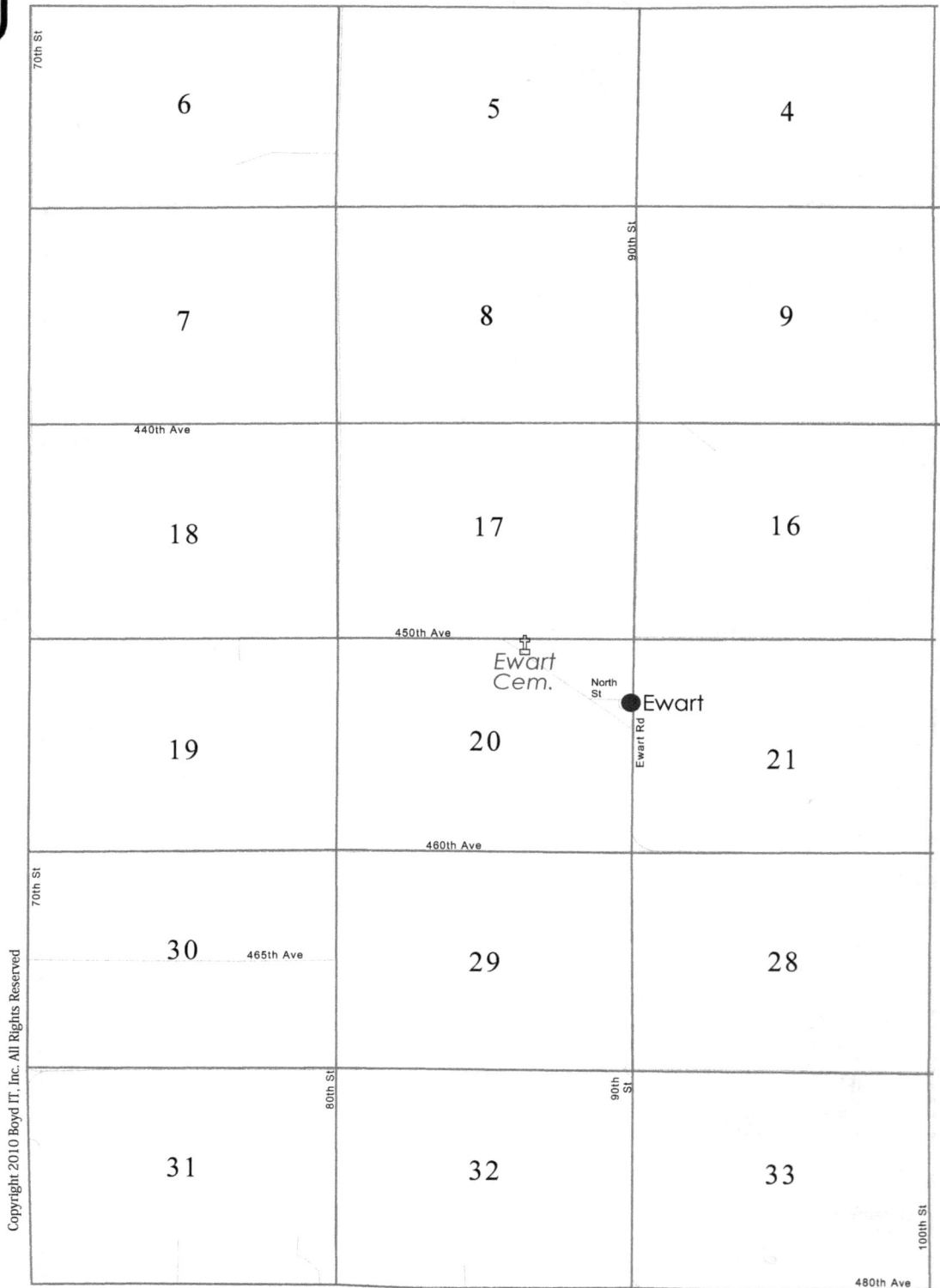

6	5	4
7	8	9
18	17	16
19	20	21
30	29	28
31	32	33

70th St · 90th St · 440th Ave · 450th Ave · Ewart Cem. · North St · Ewart Rd · Ewart · 460th Ave · 70th St · 465th Ave · 80th St · 90th St · 100th St · 480th Ave

3	2	1
10	11	12
15	14	13
22	23	24
27	26	25
34	35	36

110th St

430th Ave

440th Ave

130th St

450th Ave

460th Ave · 460th St

US Hwy 63

115th St

470th Ave

110th St

125th St

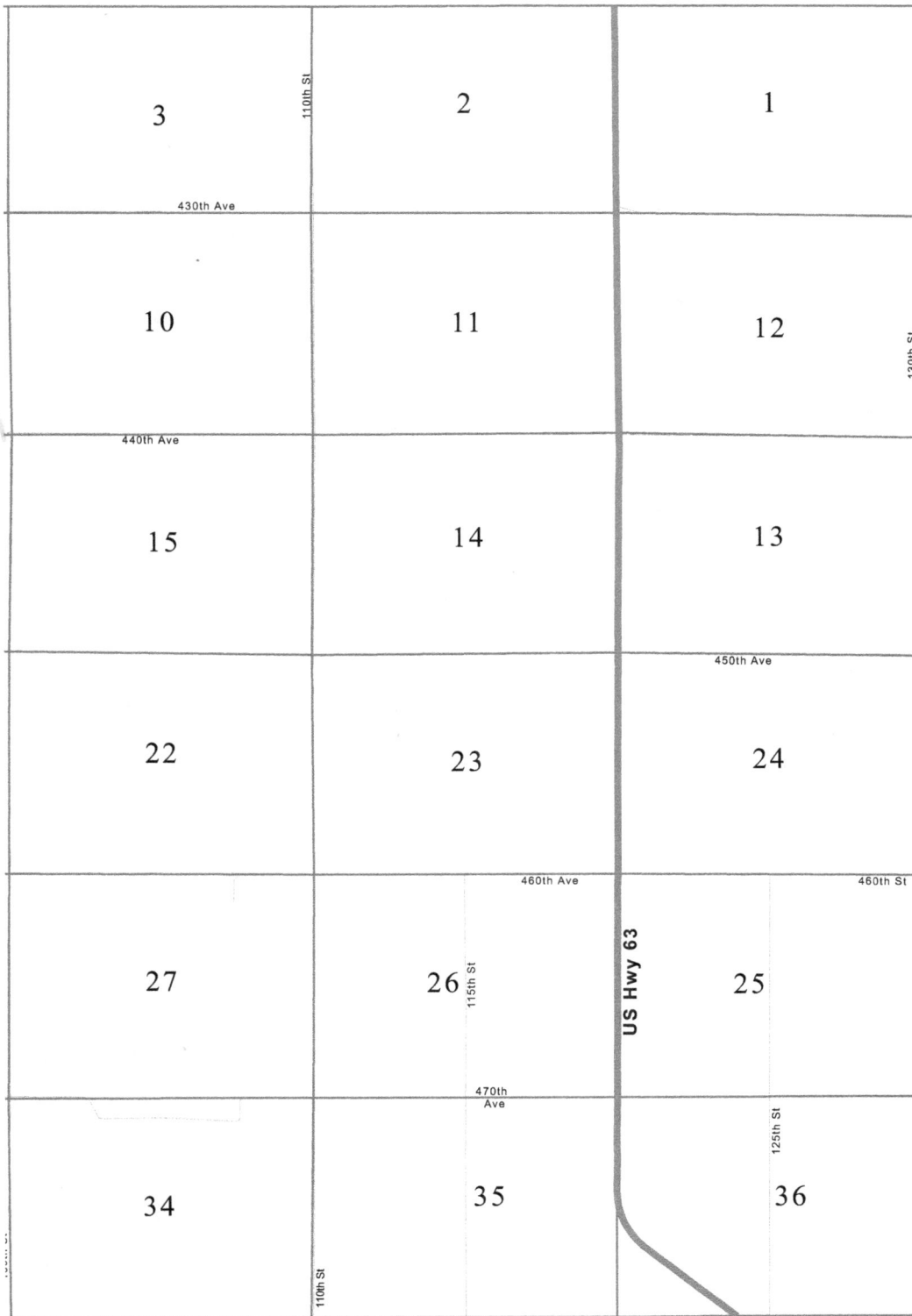

Helpful Hints

1. This road map has a number of uses, but primarily it is to help you: a) find the present location of land owned by your ancestors (at least the general area), b) find cemeteries and city-centers, and c) estimate the route/roads used by Census-takers & tax-assessors.

2. If you plan to travel to Poweshiek County to locate cemeteries or land parcels, please pick up a modern travel map for the area before you do. Mapping old land parcels on modern maps is not as exact a science as you might think. Just the slightest variations in public land survey coordinates, estimates of parcel boundaries, or road-map deviations can greatly alter a map's representation of how a road either does or doesn't cross a particular parcel of land.

Legend

————————	Section Lines
════════	Interstates
━━━━━━	Highways
————————	Other Roads
●	Cities/Towns
✝	Cemeteries

Scale: Section = 1 mile X 1 mile
(generally, with some exceptions)

157

Historical Map

T79-N R15-W
5th PM Meridian

Map Group 10

Cities & Towns
Ewart

Cemeteries
Ewart Cemetery

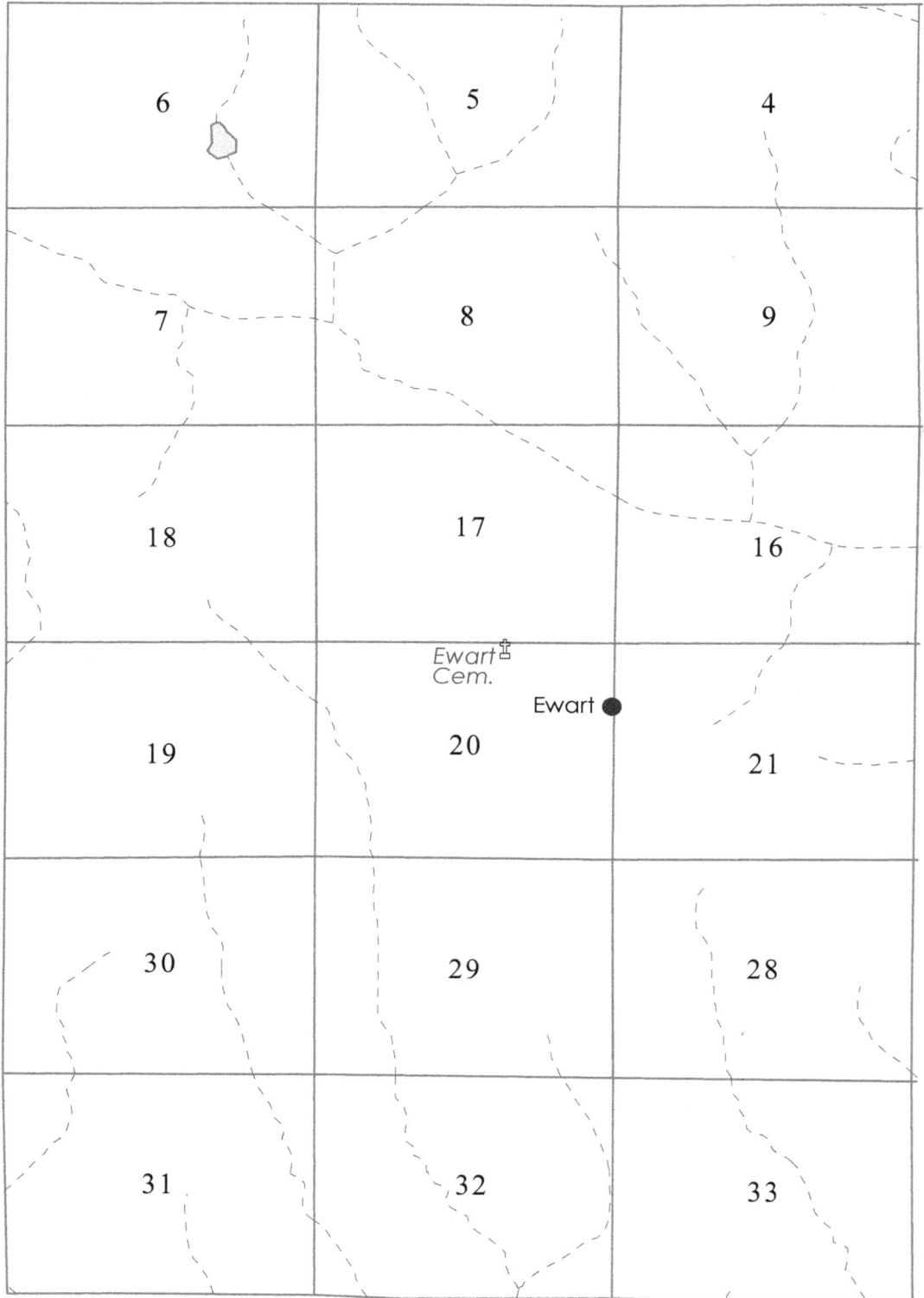

6	5	4
7	8	9
18	17	16
19	20	21
30	29	28
31	32	33

Ewart Cem.

Ewart ●

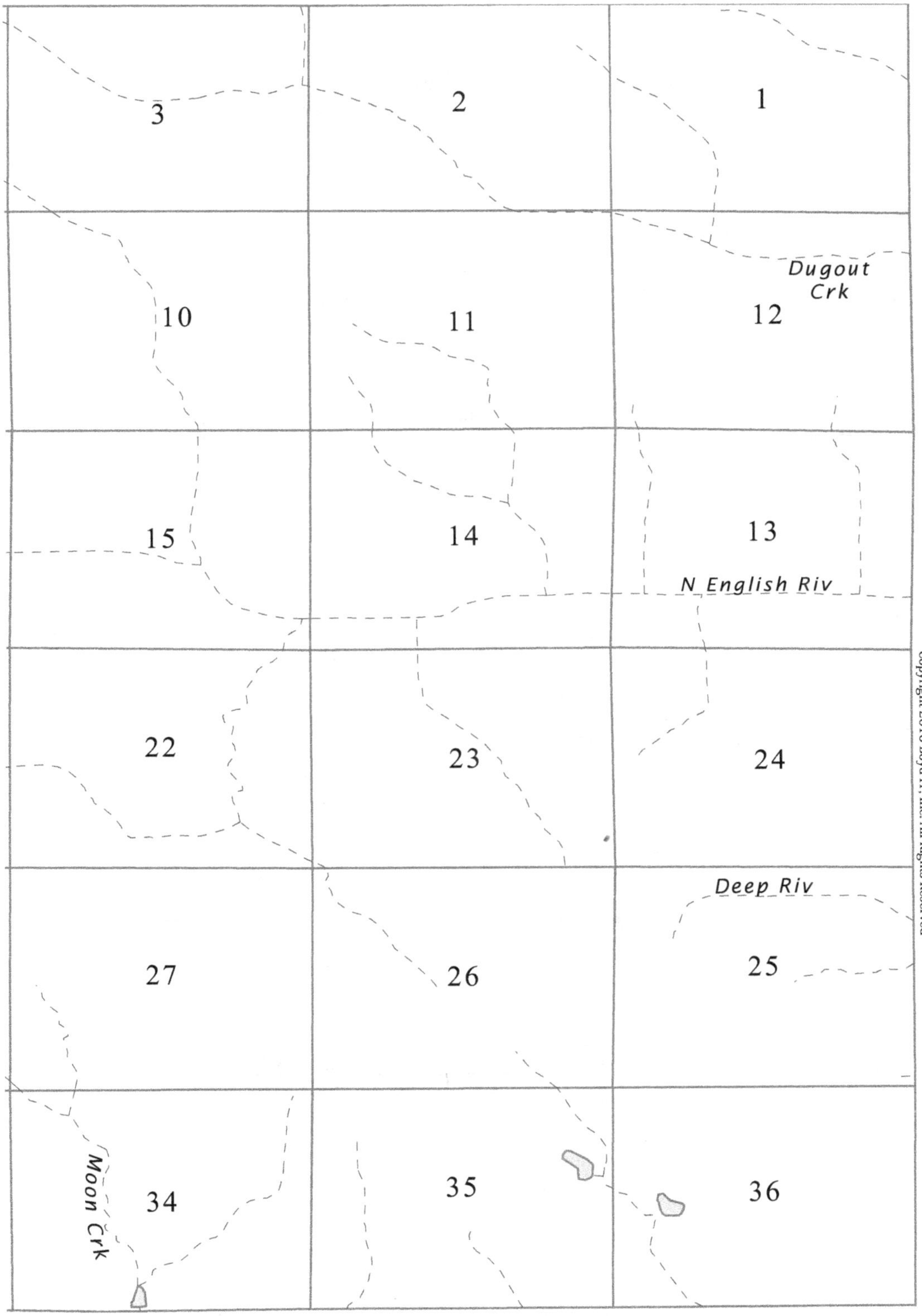

3
2
1
10
11
12
Dugout Crk
15
14
13
N English Riv
22
23
24
27
26
25
Deep Riv
34
35
36
Moon Crk

Helpful Hints

1. This Map takes a different look at the same Congressional Township displayed in the preceding two maps. It presents features that can help you better envision the historical development of the area: a) Water-bodies (lakes & ponds), b) Water-courses (rivers, streams, etc.), c) Railroads, d) City/town center-points (where they were oftentimes located when first settled), and e) Cemeteries.

2. Using this "Historical" map in tandem with this Township's Patent Map and Road Map, may lead you to some interesting discoveries. You will often find roads, towns, cemeteries, and waterways are named after nearby landowners: sometimes those names will be the ones you are researching. See how many of these research gems you can find here in Poweshiek County.

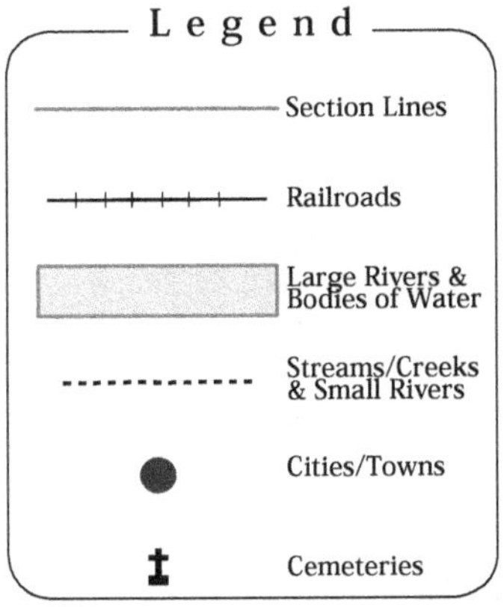

Legend
Section Lines
Railroads
Large Rivers & Bodies of Water
Streams/Creeks & Small Rivers
Cities/Towns
Cemeteries

Scale: Section = 1 mile X 1 mile
(there are some exceptions)

Map Group 11: Index to Land Patents

Township 79-North Range 14-West (5th PM)

After you locate an individual in this Index, take note of the Section and Section Part then proceed to the Land Patent map on the pages immediately following. You should have no difficulty locating the corresponding parcel of land.

The "For More Info" Column will lead you to more information about the underlying Patents. See the *Legend* at right, and the "How to Use this Book" chapter, for more information.

```
                    LEGEND
         "For More Info . . . " column
A = Authority (Legislative Act, See Appendix "A")
B = Block or Lot (location in Section unknown)
C = Cancelled Patent
F = Fractional Section
G = Group  (Multi-Patentee Patent, see Appendix "C")
V = Overlaps another Parcel
R = Re-Issued (Parcel patented more than once)

(A & G items require you to look in the Appendixes referred
to above. All other Letter-designations followed by a number
require you to locate line-items in this index that possess
the ID number found after the letter).
```

ID	Individual in Patent	Sec.	Sec. Part	Date Issued	Other Counties	For More Info . . .
2321	ALLEN, Lyman	2	N½SW	1855-05-10		A1
2370	ALLEN, William	11	NENW	1855-01-01		A6
2371	" "	2	SESW	1855-01-01		A6 G3
2248	BERRYHILL, Charles H	36	S½SE	1853-09-10		A6 G15
2249	" "	15	NESW	1854-03-01		A6 G12
2247	" "	19	NESW	1854-07-01		A6 G11
2244	" "	19	NWSW	1854-10-02		A6 F
2246	" "	19	SWNW	1854-10-02		A6 F
2245	" "	19	SWNE	1854-11-01		A4
2242	" "	18	SESW	1855-02-01		A6 F
2243	" "	18	SWSE	1855-02-01		A6
2339	BIRD, Roderick D	19	S½SE	1854-05-01		A1
2340	" "	30	N½SE	1854-05-01		A1
2341	" "	30	NE	1854-05-01		A1
2342	" "	36	SWSW	1854-05-01		A1
2316	BLOUNT, Nancy	36	NE	1855-02-01		A6 G193
2317	BONE, Joseph	32	SESW	1854-05-01		A1
2265	BREWSTER, James	18	NESW	1918-11-11		A2 F
2266	" "	18	W½SW	1918-11-11		A2 F
2267	" "	19	NWNW	1918-11-11		A2 F
2334	BRICK, Elizabeth	31	S½NE	1854-10-02		A6 G36 V2282
2334	BRICK, Priscilla	31	S½NE	1854-10-02		A6 G36 V2282
2334	BRICK, Rebecca Paulina	31	S½NE	1854-10-02		A6 G36 V2282
2237	BRYAN, Alanson	31	W½SW	1854-05-01		A1 F
2324	BRYAN, Neri	31	NESW	1853-11-01		A1 F
2325	" "	31	SESW	1854-03-01		A6 F
2347	CHIPMAN, Silas W	8	E½SW	1856-09-01		A1
2348	" "	8	SE	1856-09-01		A1
2369	CLARK, Wesley C	18	N½	1855-05-01		A1 F
2309	CLEMENS, John	32	N½SW	1852-05-01		A6 G53
2309	CLEMENTS, John	32	N½SW	1852-05-01		A6 G53
2306	CUSHMAN, Job	17	NE	1855-05-10		A1
2367	DAVIS, Sally	1	SESW	1855-01-01		A6 G126
2322	DEPEW, Mildred	25	E½SW	1854-05-01		A1
2323	" "	25	W½SW	1854-10-02		A6
2362	DIKEMAN, Freelove	1	SENW	1855-01-01		A6 G127 F
2247	DOBBIN, Julia Ann	19	NESW	1854-07-01		A6 G11
2263	DOWNEY, Hugh D	9	SW	1855-05-01		A1
2302	EASLEY, James S	14	N½SW	1855-01-01		A6 G115
2300	" "	14	S½SW	1855-01-01		A6
2303	" "	36	NENW	1855-05-01		A6 G120 C
2301	" "	14	SE	1855-05-10		A1
2304	" "	36	NESW	1873-05-27		A6 G120
2354	EDWARDS, Thomas M	1	NESE	1855-01-01		A6
2366	" "	1	NESW	1855-01-01		A6 G130
2364	" "	1	NWSE	1855-01-01		A6 G131 C F R2368

ID	Individual in Patent	Sec.	Sec. Part	Date Issued	Other Counties	For More Info . . .
2368	EDWARDS, Thomas M (Cont'd)	1	NWSE	1855-01-01		A6 G128 R2364
2355	"	"	1	NWSW	1855-01-01		A6
2356	"	"	1	SENE	1855-01-01		A6 F
2362	"	"	1	SENW	1855-01-01		A6 G127 F
2363	"	"	1	SESE	1855-01-01		A6 G132
2367	"	"	1	SESW	1855-01-01		A6 G126
2357	"	"	1	SWNW	1855-01-01		A6 F
2358	"	"	1	SWSE	1855-01-01		A6
2359	"	"	1	SWSW	1855-01-01		A6
2361	"	"	2	S½NE	1855-01-01		A6 G129 F
2352	"	"	1	N½NE	1855-05-01		A1 F
2353	"	"	1	N½NW	1855-05-01		A1 F
2360	"	"	2	N½NE	1855-05-01		A1 F
2365	"	"	1	SWNE	1915-03-30		A6 G131
2368	EWERS, Sarah	1	NWSE	1855-01-01		A6 G128 R2364
2361	FLOYD, Abraham	2	S½NE	1855-01-01		A6 G129 F
2259	FOLSOM, Gilman	7	SE	1855-05-01		A1
2260	"	"	8	W½SW	1855-05-01		A1
2335	GATLING, Richard J	22	SW	1854-05-01		A1
2336	"	"	32	NE	1854-12-01		A6
2337	"	"	32	SE	1854-12-01		A6
2372	GATLING, William J	27	NW	1854-05-01		A1
2302	GOODE, Elizabeth	14	N½SW	1855-01-01		A6 G115
2271	GOWER, James H	15	W½NW	1857-02-20		A5
2268	"	"	11	NWNE	1857-03-10		A1
2269	"	"	11	SENW	1857-03-10		A1
2270	"	"	11	SWSW	1857-03-10		A1
2272	"	"	2	SWSW	1857-03-10		A1
2315	GRUB, Elizabeth	25	NW	1855-01-01		A6 G194
2311	HADDEN, John	9	NW	1856-06-16		A6
2318	HILL, Joseph	11	NENE	1855-01-01		A6
2319	"	"	12	NW	1855-03-01		A6
2249	HUMMEL, Susannah	15	NESW	1854-03-01		A6 G12
2349	IOWA, State Of	16		1937-08-26		A3
2366	JENNINGS, Polly	1	NESW	1855-01-01		A6 G130
2273	JOHNSON, James	19	NWSE	1854-12-01		A1
2274	"	"	19	SESW	1854-12-01		A1 F
2275	"	"	20	E½NW	1854-12-01		A1
2276	"	"	20	E½SW	1854-12-01		A1
2277	"	"	20	NE	1854-12-01		A1
2278	"	"	22	N½	1854-12-01		A1
2279	"	"	23		1854-12-01		A1
2280	"	"	24		1854-12-01		A1
2281	"	"	30	S½SE	1854-12-01		A1
2282	"	"	31	E½	1854-12-01		A1
2283	"	"	31	NW	1854-12-01		A1 R2241
2284	"	"	32	N½NW	1854-12-01		A1
2285	"	"	33	E½SW	1854-12-01		A1
2286	"	"	33	NESE	1854-12-01		A1
2287	"	"	33	SWSW	1854-12-01		A1
2288	"	"	33	W½SE	1854-12-01		A1
2289	"	"	34	NWSW	1854-12-01		A1
2290	"	"	34	SE	1854-12-01		A1
2291	"	"	34	SESW	1854-12-01		A1
2292	"	"	35	SESW	1854-12-01		A1
2293	"	"	35	SWSE	1854-12-01		A1
2294	"	"	35	W½SW	1854-12-01		A1
2295	"	"	36	N½SE	1854-12-01		A1
2313	LISTON, Jonathan A	22	SE	1854-12-01		A1
2315	"	"	25	NW	1855-01-01		A6 G194
2314	"	"	26	NE	1855-01-01		A6
2316	"	"	36	NE	1855-02-01		A6 G193
2258	LOTT, Bartholomew	2	S½NW	1855-03-01		A6 G284 F
2258	LOTT, Loraina Jane	2	S½NW	1855-03-01		A6 G284 F
2258	LOTT, Mary B	2	S½NW	1855-03-01		A6 G284 F
2350	MCVAY, Thomas F	31	N½SE	1854-05-01		A6 V2282
2351	"	"	32	S½NW	1854-05-01		A6
2364	NEWKIRK, Martha	1	NWSE	1855-01-01		A6 G131 C F R2368
2365	"	"	1	SWNE	1915-03-30		A6 G131
2264	NEWSHELL, Isaac	36	SESW	1853-10-01		A6
2250	PATTERSON, David W	29	SW	1854-05-01		A1
2296	PATTERSON, James M	29	NW	1854-05-01		A1
2303	PEGRAM, Rebecca	36	NENW	1855-05-01		A6 G120 C

ID	Individual in Patent	Sec.	Sec. Part	Date Issued	Other Counties	For More Info . . .
2304	PEGRAM, Rebecca (Cont'd)	36	NESW	1873-05-27		A6 G120
2297	PITT, James	17	SE	1855-05-01		A1
2298	" "	17	W½	1855-05-01		A1
2238	PORTER, Albert G	33	N½	1854-05-01		A1
2239	" "	33	NWSW	1854-05-01		A1
2312	REYNOLDS, George W	3	N½	1854-05-01		A1 G240 F
2299	REYNOLDS, James	4		1854-05-01		A1 F
2312	REYNOLDS, John	3	N½	1854-05-01		A1 G240 F
2332	ROBERTS, Porteus B	12	E½	1855-05-10		A1
2333	" "	13	S½	1855-05-10		A1
2371	ROBINSON, Mary	2	SESW	1855-01-01		A6 G3
2248	RYAN, Mary	36	S½SE	1853-09-10		A6 G15
2253	SANXAY, Frederic	15	NWSW	1854-08-01		A6
2251	ST JOHN, DUBOIS	11	E½SW	1855-05-10		A1
2252	" "	11	W½SE	1855-05-10		A1
2240	STANLEY, Annette	31	NWNE	1854-05-01		A1 V2282
2241	STANLEY, Asel	31	NW	1854-02-01		A6 F R2283
2338	SWIFT, Richard K	14	NW	1855-05-10		A1
2305	TAYLOR, James	12	SW	1855-01-01		A6
2343	TIBBALS, Samuel W	18	N½SE	1855-05-10		A1
2344	" "	18	SESE	1855-05-10		A1
2345	" "	30	SW	1855-05-10		A1 F
2346	" "	30	SWNW	1855-05-10		A1 F
2373	TIBBALS, William J	15	S½SW	1855-05-10		A1
2374	" "	19	SENE	1855-05-10		A1
2375	" "	31	NENE	1855-05-10		A1 V2282
2326	TOUSEY, Omer	26	S½	1854-05-01		A1
2327	" "	27	S½	1854-05-01		A1
2328	" "	34	N½	1854-05-01		A1
2329	" "	34	NESW	1854-05-01		A1
2330	" "	35	N½	1854-05-01		A1
2331	" "	35	NESW	1854-05-01		A1
2262	TRACY, Guy	7	W½SW	1854-05-01		A1 F
2261	" "	7	E½SW	1855-12-15		A1 F
2363	WASSON, Jollina	1	SESE	1855-01-01		A6 G132
2320	WATSON, Leander	20	SWSW	1856-06-16		A6
2258	WILLIAMS, George C	2	S½NW	1855-03-01		A6 G284 F
2254	" "	2	E½SE	1855-05-01		A1
2255	" "	2	N½NW	1855-05-01		A1 F
2256	" "	2	NWSE	1855-05-01		A6
2257	" "	2	SWSE	1866-06-01		A6
2376	WILLIAMS, William P	3	SW	1855-03-01		A6
2310	WILSON, John D	10	E½NW	1855-05-10		A1
2307	WOODWARD, Job M	13	NE	1855-03-01		A6
2308	" "	13	NW	1855-03-01		A6

Patent Map

T79-N R14-W
5th PM Meridian

Map Group 11

Township Statistics

Parcels Mapped	:	140
Number of Patents	:	116
Number of Individuals	:	72
Patentees Identified	:	66
Number of Surnames	:	59
Multi-Patentee Parcels	:	21
Oldest Patent Date	:	5/1/1852
Most Recent Patent	:	8/26/1937
Block/Lot Parcels	:	0
Parcels Re - Issued	:	2
Parcels that Overlap	:	4
Cities and Towns	:	0
Cemeteries	:	1

Section 6

Section 5

Section 4
REYNOLDS James 1854

Section 7
TRACY Guy 1854
TRACY Guy 1855
FOLSOM Gilman 1855

Section 8
FOLSOM Gilman 1855
CHIPMAN Silas W 1856
CHIPMAN Silas W 1856

Section 9
HADDEN John 1856
DOWNEY Hugh D 1855

Section 18
CLARK Wesley C 1855
BREWSTER James 1918
BREWSTER James 1918
TIBBALS Samuel W 1855
BERRYHILL Charles H 1855
BERRYHILL Charles H 1855
TIBBALS Samuel W 1855

Section 17
PITT James 1855
CUSHMAN Job 1855
PITT James 1855

Section 16
IOWA State Of 1937

Section 19
BREWSTER James 1918
BERRYHILL Charles H 1854
BERRYHILL Charles H 1854
BERRYHILL [11] Charles H 1854
BERRYHILL Charles H 1854
TIBBALS William J 1855
JOHNSON James 1854
JOHNSON James 1854
BIRD Roderick D 1854

Section 20
JOHNSON James 1854
JOHNSON James 1854
JOHNSON James 1854
WATSON Leander 1856

Section 21
JOHNSON James 1854

Section 30
TIBBALS Samuel W 1855
BIRD Roderick D 1854
BIRD Roderick D 1854
TIBBALS Samuel W 1855
JOHNSON James 1854

Section 29
PATTERSON James M 1854
PATTERSON David W 1854

Section 28

Section 31
STANLEY Asel 1854
STANLEY Annette 1854
TIBBALS William J 1855
JOHNSON James 1854
BRICK [36] Priscilla 1854
BRYAN Alanson 1854
BRYAN Neri 1853
MCVAY Thomas F 1854
BRYAN Neri 1854
JOHNSON James 1854

Section 32
JOHNSON James 1854
MCVAY Thomas F 1854
CLEMENS [53] John 1852
BONE Joseph 1854
GATLING Richard J 1854
GATLING Richard J 1854

Section 33
PORTER Albert G 1854
PORTER Albert G 1854
JOHNSON James 1854
JOHNSON James 1854
JOHNSON James 1854
JOHNSON James 1854

REYNOLDS [240] John 1854	WILLIAMS George C 1855	EDWARDS Thomas M 1855	EDWARDS Thomas M 1855	EDWARDS Thomas M 1855

Helpful Hints

1. This Map's INDEX can be found on the preceding pages.

2. Refer to Map "C" to see where this Township lies within Poweshiek County, Iowa.

3. Numbers within square brackets [ ] denote a multi-patentee land parcel (multi-owner). Refer to Appendix "C" for a full list of members in this group.

4. Areas that look to be crowded with Patentees usually indicate multiple sales of the same parcel (Re-issues) or Overlapping parcels. See this Township's Index for an explanation of these and other circumstances that might explain "odd" groupings of Patentees on this map.

Section 1:
WILLIAMS [284] George C 1855
EDWARDS [129] Thomas M 1855
EDWARDS Thomas M 1855
EDWARDS [127] Thomas M 1855
EDWARDS [131] Thomas M 1915
EDWARDS Thomas M 1855
1
ALLEN Lyman 1855
WILLIAMS George C 1855
WILLIAMS George C 1855
EDWARDS Thomas M 1855
EDWARDS [130] Thomas M 1855
EDWARDS [128] Thomas M 1855
EDWARDS [131] Thomas M 1855
EDWARDS Thomas M 1855
GOWER James H 1857
ALLEN [3] William 1855
WILLIAMS George C 1866
EDWARDS Thomas M 1855
EDWARDS [126] Thomas M 1855
EDWARDS Thomas M 1855
EDWARDS [132] Thomas M 1855

3 WILLIAMS William P 1855

2

Section 10:
WILSON John D 1855
10

Section 11:
ALLEN William 1855
GOWER James H 1857
HILL Joseph 1855
GOWER James H 1857
11
JOHN Dubois St 1855
GOWER James H 1857
JOHN Dubois St 1855

Section 12:
HILL Joseph 1855
12
TAYLOR James 1855
ROBERTS Porteus B 1855

Section 15:
GOWER James H 1857
15
SANXAY Frederic 1854
BERRYHILL [12] Charles H 1854
TIBBALS William J 1855

Section 14:
SWIFT Richard K 1855
14
EASLEY [115] James S 1855
EASLEY James S 1855
EASLEY James S 1855

Section 13:
WOODWARD Job M 1855
WOODWARD Job M 1855
13
ROBERTS Porteus B 1855

Section 22:
JOHNSON James 1854
22
GATLING Richard J 1854
LISTON Jonathan A 1854

Section 23:
23
JOHNSON James 1854

Section 24:
24
JOHNSON James 1854

Section 27:
GATLING William J 1854
27
TOUSEY Omer 1854

Section 26:
26
LISTON Jonathan A 1855
TOUSEY Omer 1854

Section 25:
LISTON [194] Jonathan A 1855
25
DEPEW Mildred 1854
DEPEW Mildred 1854

Section 34:
TOUSEY Omer 1854
34
JOHNSON James 1854
TOUSEY Omer 1854
JOHNSON James 1854
JOHNSON James 1854

Section 35:
TOUSEY Omer 1854
35
JOHNSON James 1854
TOUSEY Omer 1854
JOHNSON James 1854
JOHNSON James 1854

Section 36:
EASLEY [120] James S 1855
LISTON [193] Jonathan A 1855
36
EASLEY [120] James S 1873
JOHNSON James 1854
BIRD Roderick D 1854
NEWSHELL Isaac 1853
BERRYHILL [15] Charles H 1853

Legend

——— Patent Boundary

━━━ Section Boundary

No Patents Found (or Outside County)

1., 2., 3., ... Lot Numbers (when beside a name)

[ ] Group Number (see Appendix "C")

Scale: Section = 1 mile X 1 mile (generally, with some exceptions)

Road Map

T79-N R14-W
5th PM Meridian

Map Group 11

Cities & Towns
None

Cemeteries
Lytle Cemetery

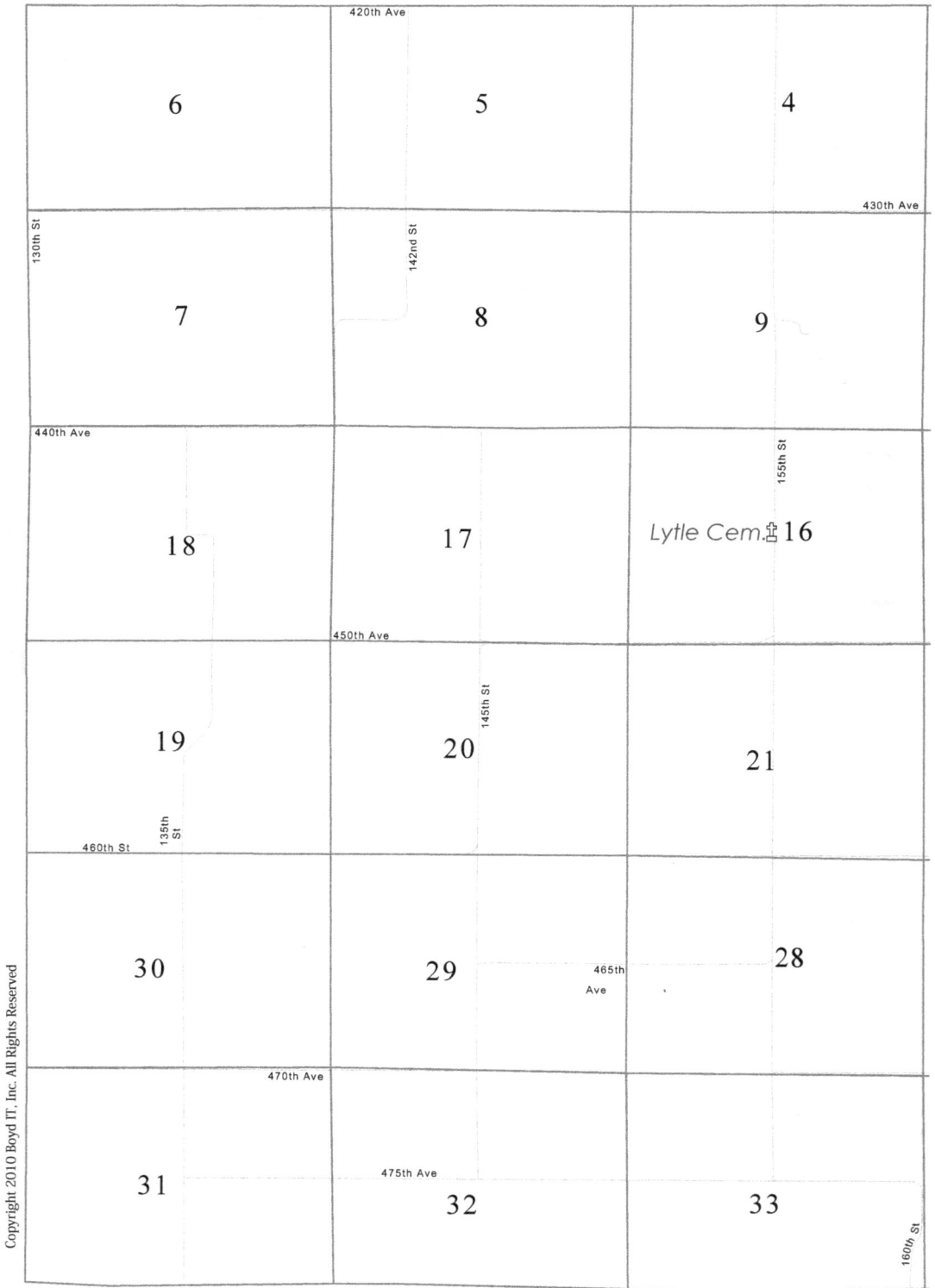

6	5	4
7	8	9
18	17	Lytle Cem. 16
19	20	21
30	29	28
31	32	33

420th Ave
430th Ave
130th St
142nd St
440th Ave
155th St
450th Ave
145th St
135th St
460th St
465th Ave
470th Ave
475th Ave
160th St

Copyright 2010 Boyd IT, Inc. All Rights Reserved

3	2	1
10	11	12
15	14	13
22	23	24
27	26	25
34	35	36

175th St

420th Ave

V18 Rd

190th St

165th St

180th St

440th Ave

450th Ave

460th Ave

470th Ave

480th Ave

V18 Rd

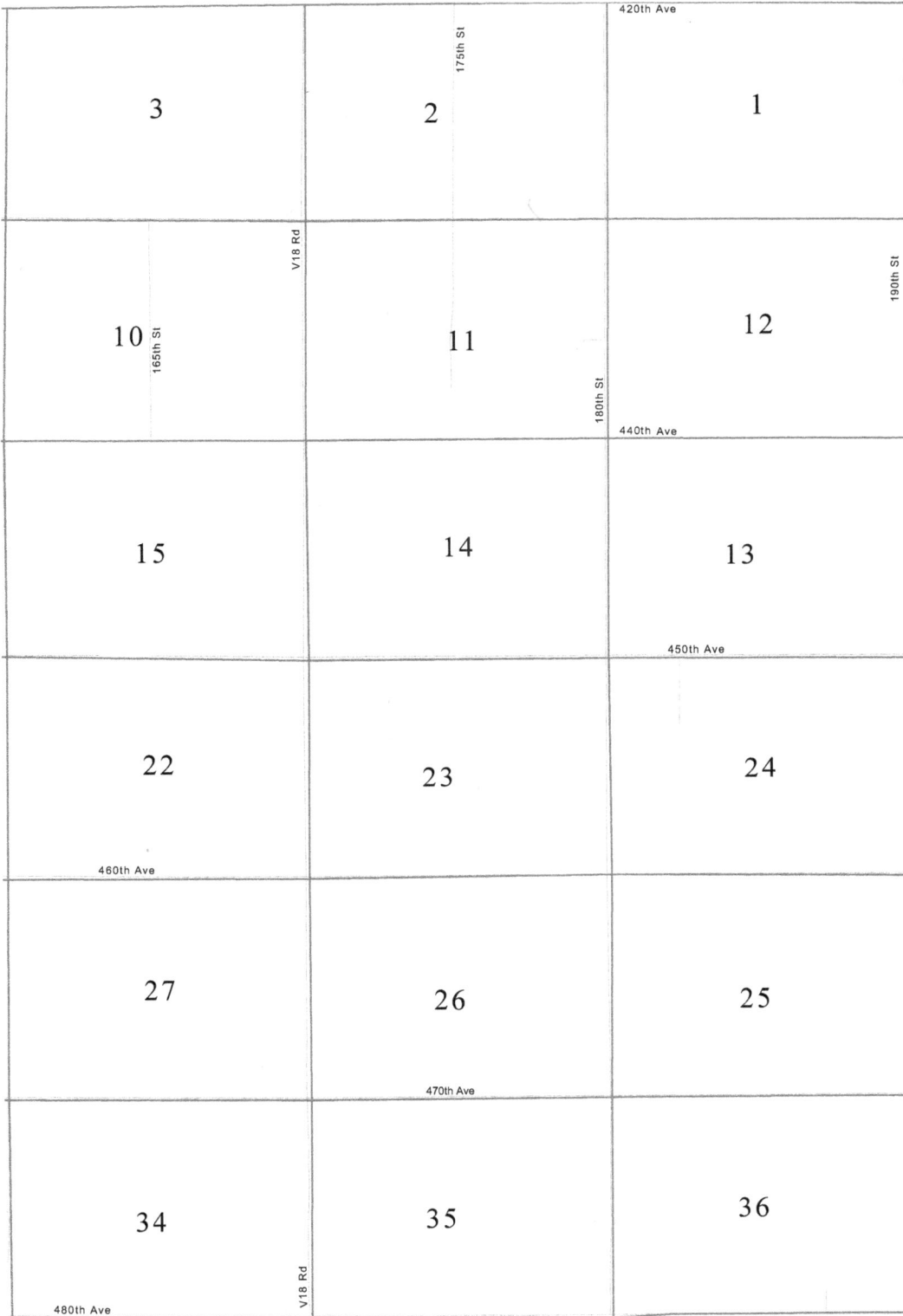

Helpful Hints

1. This road map has a number of uses, but primarily it is to help you: a) find the present location of land owned by your ancestors (at least the general area), b) find cemeteries and city-centers, and c) estimate the route/roads used by Census-takers & tax-assessors.

2. If you plan to travel to Poweshiek County to locate cemeteries or land parcels, please pick up a modern travel map for the area before you do. Mapping old land parcels on modern maps is not as exact a science as you might think. Just the slightest variations in public land survey coordinates, estimates of parcel boundaries, or road-map deviations can greatly alter a map's representation of how a road either does or doesn't cross a particular parcel of land.

Legend

————————	Section Lines
════════	Interstates
━━━━━━━	Highways
————————	Other Roads
●	Cities/Towns
✝	Cemeteries

Scale: Section = 1 mile X 1 mile
(generally, with some exceptions)

Historical Map

T79-N R14-W
5th PM Meridian

Map Group 11

Cities & Towns
None

Cemeteries
Lytle Cemetery

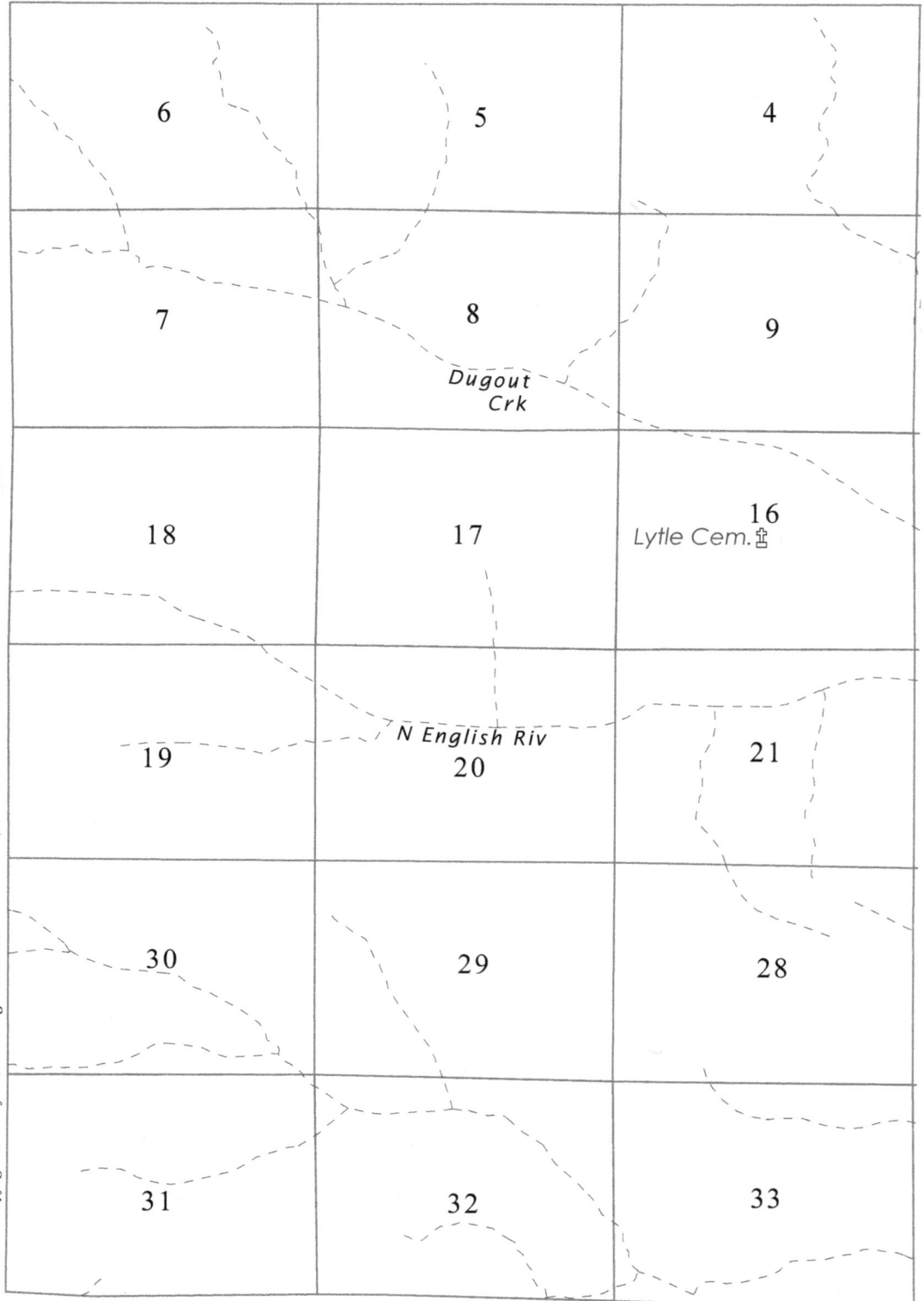

6	5	4
7	8 *Dugout Crk*	9
18	17	16 *Lytle Cem.*
19	20 *N English Riv*	21
30	29	28
31	32	33

3

2

1

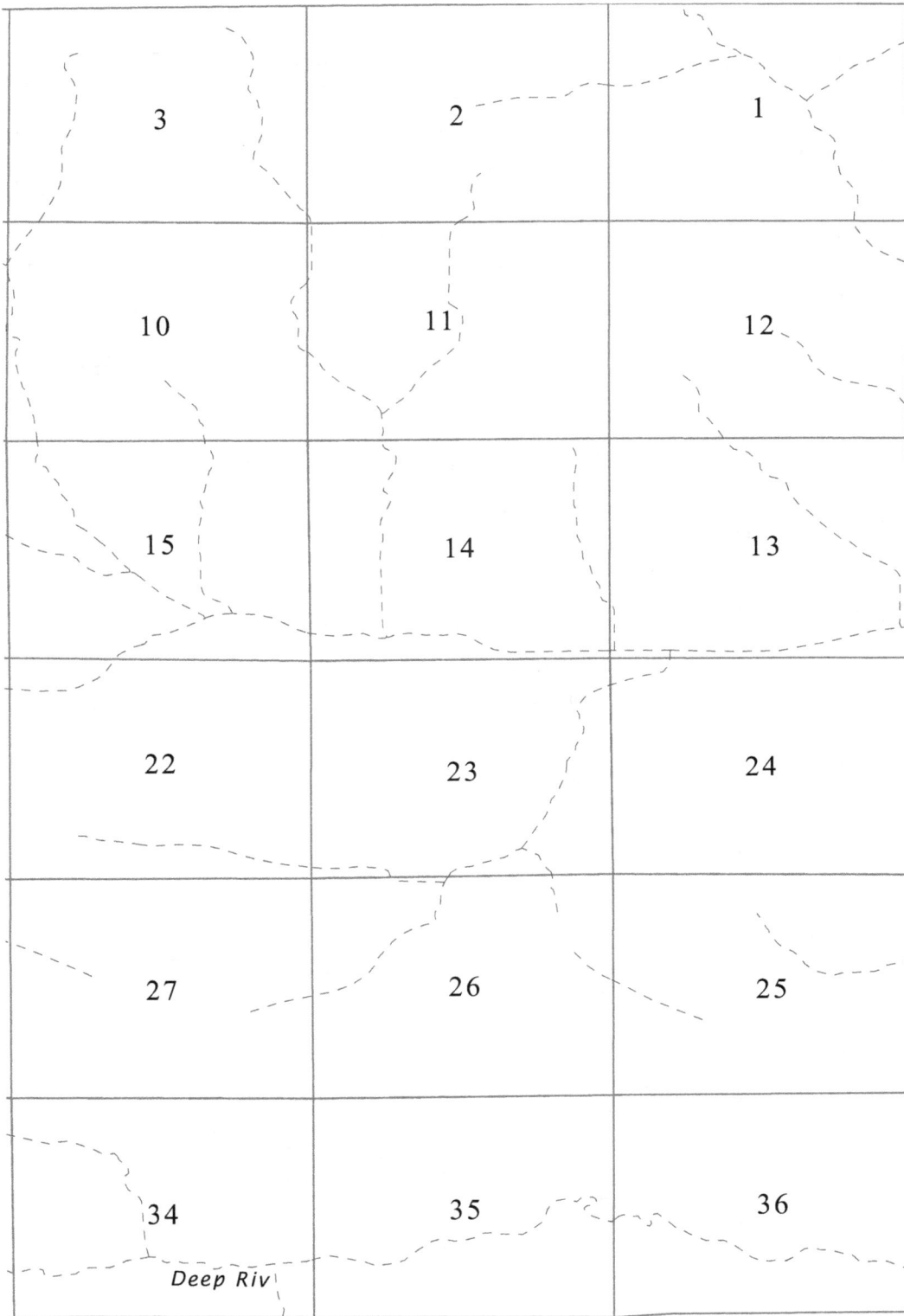

10

11

12

15

14

13

22

23

24

27

26

25

34

35

36

Deep Riv

Scale: Section = 1 mile X 1 mile
(there are some exceptions)

Map Group 12: Index to Land Patents

Township 79-North Range 13-West (5th PM)

After you locate an individual in this Index, take note of the Section and Section Part then proceed to the Land Patent map on the pages immediately following. You should have no difficulty locating the corresponding parcel of land.

The "For More Info" Column will lead you to more information about the underlying Patents. See the *Legend* at right, and the "How to Use this Book" chapter, for more information.

```
                    LEGEND
           "For More Info . . . " column
A = Authority (Legislative Act, See Appendix "A")
B = Block or Lot (location in Section unknown)
C = Cancelled Patent
F = Fractional Section
G = Group  (Multi-Patentee Patent, see Appendix "C")
V = Overlaps another Parcel
R = Re-Issued (Parcel patented more than once)

(A & G items require you to look in the Appendixes referred
to above. All other Letter-designations followed by a number
require you to locate line-items in this index that possess
the ID number found after the letter).
```

ID	Individual in Patent	Sec.	Sec. Part	Date Issued	Other Counties	For More Info . . .
2519	ADAMS, Margaret	4	NESE	1863-09-24		A5 G243
2398	ASKEW, Cyrus H	18	E½SE	1855-12-15		A1
2399	" "	18	NWSE	1855-12-15		A1
2400	" "	18	SENE	1855-12-15		A1
2401	" "	31	W½NW	1855-12-15		A1 F
2454	BALSLEY, Mary E	28	SWNW	1854-08-01		A6 G97
2456	BARKER, James	35	S½SE	1857-03-10		A1
2581	BEEBE, Walter B	1	N½NE	1855-05-01		A6 F
2396	BERRYHILL, Charles H	18	NWNW	1857-02-20		A5 G13 F
2397	" "	7	SWSW	1857-02-20		A5 G13 F
2455	BERRYHILL, James B	21	NESE	1853-07-02		A6
2566	BRADY, Samuel W	31	NE	1852-04-01		A6
2424	BRAMER, George L	9	E½NW	1855-05-01		A1
2425	" "	9	SW	1855-05-01		A1
2426	" "	9	SWNW	1855-05-01		A1
2440	CANNON, Hugh	18	E½NW	1857-03-10		A1 F
2441	" "	18	N½SW	1857-03-10		A1 F
2442	" "	18	SWNE	1857-03-10		A1
2443	" "	18	SWNW	1857-03-10		A1 F
2444	" "	7	SESW	1857-03-10		A1
2394	CAREY, Bernard	8	W½SE	1855-12-15		A1
2422	CARPENTER, George F	33	NE	1855-05-10		A1
2423	" "	34	NW	1855-05-10		A1
2433	CHITTENDEN, Henry	10	NE	1855-12-15		A1 G48
2434	" "	10	S½NW	1855-12-15		A1 G48
2435	" "	17	S½NW	1855-12-15		A1 G48
2436	" "	17	SW	1855-12-15		A1 G48
2437	" "	9	NE	1855-12-15		A1 G48
2395	CLOSE, Chalmer D	13	N½SE	1855-12-15		A1
2438	COLEY, Henry	9	SESE	1855-12-15		A1
2431	COLLINS, Murzey	1	SWNE	1854-11-01		A4 G144 F
2551	COOK, Ralph P	23	S½NE	1855-05-01		A1 G57
2552	" "	23	SENW	1855-05-01		A1 G57
2584	COOLEY, William	5	E½SE	1855-12-15		A1
2457	COOPER, James D	1	NW	1854-12-01		A1 F
2574	COX, Thomas J	29	NWNW	1855-12-15		A1
2513	CRUM, John H	33	W½NW	1855-02-01		A6 G64
2499	CULBERTSON, John C	21	SENW	1853-07-13		A6
2502	" "	21	SWNW	1854-10-02		A6 G78
2501	" "	32	SE	1854-10-02		A6
2500	" "	21	SESW	1855-01-01		A6
2503	" "	28	NWNW	1855-01-01		A6 G67
2504	" "	29	NENE	1855-01-01		A6 G67
2506	CURRAN, John	7	S½SE	1857-03-10		A1
2507	" "	8	NWSW	1857-03-10		A1
2551	CUTTING, James C	23	S½NE	1855-05-01		A1 G57

ID	Individual in Patent	Sec.	Sec. Part	Date Issued	Other Counties	For More Info . . .
2552	CUTTING, James C (Cont'd)	23	SENW	1855-05-01		A1 G57
2585	DAVIS, William	1	SW	1854-05-01		A1 G89
2586	"	2	N½	1854-05-01		A1 G89 F
2587	"	22	NW	1854-05-01		A1 G89
2588	"	24	S½SW	1854-05-01		A1 G89
2589	"	24	SWSE	1854-05-01		A1 G89
2590	"	25	N½NE	1854-05-01		A1 G89
2591	"	25	NW	1854-05-01		A1 G89
2592	"	25	SWNE	1854-05-01		A1 G89
2593	"	3	NE	1854-05-01		A1 G89 F
2594	"	36	NW	1854-05-01		A1 G89
2513	DAVISON, Henry	33	W½NW	1855-02-01		A6 G64
2410	DEARBORN, Lucy	36	SW	1855-05-01		A6 G209
2503	DENINGTON, Elizabeth	28	NWNW	1855-01-01		A6 G67
2504	"	29	NENE	1855-01-01		A6 G67
2454	DOWNEY, Hugh D	28	SWNW	1854-08-01		A6 G97
2446	"	21	NENW	1856-01-15		A6
2448	"	22	NESW	1856-01-15		A6 G104
2447	"	23	SESE	1856-01-15		A6
2453	"	24	SESE	1856-01-15		A6 G110
2449	"	13	S½SE	1857-02-16		A5 G106
2450	"	24	N½NE	1857-02-16		A5 G106
2451	"	30	W½NW	1857-02-16		A5 G102 F
2452	"	30	W½SW	1857-02-16		A5 G102 F
2445	"	13	N½SW	1857-03-10		A1
2484	EASLEY, James S	21	W½SW	1855-12-15		A1
2407	EDWARDS, Ebenezer	4	NESW	1855-12-15		A1
2408	"	4	SESE	1855-12-15		A1
2409	"	4	W½SE	1855-12-15		A1
2557	FERGUSON, Samuel	25	SW	1855-12-15		A1
2558	"	25	W½SE	1855-12-15		A1
2427	FOLSOM, Gilman	17	NENW	1854-05-01		A1
2428	"	21	NESW	1854-05-01		A1
2429	"	29	S½NW	1854-05-01		A1
2595	FORBY, William F	26		1855-05-01		A1
2545	GALLAGHER, Patrick	17	NWNW	1857-03-10		A1
2546	"	8	E½SW	1857-03-10		A1
2547	"	8	SWSW	1857-03-10		A1
2451	GARDINER, Ellen	30	W½NW	1857-02-16		A5 G102 F
2452	"	30	W½SW	1857-02-16		A5 G102 F
2585	GIFFORD, Henry B	1	SW	1854-05-01		A1 G89
2586	"	2	N½	1854-05-01		A1 G89 F
2587	"	22	NW	1854-05-01		A1 G89
2588	"	24	S½SW	1854-05-01		A1 G89
2589	"	24	SWSE	1854-05-01		A1 G89
2590	"	25	N½NE	1854-05-01		A1 G89
2591	"	25	NW	1854-05-01		A1 G89
2592	"	25	SWNE	1854-05-01		A1 G89
2593	"	3	NE	1854-05-01		A1 G89 F
2594	"	36	NW	1854-05-01		A1 G89
2432	"	1	SE	1854-10-02		A6 G145
2430	"	1	SENE	1854-10-02		A6 F
2431	"	1	SWNE	1854-11-01		A4 G144 F
2458	GILL, James H	3	SE	1855-05-01		A1
2512	GOUGH, John	8	E½SE	1855-12-15		A1
2459	GOWER, James H	18	S½SW	1857-02-16		A5 F
2460	"	18	SWSE	1857-02-16		A5
2461	"	7	NWSW	1857-02-16		A5 F
2462	"	7	W½NW	1857-02-16		A5 F
2406	GREEN, Dennis	5	E½NE	1854-12-01		A1 F
2543	GRIDER, Nicholas	6	NE	1859-11-19		A1 F
2569	GRIER, Thomas	15	NENW	1855-12-15		A1
2570	"	15	SW	1855-12-15		A1
2571	"	15	W½NW	1855-12-15		A1
2572	"	17	SE	1855-12-15		A1
2573	"	34	SW	1855-12-15		A1
2596	HARKLEROAD, William	21	NENE	1851-04-01		A1
2495	HARRY, Jane	3	W½NW	1854-12-01		A1 F
2382	HASTINGS, Andrew F	34	E½	1855-05-10		A1
2383	"	35	W½	1855-05-10		A1
2577	HAWKS, Thomas S	10	NESW	1857-02-16		A5
2578	"	10	W½SW	1857-02-16		A5
2463	HILLMAN, James	23	NESE	1854-12-01		A1

ID	Individual in Patent	Sec.	Sec. Part	Date Issued	Other Counties	For More Info . . .
2464	HILLMAN, James (Cont'd)	35	N½SE	1854-12-01		A1
2465	" "	35	S½NE	1854-12-01		A1
2378	HOOK, Margaret	29	S½NE	1854-10-02		A6 G219
2396	INGMOND, Mary	18	NWNW	1857-02-20		A5 G13 F
2397	" "	7	SWSW	1857-02-20		A5 G13 F
2568	IOWA, State Of	16		1937-08-26		A3
2519	JAMISON, Granville E	4	NESE	1863-09-24		A5 G243
2448	JOHNSON, Anna	22	NESW	1856-01-15		A6 G104
2466	JOHNSON, James	19	E½	1854-12-01		A1
2468	" "	19	E½SW	1854-12-01		A1 F
2469	" "	20	N½SW	1854-12-01		A1
2470	" "	20	S½NE	1854-12-01		A1
2471	" "	20	S½NW	1854-12-01		A1
2472	" "	20	SE	1854-12-01		A1
2477	" "	31	SE	1854-12-01		A1
2467	" "	19	E½NW	1855-02-01		A6 F
2473	" "	30	E½NW	1855-02-01		A6 F
2474	" "	30	E½SW	1855-02-01		A6 F
2475	" "	31	E½NW	1855-02-01		A6 F
2476	" "	31	E½SW	1855-02-01		A6 F
2517	JONES, John	25	SENE	1855-12-15		A1
2510	KERSTEN, John F L	7	NESE	1857-03-10		A1
2511	" "	7	SENE	1857-03-10		A1
2553	KIRKPATRICK, Richard	25	SESE	1855-12-15		A1
2560	KIRKWOOD, Samuel J	21	NWNE	1857-03-10		A1
2559	" "	20	S½SW	1857-04-01		A6
2561	KNEPPER, Samuel	5	W½NW	1855-05-01		A1
2563	" "	6	E½SE	1855-05-01		A1
2562	" "	5	W½SW	1953-10-22		A1
2449	LANE, Elizabeth	13	S½SE	1857-02-16		A5 G106
2450	" "	24	N½NE	1857-02-16		A5 G106
2386	LAYTEN, Andrew	7	NWNE	1856-09-01		A1
2387	LAYTON, Andrew	6	W½SE	1855-12-15		A1
2389	" "	7	NESW	1855-12-15		A1 F
2390	" "	7	SENW	1855-12-15		A1 F
2388	" "	7	NENW	1856-01-15		A6 F
2439	LEHMAN, Henry	35	N½NE	1857-02-20		A5
2391	LEMMON, Archibald	15	SENW	1855-12-15		A1
2597	LESLIE, William	18	N½NE	1855-12-15		A1
2598	" "	5	W½NE	1855-12-15		A1 F
2599	" "	9	N½SE	1855-12-15		A1
2600	" "	9	SWSE	1855-12-15		A1
2432	LONG, Susanna	1	SE	1854-10-02		A6 G145
2532	MAHON, Miles	7	NWSE	1857-03-10		A1
2533	" "	7	SWNE	1857-03-10		A1
2548	MARSH, Peter	31	W½SW	1855-05-01		A1 F
2392	MATHEWS, Archibald	10	SESW	1855-12-15		A1
2393	MEAD, Benjamin L	36	SE	1855-12-15		A1
2410	MEAD, Enfield S	36	SW	1855-05-01		A6 G209
2538	MEEKER, Elizabeth	23	NESW	1853-10-01		A6 G231
2539	" "	23	NWSE	1853-10-01		A6 G231
2514	MERCER, John H	11	E½SE	1855-05-01		A1
2515	" "	12	SW	1855-05-01		A1
2411	MICHAEL, Ethan	32	N½	1854-05-01		A1
2534	MORGAN, Milo	36	E½NE	1853-11-01		A1
2535	" "	36	W½NE	1855-12-15		A1
2518	MORISON, John	4	S½SW	1855-05-01		A1
2522	MORRIS, Eatten	8	NE	1855-05-01		A6 G281 R2523
2523	" "	8	NE	1857-04-10		A6 G281 R2522
2522	MORRIS, Eliza	8	NE	1855-05-01		A6 G281 R2523
2523	" "	8	NE	1857-04-10		A6 G281 R2522
2522	MORRIS, James	8	NE	1855-05-01		A6 G281 R2523
2523	" "	8	NE	1857-04-10		A6 G281 R2522
2522	MORRIS, Matthew	8	NE	1855-05-01		A6 G281 R2523
2523	" "	8	NE	1857-04-10		A6 G281 R2522
2522	MORRIS, Nathaniel	8	NE	1855-05-01		A6 G281 R2523
2523	" "	8	NE	1857-04-10		A6 G281 R2522
2542	MORTON, Morris	15	E½	1855-12-15		A1
2575	MURDOCK, Thomas	11	N½NE	1855-05-01		A1
2576	" "	2	SE	1855-05-01		A1
2554	NEAL, Robert	30	SE	1852-03-15		A6 R2555
2555	" "	30	SE	1918-06-22		A6 R2554
2377	NUSSBAUM, Abraham	6	NW	1855-05-01		A1 F

ID	Individual in Patent	Sec.	Sec. Part	Date Issued	Other Counties	For More Info . . .
2544	NUSSBAUM, Nicholas	9	NWNW	1855-05-01		A1
2416	PAYNE, Nancy	28	SENE	1854-10-02		A6 G245
2378	PETERS, Adam	29	S½NE	1854-10-02		A6 G219
2529	PINNEY, Marcellus	19	NWNW	1856-01-15		A6 F
2531	" "	19	SWNW	1856-01-15		A6 G222 F
2530	" "	19	W½SW	1856-01-15		A6 F
2601	PRICE, William	12	SE	1855-05-01		A1
2536	RENO, Morgan	22	W½SW	1853-07-01		A6
2537	" "	28	NENE	1853-07-01		A6
2538	" "	23	NESW	1853-10-01		A6 G231
2539	" "	23	NWSE	1853-10-01		A6 G231
2540	" "	20	N½NE	1854-10-02		A6 G236
2541	" "	20	N½NW	1854-10-02		A6 G236
2564	ROBBINS, Samuel M	17	NWNE	1855-05-10		A1
2565	" "	17	SENE	1855-05-10		A1
2502	ROBERTSON, Christina	21	SWNW	1854-10-02		A6 G78
2478	ROBINSON, James	13	S½SW	1855-05-01		A1
2479	" "	14	SE	1855-05-01		A1
2480	" "	23	N½NE	1855-05-01		A1
2481	" "	24	N½SW	1855-05-01		A1
2482	" "	24	NW	1855-05-01		A1
2483	" "	24	S½NE	1855-05-01		A1
2519	ROGERS, John N	4	NESE	1863-09-24		A5 G243
2381	ROUSSEAU, Alexander S	27	SE	1855-05-01		A1
2421	SANDERS, George E	33	S½	1855-11-01		A1
2582	SANFORD, Whitfield	4	E½NW	1854-12-01		A1 F
2583	" "	4	W½NE	1854-12-01		A1 F
2414	SANXAY, Frederic	17	SWNE	1854-05-01		A1
2416	" "	28	SENE	1854-10-02		A6 G245
2415	" "	32	SW	1854-10-02		A6
2433	SEARS, Walter S	10	NE	1855-12-15		A1 G48
2434	" "	10	S½NW	1855-12-15		A1 G48
2435	" "	17	S½NW	1855-12-15		A1 G48
2436	" "	17	SW	1855-12-15		A1 G48
2437	" "	9	NE	1855-12-15		A1 G48
2380	SHERWOOD, Albert	29	S½	1854-05-01		A1
2379	" "	28	SW	1854-10-02		A6
2413	SIMMONS, Frances	11	S½NE	1855-05-01		A1
2540	SMITH, Margaret	20	N½NE	1854-10-02		A6 G236
2541	" "	20	N½NW	1854-10-02		A6 G236
2384	SNYDER, Andrew J	24	N½SE	1855-05-01		A1
2385	" "	3	SW	1855-05-01		A1
2519	" "	4	NESE	1863-09-24		A5 G243
2527	SNYDER, Lewis S	17	NENE	1857-03-10		A1
2528	" "	7	NENE	1857-03-10		A1
2485	STOCKDALE, James	14	SW	1855-12-15		A1
2486	" "	22	E½	1855-12-15		A1
2487	" "	22	SESW	1855-12-15		A1
2488	" "	23	W½NW	1855-12-15		A1
2489	" "	27	SW	1855-12-15		A1
2490	" "	27	SWNW	1855-12-15		A1
2491	" "	28	SE	1855-12-15		A1
2492	" "	28	SWNE	1855-12-15		A1
2496	SUTTON, Jehu B	27	SENW	1855-12-15		A1
2497	" "	33	E½NW	1855-12-15		A1
2498	SUTTON, John B	28	SENW	1856-05-01		A1
2405	UPDEGRAFF, David	11	NW	1855-05-01		A1
2402	UPDEGRAFF, David B	12	NW	1855-05-01		A1
2403	" "	12	W½NE	1855-05-01		A1
2404	" "	2	SW	1855-05-01		A1
2505	WARD, John C	12	E½NE	1854-12-01		A1
2453	WEISER, Mary C	24	SESE	1856-01-15		A6 G110
2549	WEIST, Philip	28	NENW	1854-05-01		A1
2550	" "	28	NWNE	1854-05-01		A1
2567	WEIST, Samuel	27	N½NW	1854-05-01		A1
2604	WELCH, William	4	NWSW	1854-05-01		A1
2605	" "	4	W½NW	1854-05-01		A1 F
2412	WELLER, Fidelia	3	SENW	1855-05-01		A1 F
2493	WHERRY, James	13	N½	1855-12-15		A1
2494	" "	14	N½	1855-12-15		A1
2524	WHERRY, Joseph	10	SE	1855-12-15		A1
2526	" "	5	W½SE	1855-12-15		A1
2525	" "	11	SW	1940-04-11		A1

ID	Individual in Patent	Sec.	Sec. Part	Date Issued	Other Counties	For More Info . . .
2520	WHITE, Albert S	5	E½SW	1855-05-01		A6 G280
2522	" "	8	NE	1855-05-01		A6 G281 R2523
2521	" "	8	NW	1857-04-01		A4 G280
2523	" "	8	NE	1857-04-10		A6 G281 R2522
2520	WHITE, James L	5	E½SW	1855-05-01		A6 G280
2522	" "	8	NE	1855-05-01		A6 G281 R2523
2521	" "	8	NW	1857-04-01		A4 G280
2523	" "	8	NE	1857-04-10		A6 G281 R2522
2520	WHITE, John W	5	E½SW	1855-05-01		A6 G280
2522	" "	8	NE	1855-05-01		A6 G281 R2523
2521	" "	8	NW	1857-04-01		A4 G280
2523	" "	8	NE	1857-04-10		A6 G281 R2522
2556	WHITE, Rufus G	10	N½NW	1855-05-10		A1
2580	WILDEN, Vincen	21	SESE	1851-04-01		A1
2579	" "	21	NWNW	1855-03-01		A6
2419	WILLIAMS, George C	4	SENE	1855-03-01		A4 F
2417	" "	3	NENW	1855-05-01		A1 F
2418	" "	4	NENE	1855-05-01		A1 F
2420	" "	6	SW	1855-05-01		A1 F
2531	WILLIAMSON, Hetty	19	SWNW	1856-01-15		A6 G222 F
2602	WILLINGHAM, William W	29	NENW	1855-12-15		A1
2603	" "	29	NWNE	1855-12-15		A1
2516	WILSEY, John H	5	NW	1855-05-01		A6 F
2508	WOLFE, John D	11	W½SE	1855-12-15		A1
2509	" "	23	NENW	1855-12-15		A1

Patent Map

T79-N R13-W
5th PM Meridian

Map Group 12

Township Statistics

Parcels Mapped	:	229
Number of Patents	:	179
Number of Individuals	:	128
Patentees Identified	:	114
Number of Surnames	:	112
Multi-Patentee Parcels	:	45
Oldest Patent Date	:	4/1/1851
Most Recent Patent	:	10/22/1953
Block/Lot Parcels	:	0
Parcels Re - Issued	:	2
Parcels that Overlap	:	0
Cities and Towns	:	1
Cemeteries	:	3

Section 6
NUSSBAUM Abraham 1855
GRIDER Nicholas 1859
WILLIAMS George C 1855
LAYTON Andrew 1855
KNEPPER Samuel 1855

Section 5
KNEPPER Samuel 1855
WILSEY John H 1855
LESLIE William 1855
GREEN Dennis 1854
KNEPPER Samuel 1953
WHITE [280] John W 1855
WHERRY Joseph 1855
COOLEY William 1855

Section 4
WELCH William 1854
SANFORD Whitfield 1854
SANFORD Whitfield 1854
WILLIAMS George C 1855
WILLIAMS George C 1855
WELCH William 1854
EDWARDS Ebenezer 1855
ROGERS [243] John N 1863
MORISON John 1855
EDWARDS Ebenezer 1855
EDWARDS Ebenezer 1855

Section 7
GOWER James H 1857
LAYTON Andrew 1856
LAYTEN Andrew 1856
SNYDER Lewis S 1857
LAYTON Andrew 1855
MAHON Miles 1857
KERSTEN John F L 1857
GOWER James H 1857
LAYTON Andrew 1855
MAHON Miles 1857
KERSTEN John F L 1857
BERRYHILL [13] Charles H 1857
CANNON Hugh 1857

Section 8
WHITE [281] John W 1857
WHITE [280] John W 1857
WHITE [281] John W 1855
CURRAN John 1857
CAREY Bernard 1855
GOUGH John 1855
GALLAGHER Patrick 1857
GALLAGHER Patrick 1857
CURRAN John 1857

Section 9
NUSSBAUM Nicholas 1855
BRAMER George L 1855
BRAMER George L 1855
CHITTENDEN [48] Henry 1855
BRAMER George L 1855
LESLIE William 1855
LESLIE William 1855
COLEY Henry 1855

Section 18
BERRYHILL [13] Charles H 1857
CANNON Hugh 1857
LESLIE William 1855
CANNON Hugh 1857
CANNON Hugh 1857
ASKEW Cyrus H 1855
CANNON Hugh 1857
ASKEW Cyrus H 1855
ASKEW Cyrus H 1855
GOWER James H 1857
GOWER James H 1857

Section 17
GALLAGHER Patrick 1857
FOLSOM Gilman 1854
ROBBINS Samuel M 1855
SNYDER Lewis S 1857
CHITTENDEN [48] Henry 1855
SANXAY Frederic 1854
ROBBINS Samuel M 1855
CHITTENDEN [48] Henry 1855
GRIER Thomas 1855

Section 16
IOWA State Of 1937

Section 19
PINNEY Marcellus 1856
PINNEY [222] Marcellus 1856
JOHNSON James 1855
PINNEY Marcellus 1856
JOHNSON James 1854
JOHNSON James 1854

Section 20
RENO [236] Morgan 1854
RENO [236] Morgan 1854
JOHNSON James 1854
JOHNSON James 1854
JOHNSON James 1854
JOHNSON James 1854
KIRKWOOD Samuel J 1857

Section 21
WILDEN Vincen 1855
DOWNEY Hugh D 1856
KIRKWOOD Samuel J 1857
HARKLEROAD William 1851
CULBERTSON [78] John C 1854
CULBERTSON John C 1853
EASLEY James S 1855
FOLSOM Gilman 1854
BERRYHILL James B 1853
CULBERTSON John C 1855
WILDEN Vincen 1851

Section 30
DOWNEY [102] Hugh D 1857
JOHNSON James 1855
DOWNEY [102] Hugh D 1857
JOHNSON James 1855
NEAL Robert 1852
NEAL Robert 1918

Section 29
COX Thomas J 1855
WILLINGHAM William W 1855
WILLINGHAM William W 1855
CULBERTSON [87] John C 1855
FOLSOM Gilman 1854
PETERS [219] Adam 1854
SHERWOOD Albert 1854

Section 28
CULBERTSON [87] John C 1855
WEIST Philip 1854
WEIST Philip 1854
RENO Morgan 1853
DOWNEY [97] Hugh D 1854
SUTTON John B 1856
STOCKDALE James 1855
SANXAY [245] Frederic 1854
SHERWOOD Albert 1854
STOCKDALE James 1855

Section 31
ASKEW Cyrus H 1855
JOHNSON James 1855
BRADY Samuel W 1852
MARSH Peter 1855
JOHNSON James 1855
JOHNSON James 1854

Section 32
MICHAEL Ethan 1854
SANXAY Frederic 1854
CULBERTSON John C 1854

Section 33
CRUM [64] John H 1855
SUTTON Jehu B 1855
CARPENTER George F 1855
SANDERS George E 1855

Map of land patents showing sections 1, 2, 3, 10, 11, 12, 13, 14, 15, 22, 23, 24, 25, 26, 27, 34, 35, 36.

Helpful Hints

1. This Map's INDEX can be found on the preceding pages.

2. Refer to Map "C" to see where this Township lies within Poweshiek County, Iowa.

3. Numbers within square brackets [ ] denote a multi-patentee land parcel (multi-owner). Refer to Appendix "C" for a full list of members in this group.

4. Areas that look to be crowded with Patentees usually indicate multiple sales of the same parcel (Re-issues) or Overlapping parcels. See this Township's Index for an explanation of these and other circumstances that might explain "odd" groupings of Patentees on this map.

Copyright 2010 Boyd IT, Inc. All Rights Reserved

Legend

—— Patent Boundary

—— Section Boundary

No Patents Found (or Outside County)

1., 2., 3., ... Lot Numbers (when beside a name)

[ ] Group Number (see Appendix "C")

Scale: Section = 1 mile X 1 mile (generally, with some exceptions)

Road Map

T79-N R13-W
5th PM Meridian

Map Group 12

Cities & Towns
Guernsey

Cemeteries
Guernsey Cemetery
Harmony Cemetery
Morrison Cemetery

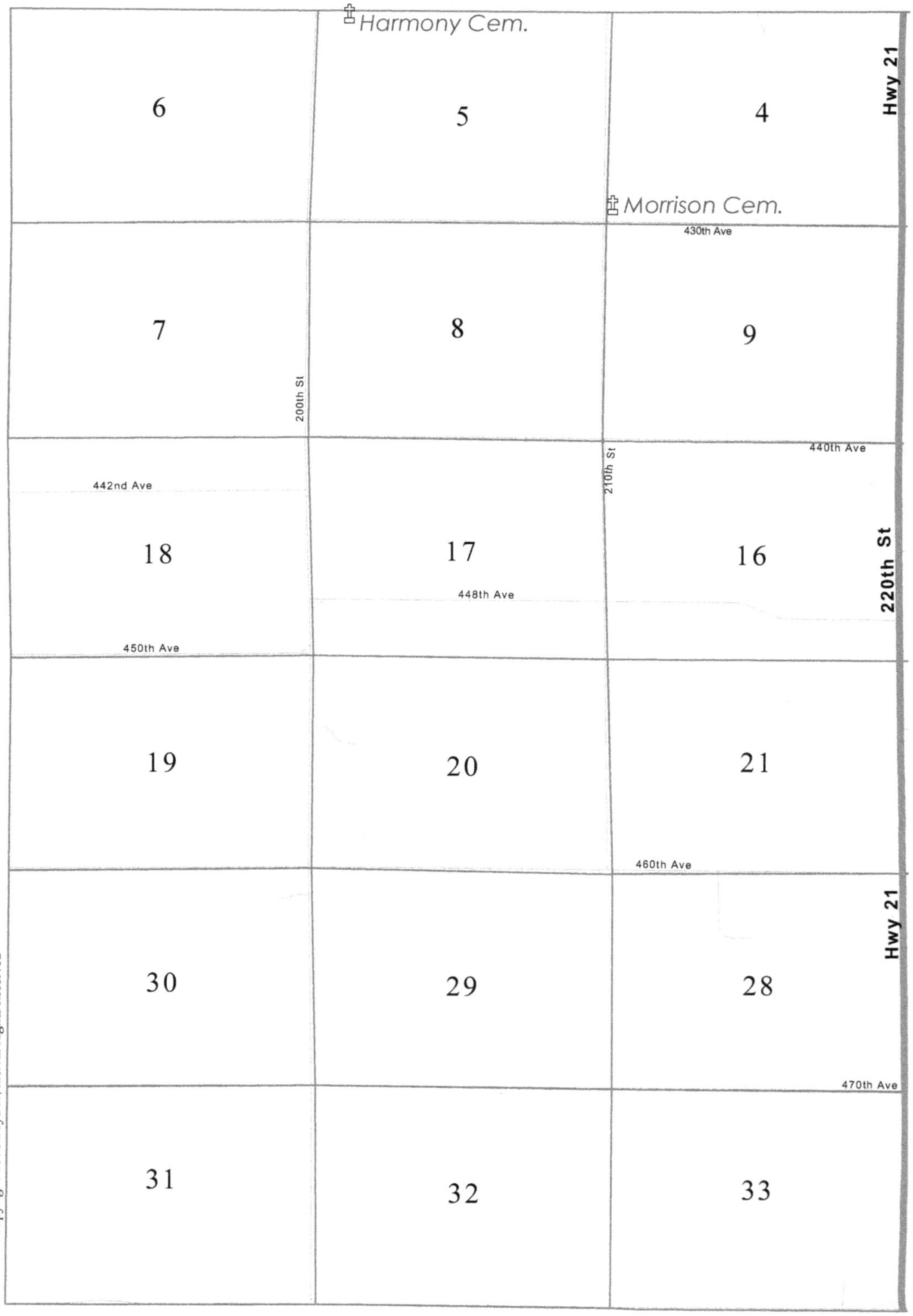

⚱ *Harmony Cem.*

| 6 | 5 | 4 |

⚱ *Morrison Cem.*

430th Ave

| 7 | 8 | 9 |

200th St

210th St

440th Ave

442nd Ave

| 18 | 17 | 16 |

448th Ave

450th Ave

220th St

| 19 | 20 | 21 |

460th Ave

Hwy 21

| 30 | 29 | 28 |

470th Ave

| 31 | 32 | 33 |

420th Ave

240th St

| 3 | 2 | 1 |

225th St

| 10 | 11 | 12 |

445th Ave

E Water

Butler

Blaine St

Lockwood St

Poweshiek-Iowa Rd

| 15 Guernsey● | 14 | 13 |

450th Ave

230th St

235th St

240th St

| 22 | 23 | 24 |

✝ Guernsey Cem.

| 27 | 26 | 25 |

| 34 | 35 | 36 |

480th Ave

Helpful Hints

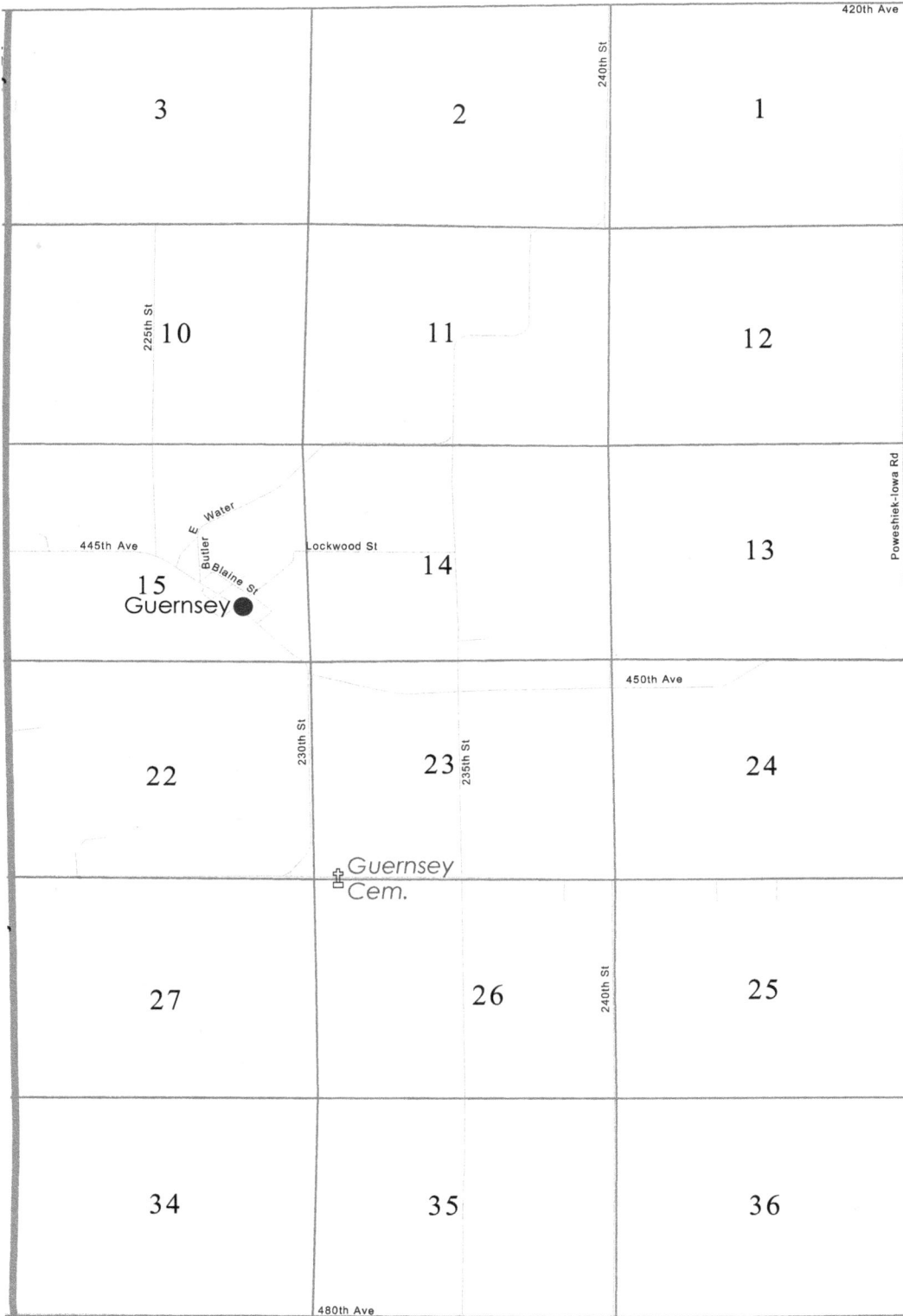

1. This road map has a number of uses, but primarily it is to help you: a) find the present location of land owned by your ancestors (at least the general area), b) find cemeteries and city-centers, and c) estimate the route/roads used by Census-takers & tax-assessors.

2. If you plan to travel to Poweshiek County to locate cemeteries or land parcels, please pick up a modern travel map for the area before you do. Mapping old land parcels on modern maps is not as exact a science as you might think. Just the slightest variations in public land survey coordinates, estimates of parcel boundaries, or road-map deviations can greatly alter a map's representation of how a road either does or doesn't cross a particular parcel of land.

Legend

————————	Section Lines
≡≡≡≡≡≡≡	Interstates
▬▬▬▬▬▬	Highways
————————	Other Roads
●	Cities/Towns
✝	Cemeteries

Scale: Section = 1 mile X 1 mile
(generally, with some exceptions)

Historical Map

T79-N R13-W
5th PM Meridian

Map Group 12

Cities & Towns

Guernsey

Cemeteries

Guernsey Cemetery
Harmony Cemetery
Morrison Cemetery

⛪ Harmony Cem.

| 6 | 5 | 4 |

⛪ Morrison Cem.

| 7 | 8 | 9 |

| 18 | 17 | 16 |

| 19 | 20 | 21 |

| 30 | 29 | 28 |

Jordan Crk

| 31 | 32 | 33 |

Deep Riv

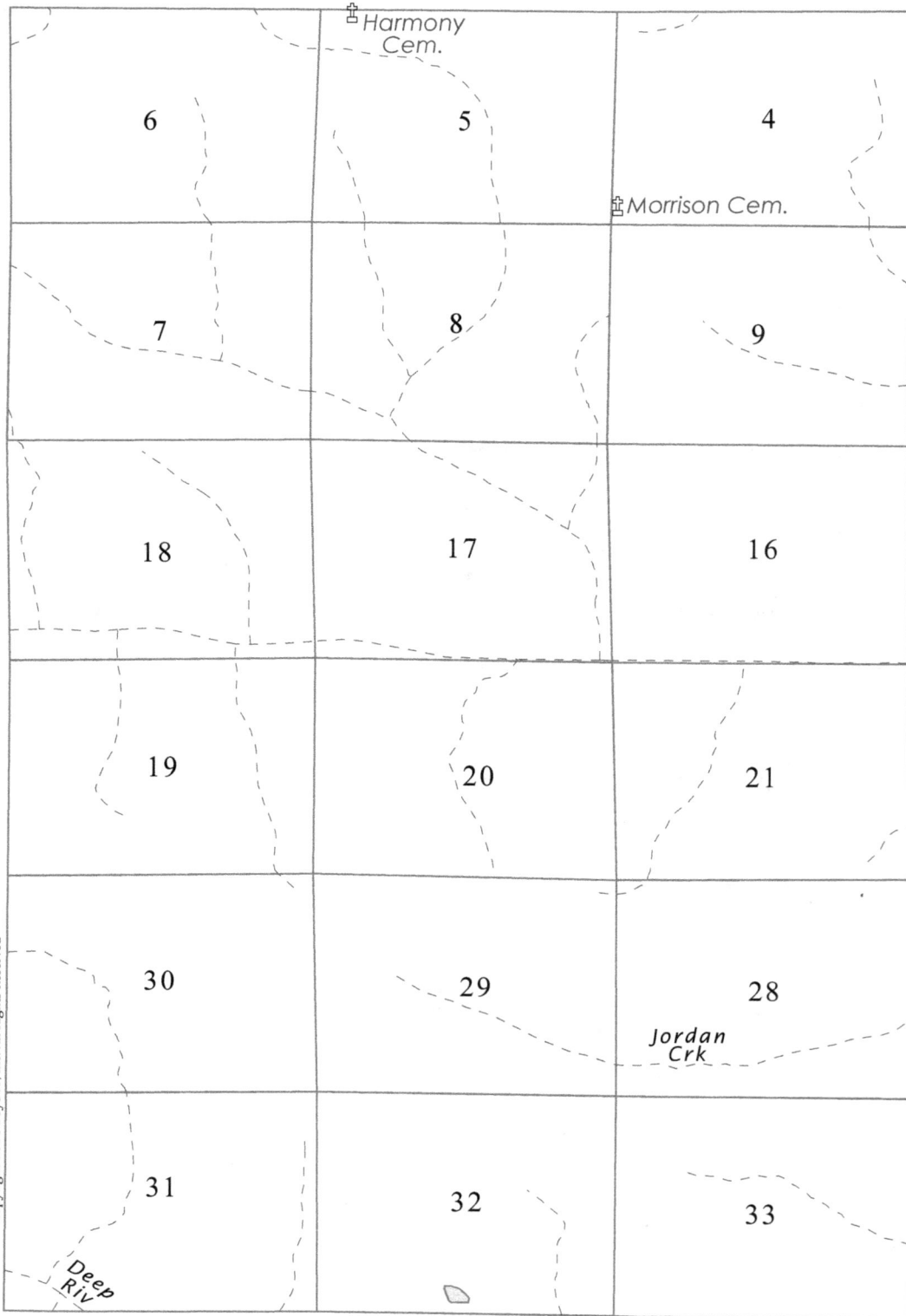

3

2

1

10

11

12

15

Guernsey ●

14

13

22

23

24

N English Riv

Guernsey Cem.

27

26

25

34

35

36

Helpful Hints

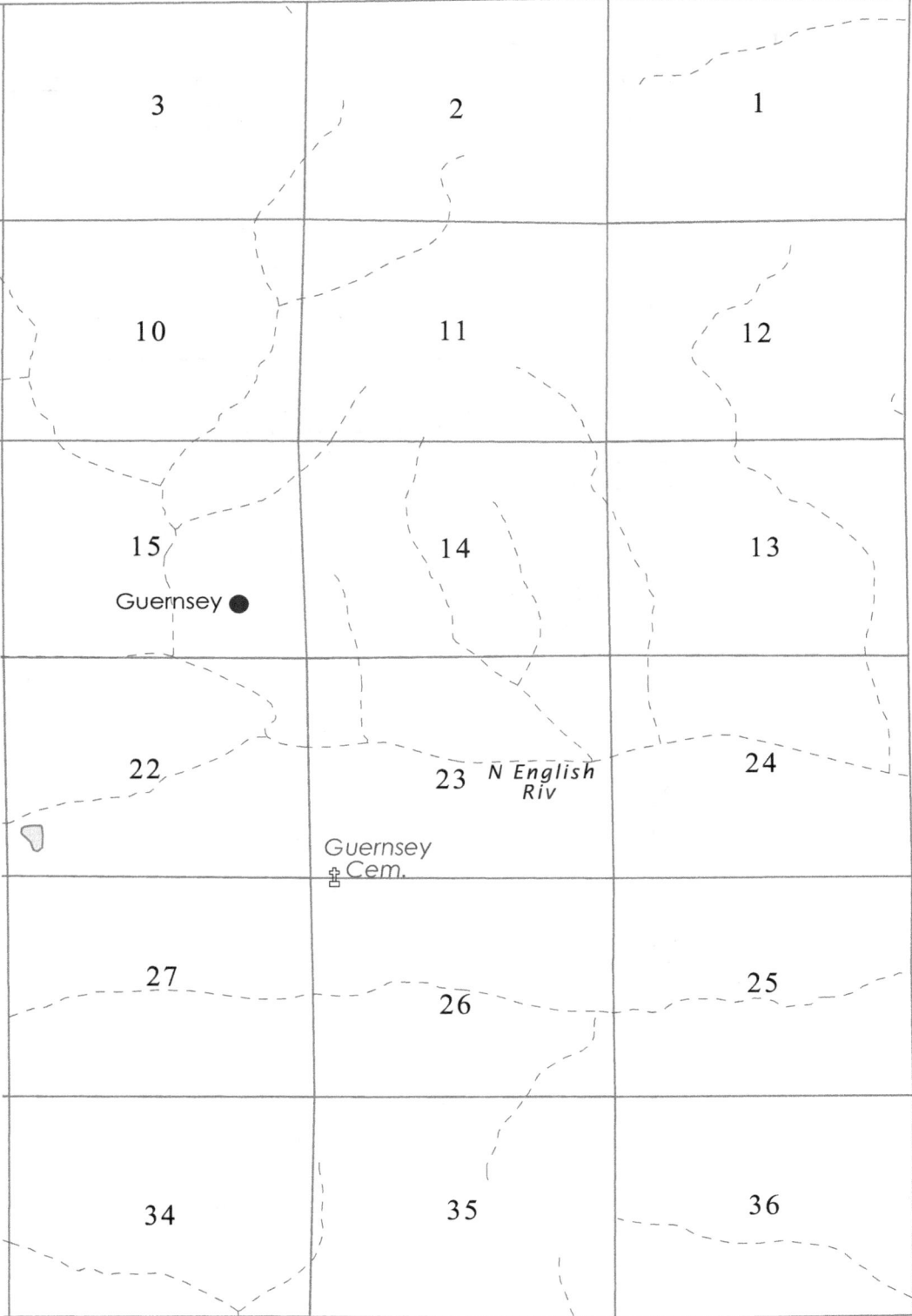

1. This Map takes a different look at the same Congressional Township displayed in the preceding two maps. It presents features that can help you better envision the historical development of the area: a) Water-bodies (lakes & ponds), b) Water-courses (rivers, streams, etc.), c) Railroads, d) City/town center-points (where they were oftentimes located when first settled), and e) Cemeteries.

2. Using this "Historical" map in tandem with this Township's Patent Map and Road Map, may lead you to some interesting discoveries. You will often find roads, towns, cemeteries, and waterways are named after nearby landowners: sometimes those names will be the ones you are researching. See how many of these research gems you can find here in Poweshiek County.

Legend

—————	Section Lines
+++++++	Railroads
▭	Large Rivers & Bodies of Water
- - - - - -	Streams/Creeks & Small Rivers
●	Cities/Towns
⚓	Cemeteries

Scale: Section = 1 mile X 1 mile
(there are some exceptions)

Map Group 13: Index to Land Patents

Township 78-North Range 16-West (5th PM)

After you locate an individual in this Index, take note of the Section and Section Part then proceed to the Land Patent map on the pages immediately following. You should have no difficulty locating the corresponding parcel of land.

The "For More Info" Column will lead you to more information about the underlying Patents. See the *Legend* at right, and the "How to Use this Book" chapter, for more information.

<table>
<tr><td colspan="5">LEGEND</td></tr>
<tr><td colspan="5">"For More Info . . . " column</td></tr>
<tr><td colspan="5">A = Authority (Legislative Act, See Appendix "A")</td></tr>
<tr><td colspan="5">B = Block or Lot (location in Section unknown)</td></tr>
<tr><td colspan="5">C = Cancelled Patent</td></tr>
<tr><td colspan="5">F = Fractional Section</td></tr>
<tr><td colspan="5">G = Group (Multi-Patentee Patent, see Appendix "C")</td></tr>
<tr><td colspan="5">V = Overlaps another Parcel</td></tr>
<tr><td colspan="5">R = Re-Issued (Parcel patented more than once)</td></tr>
</table>

(A & G items require you to look in the Appendixes referred to above. All other Letter-designations followed by a number require you to locate line-items in this index that possess the ID number found after the letter).

ID	Individual in Patent	Sec.	Sec. Part	Date Issued	Other Counties	For More Info . . .
2611	ALLOWAY, Abraham	33	NENW	1855-05-10		A1
2853	APPLEGATE, Joseph	24	NESW	1855-05-01		A1
2854	" "	24	NWSE	1855-05-10		A1
2967	APPLEGATE, Thomas S	24	NWSW	1857-03-10		A1
2634	ARMITAGE, Ann	35	SWNW	1852-09-01		A6
2649	ARNOLD, David	20	NENE	1852-09-01		A6
2650	" "	21	NWNW	1852-09-01		A6
2798	BAILEY, Jesse	35	SW	1855-12-15		A1
2799	" "	35	SWNE	1855-12-15		A1
2794	" "	3	12	1857-03-10		A1
2795	" "	3	3	1857-03-10		A1
2796	" "	3	4	1857-03-10		A1
2797	" "	3	5	1857-03-10		A1
2880	BALDWIN, Mary	33	NESW	1852-09-10		A6
2873	BENNETT, Frances	25	E½SW	1855-05-01		A6 G180
2641	BERRYHILL, Charles H	13	SESE	1853-10-01		A6 G9
2751	BERRYHILL, James B	14	NW	1855-12-15		A1
2752	" "	15	NE	1855-12-15		A1
2753	" "	22	NENW	1857-03-10		A1
2829	BERRYHILL, John H	9	NESE	1855-01-01		A6 G24
2827	" "	9	SENE	1855-01-01		A6
2830	" "	9	SESE	1855-01-01		A6 G22
2828	" "	9	SWSE	1855-01-01		A6 G23
2984	BERRYHILL, William D	14	N½SW	1855-12-15		A1
2985	" "	15	NWSW	1855-12-15		A1
2986	" "	15	SWNW	1855-12-15		A1
2606	BETTS, Aaron	31	N½SE	1855-12-15		A1
2607	" "	31	S½NE	1855-12-15		A1
2608	" "	32	NWSW	1855-12-15		A1
2810	BINFORD, John	18	NESW	1855-05-01		A1 F
2811	" "	18	SE	1855-05-01		A1
2812	" "	19	E½NW	1855-05-01		A1 F
2813	" "	19	SENE	1855-05-01		A1
2814	" "	19	W½NE	1855-05-01		A1
2879	BIXLER, Magdalene	34	SWSW	1852-09-10		A6
2641	BOONE, Eleanor	13	SESE	1853-10-01		A6 G9
2636	BOWMAN, Benjamin	35	W½SE	1855-12-15		A1
2960	BOYER, Theodore F	29	NWSW	1855-02-01		A6
2961	" "	29	SWSW	1855-05-01		A1
2926	BRACKENRIDGE, Robert B	4	11	1855-12-15		A1
2927	" "	4	NESW	1855-12-15		A1
2928	" "	5	E½SE	1855-12-15		A1
2897	BRAINARD, Nelson	31	SESW	1855-05-01		A1 F
2898	" "	31	SWSE	1855-05-01		A1
2899	" "	32	S½SE	1855-05-01		A1
2895	BREED, Nathan	6	8	1854-12-01		A1

ID	Individual in Patent	Sec.	Sec. Part	Date Issued	Other Counties	For More Info ...
2896	BREED, Nathan (Cont'd)	6	9	1854-12-01		A1
2754	BRIDGES, James	22	SWNE	1855-12-15		A1
2911	BRIDGES, Rezin	17	NWNE	1854-05-01		A1
2913	" "	21	SWNW	1854-05-01		A1
2912	" "	20	SENE	1854-12-01		A1
2628	BROWNLEE, Andrew	35	NESE	1855-12-15		A1
2660	BUTLER, Edward	3	SWSW	1855-12-15		A1
2693	BYERS, William	19	S½SE	1855-05-01		A1 G187
2694	" "	30	N½NE	1855-05-01		A1 G187
2869	BYINGTON, Legrand	27	SESW	1854-05-01		A6 G43
2870	" "	27	SWSE	1854-05-01		A6 G43
2902	CANTRIL, Newton S	28	SWSE	1854-05-01		A1
2708	CARPENTER, Hiram M	22	SESW	1852-11-01		A1
2980	CARTER, Wesley	19	NENE	1853-07-13		A6 G46
2924	CASE, Riley	31	E½NW	1855-05-10		A1 F
2925	" "	31	NESW	1855-05-10		A1 F
2981	CASTOR, Wesley	20	NWNW	1854-12-01		A1
2846	CHESHIRE, John W	21	SWSW	1855-12-15		A1
2847	" "	4	7	1855-12-15		A1
2848	" "	5	6	1855-12-15		A1
2979	CLARK, Wesley C	25	N½SE	1856-09-01		A1
2821	CLAXTON, Elizabeth	1	E½SE	1855-05-01		A6 G66
2908	CLOUD, Peter C	4	5	1855-12-15		A1
2937	CLOUD, Seth	11	W½NE	1855-12-15		A1
2943	CLUTE, Solomon J	27	N½SW	1857-03-10		A1
2944	" "	27	NWSE	1857-03-10		A1
2945	" "	27	S½NW	1857-03-10		A1
2946	" "	28	NESE	1857-03-10		A1
2965	COX, Thomas J	3	1	1855-12-15		A1
2966	" "	3	2	1855-12-15		A1
2963	" "	1	NWSW	1857-03-10		A1
2964	" "	2	11	1857-05-01		A1
2749	CRAVER, James A	15	SESE	1856-01-15		A6 G60
2750	" "	22	NENE	1856-01-15		A6 G60
2747	" "	24	NESE	1856-01-15		A6
2748	" "	24	SWSE	1856-01-15		A6 G61
2823	CRILL, John	34	NWNE	1852-03-10		A1
2824	" "	34	SWSE	1852-03-10		A1
2904	CRISMAN, Obed	28	SWNW	1855-12-15		A1
2820	CULBERTSON, John C	6	NESE	1854-12-01		A1
2821	" "	1	E½SE	1855-05-01		A6 G66
2819	" "	4	N½SE	1855-12-15		A1
2815	" "	12	NENE	1856-01-15		A6
2816	" "	20	NENW	1857-03-10		A1
2817	" "	3	11	1857-03-10		A1
2818	" "	3	6	1857-03-10		A1
2822	" "	17	W½SW	1860-11-01		A5 G73
2825	DEVRICKSON, John	12	SESE	None-NA-NA		A6 R2620
2657	DEWEY, Dwight C	17	NENE	1856-09-01		A1
2658	" "	34	E½SE	1857-02-16		A5
2659	" "	34	SENE	1857-02-16		A5
2737	DOWNEY, Hugh D	32	NWSE	1855-01-01		A6 G103
2721	" "	33	NWNW	1855-01-01		A6
2712	" "	21	NENE	1855-03-01		A4
2713	" "	21	SWNE	1855-03-01		A4
2717	" "	31	SESE	1855-05-01		A1
2718	" "	32	NESE	1855-05-01		A1
2719	" "	32	S½NE	1855-05-01		A1
2720	" "	32	SWSW	1855-05-01		A1
2722	" "	33	SWNW	1855-05-01		A1
2711	" "	19	SW	1855-05-10		A1 F
2714	" "	30	S½SE	1855-05-10		A1
2715	" "	30	SW	1855-05-10		A1 F
2716	" "	31	N½NE	1855-05-10		A1
2710	" "	10	SWNW	1855-12-15		A1
2724	" "	4	1	1855-12-15		A1
2725	" "	4	12	1855-12-15		A1
2726	" "	4	8	1855-12-15		A1
2727	" "	4	9	1855-12-15		A1
2728	" "	4	NWSW	1855-12-15		A1
2729	" "	5	11	1855-12-15		A1
2730	" "	5	7	1855-12-15		A1
2731	" "	5	8	1855-12-15		A1

ID	Individual in Patent	Sec.	Sec. Part	Date Issued	Other Counties	For More Info . . .
2732	DOWNEY, Hugh D (Cont'd)	5	SESW	1855-12-15		A1
2733	" "	8	NESW	1855-12-15		A1
2734	" "	8	NWNE	1855-12-15		A1
2735	" "	8	NWSE	1855-12-15		A1
2736	" "	9	NWSE	1855-12-15		A1
2723	" "	35	SESE	1857-02-16		A5
3001	DUGGAR, William S	8	SENE	1855-12-15		A1
3002	" "	9	SWNW	1855-12-15		A1
2745	DUNGAN, Sarah	24	NENW	1854-10-02		A6 G278
2746	" "	24	NWNE	1854-10-02		A6 G278
2635	DUPREE, Banister	35	NWNW	1852-09-10		A6
2790	EASLEY, James S	22	NESW	1855-01-01		A6
2791	" "	22	NWSE	1855-01-01		A6
2742	EBY, Jacob R	29	NENE	1855-05-01		A6
2637	" "	29	NW	1855-05-01		A1 G188
2940	EDWARDS, Solomon	18	NWNE	1854-05-01		A1
2941	" "	33	SWSW	1854-05-01		A1
2942	" "	8	W½SW	1854-05-01		A1
2865	EGERTON, Martha	36	NENW	1854-03-01		A6 G242
2619	ELLIOTT, Allen	26	NESW	1852-09-10		A6
2989	ENGLISH, William	22	NWNE	1849-04-10		A1
2991	" "	26	SENW	1849-06-01		A2
2992	" "	26	SWNE	1849-06-01		A2
2993	" "	26	W½NW	1849-06-01		A2
2990	" "	26	NENW	1855-12-15		A1
2740	FARMER, Irvin	24	SESW	1853-07-02		A6 G134
2938	FARMER, Silas F	24	SWSW	1854-12-01		A6
2855	FOSS, Joseph B	4	S½SE	1855-12-15		A1
2856	" "	4	S½SW	1855-12-15		A1
2857	" "	9	E½NW	1855-12-15		A1
2858	" "	9	N½NE	1855-12-15		A1
2826	FOWLER, John	22	SESE	1852-10-01		A6
2688	FRIEND, Franklin	6	5	1854-12-01		A1
2702	FULKER, Henry	17	N½SE	1853-06-01		A6
2703	" "	17	NESW	1853-06-01		A6
2705	" "	17	SWSE	1853-06-01		A6
2704	" "	17	SESW	1855-12-15		A1
2669	GAUSE, Eli C	6	NWSE	1856-01-15		A6
2670	" "	6	SWSE	1856-01-15		A6
2859	GOSNELL, Joseph	34	SESW	1852-09-10		A6
2771	GOWER, James H	8	SWSE	1854-05-01		A1
2764	" "	21	SENW	1854-10-02		A6
2774	" "	8	SESE	1854-10-02		A6 G151
2765	" "	22	NWSW	1854-11-01		A4
2763	" "	21	E½SE	1854-12-01		A1
2767	" "	4	10	1855-01-01		A6
2758	" "	15	NWNW	1855-05-10		A1
2770	" "	8	NENE	1855-05-10		A1
2772	" "	9	NWNW	1855-05-10		A1
2773	" "	9	SWNE	1855-05-10		A1
2759	" "	15	SWSE	1855-12-15		A1
2760	" "	17	SWNW	1855-12-15		A1
2761	" "	20	NWNE	1855-12-15		A1
2762	" "	20	SWNE	1855-12-15		A1
2766	" "	22	SENW	1855-12-15		A1
2768	" "	7	NESE	1855-12-15		A1
2769	" "	7	SESW	1855-12-15		A1 F
2755	" "	1	1	1857-03-10		A1
2756	" "	11	SWSW	1857-03-10		A1
2757	" "	14	NWNE	1857-03-10		A1
2706	GRAVES, Henry S	20	N½SE	1856-06-16		A6
2738	HAINES, Hyman	32	NESW	1855-05-01		A1
2739	" "	32	SESW	1855-05-01		A1
2874	HAMBLETON, Levi	2	3	1855-12-15		A1
2875	" "	2	4	1855-12-15		A1
2876	" "	2	6	1855-12-15		A1
2881	HAMBLETON, Mary H	2	E½SW	1855-12-15		A1
2882	" "	2	NWSW	1855-12-15		A1
2883	" "	2	SWSE	1855-12-15		A1
2906	HAMBLETON, Osborn	11	SENE	1855-12-15		A1
2907	" "	12	SWNW	1855-12-15		A1
2737	HARRIS, Suckey	32	NWSE	1855-01-01		A6 G103
2644	HASE, Clayburn	13	SWNW	1855-01-01		A6

ID	Individual in Patent	Sec.	Sec. Part	Date Issued	Other Counties	For More Info . . .
2962	HATHAWAY, Thomas F	25	NW	1855-05-10		A1
2994	HAYTER, William	25	S½NE	1855-05-01		A1
2900	HAZLETON, Newton	22	NESE	1855-12-15		A1
2692	" "	22	SENE	1855-12-15		A1 G171
2901	" "	23	NWSW	1855-12-15		A1
2877	HECK, Lewis	32	NW	1855-05-01		A1
2861	HEILMAYER, Joseph	20	SESW	1855-05-01		A1
2860	"	17	NENW	1856-05-01		A1
2862	HEILMYER, Joseph	8	SESW	1855-05-01		A1
2622	HIATT, Amos	1	2	1855-05-01		A1
2623	" "	1	3	1855-05-01		A1
2866	HIATT, Josiah	4	3	1855-12-15		A1
2867	" "	4	4	1855-12-15		A1
2868	" "	4	6	1855-12-15		A1
2749	HIGGINBOTHAM, Sarah	15	SESE	1856-01-15		A6 G60
2750	" "	22	NENE	1856-01-15		A6 G60
2689	HITCHCOCK, Frances P	6	11	1855-01-01		A6 G244
2692	HOBART, George	22	SENE	1855-12-15		A1 G171
2691	" "	23	S½NW	1855-12-15		A1
2841	HOKE, Mary E	28	NWSE	1855-03-01		A4 G212
2787	HOLLEY, James N	3	SE	1855-05-01		A1
2995	HOLLOPETER, William	34	NENE	1854-05-01		A1
2788	HOLLY, James N	10	SENE	1855-12-15		A1
2789	" "	10	W½NE	1855-12-15		A1
2777	HOOVER, James M	7	NENW	1855-01-01		A6
2778	"	7	W½NE	1855-01-01		A6
2830	HOVERSTICK, Susannah	9	SESE	1855-01-01		A6 G22
2741	HURST, Jacob	34	NWSW	1852-09-10		A6
2957	IOWA, State Of	16		1937-08-26		A3
2678	IRELAND, Enoch	34	SWNW	1852-08-04		A6
2873	JEROME, Lesbia P	25	E½SW	1855-05-01		A6 G180
2871	"	25	NWSW	1857-04-01		A4
2872	"	26	NWNE	1857-04-01		A4
2792	JOHNSON, Jervis	5	12	1853-08-01		A1
2793	" "	5	NWSW	1853-08-01		A1
2863	JOHNSON, Joseph	6	W½SW	1854-12-01		A1 F
2930	JONES, Robert T	36	NWSW	1855-12-15		A1
2931	" "	36	SESW	1855-12-15		A1
2624	KENWORTHY, Amos M	5	NESW	1855-05-10		A1
2625	" "	5	SWSW	1855-05-10		A1
2626	" "	6	6	1855-05-10		A1
2627	" "	6	SESE	1855-05-10		A1
2800	KENWORTHY, Jesse W	5	W½SE	1855-05-10		A1
2801	" "	6	2	1855-05-10		A1
2802	" "	6	3	1855-05-10		A1
2803	" "	6	7	1855-05-10		A1
2693	KRIDLER, George	19	S½SE	1855-05-01		A1 G187
2694	" "	30	N½NE	1855-05-01		A1 G187
2637	KUNKEL, Benjamin	29	NW	1855-05-01		A1 G188
2638	" "	29	NWNE	1856-03-24		A6 G189
2774	LENTZ, Hannah	8	SESE	1854-10-02		A6 G151
2616	LINSTED, Alfred	31	W½NW	1855-05-10		A1 F
2617	" "	31	W½SW	1855-05-10		A1 F
2831	MCBRIDE, John	11	SESW	1855-12-15		A1
2832	" "	11	SWSE	1855-12-15		A1
2833	" "	28	E½NE	1855-12-15		A1
2822	MCCLURE, Lydia	17	W½SW	1860-11-01		A5 G73
2621	MCDONALD, Allen F	13	NWNW	1853-10-01		A6
2620	" "	12	SESE	1856-06-16		A6 R2825
2651	MCDONNALD, David	13	SENE	1855-05-01		A1
2629	MCDOWELL, Andrew J	22	SWSE	1853-07-01		A6
2630	" "	27	NWNE	1853-07-01		A6
2834	MCDOWELL, John	22	SWSW	1849-04-10		A1
2835	" "	27	NWNW	1849-04-10		A1
2836	" "	27	SWSW	1849-04-10		A1
2837	" "	28	SESE	1849-04-10		A1
2838	" "	36	SWSW	1855-05-10		A1
2642	MCKEAN, Charles	26	E½SE	1855-12-15		A1
2779	MCLAIN, James	1	10	1855-05-01		A1
2780	" "	1	7	1855-05-01		A1
2781	" "	1	8	1855-05-01		A1
2782	" "	1	9	1855-05-01		A1
2783	" "	2	10	1855-05-01		A1

ID	Individual in Patent	Sec.	Sec. Part	Date Issued	Other Counties	For More Info . . .
2784	MCLAIN, James (Cont'd)	2	7	1855-05-01		A1
2785	" "	2	8	1855-05-01		A1
2786	" "	2	9	1855-05-01		A1
2637	MEILY, Samuel	29	NW	1855-05-01		A1 G188
2776	MOODY, Ann S	26	SWSE	1853-10-01		A6 G275
2839	MORGAN, John	28	E½SW	1854-10-02		A6
2840	" "	28	SENW	1854-10-02		A6
2841	" "	28	NWSE	1855-03-01		A4 G212
2932	MOSSER, Samuel	27	E½NE	1855-12-15		A1
2933	" "	27	SWNE	1855-12-15		A1
2934	" "	28	W½NE	1855-12-15		A1
2935	" "	28	W½SW	1855-12-15		A1
2652	MYERS, David	14	E½NE	1855-12-15		A1
2740	NEWTON, Francis	24	SESW	1853-07-02		A6 G134
2647	ORCUTT, Daniel D	33	NESE	1854-05-01		A1
2648	" "	33	NWNE	1854-05-01		A1
2958	OSBORN, Stephen	30	NW	1855-05-10		A1 F
2997	PARKER, William	8	SENW	1854-05-01		A1
2998	" "	8	SWNE	1854-05-01		A1
2999	" "	8	W½NW	1854-05-01		A1
2996	" "	7	W½NW	1854-12-01		A1 F
2682	PARKS, Ephraim	36	NWNE	1855-05-10		A1
2680	PARKS, Ephraim M	36	NESW	1853-10-01		A6
2681	" "	36	SWNE	1853-10-01		A6
2679	" "	36	E½NE	1854-07-01		A6
2980	PIERSOL, Ellen	19	NENE	1853-07-13		A6 G46
2980	PIERSOL, Sarah	19	NENE	1853-07-13		A6 G46
2612	PIKE, Albert	15	NESW	1855-12-15		A1
2653	PIKE, David	6	E½SW	1855-05-10		A1 F
2905	PIKE, Orlando	15	NENW	1853-07-13		A6
2609	PLEAS, Aaron L	18	NENW	1855-12-15		A1 F
2610	" "	6	10	1855-12-15		A1
2632	POWER, Andrew	11	NWSE	1853-11-01		A1
2633	" "	11	SENW	1853-11-01		A1
2631	" "	11	NESW	1855-12-15		A1
2864	POWER, Joseph	10	NWNW	1855-05-01		A1
2640	RAGADALE, Camma R	34	NENW	1853-08-01		A6
2909	REED, Philip T	15	N½SE	1855-12-15		A1
2890	RENO, Morgan	33	NWSW	1852-09-10		A6
2887	" "	17	NWNW	1853-07-01		A6
2888	" "	18	NENE	1853-07-01		A6
2894	" "	7	S½SE	1853-07-01		A6
2889	" "	18	W½NW	1855-05-10		A1 F
2893	" "	5	5	1855-05-10		A1
2892	" "	4	2	1855-12-15		A1
2891	" "	34	NWSE	1856-10-10		A2
2618	REYNOLDS, Alfred	1	6	1854-12-01		A1
2654	REYNOLDS, David	5	10	1855-12-15		A1
2655	" "	5	9	1855-12-15		A1
2656	RICKEY, David T	30	S½NE	1855-05-10		A1
2921	RIVERS, Richard	12	SWSW	1853-07-01		A6
2917	" "	11	NESE	1854-12-01		A1
2918	" "	11	SESE	1855-05-01		A1
2919	" "	12	NESW	1855-05-01		A1
2920	" "	12	NWSW	1856-05-01		A1
3000	RIVERS, William	12	SENE	1853-11-01		A1
2748	ROBERTS, Ada	24	SWSE	1856-01-15		A6 G61
2959	ROBERTS, Stephen	6	12	1853-11-01		A1
2865	ROBERTSON, Joseph	36	NENW	1854-03-01		A6 G242
2615	ROBISON, Alexander	35	SENW	1852-11-01		A1
2638	ROGERS, Mary	29	NWNE	1856-03-24		A6 G189
2689	SANXAY, Frederic	6	11	1855-01-01		A6 G244
2842	SHAY, John	8	NENW	1855-12-15		A1
2878	SHEPHARD, Lucius	15	SESW	1854-05-01		A1
2885	SIGLER, Michael	3	10	1855-12-15		A1
2886	" "	3	7	1855-12-15		A1
2903	SMITH, Nicholas	27	NENW	1852-05-01		A6
2936	SMITH, Samuel	35	NWNE	1854-07-01		A6
2843	SNODDY, John	15	SWSW	1852-09-01		A6
2844	" "	21	SENE	1852-09-01		A6
2845	" "	22	W½NW	1852-09-01		A6
2929	SNODGRASS, Robert	34	NESW	1853-05-10		A6
2639	SNOW, Benjamin	34	NWNW	1850-03-01		A1

ID	Individual in Patent	Sec.	Sec. Part	Date Issued	Other Counties	For More Info . . .
2809	SNOW, John B	28	NWNW	1853-05-03		A6
2804	" "	20	S½SE	1853-06-01		A6
2805	" "	21	N½SW	1854-05-01		A1
2806	" "	21	SESW	1855-05-10		A1
2807	" "	23	SWSW	1855-12-15		A1
2808	" "	26	E½NE	1855-12-15		A1
2922	SPURRIER, Richard	19	N½SE	1855-12-15		A1
2923	" "	30	N½SE	1855-12-15		A1
2910	STIVENS, Prince	35	NENW	1854-05-01		A1
2643	STUBBINS, Charles	34	SENW	1852-10-01		A6
2667	SWAIM, Edwin W	5	3	1855-12-15		A1
2668	" "	5	4	1855-12-15		A1
2675	SWAIM, Elihu	5	1	1855-12-15		A1
2676	" "	5	2	1855-12-15		A1
2974	SWAIN, Timothy	17	SESE	1854-05-01		A1
2645	SWANEY, Conrad	21	SWSE	1854-02-01		A6 G263
2646	SWANEY, Conrod	21	NWSE	1849-04-10		A1
2914	SYLVESTER, Richard H	10	NENE	1857-04-10		A6
2915	" "	11	NENW	1857-04-10		A6
2916	" "	11	W½NW	1857-04-10		A6
3003	TAYLOR, William S	25	N½NE	1855-05-01		A1
2987	TERRY, William D	18	S½NE	1857-02-20		A5
2988	" "	18	SENW	1857-02-20		A5 F
2968	THOMPSON, Thomas	20	SWSW	1855-05-01		A1
2969	" "	29	E½SW	1855-05-01		A1
2970	" "	29	S½NE	1855-05-01		A1
2971	" "	29	SE	1855-05-01		A1
2972	" "	32	N½NE	1855-05-01		A1
2775	TOMPKINS, James J	26	NWSE	1853-10-01		A6
2776	" "	26	SWSE	1853-10-01		A6 G275
2661	TRUMAN, Edward D	14	SWSE	1855-12-15		A1
2662	" "	17	S½NE	1855-12-15		A1
2663	" "	21	NENW	1855-12-15		A1
2664	" "	21	NWNE	1855-12-15		A1
2665	" "	23	NWNE	1855-12-15		A1
2666	" "	23	S½NE	1855-12-15		A1
2978	TURNER, Walter	6	4	1848-07-01		A1
2828	UNGER, Catharine	9	SWSE	1855-01-01		A6 G23
3004	WADE, William	26	W½SW	1852-09-01		A6
3005	" "	27	E½SE	1852-09-01		A6
2690	WALKER, George B	26	SESW	1855-05-01		A1
2695	WATSON, George	14	NWSE	1853-10-01		A6
2697	" "	14	SWNE	1853-10-01		A6
2700	" "	24	SENW	1853-10-01		A6
2699	" "	24	NENE	1853-11-01		A1
2701	" "	24	W½NW	1854-02-01		A6
2696	" "	14	SESE	1854-11-01		A4
2698	" "	23	NENE	1855-05-01		A1
2743	WATSON, Jacob	13	N½SE	1854-05-01		A1
2744	" "	13	SWSE	1854-10-02		A6
2745	" "	24	NENW	1854-10-02		A6 G278
2746	" "	24	NWNE	1854-10-02		A6 G278
2829	WATSON, Margaret	9	NESE	1855-01-01		A6 G24
2939	WATSON, Simon	1	12	1855-12-15		A1
2948	WATSON, Solomon	1	4	1853-11-01		A1
2953	" "	2	1	1853-11-01		A1
2954	" "	2	2	1855-05-01		A1
2955	" "	2	E½SE	1855-05-01		A1
2947	" "	1	11	1855-05-10		A1
2949	" "	1	5	1855-05-10		A1
2950	" "	1	SWSW	1855-05-10		A1
2951	" "	11	NENE	1855-05-10		A1
2952	" "	12	NWNW	1855-05-10		A1
2956	" "	2	NWSE	1855-05-10		A1
2973	WEST, Thomas	10	S½	1855-12-15		A1
2683	WHEATLEY, Francis	14	NESE	1855-12-15		A1
2684	" "	14	SWSW	1855-12-15		A1
2685	" "	23	NWNW	1855-12-15		A1
2686	" "	24	SESE	1855-12-15		A1
2687	" "	24	SWNE	1855-12-15		A1
2613	WHITE, Albert	3	E½SW	1855-12-15		A1
2614	" "	3	NWSW	1855-12-15		A1
2672	WHITE, Eli	7	NESW	1855-01-01		A6

ID	Individual in Patent	Sec.	Sec. Part	Date Issued	Other Counties	For More Info . . .
2671	WHITE, Eli (Cont'd)	7	E½NE	1855-05-10		A1
2673	" "	7	NWSE	1855-05-10		A1
2850	WHITE, John	23	E½SW	1855-12-15		A1
2851	" "	23	SE	1855-12-15		A1
2852	" "	34	SWNE	1855-12-15		A1
2975	WHITE, Timothy	14	SESW	1855-12-15		A1
2976	" "	23	NENW	1855-12-15		A1
2977	" "	28	NENW	1855-12-15		A1
2982	WHITE, William C	10	E½NW	1855-12-15		A1
2983	" "	11	NWSW	1855-12-15		A1
2709	WHITNEY, Hiram	35	SENE	1855-12-15		A1
2674	WILLIAMS, Elias J	36	SENW	1855-12-15		A1
2645	WILLIAMS, Elizabeth	21	SWSE	1854-02-01		A6 G263
2849	WILLIAMS, John W	8	NESE	1855-12-15		A1
2884	WILLIAMS, Micajah T	7	SENW	1855-03-01		A4 F
2677	WILTSE, Elizabeth	6	1	1855-12-15		A1
2869	WOOLARD, Letitia	27	SESW	1854-05-01		A6 G43
2870	" "	27	SWSE	1854-05-01		A6 G43
2707	ZIMMERMAN, Henry	7	W½SW	1854-05-01		A1 F

Patent Map

T78-N R16-W
5th PM Meridian

Map Group 13

Township Statistics

Parcels Mapped	:	400
Number of Patents	:	312
Number of Individuals	:	189
Patentees Identified	:	180
Number of Surnames	:	153
Multi-Patentee Parcels	:	28
Oldest Patent Date	:	7/1/1848
Most Recent Patent	:	8/26/1937
Block/Lot Parcels	:	68
Parcels Re-Issued	:	1
Parcels that Overlap	:	0
Cities and Towns	:	2
Cemeteries	:	4

Lots-Sec. 6
1 WILTSE, Elizabeth 1855
2 KENWORTHY, Jesse W 1855
3 KENWORTHY, Jesse W 1855
4 TURNER, Walter 1848
5 FRIEND, Franklin 1854
6 KENWORTHY, Amos M 1855
7 KENWORTHY, Jesse W 1855
8 BREED, Nathan 1854
9 BREED, Nathan 1854
10 PLEAS, Aaron L 1855
11 SANXAY, Frederi[244]1855
12 ROBERTS, Stephen 1853

Lots-Sec. 5
1 SWAIM, Elihu 1855
2 SWAIM, Elihu 1855
3 SWAIM, Edwin W 1855
4 SWAIM, Edwin W 1855
5 RENO, Morgan 1855
6 CHESHIRE, John W 1855
7 DOWNEY, Hugh D 1855
8 DOWNEY, Hugh D 1855
9 REYNOLDS, David 1855
10 REYNOLDS, David 1855
11 DOWNEY, Hugh D 1855
12 JOHNSON, Jervis 1853

Lots-Sec. 4
1 DOWNEY, Hugh D 1855
2 RENO, Morgan 1855
3 HIATT, Josiah 1855
4 HIATT, Josiah 1855
5 CLOUD, Peter C 1855
6 HIATT, Josiah 1855
7 CHESHIRE, John W 1855
8 DOWNEY, Hugh D 1855
9 DOWNEY, Hugh D 1855
10 GOWER, James H 1855
11 BRACKENRIDGE, Robert1855
12 DOWNEY, Hugh D 1855

Lots-Sec. 3

1	COX, Thomas J	1855
2	COX, Thomas J	1855
3	BAILEY, Jesse	1857
4	BAILEY, Jesse	1857
5	BAILEY, Jesse	1857
6	CULBERTSON, John C	1857
7	SIGLER, Michael	1855
10	SIGLER, Michael	1855
11	CULBERTSON, John C	1857
12	BAILEY, Jesse	1857

Lots-Sec. 2

1	WATSON, Solomon	1853
2	WATSON, Solomon	1853
3	HAMBLETON, Levi	1855
4	HAMBLETON, Levi	1855
6	HAMBLETON, Levi	1855
7	MCLAIN, James	1855
8	MCLAIN, James	1855
9	MCLAIN, James	1855
10	MCLAIN, James	1855
11	COX, Thomas J	1857

Lots-Sec. 1

1	GOWER, James H	1857
2	HIATT, Amos	1855
3	HIATT, Amos	1855
4	WATSON, Solomon	1853
5	WATSON, Solomon	1855
6	REYNOLDS, Alfred	1854
7	MCLAIN, James	1855
8	MCLAIN, James	1855
9	MCLAIN, James	1855
10	MCLAIN, James	1855
11	WATSON, Solomon	1855
12	WATSON, Simon	1855

Helpful Hints

1. This Map's INDEX can be found on the preceding pages.

2. Refer to Map "C" to see where this Township lies within Poweshiek County, Iowa.

3. Numbers within square brackets [ ] denote a multi-patentee land parcel (multi-owner). Refer to Appendix "C" for a full list of members in this group.

4. Areas that look to be crowded with Patentees usually indicate multiple sales of the same parcel (Re-issues) or Overlapping parcels. See this Township's Index for an explanation of these and other circumstances that might explain "odd" groupings of Patentees on this map.

Section 3 / 2 / 1

3 — WHITE Albert 1855; WHITE Albert 1855; HOLLEY James N 1855; BUTLER Edward 1855

2 — HAMBLETON Mary H 1855; WATSON Solomon 1855; WATSON Solomon 1855; HAMBLETON Mary H 1855; HAMBLETON Mary H 1855

1 — COX Thomas J 1857; WATSON Solomon 1855; CULBERTSON [66] John C 1855

Section 10 / 11 / 12

10 — POWER Joseph 1855; WHITE William C 1855; HOLLY James N 1855; SYLVESTER Richard H 1857; DOWNEY Hugh D 1855; HOLLY James N 1855; WEST Thomas 1855

11 — SYLVESTER Richard H 1857; SYLVESTER Richard H 1857; CLOUD Seth 1855; POWER Andrew 1853; WATSON Solomon 1855; HAMBLETON Osborn 1855; WHITE William C 1855; POWER Andrew 1855; POWER Andrew 1853; RIVERS Richard 1854; GOWER James H 1857; MCBRIDE John 1855; MCBRIDE John 1855; RIVERS Richard 1855

12 — WATSON Solomon 1855; HAMBLETON Osborn 1855; RIVERS Richard 1856; RIVERS Richard 1855; RIVERS Richard 1853; CULBERTSON John C 1856; RIVERS William 1853; DEVRICKSON John None; MCDONALD Allen F 1855

Section 15 / 14 / 13

15 — GOWER James H 1855; PIKE Orlando 1853; BERRYHILL James B 1855; BERRYHILL William D 1855; BERRYHILL William D 1855; PIKE Albert 1855; REED Philip T 1855

14 — BERRYHILL James B 1855; GOWER James H 1857; WATSON George 1853; BERRYHILL William D 1855; WATSON George 1853; WHEATLEY Francis 1855; MYERS David 1855

13 — MCDONALD Allen F 1853; HASE Clayburn 1855; MCDONNALD David 1855; WATSON Jacob 1854; WATSON Jacob 1854; BERRYHILL [9] Charles H 1853

Section 22 / 23 / 24

22 — SNODDY John 1852; SHEPHARD Lucius 1854; GOWER James H 1855; CRAVER [60] James A 1856; BERRYHILL James B 1857; ENGLISH William 1849; CRAVER [60] James A 1856; GOWER James H 1855; BRIDGES James 1855; HOBART [171] George 1855; GOWER James H 1854; EASLEY James S 1855; EASLEY James S 1855; HAZLETON Newton 1855; MCDOWELL John 1849; CARPENTER Hiram M 1852; MCDOWELL Andrew J 1853; FOWLER John 1852

23 — SNODDY John 1852; WHEATLEY Francis 1855; WHITE Timothy 1855; TRUMAN Edward D 1855; WATSON George 1854; WHEATLEY Francis 1855; WHITE Timothy 1855; TRUMAN Edward D 1855; WATSON George 1855; HOBART George 1855; TRUMAN Edward D 1855; HAZLETON Newton 1855; SNOW John B 1855; WHITE John 1855; WHITE John 1855

24 — WATSON Jacob 1854; WATSON Jacob 1854; WATSON George 1853; WATSON George 1854; WATSON George 1853; WHEATLEY Francis 1855; APPLEGATE Thomas S 1857; APPLEGATE Joseph 1855; APPLEGATE Joseph 1855; CRAVER James A 1856; FARMER Silas F 1854; FARMER [134] Irvin 1853; CRAVER [61] James A 1856; WHEATLEY Francis 1855

Section 27 / 26 / 25

27 — MCDOWELL John 1849; SMITH Nicholas 1852; MCDOWELL Andrew J 1853; MOSSER Samuel 1855; CLUTE Solomon J 1857; MOSSER Samuel 1855; CLUTE Solomon J 1857; CLUTE Solomon J 1857; WADE William 1852; MCDOWELL John 1849; BYINGTON [43] Legrand 1854; BYINGTON [43] Legrand 1854

26 — ENGLISH William 1849; ENGLISH Lesbia P 1857; JEROME Lesbia P 1857; SNOW John B 1855; ENGLISH William 1849; ENGLISH William 1849; ELLIOTT Allen 1852; TOMPKINS James J 1853; ENGLISH William 1849; MCKEAN Charles 1855; WADE William 1852; WALKER George B 1855; TOMPKINS [275] James J 1853

25 — HATHAWAY Thomas F 1855; TAYLOR William S 1855; HAYTER William 1855; JEROME Lesbia P 1857; CLARK Wesley C 1856; JEROME [180] Lesbia P 1855

Section 34 / 35 / 36

34 — SNOW Benjamin 1850; RAGADALE Camma R 1853; CRILL John 1852; HOLLOPETER William 1854; IRELAND Enoch 1852; STUBBINS Charles 1852; WHITE John 1855; DEWEY Dwight C 1857; HURST Jacob 1852; SNODGRASS Robert 1853; RENO Morgan 1856; DEWEY Dwight C 1857; BIXLER Magdalene 1852; GOSNELL Joseph 1852; CRILL John 1852

35 — DUPREE Banister 1852; STIVENS Prince 1854; SMITH Samuel 1854; ARMITAGE Ann 1852; ROBISON Alexander 1852; BAILEY Jesse 1855; WHITNEY Hiram 1855; BAILEY Jesse 1855; BOWMAN Benjamin 1855; BROWNLEE Andrew 1855; DOWNEY Hugh D 1857

36 — ROBERTSON [242] Joseph 1854; PARKS Ephraim 1855; WILLIAMS Elias J 1855; PARKS Ephraim M 1853; PARKS Ephraim M 1854; JONES Robert T 1855; PARKS Ephraim M 1853; JONES Robert T 1855; MCDOWELL John 1855

Legend

——— Patent Boundary

━━━ Section Boundary

No Patents Found (or Outside County)

1., 2., 3., ... Lot Numbers (when beside a name)

[ ] Group Number (see Appendix "C")

Scale: Section = 1 mile X 1 mile (generally, with some exceptions)

Road Map

T78-N R16-W
5th PM Meridian

Map Group 13

Cities & Towns
Searsboro
Stillwell

Cemeteries
Cemetery Hill Cemetery
Mill Grove Cemetery
Searsboro International Order
 of Odd Fellows Cemetery
West Liberty Cemetery

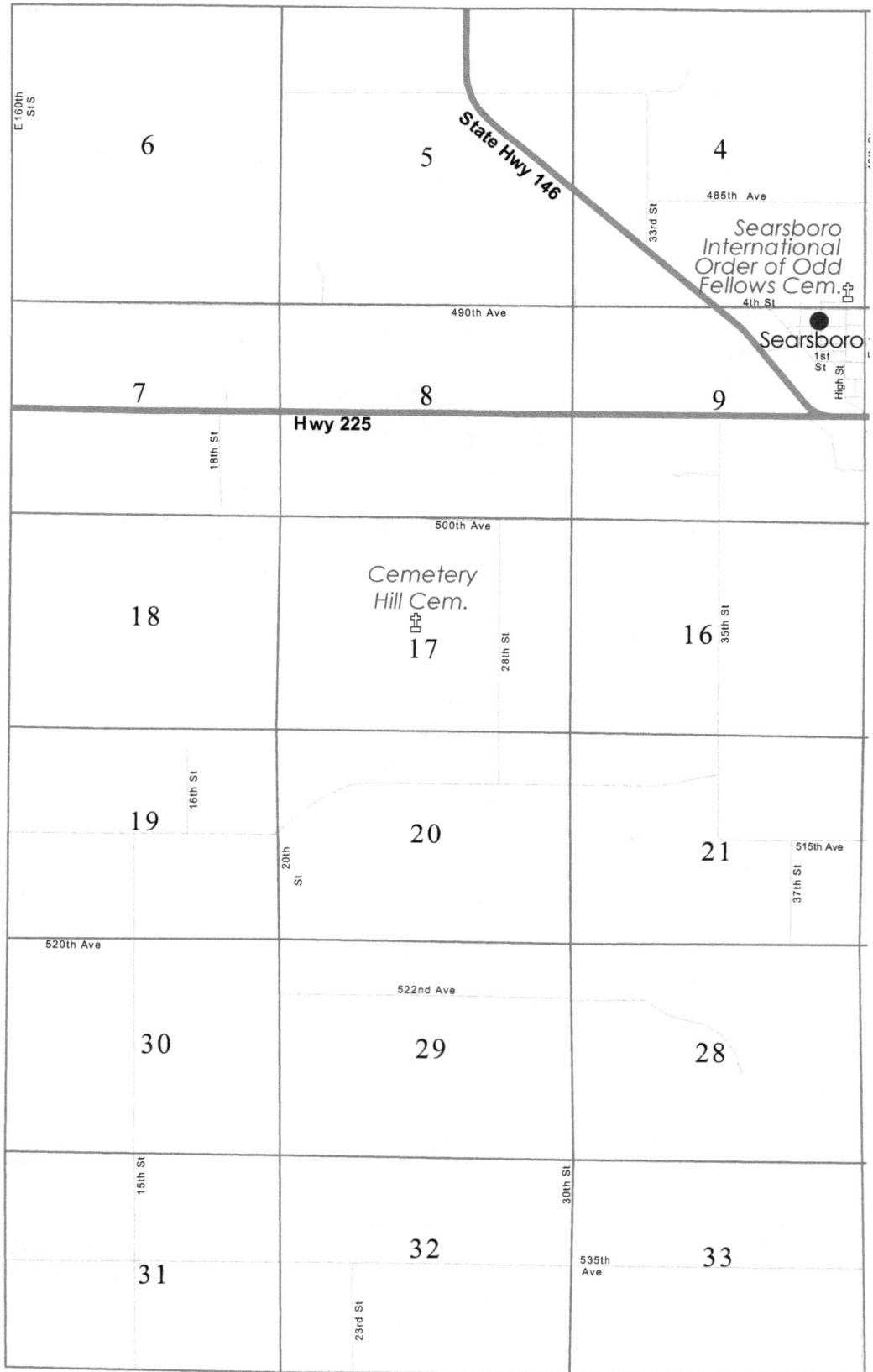

6

5

State Hwy 146

4

485th Ave

33rd St

Searsboro
International
Order of Odd
Fellows Cem.

490th Ave

4th St

Searsboro

1st
St

High St

7

18th St

8

Hwy 225

9

500th Ave

18

Cemetery
Hill Cem.

17

28th St

16

35th St

19

16th St

20

20th
St

21

515th Ave

37th St

520th Ave

30

522nd Ave

29

28

15th St

31

23rd St

32

30th St

535th
Ave

33

E 160th St S

40th St

55th St

480th Ave

3

2

1

60th St

68th St

East St

10

11

State Hwy 146

Diamond Trail Rd

West Liberty Cem.

12

502nd St

50th St

15

14

505th Ave

13

510th Ave

512th Ave

22

23

24

520th Ave

Forest Home Rd

27

26

25

Mill Grove Cem.

Stillwell

River Rd

40th St

70th St

34

35

State Hwy 146

36

Jewell Ave

540th Ave

Copyright 2010 Boyd IT, Inc. All Rights Reserved

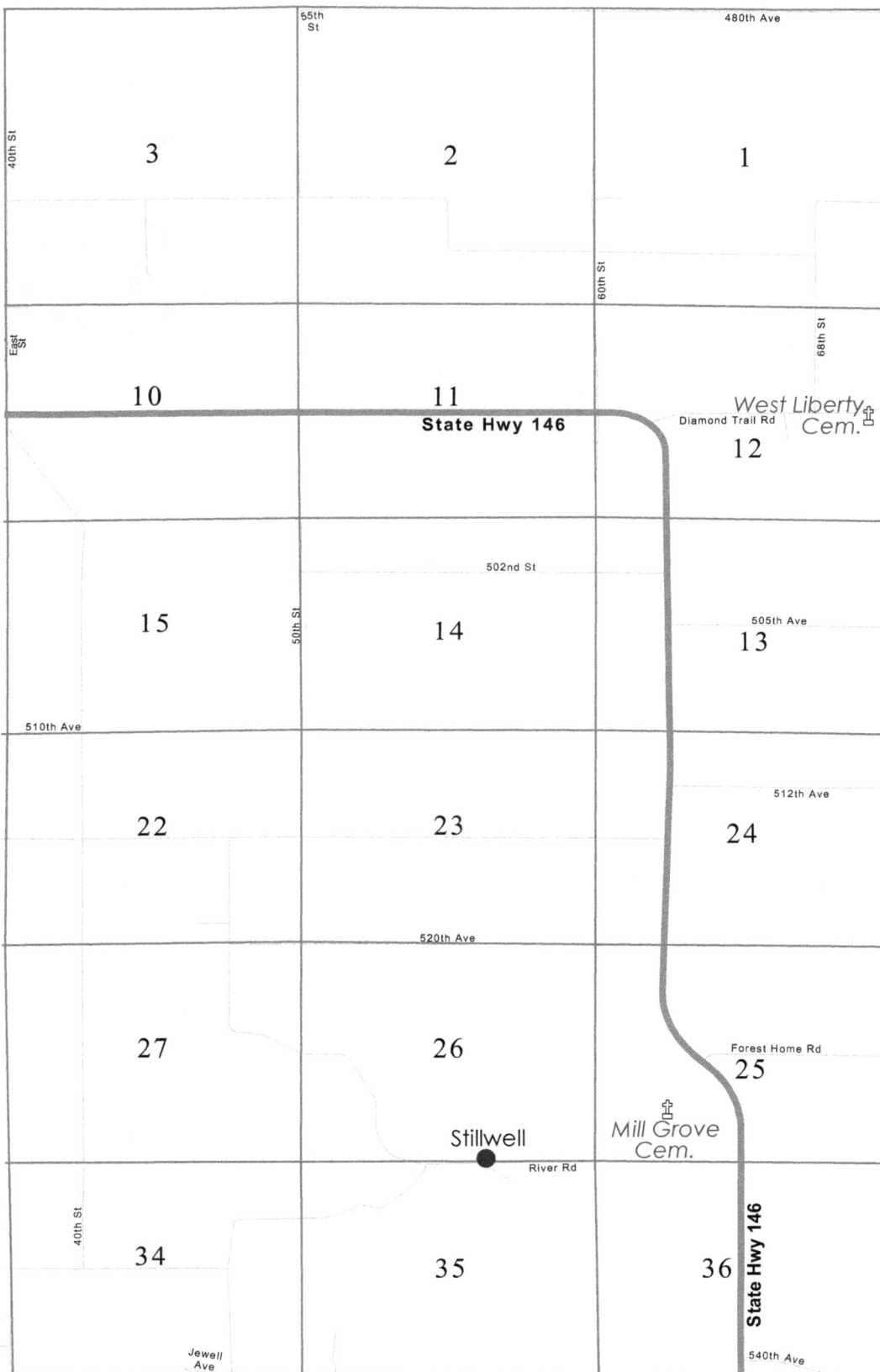

Legend

————	Section Lines
≡≡≡≡	Interstates
▬▬▬▬	Highways
————	Other Roads
●	Cities/Towns
☩	Cemeteries

Scale: Section = 1 mile X 1 mile
(generally, with some exceptions)

Historical Map

T78-N R16-W
5th PM Meridian

Map Group 13

Cities & Towns
Searsboro
Stillwell

Cemeteries
Cemetery Hill Cemetery
Mill Grove Cemetery
Searsboro International Order
 of Odd Fellows Cemetery
West Liberty Cemetery

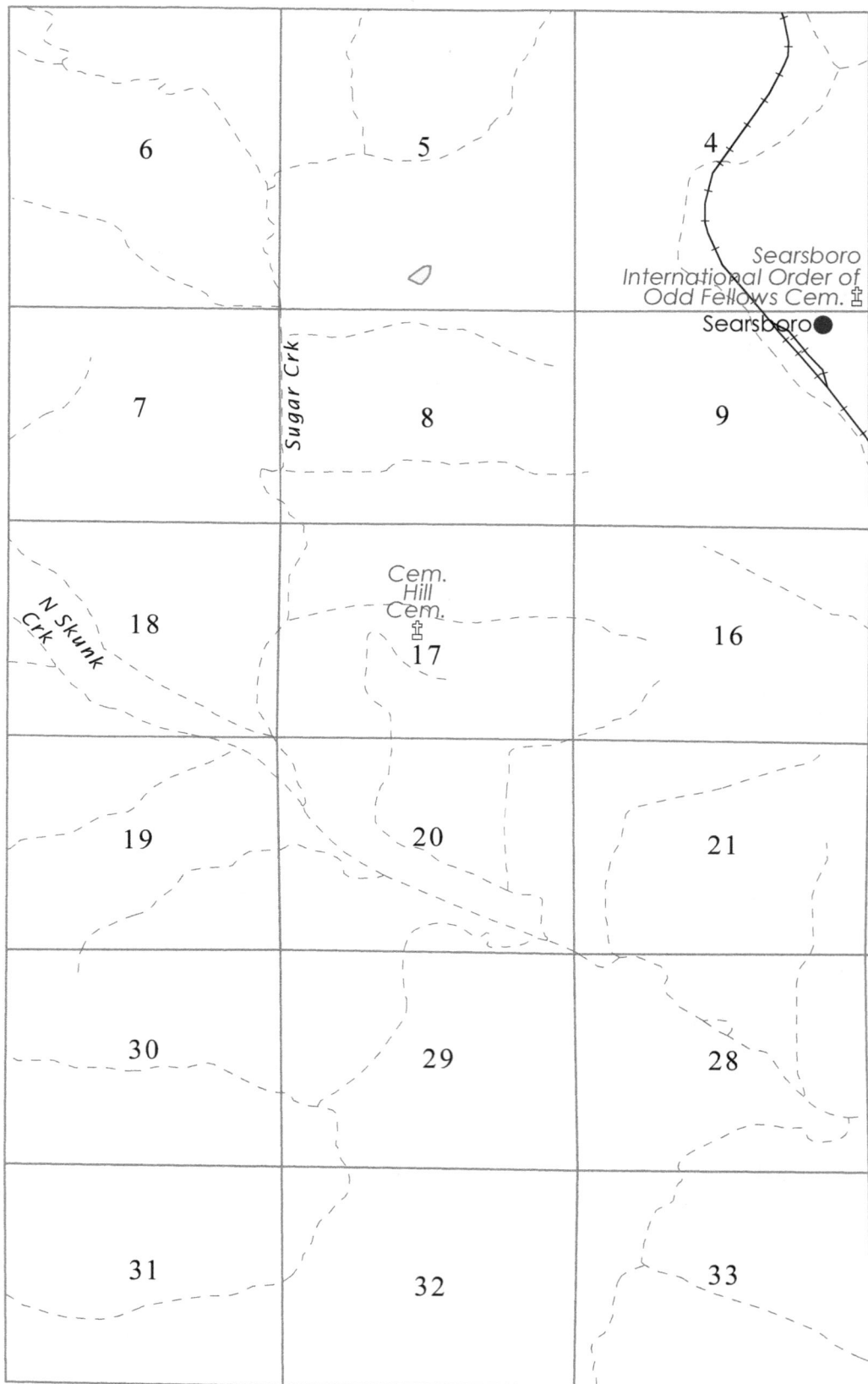

6

5

4

*Searsboro
International Order of
Odd Fellows Cem.*

Searsboro ●

Sugar Crk

7

8

9

N Skunk Crk

18

*Cem.
Hill
Cem.*

17

16

19

20

21

30

29

28

31

32

33

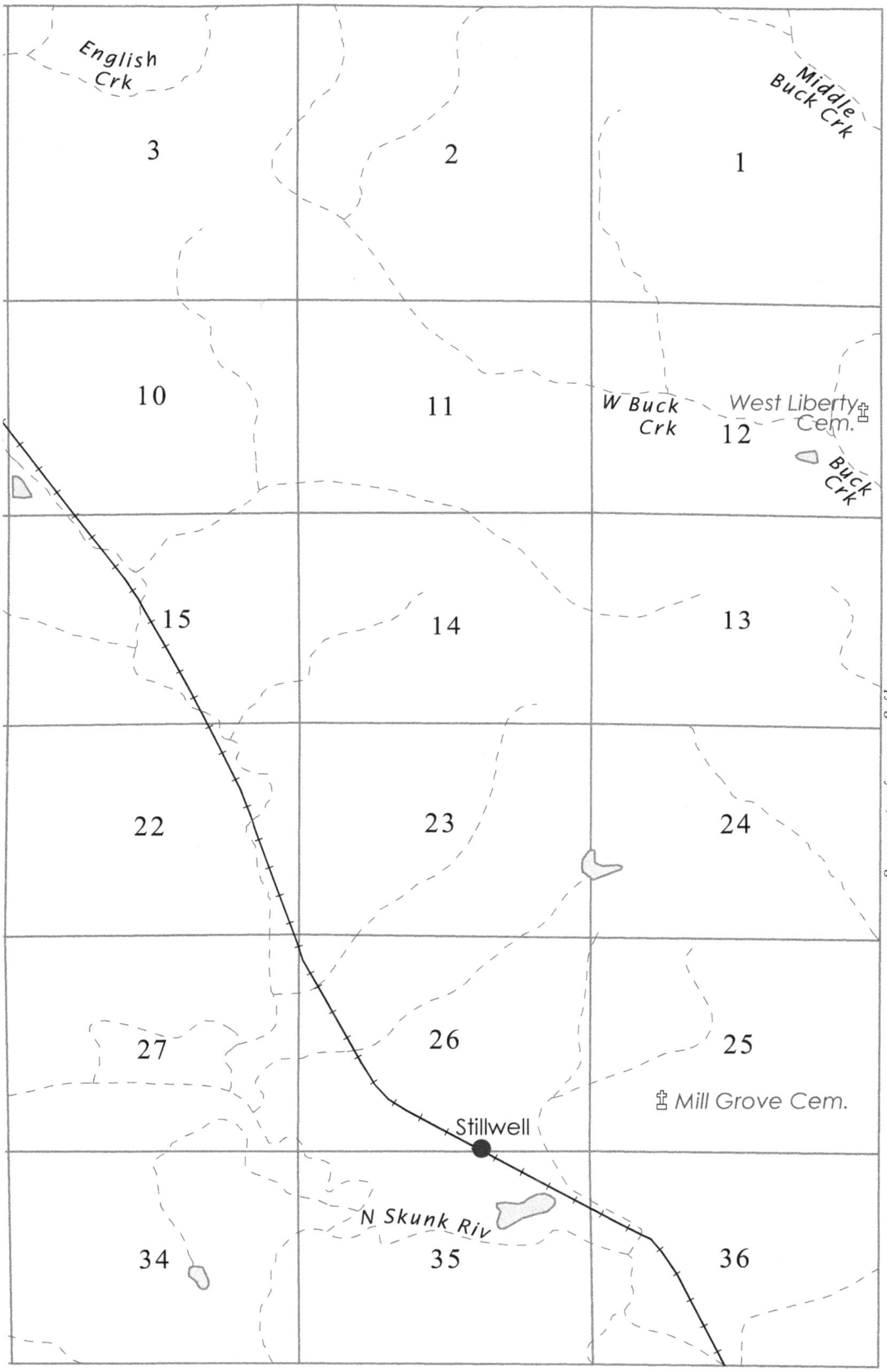
English Crk
Middle Buck Crk
3
2
1
10
11
W Buck Crk
West Liberty Cem.
12
Buck Crk
15
14
13
22
23
24
27
26
25
Mill Grove Cem.
Stillwell
N Skunk Riv
34
35
36

Helpful Hints

1. This Map takes a different look at the same Congressional Township displayed in the preceding two maps. It presents features that can help you better envision the historical development of the area: a) Water-bodies (lakes & ponds), b) Water-courses (rivers, streams, etc.), c) Railroads, d) City/town center-points (where they were oftentimes located when first settled), and e) Cemeteries.

2. Using this "Historical" map in tandem with this Township's Patent Map and Road Map, may lead you to some interesting discoveries. You will often find roads, towns, cemeteries, and waterways are named after nearby landowners: sometimes those names will be the ones you are researching. See how many of these research gems you can find here in Poweshiek County.

Legend

- Section Lines
- Railroads
- Large Rivers & Bodies of Water
- Streams/Creeks & Small Rivers
- Cities/Towns
- Cemeteries

Scale: Section = 1 mile X 1 mile
(there are some exceptions)

Map Group 14: Index to Land Patents

Township 78-North Range 15-West (5th PM)

After you locate an individual in this Index, take note of the Section and Section Part then proceed to the Land Patent map on the pages immediately following. You should have no difficulty locating the corresponding parcel of land.

The "For More Info" Column will lead you to more information about the underlying Patents. See the *Legend* at right, and the "How to Use this Book" chapter, for more information.

```
┌────────────────────────────────────────────────────────────┐
│                        LEGEND                                │
│           "For More Info . . . " column                      │
│ ─────────────────────────────────────────────────           │
│ A = Authority (Legislative Act, See Appendix "A")            │
│ B = Block or Lot (location in Section unknown)               │
│ C = Cancelled Patent                                         │
│ F = Fractional Section                                       │
│ G = Group  (Multi-Patentee Patent, see Appendix "C")         │
│ V = Overlaps another Parcel                                  │
│ R = Re-Issued (Parcel patented more than once)               │
│                                                              │
│ (A & G items require you to look in the Appendixes referred  │
│ to above. All other Letter-designations followed by a number │
│ require you to locate line-items in this index that possess  │
│ the ID number found after the letter).                       │
└────────────────────────────────────────────────────────────┘
```

ID	Individual in Patent	Sec.	Sec. Part	Date Issued	Other Counties	For More Info . . .
3090	ALLEN, Isam P	26	SESE	1853-10-01		A6
3184	APPLEGATE, Joseph	19	W½NW	1855-05-01		A1 F
3182	BARBOUR, Catharine	31	SE	1855-07-02		A6 G282
3272	BARNES, William H	22	SESW	1854-08-01		A6
3274	"	27	NWNE	1854-08-01		A6
3273	"	22	SWSE	1855-05-01		A1
3267	BEASON, William	26	SWNW	1854-05-01		A1
3061	BEELER, George M	7	SWSE	1855-05-10		A1
3039	BERRYHILL, Charles H	11	SWNW	1854-08-01		A6 G14
3040	"	33	NWSE	1855-05-01		A6 G16
3037	"	33	SWNE	1855-05-01		A6
3031	"	19	SENW	1855-05-10		A1 F
3032	"	2	10	1855-05-10		A1
3033	"	2	9	1855-05-10		A1
3036	"	31	NENE	1855-05-10		A1
3038	"	6	1	1855-05-10		A1
3035	"	30	S½SE	1855-12-15		A1
3030	"	19	SENE	1857-04-01		A4
3034	"	20	SWNW	1857-04-01		A4
3270	BERRYHILL, William D	9	N½NW	1853-06-01		A6
3020	BINEGAR, Andrew J	28	NWSW	1853-10-01		A6
3258	BONE, Valentine	15	SENW	1852-03-10		A1 R3014
3259	"	15	SWNW	1853-07-20		A6
3098	BORLAND, James	3	12	1853-06-01		A6
3246	BOSLEY, Samuel W	35	SESW	1853-09-10		A6
3255	BROOKS, Thomas L	36	NWNE	1855-07-02		A6 G37
3256	BROPLEY, Thomas L	24	E½NE	1855-05-10		A1
3007	BRYAN, Alanson	12	NWNE	1854-05-01		A1
3008	"	14	NWNW	1854-05-01		A6
3009	"	17	NESE	1854-05-01		A1
3010	"	18	E½SE	1854-05-01		A1
3011	"	23	NWNW	1854-05-01		A1
3013	"	34	NESW	1855-07-02		A6 G39
3012	"	27	E½NE	1855-12-15		A1
3193	BYINGTON, Legrand	27	SWSE	1854-05-01		A1
3194	"	34	SESW	1855-03-01		A6 G42
3015	CALDWELL, Alexander	26	NENE	1853-11-01		A1
3195	CARPENTER, Levi	18	NESW	1852-09-01		A6 F
3196	"	18	NWSE	1852-09-01		A6
3197	"	18	SWSE	1853-06-01		A6
3199	"	6	5	1853-06-01		A6
3200	"	6	W½SW	1853-06-01		A6 F
3201	"	7	SESW	1854-05-01		A1 F
3198	"	18	W½SW	1857-05-01		A1 F
3242	CHAMBERLAIN, Rosannah	1	1	1854-12-01		A1
3243	"	1	2	1854-12-01		A1

ID	Individual in Patent	Sec.	Sec. Part	Date Issued	Other Counties	For More Info . . .
3162	CHAMBERLIN, John	1	7	1854-12-01		A1
3163	" "	1	8	1854-12-01		A1
3081	CHASE, Hannah	2	1	1854-12-01		A6 G99
3082	" "	2	2	1854-12-01		A6 G99
3083	" "	2	8	1854-12-01		A6 G99
3052	CHEESMAN, Felix	15	S½NE	1850-03-01		A1
3164	COFFEE, John	22	NWNE	1855-05-01		A1
3249	COMBE, Thomas	36	E½NE	1855-05-10		A1
3277	COPE, William R	11	NESW	1855-05-01		A1
3278	" "	11	NWSE	1855-05-01		A1
3279	" "	11	S½NE	1855-05-01		A1
3251	COX, Thomas J	11	N½NE	1855-05-01		A1
3254	" "	3	SESW	1855-12-15		A1
3252	" "	19	NWSE	1857-03-10		A1
3253	" "	23	SESW	1857-03-10		A1
3097	CRAVER, James A	19	W½SW	1855-12-15		A1 F
3096	" "	19	SESW	1858-06-10		A6 F
3146	CROOKHAM, John A L	1	5	1857-04-01		A6 G62 C R3147
3147	" "	1	5	1857-11-06		A6 G63 R3146
3148	CULBERTON, John C	4	2	1857-04-01		A4 R3152
3156	CULBERTSON, John C	2	7	1855-01-01		A6 G74
3149	" "	19	NENW	1855-05-01		A6 F
3150	" "	19	SWNE	1855-05-01		A6
3157	" "	3	2	1855-05-01		A6 G83
3158	" "	10	10	1856-01-15		A6 G79 C
3159	" "	10	NWSE	1856-01-15		A6 G79 C
3151	" "	4	11	1857-02-16		A5
3153	" "	4	6	1857-02-16		A5
3154	" "	4	7	1857-02-16		A5
3160	" "	4	10	1857-04-04		A6 G80
3161	" "	4	NWSE	1857-04-04		A6 G80
3155	" "	6	4	1857-04-10		A6
3152	" "	4	2	1931-07-28		A4 R3148
3202	DAVIS, Michael	3	1	1855-12-15		A1
3108	DEAN, Amanda	31	SENW	1854-10-02		A6 G149 F
3087	DEMENT, Isaac G	21	SESE	1853-08-01		A6 G93
3088	" "	22	SWSW	1853-08-01		A6 G93
3087	DEMENT, Sarah	21	SESE	1853-08-01		A6 G93
3088	" "	22	SWSW	1853-08-01		A6 G93
3076	DOWNEY, Hugh D	29	NWSW	1854-08-01		A6
3077	" "	29	SWNW	1854-08-01		A6
3081	" "	2	1	1854-12-01		A6 G99
3082	" "	2	2	1854-12-01		A6 G99
3083	" "	2	8	1854-12-01		A6 G99
3074	" "	11	NWSW	1855-12-15		A1
3079	" "	3	SWSW	1855-12-15		A1
3080	" "	9	NWNE	1855-12-15		A1
3073	" "	11	NWNW	1856-01-15		A6
3075	" "	2	SWSW	1856-01-15		A6
3078	" "	3	SESE	1856-01-15		A6
3126	EASLEY, James S	19	S½SE	1855-01-01		A6
3138	" "	2	12	1855-01-01		A6 G119
3139	" "	2	5	1855-01-01		A6 G119
3127	" "	3	10	1855-01-01		A6
3130	" "	3	9	1855-01-01		A6
3142	" "	3	N½SE	1855-01-01		A6 G121
3131	" "	30	N½NE	1855-01-01		A6
3132	" "	4	NESW	1855-01-01		A6
3140	" "	5	10	1855-01-01		A6 G118
3141	" "	5	7	1855-01-01		A6 G118
3133	" "	6	10	1855-03-01		A4 R3134
3136	" "	6	9	1855-03-01		A4 R3137
3135	" "	6	3	1855-05-10		A1
3128	" "	3	7	1856-01-15		A6
3129	" "	3	8	1856-01-15		A6
3134	" "	6	10	1950-04-25		A4 R3133
3137	" "	6	9	1950-04-25		A4 R3136
3016	EASON, Alexander	4	S½SE	1855-05-01		A1
3084	FARMER, Irvin	31	NENW	1853-07-02		A6 F
3086	FARMER, Isaac	29	NESE	1854-11-01		A4
3085	FARMER, Isaac D	29	SWSW	1855-05-10		A1
3239	FARNHAM, Anna	8	SWSE	1853-06-01		A6 G256
3106	GOWER, James H	31	SWNE	1853-07-20		A6

ID	Individual in Patent	Sec.	Sec. Part	Date Issued	Other Counties	For More Info . . .
3107	GOWER, James H (Cont'd)	31	W½SW	1853-07-20		A6 F
3108	" "	31	SENW	1854-10-02		A6 G149 F
3104	" "	29	NESW	1854-11-01		A4
3103	" "	26	SWNE	1855-12-15		A1
3105	" "	30	W½SW	1857-03-10		A1 F
3109	" "	31	SENE	1857-04-01		A6 G153
3063	GRAHAM, Giles S	24	S½SW	1854-12-01		A6 G202
3174	HALL, John W	26	SENW	1853-07-02		A6
3185	HALL, Joseph	4	12	1853-11-01		A1
3018	HARNER, Andrew	23	NWSE	1855-05-10		A1
3019	" "	23	SWNE	1855-05-10		A1
3168	HART, John	19	NESE	1854-02-01		A6 R3228
3228	HART, Moses	19	NESE	1853-04-15		A6 R3168
3250	HATHAWAY, Thomas F	24	W½NE	1854-12-01		A1
3066	HAY, Henry	30	N½SE	1855-12-15		A1
3091	HAY, Jackson	30	S½NE	1855-12-15		A1
3092	" "	5	3	1855-12-15		A1
3093	" "	5	4	1855-12-15		A1
3271	HAYS, William F	5	12	1854-12-01		A6
3275	HAYTER, William	30	E½NW	1855-05-01		A1 F
3144	HUTCHENS, Jeremiah J	13	SESW	1855-05-10		A1
3022	HUTCHINS, Asa B	3	11	1855-05-01		A1
3023	" "	3	N½SW	1855-05-01		A1
3024	" "	4	1	1855-05-01		A1
3025	" "	4	NESE	1855-05-01		A1
3247	IOWA, State Of	16		1937-08-26		A3
3068	JAMES, Henry	6	8	1853-06-01		A6
3067	" "	6	7	1854-12-01		A1
3110	JOHNSON, James	12	W½NW	1854-12-01		A1
3111	" "	13	E½SE	1854-12-01		A1
3112	" "	13	W½NW	1854-12-01		A1
3113	" "	13	W½SW	1854-12-01		A1
3269	JOHNSON, William C	36	N½SW	1853-09-10		A6
3268	" "	35	NESE	1853-11-01		A1
3114	KESTER, James L	2	SE	1855-05-01		A1
3260	LAMSON, Ward	35	NWSW	1854-01-10		A6 R3102
3261	" "	35	SWNW	1854-01-10		A6 V3192
3266	LONG, Wiley	9	NENE	1853-07-20		A6 G196
3263	" "	4	5	1873-06-10		A6
3264	" "	5	8	1873-06-10		A6
3265	" "	5	9	1873-06-10		A6
3124	LOONEY, James P	24	NW	1855-05-10		A1
3039	LYON, Alfred	11	SWNW	1854-08-01		A6 G14
3140	MARSHALL, Mary Ann	5	10	1855-01-01		A6 G118
3141	" "	5	7	1855-01-01		A6 G118
3063	MARTIN, Giles S	24	S½SW	1854-12-01		A6 G202
3146	MASAY,	1	5	1857-04-01		A6 G62 C R3147
3147	MASUY,	1	5	1857-11-06		A6 G63 R3146
3138	MCCARTY, Catharine	2	12	1855-01-01		A6 G119
3139	" "	2	5	1855-01-01		A6 G119
3070	MCDONALD, Henry	5	SESE	1853-07-01		A6
3069	" "	4	S½SW	1853-10-01		A6
3017	MCDONNALD, Allen	7	NESW	1853-11-01		A1 F
3041	MCKEAN, Charles	31	W½NW	1855-12-15		A1 F
3165	MCVAY, John H	21	NESE	1850-04-10		A1
3166	" "	22	NWSW	1850-04-10		A1
3167	" "	22	SWNW	1854-10-02		A6
3116	MCVEY, James O	11	E½NW	1855-05-10		A1
3119	" "	23	NWNE	1855-05-10		A1
3120	" "	36	NW	1855-05-10		A1
3117	" "	15	E½SW	1855-12-15		A1
3118	" "	15	SE	1855-12-15		A1
3121	" "	6	11	1855-12-15		A1
3122	" "	6	6	1855-12-15		A1
3123	" "	6	W½SE	1857-03-10		A1
3262	MCVEY, Wesley	8	NENW	1850-03-01		A1
3013	MILLER, Rachel	34	NESW	1855-07-02		A6 G39
3169	MOORE, John	26	NWNW	1850-12-02		A1
3248	MOORE, Stephen	33	SWSE	1850-12-02		A1
3072	MORRISON, Elizabeth	30	NESW	1857-04-10		A6 G259 F
3229	MORSMAN, Moses J	36	NWSE	1854-08-01		A6 G213
3089	MYERS, Isaac	34	SWNW	1855-12-15		A1
3045	NICHOLS, Daniel Webster	31	SESW	1854-08-01		A6 F

ID	Individual in Patent	Sec.	Sec. Part	Date Issued	Other Counties	For More Info . . .
3231	NICHOLS, Peter	17	SESE	1852-11-01		A1
3232	OGDEN, Richard B	12	NENE	1852-11-01		A1
3156	PAGE, Betsey	2	7	1855-01-01		A6 G74
3276	PHILLIPS, William	12	SWSE	1855-05-10		A1
3125	PIERCE, James	10	NENE	1853-11-01		A1
3014	PIKE, Albert	15	SENW	1852-11-01		A1 R3258
3021	POWER, Andrew	18	SESW	1853-11-01		A1 F
3194	QUACKENBUSH, Mary	34	SESW	1855-03-01		A6 G42
3170	REDMAN, John	25	NENE	1855-12-15		A1
3215	RENO, Morgan	29	NWSE	1853-07-13		A6
3207	" "	10	E½NW	1853-10-01		A6
3216	" "	29	SESE	1853-10-01		A6
3214	" "	28	SWSW	1854-07-01		A2
3225	" "	7	NWSE	1854-10-02		A6
3204	" "	1	3	1854-12-01		A1
3208	" "	22	NENE	1855-01-01		A6
3226	" "	22	SENE	1855-01-01		A6 G234
3220	" "	4	NWSW	1855-03-01		A4
3223	" "	5	NESE	1855-03-01		A4
3209	" "	22	SENW	1855-05-01		A6
3210	" "	22	SWNE	1855-05-01		A6
3217	" "	32	SENE	1855-05-01		A6
3224	" "	6	2	1855-05-01		A1
3205	" "	1	4	1855-05-10		A1
3206	" "	1	6	1855-05-10		A1
3218	" "	4	3	1855-12-15		A1
3219	" "	4	4	1855-12-15		A1
3221	" "	5	1	1855-12-15		A1
3222	" "	5	2	1855-12-15		A1
3211	" "	24	E½SE	1856-01-15		A6
3212	" "	24	NESW	1856-01-15		A6
3213	" "	24	NWSW	1856-01-15		A6
3094	RIVERS, Jacob	7	W½NW	1853-07-01		A6 F
3095	" "	7	W½SW	1853-11-01		A1 F
3234	RIVERS, Richard	18	W½NW	1853-11-01		A1 F
3235	" "	19	NWNE	1857-05-01		A1
3142	ROARK, Mary Melana	3	N½SE	1855-01-01		A6 G121
3186	ROBERTSON, Joseph	31	NESW	1854-03-01		A6 F
3183	ROBINS, Julia	17	SENW	1855-07-02		A6 G283
3226	RUCKER, Emeline	22	SENE	1855-01-01		A6 G234
3240	SANBORN, Phebe	6	SESW	1853-06-01		A6 G257 F
3006	SANDERS, Aaron A	21	N½SW	1853-09-10		A6
3054	SANXAY, Frederic	13	NENE	1854-05-01		A1
3056	" "	23	NESW	1854-05-01		A1
3059	" "	12	NWSE	1854-08-01		A6 G246
3055	" "	13	SENE	1854-10-02		A6
3057	" "	3	3	1855-12-15		A1
3058	" "	3	4	1855-12-15		A1
3192	SATCHELL, Joseph W	35	S½NW	1850-12-02		A1 V3261
3102	SAUNDERS, James F	35	NWSW	1854-07-01		A6 R3260
3227	SAUNDERS, Moses G	34	N½SE	1851-04-01		A1
3143	SAVILLE, Jane	32	SWNE	1855-05-01		A6
3071	SHARP, Henry	32	SESW	1855-12-15		A1
3171	SHARRITT, John	9	E½SW	1854-08-01		A6
3172	" "	9	SENW	1854-08-01		A6
3173	" "	9	SWSW	1854-08-01		A6
3158	SHEFFER, Sarah	10	10	1856-01-15		A6 G79 C
3159	" "	10	NWSE	1856-01-15		A6 G79 C
3029	SHELEY, Beverly	34	SWSE	1851-04-01		A1
3281	SHELEY, William	34	SESE	1855-07-02		A6
3160	SHIFFER, Sarah	4	10	1857-04-04		A6 G80
3161	" "	4	NWSE	1857-04-04		A6 G80
3048	SKINNER, Edward	14	NENE	1855-05-01		A1
3062	SMITH, George	35	NESW	1854-11-01		A4
3245	SMITH, Samuel	34	SENE	1850-12-02		A1
3244	" "	26	W½SW	1853-08-01		A6
3040	SOHN, Hannah	33	NWSE	1855-05-01		A6 G16
3026	STANLEY, Asel	11	SWSW	1853-11-01		A1
3236	STEEL, Robert F	8	SENW	1850-04-10		A1
3241	STEEL, Robert Franklin	8	NWSE	1850-03-01		A1
3240	STEELE, Robert F	6	SESW	1853-06-01		A6 G257 F
3237	" "	8	NESW	1853-06-01		A6
3239	" "	8	SWSE	1853-06-01		A6 G256

ID	Individual in Patent	Sec.	Sec. Part	Date Issued	Other Counties	For More Info . . .
3238	STEELE, Robert F (Cont'd)	8	SESW	1855-05-01		A1
3072	STIX, Henry	30	NESW	1857-04-10		A6 G259 F
3187	STONEHOCKER, Joseph	23	E½NE	1855-12-15		A1
3188	" "	29	NWNW	1855-12-15		A1
3189	" "	5	11	1855-12-15		A1
3190	" "	5	5	1855-12-15		A1
3191	" "	5	6	1855-12-15		A1
3065	SUTTON, Hannibal	4	9	1850-04-10		A1
3064	" "	4	8	1853-07-20		A6
3233	SYLVESTER, Richard H	32	N½NE	1855-12-15		A1
3229	TAYLOR, Eliza	36	NWSE	1854-08-01		A6 G213
3099	TAYLOR, James D	2	11	1855-05-01		A1
3100	" "	2	E½SW	1855-05-01		A1
3101	" "	2	NWSW	1855-05-01		A1
3280	TAYLOR, William S	19	NESW	1855-05-01		A1
3257	THOMPSON, Thomas	27	SWNE	1855-05-01		A1
3059	TRACY, Clarissa	12	NWSE	1854-08-01		A6 G246
3027	VESTAL, Bartholomew	3	5	1855-07-02		A6
3028	" "	3	6	1855-07-02		A6
3145	WATSON, Jesse	6	NESW	1855-05-10		A1 F
3266	WEAVER, Elizabeth	9	NENE	1853-07-20		A6 G196
3255	WELLS, Nachi	36	NWNE	1855-07-02		A6 G37
3230	WEST, Nathan A	14	S½NE	1850-03-01		A1
3053	WHEATLEY, Francis	30	W½NW	1855-12-15		A1 F
3042	WHITCOMB, Charles S	23	SWSW	1855-05-10		A1
3157	WHITE, Elizabeth	3	2	1855-05-01		A6 G83
3175	WHITE, John	15	W½SW	1854-10-02		A6
3177	" "	22	N½NW	1854-10-02		A6
3178	" "	24	W½SE	1855-05-01		A1
3179	" "	33	NWNE	1855-05-01		A6
3176	" "	17	NENW	1855-07-02		A6
3183	" "	17	SENW	1855-07-02		A6 G283
3182	" "	31	SE	1855-07-02		A6 G282
3181	" "	35	W½NE	1855-07-02		A6
3180	" "	35	SENE	1857-04-01		A4
3203	WHITE, Miles	32	SWSW	1855-05-10		A1
3051	WILLIAMS, Elias J	31	NWNE	1855-12-15		A1
3050	" "	30	SESW	1857-03-10		A1 F
3282	WILLINGHAM, William W	36	SWNE	1855-07-02		A6
3109	WIMER, Elizabeth	31	SENE	1857-04-01		A6 G153
3049	WINN, Edward	35	SWSW	1855-07-02		A6
3046	WOODWARD, Davis M	13	SWNE	1854-05-01		A1
3047	" "	13	W½SE	1854-05-01		A1
3060	WOOLVERTON, Garrett R	23	NESE	1855-05-01		A1
3044	WRIGHT, Christopher	28	SESW	1854-02-01		A6
3043	" "	28	NESW	1854-05-01		A1
3115	WYMORE, James M	35	NENE	1853-10-01		A6

Patent Map

T78-N R15-W
5th PM Meridian

Map Group 14

Township Statistics

Parcels Mapped	:	277
Number of Patents	:	230
Number of Individuals	:	146
Patentees Identified	:	140
Number of Surnames	:	126
Multi-Patentee Parcels	:	35
Oldest Patent Date	:	3/1/1850
Most Recent Patent	:	4/25/1950
Block/Lot Parcels	:	69
Parcels Re - Issued	:	7
Parcels that Overlap	:	2
Cities and Towns	:	2
Cemeteries	:	9

Lots-Sec. 6
1. BERRYHILL, Charles H 1855
2. RENO, Morgan 1855
3. EASLEY, James S 1855
4. CULBERTSON, John C 1857
5. CARPENTER, Levi 1853
6. MCVEY, James O 1855
7. JAMES, Henry 1854
8. JAMES, Henry 1853
9. EASLEY, James S 1950
9. EASLEY, James S 1855
10. EASLEY, James S 1855
10. EASLEY, James S 1950
11. MCVEY, James O 1855

Lots-Sec. 5
1. RENO, Morgan 1855
2. RENO, Morgan 1855
3. HAY, Jackson 1855
4. HAY, Jackson 1855
5. STONEHOCKER, Joseph 1855
6. STONEHOCKER, Joseph 1855
7. EASLEY, James S [118] 1855
8. LONG, Wiley 1873
9. LONG, Wiley 1873
10. EASLEY, James S [118] 1855
11. STONEHOCKER, Joseph 1855
12. HAYS, William F 1854

Lots-Sec. 4
1. HUTCHINS, Asa B 1855
2. CULBERTSON, John C 1857
2. CULBERTSON, John C 1931
3. RENO, Morgan 1855
4. RENO, Morgan 1855
5. LONG, Wiley 1873
6. CULBERTSON, John C 1857
7. CULBERTSON, John C 1857
8. SUTTON, Hannibal 1853
9. SUTTON, Hannibal 1850
10. CULBERTSON, John [80] 1857
11. CULBERTSON, John C 1857
12. HALL, Joseph 1853

Section 6
CARPENTER Levi 1853
WATSON Jesse 1855
STEELE [257] Robert F 1853
MCVEY James O 1857

Section 5

Section 4
RENO Morgan 1855
RENO Morgan 1855
EASLEY James S 1855
MCDONALD Henry 1853
MCDONALD Henry 1853
CULBERTSON [80] John C 1857
HUTCHINS Asa B 1855
EASON Alexander 1855

Section 7
RIVERS Jacob 1853
RIVERS Jacob 1853
MCDONNALD Allen 1853
RENO Morgan 1854
CARPENTER Levi 1854
BEELER George M 1855

Section 8
MCVEY Wesley 1850
STEEL Robert F 1850
STEELE Robert F 1853
STEEL Robert Franklin 1850
STEELE Robert F 1855
STEELE [256] Robert F 1853

Section 9
BERRYHILL William D 1853
DOWNEY Hugh D 1855
LONG [196] Wiley 1853
SHARRITT John 1854
SHARRITT John 1854
SHARRITT John 1854
SHARRITT John 1854

Section 18
RIVERS Richard 1853
CARPENTER Levi 1857
CARPENTER Levi 1852
CARPENTER Levi 1852
POWER Andrew 1853
CARPENTER Levi 1853
BRYAN Alanson 1854

Section 17
WHITE John 1855
WHITE [283] John 1855
BRYAN Alanson 1854
NICHOLS Peter 1852

Section 16
IOWA State Of 1937

Section 19
APPLEGATE Joseph 1855
CULBERTSON John C 1855
RIVERS Richard 1857
BERRYHILL Charles H 1855
CULBERTSON John C 1855
BERRYHILL Charles H 1857
BERRYHILL Charles H 1857
TAYLOR William S 1855
COX Thomas J 1857
HART John 1854
HART Moses 1853
CRAVER James A 1855
CRAVER James A 1858
EASLEY James S 1855

Section 20

Section 21
SANDERS Aaron A 1853
MCVAY John H 1850
DEMENT [93] Isaac G 1853

Section 30
WHEATLEY Francis 1855
HAYTER William 1855
EASLEY James S 1855
STONEHOCKER Joseph 1855
GOWER James H 1857
STIX [259] Henry 1857
HAY Henry 1855
HAY Jackson 1855
DOWNEY Hugh D 1854
WILLIAMS Elias J 1857
BERRYHILL Charles H 1855

Section 29
DOWNEY Hugh D 1854
GOWER James H 1854
RENO Morgan 1853
FARMER Isaac 1854
FARMER Isaac D 1855
RENO Morgan 1854

Section 28
BINEGAR Andrew J 1853
WRIGHT Christopher 1854
RENO Morgan 1854
WRIGHT Christopher 1854

Section 31
MCKEAN Charles 1855
FARMER Irvin 1853
WILLIAMS Elias J 1855
BERRYHILL Charles H 1855
GOWER [149] James H 1854
GOWER James H 1853
GOWER [153] James H 1857
GOWER James H 1853
ROBERTSON Joseph 1854
NICHOLS Daniel Webster 1854
WHITE [282] John 1855

Section 32
SYLVESTER Richard H 1855
SAVILLE Jane 1855
RENO Morgan 1855
WHITE Miles 1855
SHARP Henry 1855

Section 33
WHITE John 1855
BERRYHILL Charles H 1855
BERRYHILL [16] Charles H 1855
MOORE Stephen 1850

Lots-Sec. 3

1	DAVIS, Michael	1855
2	CULBERTSON, John[83]1855
3	SANXAY, Frederic	1855
4	SANXAY, Frederic	1855
5	VESTAL, Bartholomew 1855
6	VESTAL, Bartholomew 1855
7	EASLEY, James S	1856
8	EASLEY, James S	1856
9	EASLEY, James S	1855
10	EASLEY, James S	1855
11	HUTCHINS, Asa B	1855
12	BORLAND, James	1853

Lots-Sec. 2

1	DOWNEY, Hugh D [99]1854
2	DOWNEY, Hugh D [99]1854
5	EASLEY, James S[119]1855
7	CULBERTSON, John[74]1855
8	DOWNEY, Hugh D [99]1854
9	BERRYHILL, Charles H1855
10	BERRYHILL, Charles H1855
11	TAYLOR, James D	1855
12	EASLEY, James S[119]1855

Lots-Sec. 1

1	CHAMBERLAIN, Rosanna1854
2	CHAMBERLAIN, Rosanna1854
3	RENO, Morgan	1854
4	RENO, Morgan	1854
5	CROOKHAM, John A[63]1857
5	CROOKHAM, John A[62]1857
6	RENO, Morgan	1855
7	CHAMBERLIN, John	1854
8	CHAMBERLIN, John	1854

3
HUTCHINS Asa B 1855
EASLEY [121] James S 1855

2
TAYLOR James D 1855
KESTER James L 1855

1

DOWNEY Hugh D 1855
COX Thomas J 1855
DOWNEY Hugh D 1856
DOWNEY Hugh D 1856
TAYLOR James D 1855

10
RENO Morgan 1853
PIERCE James 1853
DOWNEY Hugh D 1856
BERRYHILL [14] Charles H 1854
MCVEY James O 1855
11
COX Thomas J 1855
COPE William R 1855
JOHNSON James 1854
BRYAN Alanson 1854
OGDEN Richard B 1852
12

CULBERTSON [79] John C 1856
DOWNEY Hugh D 1855
COPE William R 1855
COPE William R 1855
SANXAY [246] Frederic 1854

Lots-Sec. 10

| 10 | CULBERTSON, John[79]1856 |

STANLEY Asel 1853
PHILLIPS William 1855

BRYAN Alanson 1854
SKINNER Edward 1855
SANXAY Frederic 1854

15
BONE Valentine 1853
BONE Valentine 1852
PIKE Albert 1852
CHEESMAN Felix 1850
WEST Nathan A 1850
JOHNSON James 1854
WOODWARD Davis M 1854
SANXAY Frederic 1854

14

13

WHITE John 1854
MCVEY James O 1855
MCVEY James O 1855
JOHNSON James 1854
HUTCHENS Jeremiah J 1855
WOODWARD Davis M 1854
JOHNSON James 1854

WHITE John 1854
COFFEE John 1855
RENO Morgan 1855
BRYAN Alanson 1854
MCVEY James O 1855
STONEHOCKER Joseph 1855
LOONEY James P 1855
HATHAWAY Thomas F 1854
BROPLEY Thomas L 1855

MCVAY John H 1854
RENO Morgan 1855
RENO Morgan 1855
RENO [234] Morgan 1855
HARNER Andrew 1855

24

22
SANXAY Frederic 1854
HARNER Andrew 1855
WOOLVERTON Garrett R 1855
RENO Morgan 1856
RENO Morgan 1856
WHITE John 1855
RENO Morgan 1856

MCVAY John H 1850

DEMENT [93] Isaac G 1853
BARNES William H 1854
BARNES William H 1855
WHITCOMB Charles S 1855
COX Thomas J 1857
MARTIN [202] Giles S 1854

BARNES William H 1854
BRYAN Alanson 1855
MOORE John 1850
CALDWELL Alexander 1853
REDMAN John 1855

THOMPSON Thomas 1855
BEASON William 1854
HALL John W 1853
GOWER James H 1855

27
26
25

BYINGTON Legrand 1854
SMITH Samuel 1853
ALLEN Isam P 1853

WHITE John 1855
WYMORE James M 1853
MCVEY James O 1855
BROOKS [37] Thomas L 1855
COMBE Thomas 1855

34
MYERS Isaac 1855
SMITH Samuel 1850
LAMSON Ward 1854
SATCHELL Joseph W 1850
WHITE John 1857
WILLINGHAM William W 1855

BRYAN [39] Alanson 1855
SAUNDERS Moses G 1851
SAUNDERS James F 1854
LAMSON Ward 1854
SMITH George 1854
35
JOHNSON William C 1853
JOHNSON William C 1853
MORSMAN [213] Moses J 1854
36

BYINGTON [42] Legrand 1855
SHELEY Beverly 1851
SHELEY William 1855
WINN Edward 1855
BOSLEY Samuel W 1853

Helpful Hints

1. This Map's INDEX can be found on the preceding pages.

2. Refer to Map "C" to see where this Township lies within Poweshiek County, Iowa.

3. Numbers within square brackets [ ] denote a multi-patentee land parcel (multi-owner). Refer to Appendix "C" for a full list of members in this group.

4. Areas that look to be crowded with Patentees usually indicate multiple sales of the same parcel (Re-issues) or Overlapping parcels. See this Township's Index for an explanation of these and other circumstances that might explain "odd" groupings of Patentees on this map.

Legend

——————— Patent Boundary

━━━━━━━ Section Boundary

No Patents Found (or Outside County)

1., 2., 3., ... Lot Numbers (when beside a name)

[ ] Group Number (see Appendix "C")

Scale: Section = 1 mile X 1 mile (generally, with some exceptions)

Road Map

T78-N R15-W
5th PM Meridian

Map Group 14

Cities & Towns
Brownsville
Montezuma

Cemeteries
Beason Cemetery
Bone Cemetery
Forest Home Cemetery
Jackson Township Cemetery
Little Mount Baptist Cemetery
Masonic IOOF Cemetery
McCoy Cemetery
McDonald Cemetery
Sheley Cemetery

480th Ave

Falcon Dr

W Woodland Rd

Crabtree Rd

Horseshoe Dr

Ivy Dr

Vine Dr

Lakeview Dr

6

5

4

† McDonald Cem.

Elm Rd Rd

Valley

Woodland Rd

Oak Rd

90th St

490th Ave

S Shore Dr

Diamond Trail Rd

7

8

9

495th Ave

Little
† *Mount Baptist Cem.*

80th St

500th Ave

18

17

16

505th Ave

510th Ave

512th Ave

19

20

21

520th Ave

Forest Home Rd

†

Forest Home Cem.

30

29

525th Ave

28

70th St

Sawmill Rd

31

32

33

90th St

100th St

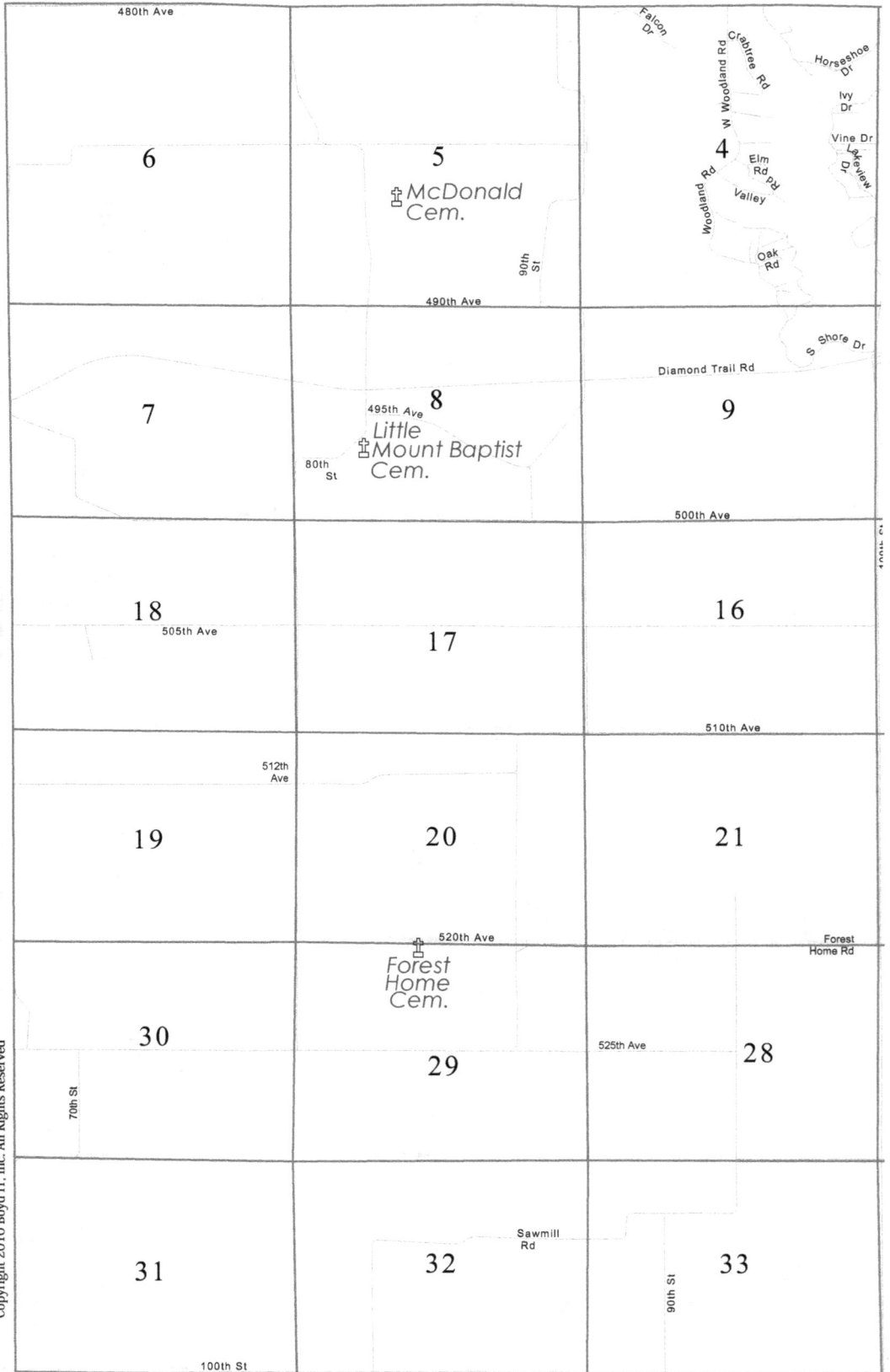

3

2

1

103rd St

480th Ave

US Hwy 63

Hillcrest Ridge

110th St

Cottage Ln

W Madison St
W Jefferson St

Main St

Montezuma

S High St

W Dallas St
W Cass St

Masonic IOOF Cem.

W Wood St

106th St

Jackson Township Cem.

10

11

12

100th St

Bone Cem.

McCoy Cem.

15

14

Hwy 63

13

510th Ave

22

23

24

Beason Cem.

27

26

525th Ave

25

110th St

530th Ave

34

35

Brownsville

36

537th Ave

Sheley Cem.

130th St

Helpful Hints

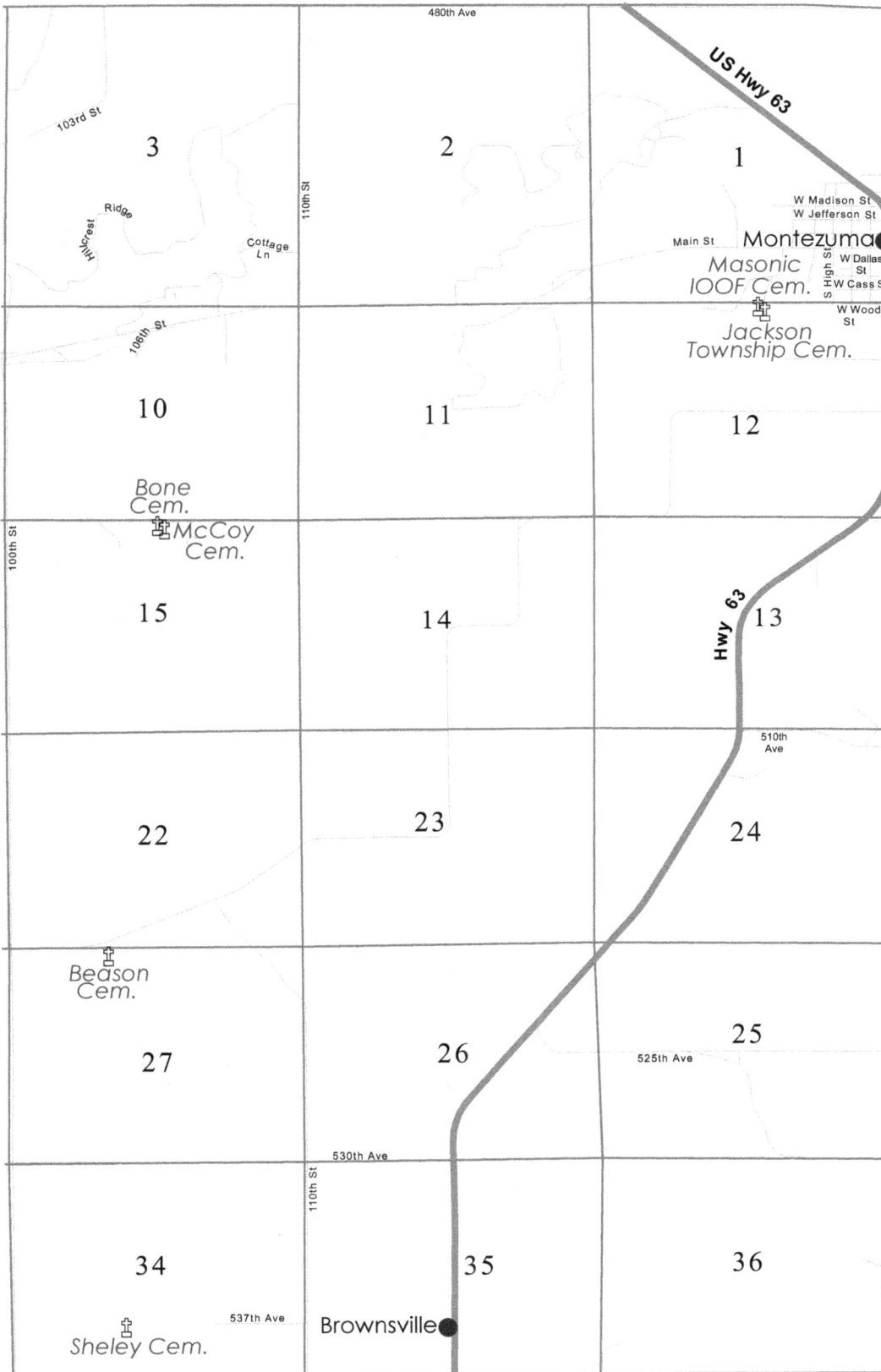

1. This road map has a number of uses, but primarily it is to help you: a) find the present location of land owned by your ancestors (at least the general area), b) find cemeteries and city-centers, and c) estimate the route/roads used by Census-takers & tax-assessors.

2. If you plan to travel to Poweshiek County to locate cemeteries or land parcels, please pick up a modern travel map for the area before you do. Mapping old land parcels on modern maps is not as exact a science as you might think. Just the slightest variations in public land survey coordinates, estimates of parcel boundaries, or road-map deviations can greatly alter a map's representation of how a road either does or doesn't cross a particular parcel of land.

Legend

——————— Section Lines

═══════ Interstates

━━━━━━━ Highways

——————— Other Roads

● Cities/Towns

✝ Cemeteries

Scale: Section = 1 mile X 1 mile
(generally, with some exceptions)

Historical Map

T78-N R15-W
5th PM Meridian

Map Group 14

Cities & Towns
Brownsville
Montezuma

Cemeteries
Beason Cemetery
Bone Cemetery
Forest Home Cemetery
Jackson Township Cemetery
Little Mount Baptist Cemetery
Masonic IOOF Cemetery
McCoy Cemetery
McDonald Cemetery
Sheley Cemetery

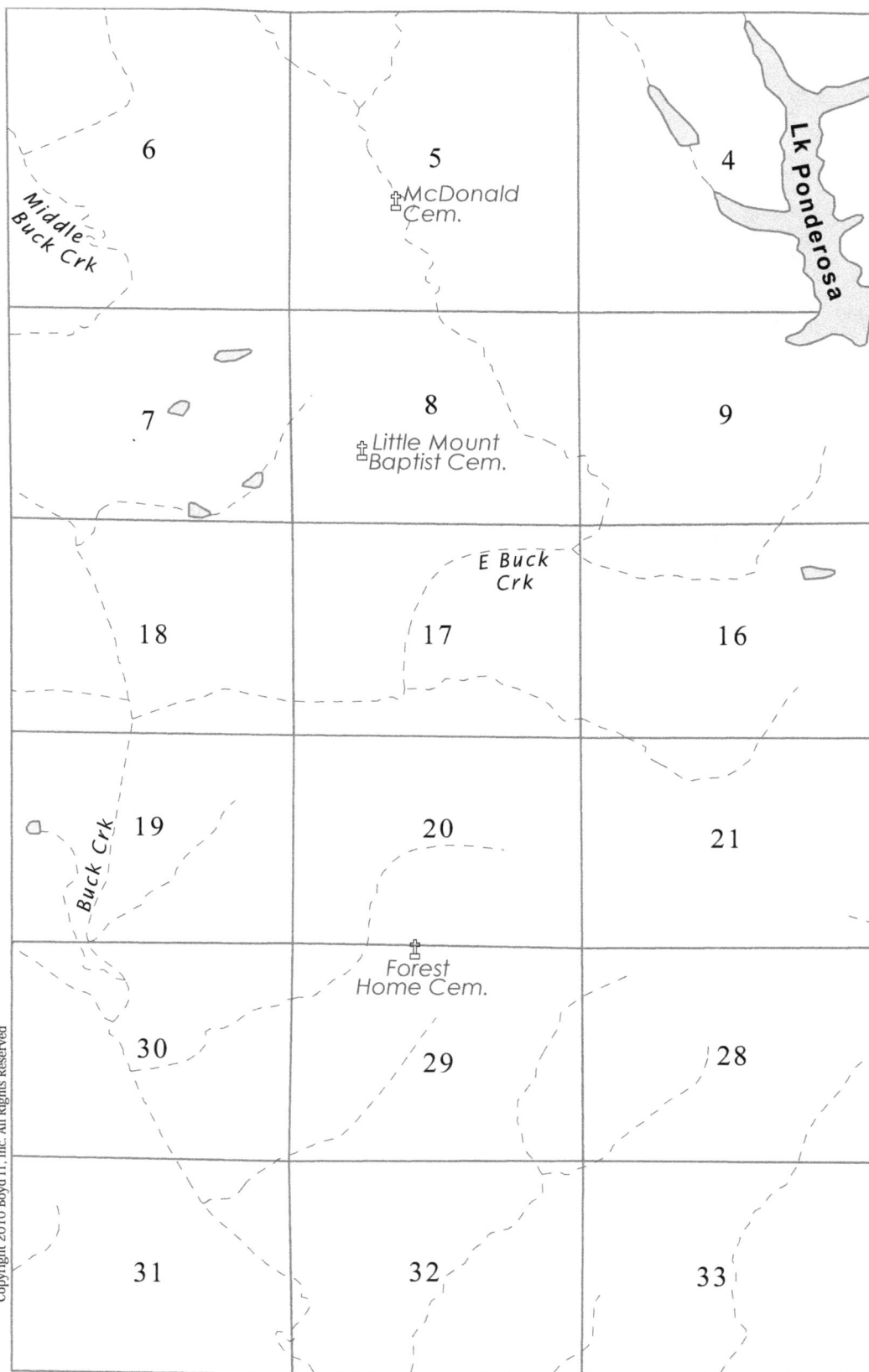

6

5

☩ McDonald
Cem.

4

Lk Ponderosa

Middle Buck Crk

7

8

☩ Little Mount
Baptist Cem.

9

E Buck
Crk

18

17

16

Buck Crk

19

20

21

☩ Forest
Home Cem.

30

29

28

31

32

33

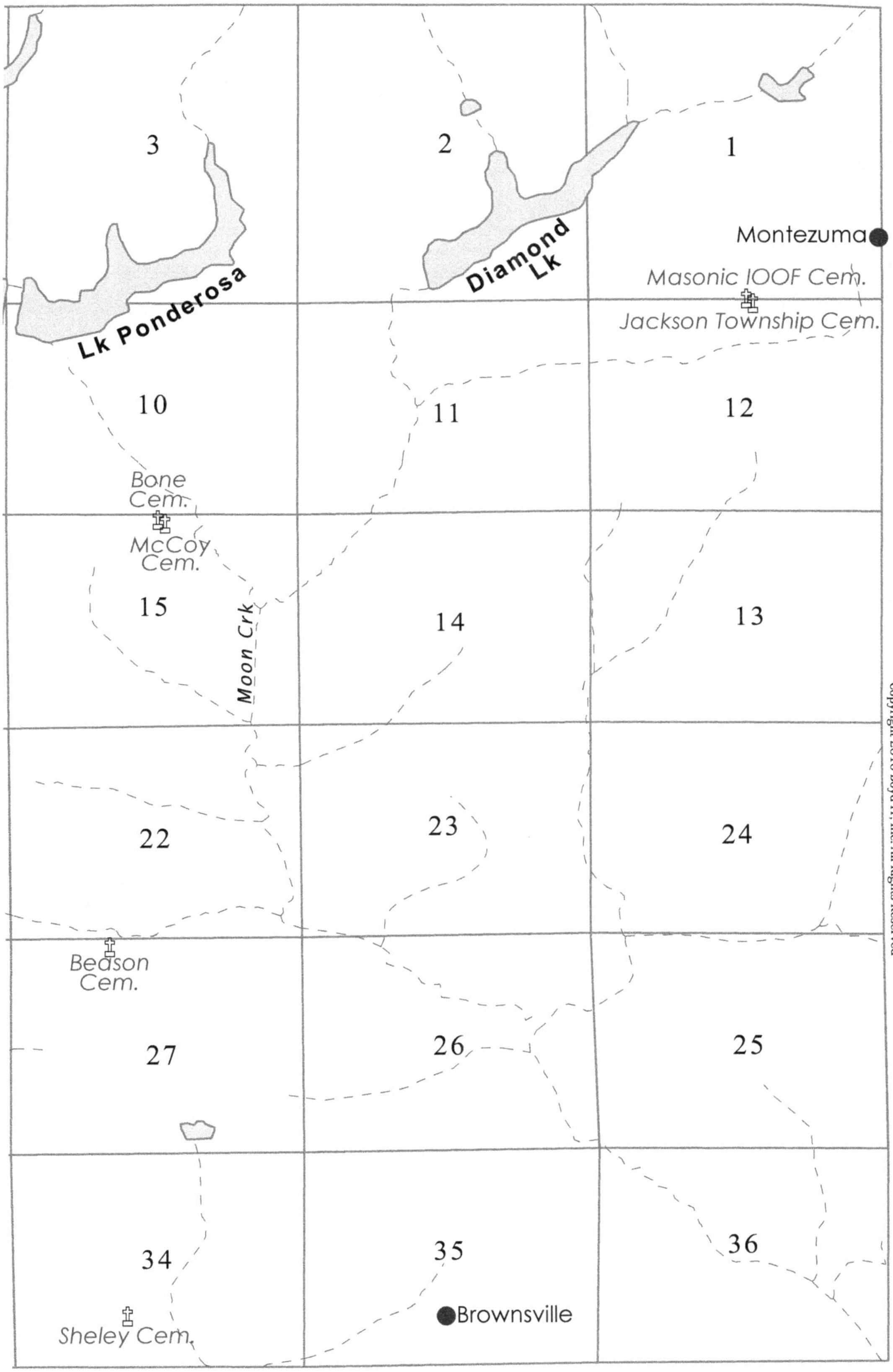
3
2
1
Lk Ponderosa
Diamond Lk
Montezuma
Masonic IOOF Cem.
Jackson Township Cem.
10
11
12
Bone Cem.
McCoy Cem.
15
14
13
Moon Crk
22
23
24
Beason Cem.
27
26
25
34
35
36
Sheley Cem.
Brownsville

Helpful Hints

1. This Map takes a different look at the same Congressional Township displayed in the preceding two maps. It presents features that can help you better envision the historical development of the area: a) Water-bodies (lakes & ponds), b) Water-courses (rivers, streams, etc.), c) Railroads, d) City/town center-points (where they were oftentimes located when first settled), and e) Cemeteries.
2. Using this "Historical" map in tandem with this Township's Patent Map and Road Map, may lead you to some interesting discoveries. You will often find roads, towns, cemeteries, and waterways are named after nearby landowners: sometimes those names will be the ones you are researching. See how many of these research gems you can find here in Poweshiek County.

Legend

- Section Lines
- Railroads
- Large Rivers & Bodies of Water
- Streams/Creeks & Small Rivers
- Cities/Towns
- Cemeteries

Scale: Section = 1 mile X 1 mile
(there are some exceptions)

Map Group 15: Index to Land Patents

Township 78-North Range 14-West (5th PM)

After you locate an individual in this Index, take note of the Section and Section Part then proceed to the Land Patent map on the pages immediately following. You should have no difficulty locating the corresponding parcel of land.

The "For More Info" Column will lead you to more information about the underlying Patents. See the *Legend* at right, and the "How to Use this Book" chapter, for more information.

```
                        LEGEND
              "For More Info . . . " column
A = Authority (Legislative Act, See Appendix "A")
B = Block or Lot (location in Section unknown)
C = Cancelled Patent
F = Fractional Section
G = Group  (Multi-Patentee Patent, see Appendix "C")
V = Overlaps another Parcel
R = Re-Issued (Parcel patented more than once)

(A & G items require you to look in the Appendixes referred
to above. All other Letter-designations followed by a number
require you to locate line-items in this index that possess
the ID number found after the letter).
```

ID	Individual in Patent	Sec.	Sec. Part	Date Issued	Other Counties	For More Info . . .
3348	ADAMS, Jackey P	34	SESW	1854-10-02		A6 G18
3343	ALLEN, Iram P	29	NENW	1854-05-01		A1
3344	ALLEN, Isaac	32	NWSE	1854-11-01		A4
3320	BACON, Elizabeth	8	SESW	1852-05-10		A6
3322	BARNES, Garter S	4	S½SW	1852-03-15		A6
3394	BARNES, John H	28	NWNE	1854-12-01		A1
3484	BARNES, Mary	32	E½SE	1855-07-02		A6 G29
3485	" "	33	W½SW	1855-07-02		A6 G29
3452	BARNES, Robert G	29	NENE	1854-12-01		A1
3486	BARNES, William G P	29	NESW	1854-05-01		A1
3487	" "	29	NWSE	1854-05-01		A1
3299	BERRYHILL, Charles H	1	8	1853-09-10		A6 G17
3298	" "	3	9	1854-07-01		A6
3296	" "	2	12	1854-11-01		A4
3297	" "	2	5	1854-11-01		A4
3295	" "	12	N½NW	1855-05-10		A1
3294	" "	1	12	1857-04-01		A4
3348	BERRYHILL, James B	34	SESW	1854-10-02		A6 G18
3349	" "	34	SWSE	1854-10-02		A6 G20
3346	" "	1	5	1855-12-15		A1
3347	" "	32	SENW	1855-12-15		A1
3460	BIRD, Roderick D	3	SESW	1854-05-01		A1
3461	" "	3	SWSE	1854-05-01		A1
3459	" "	10	NENW	1854-08-01		A6
3467	" "	10	NWNE	1854-08-01		A6 G26
3462	" "	4	NESE	1854-08-01		A6
3463	" "	4	NWSE	1854-08-01		A6
3464	" "	4	SESE	1854-08-01		A6
3465	" "	4	SWSE	1854-08-01		A6
3466	" "	9	NENE	1854-11-01		A4 V3354
3484	BOSWELL, William	32	E½SE	1855-07-02		A6 G29
3485	" "	33	W½SW	1855-07-02		A6 G29
3291	BOYDSTON, Benjamin F	18	NWNE	1854-12-01		A1
3293	BRACKEN, Caleb H	36	NW	1855-05-01		A1
3350	BRIDGES, James	5	SESW	1854-08-01		A6
3389	CAMPBELL, John	31	NE	1855-05-10		A1
3475	CARBERY, Thomas	22	E½SE	1855-05-01		A1
3476	" "	22	NWSE	1855-05-01		A1
3328	CHESNUT, Nancy	17	NW	1854-03-01		A6 G277
3467	CHRISTAIN, Sarah	10	NWNE	1854-08-01		A6 G26
3318	CLEAVER, Eli V	31	NENW	1855-12-15		A1 F
3477	COMBE, Thomas	13	S½SW	1855-05-10		A1
3478	" "	31	SW	1855-05-10		A1 F
3309	CONNELLY, Edward	28	N½SW	1854-10-02		A6
3314	" "	33	E½SW	1854-10-02		A6
3315	" "	33	W½SE	1854-10-02		A6

ID	Individual in Patent	Sec.	Sec. Part	Date Issued	Other Counties	For More Info . . .
3308	CONNELLY, Edward (Cont'd)	20	SWSE	1854-12-01		A6
3310	" "	32	E½SW	1855-05-01		A6
3311	" "	32	NWSW	1855-05-01		A1
3312	" "	32	SWNW	1855-05-01		A1
3313	" "	32	SWSW	1855-12-15		A1
3502	COPE, William R	32	SWSE	1855-05-01		A1
3503	" "	34	NWSW	1855-05-01		A1
3504	" "	36	SW	1855-05-01		A1
3469	COWGILL, Sarah	36	S½SE	1855-05-01		A1
3285	CRADDOCK, Mary A	29	SENW	1854-10-02		A6 G214
3286	" "	29	SWNE	1854-10-02		A6 G214
3388	CULBERTSON, John C	30	SWNE	1855-05-01		A6
3284	CURRY, Andrew	8	E½NE	1852-03-01		A6
3391	DARLAND, John	28	W½NW	1854-10-02		A6 G87
3390	" "	28	E½NW	1855-01-01		A6
3408	DARLAND, Lambert	28	S½SW	1854-08-01		A6 G88
3323	DORLING, George	33	NESE	1854-10-02		A6
3342	DOWNEY, Hugh D	12	NWNE	1855-03-01		A4
3341	" "	1	1	1855-12-15		A1
3283	EASON, Alexander	4	4	1855-05-01		A1
3472	EDDY, Stephen	8	SE	1852-05-10		A6
3439	GATLING, Richard J	2	SW	1854-05-01		A1
3441	" "	21	SW	1854-05-01		A1
3440	" "	21	NW	1854-10-02		A6
3437	" "	12	S½SE	1855-02-01		A6 C R3492
3438	" "	13	N½NE	1855-02-01		A6 C R3493
3451	" "	24	E½SE	1855-02-01		A6 G142
3445	" "	24	NE	1855-02-01		A6
3447	" "	24	W½SE	1855-02-01		A6
3448	" "	25	NW	1855-02-01		A6 C R3449
3450	" "	25	SE	1855-02-01		A6
3446	" "	24	NW	1855-03-01		A4
3442	" "	23	S½	1855-05-01		A1
3443	" "	23	S½NE	1855-05-01		A1
3444	" "	23	S½NW	1855-05-01		A1
3449	" "	25	NW	1879-12-30		A1 R3448
3496	GATLING, William J	17	E½	1854-05-01		A1
3497	" "	2	SE	1854-05-01		A1
3490	" "	11	N½NE	1854-10-02		A6
3491	" "	11	N½NW	1854-10-02		A6
3498	" "	3	E½SE	1854-10-02		A6
3489	" "	10	NENE	1854-11-01		A4
3494	" "	13	S½NE	1855-01-01		A6
3495	" "	13	S½NW	1855-01-01		A6
3492	" "	12	S½SE	1918-10-19		A6 R3437
3493	" "	13	N½NE	1918-10-19		A6 R3438
3356	GOWER, James H	25	SW	1855-05-01		A1
3357	" "	3	NESW	1855-05-01		A1
3358	" "	3	NWSE	1855-05-01		A1
3359	" "	31	SENW	1855-05-10		A1 F
3360	" "	31	W½NW	1855-05-10		A1 F
3396	GUILD, John M	27	S½	1855-05-01		A1
3324	HAGERTY, George J	4	3	1854-05-01		A1
3319	HALL, Eliza	26	SE	1855-05-01		A1
3395	HALL, John	26	SW	1855-05-01		A1
3351	HAMILTON, James C	26	NW	1855-05-01		A1
3411	HARDEN, Matthew	1	2	1854-12-01		A1
3488	HARKLEROAD, William	1	3	1850-04-10		A1
3387	HINER, Joel	20	NWSW	1854-05-01		A1
3453	HUTCHESON, Robert	35		1855-05-01		A1
3454	" "	36	NE	1855-05-01		A1
3471	IOWA, State Of	16		1937-08-26		A3
3361	JOHNSON, James	17	E½SW	1854-12-01		A1
3362	" "	18	NENW	1854-12-01		A1 F
3363	" "	18	SESW	1854-12-01		A1 F
3364	" "	19	NENE	1854-12-01		A1
3365	" "	19	NESE	1854-12-01		A1
3366	" "	20	E½NW	1854-12-01		A1
3367	" "	20	N½NE	1854-12-01		A1
3368	" "	20	NWNW	1854-12-01		A1
3369	" "	20	S½SW	1854-12-01		A1
3370	" "	20	SESE	1854-12-01		A1
3371	" "	3	10	1854-12-01		A1

ID	Individual in Patent	Sec.	Sec. Part	Date Issued	Other Counties	For More Info . . .
3372	JOHNSON, James (Cont'd)	3	11	1854-12-01		A1
3373	" "	3	12	1854-12-01		A1
3374	" "	3	5	1854-12-01		A1
3375	" "	3	6	1854-12-01		A1
3376	" "	3	7	1854-12-01		A1
3307	KNOTT, Dorothy	8	NESW	1852-05-10		A6
3434	LANDEN, Orey	33	SWNW	1854-05-01		A1
3336	LAWRENCE, Christian	1	10	1854-12-01		A6 G217
3337	" "	1	9	1854-12-01		A6 G217
3338	" "	1	E½SE	1854-12-01		A6 G217
3300	LISOR, Clement H	21	SE	1855-05-01		A1
3301	"	22	SW	1855-05-01		A1
3501	LYNN, William	4	2	1854-05-01		A1
3321	LYTLE, Enos M	12	NENE	1855-05-10		A1
3290	MALONE, Benjamin C	17	W½SW	1854-05-01		A1
3470	MARKS, Sarah	8	SWNW	1852-04-01		A6
3352	MARTIN, James D	28	E½NE	1855-05-01		A1
3353	" "	28	SWNE	1855-05-01		A1
3382	MCVEY, James O	18	W½NW	1854-12-01		A1 F
3383	" "	22	S½NE	1855-05-10		A1
3384	" "	26	NE	1855-05-10		A1
3480	MCVEY, Wesley	3	NWSW	1855-05-01		A1
3479	" "	19	W½SW	1855-12-15		A1 F
3481	MCVEY, Westley	29	NWNE	1855-12-15		A1
3482	" "	29	SENE	1855-12-15		A1
3483	" "	3	8	1855-12-15		A1
3435	MORGAN, Peter	1	11	1855-05-01		A1
3436	" "	1	6	1855-05-01		A1
3379	MURRAY, James	2	11	1855-05-01		A1
3380	" "	2	6	1855-05-01		A1
3381	" "	4	9	1855-05-01		A1
3285	MUSGROVE, Andrew J	29	SENW	1854-10-02		A6 G214
3286	" "	29	SWNE	1854-10-02		A6 G214
3292	MUSGROVE, Benjamin	29	NWSW	1855-01-01		A6 G215
3377	MUSGROVE, James M	29	E½SE	1854-05-01		A1
3349	NELSON, Sheney	34	SWSE	1854-10-02		A6 G20
3345	NEWHALL, Isaac	1	4	1854-05-01		A1
3339	NIXON, Orvill A	10	S½NW	1854-12-01		A6 G218
3451	PARKER, Tempy	24	E½SE	1855-02-01		A6 G142
3292	PAROTT, Mary	29	NWSW	1855-01-01		A6 G215
3336	PARRISH, Hardin	1	10	1854-12-01		A6 G217
3337	" "	1	9	1854-12-01		A6 G217
3338	" "	1	E½SE	1854-12-01		A6 G217
3339	" "	10	S½NW	1854-12-01		A6 G218
3329	" "	10	SW	1854-12-01		A1
3330	" "	15	E½NW	1854-12-01		A6
3331	" "	15	W½NW	1854-12-01		A6
3332	" "	9	E½NW	1854-12-01		A1
3333	" "	9	SE	1854-12-01		A1
3334	" "	9	SENE	1854-12-01		A1
3335	" "	9	SWNW	1854-12-01		A1
3401	PORTER, John	10	NWNW	1854-05-01		A1
3402	" "	3	SWSW	1854-05-01		A1
3354	RANKIN, James F	9	N½NE	1854-05-01		A1 V3466
3355	" "	9	NWNW	1854-05-01		A1
3403	REDMAN, John	30	NWNW	1855-12-15		A1 F
3406	REDMOND, John	30	S½NW	1853-07-20		A6 F
3404	" "	20	NESW	1854-12-01		A1
3405	" "	20	SWNW	1855-01-01		A6 F
3287	REED, Andrew R	18	W½SW	1855-05-10		A1 F
3415	RENO, Morgan	2	7	1855-01-01		A6
3416	" "	22	SWSE	1855-01-01		A6
3422	" "	30	E½SW	1855-01-01		A6 F
3423	" "	31	SE	1855-03-01		A4 G235
3413	" "	2	3	1855-05-10		A1
3414	" "	2	4	1855-05-10		A1
3418	" "	3	1	1855-05-10		A1
3419	" "	3	2	1855-05-10		A1
3417	" "	29	SWSW	1855-12-15		A1
3420	" "	3	3	1855-12-15		A1
3421	" "	3	4	1855-12-15		A1
3408	REVERE, Judith	28	S½SW	1854-08-01		A6 G88
3407	ROBERTS, John	27	NW	1855-05-01		A1

ID	Individual in Patent	Sec.	Sec. Part	Date Issued	Other Counties	For More Info . . .
3302	RORTY, Daniel	30	SE	1855-05-10		A1
3391	RUSSELL, Phebe M	28	W½NW	1854-10-02		A6 G87
3423	SCRUGS, Amelia L	31	SE	1855-03-01		A4 G235
3392	SEARIGHT, John F	4	5	1854-05-01		A1
3393	" "	4	6	1854-05-01		A1
3327	SHARP, George	33	NENW	1854-08-01		A6 G249
3325	" "	33	NWNW	1854-08-01		A6
3326	" "	33	SENW	1854-08-01		A6
3409	SHEPARD, Levi	29	NWNW	1854-05-01		A1
3410	" "	29	SWNW	1854-10-02		A6
3316	SKINNER, Edward	34	N½	1855-05-01		A1
3317	" "	34	NESW	1855-05-10		A1
3455	SKINNER, Robert S	5	1	1854-05-01		A1
3456	" "	5	2	1854-05-01		A1
3457	" "	5	3	1854-05-01		A1
3458	" "	5	4	1854-05-01		A1
3397	SMITH, John P	13	N½SW	1855-05-01		A1
3398	" "	34	N½SE	1855-05-01		A1
3399	" "	34	SESE	1855-05-01		A1
3400	" "	36	N½SE	1855-05-01		A1
3327	SNOWDEN, Elizabeth W	33	NENW	1854-08-01		A6 G249
3303	SNYDER, David	21	NE	1855-05-01		A1
3304	" "	22	NW	1855-05-01		A1
3340	SWEET, Henry C	27	NE	1855-05-01		A1
3288	TEEL, Asa	4	10	1854-05-01		A1
3289	" "	4	7	1854-05-01		A1
3499	TIBBALS, William J	2	10	1855-05-10		A1
3500	" "	2	9	1855-05-10		A1
3505	TIBBALS, William T	1	W½SW	1855-12-15		A1
3305	TOSSE, Dominick	8	E½NW	1852-04-01		A6
3306	" "	8	W½NE	1852-04-01		A6
3424	TOUSEY, Omer	10	S½NE	1854-05-01		A1
3425	" "	10	SE	1854-05-01		A1
3426	" "	11	S½	1854-05-01		A1
3427	" "	11	S½NE	1854-05-01		A1
3428	" "	11	S½NW	1854-05-01		A1
3429	" "	14		1854-05-01		A1
3430	" "	15	E½	1854-05-01		A1
3431	" "	22	N½NE	1854-05-01		A1
3432	" "	23	N½NE	1854-05-01		A1
3433	" "	23	N½NW	1854-05-01		A1
3473	WALKER, Thomas C	20	N½SE	1854-05-01		A1
3474	" "	20	S½NE	1854-05-01		A1
3328	WASSON, George W	17	NW	1854-03-01		A6 G277
3299	WEBBER, Mary	1	8	1853-09-10		A6 G17
3412	WHITE, Miles	34	SWSW	1854-05-01		A1
3385	WILSON, James W	1	7	1854-12-01		A1
3386	WOOD, James	30	SWSW	1855-12-15		A1 F
3378	WYMORE, James M	33	SESE	1854-08-01		A6
3468	ZEIGLER, Samuel P	13	SE	1855-05-01		A1

Patent Map

T78-N R14-W
5th PM Meridian

Map Group 15

Township Statistics

Parcels Mapped	:	223
Number of Patents	:	170
Number of Individuals	:	104
Patentees Identified	:	99
Number of Surnames	:	89
Multi-Patentee Parcels	:	19
Oldest Patent Date	:	4/10/1850
Most Recent Patent	:	8/26/1937
Block/Lot Parcels	:	45
Parcels Re-Issued	:	3
Parcels that Overlap	:	2
Cities and Towns	:	0
Cemeteries	:	2

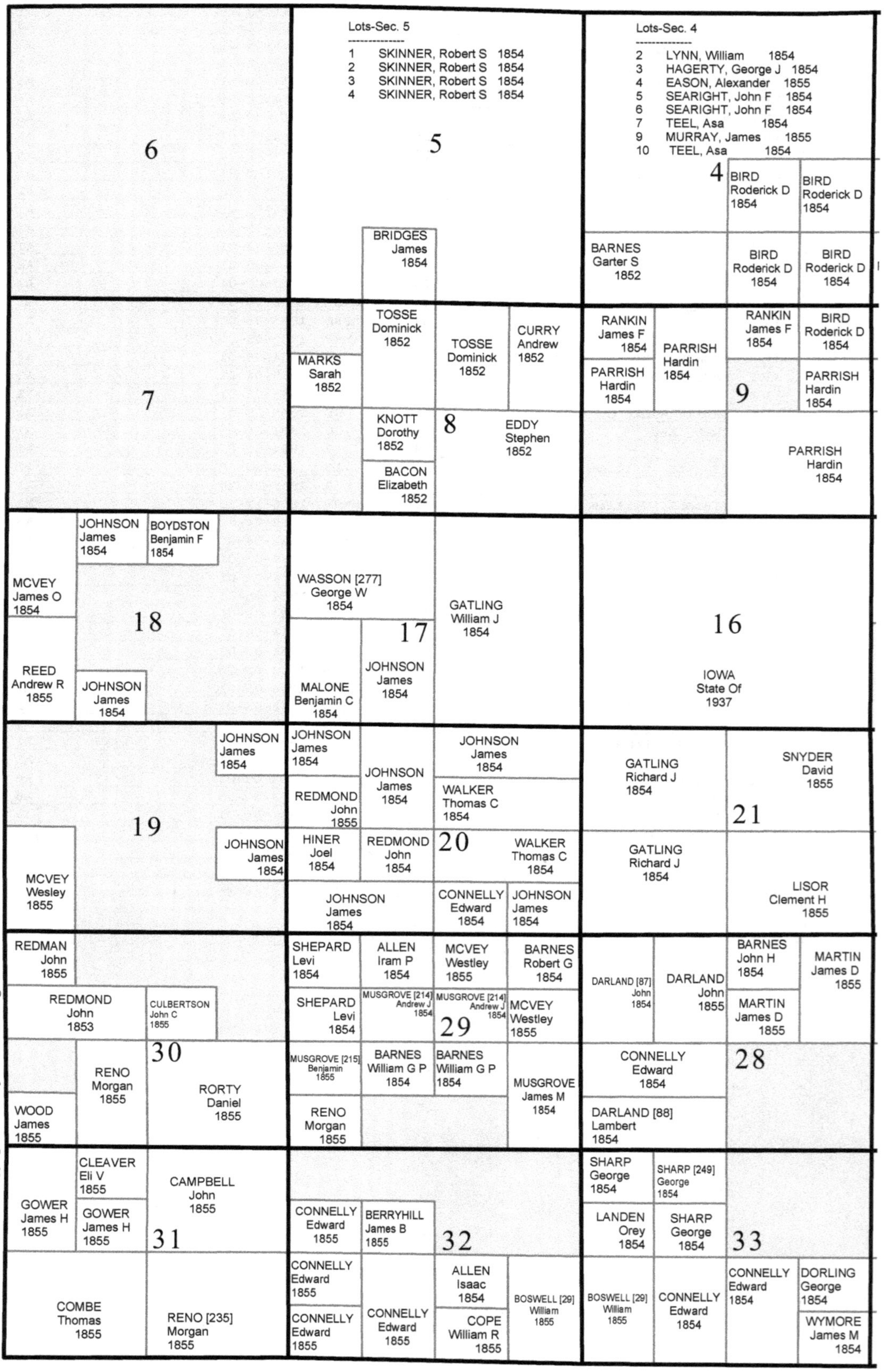

Lots-Sec. 5
1 SKINNER, Robert S 1854
2 SKINNER, Robert S 1854
3 SKINNER, Robert S 1854
4 SKINNER, Robert S 1854

Lots-Sec. 4
2 LYNN, William 1854
3 HAGERTY, George J 1854
4 EASON, Alexander 1855
5 SEARIGHT, John F 1854
6 SEARIGHT, John F 1854
7 TEEL, Asa 1854
9 MURRAY, James 1855
10 TEEL, Asa 1854

Patent map grid showing sections 4-9, 16-21, 28-33 with landowner names.

Lots-Sec. 3

1	RENO, Morgan	1855
2	RENO, Morgan	1855
3	RENO, Morgan	1855
4	RENO, Morgan	1855
5	JOHNSON, James	1854
6	JOHNSON, James	1854
7	JOHNSON, James	1854
8	MCVEY, Westley	1855
9	BERRYHILL, Charles H	1854
10	JOHNSON, James	1854
11	JOHNSON, James	1854
12	JOHNSON, James	1854

Lots-Sec. 2

3	RENO, Morgan	1855
4	RENO, Morgan	1854
5	BERRYHILL, Charles H	1854
6	MURRAY, James	1855
7	RENO, Morgan	1855
9	TIBBALS, William J	1855
10	TIBBALS, William J	1855
11	MURRAY, James	1855
12	BERRYHILL, Charles H	1854

Lots-Sec. 1

1	DOWNEY, Hugh D	1855
2	HARDEN, Matthew	1854
3	HARKLEROAD, William	1850
4	NEWHALL, Isaac	1854
5	BERRYHILL, James B	1855
6	MORGAN, Peter	1855
7	WILSON, James W	1854
8	BERRYHILL, Charl[17]	1853
9	PARRISH, Hardin[217]	1854
10	PARRISH, Hardin[217]	1854
11	MORGAN, Peter	1855
12	BERRYHILL, Charles H	1857

Copyright 2010 Boyd IT, Inc. All Rights Reserved

Helpful Hints

1. This Map's INDEX can be found on the preceding pages.

2. Refer to Map "C" to see where this Township lies within Poweshiek County, Iowa.

3. Numbers within square brackets [ ] denote a multi-patentee land parcel (multi-owner). Refer to Appendix "C" for a full list of members in this group.

4. Areas that look to be crowded with Patentees usually indicate multiple sales of the same parcel (Re-issues) or Overlapping parcels. See this Township's Index for an explanation of these and other circumstances that might explain "odd" groupings of Patentees on this map.

Legend

————————	Patent Boundary
▬▬▬▬▬▬▬	Section Boundary
	No Patents Found (or Outside County)
1., 2., 3., ...	Lot Numbers (when beside a name)
[ ]	Group Number (see Appendix "C")

Scale: Section = 1 mile X 1 mile (generally, with some exceptions)

Map details:

Section 3: MCVEY Wesley 1855; GOWER James H 1855; GOWER James H 1854; GATLING William J 1854; PORTER John 1854; BIRD Roderick D 1854; BIRD Roderick D 1854; PORTER John 1854; BIRD Roderick D 1854; BIRD [26] Roderick D 1854; GATLING William J 1854

Section 2: GATLING Richard J 1854; GATLING William J 1854

Section 1: TIBBALS William T 1855; PARRISH [217] Hardin 1854

Section 10: PARRISH [218] Hardin 1854; TOUSEY Omer 1854; PARRISH Hardin 1854; TOUSEY Omer 1854

Section 11: GATLING William J 1854; GATLING William J 1854; TOUSEY Omer 1854; TOUSEY Omer 1854; TOUSEY Omer 1854

Section 12: GATLING Richard J 1855; GATLING William J 1918

Section 15: PARRISH Hardin 1854; PARRISH Hardin 1854; TOUSEY Omer 1854

Section 14: TOUSEY Omer 1854

Section 13: GATLING Richard J 1855; GATLING William J 1918; GATLING William J 1855; GATLING William J 1855; SMITH John P 1855; ZEIGLER Samuel P 1855; COMBE Thomas 1855

Section 22: SNYDER David 1855; TOUSEY Omer 1854; MCVEY James O 1855; CARBERY Thomas 1855; CARBERY Thomas 1855; RENO Morgan 1855; LISOR Clement H 1855

Section 23: TOUSEY Omer 1854; TOUSEY Omer 1854; GATLING Richard J 1855; GATLING Richard J 1855; GATLING Richard J 1855

Section 24: GATLING Richard J 1855; GATLING [142] Richard J 1855; GATLING Richard J 1855

Section 27: ROBERTS John 1855; SWEET Henry C 1855; GUILD John M 1855

Section 26: HAMILTON James C 1855; MCVEY James O 1855; HALL John 1855; HALL Eliza 1855

Section 25: GATLING Richard J 1879; GATLING Richard J 1855; GOWER James H 1855; GATLING Richard J 1855

Section 34: SKINNER Edward 1855; COPE William R 1855; SKINNER Edward 1855; SMITH John P 1855; WHITE Miles 1854; BERRYHILL [18] James B 1854; BERRYHILL [20] James B 1854; SMITH John P 1855

Section 35: HUTCHESON Robert 1855

Section 36: BRACKEN Caleb H 1855; HUTCHESON Robert 1855; COPE William R 1855; SMITH John P 1855; COWGILL Sarah 1855

Road Map

T78-N R14-W
5th PM Meridian

Map Group 15

Cities & Towns
None

Cemeteries
Harper Cemetery
Lisor Cemetery

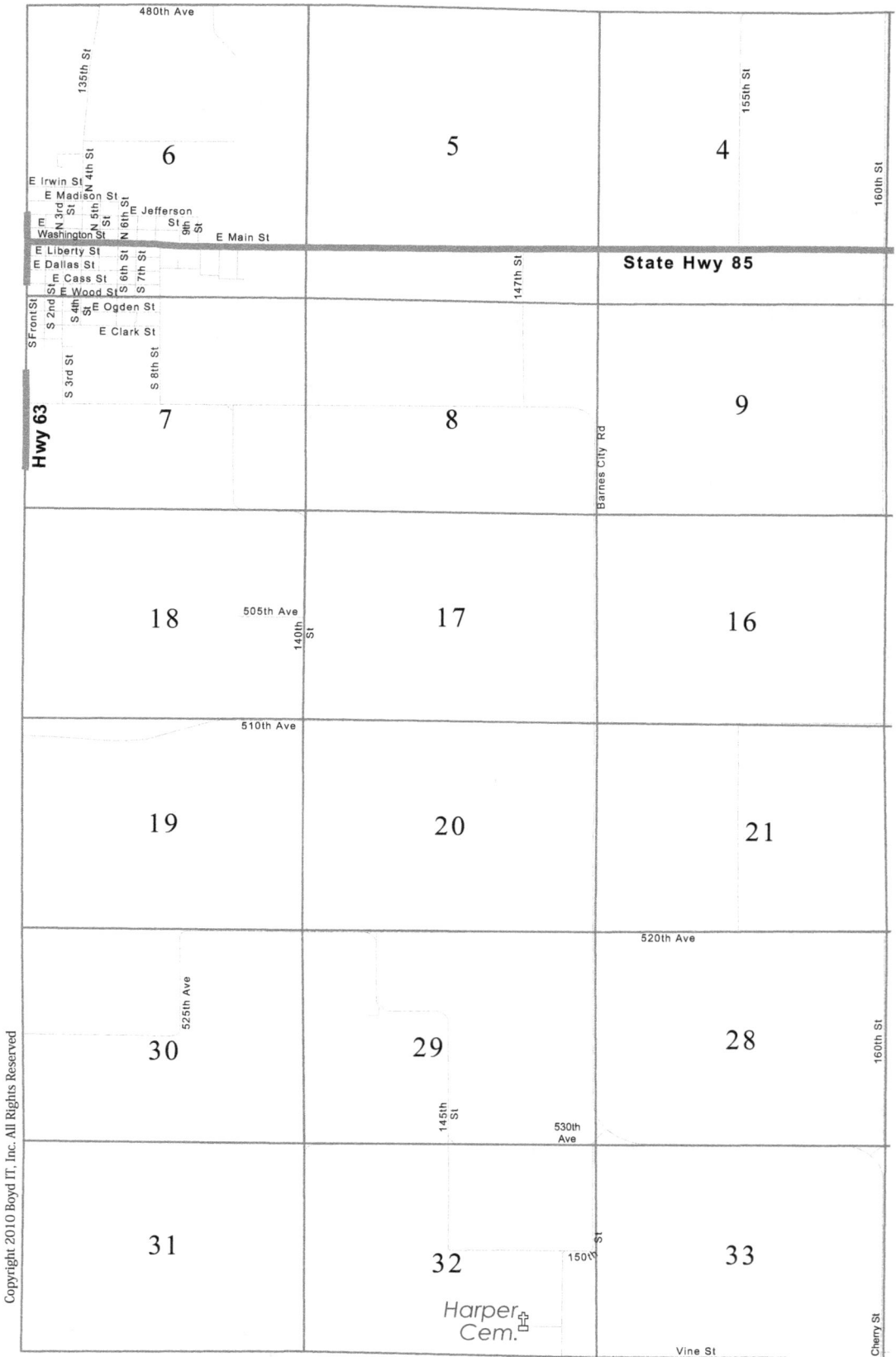

480th Ave

135th St

155th St

160th St

6

5

4

E Irwin St
N 4th St
E Madison St
N 3rd St
N 5th St
E
E Jefferson
Washington St
N 6th St
9th St
St
E Main St

E Liberty St
E Dallas St
S 6th St
147th St
State Hwy 85
E Cass St
S 7th St
S 2nd St
S 4th St
E Wood St
S Front St
E Ogden St
E Clark St
S 3rd St
S 8th St

Hwy 63

7

8

Barnes City Rd

9

18

505th Ave
140th St

17

16

510th Ave

19

20

21

525th Ave

520th Ave

30

29

145th St

530th Ave

28

160th St

Copyright 2010 Boyd IT, Inc. All Rights Reserved

31

32

150th St

Harper
Cem.

33

Cherry St

Vine St

3

2

1

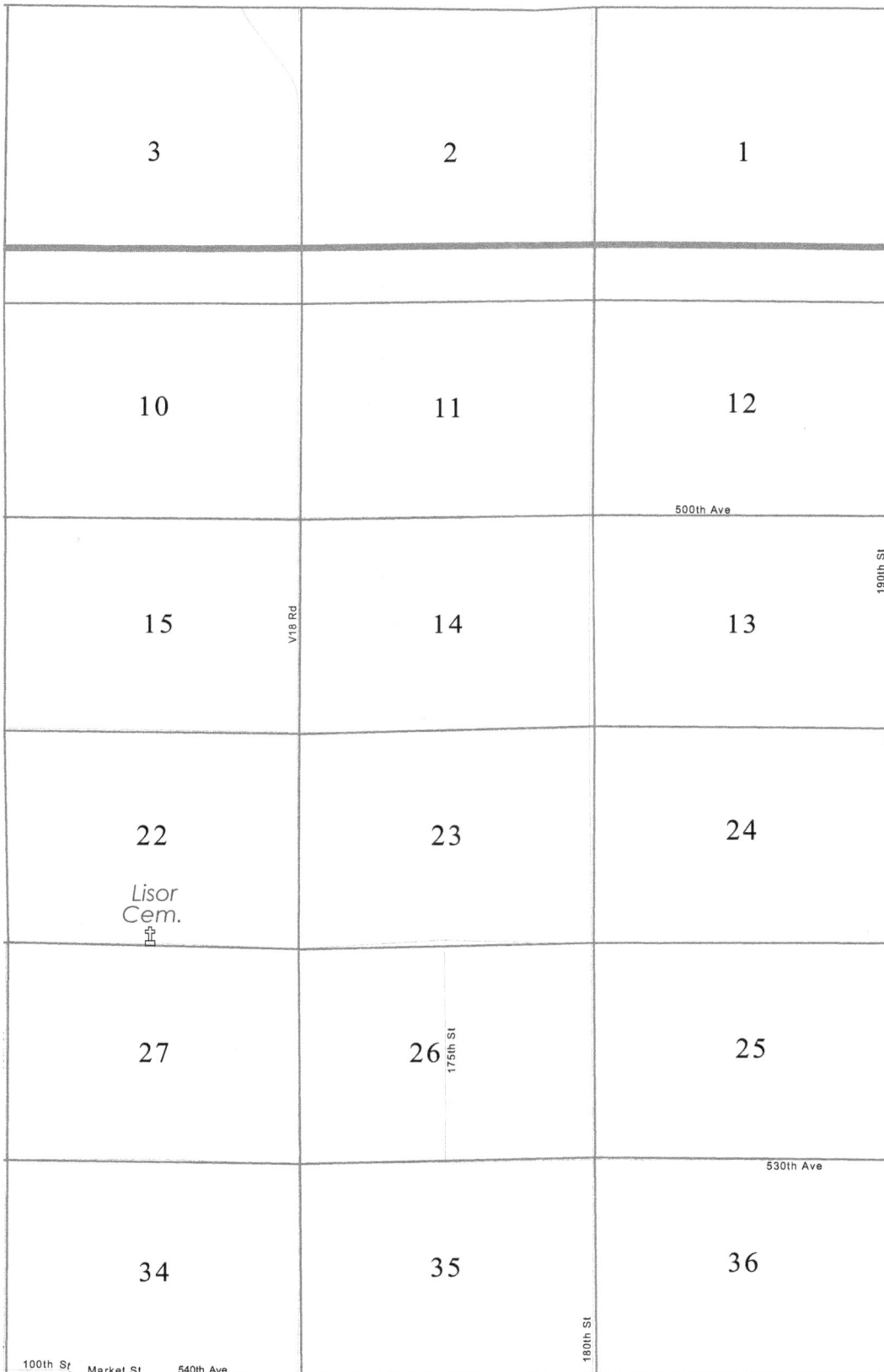

10

11

12

500th Ave

15

V18 Rd

14

13

190th St

22

Lisor Cem.

23

24

27

26

175th St

25

530th Ave

34

35

36

100th St   Market St   540th Ave

180th St

Scale: Section = 1 mile X 1 mile
(generally, with some exceptions)

Historical Map

T78-N R14-W
5th PM Meridian

Map Group 15

<u>Cities & Towns</u>
None

<u>Cemeteries</u>
Harper Cemetery
Lisor Cemetery

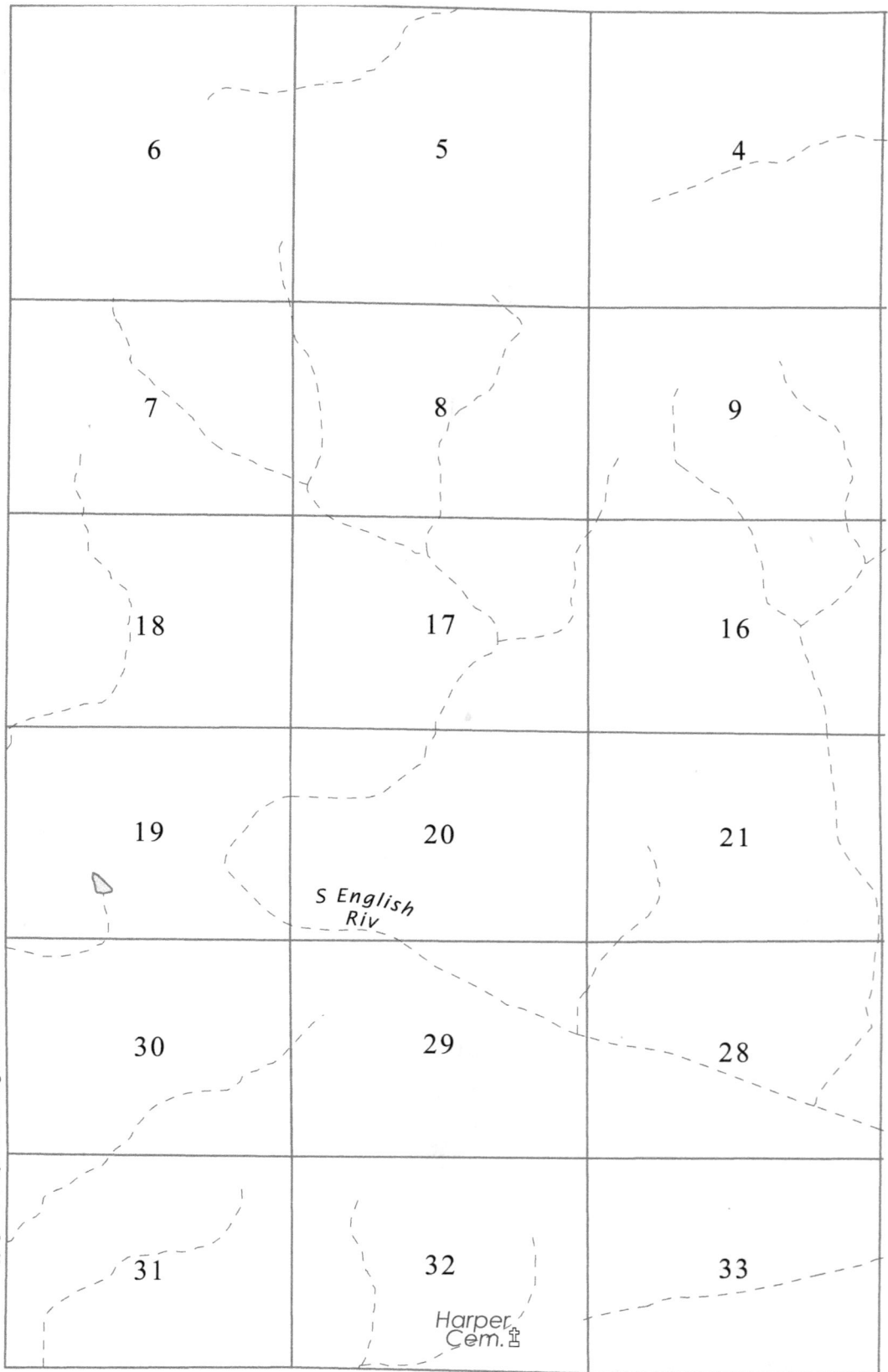

6	5	4
7	8	9
18	17	16
19	20	21
30	29	28
31	32	33

S English Riv

Harper Cem.

3	2	1
10	11	12
15	14	13
22	23	24
27	26	25
34	35	36

Lisor Cem. ☩

Copyright 2010 Boyd IT, Inc. All Rights Reserved

Helpful Hints

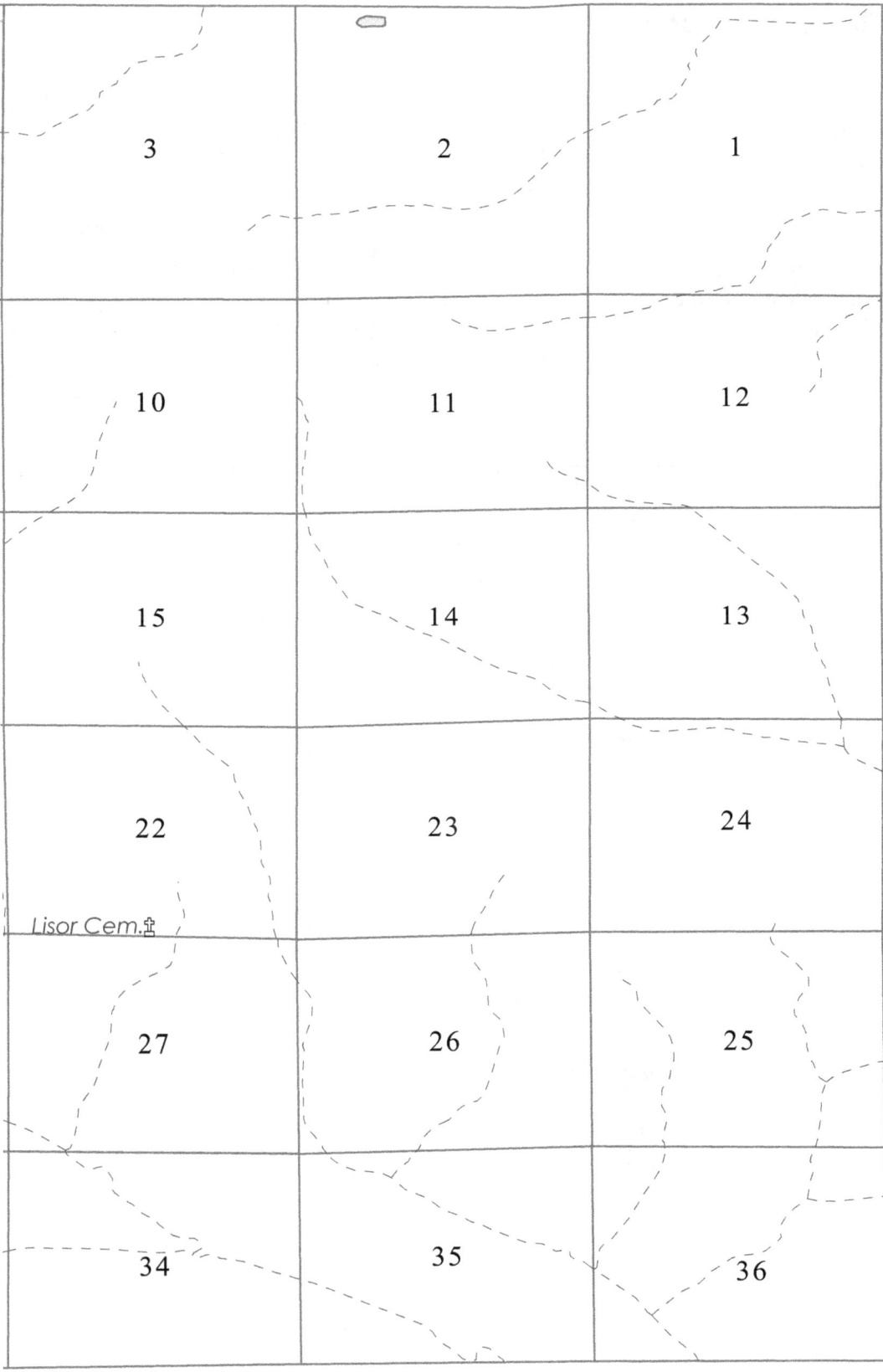

1. This Map takes a different look at the same Congressional Township displayed in the preceding two maps. It presents features that can help you better envision the historical development of the area: a) Water-bodies (lakes & ponds), b) Water-courses (rivers, streams, etc.), c) Railroads, d) City/town center-points (where they were oftentimes located when first settled), and e) Cemeteries.

2. Using this "Historical" map in tandem with this Township's Patent Map and Road Map, may lead you to some interesting discoveries. You will often find roads, towns, cemeteries, and waterways are named after nearby landowners: sometimes those names will be the ones you are researching. See how many of these research gems you can find here in Poweshiek County.

Legend

———————	Section Lines
—+—+—+—+—	Railroads
▢	Large Rivers & Bodies of Water
- - - - - - -	Streams/Creeks & Small Rivers
●	Cities/Towns
☩	Cemeteries

Scale: Section = 1 mile X 1 mile
(there are some exceptions)

Map Group 16: Index to Land Patents

Township 78-North Range 13-West (5th PM)

After you locate an individual in this Index, take note of the Section and Section Part then proceed to the Land Patent map on the pages immediately following. You should have no difficulty locating the corresponding parcel of land.

The "For More Info" Column will lead you to more information about the underlying Patents. See the *Legend* at right, and the "How to Use this Book" chapter, for more information.

```
                        LEGEND
             "For More Info . . . " column
A = Authority (Legislative Act, See Appendix "A")
B = Block or Lot (location in Section unknown)
C = Cancelled Patent
F = Fractional Section
G = Group  (Multi-Patentee Patent, see Appendix "C")
V = Overlaps another Parcel
R = Re-Issued (Parcel patented more than once)

(A & G items require you to look in the Appendixes referred
to above. All other Letter-designations followed by a number
require you to locate line-items in this index that possess
the ID number found after the letter).
```

ID	Individual in Patent	Sec.	Sec. Part	Date Issued	Other Counties	For More Info . . .
3599	ALEXANDER, Margaret	3	SESW	1855-03-01		A4 G95
3665	ANDREWS, John L	31	SE	1855-05-01		A1
3730	BAKER, Willard W	4	5	1855-01-01		A6
3731	" "	4	6	1855-01-01		A6
3705	BALL, Nathan	29	W½SW	1855-05-10		A1
3706	" "	30	SE	1855-05-10		A1
3616	BARKER, James	2	1	1857-03-10		A1 R3571
3617	" "	2	2	1857-03-10		A1
3618	" "	2	3	1857-03-10		A1
3619	" "	2	4	1857-03-10		A1
3620	" "	3	1	1857-03-10		A1
3518	BERRYHILL, Charles H	6	4	1853-09-10		A6 G10
3519	" "	6	5	1853-09-10		A6 G10
3516	" "	2	6	1854-07-01		A6
3517	" "	22	NW	1854-12-01		A1
3611	BERRYHILL, James B	5	NESW	1853-07-02		A6
3612	" "	5	NWSE	1853-07-02		A6
3607	" "	11	NWNE	1853-10-01		A6
3609	" "	4	SESW	1854-05-01		A1
3614	" "	9	NENE	1854-05-01		A1
3608	" "	11	SWNE	1854-08-01		A6
3610	" "	5	6	1855-12-15		A1
3613	" "	7	N½NE	1855-12-15		A1
3742	BERRYHILL, William D	4	NESW	1854-05-01		A1
3743	" "	4	SWSW	1854-05-01		A1
3744	" "	5	SESE	1854-05-01		A1
3745	" "	9	N½NW	1854-05-01		A1
3666	BOYLE, John R	17	NENW	1857-03-10		A1
3520	BRACKIN, Clarrissa	33	N½NW	1855-12-15		A1
3543	BUCKINGHAM, Esau	3	2	1855-05-01		A1
3680	BYINGTON, Legrand	4	10	1853-07-20		A6
3681	" "	4	9	1853-07-20		A6
3682	" "	4	N½SE	1853-07-20		A6
3548	CARPENTER, George F	26	SW	1855-05-10		A1
3562	CARVER, Harrison	19	S½	1855-05-10		A1 G47 F
3563	" "	19	SENW	1855-05-10		A1 G47 F
3562	CARVER, Thomas P	19	S½	1855-05-10		A1 G47 F
3563	" "	19	SENW	1855-05-10		A1 G47 F
3732	CLARK, William A	1	SWSE	1854-05-01		A1
3733	" "	1	SWSW	1854-05-01		A1
3741	" "	2	SESE	1854-05-01		A1
3734	" "	10	N½NW	1854-12-01		A1
3735	" "	10	N½SE	1854-12-01		A1
3736	" "	2	10	1854-12-01		A1
3737	" "	2	7	1854-12-01		A1
3738	" "	2	8	1854-12-01		A1

ID	Individual in Patent	Sec.	Sec. Part	Date Issued	Other Counties	For More Info . . .
3739	CLARK, William A (Cont'd)	2	9	1854-12-01		A1
3740	" "	2	NESE	1854-12-01		A1
3538	CLEAVER, Eli V	36	W½NE	1855-12-15		A1
3539	CLEVER, Eli V	33	S½NW	1856-01-15		A6
3514	CLOSE, Chalmer D	35	SW	1855-12-15		A1
3532	CONNELLY, Edward	11	NENE	1854-03-01		A6 G56
3533	" "	12	NWNW	1854-03-01		A6 G56
3531	" "	3	NESW	1854-10-02		A6
3637	COOK, James L	2	5	1855-12-15		A1
3638	" "	24	E½NW	1855-12-15		A1
3639	" "	24	N½SW	1855-12-15		A1
3713	COOK, Ralph P	23		1855-05-01		A1 G57
3775	COPE, William R	28	W½SE	1855-05-10		A1
3776	" "	33	SENE	1855-05-10		A1
3777	" "	33	W½NE	1855-05-10		A1
3778	" "	34	SWNW	1855-05-10		A1
3675	CORNWELL, Joseph H	10	SESE	1855-05-01		A1
3676	" "	11	S½SW	1855-05-01		A1
3677	" "	9	S½NW	1855-05-01		A1
3678	" "	9	SW	1855-05-01		A1
3541	COX, Ephraim	15	S½NW	1854-12-01		A1
3542	" "	15	SW	1854-12-01		A1
3512	CRANAGE, Benjamin	34	NENW	1857-05-21		A6 R3762
3647	CRAWFORD, Susan W	5	SWSE	1855-01-01		A6 G114
3506	CROSS, Albert T	10	NESW	1856-05-01		A1
3656	CULBERTSON, John C	6	11	1853-07-01		A6
3659	" "	5	10	1853-07-02		A6 G68
3660	" "	5	11	1853-07-02		A6 G68
3655	" "	6	10	1853-07-02		A6
3657	" "	6	SESE	1855-01-01		A6
3658	" "	8	S½NE	1855-05-01		A6
3653	" "	5	4	1857-02-20		A5
3654	" "	6	1	1857-02-20		A5
3561	CUNNINGHAM, Hannah	24	N½NE	1855-12-15		A1
3713	CUTTING, James C	23		1855-05-01		A1 G57
3518	DAVIS, Eliza L	6	4	1853-09-10		A6 G10
3519	" "	6	5	1853-09-10		A6 G10
3746	DAVIS, William	1	11	1854-05-01		A1 G89
3747	" "	1	12	1854-05-01		A1 G89
3748	" "	1	5	1854-05-01		A1 G89
3749	" "	1	6	1854-05-01		A1 G89
3750	" "	1	7	1854-05-01		A1 G89
3751	" "	1	8	1854-05-01		A1 G89
3510	DEITRICH, Anthony	31	W½NW	1855-05-10		A1 F
3511	" "	31	W½SW	1855-05-10		A1 F
3661	DILLON, John	24	N½SE	1855-12-15		A1
3662	" "	24	S½NE	1855-12-15		A1
3766	DODDS, William J	17	E½	1855-05-01		A1
3767	" "	17	SENW	1855-05-01		A1
3573	DOUNEY, Hugh D	7	W½NW	1854-12-01		A1 F
3574	" "	7	W½SW	1854-12-01		A1 F
3594	DOWNEY, Hugh D	7	SENE	1854-12-01		A6
3599	" "	3	SESW	1855-03-01		A4 G95
3591	" "	6	NESW	1855-04-04		A2 F
3578	" "	3	3	1855-05-01		A1
3579	" "	3	4	1855-05-01		A1
3580	" "	3	5	1855-05-01		A1
3582	" "	32	E½NW	1855-05-01		A1
3583	" "	4	1	1855-05-01		A1
3584	" "	4	2	1855-05-01		A1
3585	" "	4	3	1855-05-01		A1
3586	" "	4	4	1855-05-01		A1
3587	" "	4	7	1855-05-01		A1
3593	" "	7	NESW	1855-05-01		A6 F
3595	" "	7	SENW	1855-05-01		A6 F
3597	" "	4	11	1855-06-01		A6 G109
3598	" "	4	12	1855-06-01		A6 G109
3589	" "	5	9	1855-06-01		A6
3588	" "	5	3	1855-12-15		A1
3590	" "	6	12	1855-12-15		A1
3596	" "	8	NWNW	1855-12-15		A1
3575	" "	28	E½NE	1856-01-15		A6
3577	" "	28	W½NE	1856-01-15		A6

ID	Individual in Patent	Sec.	Sec. Part	Date Issued	Other Counties	For More Info . . .
3581	DOWNEY, Hugh D (Cont'd)	3	SESE	1856-01-15		A6
3592	" "	6	NWSE	1857-04-01		A4
3576	" "	28	SESE	1904-06-22		A6
3640	EASLEY, James S	12	NENE	1854-07-01		A6
3641	" "	31	E½NW	1855-01-01		A6
3645	" "	5	S½SW	1855-01-01		A6 G117
3647	" "	5	SWSE	1855-01-01		A6 G114
3642	" "	8	NENW	1855-01-01		A6
3643	" "	8	NWNE	1855-01-01		A6
3644	" "	8	S½NW	1855-01-01		A6
3646	" "	4	8	1855-05-01		A6 G122
3752	EHRET, William	30	NE	1855-05-10		A1
3509	FAHRNEY, Andrew	27	NW	1855-05-01		A1
3513	FAHRNEY, Benjamin	22	S½NE	1855-05-01		A1
3544	FAHRNEY, Ezra	14	N½SW	1854-12-01		A1 V3722, 3723
3545	" "	14	S½NW	1854-12-01		A1 V3724
3602	FAHRNEY, Jacob	14	S½SW	1855-05-01		A1 V3722
3603	" "	22	S½	1855-05-01		A1
3720	FAHRNEY, Samuel	27	NE	1855-05-01		A1
3549	FISHER, George	1	10	1855-12-15		A1 C R3550
3551	" "	1	9	1855-12-15		A1 C R3552
3553	" "	1	N½NE	1855-12-15		A1 C
3555	" "	1	NWSW	1855-12-15		A1 C R3556
3550	" "	1	10	1913-11-07		A1 R3549
3552	" "	1	9	1913-11-07		A1 R3551
3554	" "	1	N½SE	1913-11-07		A1
3556	" "	1	NWSW	1913-11-07		A1 R3555
3685	FLATTERY, Lucus	12	E½SW	1855-05-01		A1
3686	" "	12	W½SE	1855-05-01		A1
3525	FUNK, Daniel	13	NE	1855-05-01		A1
3696	FUNK, Michael	10	SWSE	1854-12-01		A1
3697	" "	14	N½NW	1854-12-01		A1
3698	" "	15	N½NE	1854-12-01		A1
3564	GALLEY, Henry	13	E½SW	1855-05-01		A1 V3652
3565	" "	13	NWSE	1855-05-01		A1
3663	GANTZ, John	14	SE	1855-05-01		A1
3664	" "	21	NE	1855-05-01		A1
3605	GARDNER, Jacob M	13	NW	1855-05-01		A1
3606	" "	14	NE	1855-05-01		A1
3746	GIFFORD, Henry B	1	11	1854-05-01		A1 G89
3747	" "	1	12	1854-05-01		A1 G89
3748	" "	1	5	1854-05-01		A1 G89
3749	" "	1	6	1854-05-01		A1 G89
3750	" "	1	7	1854-05-01		A1 G89
3751	" "	1	8	1854-05-01		A1 G89
3659	GORDON, Lavina	5	10	1853-07-02		A6 G68
3660	" "	5	11	1853-07-02		A6 G68
3624	GOWER, James H	1	E½SW	1853-10-01		A6
3628	" "	2	W½SE	1853-10-01		A6
3625	" "	11	NWNW	1854-12-01		A6
3631	" "	32	E½	1855-05-01		A1
3629	" "	30	NW	1855-05-10		A1 F
3630	" "	30	W½SW	1855-05-10		A1 F
3621	" "	1	2	1855-12-15		A1
3622	" "	1	3	1855-12-15		A1
3623	" "	1	4	1855-12-15		A1
3626	" "	19	NENW	1856-09-01		A1 F
3627	" "	19	W½NW	1856-09-01		A1 F
3632	GRAHAM, James H	18	NW	1855-05-01		A1 F
3633	" "	18	W½NE	1855-05-01		A1
3634	" "	7	SESW	1855-05-01		A1 F
3635	" "	7	SWSE	1855-05-01		A1
3764	HAPGOOD, William	34	SW	1855-05-10		A1
3761	" "	25	SW	1855-12-15		A1
3763	" "	34	SENW	1855-12-15		A1
3762	" "	34	NENW	1856-01-15		A6 C R3512
3765	HARKLEROAD, William	6	6	1850-04-10		A1
3636	HICKMAN, James H	12	NWNE	1854-05-01		A1
3526	HOYT, Daniel S	8	NENE	1854-05-01		A1
3648	ILES, Jeremiah	36	N½NW	1855-12-15		A1
3728	IOWA, State Of	16		1937-08-26		A3
3679	JAMES, Lavina	6	NESE	1852-09-01		A6
3566	JARRETT, Henry	1	1	1857-03-10		A1

ID	Individual in Patent	Sec.	Sec. Part	Date Issued	Other Counties	For More Info . . .
3717	JOHNSTON, Robert T	20	SE	1855-05-01		A1
3718	" "	28	W½	1855-05-01		A1
3719	" "	29	NE	1855-05-01		A1
3547	JONES, George A	26	NE	1855-01-01		A6
3546	" "	24	S½SE	1855-05-01		A1
3645	JONES, Mary	5	S½SW	1855-01-01		A6 G117
3687	KIRK, Mark	21	SE	1855-12-15		A1
3688	" "	29	E½SW	1855-12-15		A1
3689	" "	29	N½SE	1855-12-15		A1
3721	KIRKWOOD, Samuel J	36	NWSE	1857-03-10		A1
3770	LADELEY, William	25	NE	1855-05-01		A1
3690	LIGHT, Matthew	7	NENW	1854-12-01		A1 F
3691	LIGHT, Matthias	6	SESW	1854-12-01		A6 F
3692	" "	6	SWSE	1854-12-01		A6
3572	LITTLE, Hiram H	8	E½SW	1855-05-01		A6
3704	LOGAN, Sarah M	21	SW	1855-03-01		A4 G230
3537	LUCAS, Edward W	27	NWSW	1854-05-01		A1 G197
3534	" "	28	NESE	1854-05-01		A1
3535	" "	33	NENE	1855-05-01		A1
3536	" "	34	NWNW	1855-05-01		A1
3537	LUCAS, Robert S	27	NWSW	1854-05-01		A1 G197
3716	" "	27	SWSW	1854-12-01		A1
3714	MAY, Richard L	5	NWSW	1852-11-01		A1
3529	MCCULLOUGH, David	25	SE	1855-05-10		A1
3540	MEAD, Enfield S	36	SWSE	1855-05-01		A6
3693	MEAD, Meril	8	NESE	1855-01-01		A6
3694	" "	8	SESE	1855-01-01		A6
3695	" "	8	W½SE	1855-01-01		A6
3651	MERCER, Jessee	13	E½SE	1855-12-15		A1
3652	" "	13	SW	1855-12-15		A1 V3564, 3604
3567	MIDDLEKAUFF, Henry	15	N½SE	1854-12-01		A1
3568	" "	15	S½NE	1854-12-01		A1
3532	MILLIKEN, Mary	11	NENE	1854-03-01		A6 G56
3533	" "	12	NWNW	1854-03-01		A6 G56
3729	MORLAND, Theopholis	29	S½SE	1855-05-10		A1
3707	MOUSER, Nicholas	10	W½SW	1856-01-15		A6
3708	" "	9	NESE	1856-01-15		A6
3709	" "	9	SENE	1856-01-15		A6
3772	MUMMA, William	35	NW	1855-01-01		A6 C R3773
3771	" "	27	E½SW	1855-05-01		A1
3773	MUMMRA, William	35	NW	1876-08-30		A1 R3772
3530	MURPHY, David	11	SE	1855-05-01		A1
3604	MYERS, Jacob L	13	W½SW	1855-12-15		A1 V3652
3711	OLIPHANT, Rachel B	32	W½NW	1855-05-01		A1
3507	PARSONS, Amos M	20	SW	1855-05-10		A1
3508	" "	29	NW	1855-05-10		A1
3715	PASSON, Richard M	6	W½SW	1855-05-01		A1 F
3570	POWELL, Henry S	34	NE	1855-05-10		A1
3601	PRESTON, Isaac	31	NE	1855-05-01		A1
3673	PUGH, Jonathan G	33	S½	1855-05-10		A1
3674	" "	34	SE	1855-05-10		A1
3699	RENO, Morgan	10	S½NW	1852-12-10		A6
3701	" "	7	NWSE	1853-07-01		A6
3702	" "	7	SWNE	1853-07-01		A6
3700	" "	11	NENW	1855-03-01		A6
3704	" "	21	SW	1855-03-01		A4 G230
3703	" "	3	7	1855-05-01		A6 G238
3569	ROHRER, Henry	27	SE	1855-05-10		A1
3683	ROWLAND, Levi	15	NWNW	1855-05-01		A1
3684	" "	24	W½NW	1855-05-01		A1
3571	SANDERS, Henry	2	1	1857-03-10		A1 R3616
3667	SARGOOD, John	10	SESW	1852-11-01		A1
3668	" "	15	NENW	1853-10-01		A6
3669	" "	4	SESE	1853-10-01		A6
3600	SAXTON, Isaac A	20	NE	1855-05-10		A1
3712	SCHOOLEY, Rachel H	31	E½SW	1855-05-01		A1 F
3521	SEVERNS, Daniel A	4	NWSW	1853-07-20		A6 G248
3522	" "	5	NESE	1853-07-20		A6 G248
3557	SHAUL, George	9	SESE	1853-07-01		A6
3558	" "	9	SWNE	1853-07-01		A6
3559	" "	9	W½SE	1853-07-01		A6
3670	SLACK, John	24	S½SW	1855-05-01		A1
3671	" "	25	NW	1855-05-01		A1

ID	Individual in Patent	Sec.	Sec. Part	Date Issued	Other Counties	For More Info . . .
3753	SMITH, William H	11	SENE	1855-05-01		A1
3754	" "	12	SWNW	1855-05-01		A1
3755	" "	12	W½SW	1855-05-01		A1
3756	" "	17	SW	1855-05-01		A1
3757	" "	20	NW	1855-05-01		A1
3758	" "	7	E½SE	1855-05-01		A1
3759	" "	8	W½SW	1855-05-01		A1
3597	SMOTHERS, Elizabeth	4	11	1855-06-01		A6 G109
3598	" "	4	12	1855-06-01		A6 G109
3710	STACY, Pelatiah	35	SE	1855-01-01		A6
3779	STEWART, William	21	NW	1855-05-10		A1
3672	STROUSE, John	12	E½SE	1855-05-01		A1
3527	STRUBLE, Daniel	18	SE	1855-05-01		A1
3528	" "	19	NE	1855-05-01		A1
3523	STRUBLE, Daniel D	17	W½NW	1855-05-01		A1
3524	" "	18	E½NE	1855-05-01		A1
3649	STUFF, Jeremiah	15	S½SE	1854-12-01		A1
3650	" "	22	N½NE	1854-12-01		A1
3726	TAYLOR, Sanford	11	N½SW	1855-05-01		A1
3727	" "	3	8	1857-04-01		A4
3768	TIBBALS, William J	4	SWSE	1855-05-10		A1
3769	" "	9	NWNE	1855-05-10		A1
3703	TUTHILL, Elizabeth	3	7	1855-05-01		A6 G238
3521	VERNON, Mary Ann	4	NWSW	1853-07-20		A6 G248
3522	" "	5	NESE	1853-07-20		A6 G248
3646	WARD, Sarah	4	8	1855-05-01		A6 G122
3615	WHERRY, James B	36	E½SE	1855-12-15		A1
3788	WHERRY, William	36	E½NE	1855-12-15		A1
3774	WHITLOCK, William N	3	6	1855-12-15		A1
3780	WILLINGHAM, William W	1	SESE	1854-08-01		A6
3781	" "	11	SENW	1854-08-01		A6
3782	" "	12	E½NW	1854-08-01		A6
3783	" "	12	SWNE	1854-08-01		A6
3784	" "	5	1	1855-12-15		A1
3785	" "	5	2	1855-12-15		A1
3786	" "	5	7	1855-12-15		A1
3787	" "	5	8	1855-12-15		A1
3722	WILSON, Samuel M	14	E½SW	1855-10-15		A1 V3544, 3602
3723	" "	14	NWSW	1855-10-15		A1 V3544
3724	" "	14	SENW	1855-10-15		A1 V3545
3515	WOLCOTT, Chancy W	12	SENE	1855-12-15		A1
3760	WRIGHT, William H	30	E½SW	1855-01-01		A6 F
3560	YATES, George	26	SE	1855-05-10		A1
3725	ZEIGLER, Samuel P	18	SW	1855-05-01		A1 F

Patent Map

T78-N R13-W
5th PM Meridian

Map Group 16

Township Statistics

Parcels Mapped	:	283
Number of Patents	:	214
Number of Individuals	:	127
Patentees Identified	:	124
Number of Surnames	:	111
Multi-Patentee Parcels	:	26
Oldest Patent Date	:	4/10/1850
Most Recent Patent	:	8/26/1937
Block/Lot Parcels	:	62
Parcels Re - Issued	:	6
Parcels that Overlap	:	9
Cities and Towns	:	3
Cemeteries	:	3

Lots-Sec. 6
- 1 CULBERTSON, John C 1857
- 4 BERRYHILL, Charl[10]1853
- 5 BERRYHILL, Charl[10]1853
- 6 HARKLEROAD, William 1850
- 10 CULBERTSON, John C 1853
- 11 CULBERTSON, John C 1853
- 12 DOWNEY, Hugh D 1855

Lots-Sec. 5
- 1 WILLINGHAM, William 1855
- 2 WILLINGHAM, William 1855
- 3 DOWNEY, Hugh D 1855
- 4 CULBERTSON, John C 1857
- 6 BERRYHILL, James B 1855
- 7 WILLINGHAM, William 1855
- 8 WILLINGHAM, William 1855
- 9 DOWNEY, Hugh D 1855
- 10 CULBERTSON, John[68]1853
- 11 CULBERTSON, John[68]1853

Lots-Sec. 4
- 1 DOWNEY, Hugh D 1855
- 2 DOWNEY, Hugh D 1855
- 3 DOWNEY, Hugh D 1855
- 4 DOWNEY, Hugh D 1855
- 5 BAKER, Willard W 1855
- 6 BAKER, Willard W 1855
- 7 DOWNEY, Hugh D 1855
- 8 EASLEY, James S[122]1855
- 9 BYINGTON, Legrand 1853
- 10 BYINGTON, Legrand 1853
- 11 DOWNEY, Hugh D [109]1855
- 12 DOWNEY, Hugh D [109]1855

Section 6
- PASSON Richard M 1855
- DOWNEY Hugh D 1855
- DOWNEY Hugh D 1857
- JAMES Lavina 1852
- LIGHT Matthias 1854
- LIGHT Matthias 1854
- CULBERTSON John C 1855

Section 5
- MAY Richard L 1852
- BERRYHILL James B 1853
- BERRYHILL James B 1853
- SEVERNS [248] Daniel A 1853
- EASLEY [117] James S 1855
- EASLEY [114] James S 1855
- BERRYHILL William D 1854

Section 4
- SEVERNS [248] Daniel A 1853
- BERRYHILL William D 1854
- BYINGTON Legrand 1853
- BERRYHILL William D 1854
- BERRYHILL James B 1854
- TIBBALS William J 1855
- SARGOOD John 1853

Section 7
- DOUNEY Hugh D 1854
- LIGHT Matthew 1854
- BERRYHILL James B 1855
- DOWNEY Hugh D 1855
- RENO Morgan 1853
- DOWNEY Hugh D 1854
- DOUNEY Hugh D 1854
- DOWNEY Hugh D 1855
- RENO Morgan 1853
- SMITH William H 1855
- GRAHAM James H 1855
- GRAHAM James H 1855

Section 8
- DOWNEY Hugh D 1855
- EASLEY James S 1855
- EASLEY James S 1855
- HOYT Daniel S 1854
- EASLEY James S 1855
- CULBERTSON John C 1855
- SMITH William H 1855
- LITTLE Hiram H 1855
- MEAD Meril 1855
- MEAD Meril 1855
- MEAD Meril 1855

Section 9
- BERRYHILL William D 1854
- BERRYHILL William D 1854
- TIBBALS William J 1855
- BERRYHILL James B 1854
- CORNWELL Joseph H 1855
- SHAUL George 1853
- MOUSER Nicholas 1856
- CORNWELL Joseph H 1855
- SHAUL George 1853
- MOUSER Nicholas 1856
- SHAUL George 1853

Section 18
- GRAHAM James H 1855
- GRAHAM James H 1855
- STRUBLE Daniel D 1855
- ZEIGLER Samuel P 1855
- STRUBLE Daniel 1855

Section 17
- STRUBLE Daniel D 1855
- BOYLE John R 1857
- DODDS William J 1855
- SMITH William H 1855

Section 16
- DODDS William J 1855
- IOWA State Of 1937

Section 19
- GOWER James H 1856
- GOWER James H 1856
- CARVER [47] Harrison 1855
- STRUBLE Daniel 1855
- CARVER [47] Harrison 1855

Section 20
- SMITH William H 1855
- PARSONS Amos M 1855

Section 21
- SAXTON Isaac A 1855
- JOHNSTON Robert T 1855
- STEWART William 1855
- RENO [230] Morgan 1855
- GANTZ John 1855
- KIRK Mark 1855

Section 30
- GOWER James H 1855
- EHRET William 1855
- WRIGHT William H 1855
- BALL Nathan 1855
- GOWER James H 1855

Section 29
- PARSONS Amos M 1855
- BALL Nathan 1855
- KIRK Mark 1855
- JOHNSTON Robert T 1855
- KIRK Mark 1855
- MORLAND Theopholis 1855

Section 28
- JOHNSTON Robert T 1855
- DOWNEY Hugh D 1856
- DOWNEY Hugh D 1856
- COPE William R 1855
- LUCAS Edward W 1854
- DOWNEY Hugh D 1904

Section 31
- DEITRICH Anthony 1855
- EASLEY James S 1855
- PRESTON Isaac 1855
- SCHOOLEY Rachel H 1855
- DEITRICH Anthony 1855
- ANDREWS John L 1855

Section 32
- OLIPHANT Rachel B 1855
- DOWNEY Hugh D 1855
- GOWER James H 1855

Section 33
- BRACKIN Clarrissa 1855
- CLEVER Eli V 1856
- COPE William R 1855
- LUCAS Edward W 1855
- COPE William R 1855
- PUGH Jonathan G 1855

Lots-Sec. 3
1	BARKER, James	1857
2	BUCKINGHAM, Esau	1855
3	DOWNEY, Hugh D	1855
4	DOWNEY, Hugh D	1855
5	DOWNEY, Hugh D	1855
6	WHITLOCK, William N	1855
7	RENO, Morgan [238]	1855
8	TAYLOR, Sanford	1857

Lots-Sec. 2
1	BARKER, James	1857
1	SANDERS, Henry	1857
2	BARKER, James	1857
3	BARKER, James	1857
4	BARKER, James	1857
5	COOK, James L	1855
6	BERRYHILL, Charles H	1854
7	CLARK, William A	1854
8	CLARK, William A	1854
9	CLARK, William A	1854
10	CLARK, William A	1854

Lots-Sec. 1
1	JARRETT, Henry	1857
2	GOWER, James H	1855
3	GOWER, James H	1855
4	GOWER, James H	1855
5	DAVIS, William [89]	1854
6	DAVIS, William [89]	1854
7	DAVIS, William [89]	1854
8	DAVIS, William [89]	1854
9	FISHER, George	1913
9	FISHER, George	1855
10	FISHER, George	1913
10	FISHER, George	1855
11	DAVIS, William [89]	1854
12	DAVIS, William [89]	1854

FISHER George 1855

3
CONNELLY Edward 1854
DOWNEY [95] Hugh D 1855
DOWNEY Hugh D 1856

2
GOWER James H 1853
CLARK William A 1854
CLARK William A 1854

1
FISHER George 1855
FISHER George 1913
GOWER James H 1853
FISHER George 1913
CLARK William A 1854
CLARK William A 1854
WILLINGHAM William W 1854

CLARK William A 1854
RENO Morgan 1852
10
GOWER James H 1854
RENO Morgan 1855
BERRYHILL James B 1853
CONNELLY [56] Edward 1854
CONNELLY [56] Edward 1854
HICKMAN James H 1854
EASLEY James S 1854
WILLINGHAM William W 1854

MOUSER Nicholas 1856
CROSS Albert T 1856
CLARK William A 1854
WILLINGHAM William W 1854
BERRYHILL James B 1854
SMITH William H 1855
SMITH William H 1855
WILLINGHAM William W 1854
WOLCOTT Chancy W 1855
SARGOOD John 1852
FUNK Michael 1854
CORNWELL Joseph H 1855
TAYLOR Sanford 1855
11
SMITH William H 1855
FLATTERY Lucus 1855
12
STROUSE John 1855
CORNWELL Joseph H 1855
MURPHY David 1855
FLATTERY Lucus 1855

ROWLAND Levi 1855
SARGOOD John 1853
FUNK Michael 1854
FUNK Michael 1854
GARDNER Jacob M 1855
FUNK Daniel 1855
COX Ephraim 1854
MIDDLEKAUFF Henry 1854
FAHRNEY Ezra 1854
WILSON Samuel M 1855
GARDNER Jacob M 1855
13
15
MIDDLEKAUFF Henry 1854
WILSON Samuel M 1855
FAHRNEY Ezra 1854
14
MERCER Jessee 1855
GALLEY Henry 1855
GALLEY Henry 1855
MERCER Jessee 1855
COX Ephraim 1854
STUFF Jeremiah 1854
FAHRNEY Jacob 1855
WILSON Samuel M 1855
GANTZ John 1855
MYERS Jacob L 1855

BERRYHILL Charles H 1854
STUFF Jeremiah 1854
FAHRNEY Benjamin 1855
CUNNINGHAM Hannah 1855
ROWLAND Levi 1855
COOK James L 1855
DILLON John 1855
22
23
COOK James L 1855
24
DILLON John 1855
FAHRNEY Jacob 1855
COOK [57] Ralph P 1855
SLACK John 1855
JONES George A 1855

FAHRNEY Samuel 1855
JONES George A 1855
SLACK John 1855
LADELEY William 1855
FAHRNEY Andrew 1855
27
26
25
LUCAS [197] Edward W 1854
LUCAS Robert S 1854
MUMMA William 1855
ROHRER Henry 1855
CARPENTER George F 1855
YATES George 1855
HAPGOOD William 1855
MCCULLOUGH David 1855

LUCAS Edward W 1855
CRANAGE Benjamin 1857
HAPGOOD William 1856
POWELL Henry S 1855
MUMMA William 1855
ILES Jeremiah 1855
CLEAVER Eli V 1855
WHERRY William 1855
COPE William R 1855
HAPGOOD William 1855
MUMMRA William 1876
35
36
34
PUGH Jonathan G 1855
STACY Pelatiah 1855
KIRKWOOD Samuel J 1857
WHERRY James B 1855
HAPGOOD William 1855
CLOSE Chalmer D 1855
MEAD Enfield S 1855

Copyright 2010 Boyd IT, Inc. All Rights Reserved

Helpful Hints

1. This Map's INDEX can be found on the preceding pages.

2. Refer to Map "C" to see where this Township lies within Poweshiek County, Iowa.

3. Numbers within square brackets [ ] denote a multi-patentee land parcel (multi-owner). Refer to Appendix "C" for a full list of members in this group.

4. Areas that look to be crowded with Patentees usually indicate multiple sales of the same parcel (Re-issues) or Overlapping parcels. See this Township's Index for an explanation of these and other circumstances that might explain "odd" groupings of Patentees on this map.

Legend

———— Patent Boundary

━━━━ Section Boundary

No Patents Found (or Outside County)

1., 2., 3., ... Lot Numbers (when beside a name)

[ ] Group Number (see Appendix "C")

Scale: Section = 1 mile X 1 mile (generally, with some exceptions)

Road Map

T78-N R13-W
5th PM Meridian

Map Group 16

Cities & Towns
Deep River
Dresden
Tilton

Cemeteries
Deep River Cemetery
Dresden Cemetery
Light Cemetery

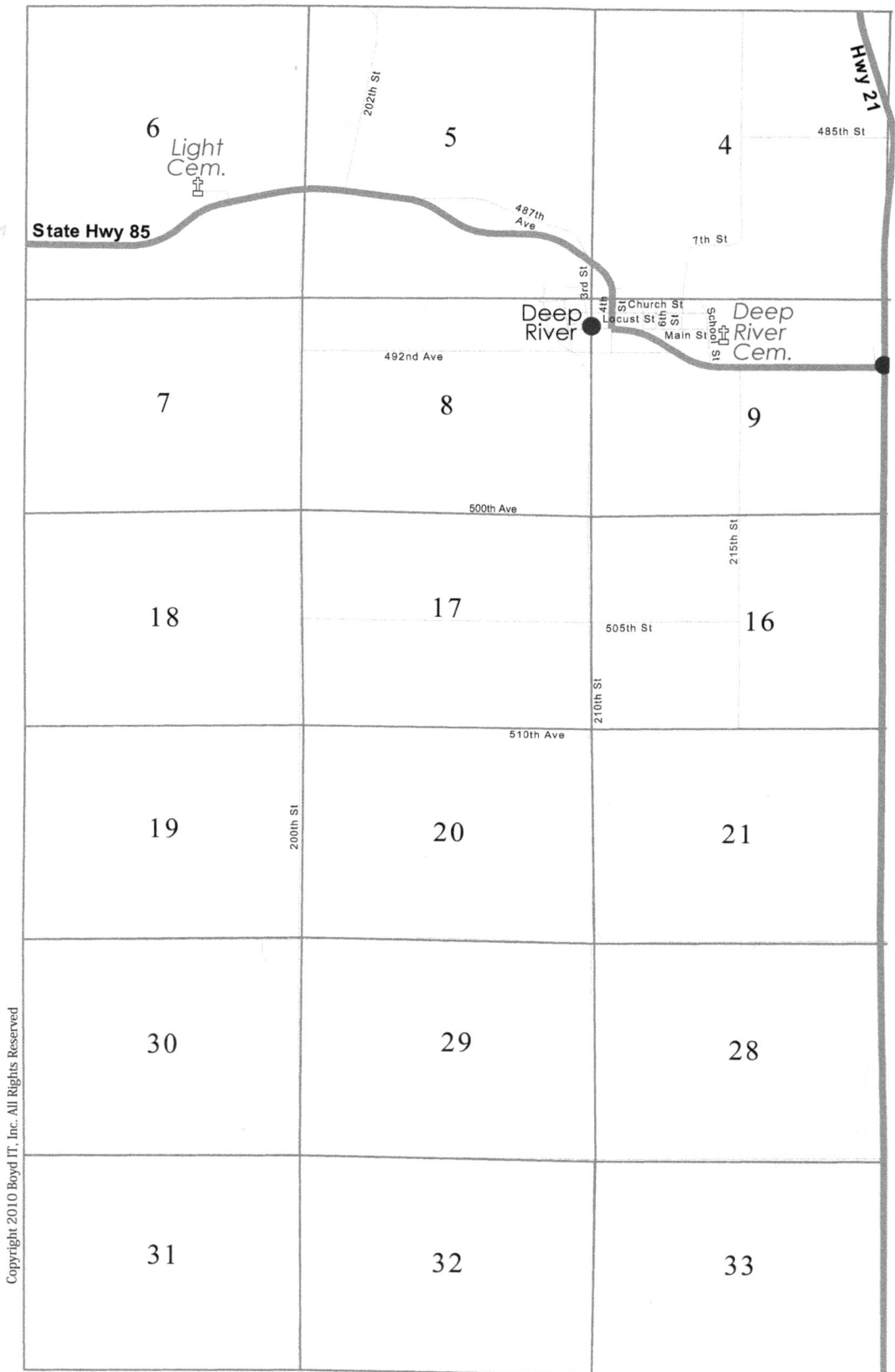

Hwy 21

202th St

485th St

6
Light
Cem.

5

4

State Hwy 85

487th
Ave

7th St

3rd St

4th St

Church St
Locust St

6th St

School St

Main St

Deep
River

Deep
River
Cem.

492nd Ave

7

8

9

500th Ave

215th St

18

17

505th St

16

210th St

510th Ave

200th St

19

20

21

30

29

28

31

32

33

3

2

1

480th Ave

Diamond Trail Rd

●Dresden

230th St

225th St

240th St

10

11

12

500th Ave

220th St

15

14

13

✝
Dresden Cem.

510th Ave

Poweshiek-Iowa Rd

22

23

235th St

24

520th Ave

27

26

25

530th Ave

Hwy 21

230th St

34

35

36

1st St

●Tilton

540th Ave

Keokuk Iowa Rd

Legend

———— Section Lines

━━━━ Interstates

━━━━ Highways

———— Other Roads

● Cities/Towns

✝ Cemeteries

Scale: Section = 1 mile X 1 mile
(generally, with some exceptions)

Historical Map

T78-N R13-W
5th PM Meridian

Map Group 16

Cities & Towns
Deep River
Dresden
Tilton

Cemeteries
Deep River Cemetery
Dresden Cemetery
Light Cemetery

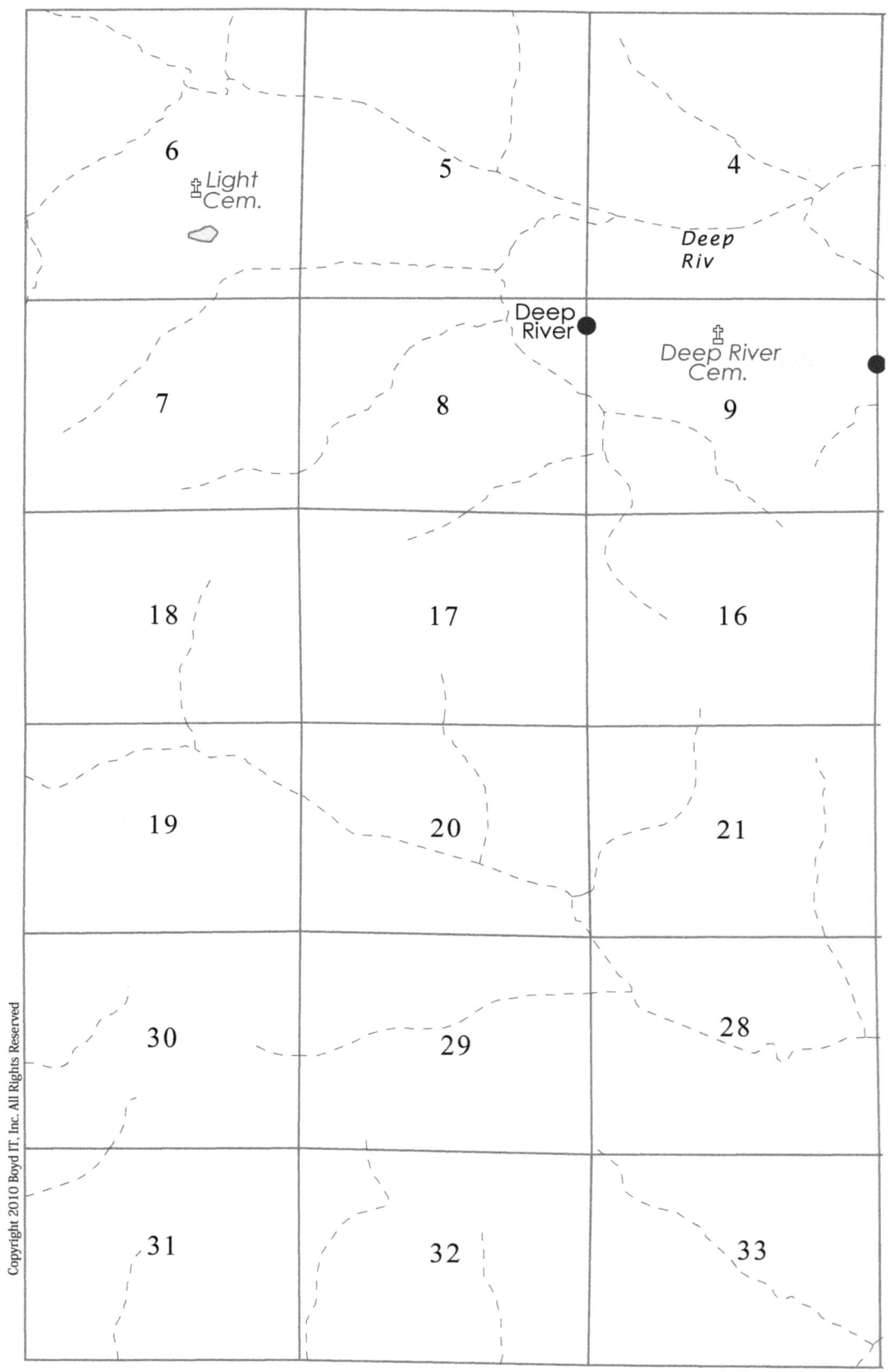

6 Light Cem.	5	4 Deep Riv
7	8 Deep River	9 Deep River Cem.
18	17	16
19	20	21
30	29	28
31	32	33

3

2

1

● Dresden

10

11

12

15 ‡ Dresden
        Cem.

14

13

Middle
English Riv

22

23

24

27

26

25

34

35

36

● Tilton

Helpful Hints

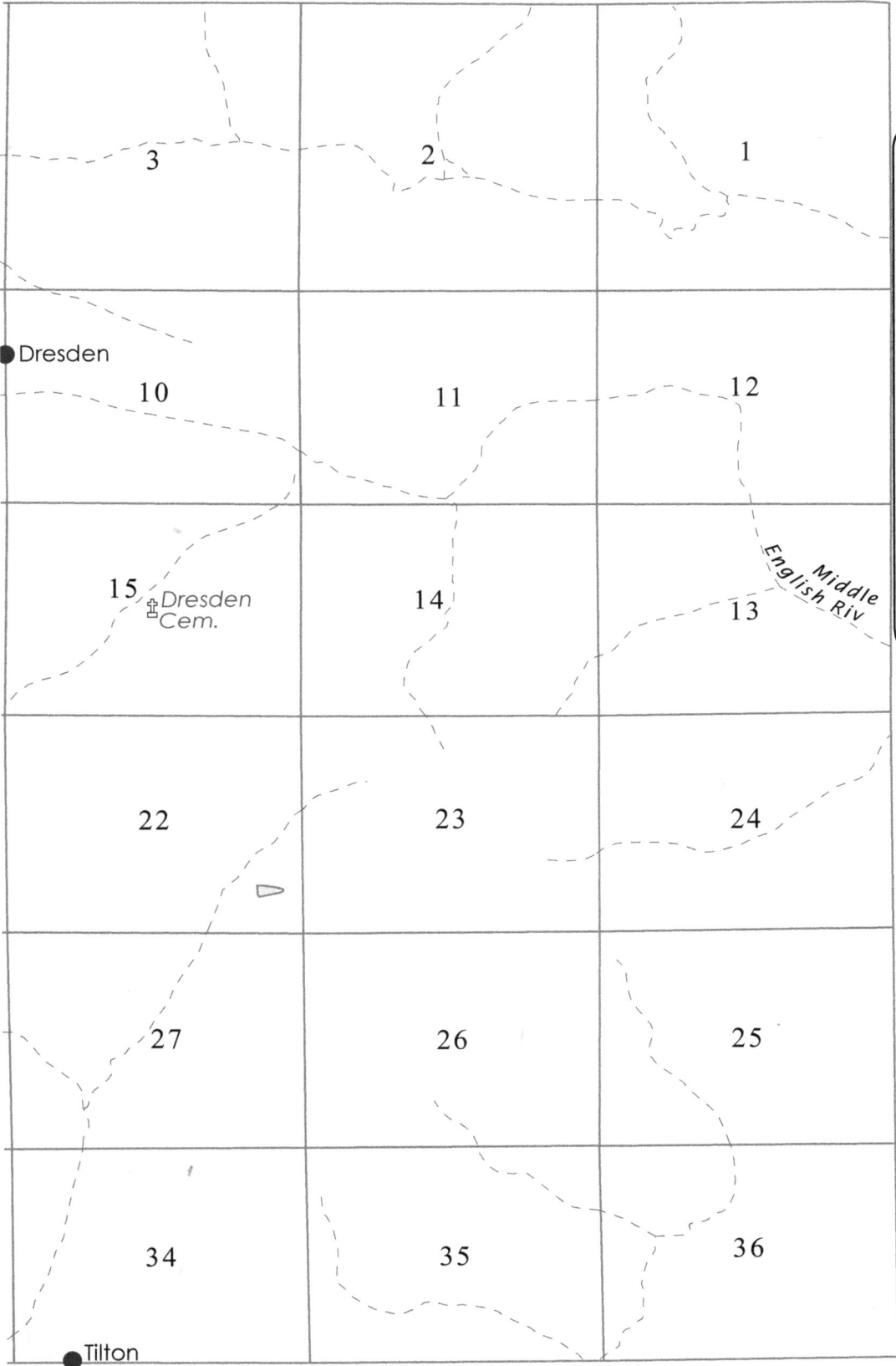

1. This Map takes a different look at the same Congressional Township displayed in the preceding two maps. It presents features that can help you better envision the historical development of the area: a) Water-bodies (lakes & ponds), b) Water-courses (rivers, streams, etc.), c) Railroads, d) City/town center-points (where they were oftentimes located when first settled), and e) Cemeteries.

2. Using this "Historical" map in tandem with this Township's Patent Map and Road Map, may lead you to some interesting discoveries. You will often find roads, towns, cemeteries, and waterways are named after nearby landowners: sometimes those names will be the ones you are researching. See how many of these research gems you can find here in Poweshiek County.

Legend

————————	Section Lines
—+—+—+—+—	Railroads
▭	Large Rivers & Bodies of Water
- - - - - - - -	Streams/Creeks & Small Rivers
●	Cities/Towns
‡	Cemeteries

Scale: Section = 1 mile X 1 mile
(there are some exceptions)

Appendices

Appendix A - Acts of Congress Authorizing the Patents Contained in this Book

The following Acts of Congress are referred to throughout the Indexes in this book. The text of the Federal Statutes referred to below can usually be found on the web. For more information on such laws, check out the publishers's web-site at *www.arphax.com,* go to the "Research" page, and click on the "Land-Law" link.

Ref. No.	Date and Act of Congress	Number of Parcels of Land
1	April 24, 1820: Sale-Cash Entry (3 Stat. 566)	2539
2	February 11, 1847: ScripWarrant Act of 1847 (9 Stat. 123)	23
3	June 21, 1934: State Grant-School Sec Patent (48 Stat. 1185)	16
4	March 22, 1852: ScripWarrant Act of 1852 (10 Stat. 3)	107
5	March 3, 1855: ScripWarrant Act of 1855 (10 Stat. 701)	102
6	September 28, 1850: ScripWarrant Act of 1850 (9 Stat. 520)	1001

Appendix B - Section Parts (Aliquot Parts)

The following represent the various abbreviations we have found thus far in describing the parts of a Public Land Section. Some of these are very obscure and rarely used, but we wanted to list them for just that reason. A full section is 1 square mile or 640 acres.

Section Part	Description	Acres
\<none\>	Full Acre (if no Section Part is listed, presumed a full Section)	640
\<1-??\>	A number represents a Lot Number and can be of various sizes	?
E½	East Half-Section	320
E½E½	East Half of East Half-Section	160
E½E½SE	East Half of East Half of Southeast Quarter-Section	40
E½N½	East Half of North Half-Section	160
E½NE	East Half of Northeast Quarter-Section	80
E½NENE	East Half of Northeast Quarter of Northeast Quarter-Section	20
E½NENW	East Half of Northeast Quarter of Northwest Quarter-Section	20
E½NESE	East Half of Northeast Quarter of Southeast Quarter-Section	20
E½NESW	East Half of Northeast Quarter of Southwest Quarter-Section	20
E½NW	East Half of Northwest Quarter-Section	80
E½NWNE	East Half of Northwest Quarter of Northeast Quarter-Section	20
E½NWNW	East Half of Northwest Quarter of Northwest Quarter-Section	20
E½NWSE	East Half of Northwest Quarter of Southeast Quarter-Section	20
E½NWSW	East Half of Northwest Quarter of Southwest Quarter-Section	20
E½S½	East Half of South Half-Section	160
E½SE	East Half of Southeast Quarter-Section	80
E½SENE	East Half of Southeast Quarter of Northeast Quarter-Section	20
E½SENW	East Half of Southeast Quarter of Northwest Quarter-Section	20
E½SESE	East Half of Southeast Quarter of Southeast Quarter-Section	20
E½SESW	East Half of Southeast Quarter of Southwest Quarter-Section	20
E½SW	East Half of Southwest Quarter-Section	80
E½SWNE	East Half of Southwest Quarter of Northeast Quarter-Section	20
E½SWNW	East Half of Southwest Quarter of Northwest Quarter-Section	20
E½SWSE	East Half of Southwest Quarter of Southeast Quarter-Section	20
E½SWSW	East Half of Southwest Quarter of Southwest Quarter-Section	20
E½W½	East Half of West Half-Section	160
N½	North Half-Section	320
N½E½NE	North Half of East Half of Northeast Quarter-Section	40
N½E½NW	North Half of East Half of Northwest Quarter-Section	40
N½E½SE	North Half of East Half of Southeast Quarter-Section	40
N½E½SW	North Half of East Half of Southwest Quarter-Section	40
N½N½	North Half of North Half-Section	160
N½NE	North Half of Northeast Quarter-Section	80
N½NENE	North Half of Northeast Quarter of Northeast Quarter-Section	20
N½NENW	North Half of Northeast Quarter of Northwest Quarter-Section	20
N½NESE	North Half of Northeast Quarter of Southeast Quarter-Section	20
N½NESW	North Half of Northeast Quarter of Southwest Quarter-Section	20
N½NW	North Half of Northwest Quarter-Section	80
N½NWNE	North Half of Northwest Quarter of Northeast Quarter-Section	20
N½NWNW	North Half of Northwest Quarter of Northwest Quarter-Section	20
N½NWSE	North Half of Northwest Quarter of Southeast Quarter-Section	20
N½NWSW	North Half of Northwest Quarter of Southwest Quarter-Section	20
N½S½	North Half of South Half-Section	160
N½SE	North Half of Southeast Quarter-Section	80
N½SENE	North Half of Southeast Quarter of Northeast Quarter-Section	20
N½SENW	North Half of Southeast Quarter of Northwest Quarter-Section	20
N½SESE	North Half of Southeast Quarter of Southeast Quarter-Section	20

Section Part	Description	Acres
N½SESW	North Half of Southeast Quarter of Southwest Quarter-Section	20
N½SESW	North Half of Southeast Quarter of Southwest Quarter-Section	20
N½SW	North Half of Southwest Quarter-Section	80
N½SWNE	North Half of Southwest Quarter of Northeast Quarter-Section	20
N½SWNW	North Half of Southwest Quarter of Northwest Quarter-Section	20
N½SWSE	North Half of Southwest Quarter of Southeast Quarter-Section	20
N½SWSE	North Half of Southwest Quarter of Southeast Quarter-Section	20
N½SWSW	North Half of Southwest Quarter of Southwest Quarter-Section	20
N½W½NW	North Half of West Half of Northwest Quarter-Section	40
N½W½SE	North Half of West Half of Southeast Quarter-Section	40
N½W½SW	North Half of West Half of Southwest Quarter-Section	40
NE	Northeast Quarter-Section	160
NEN½	Northeast Quarter of North Half-Section	80
NENE	Northeast Quarter of Northeast Quarter-Section	40
NENENE	Northeast Quarter of Northeast Quarter of Northeast Quarter	10
NENENW	Northeast Quarter of Northeast Quarter of Northwest Quarter	10
NENESE	Northeast Quarter of Northeast Quarter of Southeast Quarter	10
NENESW	Northeast Quarter of Northeast Quarter of Southwest Quarter	10
NENW	Northeast Quarter of Northwest Quarter-Section	40
NENWNE	Northeast Quarter of Northwest Quarter of Northeast Quarter	10
NENWNW	Northeast Quarter of Northwest Quarter of Northwest Quarter	10
NENWSE	Northeast Quarter of Northwest Quarter of Southeast Quarter	10
NENWSW	Northeast Quarter of Northwest Quarter of Southwest Quarter	10
NESE	Northeast Quarter of Southeast Quarter-Section	40
NESENE	Northeast Quarter of Southeast Quarter of Northeast Quarter	10
NESENW	Northeast Quarter of Southeast Quarter of Northwest Quarter	10
NESESE	Northeast Quarter of Southeast Quarter of Southeast Quarter	10
NESESW	Northeast Quarter of Southeast Quarter of Southwest Quarter	10
NESW	Northeast Quarter of Southwest Quarter-Section	40
NESWNE	Northeast Quarter of Southwest Quarter of Northeast Quarter	10
NESWNW	Northeast Quarter of Southwest Quarter of Northwest Quarter	10
NESWSE	Northeast Quarter of Southwest Quarter of Southeast Quarter	10
NESWSW	Northeast Quarter of Southwest Quarter of Southwest Quarter	10
NW	Northwest Quarter-Section	160
NWE½	Northwest Quarter of Eastern Half-Section	80
NWN½	Northwest Quarter of North Half-Section	80
NWNE	Northwest Quarter of Northeast Quarter-Section	40
NWNENE	Northwest Quarter of Northeast Quarter of Northeast Quarter	10
NWNENW	Northwest Quarter of Northeast Quarter of Northwest Quarter	10
NWNESE	Northwest Quarter of Northeast Quarter of Southeast Quarter	10
NWNESW	Northwest Quarter of Northeast Quarter of Southwest Quarter	10
NWNW	Northwest Quarter of Northwest Quarter-Section	40
NWNWNE	Northwest Quarter of Northwest Quarter of Northeast Quarter	10
NWNWNW	Northwest Quarter of Northwest Quarter of Northwest Quarter	10
NWNWSE	Northwest Quarter of Northwest Quarter of Southeast Quarter	10
NWNWSW	Northwest Quarter of Northwest Quarter of Southwest Quarter	10
NWSE	Northwest Quarter of Southeast Quarter-Section	40
NWSENE	Northwest Quarter of Southeast Quarter of Northeast Quarter	10
NWSENW	Northwest Quarter of Southeast Quarter of Northwest Quarter	10
NWSESE	Northwest Quarter of Southeast Quarter of Southeast Quarter	10
NWSESW	Northwest Quarter of Southeast Quarter of Southwest Quarter	10
NWSW	Northwest Quarter of Southwest Quarter-Section	40
NWSWNE	Northwest Quarter of Southwest Quarter of Northeast Quarter	10
NWSWNW	Northwest Quarter of Southwest Quarter of Northwest Quarter	10
NWSWSE	Northwest Quarter of Southwest Quarter of Southeast Quarter	10
NWSWSW	Northwest Quarter of Southwest Quarter of Southwest Quarter	10
S½	South Half-Section	320
S½E½NE	South Half of East Half of Northeast Quarter-Section	40
S½E½NW	South Half of East Half of Northwest Quarter-Section	40
S½E½SE	South Half of East Half of Southeast Quarter-Section	40

Section Part	Description	Acres
S½E½SW	South Half of East Half of Southwest Quarter-Section	40
S½N½	South Half of North Half-Section	160
S½NE	South Half of Northeast Quarter-Section	80
S½NENE	South Half of Northeast Quarter of Northeast Quarter-Section	20
S½NENW	South Half of Northeast Quarter of Northwest Quarter-Section	20
S½NESE	South Half of Northeast Quarter of Southeast Quarter-Section	20
S½NESW	South Half of Northeast Quarter of Southwest Quarter-Section	20
S½NW	South Half of Northwest Quarter-Section	80
S½NWNE	South Half of Northwest Quarter of Northeast Quarter-Section	20
S½NWNW	South Half of Northwest Quarter of Northwest Quarter-Section	20
S½NWSE	South Half of Northwest Quarter of Southeast Quarter-Section	20
S½NWSW	South Half of Northwest Quarter of Southwest Quarter-Section	20
S½S½	South Half of South Half-Section	160
S½SE	South Half of Southeast Quarter-Section	80
S½SENE	South Half of Southeast Quarter of Northeast Quarter-Section	20
S½SENW	South Half of Southeast Quarter of Northwest Quarter-Section	20
S½SESE	South Half of Southeast Quarter of Southeast Quarter-Section	20
S½SESW	South Half of Southeast Quarter of Southwest Quarter-Section	20
S½SESW	South Half of Southeast Quarter of Southwest Quarter-Section	20
S½SW	South Half of Southwest Quarter-Section	80
S½SWNE	South Half of Southwest Quarter of Northeast Quarter-Section	20
S½SWNW	South Half of Southwest Quarter of Northwest Quarter-Section	20
S½SWSE	South Half of Southwest Quarter of Southeast Quarter-Section	20
S½SWSE	South Half of Southwest Quarter of Southeast Quarter-Section	20
S½SWSW	South Half of Southwest Quarter of Southwest Quarter-Section	20
S½W½NE	South Half of West Half of Northeast Quarter-Section	40
S½W½NW	South Half of West Half of Northwest Quarter-Section	40
S½W½SE	South Half of West Half of Southeast Quarter-Section	40
S½W½SW	South Half of West Half of Southwest Quarter-Section	40
SE	Southeast Quarter Section	160
SEN½	Southeast Quarter of North Half-Section	80
SENE	Southeast Quarter of Northeast Quarter-Section	40
SENENE	Southeast Quarter of Northeast Quarter of Northeast Quarter	10
SENENW	Southeast Quarter of Northeast Quarter of Northwest Quarter	10
SENESE	Southeast Quarter of Northeast Quarter of Southeast Quarter	10
SENESW	Southeast Quarter of Northeast Quarter of Southwest Quarter	10
SENW	Southeast Quarter of Northwest Quarter-Section	40
SENWNE	Southeast Quarter of Northwest Quarter of Northeast Quarter	10
SENWNW	Southeast Quarter of Northwest Quarter of Northwest Quarter	10
SENWSE	Souteast Quarter of Northwest Quarter of Southeast Quarter	10
SENWSW	Southeast Quarter of Northwest Quarter of Southwest Quarter	10
SESE	Southeast Quarter of Southeast Quarter-Section	40
SESENE	SoutheastQuarter of Southeast Quarter of Northeast Quarter	10
SESENW	Southeast Quarter of Southeast Quarter of Northwest Quarter	10
SESESE	Southeast Quarter of Southeast Quarter of Southeast Quarter	10
SESESW	Southeast Quarter of Southeast Quarter of Southwest Quarter	10
SESW	Southeast Quarter of Southwest Quarter-Section	40
SESWNE	Southeast Quarter of Southwest Quarter of Northeast Quarter	10
SESWNW	Southeast Quarter of Southwest Quarter of Northwest Quarter	10
SESWSE	Southeast Quarter of Southwest Quarter of Southeast Quarter	10
SESWSW	Southeast Quarter of Southwest Quarter of Southwest Quarter	10
SW	Southwest Quarter-Section	160
SWNE	Southwest Quarter of Northeast Quarter-Section	40
SWNENE	Southwest Quarter of Northeast Quarter of Northeast Quarter	10
SWNENW	Southwest Quarter of Northeast Quarter of Northwest Quarter	10
SWNESE	Southwest Quarter of Northeast Quarter of Southeast Quarter	10
SWNESW	Southwest Quarter of Northeast Quarter of Southwest Quarter	10
SWNW	Southwest Quarter of Northwest Quarter-Section	40
SWNWNE	Southwest Quarter of Northwest Quarter of Northeast Quarter	10
SWNWNW	Southwest Quarter of Northwest Quarter of Northwest Quarter	10

Section Part	Description	Acres
SWNWSE	Southwest Quarter of Northwest Quarter of Southeast Quarter	10
SWNWSW	Southwest Quarter of Northwest Quarter of Southwest Quarter	10
SWSE	Southwest Quarter of Southeast Quarter-Section	40
SWSENE	Southwest Quarter of Southeast Quarter of Northeast Quarter	10
SWSENW	Southwest Quarter of Southeast Quarter of Northwest Quarter	10
SWSESE	Southwest Quarter of Southeast Quarter of Southeast Quarter	10
SWSESW	Southwest Quarter of Southeast Quarter of Southwest Quarter	10
SWSW	Southwest Quarter of Southwest Quarter-Section	40
SWSWNE	Southwest Quarter of Southwest Quarter of Northeast Quarter	10
SWSWNW	Southwest Quarter of Southwest Quarter of Northwest Quarter	10
SWSWSE	Southwest Quarter of Southwest Quarter of Southeast Quarter	10
SWSWSW	Southwest Quarter of Southwest Quarter of Southwest Quarter	10
W½	West Half-Section	320
W½E½	West Half of East Half-Section	160
W½N½	West Half of North Half-Section (same as NW)	160
W½NE	West Half of Northeast Quarter	80
W½NENE	West Half of Northeast Quarter of Northeast Quarter-Section	20
W½NENW	West Half of Northeast Quarter of Northwest Quarter-Section	20
W½NESE	West Half of Northeast Quarter of Southeast Quarter-Section	20
W½NESW	West Half of Northeast Quarter of Southwest Quarter-Section	20
W½NW	West Half of Northwest Quarter-Section	80
W½NWNE	West Half of Northwest Quarter of Northeast Quarter-Section	20
W½NWNW	West Half of Northwest Quarter of Northwest Quarter-Section	20
W½NWSE	West Half of Northwest Quarter of Southeast Quarter-Section	20
W½NWSW	West Half of Northwest Quarter of Southwest Quarter-Section	20
W½S½	West Half of South Half-Section	160
W½SE	West Half of Southeast Quarter-Section	80
W½SENE	West Half of Southeast Quarter of Northeast Quarter-Section	20
W½SENW	West Half of Southeast Quarter of Northwest Quarter-Section	20
W½SESE	West Half of Southeast Quarter of Southeast Quarter-Section	20
W½SESW	West Half of Southeast Quarter of Southwest Quarter-Section	20
W½SW	West Half of Southwest Quarter-Section	80
W½SWNE	West Half of Southwest Quarter of Northeast Quarter-Section	20
W½SWNW	West Half of Southwest Quarter of Northwest Quarter-Section	20
W½SWSE	West Half of Southwest Quarter of Southeast Quarter-Section	20
W½SWSW	West Half of Southwest Quarter of Southwest Quarter-Section	20
W½W½	West Half of West Half-Section	160

Appendix C - Multi-Patentee Groups

The following index presents groups of people who jointly received patents in Poweshiek County, Iowa. The Group Numbers are used in the Patent Maps and their Indexes so that you may then turn to this Appendix in order to identify all the members of the each buying group.

Group Number 1
ADAIR, Byers; ADAIR, Samuel C

Group Number 2
ALEXANDER, Robert; ALEXANDER, James

Group Number 3
ALLEN, William; ROBINSON, Mary

Group Number 4
ANTHONY, John P; LYNASON, Jane

Group Number 5
BADGER, Lewis; PELTON, Dolly T

Group Number 6
BEADLESTON, Ebenezer; CUMMINGS, Elizabeth

Group Number 7
BEADLESTON, Ebenezer; RICE, Amanda

Group Number 8
BERRYHILL, Charles H; ATCHISON, Nancy

Group Number 9
BERRYHILL, Charles H; BOONE, Eleanor

Group Number 10
BERRYHILL, Charles H; DAVIS, Eliza L

Group Number 11
BERRYHILL, Charles H; DOBBIN, Julia Ann

Group Number 12
BERRYHILL, Charles H; HUMMEL, Susannah

Group Number 13
BERRYHILL, Charles H; INGMOND, Mary

Group Number 14
BERRYHILL, Charles H; LYON, Alfred

Group Number 15
BERRYHILL, Charles H; RYAN, Mary

Group Number 16
BERRYHILL, Charles H; SOHN, Hannah

Group Number 17
BERRYHILL, Charles H; WEBBER, Mary

Group Number 18
BERRYHILL, James B; ADAMS, Jackey P

Group Number 19
BERRYHILL, James B; BERRYHILL, William D

Group Number 20
BERRYHILL, James B; NELSON, Sheney

Group Number 21
BERRYHILL, James B; OTTO, Susanna

Group Number 22
BERRYHILL, John H; HOVERSTICK, Susannah

Group Number 23
BERRYHILL, John H; UNGER, Catharine

Group Number 24
BERRYHILL, John H; WATSON, Margaret

Group Number 25
BERRYHILL, William D; BERRYHILL, James B

Group Number 26
BIRD, Roderick D; CHRISTAIN, Sarah

Group Number 27
BLAKE, Lewis; POOLE, Sarah

Group Number 28
BORLAND, James; MENARY, Betsy

Group Number 29
BOSWELL, William; BARNES, Mary

Group Number 30
BOTTS, William S; HONICON, Alcey

Group Number 31
BOTTS, William S; HONOCOL, Aley

Group Number 32
BOYD, John W; FREANER, William

Group Number 33
BRABROOK, George; BATES, Calista B

Group Number 34
BRAYTON, Benjamin B; DRURY, Rachael

Group Number 35
BRAYTON, Benjamin B; MITCHELL, Emily

Group Number 36
BRICK, Priscilla; BRICK, Elizabeth; BRICK, Rebecca Paulina

Group Number 37
BROOKS, Thomas L; WELLS, Nachi

Group Number 38
BRYAN, Alanson; EARLEY, Andasire

Group Number 39
BRYAN, Alanson; MILLER, Rachel

Group Number 40
BRYAN, Alanson; MITCHELL, Elizabeth

Group Number 41
BUDD, Edward; PARKER, Elizabeth H

Group Number 42
BYINGTON, Legrand; QUACKENBUSH, Mary

Group Number 43
BYINGTON, Legrand; WOOLARD, Letitia

Group Number 44
CALDWELL, John; SANDERS, William

Group Number 45
CAMPBELL, Jacob; BRYAN, Jane

Group Number 46
CARTER, Wesley; PIERSOL, Sarah; PIERSOL, Ellen

Group Number 47
CARVER, Harrison; CARVER, Thomas P

Group Number 48
CHITTENDEN, Henry; SEARS, Walter S

Group Number 49
CHOUTEAU, Edward A; PLUM, Catharine

Group Number 50
CLARK, Josiah W; HUNT, Mornan

Group Number 51
CLARK, Josiah W; TYSON, Ann

Group Number 52
CLARK, William; PATTERSON, Rachel

Group Number 53
CLEMENS, John; CLEMENTS, John

Group Number 54
CODDINGTON, James; ESTES, Beulah

Group Number 55
CONNELLY, Edward; BEAN, Silva

Group Number 56
CONNELLY, Edward; MILLIKEN, Mary

Group Number 57
COOK, Ralph P; CUTTING, James C

Group Number 58
CORBIN, Austin; WYATT, Sally

Group Number 59
COULTER, John Alexander; CYPHER, Elizabeth

Group Number 60
CRAVER, James A; HIGGINBOTHAM, Sarah

Group Number 61
CRAVER, James A; ROBERTS, Ada

Group Number 62
CROOKHAM, John A L; MASAY,

Group Number 63
CROOKHAM, John A L; MASUY,

Group Number 64
CRUM, John H; DAVISON, Henry

Group Number 65
CULBERTSON, John C; CASWELL, Elanor

Group Number 66
CULBERTSON, John C; CLAXTON, Elizabeth

Group Number 67
CULBERTSON, John C; DENINGTON, Elizabeth

Group Number 68
CULBERTSON, John C; GORDON, Lavina

Group Number 69
CULBERTSON, John C; GRIDLEY, Millicent

Group Number 70
CULBERTSON, John C; HARRINGTON, Abigail

Group Number 71
CULBERTSON, John C; HAVELY, Elizabeth

Group Number 72
CULBERTSON, John C; HOLMES, Keren H

Group Number 73
CULBERTSON, John C; MCCLURE, Lydia

Group Number 74
CULBERTSON, John C; PAGE, Betsey

Group Number 75
CULBERTSON, John C; PAUL, Elizabeth D

Group Number 76
CULBERTSON, John C; QUIGGINS, Mary; QUIGGINS, Eliza; QUIGGINS, Nancy

Group Number 77
CULBERTSON, John C; RENO, Morgan

Group Number 78
CULBERTSON, John C; ROBERTSON, Christina

Group Number 79
CULBERTSON, John C; SHEFFER, Sarah

Group Number 80
CULBERTSON, John C; SHIFFER, Sarah

Group Number 81
CULBERTSON, John C; SPONSLER, Anna

Group Number 82
CULBERTSON, John C; TAYLOR, Sally

Group Number 83
CULBERTSON, John C; WHITE, Elizabeth

Group Number 84
CUSHMAN, Job; ROBERTS, Mary A

Group Number 85
DANIELS, Francis; COLLINS, Phebe

Group Number 86
DANIELS, Francis; SCHNEIDER, Catharine

Group Number 87
DARLAND, John; RUSSELL, Phebe M

Group Number 88
DARLAND, Lambert; REVERE, Judith

Group Number 89
DAVIS, William; GIFFORD, Henry B

Group Number 90
DEEMER, Daniel; MCROY, Susannah

Group Number 91
DELAHOYDE, John; BONNEY, Lucinda

Group Number 92
DELAHOYDE, John; VOUGHT, Jane

Group Number 93
DEMENT, Isaac G; DEMENT, Sarah

Group Number 94
DIX, John A; WILSON, Matilda J

Group Number 95
DOWNEY, Hugh D; ALEXANDER, Margaret

Group Number 96
DOWNEY, Hugh D; ATWELL, Dorothy J

Group Number 97
DOWNEY, Hugh D; BALSLEY, Mary E

Group Number 98
DOWNEY, Hugh D; CHANDLER, Margaret

Group Number 99
DOWNEY, Hugh D; CHASE, Hannah

Group Number 100
DOWNEY, Hugh D; EVANS, Mary

Group Number 101
DOWNEY, Hugh D; FISHER, Hannah L

Group Number 102
DOWNEY, Hugh D; GARDINER, Ellen

Group Number 103
DOWNEY, Hugh D; HARRIS, Suckey

Group Number 104
DOWNEY, Hugh D; JOHNSON, Anna

Group Number 105
DOWNEY, Hugh D; KERN, Gertrude

Group Number 106
DOWNEY, Hugh D; LANE, Elizabeth

Group Number 107
DOWNEY, Hugh D; PARCEL, Jane

Group Number 108
DOWNEY, Hugh D; RICHARDSON, Bridges

Group Number 109
DOWNEY, Hugh D; SMOTHERS, Elizabeth

Group Number 110
DOWNEY, Hugh D; WEISER, Mary C

Group Number 111
DOWNEY, Hugh D; WILSON, Ann

Group Number 112
DRUMMOND, Samuel; GRANT, Abigail

Group Number 113
DUFFIELD, James R; LITTLE, Nancy

Group Number 114
EASLEY, James S; CRAWFORD, Susan W

Group Number 115
EASLEY, James S; GOODE, Elizabeth

Group Number 116
EASLEY, James S; JACKSON, Elizabeth

Group Number 117
EASLEY, James S; JONES, Mary

Group Number 118
EASLEY, James S; MARSHALL, Mary Ann

Group Number 119
EASLEY, James S; MCCARTY, Catharine

Group Number 120
EASLEY, James S; PEGRAM, Rebecca

Group Number 121
EASLEY, James S; ROARK, Mary Melana

Group Number 122
EASLEY, James S; WARD, Sarah

Group Number 123
EASLEY, James S; WATKINS, Elizabeth

Group Number 124
EASLEY, James S; WHITE, Penelope

Group Number 125
EBERHART, Margaret L; SMITH, Polly

Group Number 126
EDWARDS, Thomas M; DAVIS, Sally

Group Number 127
EDWARDS, Thomas M; DIKEMAN, Freelove

Group Number 128
EDWARDS, Thomas M; EWERS, Sarah

Group Number 129
EDWARDS, Thomas M; FLOYD, Abraham

Group Number 130
EDWARDS, Thomas M; JENNINGS, Polly

Group Number 131
EDWARDS, Thomas M; NEWKIRK, Martha

Group Number 132
EDWARDS, Thomas M; WASSON, Jollina

Group Number 133
ESTLICK, Elizabeth; LOVE, Agnes H

Group Number 134
FARMER, Irvin; NEWTON, Francis

Group Number 135
FISHER, George S; DAINGERFIELD, Mariah H

Group Number 136
FORSYTHE, Mathew; BRAUGHTON, Sarah H

Group Number 137
FRANCIS, George M; GARRETT, Eliza L

Group Number 138
FRAZIER, William; JOHNSTON, Margaret

Group Number 139
FRYAR, Daniel; BLACK, Nancy

Group Number 140
FULTON, Francis M; CUNNINGHAM, Mary

Group Number 141
GATES, Samuel; ATWOOD, Nancy

Group Number 142
GATLING, Richard J; PARKER, Tempy

Group Number 143
GATTRELL, Nathan; BEAN, Silas T; BEAN, Betsy L;
BEAN, Mary Jane

Group Number 144
GIFFORD, Henry B; COLLINS, Murzey

Group Number 145
GIFFORD, Henry B; LONG, Susanna

Group Number 146
GILLETT, Samuel N; GILLETT, Simeon B

Group Number 147
GILLETT, Samuel; GILLETT, Simeon

Group Number 148
GILMORE, Quincy A; SHAYLER, Lucinda

Group Number 149
GOWER, James H; DEAN, Amanda

Group Number 150
GOWER, James H; DOUGLASS, Anne E

Group Number 151
GOWER, James H; LENTZ, Hannah

Group Number 152
GOWER, James H; RAMAY, Elizabeth

Group Number 153
GOWER, James H; WIMER, Elizabeth

Group Number 154
GRAHAM, Jacob V B; LYNASON, Jane

Group Number 155
GRINNELL, Josiah B; WILSON, Mary Ann

Group Number 156
GUNNELL, Josiah B; SILPATH, Julia Ann

Group Number 157
GWIN, Jacob; IS-FI-KE,

Group Number 158
HAMILTON, George A; COLE, Addison G; COLE, Mary L

Group Number 159
HAMILTON, George A; PARMER, Jerusha

Group Number 160
HAMILTON, George A; STOKES, Elinira

Group Number 161
HAMMOND, George; HAMMOND, Hiram

Group Number 162
HAND, Seneca L; KING, Sally

Group Number 163
HANES, Henry; POLLARD, Jane

Group Number 164
HART, Anson; HARRINGTON, Clarissa

Group Number 165
HASTINGS, Walter; TILL, Libby

Group Number 166
HATFIELD, Amos F; ARCHER, Mary

Group Number 167
HIGGINSON, John C; PARSONS, Nancy

Group Number 168
HIGGINSON, John C; WHITE, Sarah

Group Number 169
HILL, Samuel; HOSICK, Susan

Group Number 170
HILL, Samuel; RILEY, Elcy

Group Number 171
HOBART, George; HAZLETON, Newton

Group Number 172
HOLLENBACK, John; MAHAN, Maria

Group Number 173
HOLLENBECK, Jerome W; JACKSON, Elizabeth

Group Number 174
HOLLENBECK, Jerome W; PERCY, Content

Group Number 175
HOLLENBECK, Jerome W; TARR, Lettice

Group Number 176
HOLLENBECK, Jerome W; WILDER, Prudence

Group Number 177
HOLYOKE, Thomas; KINGSMORE, Catharine

Group Number 178
HOWARD, Mark; CROCKER, Dorothy

Group Number 179
JENNINGS, James H; KENNEDY, Mary

Group Number 180
JEROME, Lesbia P; BENNETT, Frances

Group Number 181
JOHNSON, Archibald; GILLELAND, Nancy G

Group Number 182
JUDD, Eli P; MOSELY, Frederick; SMITH, Benjamin L

Group Number 183
KAUFFMAN, Christian; MARVIN, Olivia

Group Number 184
KIRKWOOD, Samuel J; BENNETT, Hannah

Group Number 185
KIRKWOOD, Samuel J; JONES, Leanah

Group Number 186
KIRKWOOD, Samuel J; LANE, Miranda

Group Number 187
KRIDLER, George; BYERS, William

Group Number 188
KUNKEL, Benjamin; EBY, Jacob R; MEILY, Samuel

Group Number 189
KUNKEL, Benjamin; ROGERS, Mary

Group Number 190
LARREW, James; HULL, Elizabeth S

Group Number 191
LAYLANDER, James; LALANDER, Mary

Group Number 192
LEE, James; TRACY, Sicha

Group Number 193
LISTON, Jonathan A; BLOUNT, Nancy

Group Number 194
LISTON, Jonathan A; GRUB, Elizabeth

Group Number 195
LOESCH, Henry; SPANGLER, Philip

Group Number 196
LONG, Wiley; WEAVER, Elizabeth

Group Number 197
LUCAS, Edward W; LUCAS, Robert S

Group Number 198
MANAT, William; MANAT, Mary Ann

Group Number 199
MANN, Charles A; KAPLE, Martha

Group Number 200
MARK, Levi G; LAITON, Mercy

Group Number 201
MARK, Levi G; MUIRHIRD, Sarah

Group Number 202
MARTIN, Giles S; GRAHAM, Giles S

Group Number 203
MCCLELLAN, John H; CROMER, Elizabeth

Group Number 204
MCCLELLAN, John H; MCCLEIF, Catharine

Group Number 205
MCCLELLAN, John H; WILSON, Maria

Group Number 206
MCCORKLE, Milton E; PROPST, Nancy

Group Number 207
MCKENZIE, Lewis; JAMIESON, Maria C

Group Number 208
MEAD, Benjamin L; MEAD, Enfield S

Group Number 209
MEAD, Enfield S; DEARBORN, Lucy

Group Number 210
MERWIN, Phineas; WITHROW, Mary

Group Number 211
MONSON, Henry L; POTTER, Reuben; POTTER, Jesse A; POTTER, David W

Group Number 212
MORGAN, John; HOKE, Mary E

Group Number 213
MORSMAN, Moses J; TAYLOR, Eliza

Group Number 214
MUSGROVE, Andrew J; CRADDOCK, Mary A

Group Number 215
MUSGROVE, Benjamin; PAROTT, Mary

Group Number 216
PARKS, George W; SANDERS, Elizabeth W

Group Number 217
PARRISH, Hardin; LAWRENCE, Christian

Group Number 218
PARRISH, Hardin; NIXON, Orvill A

Group Number 219
PETERS, Adam; HOOK, Margaret

Group Number 220
PHELPS, Frederick; BOTTOMS, Mary

Group Number 221
PHELPS, Frederick; EASTER,

Group Number 222
PINNEY, Marcellus; WILLIAMSON, Hetty

Group Number 223
PLYMPTON, Jeremiah; CLARK, Sally

Group Number 224
PUSEY, William H M; BAIL, Rebecca

Group Number 225
PUSEY, William H M; LANGFORD, Naomi R

Group Number 226
PUTNAM, Harvey C; GLADSON, Rebecca

Group Number 227
REED, Julius A; ADKINS, Mary

Group Number 228
RENO, Morgan; ASKINS, Isabella

Group Number 229
RENO, Morgan; COVINGTON, Elizabeth

Group Number 230
RENO, Morgan; LOGAN, Sarah M

Group Number 231
RENO, Morgan; MEEKER, Elizabeth

Group Number 232
RENO, Morgan; NEAL, Milly

Group Number 233
RENO, Morgan; PARKS, Nancy

Group Number 234
RENO, Morgan; RUCKER, Emeline

Group Number 235
RENO, Morgan; SCRUGS, Amelia L

Group Number 236
RENO, Morgan; SMITH, Margaret

Group Number 237
RENO, Morgan; STILES, Jerusha

Group Number 238
RENO, Morgan; TUTHILL, Elizabeth

Group Number 239
RENO, Morgan; UNDERWOOD, Sarah

Group Number 240
REYNOLDS, John; REYNOLDS, George W

Group Number 241
RIGGS, Jetur R; DUNNING, Abigail P

Group Number 242
ROBERTSON, Joseph; EGERTON, Martha

Group Number 243
ROGERS, John N; ADAMS, Margaret; JAMISON, Granville E; SNYDER, Andrew J

Group Number 244
SANXAY, Frederic; HITCHCOCK, Frances P

Group Number 245
SANXAY, Frederic; PAYNE, Nancy

Group Number 246
SANXAY, Frederic; TRACY, Clarissa

Group Number 247
SARGENT, George B; BARRETT, Bethiah

Group Number 248
SEVERNS, Daniel A; VERNON, Mary Ann

Group Number 249
SHARP, George; SNOWDEN, Elizabeth W

Group Number 250
SHERMAN, William; HERRON, Sarah

Group Number 251
SHERWOOD, Albert; FAIRBANK, Betsey

Group Number 252
SKINNER, Franklin; DOBYNS, Duly

Group Number 253
SLADDEN, John; MCMILLAN, Margaret

Group Number 254
SMITH, Lander; WRENN, Ann

Group Number 255
SNYDER, Lewis S; GRAYUM, Polly

Group Number 256
STEELE, Robert F; FARNHAM, Anna

Group Number 257
STEELE, Robert F; SANBORN, Phebe

Group Number 258
STERRET, James P; MCGARY, Elizabeth

Group Number 259
STIX, Henry; MORRISON, Elizabeth

Group Number 260
STODDARD, Charles H; NICHOLAS, Hester

Group Number 261
STRONG, John C; STRONG, Charles; STRONG, Emily

Group Number 262
STROW, John; STROW, Perry

Group Number 263
SWANEY, Conrad; WILLIAMS, Elizabeth

Group Number 264
SWITZER, Tavner B; BOGGS, Mary

Group Number 265
TALBOTT, Joseph; ANDERSON, Jane

Group Number 266
TALBOTT, Joshua C; TRICKER, Lucinda

Group Number 267
TAYLOR, Lorenzo M; GRIFFIN, Sophia

Group Number 268
TAYLOR, Lorenzo M; MONTGOMERY, Mary

Group Number 269
TAYLOR, Lorenzo M; PHILLIPS, Phebe

Group Number 270
TAYLOR, Lorenzo M; WESTCOTT, Sarah

Group Number 271
THORN, William; WILLIAMS, Jesee S

Group Number 272
THORN, William; WILLIAMS, Jesse L

Group Number 273
THORN, William; WILLIAMS, Jesse L; CARBERRY, Jonathan

Group Number 274
THORN, William; WILLIAMS, Jesse L; KELLY, Nancy

Group Number 275
TOMPKINS, James J; MOODY, Ann S

Group Number 276
TUCKER, Jacob T; CAPLES, Mary

Group Number 277
WASSON, George W; CHESNUT, Nancy

Group Number 278
WATSON, Jacob; DUNGAN, Sarah

Group Number 279
WHITE, Elias A; MCCURTAIN, Judy

Group Number 280
WHITE, John W; WHITE, James L; WHITE, Albert S

Group Number 281
WHITE, John W; WHITE, James L; WHITE, Albert S;
MORRIS, Eatten; MORRIS, Eliza; MORRIS, James;
MORRIS, Nathaniel; MORRIS, Matthew

Group Number 282
WHITE, John; BARBOUR, Catharine

Group Number 283
WHITE, John; ROBINS, Julia

Group Number 284
WILLIAMS, George C; LOTT, Bartholomew; LOTT,
Mary B; LOTT, Loraina Jane

Group Number 285
WILLINGHAM, William W; BEAN, Mary

Group Number 286
WILLINGHAM, William W; CRENSHAW, Elizabeth

Group Number 287
WILLINGHAM, William W; HOOPER, Lucinda

Group Number 288
WILLINGHAM, William W; HUTCHINS, Caroline R

Group Number 289
WILLINGHAM, William W; WOODWARD, John P

Group Number 290
WILSON, George W; STEVENSON, Mary

Group Number 291
WISDEN, Thomas W; GINN, Jane H

Group Number 292
WOLFE, Peter; FLESHER, Lucinda

Group Number 293
WOODWARD, John B; EVANS, George W

Group Number 294
WRIGHT, Lewis; NOLAND, Mary

Group Number 295
YOUNG, Stephen; ALEXANDER, Catharine F

Extra! Extra! (about our Indexes)

We purposefully do not have an all-name index in the back of this volume so that our readers do not miss one of the best uses of this book: finding misspelled names among more specialized indexes.

Without repeating the text of our "How-to" chapter, we have nonetheless tried to assist our more anxious researchers by delivering a short-cut to the two county-wide Surname Indexes, the second of which will lead you to all-name indexes for each Congressional Township mapped in this volume :

For your convenience, the "How To Use this Book" Chart on page 2 is repeated on the reverse of this page.

We should be releasing new titles every week for the foreseeable future. We urge you to write, fax, call, or email us any time for a current list of titles. Of course, our web-page will always have the most current information about current and upcoming books.

Arphax Publishing Co.
2210 Research Park Blvd.
Norman, Oklahoma 73069
(800) 681-5298 toll-free
(405) 366-6181 local
(405) 366-8184 fax
info@arphax.com

www.arphax.com

How to Use This Book - A Graphical Summary

Part I
"The Big Picture"

Map A *Counties in the State*
Map B *Surrounding Counties*
Map C *Congressional Townships (Map Groups) in the County*
Map D *Cities & Towns in the County*
Map E *Cemeteries in the County*
Surnames in the County *Number of Land-Parcels for Each Surname*
Surname/Township Index Directs you to Township Map Groups in Part II

The Surname/Township Index can direct you to any number of **Township Map Groups**

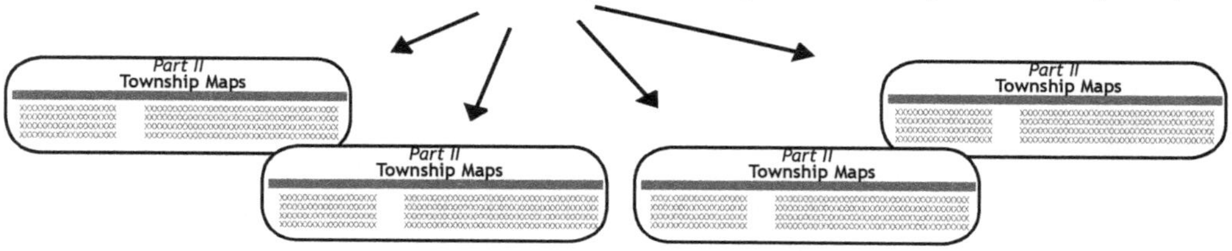

Part II
Township Map Groups
(1 for each Township in the County)

Each Township Map Group contains all four of of the following tools . . .

Land Patent Index *Every-name Index of Patents Mapped in this Township*
Land Patent Map *Map of Patents as listed in above Index*
Road Map *Map of Roads, City-centers, and Cemeteries in the Township*
Historical Map *Map of Railroads, Lakes, Rivers, Creeks, City-Centers, and Cemeteries*

Appendices

Appendix A *Congressional Authority enabling Patents within our Maps*
Appendix B *Section-Parts / Aliquot Parts (a comprehensive list)*
Appendix C *Multi-patentee Groups (Individuals within Buying Groups)*

(This page is a repeat of page 2 in the text)

www.ingramcontent.com/pod-product-compliance
Lightning Source LLC
Chambersburg PA
CBHW080234270326
41926CB00020B/4235